more excellent
HTML

< P.RE >
< \PRE > give you line space

more excellent

with an introduction to JavaScript

Timothy T. Gottleber
North Lake College
Irving, Texas

Timothy N. Trainor
Muskegon Community College
Muskegon, Michigan

Boston, MA   Burr Ridge, IL   Dubuque, IA   Madison, WI   New York, NY   San Francisco, CA   St. Louis, MO
Bangkok   Bogotá   Caracas   Lisbon   London   Madrid
Mexico City   Milan   New Delhi   Seoul   Singapore   Sydney   Taipei   Toronto

McGraw-Hill Higher Education

A Division of The **McGraw-Hill** Companies

MORE EXCELLENT HTML WITH AN INTRODUCTION
TO JAVASCRIPT

This book is printed on acid-free paper.

2 3 4 5 6 7 8 9 0 QPD/QPD 9 0 9 8 7 6 5 4 3 2 1 0 9

ISBN 0-07-233745-1

Vice president/Editor-in-chief: *Michael W. Junior*
Publisher: *David Brake*
Associate sponsoring editor: *Scott M. Hamilton*
Senior marketing manager: *Jodi McPherson*
Project manager: *Carrie Sestak*
Senior production supervisor: *Kari Geltemeyer*
Designer: *Mary Christianson*
Freelance cover designer: *TopDesk Publisher's Group*
Cover images: © *Arthur S. Aubry/PhotoDisc, Industrial Sidestreets*
Compositor: *Shepherd Incorporated*
Typeface: *11/12 Bembo*
Printer: *Quebecor Printing Book Group/Dubuque*

Library of Congress Cataloging-in Publication Data

Gottleber, Timothy T.
    More excellent HTML with an introduction to JavaScript / Timothy
T. Gottleber. Timothy N. Trainor.
      p.   cm.
    ISBN 0-07-233745-1
    1. HTML (Document markup language) 2. JavaScript (Computer
program language) I. Trainor, Timothy N., 1953–   . II. Title.
QA76.76.H94G69   2000
005.7'2—dc21   99–15468

http://www.mhhe.com

table of contents

preface

To the Student

This book was written for you. You want to learn how to build and maintain Web pages. You have the tool to help you do that in your hands. When I began to design the HTML course I teach, I couldn't find a book that would work well as a text for the class. There were many technical books and reference manuals available, but none of them written for students, and none were designed to be an aid in learning how to build Web pages. They were, and remain, excellent references once you know what you are doing, but they are not textbooks. I also talked with my students about what they wanted in a text. As a result of all those discussions, I wrote *Excellent HTML with an Introduction to Java Applets.*

After I finished that book, the W^{3}C (World Wide Web Consortium) revised the HTML standard and released HTML 4.0, the current standard. In addition, the world moved away from considering Java applets as the ideal "dynamic" inclusion into Web pages, and JavaScript has come into favor. As the new book began to take shape, Dr. Tim Trainor came on board as co-author, providing new ideas and vision. This created a very dynamic team that has been responsible for this new text. We also had the opportunity to talk to students about what they wanted or needed to learn in order to create their personal and/or commercial Web pages.

There are two ways to approach learning how to code the HyperText Markup Language (HTML) used to create Web pages. **The first way is to just jump in and see what you can hack together through trial and error.** HTML isn't that complex, and it isn't that difficult to create some, well at least fair, pages that way. However, there are two distinct disadvantages to that approach:

- You can learn some awful habits.
- You miss out on some great techniques.

The second way to learn HTML is to follow a more structured approach:

- First, learning how to use simple tags.
- Then moving on to the more complex ones.

It is very useful and productive to see what you can do with just a handful of selected tags before you start using the really "slick" ones like frames or tables.

This book uses the second approach. You will begin building Web pages in Chapter 2, and keep building more and more complex pages as you work through the text. If you have a special need, feel free to look ahead. Remember, however, we created the exercises at the end of each chapter to give you a chance to gain experience with the new tags you learned in that chapter and refresh your memory on the tags you have already learned.

Welcome to the wonderful world of HTML; it is an exciting place that is changing even as you read this. And one final note: you will read this many times throughout the text, but we would like to focus your attention upon it at the very beginning of your study of HTML. Your job is to provide new and exciting content to the community we call the World Wide Web. Concentrate on the content, and let the browsers that load your pages worry about the formatting. Go play on the Web, and if you want to see what our students are doing, come visit us at **http://phred.dcccd.edu** and **http://student.muskegon. cc.mi.us** and take a look at the student pages hosted there. They have done and are doing some wonderful things.

To the Instructor

Teaching HTML is challenging and exciting. In part, I developed my first book because I was frustrated with the texts currently being used to teach HTML. There were reference books and technical manuals available, but nothing designed to be used in the classroom. My students come to the class with a wide range of computer expertise, from the absolute novice to the professional programmer. I wrote my first book to make it easier to teach HTML, and to give the students the text they needed to succeed.

Then the World Wide Web Consortium (W^3C) revised the HTML standard and released HTML 4.0. In addition, my students and instructors around the country began expressing a stronger interest in JavaScript than in Java applets. Here was a chance for me to take a fresh look at Web page creation. Dr. Tim Trainor joined the project bringing his years of HTML teaching experience, his wit, and his wonderful ideas.

The book you hold in your hands has been tweaked and refined in the crucible of the classroom. It is designed to take the student from an overview of the history and origins of HTML through the design and development of clean, easy to maintain Web pages using stylesheets, JavaScript, and other dynamic HTML features. We have woven the new specifications throughout the text. Unlike many of the texts on the market that address Dynamic HTML and the 4.0 standard in just a chapter or two, we have built them into this text from the beginning. The first seven chapters have very few examples of styles and stylesheets, because we want the student to learn how to use the inline tags first. Starting in Chapter 8, where we introduce styles, and continuing throughout the rest of the book, the examples use style elements. The chapters about JavaScript and the other features of Dynamic HTML provide the students with a solid grounding in those techniques as well.

In writing this book we have not assumed the reader, your student, has an in-depth background with computers, but it would be a good idea if the student were minimally computer literate. We ourselves have had a couple of students who were new to computing and they succeeded, albeit by putting in some serious work.

The text is laid out in the order we teach our own classes. It starts with some simple tags, and progresses into the more sophisticated tags as the students become comfortable with the format and syntax of HTML. Although you don't have to follow any particular order (since most chapters can pretty much stand alone), there are a few back references that give the students grounding and re-fresh concepts. As each new tag is introduced, there are both examples of the HTML code and screen captures showing what that code generates. This allows the students to play with HTML and compare their results to those shown in the text. At the end of the chapter, there are sets of exercises that enable the student to create pages using the tags they have learned. The design process (and some of the exercises) build from chapter to chapter. In our experience, this is the best way to teach HTML. Give the students a tag, tell them how it works, and then let them use it. That way they can have actual hands-on experience with the tags and they tend to learn more quickly.

The physical layout of the content is geared to serve the student as a reference, but also to provide an advanced organizer for your lecture. Each new tag is enclosed within a graphical element showing the tag name, type of tag, a list of its attributes, and special notes on the use of that tag. You don't have to have several texts open at the same time, as you lecture; all the information is right there for you.

There is a wealth of ancillary tools that come with the text as well. They include:

1. A Web site that contains the JavaScript and most of the HTML examples from the book as well as Instructor notes, suggestions, and a sample syllabus.
2. A CD, included with the book that contains
   - Most of the HTML examples from the text.
   - All the JavaScripts used in the book, with a simple HTML page to drive each.
   - A selection of buttons, backgrounds, and lines for use on Web pages.
   - CuteFTP, a handy file transfer protocol tool to move data across the Web.
   - HomeSite, a powerful HTML editor.
   - ColdFusion, a Web site design tool.
   - HotDog, another HTML editor. (There are some examples that use HotDog in the text.)
   - MapEdit, a wonderful tool for producing image maps easily and quickly.
   - Scriptbuilder, a great way to create JavaScripts easily.
   - PaintShop Pro to create art for the pages.
   - WinZip, a useful tool for compressing HTML and images before ship-ping them across the Web.
   - CSE HTML Validator, a really neat HTML validation program that will check for both required and recommended HTML syntax.

You and your students can access the HTML examples by pointing your browser at D:/html/index.html—this assumes that D: is your CD-ROM drive.

## CHAPTER one

AN HTML OVERVIEW

The first part of this book focuses on *HyperText Markup Language (HTML)*, the set of codes used to build Web pages. After studying HTML, you will be able to build, change, and maintain your own pages on the Internet's *World Wide Web*, also called the *Net*. As in almost any aspect of the world of computing, HTML authors use some special vocabulary. If you find a word that you don't understand, please check in the glossary at the end of this book. Knowing the meaning of the special terms used with HTML is very important. Often half the battle in learning a new skill is learning the vocabulary of that skill.

What HTML Isn't

Before we look at what HTML is, it is important to make sure you understand what HTML isn't. First, HTML isn't hard to learn or use! Just like anything new, it looks a little strange when you first see it, but in a short time you can be reading and writing HTML like a pro. Second, HTML isn't a true programming language. In other words, it is not a language used to write Web programs. We will get into programming when we explore Common Gateway Interface scripts in Chapter 11 and JavaScript in Chapter 13. HTML also isn't a page description language, or a *WYSIWYG* (*What You See Is What You Get*) word processor or a desktop publishing tool. HTML is used primarily to define the content of a document (what it says) and only secondarily to describe the page layout (how it looks). You can determine exactly what the document says, but not precisely how it looks when displayed.

The terms *document* and *page* are often used interchangeably when talking about the World Wide Web. They don't mean exactly the same thing. HTML is used to create electronic documents that can be read on many different systems using software called a **browser.** The browser translates the HTML codes into a presentation on the screen. Technically, the **document** is the actual HTML codes and text you write (Figure 1.1), and the **page** is how it looks when viewed (see Figure 1.6 later in this chapter). Most Net cruisers don't make that distinction, so you may see the terms used interchangeably.

One fundamental fact of HTML is that although the author controls the content, the browser controls the layout of a document (with one exception that we will look at later). You can spend lots of time hand-editing (inserting extra spaces, tabs, blank lines, and such) to make your page look great, but most browsers will remove all those spaces, and all your careful work will be lost. The HTML term for extra spaces, tabs, and carriage returns is **white space.** HTML browsers usually compress all the white space into a single space.

What's in a Name?

Now that we know what it is not, let's look at what HTML is. We will start with the name. The H stands for "hyper." A **hyper document** is one that contains links to other "things" or places either within or outside the document. A **link** is the general term for a specially marked place on the screen that will cause something to happen when you activate it. Clicking (with a mouse button) on a link can open another HTML document, move you to another place in the current document, display a picture, play a sound, or run a video clip.

As you move from hyper document to hyper document, the browser builds a chain of the pages you have visited so that you can easily go back and revisit one. Since the browser builds a chain, each page you have visited could be called a link in that chain. As an HTML author, or *Web weaver,* you will code links from your documents to other documents, both on your computer and across the world. For example, if this were a hyper document, and if the author

```
<HTML>
<HEAD>
<TITLE>Example HTML Document</TITLE>
</HEAD>
<BODY>

<H1>Level-1 Heading</H1>
<P>The elements of an HTML document
and the resulting Web page are the
same as those found in any written document.
For example, a paragraph like this one is a
common design element.
</P>

<H2>Level-2 Heading</H2>
<P>There are ordered lists: </P>
<OL>
  <LI>This </LI>
  <LI>That </LI>
  <LI>Another thing </LI>
</OL>

<H3>Level-3 Heading</H3>
<P>There are unordered (bulleted) lists: </P>
<UL>
  <LI>This </LI>
  <LI>That </LI>
  <LI>Another thing </LI>
</UL>

</BODY>
</HTML>
```

Figure 1.1 Example of HTML document (Figure 1.6 shows resulting Web page).

had built in a link that defined the word Internet, that word may appear in a different font from the rest of the document. It could be underlined and/or in a different color. By moving your screen pointer to that spot on the page and clicking the mouse button, you would cause the link to open a small page that defined the word "Internet."

Here is another example: Suppose you go to the University of Virginia's Electronic Text Center, where many books are online. At that site you see the screen presented at the top of Figure 1.2. You want to read *Alice in Wonderland,* so you move your mouse pointer to that title (the fifth entry on the screen), and press the left mouse button. The next thing that appears on your screen is the first page of the electronic text, as shown at the bottom of Figure 1.2 on page 4. The title on the previous page was a link to the actual document.

Hyper documents are often considered more useful than standard text documents because the user can explore relationships among the ideas, or get

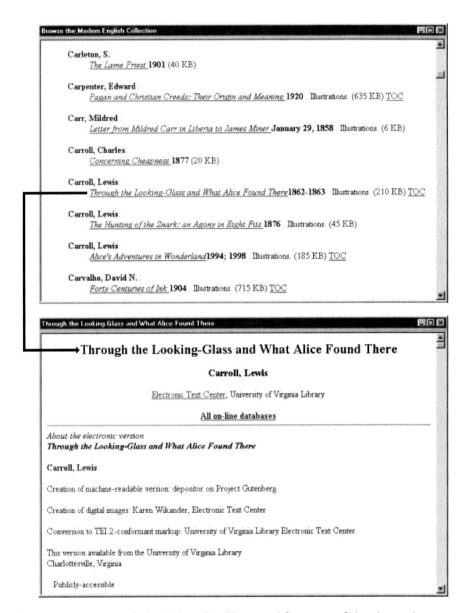

Figure 1.2 University of Virginia's online library and first page of the electronic version of *Alice in Wonderland* by Lewis Carroll.

definitions by clicking on the links the author provides. Some people predict that in the future you will be reading books like this one over the World Wide Web rather than on paper.

Let's continue with the meaning of the letters in HTML. The T stands for "text." These are the words you want to display on the computer's screen. HTML evolved as a screen-oriented subset of the *Standard Generalized Markup Language* (*SGML*). It allows "*portability* across platforms," meaning it allows all sorts of computers, anywhere in the world, to view documents containing HTML codes. The term **platform** refers to the combination of the type of computer and its operating system, browser, and so on. For example, an Intel-based personal computer (PC) running Microsoft's Windows operating system and Internet Explorer browser is one type of platform. A Macintosh running the System 8 operating system and Netscape's Navigator browser is a different type of platform.

The ML in HTML stands for "markup language." This term comes from the publishing industry and its proofreaders' marks. Editors use symbols like ¶, the paragraph mark, to indicate a change in the way the text appears on the page. Instead of symbols, HTML uses letters bracketed in the less-than (<) and greater-than (>) signs, also called angle brackets. For example, HTML uses <P> to indicate the start of a new paragraph.

We can use HTML to change the general way the text is laid out, but we are always at the mercy of the browser used to view our HTML document for the exact format. Some browsers recognize only a subset of the HTML codes and ignore the others. There is little consistency among the various browsers. Some will display headings like this:

This is a heading

Others will display the same heading like this:

This is a heading

Any one browser will, however, be consistent within itself in the way it displays text marked up in a particular way.

One central concept of HTML development is that *you are responsible for the content, but the browser handles the layout.* In other words, you have limited control of the format, so you should focus on the *content*—the information you are making available—and leave the formatting to the browser.

Browsers

A browser is the computer program (*interface*) you use to explore the World Wide Web. The browser program translates documents containing the HTML language into words and images on the screen. Most browsers

1. Respond to the following navigation buttons or keys (Figure 1.3, on page 6)
   - "Forward"
   - "Back"
   - "Restore" or "Refresh" (to retrieve page from Web server again)
   - "Home" (the Web page your computer system looks for first)
2. Print page (Figure 1.3, on page 6)
3. Provide a navigation line for entering a new Web address (Figure 1.4, on page 7)
4. Display images (Figure 1.5, on page 8)
5. Display translated HTML documents as pages (Figure 1.6, on page 9)
6. Display the HTML codes in a document (Figure 1.17, on page 24)

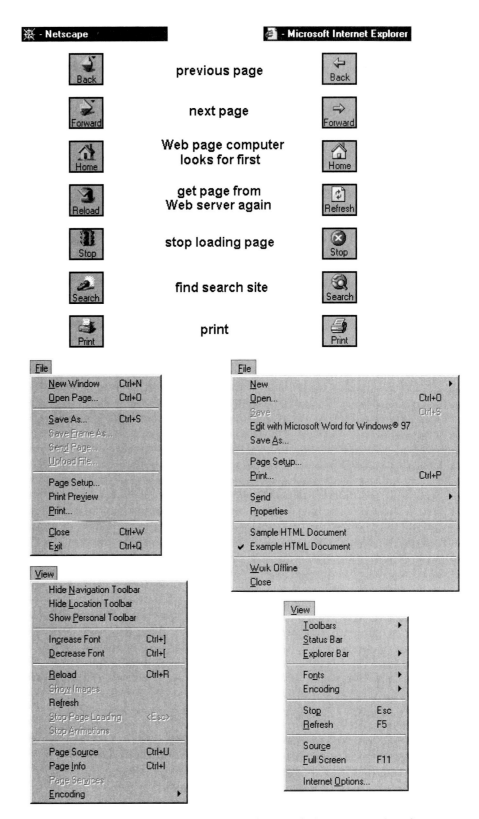

Figure 1.3 Navigation buttons, File menu options, and View menu options for popular graphical browsers.

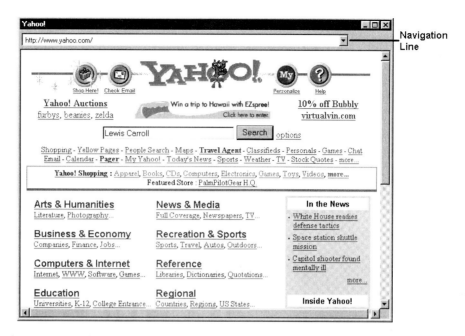

Figure 1.4 Graphical browser display with search site address in navigation line.

7. Play video and sound clips with the help of a ***plug-in,*** an independent program module that can be added to the browser

Navigator, Internet Explorer, and Lynx (pronounced "links") are three examples of browser programs. Browsers can be text-only, like Lynx, or graphical, like Navigator and Internet Explorer. Once a browser is installed, people often start their Web cruising at a ***search site***. These specialized Web pages are designed to help people find other pages by means of one or more keywords. The search site in Figure 1.4 is set to look for any Web pages that refer to Lewis Carroll. A list of popular search sites is presented at the end of this chapter.

Graphical Browsers

Graphical browsers, like Navigator (Figure 1.5) and Internet Explorer (refer again to Figure 1.6) display pictures, play sounds, and show animations. They are *multimedia* presentation tools. To take full advantage of HTML's multimedia capabilities your computer needs to have a color monitor and sound card to support speakers or headphones. Some people would say a microphone is mandatory input hardware.

Multimedia features place high demands on data transmission and storage hardware. It takes a lot of transmission time as well as disk space to utilize video and high fidelity sound. Figure 1.5 shows phred the Underground Web Server as seen with Netscape's Navigator browser.

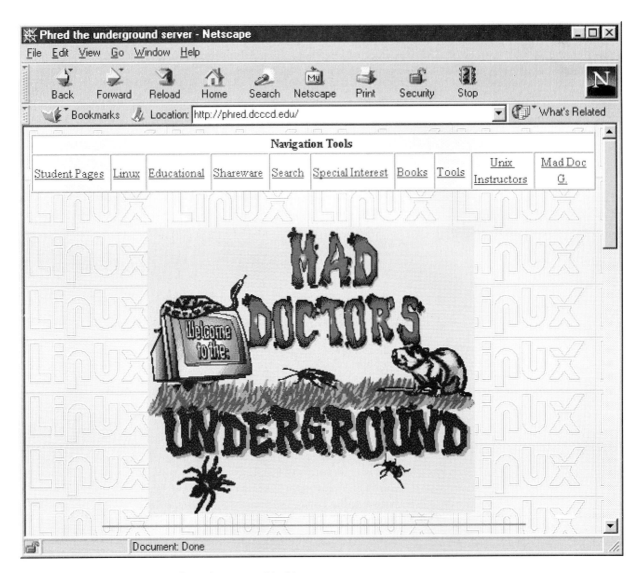

Figure 1.5 Display by Netscape's Navigator graphical browser.

Navigator

Currently Netscape's Navigator browser (Figure 1.5) is the most widely used graphical browser on the Web. The Netscape Communications Corporation, a subsidiary of America Online, also distributes Navigator as part of its Communicator package of desktop software. You will find that Navigator is always being upgraded to keep current with new HTML specifications. It is free to students and faculty.

In addition to the current release of Navigator, Netscape offers interested users access to *beta releases*. These releases are experimental versions that test new features before they become part of the current release. You can download Navigator from Netscape's home page at http://home.netscape.com. The term ***downloading*** means copying a file from another computer to your computer.

Internet Explorer

The other popular graphical browser is Microsoft's Internet Explorer (refer again to Figure 1.6). These two browsers, Netscape's Navigator and Microsoft's Internet Explorer, are major players in the current "browser wars" being fought on the Web. Microsoft is also tangling with the U.S. Justice Department as to whether a browser is independent of a computer's operating system. Microsoft claims that browsing the Internet is just another task performed by a computer's operating system. Since Microsoft sells the most popular operating system in the world, Windows, it hopes to gain an edge over Netscape by integrating Internet Explorer into the Windows package of desktop software.

Internet Explorer is also available through the Web using Microsoft's home page at http://www.microsoft.com. Beta copies of new releases are available from this Web site as well. Both companies offer online forums for discussing software problems and solutions. They also provide technical support documents for troubleshooting.

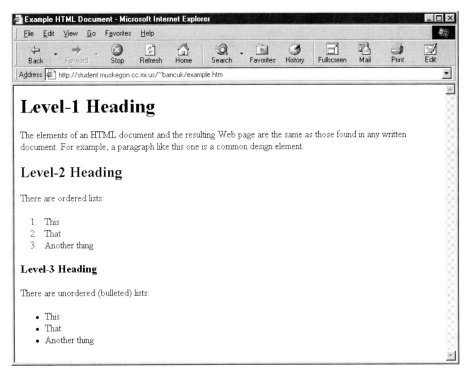

Figure 1.6 Microsoft's Internet Explorer graphical browser display of the HTML code in Figure 1.1.

Mosaic

The first popular graphical browser, called Mosaic, was developed by the National Center for Supercomputing Applications (NCSA) at the University of Illinois, Urbana-Champaign (Figure 1.7). The founding members of Netscape originally gained much of their expertise working on Mosaic. This browser is no longer being revised, but can be downloaded using the university's Web site at http://www.ncsa.uiuc.edu/SDG/Software/Mosaic/.

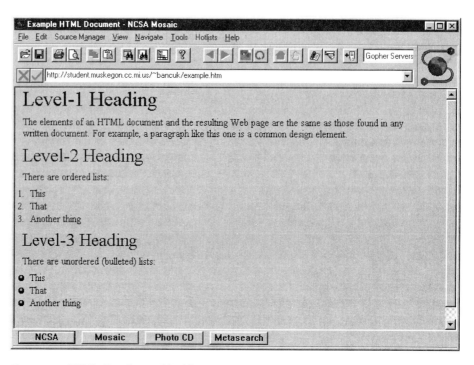

Figure 1.7 NCSA's Mosaic graphical browser display of the HTML code in Figure 1.1.

Text-Only Browsers

There is strong support for text-only browsers by the original community of Internet users. They maintain that the Web exists to share information and that most information can be more quickly shared if users don't have to wait for large graphic files to cross the Web. Many sophisticated Web cruisers use Lynx or another text-only browser when they want to access a lot of textual information quickly. They use graphical browsers only for obtaining images or for recreation on the Web.

Lynx

Lynx was developed at the University of Kansas (go Jayhawks!) for computer platforms using the UNIX operating system. It ignores all HTML references to colors, pictures, sounds, or videos. Figure 1.8 shows phred the Underground Web Server as it looks when displayed with the Lynx browser. This is the same home page shown with a graphical browser in Figure 1.5. This screen took less than a second to appear on Tim G's computer. Why did it load so fast with the Lynx browser? Because the graphic files were not transferred.

As you write HTML code, it is important to keep in mind the different ways that different browsers handle the documents you create. As a user, you can simply pick the browser you like best. But as a Web weaver, you need to try your pages with at least two different graphical browsers and a text-only browser to see how they work. Some graphical browsers have a text-only mode.

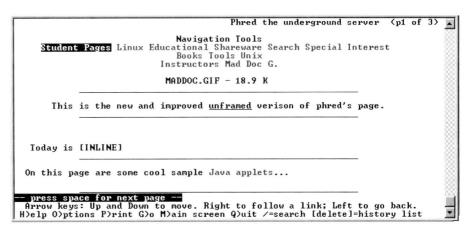

Figure 1.8 Lynx text-only browser display.

Nonvisual Browsers

Web weavers must also be aware of nonvisual applications for the Internet. A new generation of personal computer will come equipped with speech synthesizers. These systems will not only be used by visually impaired users, but by sighted people working away from their computer screens.

Audio

One new area where the popular graphical browsers can compete is in their ability to translate HTML code into sounds using the computer's speech synthesizer. The latest generation of HTML code can format sounds, called *voices.* As a Web weaver, you will be able to control the gender of the voice and even how fast it talks!

Braille

Specialized browsers are also available that convert HTML code into Braille output. These browsers have many of the same attributes and needs as text-only browsers in that they can render only text, not graphics, images, sound, or video.

What Is a URL?

Throughout our discussion of the World Wide Web, we will be using the term **URL.** URL stands for **Uniform Resource Locator.** It simply describes the location, or **Internet address,** of the specific resource we want to use for our document. The term URL is pronounced as three letters, "you are ell," not as one word, "erl." A URL can point to a different Web page, to another location in the current page, or to a component of a page, like an image. For example, http://home.netscape.com/ is the URL of the Netscape home page, and http://www.yahoo.com/ is Yahoo's home page. The **home page** is the first page or main page for a series of related Web pages called a **Web site.**

When we study links and anchors, we will be using different kinds of URLs. But every URL must conform to a set of rules. These rules allow browsers and other programs to understand the URL and use it to reliably move the data across the Internet from one location or page to another. When you create your Web page, it will have a URL that is unique to that page. That unique URL, or address, will allow anyone on the World Wide Web to find your page and view the information you place there.

The general form of a full URL is

`protocol://domain name/path/filename`.

For example, the page from the Electronic Text Library at the University of Virginia (Figure 1.2) that lets you browse for authors with a last name that starts with C is

`http://etext.lib.virginia.edu/modeng/modengC.browse.html`.

Here the protocol is `http://`, the domain name is `etext.lib.virginia.edu/`, the path is `modeng/`, and the filename is `modengC.browse.html`.

In some cases you need to specify only part of a URL. For example, to go to the Electronic Text Library at the University of Virginia, you would need to specify only the protocol and the domain name, `http://etext.lib.virgina.edu/`.

When the filename is missing, most computer systems use a filename of `index.htm` or `index.html`. Let's look at each of the three parts of the URL and see what they mean.

Protocol

The *protocol* of a URL identifies the format of the information being accessed from the Internet. The browser must know how to interpret what it finds. It is as if your browser could translate several different languages into English. Before it could translate a page, it would have to know what language it was translating. That is what the protocol tells the browser—how the information it is receiving is organized. There are seven common protocols, shown in Table 1.1. As you might expect, we will primarily use the *Hypertext Transfer Protocol* (*http*) with your browser to display the hyper documents created throughout this book.

Domain

The *domain name* is the second part of the URL. It specifies the physical location of the file or information resource. A *domain* is the computer that runs the Web server software handling the protocol specified in the first part of the URL. The domain portion of the URL starts immediately after the colon or the two slashes (//) that ends the protocol. The domain name ends with a single slash. You can specify the domain either by its IP address (discussed next) or by using a domain name that stands for the site's IP address.

Internet Protocol (**IP**) *addresses* are four sets of one, two, or three digits separated by periods. No three-digit number is ever greater than 255. An example of an IP address is 198.95.251.5. IP addresses identify specific computers on the Internet, including the World Wide Web. If you choose to use a domain name instead if an IP address, a special program called a *Domain Name Server* (*DNS*) will try to translate the domain name into the IP address. If it cannot translate the domain name, you will see the annoying "DNS unable to translate domain name" message.

PROTOCOL	EXAMPLE	DESCRIPTION
file:	file:///C|foobar.htm	The file protocol is used to locate a file you want the browser to read. Usually the file is located on the same computer as the document that points to it. Notice it has three slashes, not two, and the drive letter "C" is followed by a vertical bar, not a colon.
ftp:	ftp://ftp.fancyfoo.stuff/foobar.txt	Ftp is used to bring a resource from another computer to the user's computer. Usually ftp is used when you want your users to be able to download or copy a file to their computers.
gopher:	gopher://deep.gopher.hole/	The gopher protocol transfers control to a gopher site and allows you to display the files available on that *gopher space*, also called *gopher hole*.
http:	http://unreal.place.com/	Http is used for links that point to other Web pages.
mailto:	mailto:someone@somewhere.net	The mailto protocol will start a mail program if the browser supports mailto URLs. Mailto is often used to request feedback about a Web page. Notice there are no slashes.
news:	news:alt.some.cool.newsgroup news:C6491Rt@netplace.net	If the browser supports Usenet news URLs, the first example shown in the column to the left will open the newsreader and allow you to begin reading that newsgroup. The second example will just open the article specified from the newsgroup. Each article is given a specific number to identify it. Notice that there are no slashes.
telnet:	telnet://user:password@server:port telnet://server:port	The first example shown in the column to the left will login remotely at the computer specified, using the username and password supplied. This is a dangerous practice, because your username and password are visible in the HTML code. In the second example, the browser should prompt for a username and password before making the connection. It is a safer alternative. Always remember to tell your users what username and password to use if you don't supply one.

Table 1.1 Types of Internet protocols.

Since most people find numbers harder to remember than names, it is a better practice to tell someone to download software from home.netscape.com than from 198.95.251.53, the IP address. Domain names can be very long. They usually end in a two- or three-character extension. Common extensions are shown in Table 1.2. Some extensions also indicate the country of the domain. For example, a domain name that ends in .au indicates an Australian site, and one that ends in .fr indicates a location in France.

If you want to look at the main page for a domain, you can usually specify just the protocol and domain without specifying a path or filename. For example, if you want to see Netscape's home page, you can type the following into the navigation line for your browser: http://home.netscape.com/. If you want to look at Yahoo's home page, use http://www.yahoo.com/.

EXTENSION	MEANING
.edu	Educational site, usually a college or university
.com	Commercial site or business
.gov	Government site, like the White House or Senate
.org	Nonprofit organization
.net	Usually an ISP (Internet Service Provider)

Table 1.2 Common domain name extensions.

Path and Filename

If the resource you are connecting to is a file, then the URL will end in a filename. In the example for Figure 1.2, the URL of http://etext.lib.virgina.edu/modeng/modengC.browse.html was used. The path and filename appear after the forward slash that follows edu. The HTML document is called modengC.browse.html, and the path is called modeng, which is the name of the directory or subdirectory in which the file is located.

URLs are the heart of navigation across the World Wide Web, and we will use them throughout our exploration of HTML.

HTML Terminology

Like any other specialized skill, using HTML requires that you learn some specific terms. Some of the terms are logical, and some are, well, a little odd. If you're going to read books about HTML, talk with people about HTML, or cruise the Net to find out more about HTML, you will need to learn a handful of specialized terms.

Tags

One of the first terms you will run across is *tag.* Tags are HTML codes that are enclosed in angle brackets (< and >). These tags are used to lay out the Web page. For example, the <BR> tag adds a line break into the text. Other tags center text, insert graphics, or change the screen color. You will learn more about specific HTML tags in the chapters that follow.

Tags come in two general types: containers and empty tags. The tag <BR> is an *empty tag;* it does not hold, or surround, any text.

Containers

The other type of tag, a *container,* has both a starting tag and an ending tag. Between the starting and ending tags is information that is controlled by the container. For example, the *bold* container tag is very useful when formatting text. It looks like this in HTML:

This text is <B>bold</B>

This container would produce the following when viewed by most browsers:

This text is **bold**

The <B>bold</B> container makes the text it holds, or contains, appear in a bold font. If a bold font is not available, the browser may make the text appear in reverse video (white text on a black background) or underlined. Remember that the actual presentation of the text is up to the browser.

Notice that the bold tag starts with what looks like an empty tag (<B>) and ends with a slightly different form of that tag. The ending tag has a right, or forward, slash before the tag character (</B>). It is very important to place the ending tag correctly behind the desired text. In this case, if we left off the ending tag, the browser would bold the rest of the text in the document.

Attributes

Empty or starting container tags can contain other HTML elements called ***attributes***, which are special codes that modify the related tag. For example, the <P>paragraph<P> container identifies a paragraph of text. It has one attribute, **align,** which allows you to have the paragraph left justified, right justified, or centered in the line like this:

<P align="CENTER">Place this line in the middle of the page.</P>

Ending container tags cannot have attributes.

The browser will usually choose to align the text on the left margin unless you specify otherwise. In other words, left alignment is the default value. A ***default value*** is the option or feature a program uses when the user does not specify a particular one.

The **align** attribute is part of the starting tag. Let's look at the examples of this container in Figure 1.9 so that you can see how tags and attributes look in actual HTML code. If we put the code in Figure 1.9 (on page 16) into an HTML document, it will look like Figure 1.10 (on page 16) when displayed by a browser.

Don't worry if some of the code you see appears a little odd right now. You are just beginning your exploration of HTML. As with learning any new language, it will take a little time to figure it out.

```
<HTML>
<HEAD>
<TITLE>Paragraph Using align Attribute</TITLE>
</HEAD>
<BODY>
<P align="RIGHT">
Right is Right
</P>

<P align="CENTER">
Center is Middle
</P>

<P align="LEFT">
Left is Left
</P>

<P>
Left is also the Default
</P>

</BODY>
</HTML>
```

Figure 1.9 HTML code showing paragraph container with align attributes.

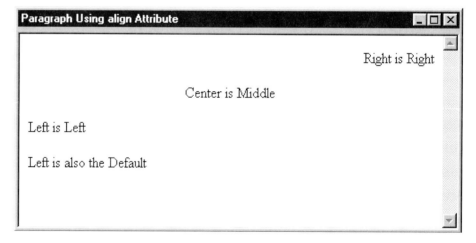

Figure 1.10 Browser display of HTML code in Figure 1.9, showing how the align attribute affects paragraph placement.

A Rule to Live By

Good HTML authors always close every container. We realize that some containers are migrating to the status of empty tags, and popular browsers no longer require the ending tag for them. HTML specifications are constantly changing; new tags are added, older tags are **deprecated,** meaning they are listed as nearing *obsolete* status, when they can no longer be used. The way tags are used evolves.

Regardless, professionals follow the rules until a tag is declared obsolete. The organization that oversees these changes is discussed in the next section.

One of the more interesting and yet confusing features of most HTML browsers is their ability to infer, or guess, when to close a container. For example, the code in Figure 1.11 will produce exactly the same results shown in Figure 1.10. Compare this poorly written HTML code with the code in Figure 1.9.

Notice that there are no closing paragraph tags in Figure 1.11. Most browsers will properly infer when you want to end one paragraph and start another, so you might be able to "get away" with using the code in Figure 1.11. But good Web weavers do not leave things to chance. One of the good coding rules to live by is to close every container, even those at the end of a document. Otherwise, you could produce some very strange-looking pages.

```
<P align="RIGHT">
Right is Right

<P align="CENTER">
Center is Middle

<P align="LEFT">
Left is Left

<P>
Left is also the Default
```

Figure 1.11 HTML code with end tags missing.

HTML Command Format

The <P> container provides a good example of the general format of an HTML command. It is used to contain the paragraphs within an HTML document. You will see exactly how to use this container when you build your first Web page in Chapter 2. For now we will use it to examine the format of an HTML command.

You can see from Figure 1.12 that there are three parts to an HTML container. The beginning tag, which may have attributes, is the first part. The text held by the container is the second part. The ending tag is the third part. If you choose not to use an attribute, the browser reading the document will choose a value, the default, for you. The general format of an empty tag is just like the starting tag of the container. We will explore both types of tags in more detail in Chapter 2.

```
<P align="RIGHT">Right is Right</P>
   |—— attribute ———|
|—— beginning tag ————|—— content of container ——|– ending tag –|
```

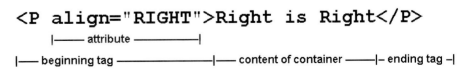

Figure 1.12 HTML command format.

World Wide Web Consortium (W³C)

You may be wondering who establishes and controls HTML protocols and tags. The *World Wide Web Consortium* (*W³C*) sets, for the most part, these standards. This international consortium was founded in 1994 to promote the evolution of the Web and to provide an open forum to organize and discuss changes. Over 200 commercial or academic members oversee W³C. It is physically hosted by the Massachusetts Institute of Technology in the United States, the Institut National de Recherche en Informatique et en Automatique in Europe, and Keio University in Japan.

Currently in force are the HTML 4.0 specifications originally published by the W³C on December 18, 1997, and revised April 24, 1998. HTML specifications developed by consortium members are first presented as a *working draft.* If the new tag or protocol has merit, it becomes part of a *proposed recommendation.* When W³C members reach consensus on a proposed recommendation, it is elevated to a *recommendation.* Software developers then design new browsers and other Internet tools using these recommendations. In some cases developers push the W³C by incorporating proposed recommendations into beta releases of their software. Once published, periodic updates then follow to correct minor problems with the recommendation. Figure 1.13 is from the April 24, 1998, revision.

Sometimes recommendations offer a new approach to an old problem. For example, the <STYLE> tag that changes font attributes has replaced the <BASEFONT> and <FONT> tags. The W³C takes a two-step approach to eliminating older tags. The first step is to list deprecated HTML tags as shown in Figure 1.13. As explained earlier, these tags are still supported by software but are designated as "on their way out." Eventually W³C members agree on when tags have become *obsolete,* meaning that they can no longer be used because the updated versions of the browsers will not recognize them.

Necessary Tools

To become a Web weaver, you need only three tools: a simple ASCII editor, an **HTML viewer** (software that lets you see what your document will look like on a browser), and an **Internet Service Provider** (**ISP**) to "host" your page. An ISP is a company or school that will put your document on a *Web server* (a computer on the Internet with a recognized domain name or IP address) so other people can browse your page from across the Internet. Making your page available on a known domain is called *hosting* your page. The **Web administrator** is the person who maintains the Web server, operating system, security, backup, and other basic computer "housekeeping." This person is not to be confused with a **Web master,** who is responsible for a collection of Web pages on a Web site.

Let's look at the three tools every Web author must have.

ASCII Editor

The first requirement for building Web pages is an editor that produces plain ASCII files as output. *ASCII* stands for *American Standard Code for Information Interchange.* An **ASCII editor** produces a standard ASCII file, meaning a file with

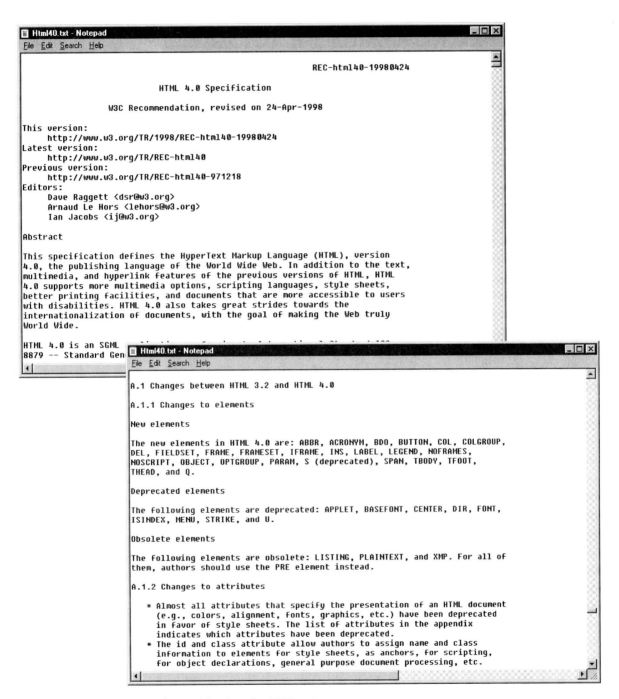

Figure 1.13 Excerpts of the W³C specifications for HTML 4.0.

just the text, no embedded word-processing codes. Most word-processing software will add formatting, font, and other types of codes to the document. Browsers don't know what to do with those extra characters. Figure 1.14 on page 20 shows some of the codes that appear in a word-processed file. As you can see, they make little sense!

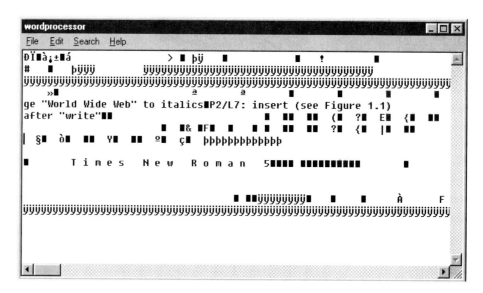

Figure 1.14 ASCII Editor displaying codes from word-processed file.

To produce HTML code, you need a simple editor. If you are using a Unix system, the vi editor is an excellent choice. The Notepad editor in Windows will also work. Most of the word processors, like Microsoft Word or WordPerfect, can save a file as plain ASCII if you specify it. You need to select the "Save as" option and ask for DOS text. Almost any word-processing or editing package can be used, but it is sometimes easier to produce HTML code with a simple editor. There are add-ons for some of the more popular word processors that enable them to act as HTML editors. Later in this chapter we will discuss specialized HTML editors.

HTML Viewer

There are three different ways you can view your document to see how it will appear on the World Wide Web. One of the easier ways to preview your documents is with your browser. Most browsers allow you to specify the source of the HTML documents you are browsing. For example, with Navigator and Internet Explorer, you can simply click on the File menu, click on Open, and type in the name of the file you just created. Or you can use the Browse feature to find your new document (touching the Control key and the O key at the same time will also invoke this option). Remember to save your document with an extension of .htm in Windows or .html in Unix so that viewer software will recognize it as an HTML document. For example, an HTML document called compare.htm on a computer running Windows would be called compare.html on a Unix system and compare.htm on Macintosh platforms.

The latest versions of most word-processing software can read HTML coding. If you are using an older word processor, check to see if you can download an HTML viewer add-on (option) for it. Several free packages add this feature to word processors, like Microsoft Word version 6.0. By using this type of viewer, you can see what your new document may look like on the page. You can check your choice of colors, fonts, and local images. But because these viewers are not connected to the Internet, they will not be able to link to other sites across the World Wide Web.

In addition to browsers and word-processor add-ons, several stand-alone HTML viewers are available for downloading from the Net. HTML Viewer is a package for Macintosh computers that allows the user to view HTML documents without having an online connection. I-View is a similar product for computers running Windows.

You should also have one of the text-only viewers so that you can see what your page will look like to users with text-only browsers like Lynx. Responsible Web weavers always produce pages of text that are accessible and usable with either graphical or nongraphical browsers.

Internet Service Provider (ISP)

Most people don't maintain a full-time, high-speed connection to the Internet. As a result, if you want to maintain a Web site, you need an organization that can store your Web pages and make them available on the Internet. As mentioned earlier, companies that host Web sites are called *ISPs* (*Internet Service Providers*). Your college may act as an ISP and host student Web sites. Or it may provide Internet access and e-mail but not the storage space or personal Internet address needed to maintain a Web site. Colleges usually ask students to pay additional fees to support these ISP capabilities. If you don't know what Internet services your college supports, ask your instructor or someone in student services.

As you might expect, services and the related fees vary among ISPs. Some charge a monthly fee for the storage space you use. Others include a fixed amount of space in their pricing but charge you for any space you use above the limit. For example, one ISP charges users $49.95 per year for Internet access. This ISP will host Web pages of up to 2 megabytes in size as part of the yearly fee. If the user needs more storage space, the cost is $1.95 per megabyte per month. There is no additional fee for connect time, e-mail messages sent or received, or any other services. However, technical support is available only during office hours, Monday through Friday.

Another ISP charges $19.95 a month. For this charge the user gets access to the Internet, an e-mail account with unlimited send and receive capabilities, a customized graphical browser, special services (like online stock portfolio management) and technical support 24 hours a day, seven days a week. If you want this ISP to host your Web site, you are charged an additional $2.50 per megabyte per month.

These two different ISPs illustrate some of the significant difference in services and price. Consider a budget-priced ISP if your are able to download your own browser and install it on your computer and don't need much technical support. If you want more support, or want to be able to just type install to load the customized browser the ISP sent you on the CD, you may wish to subscribe to a more expensive "value-added" ISP. As always, you get what you pay for.

Nice-to-Have Tools

You can get by with the tools mentioned in the previous section, but there are four other HTML tools that will make the job of building and maintaining Web pages much easier. First, although you can build Web pages with a simple ASCII editor, it is much easier and faster to use a special *HTML editor* to write your document. Second, you can take an existing file built with a word processor and run it though an *HTML text-file converter* to create an HTML document from the plain text. (Some HTML editors can also do this job.) Third, to ensure that your Web page works correctly, you can use one of the *HTML verifiers* to make sure your links are valid and your HTML syntax and grammar are correct. Fourth, you can use your Web pages to execute programs of your own creation through the use of a *JavaScript editor.* Let's look at these different tools individually.

HTML Editor

An ***HTML editor*** allows you to create an HTML document and see how the codes work. Many HTML editors are available for downloading from the Internet. Some are free, some are ***shareware,*** and others are commercial products. Don't forget that shareware is not freeware. While you can legally give copies of either to a friend, installing and using shareware obligates you to register the software and pay any registration fees.

There is quite a bit of variability in the way HTML editors work. As you can see in Figure 1.15, some editors show you all the HTML tags in the document. The user then switches to a preview screen to view the HTML document as a Web page. The advantage of this style of editor is that since you actually see the

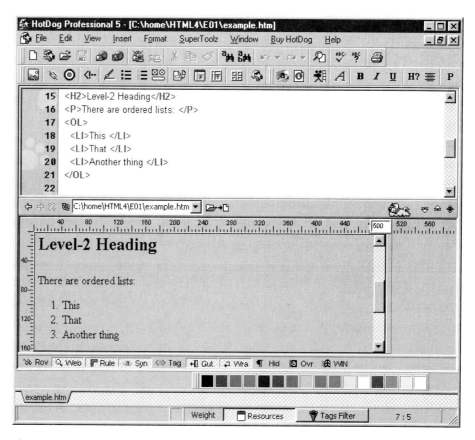

Figure 1.15 HTML code as it appears in Hotdog HTML editor.

tags and attributes, not simply the results, it is somewhat simpler to edit, or modify, the document. A disadvantage is that you need to switch back and forth between HTML view and Web view.

The editor in Figure 1.16 takes a more graphical approach to displaying the HTML tags in a document. This figure is displaying the same HTML code used in Figure 1.15. One disadvantage to this WYSIWYG approach is that the user must often infer which attributes are being used. Furthermore, you are never guaranteed that any independent HTML editor will handle the codes the same as your favorite browser. Notice how the level-2 heading is treated differently in Figures 1.15 through 1.18.

Figure 1.17 (on page 24) shows this file as it looks using Netscape's Composer, which is the HTML editor that comes with Netscape's Communicator software package. This editor allows you to bounce back and forth between the browser and editor. It shows you the HTML tags and provides a set of menus and buttons that assist you in editing the document. Buttons are used to insert new tags. Authors select attributes from pop-up menus.

The editing style you choose is a personal decision. Any of these editors will get the job done for you. However, as teachers we prefer editors that let you see as much of the code as possible. By working with HTML code at this level you get a better understanding of the relationships between the code and what ends up on the browser's screen (see Figure 1.18, on page 25).

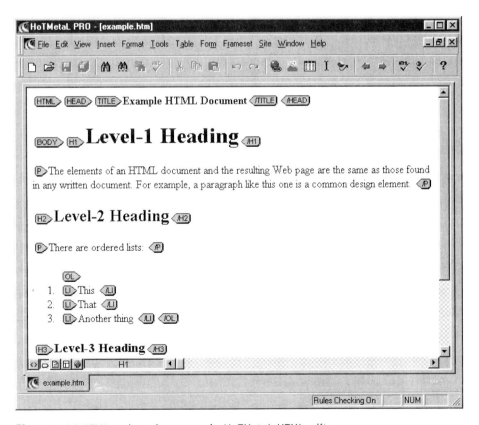

Figure 1.16 HTML code as it appears in HoTMetaL HTML editor.

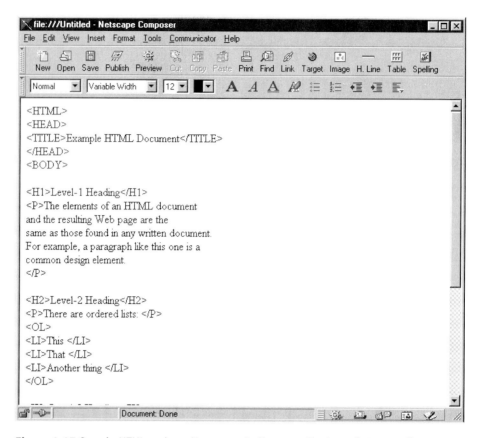

```
<HTML>
<HEAD>
<TITLE>Example HTML Document</TITLE>
</HEAD>
<BODY>

<H1>Level-1 Heading</H1>
<P>The elements of an HTML document
and the resulting Web page are the
same as those found in any written document.
For example, a paragraph like this one is a
common design element.
</P>

<H2>Level-2 Heading</H2>
<P>There are ordered lists: </P>
<OL>
<LI>This </LI>
<LI>That </LI>
<LI>Another thing </LI>
</OL>
```

Figure 1.17 Sample HTML code as it appears in Netscape Navigator's HTML editor.

HTML Text-File Converters

Several **HTML text-file converters** can be used to embed HTML codes within an existing text file and make it an HTML document. Some of these software tools are designed for the Microsoft word processor, Word, either version 2.0 or version 6.0. The ANT HTML converter and the GT_HTML converter are both available for downloading from the Internet. The latest version of Word comes with an HTML text-file converter. You convert a file by using the File menu's "Save as HTML" option. Quarter Deck Corporation produces the commercial converter, Web Author. In addition to these specialized conversion tools, most of the major HTML authoring packages can also take a text file as input and imbed HTML codes within it to make it an HTML document.

HTML Verifiers

Before publishing your page on the World Wide Web, you must make sure that it works. If you have some links that don't connect, or some containers that are left unclosed, your users may end up with results you didn't intend. To solve these problems, you can personally test each link and exercise each part of your page to ensure that it performs as expected. However, if you have a large set of

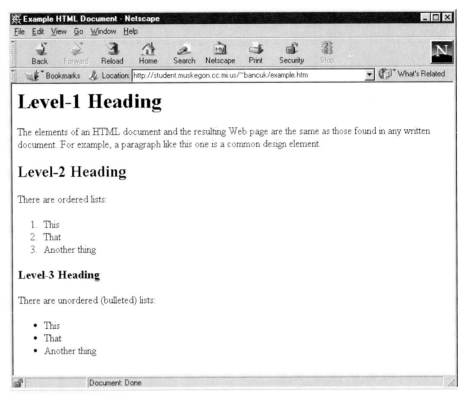

Figure 1.18 HTML code as it appears in Navigator browser.

pages with hundreds of links, it would take a lot of time to do the testing. Some tools are available on the World Wide Web that will check your pages for errors, testing each link and making sure the syntax is correct. One of the better HTML verifiers, or *verification programs,* is called Weblint (the URL is listed in this chapter). You can also visit Doctor HTML or WebTech to have your pages evaluated. If you are building a large Web site or for some other reason cannot take the time to evaluate all your links and syntax, you might want to use one of these verification services.

JavaScript Editor

Just as an HTML editor makes writing and testing HTML somewhat easier, a *JavaScript editor* can simplify the task of building and testing JavaScript code. We will provide you with an overview of JavaScript in Chapter 13. For now let's just say that the JavaScript editor helps you write your own computer programs that become part of the Web page. Figure 1.19 shows the opening screen for a popular JavaScript editor called ScriptBuilder. It shows some of the library tools available in the left frame, and the source code for an HTML page that has a JavaScript on the right. Notice how the different parts of the script look different. They are also colored differently to help the author distinguish them. If you are going to use JavaScript, investing in a good JavaScript editor can significantly lighten your load.

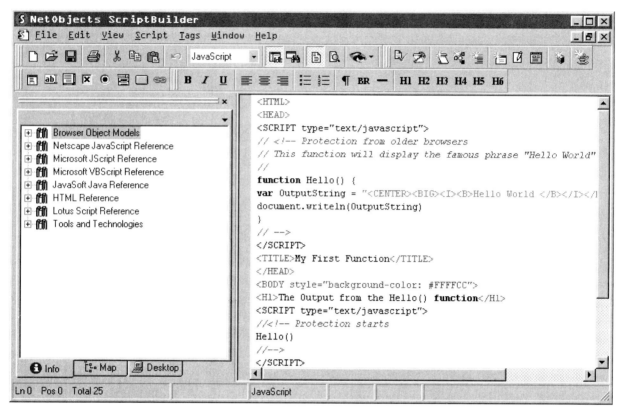

Figure 1.19 JavaScript editor.

Places to Get Neat Stuff on the Net An astounding number of Web sites provide software that works with HTML. What follows is only a partial listing of the available software. As you know, URLs change from day to day, so if one of these sites is no longer available, you can use a search site to find other sites that are more current. This list is a place to start, not an exhaustive one.

Browsers

- **Netscape** (http://home.netscape.com). This is one of the favorite browsers for the Web. You can download the most recent version of this browser, and if you are associated with a school, you can register your copy for free. From this site you can download the Navigator browser for several platforms including both Macintosh and Windows platforms.
- **Internet Explorer** (http://www.microsoft.com). This is the other "big" browser in the browser wars. You can download the most recent version of this browser free from Microsoft.
- **Lynx** (http://www.ukans.edu/about_lynx/about_lynx.htm and ftp://ftp2.cc.ukans.edu/pub/DosLynx/readme.htm). This is one of the most often used nongraphical, or text-only, browsers. You should test your

page with a nongraphical browser so you can address the needs of those users who don't believe that a picture is worth a thousand words. The first URL given here tells you about Lynx, and you can download it from the second URL.

- **Cyberdog** (http://cyberdog.apple.com). This is one of the more popular Macintosh browsers available for downloading.

HTML Editors

A wide selection of HTML editors exists. Many are shareware or freeware, and some are commercial packages. Several are tools that add features to word processors like Microsoft Word. The following list is just a small sample of the available products.

- **HotDog** (http://www.sausage.com). This one of the better HTML editors if you want to see HTML presented as the language rather than as the outcome. If you purchase the professional version, it includes a page viewer, so you don't need a browser. However, the page viewer is limited in the attributes it accepts. Therefore, it is best to have a browser available to view the page.
- **HoTMetaL** (http://www.sq.com). This editor is preferred by nearly half the HTML community because it has very strong validation, or verification, routines. It tries to be somewhat WYSIWYG, which distracts some Web weavers. You will need a browser to view your page.
- **PageSpinner** (http://www.algonet.se). This is one of the more commonly used Macintosh editors.
- **Arachnid** (http://www.uiowa.edu). This is a very popular Macintosh HTML editor. There are fewer Macintosh editors than those built for the Intel-based computers, but Macintosh users are very loyal to their particular favorite.

Conversion Programs

If you need to convert an existing electronic file into an HTML document, you can use an HTML editor or one of the following conversion tools.

- **ANT HTML** (http://www.mcia.com/ant/antdesc.htm). This tool works with both Word for Windows and Word for Macintosh.
- **WP2X** (http://www.milkyway.com/People/Michael.Richardson/wp2x.html) This tool works with WordPerfect documents
- **GT_HTML** (http://www.hatech.edu/work_html). This tool works with both the Word for Windows and Word for Macintosh.
- **Cyberleaf** (http://www.ileaf.com/ip.html). This tool works with Microsoft Word, WordPerfect, and Framemaker.

HTML Verifiers

It is important to ensure that your Web page contains valid links and correct syntax. You can use these HTML verifiers at the URLs listed.

- **MOMspider** (http://www.ics.uci.edu/pub/websoft/MOMspider). This is a commonly used verifier.

- **Doctor HTML** (http://www.sai.msu.su/admin). You need to be patient if you use Doctor HTML. It may take a little while for the analysis of your site to be sent back to you.
- **Weblint** (http://html.tqn.com/library/bl weblint.htm or http://www.weblint.com). The first address allows you to download a copy of WebLint. The second allows you to enter a URL, and the WebLint code at that site will evaluate it.
- **W³C** (http://validator.w3c.org). The validation service of the W³C!

W³ Consortium

You can find the latest HTML specifications at the W³C's Web site found at http://www.w3.org.

Additional Search Sites

Many new and better HTML tools will become available as more and more people begin to use the Web to transfer information. Following are some of the more popular search tools for exploring the Web to find additional resources.

- **Yahoo** (http://www.yahoo.com)
- **Altavista** (http://altavista.digital.com)
- **Snap** (http://www.snap.com)

Key Terms

ASCII editor
Attribute
Browser
Default value
Deprecated tags
Document
Domain name
Downloading
Home page
HTML editor
HTML text-file converter
HTML viewer
Hyper document
Hypertext Markup Language (HTML)
Internet address
Internet Protocol (IP) address
Internet Service Provider (ISP)
Link
Page
Platform
Plug-in
Protocol

Search site
Shareware
Tag
Uniform Resource Locator (URL)
Web administrator
Web master
Web site
White space

Review Questions

1. What is the definition for each of the key terms?

2. With respect to the Internet, what is the difference between a document and a page?

3. Who or what controls a Web page's content and layout?

4. Why is a hyper document considered more useful than a standard text document?

5. What five features are common to most browsers?

6. What are the names of three graphical browsers and one text-only browser?

7. How many browsers should a Web weaver use to test a newly designed Web page?

8. Identify and describe seven protocols used on the Internet.

9. List the extensions used by schools, business, ISPs, nonprofit organizations, and the government.

10. What special characters enclose HTML tags?

11. In HTML container tags what distinguishes the ending tag from the beginning tag?

12. What does the World Wide Web Consortium do?

13. Describe the five-step life cycle of an HTML tag.

14. Describe three tools every Web weaver uses.

15. What are three situations that might require additional fees from ISPs?

Exercises

1.1. Use an ASCII editor to describe the computer platform you are using for this class.

1.2. Find and print two Web site designs: one you like and one you don't like.

1.3. Find and print the latest revision to the HTML specifications. Your instructor might want to limit the number of pages you output.

1.4. Use the Internet to find a page where you can get a legal copy of your favorite browser, and employ an ASCII editor to explain how you would do it.

1.5. Print the HTML code for the home page of a Web site you like to use.

1.6. Visit two search sites on the Net, and explore pages that deal with HTML issues. Record the URLs of the pages you visit, and share them with your classmates.

## CHAPTER two

YOUR FIRST WEB PAGE

Now that you know some of the terminology used in HTML, it's time to build a simple page. The purpose of the World Wide Web is to share information. Your page should provide unique information to the users in a way that is easy to understand and pleasant to view. Remember that not all the users will have graphical browsers, so build a page in a way that is usable in both graphical and text-only modes. Let's look at the basic tags used in every HTML document.

HTML Tags

As mentioned in Chapter 1, in HTML there are two major types of markup labels: empty elements (tags) and containers. ***Empty elements*** are used for page formatting. An empty element has no closing tag and so does not enclose any text. It starts with a left angle bracket (<) followed immediately by the tag identifier, or name. Next come any ***attributes***—special words that modify the way the tag works—separated by spaces. The tag ends with a right angle bracket (>). For example, <HR width="50%"> is an empty tag that puts a line across the screen. The attribute, width="50%", determines how long the line is, in this case 50 percent of the screen width.

Container elements are used to manipulate, or control, the contents placed within them. Containers begin with a starting tag, which is formatted with angle brackets like an empty tag. They also have an ending tag that marks the end of the text they contain, or surround. The ending tag starts with a left angle bracket, has a slash (/) preceding the tag identifier, and ends with a right angle bracket. </HTML> is an example of an ending tag. There can be no attributes on an ending tag, and the tag identifier (name) must be preceded by a slash (/).

Creating an HTML Template

The starting container element that surrounds the whole Web page is <HTML>. It is closed by the </HTML> tag. All the contents of a Web page or document must be enclosed by the <HTML> *contents of page* </HTML> container. This is the beginning of your first HTML document.

There are a handful of other HTML elements along with the <HTML></HTML> container shown in Figure 2.1 that are used in almost every HTML document. We recommend that you type them into your computer using an ASCII editor and save them as `HTMLtemp.htm` or `HTMLtemp.html`. Use this file as a template whenever you create a new HTML document. Remember that when you modify this template, you need to save the new file under a different name, or you will overwrite the template.

All the elements used in Figure 2.1 are containers. Notice that a container element can contain other container elements. When this happens, Web weavers should double-check that they do not accidentally reverse the order of the ending tags. In Figure 2.1 the <TITLE> tag is inside the <HEAD> tag. Therefore, the </TITLE> ending tag must precede the </HEAD> ending tag.

What follows is an overview of how these tags work and some of the common attributes associated with each tag.

<HTML>HTML Document</HTML>

Description: first and last line in every HTML document.
Type: container.
Attributes: dir, lang, and version.
Special note: may be preceded by SGML <!DOCTYPE> tag.

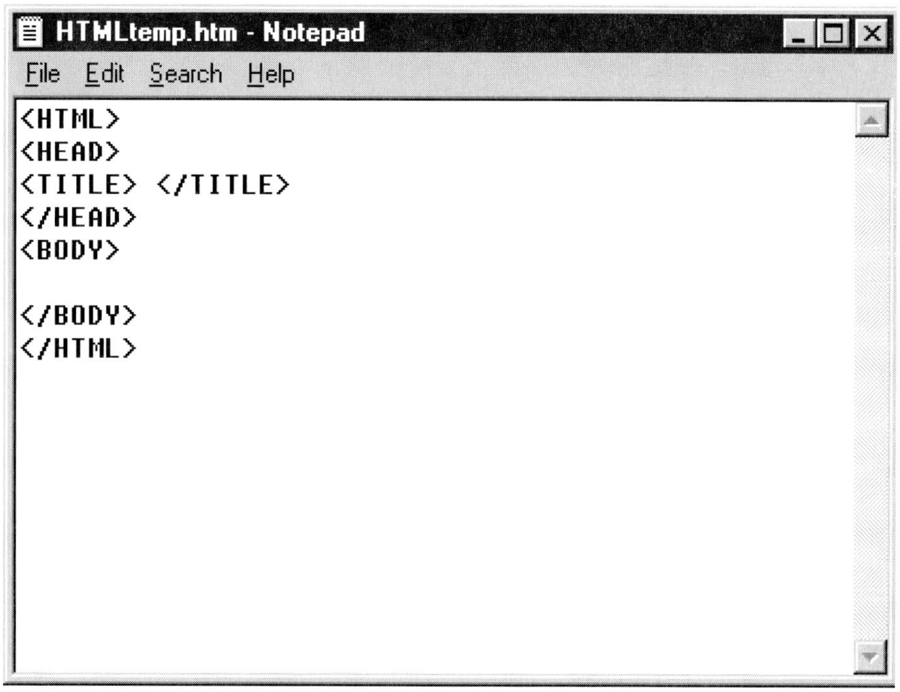

```
HTMLtemp.htm - Notepad                      _ □ ✕
File  Edit  Search  Help
<HTML>
<HEAD>
<TITLE> </TITLE>
</HEAD>
<BODY>

</BODY>
</HTML>
```

Figure 2.1 HTML template.

The <HTML> tag identifies the type of document we are creating, as well as marking the beginning and ending of our Web page. If you look at Figure 2.2 (on page 34), you will see the <HTML></HTML> container tags surround all the other tags and text that make up an HTML document. Browsers recognize HTML tags in either uppercase or lowercase; however, the specification describes them as uppercase only, so you should code them in uppercase. In this text, we will show the HTML tags in uppercase to follow the standard and to help distinguish them from the actual text. Many experienced Web weavers code their HTML like this because it makes it much easier to read and maintain. Nevertheless, as you explore the Web, you will run across pages where most or all of the tags are lowercase. This is just an author preference; browsers don't care.

version

The <HTML> tag has three attributes you can use. However, the **version** attribute was deprecated in the HTML 4.0 specifications. Interestingly, it was deprecated in favor of the *SGML* tag <!DOCTYPE> (discussed next). Both of these tags tell the browser which HTML specifications were used to create the document. For example, version="-//W3C//DTD HTML 4.0 Final//EN" indicates the document was created using the HTML 4.0 specifications for English. However, including the version attribute can cause problems with some browsers, so most experts advise against its use.

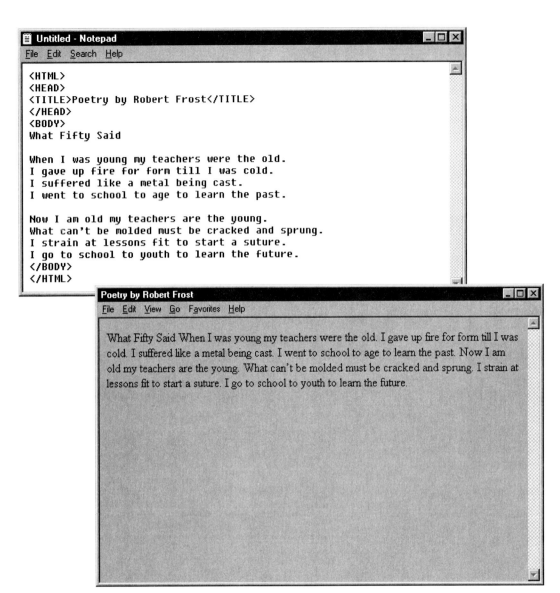

Figure 2.2 Robert Frost poem as HTML document and as displayed by a browser.

<!DOCTYPE>

Some corporate Web site administers require that authors identify in any new document which version of the HTML specifications they used. This information is beneficial when a company employs many Web weavers. The W³C now recommends that authors use the SGML <!DOCTYPE> tag when they need to identify which HTML specifications were used. As mentioned in Chapter 1, HTML is actually a subset of the universally recognized *Standard Generalized Markup Language* (*SGML*). These tags were adopted by the International Standards Organization (ISO) in 1988 to describe an electronic document.

```
<!DOCTYPE HTML PUBLIC "-//W3C//DTD HTML 4.0//EN"
"http://www.w3.org/TR/REC-html40/strict.dtd">
<HTML dir="RTL" lang="en">
<!-- Author: Your Name -->
<!-- Created: mm/dd/yy -->
<HEAD>
<TITLE>Poetry by Robert Frost</TITLE>
</HEAD dir="LTR" lang="en">
<BODY>
<H1 align="CENTER">What Fifty Said</H1>

<P>When I was young my teachers were the old.
I gave up fire for form till I was cold.
I suffered like a metal being cast.
I went to school to age to learn the past.
</P>

<P>Now I am old my teachers are the young.
What can't be molded must be cracked and sprung.
I strain at lessons fit to start a suture.
I go to school to youth to learn the future.
</P>
</BODY>
</HTML>
```

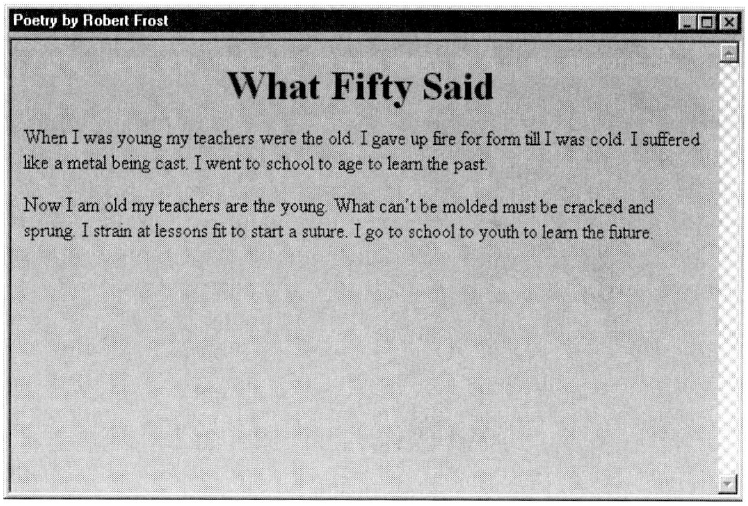

Figure 2.3 HTML document including SGML tag, comments, heading, and paragraph tags.

When used, the <!DOCTYPE> is an empty tag that precedes the <HTML></HTML> container. In other words, this is the first tag in the document. If you used the English specifications for HTML 4.0 to create the document (Figure 2.3), the following <!DOCTYPE> tag should be used:

```
<!DOCTYPE HTML PUBLIC "-//W3C//DTD HTML 4.0//EN"
"http://www.w3.org/TR/REC-html40/frameset.dtd">
```

Notice that this tag references the Web site with the HTML 4.0 specifications. Like HTML tags, this tag can be placed on one or more lines. Where the author breaks the line does not matter. Usually authors break long lines to make the code easier to read.

dir

The HTML 4.0 specifications brought with them additional emphasis on the internationalization of the Internet. Both the **dir** and **lang** (discussed next) attributes address this issue and are recognized by almost every HTML container. The **dir** attribute sets the base direction for displaying and printing text. You can set this attribute to one of two values: LTR for left-to-right and RTL for right-to-left. For example, if you were using English, Spanish, or some other Indo-European language, the following HTML code would set the directionality of a Web page to left-to-right: `<HTML dir="LTR">`. Languages like Hebrew that are read and written from right to left would utilize code that looks like this: `<HTML dir="RTL"`.

lang

The **lang** attribute specifies the base language of an element's attribute values and text content as seen in Figure 2.3. The HTML 4.0 specifications have this to say about the **lang** attribute:

> The intent of the **lang** attribute is to allow user agents [browsers] to render content more meaningfully based on accepted cultural practice for a given language. This does not imply that user agents should render characters that are atypical for a particular language in less meaningful ways; user agents must make a best attempt to render all characters, regardless of the value specified by lang (section 8.1).

While the popular browsers often default to English ("en" is the language code for English), the **lang** attribute allows the Web weaver to handle language-dependent content. Doing so will help the browser to properly render quotation marks, spacing, hyphenation, and ligatures. On a broader level, spell checkers and grammar checkers can benefit from having the language identified. Furthermore, using the **lang** attribute will help search sites document a page's content and help speech synthesizers pronounce words.

The **lang** attribute is set equal to a language code. The following HTML code sets the page's language to Spanish: `<HTML lang="es">`. The language codes can be divided into a primary code and a subcode. Two-letter primary codes are reserved for the ISO 639 standard for language abbreviations. Here are some common two-letter primary codes:

Arabic—ar	Hindi—hi
Chinese—zh	Italian—it
Dutch—nl	Japanese—ja
French—fr	Portuguese—pt
German—de	Russian—ru
Greek—el	Spanish—es
Hebrew—he	

The subcode identifies a dialect of the primary language, such as the English spoken in the United States versus the English spoken in Great Britain. In both cases the primary code is "en", but the subcode is different and is separated from the primary code by a hyphen. For U.S. English, the code is <HTML lang="en-US">. For British cockney version of English, the code is <HTML lang="en-cockney">. Some of the subcodes identify unique languages like Navajo (lang="i-navajo"), spoken by some Native Americans, or even Klingon (lang="x-klingon"), which is spoken by no one of this world.

Other than in Figure 2.3, we will forgo the use of the **lang** and **dir** attributes in order to keep our examples as simple as possible. This is not done to underplay the importance of these elements, but to focus attention on the new elements being discussed at the time and demonstrated by the related screen capture of the browser's display.

<HEAD>Header data</HEAD>

Description: provides descriptive information about a document as part of the header.
Type: container.
Attributes: dir, lang, and profile.

The <HEAD> container can include the **dir** and **lang** attributes just discussed. It primarily serves to identify the other tags that make up the header. The complete <HEAD> container is always placed between the <HTML> tag and the <BODY> tag. Because it is always located in this area of the document, the <HEAD> and </HEAD> tags can be inferred by some browsers. Therefore, you may find Web pages without a <HEAD> container. Generally, you should not depend on the browser to infer the location of a tag, because it may not guess the way you want it to. The <HEAD> container can include a variety of tags that define and manage the content of the document (Table 2.1, on page 38). The most commonly used element within the <HEAD> container is the <TITLE> tag (discussed shortly).

profile

The **profile** attribute is set to a URL that identifies information the browser should use when rendering or indexing the contents of the related Web page. The attribute is used in conjunction with the <META> tag that is discussed in detail in Chapter 12. The contents of the <META> element usually identify information about a document rather than document content. One application could be for search sites to use a common profile to identify the author, copyright information, and publication date of a collection of Web pages. The HTML code would look like this: <HEAD profile="http://www.bugsbeewee. com/profiles/catalog">. Applications for the **profile** attribute are evolving as we write this book.

TAG	FUNCTION
<BASE>	Sets the base URL for the document; used if the URL of the document is not the base for the other URL references.
<BASEFONT>	Sets the size of the font for the document. The default is 3. Deprecated in HTML 4.0 specifications.
<ISINDEX>	Indicates that the page can be searched.
<LINK>	Defines the relationship between the current document and another document on the Web.
<META>	An additional tag that can specify additional Web server name-value pairs.
<NEXTID>	An historical entry in the HTML standard—don't use it.
<STYLE>	Identifies external or document-level style sheets that control text formatting.
<SCRIPT>	Contains one or more functions written in one of the scripting languages like JavaScript or Visual Basic.
<TITLE>	The only tag that is *required* in the <HEAD> of the document. Very important because it should accurately describe your page.

Table 2.1 Tags used within the <HEAD> container.

<TITLE>Descriptive title</TITLE>

Description: provides descriptive information about the document for display at the top of the screen, not in the body of the document.
Type: container.
Attributes: dir and lang.
Special note: every HTML document must have a <TITLE> element.

The <TITLE> element can include the **dir** and **lang** attributes. It is used to identify the title of the document you are building and is required to be placed inside the <HEAD> container. If you enclose other tags in the <TITLE> element, they are ignored. See Figure 2.2 for a sample <TITLE> in the HTML code and its appearance in a browser.

Notice that the browser displays the title along the top of the screen or window. Many people confuse headings with the title and thus look for the title to be displayed in the body of the page. Most browsers, if they display the title at

all, display it outside the actual text area of the page. The title is a required part
of a Web ？？e, and it is important for three reasons:

1. ？？？？who visit your page may use the title in a *Bookmark, Favorite,* or
   ？？*try.* It should help them define the contents of the page so they
   ？？？turn to that page if they wish.

   ？？rch site or cataloging program may return only the title as
   ？？your page. People may make the decision whether to
   ？？ot based on this information.

   ？g the Net and come upon your page should have
   ？ts when they arrive.

   ？ortant to have a descriptive title. However, your
   ？many graphical browsers place the title in the
   ？ng titles may be cut off. Examples of some

？？？/TITLE>
？？ge </TITLE>
？？a Turtles </TITLE>

？ood, either because they do not give enough in-
？or because they are so long that they will be cut off

？？ </TITLE>
？My Home Page </TITLE>
？？> Really Cool Pictures of Turtles I Have Taken While On Vacation
？ITLE>

The title must be plain text. Do not use any tags within it, because they will
be ignored. Choose a title that will draw interest to your page and that accurately reflects the contents.

<BODY>Majority of document</BODY>

Description: identifies the contents of the Web page.
Type: container.
Attributes: alink, background, bgcolor, class, dir, id, lang, link,
onClick, onDblClick, onKeyDown, onKeyPress, onKeyUp, onLoad,
onMouseDown, onMouseMove, onMouseOut, onMouseOver,
onMouseUp, onUnload, style, text, title, and vlink.

Before version 3 of HTML was released, the <BODY> tag had no attributes.
Anything within the <BODY></BODY> container was called the "body content." This container holds the majority of your page. HTML version 3.0 introduced a series of attributes to give the author greater control over the appearance
of the document. Later in this chapter we will discuss the most commonly used
<BODY> attributes.

The remainder of this chapter will concentrate on the HTML tags used within the <BODY></BODY> container. These are the tags you use to render your Web page. You need to learn how to use these tags at two different levels:

1. In creating eye-catching pages that communicate the desired information to the reader.
2. In creating easy-to-read HTML documents that other Web weavers can readily understand and, if necessary, easily modify.

The mastery of both levels is what separates the amateurs from the professionals.

Two types of attributes have taken on elevated importance with the HTML 4.0 specifications: styles and events. This is a result of the increased use of mouse-controlled graphical browsers. While these attributes are discussed in detail later in the book, you need to be aware of the design issues they bring to Web page layout.

Styles

A *style* is a set of formatting rules that indicates to a browser how the author would like to display the contents of all or part of a page. The style can identify alignment, size, color, font characteristics, and so on. The HTML 4.0 specifications have introduced *cascading style sheets (CSS)*, with which the Web weaver can create several different style sheets that apply to the same document. A cascading style sheet can be either an independent document linked to the Web page or document specific and defined within the page itself. In either case the style sheet overrides the default attributes assigned to a tag. This may seem like a trivial matter to casual Web page designers. However, the proper handling of CSS can save Web masters hundreds of hours of work when modifying HTML documents.

The simplest way to change an attribute's default value is with an *inline style,* meaning one that is changed as it is being rendered by the browser. This is accomplished with the **style** attribute that sets different formatting options. For example, the level-1 heading in Figure 2.4 that defaults to a bold black font at the top of the document can be changed to a red italic font using the color and font features of the **style** attribute. The HTML code (also shown in Figure 2.4) would look like this: `<H1 style="color: red; font-style: italic">Heading 1</H1>`.

Because an inline style overrides document-level and linked style sheets, its spurious use can cause havoc on pages that need to follow a sitewide formatting standard required by many businesses.

This is not to say that inline styles should not be used. Quite the contrary, they are used to add emphasis by changing the standard presentation format. Furthermore, learning the different formatting attributes and inline style helps you explore design options that are available with different elements. In Chapters 5 and 8 we will address how style sheets are used in professional Web site development and management.

Intrinsic Events

Mouse activities, like click and double-click, and document changes, like loading or unloading a page, are called ***intrinsic events***. Moving the mouse pointer over an area of the screen, loading a picture, or performing any computer activity initiated

```
<HTML>
<HEAD>
<TITLE>Heading Tag (H1-H6) Demonstration</TITLE>
</HEAD>
<BODY>
<H1>Heading 1</H1>
<H2>Heading 2</H2>
<H3>Heading 3</H3>
<H4>Heading 4</H4>
<H5>Heading 5</H5>
<H6>Heading 6</H6>

<H1 style="color: red; font-style: italic">Heading 1</H1>
</BODY>
</HTML>
```

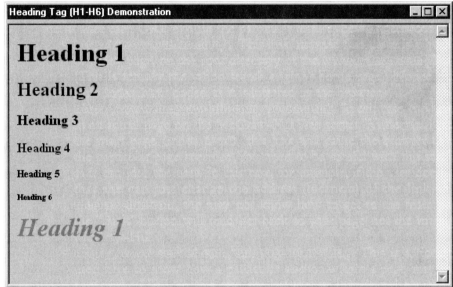

Figure 2.4 HTML code showing heading tags with and without inline styles.

by using a Web page are all considered intrinsic events. Sophisticated Web page designs can use JavaScript scripts that intercept various intrinsic events and act upon them. JavaScript event-handling code is discussed in Chapter 13. You will see attributes like onClick or onLoad listed for several tags used within the <BODY> container.

Editing an HTML Document

As you can see from the browser view of Figure 2.2, there is a lot more to HTML than placing <BODY> tags around text. We need to introduce to you some commonly used HTML tags that will make a Web page more readable. You should have open an *ASCII editor* and an *HTML viewer,* preferably a popular graphical browser, as you read the following.

Once the text and tags are entered into the ASCII editor, save the file (document) on disk with either an .htm or .html filename extension. To keep things consistent throughout this textbook, we will be using the .htm extension. After the HTML document is saved on disk, you can view it by using the browser's File menu Open option. The browser will display the contents of any .htm or .html file you load from a disk.

Once you have the document loaded into the ASCII editor and the page displayed in the browser, you can start editing the HTML tags in the editor. When you make a change to the document, you should immediately save the new version to disk. The browser will not display the changes until you refresh or reload the document. There is a "Refresh" or "Reload" button on the toolbar. An HTML editor lets you do the same jumping between the document view of HTML tags and the page view, but it may not display the rendered page exactly like a browser will.

<!-- comment -->

Description: browsers ignore any text enclosed within this tag. Authors use comment tags to annotate an HTML document.
Type: empty.
Attributes: none.
Special note: use this tag to identify the author and original creation date of the document.

Before we go on with building our first page, it is time to discuss the need to annotate your work, which involves use of the comment tag. As you write your Web page, it is important to add **comments** that identify who created it, when it was created, and, where appropriate, brief explanations of why you have done what you have done. Text enclosed in the <!-- comment --> container will not appear when your page is browsed (see Figure 2.3), but it will appear when the source document is viewed (again, see Figure 2.3). Many authors make the mistake of putting in comments that tell what they did but not why:

```
<BODY link="#FF00FF" vlink="#00FF00">.

<!-- Make the Link colors FF00FF and the vlink 00FF00 -->.
```

This comment tells what has been done, but the same information can be read from the HTML. A much better set of comments would be as follows:

```
<BODY link="#FF00FF" vlink="#00FF00">

<!-- Set LINK to Magenta and VLINK to Green -->

<!-- Use these colors to match the school's colors -->
```

Now we know not only what colors were chosen but why they were chosen instead of the default colors.

Your comments are designed as much as for you as for other Web weavers. It is very frustrating to come back to modify your page at some later date and have no earthly idea why you have built some particular elements the way you did. Well-written comments can guide you back through your logic and remind you of why you did what you did.

It is also handy to include comments on where you found the images and backgrounds you used. That way, should you lose them from your local disk, they can easily be retrieved again. Moreover, it is courteous to give credit to those other Web authors who have allowed you to use their artwork.

Comments should be only one line long and should not contain any other HTML tags. Following is an example of a comment that might follow a <HEAD> tag:

`<!-- Author: Your Name -->`

`<!-- Created: mm/dd/yy -->`

These comments will be seen only if the user elects to view the source code of the page (Figure 2.3). Careful, consistent use of comments will help you maintain your page. Comments will also help other Web weavers who want to understand how you achieved your results or who might someday work with your page.

<H1>Heading</H1> <H2></H2> <H3></H3> <H4></H4> <H5></H5> <H6></H6>

Description: identifies one of six levels of headings.
Type: container.
Attributes: align, class, dir, id, lang, onClick, onDblClick, onKeyDown, onKeyPress, onKeyUp, onMouseDown, onMouseMove, onMouseOut, onMouseOver, onMouseUp, style, and title.

A document that contains page after page of unbroken text can be very difficult for a user to read. Web pages should be broken up with appropriate headings to divide the text flow into manageable pieces. HTML allows six different levels of heading elements (<H1> </H1> . . . <H6> </H6>). The way the headings are displayed depends on the browser used to read the document. Some browsers will display the headings in different sizes of fonts. Others may indicate a header by bolding it, underlining it, moving it about the page, or changing its color. In addition, users can define how a browser will display headings as part of a style sheet. The code in Figure 2.4 specifies six different headings, which are shown the way Navigator or Internet Explorer would display them.

The headings each start a new line and provide some formatting. However, you can't rely on this feature to make your page look a certain way. If the browser used to view your page shows the different headers only by color, then your formatting will be lost. Do not attempt to use headings to control how the text looks on the page. Remember that the browser is in charge of the look— you should worry only about the content.

A level-1 heading (<H1>) is often used at the start of the body of the page or document. It should restate the title. Other headings are used to divide the text into manageable sections and to help users scan through the page to find the information they are seeking.

Remember that you must always use the closing heading tag to end your heading. The browser cannot guess where you want your heading to end, so it cannot supply the ending tag for you. If you forget to close a header, you might be unpleasantly surprised with the result. Look what happens in Figure 2.5 when a header is added without the ending tag. Without the tag that would have closed the first heading after the poem's title, the browser views the rest of the document as part of the heading. You will run across this problem from time to time as you cruise the Net.

Headings can be aligned LEFT, CENTER, or RIGHT using the **align** attribute as shown in Figure 2.3. The **class** and **style** attributes are discussed later in this text. In addition, headings can contain a wide variety of other HTML tags. For example, a heading may contain link images <IMG>, line breaks <BR>,

```
<HTML>
<HEAD>
<TITLE>Poetry by Robert Frost</TITLE>
</HEAD>
<BODY>
<H1>What Fifty Said          ┌─ missing ending tag ─┐

<P>When I was young my teachers were the old.
I gave up fire for form till I was cold.
I suffered like a metal being cast.
I went to school to age to learn the past.
</P>

<P>Now I am old my teachers are the young.
What can't be molded must be cracked and sprung.
I strain at lessons fit to start a suture.
I go to school to youth to learn the future.
</P>
</BODY>
</HTML>
```

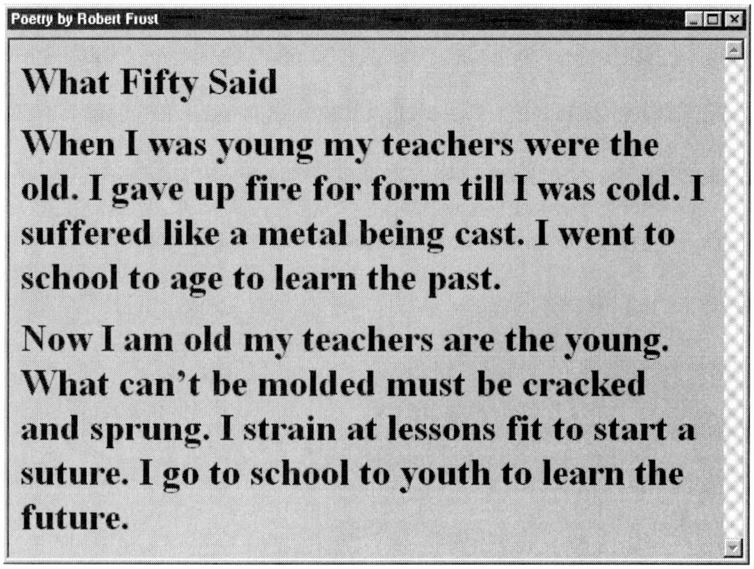

Figure 2.5 Results of HTML code when </H1> ending tag is forgotten.

horizontal rules <HR>, style changes like <STRONG>, and font modifiers like <B>or <I>. In practice, font or style changes, while allowed, are often overridden by the browser because it already prescribes the font and style of the heading text.

It is sometimes appropriate to add small images to headings. Some of the more effective ones are logos, bullets, or small icons. A document divided by easy-to-read headings helps the user identify salient points. Remember that the main reason to put a page on the Web is to provide information as quickly and efficiently as possible. Good headings help users find what they want.

<P>Paragraph</P>

Description: identifies a continuous string of text within the page.
Type: container.
Attributes: align, class, dir, id, lang, onClick, onDblClick, onKeyDown, onKeyPress, onKeyUp, onMouseDown, onMouseMove, onMouseOut, onMouseOver, onMouseUp, style, and title.

When writing a report or term paper, you divide the text into sections called paragraphs. To do that, you end the line and start the next with a tab or perhaps insert a blank line on your page like this:

The space you see above this line is called *white space.* In computer jargon, white space is defined as one or more spaces or tabs. Web browsers treat all white space the same. Therefore, if you had an HTML document with a partial line of text, three blank lines, and another partial line of text, a browser would close up the lines and make them flow into each other. For example, the HTML document with text on separate lines and a blank line between them in Figure 2.2 is displayed as a continuous line of text.

Since you can't insert tabs or blank lines to create paragraphs, you need some other tool to divide the text into logical sections. We have seen that headings can divide the text, but headings are intended to break the page into larger units than is the case for paragraphs. One way to divide text into smaller logical blocks is to use the *paragraph* (<P>) container as shown in Figure 2.3. The <P> container can be said to identify a continuous string of text within the page. Notice that the first paragraph is closed by the ending tag, </P>. A blank line between the two paragraphs would be ignored by the browser, but it automatically puts an extra line between the two paragraphs in response to the <P> container, as you can see in Figure 2.3.

As we saw in Chapter 1, many browsers can infer the ending paragraph tag. You will find some older documents on the Web that are marked in this manner. Nevertheless, it is good practice to close all your paragraph containers, even though the closing tag can be inferred in many cases.

Furthermore, we would recommend placing the ending tag on a separate line whenever text fills more than one line. It is easy to lose an ending tag in long strings of text. Placing the ending tag on a new line helps you find the ending tag and visually match it with the beginning tag.

The <P> tag recognizes the **align** attribute. Like headings, a paragraph can be aligned LEFT, CENTER, or RIGHT. Left alignment is the default; it is what the browser uses if you don't specify which type of alignment you want.

Paragraph containers often include other tags. For example, they may contain links (<A>), images (<IMG>), font changes (like <B> or <I>), line breaks (<BR>), and style changes (like <CITE> or <STRONG>). However, if the browser encounters any other tag in a paragraph, like a heading tag, that causes a break in the text flow, it assumes that the closing paragraph tag is missing and ends the paragraph for you—whether you wanted the paragraph closed there or not.

Commonly Used Empty Tags

The Robert Frost poem we have been using was actually written as two four-line stanzas as shown in Figure 2.6. We are sure Frost would agree that the way the poem is displayed affects how it is read and internalized. Good Web weavers have an eye for page layout that helps the reader get the point.

Our poem needs a *line break* (<BR>) at the end of each line. It would also help to visually separate the title from the body of the poem. This is best handled by a *horizontal rule* (<HR>) as shown in Figure 2.6. Both of these design elements are coded as HTML empty tags. Let's examine each of them.

Description: creates a line break.
Type: empty.
Attributes: class, clear, id, style, and title.

The *line break* tag (<BR>) causes the browser to stop the current line and move the cursor to the left margin of the next line. It functions like a carriage return on a typewriter or the Enter key on your keyboard when you are typing. It is often used for formatting text or inserting blank lines. For example, our poem is broken into two four-line stanzas by placing a <BR> after each period. Figure 2.6 shows the result on a browser.

<HR>

Description: creates a horizontal line on page.
Type: empty.
Attributes: align, class, id, noshade, onClick, onDblClick, onKeyDown, onKeyPress, onKeyUp, onMouseDown, onMouseMove, onMouseOut, onMouseOver, onMouseUp, size, style, title, and width.

```
<HTML>
<HEAD>
<TITLE>Poetry by Robert Frost</TITLE>
</HEAD>
<BODY>
<H1 align="CENTER">What Fifty Said</H1>
<HR align="CENTER" noshade size="4" width="50%">

<P align="CENTER">When I was young my teachers were the old.<BR>
I gave up fire for form till I was cold.<BR>
I suffered like a metal being cast.<BR>
I went to school to age to learn the past.<BR>
</P>

<P align="CENTER">Now I am old my teachers are the young.<BR>
What can't be molded must be cracked and sprung.<BR>
I strain at lessons fit to start a suture.<BR>
I go to school to youth to learn the future.<BR>
</P>

<HR align="CENTER" size="2" width="50">
</BODY>
</HTML>
```

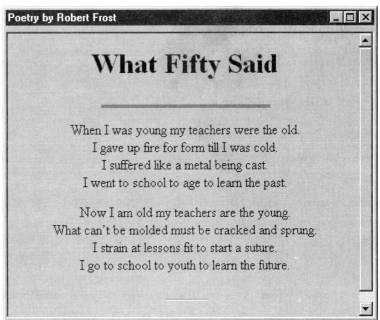

Figure 2.6 HTML code showing applications for line break <BR> and horizontal rule <HR> tags.

The *horizontal rule* element (<HR>) puts a horizontal line, or rule, across the screen. This is an empty tag. It has four attributes you can use to modify the way the line appears on the screen. Even though the tag contains attributes, it is called an empty tag because it has no closing, or ending, tag. Figure 2.6 shows how all four attributes are used.

The **align** attribute defines the horizontal placement, left, center, or right, of the line on the page. The **size** attribute determines how thick the line is. The default line is the width of the screen, side to side, 2 pixels (Internet Explorer and Mosaic) or 3 pixels (Navigator) thick. The term *pixel* stands for picture element. It is one of the many tiny dots that make up the display on your computer screen. Usually a pixel is about the size of one point of type on a standard 75 dot-per-inch display. Typical typefaces are about 12 points, or 12 pixels tall. The pixel is the smallest addressable unit of space on a screen. In Figure 2.6, the first line is 4 pixels thick, and the second line is 2 pixels thick.

The **width** attribute sets the length of the line. In Figure 2.6, the first rule is one half, 50 percent, of the screen width. The second rule is 50 pixels wide. As you can see, the **width** attribute can be expressed in either the exact number of pixels or as a percentage of the actual screen size. It is usually better to use the percentage measure because then the rule will look the same regardless of the screen size. If you use an absolute width, setting width to a fixed number of pixels, the browser will use that length regardless of screen size, and it will look different on different computers or with different browsers.

Many browsers shade a horizontal rule using some combination of black, white, dark gray, or light gray pixels to make it look like it has been chiseled into the screen. This shading is easier to see on the thick (size 5 or 6) lines. The rule is displayed as a solid color when the **noshade** attribute is present (see Figure 2.6). Notice that this attribute does not need an equal sign to change the default value. Its presence within the tag turns the shading off. Attributes like **noshade** that turn on or off a preset feature are referred to as *toggles* or *switches*.

Body Tag Attributes

You have now been introduced to a set of HTML elements that will enable you to create a wide variety of professional-looking Web pages. Before concluding this chapter we would like to expand upon some of the attributes associated with the <BODY> tag. As mentioned earlier, we will also cover some of these features as part of the introduction to style sheets in Chapters 5 and 8.

bgcolor

The **bgcolor** attribute controls the background color of the page. Like everything else that appears on your screen, it is expressed as a mixture of *red, green, and blue (RGB)*. Each of these colors has an intensity range of 0–255, with zero representing no color and 255 representing the most intense value for that color. There is a little twist with HTML, though—these color numbers must be expressed as two-digit hexadecimal (base-16) numbers. The digits in hexadecimal are 0123456789ABCDEF.

Two easy ways of converting the decimal *RGB number* to a hexadecimal are
1. Using a calculator that supports hexadecimals.
2. Using a table like the one in the back of this book.
You will find that some of the numbers are simple: 255 decimal = FF in hex, and zero decimal = 00 in hex. Here are some of the colors you can use:

White	FFFFFF
Bright red	FF0000
Bright green	00FF00
Bright blue	0000FF
Yellow	FFFF00
Magenta	FF00FF
Cyan	00FFFF
Black	000000

To make life a little easier, Navigator and the Internet Explorer support standard color names rather than just the hexadecimal numbers. A list of some of those names is included on the color insert in the back of this text. But the use of color names is not consistent from version to version of the browsers. Earlier versions of the Internet Explorer use a small subset of the names. For these reasons, we recommend that you always code colors in hexadecimal or the browser-safe standard color names shown on the color insert. The following code shows how the background color is coded:

<BODY bgcolor="yellow">

or

<BODY bgcolor="#FFFF00">

FFFF00 is the code for yellow.

Notice the octothorp, #, that is part of the color code. The octothorp tells the browser that the value following is a hexadecimal number representing the color, not a color name. Always code the octothorp as the first character of your color designators.

When you decide to add colors to your page, you can spend a significant amount of time trying to get them just the way you want them—and you can create some absolutely horrible combinations. For example, bright red letters on a bright blue background are very distracting. A background color that does not contrast well with your text color can make your page hard to read. You also need to remember that the readers of your page can configure their browsers to automatically set different colors and override all your hard work. The default background color for most browsers used to be light gray, but is white for the new browsers.

background

The **background** attribute allows you to place a picture, or image, in the background of your page. The Netscape and Internet Explorer browsers will display the image you select and will *tile,* or repeat, the image both vertically and horizontally to fill the whole background. The effect is similar to the wallpaper in Windows. You should select a dim, subtle image for your background. If the background is too intense or too bright, it will distract from or interfere with the text and other images you have on your page.

If you choose a background image, your choice of background color **(bgcolor)** will be hidden unless your background image has transparent areas. We will discuss transparent images when we look at using images in Chapter 6. The value specified in the background attribute is the path, or URL, for the background image you have selected. It should be a small image because it will need to be moved across the Internet to your viewer's location. Figure 2.7 shows the rocks.jpg background by itself, and Figure 2.8 illustrates how the page looks with that background in place.

Figure 2.7 Background image designed to be tiled on the screen.

Avoid building large, full-screen images, because they will be slow to load and will increase the congestion on the Internet. Your URL for an image should point to the Web server that hosts the page. Never use a URL that points to a file on a different Web server, because that can greatly increase the time it takes to load your page.

For example, in the HTML code in Figure 2.9 (on page 52), the image from rocks.jpg, a file that resides on the author's computer, is used. When the browser starts to build the page, it needs to look only at this file to create the background. If, instead, this file were located on another Web server, the URL would look like this: file://an.othersystem.net/pub/bground/rocks.jpg. The browser would have to establish communication with the an.othersystem.net computer, look in the /pub/bground directory, and copy the image in the file rocks.jpg back to the current computer before it could build the background for the page. This procedure would greatly increase the traffic on the Internet and would slow the browser down as it built the page.

One of the best ways to get nice backgrounds is to find them on the Net. Many sites offer *public-domain* background files, usually in *GIF (Graphic Interchange Format), JPEG (Joint Photographic Experts Group),* or *PNG (Portable Network*

Figure 2.8 Screen with little contrast between the background and text, making it difficult to read.

Graphics) format (all of which are discussed later in this book). You can use your browser to collect these backgrounds and save them on your own computer. Popular graphical browsers allow you to right-click on a background to access the "Save Background" feature. If you choose to use another Web weaver's work this way, ask permission. Usually the page will contain a way to e-mail the person who built the page. Ask the owner of the work if you can use the background on your page. Most of the time, authors are pleased that you want to use their work.

There is a cardinal rule to remember about background images: Any background image will interfere to some extent with reading the text on the page. An extreme example is shown in Figure 2.8. Make sure your background image is worth even a slight degradation of the readability of your page.

text

The **text** attribute sets the color for all the text on the page except the text enclosed in an anchor, <A>, container. We will explore anchors in the next chapter. You need to ensure that your text color works with your selected background color or background image. To help the readability of your page, it should contrast nicely and not clash. For example, the rocks.jpg choice is dark and provides a poor background for the default black text shown in Figure 2.8. A lighter text color, like white, yellow, or cyan, would provide a better contrast with this background.

```
<HTML>
<HEAD>
<TITLE>Poetry by Robert Frost</TITLE>
</HEAD>
<BODY background="rocks.jpg" text="00FFFF">
<!-- text = cyan -->
<H1 align="CENTER">What Fifty Said</H1>
<HR align="CENTER" size="4" noshade width="75%">

<P align="CENTER">When I was young my teachers were the old.<BR>
I gave up fire for form till I was cold.<BR>
I suffered like a metal being cast.<BR>
I went to school to age to learn the past.<BR>
</P>

<P align="CENTER">Now I am old my teachers are the young.<BR>
What can't be molded must be cracked and sprung.<BR>
I strain at lessons fit to start a suture.<BR>
I go to school to youth to learn the future.<BR>
</P>

<HR align="CENTER" size="2" width="50">
</BODY>
</HTML>
```

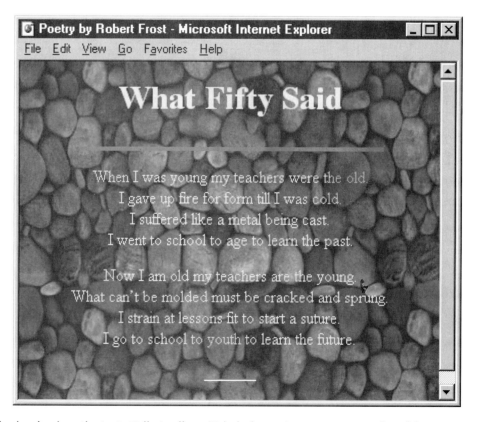

Figure 2.9 HTML code showing how the text attribute allows Web designers to contrast text color with background.

As you cruise the Net, you will come across some pages that are very difficult to read because the author of the page made a poor text-color selection. Text color is selected just like background color, using a hexadecimal value like "#FFFF00", or a color name like "yellow" if you are targeting the Netscape or Internet Explorer browsers. The following <BODY> tag establishes the text color as cyan:

```
<BODY background="rocks.jpg" text="#00FFFF">
```

Figure 2.9 shows that the cyan text is easier to read on the dark background. Figure 2.8 demonstrates how a poor choice of **background,** or **bgcolor,** with **text** can make a page almost impossible to read.

alink, link, and vlink

The following three attributes allow you to control the color of links:
  - **alink**—controls the color of the active link, or the link that is being targeted by the mouse. Only Navigator currently uses this attribute; the others ignore it.
  - **link**—controls the color of all the hyperlinks the user has not yet followed.
  - **vlink**—controls the color of all the links the user has already followed or visited at one time or another.

Keep in mind that changing these colors can confuse and frustrate your users. Most browsers keep the link colors constant, and users come to depend on those colors. As mentioned earlier, on most browsers, the links not yet chosen are blue and the links that have been visited are dark purple. Using the attributes **link** and **vlink,** you could reverse those values, making the followed links blue and those not yet visited dark purple. That could be very confusing for your users.

If you have a special need to change these colors, remember to make them different from the text color and from each other. You can specify the colors just as you did with the text and background colors, using either a hexadecimal value or a color name. The following code sets the color of the unused links as red and of those that have been visited as bright green.

```
<BODY link="#FF0000" vlink="#00FF00">
```

But remember, you should change the default colors only if you have a compelling reason to do so.

A Few Considerations

Using lots of colors and fancy images, you can produce a Web page that is a work of art. But there are some things that can go wrong with that approach:
  1. You will usually increase the time it takes to load your page. The delay not only may frustrate your users, but will also increase congestion on the Internet. If you use a large image as the background, that will substantially increase load time. Remember, not all your users are tied directly to the Internet. Some depend on 14,400 baud modems and must pay for each minute of connect time. They may not appreciate a beautiful background image that takes 10 minutes to download.

2. Your page may look wonderful on a computer with a high-resolution screen and 16 million available colors. But if your user has a machine with fewer available colors (like a 16-color VGA Windows machine), your pretty screen may become unusable. In replacing your colors with those available for that machine, the browser could set the background color and the text color to the same value, making it impossible to read! When you use colors in your page that the local computer does not have available, the local browser is forced to "dither" the image. ***Dithering*** is the process of replacing one uniform color with repeating patterns of other colors that approximate the original color. This can make your text very difficult or impossible to read, or just plain ugly. (Dithering is discussed in more detail in regard to images in Chapter 6, and you can see several examples in Figure 6.3.)

3. Even though you are using a wonderful image as your background, you might want to reconsider using an image at all. Putting text on top of an image always makes the text harder to read.

4. If you use a background image, the browser must fill in that image as the user scrolls through the page. This process by the browser can lead to slower scrolling.

5. Pages with very light text on dark backgrounds may prove difficult (if not impossible) to print.

A careful selection of colors and images can create a wonderful Web page. As you cruise the Net, you will find many examples of beautifully crafted pages. The careful use of colors and images allows you to express yourself artistically and enables you to create unique HTML documents. Playing with color and form is great fun. However, as you play, keep in mind that the real purpose for most Web pages is to transmit information. If colors and images get in the way of the transferral of information, then perhaps you need to rethink your layout.

At this point it is important to address the idea of Web page design. Usually the minds that are capable of excellent coding and HTML development aren't the same kinds of minds that are capable of excellent layout and page design. It is tempting to use all the "bells and whistles" possible when developing a page, often to the detriment of the actual content. If you are developing a professional Web page, it is almost a necessity to consult with a graphics designer. The designer can tell you which colors go together well, how much "white space" you should have on your page, where to place images for greatest effect, and so on. Your users will appreciate the result.

Key Terms

Attributes
Comments
Container element
Dithering
Empty element
Horizontal rule
Intrinsic event
Line break
Paragraph
Pixel
Style
Toggle

New Tags

```
<HTML>
<BR>
<HR>
<P>
<HEAD>
<TITLE>
<BODY>
<H1>
<H2>
<H3>
<H4>
<H5>
<H6>
```

Review Questions

1. What is the definition for each of the key terms?

2. How are each of the tags introduced in this chapter used? (Provide examples.)

3. Which HTML tags should be included in an HTML template?

4. When is the SGML <!DOCTYPE> tag used?

5. What tag must be included in every <HEAD> container element?

6. Give three reasons why the contents of the <TITLE> element should be short and descriptive.

7. What separates amateurs from professionals in regard to writing HTML code?

8. How do you update a browser's screen after changing the content or tags in the related HTML document?

9. How are comments used within an HTML document?

10. From a design point of view, what are headings used for?

11. What does a browser automatically insert between two paragraphs?

12. When and why should ending tags be placed on a new line?

13. If the **Bgcolor** and **Background** attributes both appear in a <BODY> tag, which tag takes precedence?

14. In what two ways are color attributes designated?

15. Why should a background file reside on the hosting computer instead of being referenced at another URL?

16. When using a graphical browser, how do you save background images you like?

17. Describe a situation that would require you to change the text color.

18. Give four reasons why you might choose not to use a background image.

Exercises

2.1. As a follow-up to Exercise 1.1, create a Web page that describes the computer platform you are using for this class. The HTML document should include a background color or image, comments with your name and the assignment due date, and the following information:

    a. Your name
    b. Computer's brand name
    c. Processor type and speed
    d. Screen size and resolution
    e. Audio hardware
    f. Hard disk capacity
    g. Type of removable disk or tape and associated storage capacity
    h. Hardware used to access the Internet

2.2. Create a personal Homework home page. Your instructor will use this page to link to homework assignments from this class. The HTML document should include a background color or image, comments with your name and the assignment due date, and the following information:

    a. Your name
    b. Class identifier (like "CIS 257")
    c. Class name (like "Introduction to HTML")
    d. Section number
    e. Instructor's name
    f. Instructor's office number
    g. Instructor's office telephone number
    h. Your school's name
    i. Other information specified by your instructor

Do not include personal information like an address or telephone number in order to protect your privacy.

2.3. Create a page to match the following poem by Eugene Fitch Ware. The HTML document should include a background color or image along with comments containing your name and the assignment due date. The poem's title is "He and She." It was written as two, four-line stanzas:

When I am dead you'll find it hard,
Said he,
To ever find another man
Like me.

What makes you think, as I suppose
You do,
I'd ever want another man
Like you?

2.4. Create a Web page that provides an overview of your favorite movie. The HTML document should include a background color or image, comments with your name and the assignment due date, and the following information:

a. Movie's name
b. Release date
c. Rating
d. Minutes the movie runs
e. Actors and actresses
f. Paragraph on why you like the movie

2.5. Create a Web page to sell used goods, similar to the want ads in your local paper. The HTML document should include a background color or image, comments with your name and the assignment due date, and the following information for at least five items you want to sell:

a. Item name
b. Description of the product (include dimensions when appropriate)
c. Condition: mint-in-box, excellent, good, poor, handyman's special
d. Approximate age
e. Asking price

2.6. Create a home page for your school. The HTML document should include a background color or image, comments with your name and the assignment due date, and the following information:

a. School's name
b. Address
c. Main telephone number
d. Top administrator's name and position
e. School colors
f. School mascot
g. Words to the school's fight song

## CHAPTER three

LINKS—LET'S GET HYPER

In the last chapter we built a simple, *static* Web page. A static Web page contains no links within the document or to other documents, no graphics, and no way for users to interact with the page. Now it is time to allow the users some control over where to go on the page rather than simply scrolling up and down. We also need to allow the users to move from page to page. To do this, we must incorporate links into the file, specially marked places on the screen that will perform certain actions when activated by a mouse click. Linking is an important step in Web page development because it adds the "hyper" to the term *hypertext*.

Why Is Hypertext Hyper?

A *hypertext document* is one that contains elements called *links* that allow users to activate a particular part of the screen and perform some action. The actions can include

1. Moving to another part of the document
2. Opening another document on the same Web site
3. Opening a document on a Web site somewhere else in the world

In this chapter we will deal with all three actions. In later chapters we will add links to sounds, images, and videos.

Documents having dynamic links to other documents or to places within the same document date back to the 1980s. At that time the Apple Macintosh supported *HyperCard,* which allowed users to create buttons within a document that would, when clicked, load an image, play a sound, or open and display another text file. The documents were called *stacks,* and each page or screen was a *card* in that stack. Different cards could be linked together. The main stack containing cards with links to related stacks, the table of contents, was called the *home stack.* The Hypertalk programming language used to create these buttons was a true programming language that was *interpreted* into the computer's machine language.

Similarly, HTML enables you to build documents that allow the dynamic linking of Web pages. These links should create a logical path to related information. A professional Web weaver provides links that are intuitive and help guide the user in a logical manner. In contrast, a rookie weaves a maze for the user. Links help the user pick up definitions, play sounds, view pictures and video, or move about through a collection of documents with a simple click of a mouse button.

Storyboarding Page Links

Lots of books pontificate on the subject of designing Web pages, so there is much information available on the use of fonts, color coordination, and other visual design rules. One thing all the experts agree on is that the use of links is the most important design decision you make when creating Web pages. The importance of **storyboarding** page links before you start writing becomes most evident with larger projects. A storyboard is basically a diagram that illustrates how two or more Web pages relate to one another. The links from one page to another create the "story." Figure 3.1 shows three simple storyboards. In real life these storyboards may originate on coffee-stained napkins, but eventually the Web weaver will create a more formal diagram like those shown in the figure.

Storyboards are especially important when several Web weavers are writing documents for the same Web site. Three basic Web site designs are shown by the sequential, indexed sequential, and hierarchical storyboards in Figure 3.1. These designs can spawn quite a few variations. Don't lose sight of the broader point being made here. Professional-looking and easy-to-navigate Web sites are designed before they are written.

The subject matter and target audience usually dictate how you link pages together. You can also count on the browser to provide basic navigational options like back, forward, and home.

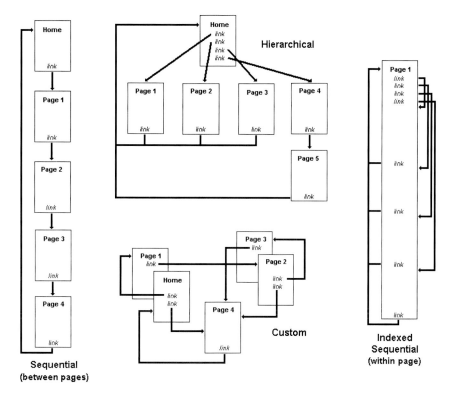

Figure 3.1 Storyboards showing three different Web site designs.

Sequential and Indexed Sequential Designs

Large amounts of related text lend themselves to a sequential design. Two variations on this theme are available to the Web weaver. When the text is limited in length and can easily be broken into headings associated with a few paragraphs, then all the text can reside in a single document (see the *indexed sequential* example in Figure 3.1). The links will then jump the user from one heading or another. For example, Figure 3.2 on page 62 shows a simple HTML document that contains four poems and links to each poem at the beginning of the document. This is an indexed sequential layout within a single Web page.

Larger bodies of text that can be read from beginning to end, like this book, often have logical subsets that stand alone. They are called sections, chapters, lessons, etc. In this case the designer might write each chapter as a separate Web page and sequentially link Chapter 1 to Chapter 2, Chapter 2 to Chapter 3, and so forth (see *sequential* example in Figure 3.1). This is a sequential design between pages. The associated links identify pages that could be stored at other sites.

```
<HTML>
<HEAD>
<TITLE>Intra-page Links</TITLE>
</HEAD>
<BODY bgcolor="#FFFFFF">
<!-- Background color = white -->
<H1>Poetry Selections</H1>
<P>This page contains some of the poetry written by some of our
favorite poets. Please take a minute to sample their work.  Most of
these poets write in one
of the recognized rhyming styles.
</P>
<P>This is a list of the poets shown on this page: </P>
<A href="#MB">Margaret E. Bruner</A><BR>
<A href="#ee">e. e. cummings</A><BR>
<A href="#RF">Robert Frost</A><BR>
<A href="#EA">Edward Arlington Robinson</A><BR>
<HR align="CENTER" noshade width="75%" size="4">

<H2><A name="RF">Robert Frost</A></H2>
<H3 align="CENTER">What Fifty Said</H3>
<P align="CENTER"> -- Text of poem omitted for clarity of example --
</P>
<HR align="CENTER" noshade width="50%" size="4">

<H2><A name="ee">e. e. cummings</A> </H2>
<H3 align="CENTER">O sweet spontaneous</H3>
<P align="CENTER"> -- Text of poem omitted for clarity of example --
</P>
<HR align="CENTER" noshade width="50%" size="4">

<H2><A name="EA">Edward A. Robinson</A></H2>
<H3 align="CENTER">Richard Cory</H3>
<P align="CENTER"> -- Text of poem omitted for clarity of example --
</P>
<HR align="CENTER" noshade width="50%" size="4">

</P>
<H2><A name="MB"> Margaret E. Bruner</A></H2>
<H3 align="CENTER">Epitaph for a Cat</H3>
<P align="CENTER"> -- Text of poem omitted for clarity of example --
</P>
<HR align="CENTER" noshade width="50%" size="4">
</BODY>
</HTML>
```

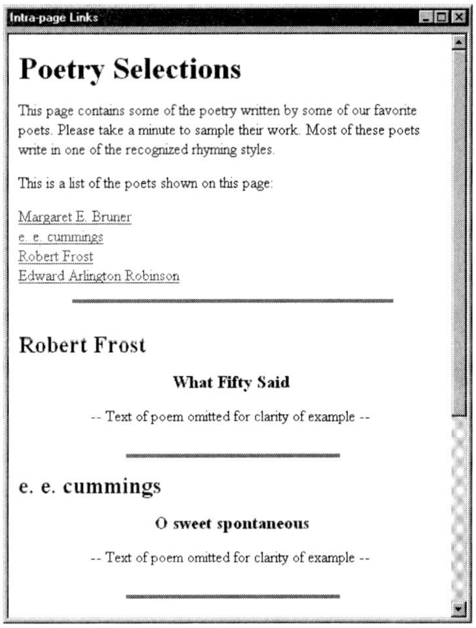

Figure 3.2 HTML code with anchor containers that create intrapage links.

Hierarchical Design

Figure 3.3 shows our favorite poems as separate pages linked hierarchically by author. A storyboard with this design is presented in Figure 3.1. It is used when related text does not need to be read in any particular order. An operations manual for your favorite word-processing program is a good example. If each

```
<HTML>
<HEAD>
<TITLE>Intra-system Links</TITLE>
</HEAD>
<BODY bgcolor="#FFFFFF">
<!-- Background color = white -->
<H1>Poetry Selections</H1>
<P>This page contains some of the poetry written by some of our
favorite poets. Please take a minute to sample their work.
Most of these poets write in one of the recognized rhyming styles.
</P>

<P>This is a list of the poets shown on this Web site: </P>
<A href="bruner.htm">Margaret E. Bruner</A><BR>
<A href="cummings.htm">e. e. cummings</A><BR>
<A href="frost.htm">Robert Frost</A><BR>
<A href="robinson.htm">Edward Arlington Robinson</A><BR>

</BODY>
</HTML>
```

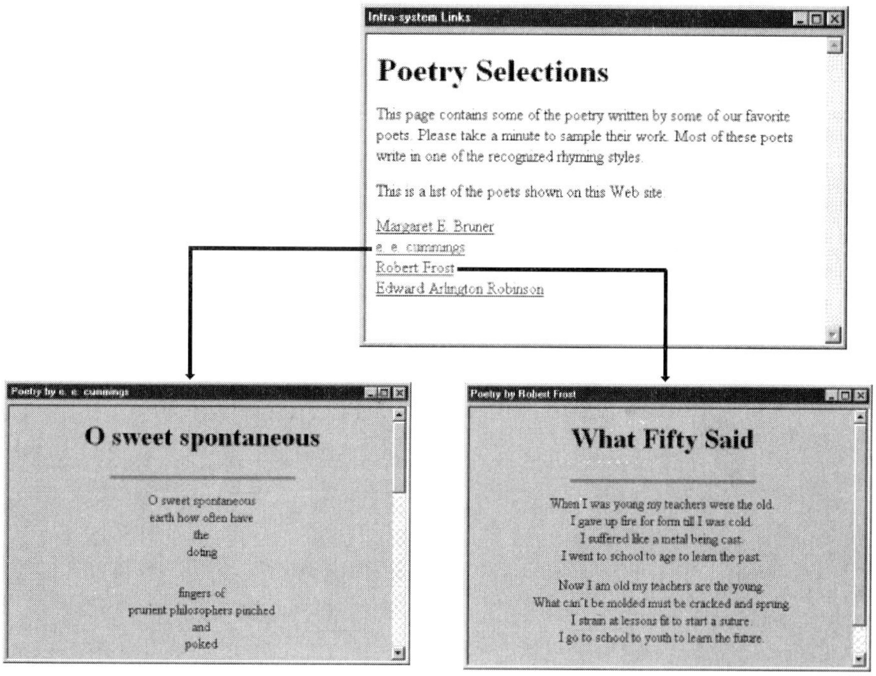

Figure 3.3 HTML code with anchor containers that create intrasystem links to independent HTML documents.

chapter of the manual described different menu options offered by the program, then you could read about the features when you needed to use them. Thus, they could be read in any order.

Custom Design

Sometimes a subject lends itself to a unique set of links (see the custom example in Figure 3.1). It is especially important to make a storyboard for sites that you think require custom links. Often creating the storyboard illustrates associations you had not considered. Better designs sometimes become apparent as the story-board unfolds. Now let's look at how we create links.

\<A\>anchor\</A\>

Description: provides data to link to images, sounds, another area within the page, or to another Internet page.
Type: container.
Attributes: accesskey, charset, coords, href, hreflang, id, name, onBlur, onClick, onDblClick, onFocus, onKeyDown, onKeyPress, onKeyUp, onMouseDown, onMouseMove, onMouseOut, onMouseOver, onMouseUp, rel, rev, shape, style, tabindex, target, title, and type.

The anchor container (\<A\>) serves as the basis for all the links we are going to create in this chapter. It is a very powerful HTML element that recognizes a variety of attributes. Since this chapter's focus is on creating links, we are deferring discussion of many of the common attributes to other chapters. Table 3.1 contains a list of some esoteric attributes recognized by the anchor tag with a brief description of how they are used.

There are several ways to refer to the relationship between the document housing the link and the document pointed to by the link. In some texts you will find the term *head* used for the place where the link starts and *tail* for the place the link points to. In others you may find the terms *start* and *destination* for these two locations. In this book we will use **source** to indicate the origin of a link and **target** to indicate the end of the link.

Source Anchors

A source anchor container is used to create the area on the page where the click of a mouse initiates the link. The following source anchor container identifies the target RF within the same document:

```
<A href="#RF">Robert Frost</A>.
```

Navigator and Internet Explorer underline the link and display related text in a different color. As mentioned in Chapter 2, this is the color controlled by the \<BODY\> container's **link** attribute. The anchor element in the previous example would look like this in most graphical browsers:

Robert Frost

Figure 3.2 shows how popular browsers would display the same HTML code. This HTML document utilizes *intrapage links* to implement the indexed sequential design. These are links to items located within a single document or page, as opposed to *intrasystem links* and *intersystem links,* which extend beyond the current document. *Intrasystem* links are within one computer system; *intersystem* links extend to other systems. Both are discussed later in this chapter.

ATTRIBUTE	DESCRIPTION
accesskey	Assigns a single-character access key to the link. Pressing this access key can initiate the link just as clicking on the link text would. For example, F could be assigned as the access key to the Robert Frost poem.
charset	Identifies the character encoding of the resource designated by the link. The charset might include special math or chemistry symbols.
coords	Identifies the position of a shape on the screen. The number and order of values depends on the shape being defined. The coords attribute can be set to one of the following values: • *circle:* center-x, center-y, radius. The radius value is a percentage value based on the associated object's width and height. The radius should be the smaller value of the two. • *poly:* x1, y1, x2, y2, . . ., xN, yN. • *rect:* left-x, top-y, right-x, bottom-y.
hreflang	Identifies the base language of the link (similar to the lang attribute) designated by the hyper reference (href) attribute and should be used only when href attribute is specified.
shape	Used with image maps to identify the shape of the map. The shape attribute can be set to one of the following values: • *default:* entire region • *circle:* circular region • *poly:* polygonal region • *rect:* rectangular region
tabindex	Identifies the position of the current element in the document's tabbing order. The tabindex can be set to any number from 0 to 32,767.

Table 3.1 Common attributes recognized by the anchor <A> tag.

Target Anchors

If we want to allow the user to jump from point to point within the same document, or to jump to a specific point in another document, we must have an element that identifies the link's *anchor name.* The <A> anchor </A> container with the **name** attribute provides an anchor name that will serve as a target.

name

The **name** attribute is used to identify a location within an HTML document. The HTML code in Figure 3.2 uses RF, ee, EA, and MB as anchor names. RF is the anchor name for the target poem by Robert Frost. The text that is contained within the anchor container, in this case Robert Frost, will be displayed on the screen in a format governed by any other containers that enclose it. When used as a <H1> element, each author's name is formatted as a level-1 heading. The HTML code that identifies the start of the Robert Frost poem in this intrapage example looks like this:

```
<A name="RF">Robert Frost</A>.
```

Each anchor name must be unique and begin with a letter of the alphabet. In other words, the name RF cannot be used again in this document. After the first letter you can use any combination of letters, digits (0-9), hyphens (-), underscores (_), colons (:), and periods (.). Do not use spaces as part of the anchor name. Furthermore, with uppercase RF already used, lower case rf is unacceptable as an anchor name within this document. Later we will explain how the anchor name is really a special URL.

This type of intrapage link is common when you are presenting a large volume of related information—for example, a large document where the table of contents contains the intrapage links. These links will allow users to select the sections they wish to view, activate them, and immediately see their selections without having to page down through the document. If you are building a menu for your page, you can also use this indexed sequential design. Remember that the user can always scroll through the whole document using the scroll bar on the right side of the page. What you are doing with this type of internal link is providing an easy way for the user to navigate around the page.

id

The HTML 4.0 specifications added the **id** attribute which, like the name attribute, can identify anchor names. It does not matter if an anchor name is created with the **name** or **id** attribute, but the name must be unique within the document. For example, the following HTML code creates the target anchor named RF: `<A id="RF">Randal, Felix</A>`.

This is the same anchor name you see used in Figure 3.2, but it could not be used in the HTML document shown in Figure 3.2 because of the following code:`<A name="RF">Robert Frost</A>`. Each anchor name must be unique within a document. You may be asking yourself why the W^{3}C would create two attributes that do the same thing. The answer is that the **id** attribute can be used in more ways than the **name** attribute, which will probably be added to the list of deprecated attributes one of these days. The 4.0 specifications identify these applications for the **id** attribute:

- Style sheet selector
- Target anchor for hypertext links
- Reference to a specific script (programming) element
- Naming <OBJECT> elements

One interesting difference between the id and name attributes is that the **name** attribute may contain character references that use an ISO-recognized code to identify special characters. For example,

```
&Uuml;
```

is the character reference for the uppercase U with an umlaut appearing over it—Ü. If we want to create the anchor name ÜN, the **id** attribute cannot be used. Only HTML code using the **name** attribute will work in this situation. It would look like this:

`<A name="&Uuml;N">Brünnhilde, Valkyrie</A>`

Other special character codes are discussed in more detail in Chapter 5 and shown in Appendix B.

So which one should you use—the **id** or the **name** attribute? It is a question you will be asking several times while reading this text. The answer depends on when you want to go with the new specifications and stop using the old ones. Anyone using Internet Explorer or Navigator versions 4 or older cannot use anchors created with the **id** attribute. In these situations, or when special characters need to be used within anchor names, the **name** attribute needs to be employed. Otherwise, the **id** attribute provides more flexibility.

Anchor Placement

It is important to remember that an anchor can be used within another container. Thus, we could put an anchor within a heading element if we wanted the header to be the target of a link. It is bad HTML style, though, to put a heading element within an anchor. Proper style would be as follows: `<H2 align="RIGHT"><A name="PP">Phred's Page</A></H2>`. Here the anchor is contained within the heading, and `Phred's Page` will appear the way the browser presents a level-2 heading. If users select a link to PP, they will be transferred to this heading.

Consider the following HTML code: `<A name="PP"><H2 align="RIGHT"> Phred's Page</H2></A>`. This code is an example of bad syntax, because the anchor contains another container, in this case a level-2 heading. Some browsers will try to close the anchor container before opening the heading container. That action could cause unpredictable results.

If you want to have working links that appear as you design them, you must maintain the integrity of your containers. In the following example, it would be easy to make the mistake of closing the heading before closing the anchor, like this:`<H2 align="RIGHT"><A name="PP">Phred's Page</H2></A>`. Notice that the heading container is closed before the anchor container. Some browsers could get confused and miss the closing anchor tag, thus keeping the anchor open. Other browsers will detect this crossed container as an error and not set up the anchor at all. In either case, the results will not be what you expect. Close your containers in the order you build them, with inner containers closed before outer containers.

Hypertext References

Figure 3.2 illustrates using the source anchors to create four intrapage links. A hypertext reference to each unique anchor name provides the information needed to update the screen display. Hypertext references to other documents maintained by the same Web server create the *intrasystem links* mentioned earlier. These references contain the HTML document's filename and a description of the hard disk directories, also called *file folders,* where the file is stored. When the hypertext reference includes a URL for another Web site, the anchor is creating an *intersystem link,* also mentioned earlier.

href

Every source anchor contains the special attribute, **href,** which stands for Hypertext REFerence. The **href** attribute identifies the pointer, or pathway, to the target of the link. An example would be <A href="#RF">Robert Frost</A>. The target of a link is a URL. In this case the URL is local to, or within, the document we have created. The URL allows the user to jump to a selected poet with the click of a mouse button. The form of the local URL is the anchor name, exactly as it appears in the **name** attribute, preceded by the octothorp, or number symbol (#).

Figure 3.3 shows the home page for a hierarchical site. This design employs separate HTML documents for each poet. For example, Robert Frost's poems are saved in frost.htm. The following anchor container creates an intrasystem link: <A href="frost.htm">Robert Frost</A>.

If the poems are maintained on other Web sites, then intersystem links are employed. The following anchor container includes a hypertext reference for Tim T's student Web site: <A href="http://student/muskegon.cc.mi.us/frost.htm">Robert Frost</A>.

Many computer systems are *case-sensitive,* so you should be careful to have the URL exactly match the target. A case-sensitive system recognizes the difference between uppercase and lowercase letters. For example, the target "RF" and the target "Rf" are different on a system that recognizes the case of the letters. If you used a target of "Rf" in your **name** or **id** attribute, you should also have an **href** of "Rf." On a case-insensitive system, like DOS, both targets are considered the same.

Always enclose the URL in quotation marks. There are some special cases when this is unnecessary, but most of the time the quotation marks are required, and it is a good habit to develop. The text between the end of the opening tag and the beginning of the ending tag is the text the user will see that indicates a link exists. Always use the closing </A> anchor tag, as it cannot be inferred by the browser. Be sure not to include leading or trailing blanks in your text. They will be underlined and look bad.

As you remember from the last chapter, the link text will be a different color and may be specified by the **link** attribute of the <BODY> container. The fact that the link text is a different color and is underlined tells the user that it is a link. Also, when the user moves the cursor over the link, it becomes a pointing finger rather than the normal arrowhead. This change in the pointer is another indication that the text under it is a link.

Intrasystem Source Anchors

If you choose to write a long hypertext document, you may be causing unnecessary problems for the user, as follows:

1. A long document is slower to download than a short one.
2. A set of short documents may be easier for users to navigate among because they can easily return to the home page or table of contents from any of the other documents.
3. One of the rules of HTML design says you should have each document focus on a single topic and do *one* thing well.

A large hypertext document providing information on 14 different topics is not doing one thing well. A more structured format for the information would be 14 smaller hypertext documents, each presenting one of the facets of the information in a well-organized fashion, and one document serving as a table of contents with a menu for the others. And in addition to being easier for the user, smaller documents will be easier for you to maintain.

Figure 3.3 presents the HTML code for poetry selections we used before, modified to reflect a hierarchical intrasystem style of development. Each **href** now points to a separate file that was created by cutting apart the previous large document. You will notice that the URL no longer starts with an octothorp (#). The missing octothorp tells the browser that the reference is to another file rather than to a target within the current document. The differences in coding an intrasystem URL rather than an intrapage URL are

1. The absence of the leading octothorp
2. The fact that the URL is now a path to a file rather than simply a target within the document

Figure 3.3 also shows how the code would look in a browser. Notice that the links are still underlined. You cannot tell just by looking at the link whether it points within the document, across documents on the same system, or across the Internet. From the browser's point of view, a link is a link.

Paths to Files

As we learned in Chapter 1, the third part of a URL is the *path* to the file. Usually the path is a set of directory names allowing the browser to find the specific HTML document referenced by the link. There are a few important considerations when building a path name. First, since the vast majority of the computers that run Web servers use the UNIX operating system, and UNIX is case-sensitive, you need to be careful with the case of your path names. If the file you want is in the path Wilbur.pages.stuff, and you code wilbur.pages.stuff as part of your link address, the link will fail. Wilbur and wilbur are two different directories on a UNIX computer.

Second, if there is no path, or if the path is simply a forward slash (/), the document you will retrieve is the highest-level HTML index document on that server. This is called the *home page*. Sometimes it is called public_html or public.htm. On UNIX computers it is usually called index.html. This document normally provides the doorway into the rest of the HTML files on that site.

Third, the shorthand use of the tilde (~) symbol is used to specify a path name to a personal HTML directory in the home directory of the individual specified. For example, the URL http://SomeCompany.Somewhere.com/~clyde/ would bring up the highest-level HTML document in Clyde's subdirectory structure. Usually this would be Clyde's index.html file, which is Clyde's home page.

This raises an interesting point. There can be a home page on SomeCompany.Somewhere.com that is the gateway into all the HTML documents on that server. Usually a well-constructed home page will provide links to all the other pages, or at least the index to each set of pages on that server. The exact location of that index.html file depends on the following:

1. The actual server software
2. The Web weaver who set up the site

The main index page for the whole server is obviously a home page. However, in the parlance of the Web, the index into Clyde's collection of HTML pages is also considered to be a home page. Generally, you should avoid coding the file name `index.html` in an URL when linking to a home page; let the browser pick the name.

When you specify the path that the browser should take to find a document, you can use either an absolute or relative path name. Both have a purpose and use, so let's discuss each of them.

Absolute Path Names

Absolute path names always start with a slash (/) and contain the full path to the document you are referencing. The browser knows that you are using an absolute path when the path name starts with the slash. There are a couple of important points about absolute path names. First, the majority of the servers on the Internet are running the Unix operating system. Therefore, the way we specify paths is more Unix-like than Windows-like. In Unix, the right, or forward, slash (/) is used to divide the parts of a path name. You will need to use this convention when coding absolute path names. In addition, when you specify a drive letter, you should follow it with the vertical bar (|) rather than the colon as you are used to in Windows. Table 3.2 provides examples of an absolute path name for three different operating systems, showing how they would be coded.

As you can see in the table, the same path name looks a little different on different operating systems. In each case, though, an absolute path tells the browser exactly where to find the file by specifying the complete path name.

Although it may seem a good idea to always specify a full path name, let's look at another way to tell the browser how to find the files it needs, using relative path names.

Relative Path Names

A relative path starts from the directory in which the browser is currently working, the directory that contains the active document. *Relative path names* must not start with a right (forward) slash, because the right slash is the first character of an absolute path name. Thus, the difference between an absolute

ABSOLUTE PATH NAME	WHAT IT TELLS THE BROWSER
href="/home/users/html/frost.html"	The file is on a Unix system, in the directory of /home/users/html. The filename is frost.html. Unix allows longer filenames.
href="/Dl/html/poems/frost.htm"	This is a Windows example. Here the file is on the D: drive, in the directory /html/poems. Note that the absolute path starts with a slash, as is required. Window uses three-character file extensions, so the .html file is saved as .htm.
href="/Hard Disk 2/HTML Poems/frost.htm"	This time the file is on a Macintosh system. It is on the second hard drive, in the directory HTML Poems.

Table 3.2 Samples of absolute path names.

and a relative path name is that the relative path name does not include the current position in the file structure, whereas the absolute path gives every directory leading to the target. The simplest relative path names point to target files contained in the same directory as the source document. This is the ideal path because it is the default. You can see examples of that type of relative link in Table 3.3. In the first example we direct the browser to look in the same directory where it found the menu page to find frost.htm. Table 3.3 provides some other examples of relative path names as well.

As you can see in comparing Table 3.2 with Table 3.3, in most cases the relative path is shorter than the absolute path. Relative path names are usually faster for the browser to use as well.

Relative versus Absolute Path Names

At first glance, it would seem much better to always use absolute path names rather than relative path names for linked material. Yet, most experts agree that just the opposite is true. To explain why, we need to first point out that whenever possible you should have all the files you are referencing in the same directory. That way the browser doesn't have far to look to find related files. Also, you can easily move the files as a group if you are changing from one server to another. If all the files are in one directory, then short, relative path names like those shown in Figure 3.3 are most efficient. Furthermore, if you use relative path names, it is easier to maintain your Web page, because you won't need to keep changing your path names when you move your files from directory to directory.

RELATIVE PATH NAME	WHAT IT TELLS THE BROWSER
href="poem.htm"	This file is in the active directory. This is the simplest relative path-naming scheme.
href="poems/poem.html"	In this case the target is in the directory or folder called poems, which is a subdirectory of the active directory.
href="lit/poetry/poem.html"	Here the target is in the subdirectory or folder called poetry, which is in the subdirectory or folder called lit, which is in the active subdirectory or folder.
href="../poem.html"	This is the way we direct the browser to move back or up one directory or folder. Here we are saying that the file we want is in the parent directory for the active directory. The .. notation says to move up or back one level.
href="../../poems/poem.htm"	Here the target is located up two levels and is in the subdirectory or folder called poems at that level.
href="../D|/English/poems/poem.htm"	Here the source document was in the directory C:/html, and the target is on the D drive on the system. In this case the absolute path would be shorter than the relative path.

Table 3.3 Samples of relative path names.

Intersystem Source Anchors

Now we need to examine intersystem links that bring data from distant machines. Linking across the World Wide Web is as easy as linking down into the same document, but it consumes Net resources and can lead to some problems that are outside the control of the Web weaver. For example, if we link to a site to bring in an audio file, that site may be down, preventing our users from hearing the audio clip. Or perhaps the site that has the clip is working just fine, but between our site and the Net a problem occurs, preventing our users from getting onto that path. Still another possibility is that the site we are linking to may change its address.

For all these reasons, wise Web weavers will regularly check to ensure that the links from their pages are valid. There are some software packages that will do this for you, but to be absolutely sure they are working, you should also check them yourself at regular intervals.

Linking Considerations

When you create a link to a page on another machine, you are giving the user's browser a different Internet address from which to download data. Often this process is referred to as "sending the user across the Net." Naturally, this is only a figure of speech, as your user stays exactly where she was but simply begins to use a different Web server. In most cases, when the user finishes accessing the distant server, she can return to your server using the "Back" button.

Domain Name or IP Address?

You can specify a hypertext reference or URL (the value of the **href** attribute to the <A> container), by either the IP or the domain name. As explained earlier, an *IP address* is a set of four numbers separated by periods or dots. For example, 204.151.55.44 is an IP address. Each device connected to the Internet has a unique IP address. The domain name describes the path to the server by giving the server's actual name and the other names of the computers that constitute the domain of the server. For example, www.McGraw-Hill.com is a domain name. Some domain names are short, and others can be quite long. The parts of domain names were discussed in Chapter 1.

If you choose to use a domain name, the browser must access a *Domain Name Service (DNS)* to translate the domain name into an IP address. Some Web weavers think that this extra step is best avoided, so they code the domain as an IP address. Although this procedure does save a little time when the browser takes the link, it is not a good practice, because the code is harder to maintain.

For example, one company decided that it needed a *firewall,* a program that protects the security of networked computers. This company had an extensive Web site and used IP addressing throughout, even to link to other pages on its own site. When it implemented the firewall computer, it had to change the IP address of its Web server. This meant going into dozens of pages and finding and changing all the addresses. After making the laborious change, the company started using a domain name instead of an IP address.

In addition to being more stable, domain names can give the user, as well as the Web weaver, an idea of where the link will go. When the user moves the mouse pointer over a link, most browsers indicate the address to which the link points. If the user sees `http://204.151.55.44/`, he has little idea where the link will take him, unless he memorizes IP addresses! However, if the user sees `http://www.McGraw-Hill.com/`, he has some idea of the kind of information he will be seeing.

In addition, the Web weaver herself, in maintaining her page, will be more likely to remember where the `www.McGraw-Hill.com` **href** points to than she would the `204.151.55.44` IP address. All things considered, it is best to use domain names rather than IP addresses as targets for links.

Sample URLs

Following are examples of URLs that point to different Web pages. The comments after each URL explain the particular features being referenced.

- **http://www.yahoo.com/.** This link assumes that there is a home page, or index page, on the root directory of the **www.yahoo.com** Web server. (This is actually the yahoo search engine's home page.) Notice that there is no `index.html` coded, as it is inferred by the browser.
- **http://www.mcgraw-hill.com/books.html.** In this case, the link points to an actual page on the McGraw-Hill Web server. Rather than retrieving the main page (`index.html`), this link will cause the browser to retrieve the particular page specified. You need to be careful with this sort of link, as it can lose the user. In this case, for example, if the user doesn't know that she can just change the address (location) of the link to **www.mcgraw-hill.com,** she may not know how to get to the main page, and the "Back" button will send her back to your page, not the main page of McGraw-Hill.
- **http://www.server.com/subpage.html#frag.** This is a fictitious site used here to show how a particular anchor within a page may appear as part of the URL. In this case, the browser will retrieve the `subpage.html` from the `server.com` site. When it begins displaying the document, it will start at the internal hyperlink target, `frag`. This address allows direct access into a longer document, allowing the user to go directly to information of interest rather than having to jump again, to the internal target, or scroll down through the document to the information wanted. To establish this sort of linkage, the Web weaver must know the target document and how it is constructed.
- **http://www.otherserver.com:80/subpage.html#frag.** This is a fictitious site used here to show the use of a *port number.* Port numbers are necessary only if the server is set up to receive http traffic on a network port other than the default port, 21. In this example, the server, `otherserver`, expects WWW requests to come into port 80. If you need to code a port number, it must follow the actual server name and be preceded by a colon, as in the example.

We have already examined the considerations involved in creating good links in your documents. When you create links across the Web, you should apply the same rules of good structure that you use for internal links. In addition, you should ensure that the links you create actually work! Think how frustrating it is for your user to try to take a link to a site you recommend only to see, "Unable to locate the server"; "The server does not have a DNS entry"; or the even more deadly message, "404 Not Found The requested URL. . . was not found on this server."

One of the most important functions you will perform for your users is to ensure that the links you provide are valid links. This means you will need to check them at regular intervals. There are some software packages that will check your links for you, but, as mentioned earlier, to make absolutely sure that they are working properly, you should check them yourself from time to time.

One-Way Streets

One of the common problems you will discover as you cruise the Web is the lack of backward pointers linking long pages back to the top or multiple pages back to a home page. The first of these two problems exists with our sequentially designed poetry selections. The menu at the top of the document helps the user link to different poems within the page. However, once the user has finished reading the poem, he must scroll back to the top. Sometimes clicking on the "Back" button will return the user to the top of a page, but this option is not reliable across browsers.

Our solution to this problem is shown in Figure 3.4. The first-level heading at the beginning of the document is assigned the anchor name Poetry using the following code: `<H1><A name="Poetry">Poetry Selections</A></H1>`. An anchor container linking the words Top of Page to the Poetry anchor name would then be placed at the end of each poem (see Figure 3.4). The source anchor container looks like this: `<A href="#Poetry">Top of Page</A>`.

The hierarchically designed poetry pages shown in Figure 3.3 need links back to the home page we called select.htm. Relying on the "Back" button can get you in trouble in this situation as well. When testing a set of pages like this, many Web weavers use the "Back" button in their browser to move from a subpage back to the home page. This works just fine if all the users will start at the home page of the series. But, this approach has a flaw if users place the URL of a target page in their Bookmarks/Favorites file. When these users come back to that page in a different browsing session, they will be unable to return to the main page. Why? Because their browser no longer holds the "Back" pages in memory. It is very frustrating to be on a subpage of the page you want, with no way to return to the home page except to either search for it again or, if you remember the URL, enter it again.

You should never create such one-way traps for your users. Always include a "Back to the home page" link in each of your documents. That way you provide linkage in both directions for your users. They may choose the "Back" feature of their browser, but they also have the opportunity to return to the main page through a designated link. The HTML code for our poetry pages looks like this: `<A href="select.htm">Return to Poetry Selections<A>`. Figure 3.5 (on page 76) illustrates how a browser handles this code.

```
<HTML>
<HEAD>
<TITLE>Intra-page Links</TITLE>
</HEAD>
<BODY bgcolor="#FFFFFF">
<!-- Background color = white -->
<H1><A name="Poetry">Poetry Selections</A></H1>
<P>This page contains some of the poetry written by some of our
favorite poets. Please take a minute to sample their work.  Most of
these poets write in one
of the recognized rhyming styles.
</P>
<P>This is a list of the poets shown on this page: </P>
<A href="#MB">Margaret E. Bruner</A><BR>
<A href="#ee">e. e. cummings</A><BR>
<A href="#RF">Robert Frost</A><BR>
<A href="#EA">Edward Arlington Robinson</A><BR>
<HR align="CENTER" noshade width="75%" size="4">

<H2><A name="RF">Robert Frost</A></H2>
<H3 align="CENTER">Fifty Said</H3>
<P align="CENTER"> -- Text of poem omitted for clarity of example --
</P>
<P align="CENTER"><A href="#Poetry">Top of Page</A>
</P>
<HR align="CENTER" noshade width="50%" size="4">
```

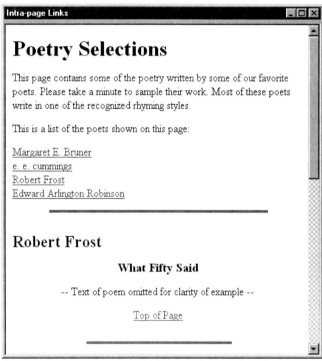

Figure 3.4 HTML code linking users to the top of a page using the name attribute.

Figure 3.5 Providing users with links back to the beginning.

The "Click Here" Faux Pas

Many new Web weavers fall victim to the "click here" faux pas, a classic error of link design in which sentences like, "<u>Click here</u> to go to the next page," or, "<u>Click here</u> to send me e-mail," are used to let the user know that there are links available on the current page. When you understand how the browser displays links, you won't feel compelled to explicitly tell the user that there are links available. It looks far more professional to say, "You can go to the <u>next page</u>," or, "See pictures of <u>my dog</u>," or even, "Send me some <u>e-mail</u>." Be subtle with your links. The users understand how their browsers display links—give them some credit.

Mailto: Protocol

This is a good time to show you how to insert a link to your e-mail system. The anchor container is also used to link the user to the computer's e-mail software. Back in Table 1.1, we listed `Mailto:` as one type of Internet protocol. Since it is an Internet protocol, it can be used as an **href** just like `http:` to link to an Internet-supported service. For example, if you were using Navigator and clicked on <u>poets'</u> e-mail address (Figure 3.5), an e-mail composition window similar to Figure 3.6 would open.

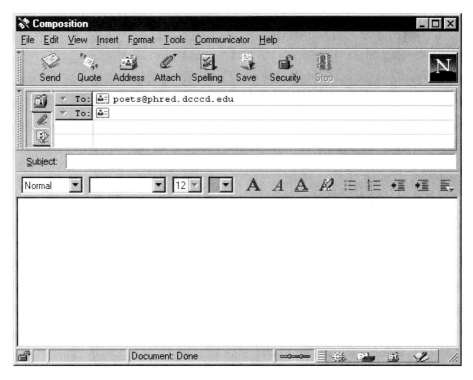

Figure 3.6 Using the `mailto:` protocol as a hypertext reference to open an e-mail composition window.

The e-mail address must be preceded by `mailto:` and be enclosed in quotes just like the other **href** attributes. However, the e-mail address does not have to be used as text as shown in Figure 3.7. The following code would open the same e-mail composition window: `<A HREF="mailto:timg@dcccd.edu">send Tim Gottleber e-mail</A>`.

Return to Poetry Selections
Please send your favorite poem and author to us at poets@phred.dcccd.edu

```
<HR align="CENTER" noshade size="2" width="50">

<P align="CENTER">
<A href="select.htm">Return to Poetry Selections</A><BR>
Please send your favorite poem and author to us at
<A href="mailto:poets@phred.dcccd.edu">poets@phred.dcccd.edu</A>
</P>
```

Figure 3.7 HTML code for page footer.

Page Footers

We are starting to accumulate an interesting list of links that must appear at the end of every HTML document. For lack of a better name, we call this information the *page footer.* Page footers usually provide, in addition to a list of the navigation links used, basic information about the creator of the page. All page footers within the same hierarchical layout share a common design. Besides a

"Back" link and e-mail address, a page footer could have all or none of the following information:

- Organization's name
- Logo
- Street address
- Telephone number
- Fax number
- Web weaver's name
- Date page was last updated
- Links to related pages

Many organizations and individual Web weavers make the page footer their signature code.

Key Terms

Absolute path name
Anchor name
Case-sensitive
Intersystem link
Intrapage link
Intrasystem link
Page footer
Path
Relative path name
Source
Static
Storyboarding
Target

New Tags

<A>

Review Questions

1. What is the definition for each of the key terms?

2. What are three different types of links found in an HTML document?

3. In what two situations are storyboards especially useful?

4. What is the most important reason to use storyboards?

5. What is the basic code for a source anchor container and a target anchor container?

6. What is the difference between a source anchor and a target anchor?

7. Why is it considered bad style to place heading tags within an anchor container?

8. What identifies a URL as an anchor name in a target anchor? What identifies it in a source anchor?

9. What <BODY> attribute changes the color of the text used in a link?

10. Why would a Web author break a long HTML document down into several short, single-topic documents?

11. What identifies an absolute path name?

12. Why is it usually better to use relative path names?

13. What are four potential problems associated with intersystem links?

14. Why is it recommended to use a domain name instead of an IP address?

15. What is the "click here" faux pas?

16. What is the basic code for an anchor container that opens the computer's e-mail composition window?

17. What type of information is found in a page footer?

Exercises

3.1. Create two storyboards. One should employ a simple sequential design and the other a hierarchical design.

3.2. Create a genealogy site that tracks at least five families. All the families must be related by blood. Every page should contain comments with your name and the assignment due date after the <HTML> tag.

    a. Draw a storyboard of the links used in this exercise.
    b. Create a home page with the family name, a general overview of the family, and links to one or more of the family pages.
    c. Each family page should contain the names of the two parents and any children. Besides the date the couple were married, provide every birthday, death day, and the town and state in which each person resides. Provide "Back" and "Forward" links to pages with related people.
    d. Create a common page footer and place it at the end of each family page. The page footer should include a horizontal rule, the family name, a link back to the home page, the date the page was last updated, your name, and a link to your e-mail address if you have one.

3.3. Retrieve the Homework home page you created in Exercise 2.2. Every page should contain comments with your name and the assignment due date after the <HTML> tag.

    a. Draw a storyboard of the links used in this exercise.

    b. Use your school's name as the text for a link to the school's home page. If your school does not have a Web site, complete Exercise 2.6, and create a link to this page.

    c. Create three documents, and use HTML Assignment #1, HTML Assignment #2, HTML Assignment #3 as the titles. Add to your Homework home page a new "Homework Assignments" heading, and place links to the three new documents under the heading.

    d. Create a page footer you can use in the new documents. The footer should contain a horizontal rule, the class identifier, a link back to the Homework home page, the date the page was last updated, your name, and a link to your e-mail address if you have one.

    e. If you completed Exercise 2.1, link the resulting page to the Homework home page, and add the new page footer to it.

3.4. Create your own Poetry Corner HTML document that uses intrapage links to connect to at least four poems. This document should contain comments with your name and the assignment due date after the <HTML> tag. If you completed Exercise 2.3, use the HTML code for one of the poems.

    a. Draw a storyboard of the links used in this exercise.

    b. The beginning of the document should contain a list of the poems by title and author. Each title should be an intrapage link to the related poem.

    c. Start each poem with a horizontal rule, the poem's title, and the author's name.

    d. After each poem there should be a "Back" link to the top of the page.

    e. Create a page footer that contains a horizontal rule, your name, a link to your e-mail address if you have one, the date the page was last updated, and a link to another Web site that displays a poem.

3.5. Retrieve the Web page about your favorite movie you created in Exercise 2.4.

    a. Add a new "What Others Think" heading to the page. Under the heading place two links to Web sites that provide information about the movie and about one of the principal actors or actresses or the director.

    b. Create at least two new HTML documents that contain biographical information about someone associated with the movie. Create links in the original page to these new pages.

    c. Create a page footer you can use in the new documents. The footer should contain a horizontal rule, the movie's name, a link back to the home page, the date the page was last updated, your name, and a link to your e-mail address if you have one.

d. Every page should contain comments with your name and the assignment due date after the <HTML> tag.

e. Draw a storyboard of the links used in this exercise.

3.6. Create an interactive glossary. Every page in the glossary should contain comments with your name and the assignment due date after the <HTML> tag.

a. The home page should provide a topic name and a heading that states "Everything You Ever Wanted To Know About ____". How many glossary pages between 5 and 26 you want to make is up to you. At a minimum, there should be five links on the home page to HTML documents with terms and their definitions in the following ranges: A–E, F–J, K–O, P–T, U–Z.

b. At least 40 definitions need to appear in the glossary.

c. Each glossary page should have a page footer that contains a horizontal rule, a "Back" link to the home page, a "Forward" link to the next alphabetical page (the page with Zs should link to the page with As), the date the page was last updated, your name, and a link to your e-mail address if you have one.

d. Draw a storyboard of the links used in this exercise.

3.7. Retrieve your school's home page created in Exercise 2.6. Every page you create should contain comments with your name and the assignment due date after the <HTML> tag.

a. Draw a storyboard of the links used in this exercise.

b. Replace the words to the school's fight song with a link to a separate page that contains the words.

c. Create a new Telephone Directory page that lists the main telephone number and at least 10 other important telephone numbers related to school. Replace the main telephone number in the home page with a link to this new page.

d. Create three new HTML documents that provide information about the school. Add links to these new pages onto the school's home page. These pages could provide biographical information about teachers, coaches, or administrators. Other pages could provide schedules for sports teams, concerts, or club activities.

e. Create a page footer you can use in the new documents. The footer should contain a horizontal rule, the school's name, the date the page was last updated, your name, and a link to your e-mail address if you have one.

## CHAPTER four

LISTS—
BRINGING
ORDER OUT OF
THE CHAOS

The main reason we build Web pages is to bring unique, easily accessed information to the world. Lists are one way to organize information for easy access. People use lists to organize information in their day-to-day lives, and we can supply that form of organizational tool to them in our Web pages.

83

Plain-Text Lists

We can build what appear to be lists of information by using the <BR> command to force a line break after each item in the list. This is a *plain-text list,* in which no list-making tags are used. To use this "brute force" method to create a list of three items, we could use the code shown in Figure 4.1. As you can see, the Web weaver must put in the numbers in the layout to make the page look like a list.

Since lists are an easy format for most people to read, HTML has special list-making tags that can be used instead of the plain-text method. There are tags for five different kinds of lists:

1. Ordered lists
2. Unordered lists
3. Definitions
4. Menus
5. Directories

The first three are the most commonly used.

<OL>ordered list</OL>

Description: identifies a numbered list of items.
Type: container.
Attributes: class, compact, dir, id, lang, onClick, onDblClick, onKeyDown, onKeyPress, onKeyUp, onMouseDown, onMouseMove, onMouseOut, onMouseOver, onMouseUp, start, style, title, type, and value.
Special note: The compact, start, type, and value attributes have been deprecated.

A simple *ordered list* (<OL>) numbers each item as shown in Figure 4.2. Two new HTML tags are involved with the ordered list: the ordered list container, <OL>. . .</OL>, which encloses the list, and the list item container, <LI>. . .</LI>, used to start each new list element.

This <OL> container is a rather sophisticated one, with some interesting attributes. The easiest way to code it is to simply enter the <OL> tag and then enter the individual list items, each enclosed within a <LI> (list item) container (discussed further later on). Some people treat the <LI> element as an empty tag because closing is inferred by all the current browsers when they find another <LI> or the end of the list. Nevertheless, we recommend closing all list items with a </LI> tag. It takes just a second longer to add the ending tag, which ensures maximum compatibility.

The simple form of the ordered list causes most browsers to put a number at the beginning of each list item. The default is for Arabic numerals, starting with number 1. Figure 4.2 shows how this list would look using a popular graphical browser. Notice that a space is automatically placed between the item number and the item. In the code shown in this figure, French Hens immediately follows the starting tag <LI>, but the browser inserts a space after the numeral.

```
<HTML>
<HEAD>
<TITLE> Plain Text List </TITLE>
</HEAD>
<BODY bgcolor="#FFFFFF">
<!-- Background color = white -->

The following shows a brute force way to build a Christmas list:<BR>
1.  Partridge in pear tree<BR>
2.  French Hens<BR>
3.  Calling Birds<BR>

</BODY>
</HTML>
```

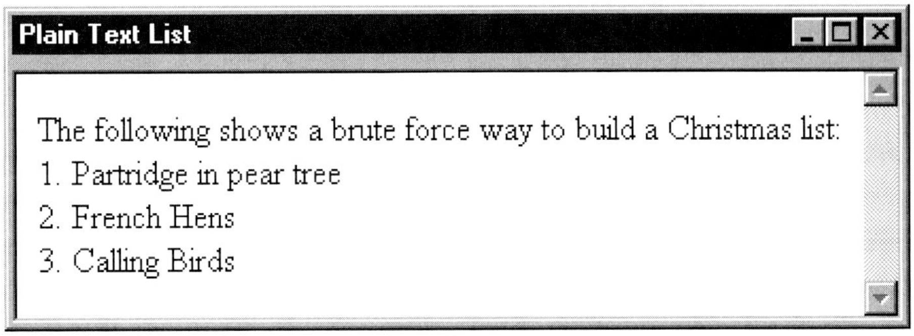

Plain Text List

The following shows a brute force way to build a Christmas list:
1. Partridge in pear tree
2. French Hens
3. Calling Birds

Figure 4.1 HTML code showing the "brute force" (plain-text) method of building a list with line breaks (<BR>).

```
<HTML>
<HEAD>
<TITLE> Ordered List </TITLE>
</HEAD>
<BODY bgcolor="#FFFFFF">
<!-- Background color = white -->

The following ordered list is a more efficient way to build the Christmas list:
<OL>
   <LI> Partridge in pear tree</LI>
   <LI>French Hens</LI>
   <LI> Calling Birds</LI>
</OL>

</BODY>
</HTML>
```

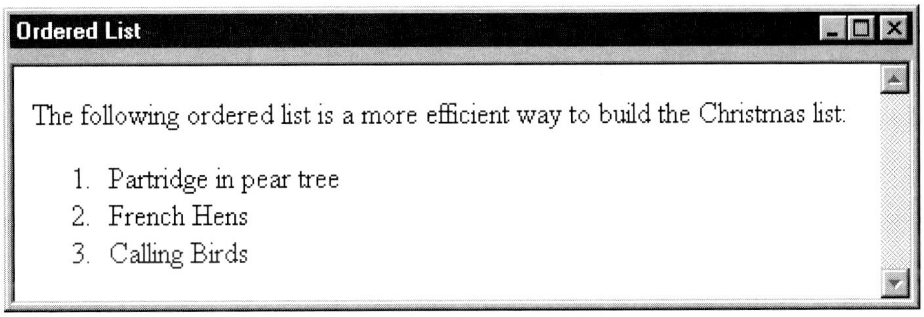

Ordered List

The following ordered list is a more efficient way to build the Christmas list:

1. Partridge in pear tree
2. French Hens
3. Calling Birds

Figure 4.2 HTML code for an ordered list.

One advantage of using the list container instead of coding a plain-text list using line breaks (<BR>) becomes obvious when you try to insert an element into the middle of the list. For example, in our Christmas list example in Figure 4.1, we were missing the turtledoves! There need to be two turtledoves before the three French hens. Using the "brute force" (plain-text) method, we would have to perform the following steps to modify the list:

1. Type in the new line between lines 1 and 2.
2. Renumber line 2 as line 3.
3. Renumber line 3 as line 4.

These corrections would result in the HTML code shown in Figure 4.3.

Bah humbug! We forgot to put the <BR> after the new entry. Now we have to edit it again. If we had used an <OL> container, all we would have had to do was insert a new <LI> container and the new entry. The browser would have updated the numbers for us, and we would not have needed to remember the <BR>, either.

Because it is easy to use the <OL> container, and because people order their worlds in lists, most Web weavers use this container a lot. The ordered list has several attributes that make it even more useful for specific tasks.

start

It is sometimes handy to have a list start at some number other than 1. The **start** attribute lets you do this. For example, you may wish to list the steps in a

```
<HTML>
<HEAD>
<TITLE> Plain Text List </TITLE>
</HEAD>
<BODY bgcolor="#FFFFFF">
<!-- Background color = white -->

The following shows a brute force way to build a Christmas list:<BR>
1. Partridge in pear tree<BR>
2. Turtledoves ─────────────────── new item
3. French Hens <BR> ┐──────────── items renumbered
4. Calling Birds<BR> ┘

</BODY>
</HTML>
```

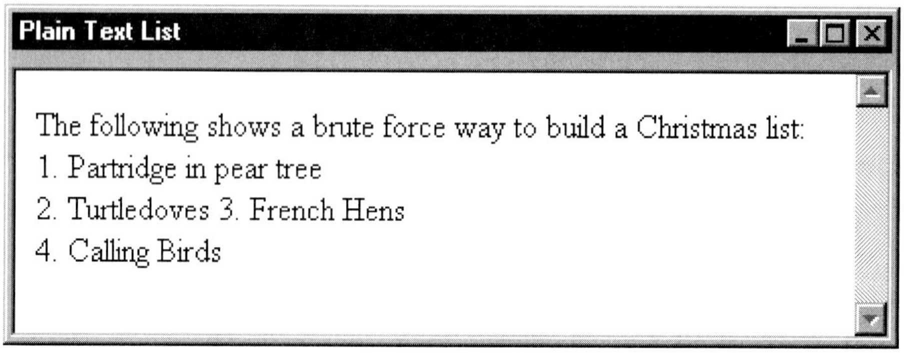

```
Plain Text List                                    _ □ ✕

The following shows a brute force way to build a Christmas list:
1. Partridge in pear tree
2. Turtledoves 3. French Hens
4. Calling Birds
```

Figure 4.3 HTML code for "brute force" list that requires renumbering when new items are inserted.

task, with some discussion interspersed among the steps. You can code the first list container that describes the first three steps, for example, then type your discussion, and then continue your list by starting a second one that begins with the number 4. Figure 4.4 shows an example. The list is restarted at item 4 using the following code: <OL start="4">.

```
<HTML>
<HEAD>
<TITLE> Ordered List Using The Start Attribute</TITLE>
</HEAD>
<BODY bgcolor="#FFFFFF">
<!-- Background color = white -->

There are 8 steps to change the oil in your Saturn:
<OL>
   <LI>Find a comfy place to park the car, in the shade in summer,
       in the sun in winter.</LI>
   <LI>Get the waste oil pan, filter wrench, and 14mm box end wrench ready.</LI>
   <LI>Find 4 quarts of 5W-30 oil and a Saturn oil filter.</LI>
</OL>

It is really important, or so the folks at Saturn tell me, to use 5W-30 oil and
genuine Saturn oil filters.
<OL start="4">
   <LI>Remove the oil drain plug, and drain the old oil into the waste oil pan.</LI>
   <LI>Remove the old filter...then clean up the mess you made.</LI>
   <LI>Replace the oil drain plug after the oil stops dripping.</LI>
   <LI>Put the new oil filter on, 1/4 turn past finger tight.</LI>
</OL>

Always remember to put just a bit of  oil on the rubber gasket before you put the
oil filter back on.  This will make a better seal, and help you get the filter
tightened correctly.
<OL start="8">
   <LI>Put 4 quarts of 5W-30 oil into the engine.</LI>
</OL>

</BODY>
</HTML>
```

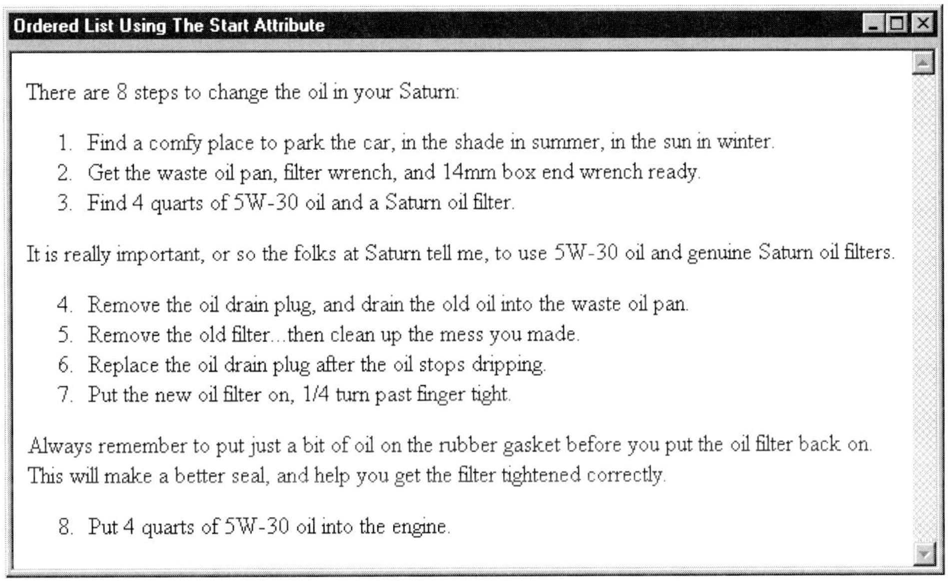

Ordered List Using The Start Attribute

There are 8 steps to change the oil in your Saturn:

1. Find a comfy place to park the car, in the shade in summer, in the sun in winter.
2. Get the waste oil pan, filter wrench, and 14mm box end wrench ready.
3. Find 4 quarts of 5W-30 oil and a Saturn oil filter.

It is really important, or so the folks at Saturn tell me, to use 5W-30 oil and genuine Saturn oil filters.

4. Remove the oil drain plug, and drain the old oil into the waste oil pan.
5. Remove the old filter...then clean up the mess you made.
6. Replace the oil drain plug after the oil stops dripping.
7. Put the new oil filter on, 1/4 turn past finger tight.

Always remember to put just a bit of oil on the rubber gasket before you put the oil filter back on. This will make a better seal, and help you get the filter tightened correctly.

8. Put 4 quarts of 5W-30 oil into the engine.

Figure 4.4 HTML code using the **start** attribute.

Notice in Figure 4.4 how the **start** attribute is used in the second and third lists. This attribute allows the browser to build the lists, but the author can still control the ordering of the numbers. It is a very handy tool. Although the **start** attribute has been deprecated for use within the <OL> container, related formatting capabilities have been incorporated into **style** attribute properties with the HTML 4.0 specifications discussed later in this chapter.

type

Besides letting you choose the number for starting your list, HTML also provides a way for you to change the style of the numbers or letters of the list elements. Table 4.1 presents the different number and letter styles provided by the **type** attribute. Figure 4.5 shows some coded examples.

This attribute will be handy for making outlines, as we will see later in the chapter, when we put lists inside lists. However, the **type** attribute, like the **start** attribute, has been deprecated in favor of the **style** attribute properties covered next.

Type	Style	Description	Examples
A	upper-alpha	Uppercase letters	A. B. C. D.
a	lower-alpha	Lowercase letters	a. b. c. d.
I	upper-roman	Uppercase Roman numerals	I. II. III. IV.
i	lower-roman	Lowercase Roman numerals	i. ii. iii. iv.
1	decimal	Arabic numerals (default)	1. 2. 3. 4

Table 4.1 List options for labeling items in an ordered list.

style

As mentioned in Chapter 2, the **style** attribute is used with a variety of HTML tags to control page layout. As shown in Figure 4.5, using this attribute to set `list-style-type` equal to **upper-alpha** produces the same results as setting the **type** attribute equal to "A". The HTML code looks like this: <OL style="list-style-type: upper-alpha">.

Not only does the **style** attribute, through the `list-style-type` property, support the styles listed in Table 4.1, it also provides the <OL> options shown in Table 4.2 (on page 90). These options in Table 4.2 are in keeping with the W[3]C's intent, along with the HTML 4.0 specifications, to support internationalism by accounting for different languages besides English.

Style versus Deprecated Attributes

An old sixties song by Bob Dylan bemoans that "the times, they are a'changin'." This could also be said about the handling of lists within the HTML 4.0 specifications. The introduction of cascading style sheets and the *inline* **style** attribute is changing the way Web weavers format a list. As we write these words, though,

type Attribute

```
Ordered list using UPPERCASE letters:
<OL type="A">
  <LI> for excellent students</LI>
  <LI> for those above average</LI>
  <LI> for the average</LI>
</OL>

Ordered list using lowercase letters:
<OL type="a">
  <LI> is for apple</LI>
  <LI> is for banana</LI>
  <LI> is for cantaloupe</LI>
</OL>

Ordered list using UPPERCASE roman numerals:
<OL type="I">
  <LI> is for first place</LI>
  <LI> is for second place</LI>
  <LI> is for third place</LI>
</OL>

Ordered list using lowercase roman numerals:
<OL type="i">
  <LI> is for the money</LI>
  <LI> is for the show</LI>
  <LI> is to get ready</LI>
</OL>
```

style Attribute

```
Ordered list using UPPERCASE letters:
<OL style="list-style-type: upper-alpha">
  <LI> for excellent students</LI>
  <LI> for those above average</LI>
  <LI> for the average</LI>
</OL>

Ordered list using lowercase letters:
<OL style="list-style-type: lower-alpha">
  <LI> is for apple</LI>
  <LI> is for banana</LI>
  <LI> is for cantaloupe</LI>
</OL>

Ordered list using UPPERCASE roman numerals:
<OL style="list-style-type: upper-roman">
  <LI> is for first place</LI>
  <LI> is for second place</LI>
  <LI> is for third place</LI>
</OL>

Ordered list using lowercase roman numerals:
<OL style="list-style-type: lower-roman">
  <LI> is for the money</LI>
  <LI> is for the show</LI>
  <LI> is to get ready</LI>
</OL>
```

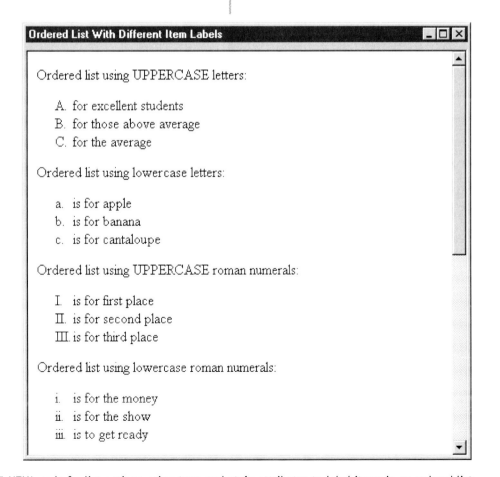

Figure 4.5 HTML code for list options using **type** and **style** attributes to label items in an ordered list.

STYLE	DESCRIPTION	EXAMPLES
Armenian	Traditional Armenian numbering	
Cjk-ideographic	Plain ideographic numbers	
Decimal-leading-zero	Decimal numbers padded by initial zeros	01. 02. 03.
Georgian	Traditional Georgian numbering	an. ban. gan.
Hebrew	Traditional Hebrew numbering	
Hiragana	Japanese style	a. i. u. e. o. ka. ki.
Katakana	Japanese style	A. I. U. E. O. KA. KI.
Hiragana-iroha	Japanese style	i. ro. ha. ni. ho. he. to.
Katakana-iroha	Japanese style	I. RO. HA. NI. HO. HE. TO.
Lower-greek	Lowercase classical Greek letters	alpha. beta. gamma.
Lower-latin	Lowercase ASCII letters	a. b. c. d.
Upper-latin	Uppercase ASCII letters	A. B. C. D.

Table 4.2 Additional label options for ordering a list using the **style** attribute.

only the latest versions of Navigator and Internet Explorer recognize some of the new **style** attributes recommended by W^{3}C. For this reason, we also explain deprecated attributes in this text, because you need to know both kinds of attributes in order to maintain backward compatibility with older browsers.

<LI>list item</LI>

Description: identifies a specific item in an ordered, unordered, menu, or directory list.
Type: container.
Attributes: class, dir, id, lang, onClick, onDblClick, onKeyDown, onKeyPress, onKeyUp, onMouseDown, onMouseMove, onMouseOut, onMouseOver, onMouseUp, style, title, type, and value.
Special note: The type and value attributes have been deprecated.

You have already seen the way the list item (<LI>) container is used to indicate elements of a list. Although the <LI> tag is really a container, browsers can always infer the end of this container by what follows. Once again we recommend using the closing tag, in this case </LI>, because we think good page design leaves the browser little to infer, or guess. Our code will, therefore, incorporate the closing tags even though the HTML specifications state that the </LI> closing tag may be omitted, and some Web weavers feel that not coding the closing tags makes it easier to modify the list. The <LI> container is an example of a container that may be evolving into an empty tag.

The <LI> container is used with ordered and unordered lists. What the <LI> tag generates depends on the type of list for which it defines an element. In an ordered list, the <LI> tag specifies a list element that is preceded by a number or letter. In an unordered list, it specifies a list element preceded by one of the different types of bullets.

The <LI> container can contain almost anything if it defines an element of an ordered or unordered list. It can contain text, images, or even other lists. If the list item is within a directory or menu list, though, that directory or menu list cannot contain other lists or ***blocked elements*** (discussed next) like paragraphs or forms.

Blocked and Inline Elements

A blocked element has a clearly defined beginning and end. It generally begins a new line and can include line breaks. It also can contain ***inline elements*** or another blocked element. Inline elements, like bold or italics, are appropriately named because they usually appear within a line of text and do not initiate line breaks. An inline element can contain other inline elements, but not a blocked element. Blocked elements are generally larger structures than inline elements. Commonly used inline elements are discussed in Chapter 5.

type

The **type** attribute of the <LI> container is very much like the **type** attribute of the <OL> container. The difference is that the <OL> **type** specifies the style of the numbers for the whole list, whereas the **type** attribute on a single <LI> changes the style of the numbering beginning with that list item and continuing until it is subsequently changed. Figure 4.6 (on page 92) shows the different values for the **type** attribute, with each list item having its own label style. This <LI> **type** attribute was deprecated in the HTML 4.0 specifications in favor of the **style** attribute's list-style-type property.

style

Both the **type** and **style** attributes can produce the same results, as shown in Figure 4.6, but a wider range of item labels is available (see Table 4.2) with the **style** attribute.

value

Like the **start** attribute of the <OL> tag, the **value** attribute of the <LI> tag can specify a particular starting value that will serve as the new base number for the rest of the items in the list—unless a subsequent item specifies another value.

Misusing the **value** attribute can cause confusing results, as shown in Figure 4.7 (on page 92). In this figure, you can see that each time **value** was changed, the change was propagated from that point down the list until there was another change. You need to be very careful when changing the **style** or **value** for list elements. It is rare that you will need to change either.

```
<HTML>
<HEAD>
<TITLE> Ordered List With Line Item Options </TITLE>
</HEAD>
<BODY bgcolor="#FFFFFF">
<!-- Background color = white -->

This list shows item options offered by type attribute:
<OL>
  <LI type="A">This element is of type A.</LI>
  <LI type="a">This element is of type a.</LI>
  <LI type="I">This element is of type I.</LI>
  <LI type="i">And this element has a type i.</LI>
</OL>

This list shows item options offered by the style attribute:
<OL>
  <LI style="list-style-type: upper-alpha">This element is upper-alpha.</LI>
  <LI style="list-style-type: lower-alpha">This element is lower-alpha.</LI>
  <LI style="list-style-type: upper-roman">This element is upper-roman.</LI>
  <LI style="list-style-type: lower-roman">And this element is lower-roman.</LI>
</OL>

</BODY>
</HTML>
```

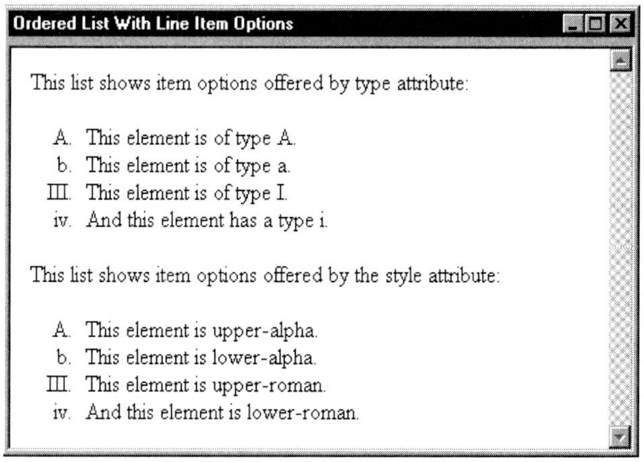

Figure 4.6 HTML code showing variations of the <LI> **type** and **style** attributes.

```
<HTML>
<HEAD>
<TITLE> Misuse of List Item value and style Attributes </TITLE>
</HEAD>
<BODY bgcolor="#FFFFFF">
<!-- Background color = white -->

The following list shows each type of list item:
<OL>
<LI value="5">This is the first element of the list.</LI>
<LI value="1"> The second element</LI>
<LI value="11"> The third element</LI>
<LI style="list-style-type: lower-roman">The fourth element changes number type,
    but not <B>value</B></LI>
<LI value="1"> and the last element has <B>value</B> 1 too,
    notice that the list-style-type back to default decimal format!</LI>
</OL>

</BODY>
</HTML>
```

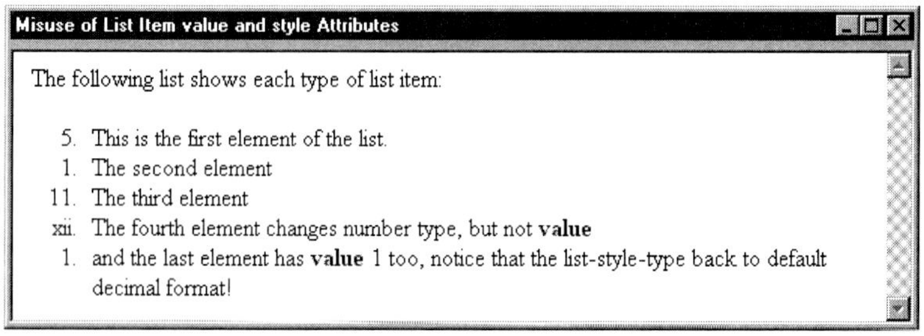

Figure 4.7 HTML code showing misuse of the <LI> **value** and **style** attributes.

If you are trying to build clean, fully HTML-compliant code, you should never embed any text or other items within a list that are not supposed to be part of the actual list. For example, Figure 4.8 shows how we could code the oil-change example that appeared earlier in Figure 4.4 without changing lists. We have included two descriptive paragraphs within the list, yet we keep them outside the actual list elements. With this noncompliant design, the browser does not need to restart the numbering on successive lists. However, unlike the first line of text, the embedded paragraphs are indented with the list items when displayed by the browser. This display is a subtle difference from the oil-changing steps created by the HTML-compliant code in Figure 4.4. Figure 4.8 is shown to illustrate a *bad* example! In other words, don't try this at home.

```
<HTML>
<HEAD>
<TITLE> Poorly Written HTML Code </TITLE>
</HEAD>
<BODY bgcolor="#FFFFFF">
<!-- Background color = white -->

There are 8 steps to change the oil in your Saturn:
<OL>
  <LI>Find a comfy place to park the car, in the shade in summer,
      in the sun in winter.</LI>
  <LI>Get the waste oil pan, filter wrench,
      and 14mm box end wrench ready.</LI>
  <LI>Find 4 quarts of 5W-30 oil and a Saturn oil filter.</LI>

<P>It is really important, or so the folks at Saturn tell me,        embedded
   to use 5W-30 oil and genuine Saturn oil filters.                  paragraph
</P>

  <LI>Remove the oil drain plug, and drain the old oil
      into the waste oil pan.</LI>
  <LI>Remove the old filter...then clean up the mess you made.</LI>
  <LI>Replace the oil drain plug after the oil stops dripping.</LI>
  <LI>Put the new oil filter on, 1/4 turn past finger tight.</LI>

<P>Always remember to put just a bit of  oil on the rubber gasket    embedded
   before you put the oil filter back on.  This will make a better seal,  paragraph
   and help you get the filter tightened correctly.
</P>

  <LI>Put 4 quarts of 5W-30 oil into the engine.</LI>
</OL>

</BODY>
</HTML>
```

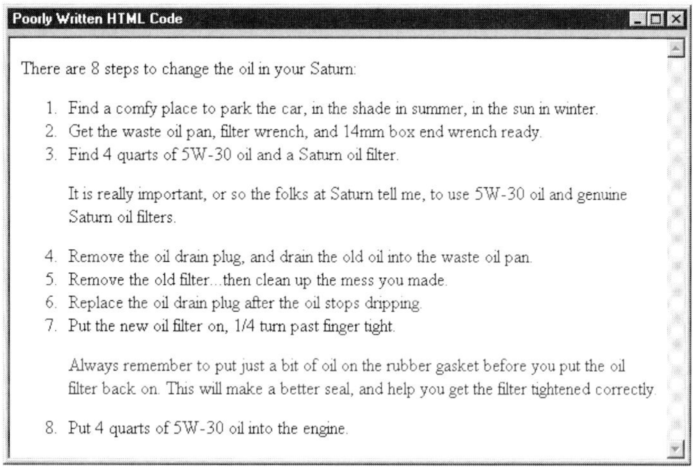

Figure 4.8 Noncompliant HTML code with paragraphs inside the ordered list—an example of what *not* to do.

<UL>unordered list</UL>

Description: identifies a list of items with no specific order implied.
Type: container.
Attributes: class, compact, dir, id, lang, onClick, onDblClick, onKeyDown, onKeyPress, onKeyUp, onMouseDown, onMouseMove, onMouseOut, onMouseOver, onMouseUp, start, style, title, and type.
Special note: The compact and type attributes have been deprecated.

The *unordered list* (<UL>) is used when you want to make a list of items that have no necessary order. It is also called a *bulleted list*. A *bullet* is the decorative label assigned to each item in a list. The W^{3}C uses the term *marker* when describing these decorative bullets used in an unordered list. A five-item unordered list is shown in Figure 4.9. Except for the fact that bullets rather than numbers or letters precede the list elements, the format of this list is very similar to that of the ordered list. Each list item in contained within an <LI>list item</LI> container.

```
<HTML>
<HEAD>
<TITLE> Unordered List </TITLE>
</HEAD>
<BODY bgcolor="#FFFFFF">
<!-- Background color = white -->

The following books usually appear on the bookshelf of Web Weavers:
<UL>
  <LI>How to Explain Obtuse Ideas to Anyone</LI>
  <LI>Charlotte's Web</LI>
  <LI>Excellent Paper Airplanes Vol. 4</LI>
  <LI>Even More Excellent HTML</LI>
  <LI>Sanity: Lost, Found,and Lost Again</LI>
</UL>
In addition, everyone should have a copy of the Boy Scout manual at hand.

</BODY>
</HTML>
```

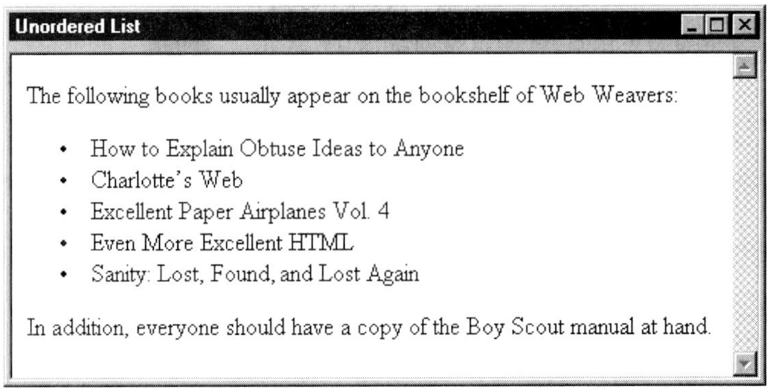

Figure 4.9 HTML code for an unordered list with five list items.

compact

Another option for both the ordered and unordered lists is the **compact** attribute. It is designed to make the list smaller by compressing line spacing between the list items. The HTML code for creating a compact unordered list looks like this: `<UL compact>`. However, most browsers ignore this attribute, so it is of little value to code it.

type or style

It is possible to change the shape of the bullets in an unordered list by using the **type** or **style** attributes. Three different marker styles are recognized by the HTML 4.0 specifications: disc, circle, or square. Disc is the default format, as shown in Figure 4.9.

In the following HTML code, the **type** attribute would establish an unordered list that uses a square as the preceding bullet for each list item: `<UL type="square">`.

As mentioned earlier in this chapter, the **type** attribute was deprecated in the most recent HTML specifications in favor of the **style** attribute. Both options are shown in Figure 4.10.

```
<HTML>
<HEAD>
<TITLE> Unordered List With Line Item Options </TITLE>
</HEAD>
<BODY bgcolor="#FFFFFF">
<!-- Background color = white -->

The marker style was originally changed using the <B>type</B> attribute.<BR>
This list uses the square bullet:
<UL type="square">
  <LI>How to Explain Obtuse Ideas to Anyone</LI>
  <LI>Charlotte's Web</LI>
  <LI>Excellent Paper Airplanes Vol. 4</LI>
  <LI>Even More Excellent HTML</LI>
  <LI>Sanity: Lost, Found, and Lost Again</LI>
</UL>

The <B>style</B> attribute provides a new way to change the marker's look.<BR>
This list uses the circle bullet:
<UL style="list-style-type: circle">
  <LI>How to Explain Obtuse Ideas to Anyone</LI>
  <LI>Charlotte's Web</LI>
  <LI>Excellent Paper Airplanes Vol. 4</LI>
  <LI>Even More Excellent HTML</LI>
  <LI>Sanity: Lost, Found, and Lost Again</LI>
</UL>
Unordered lists use the disc marker as a default bullet.

</BODY>
</HTML>
```

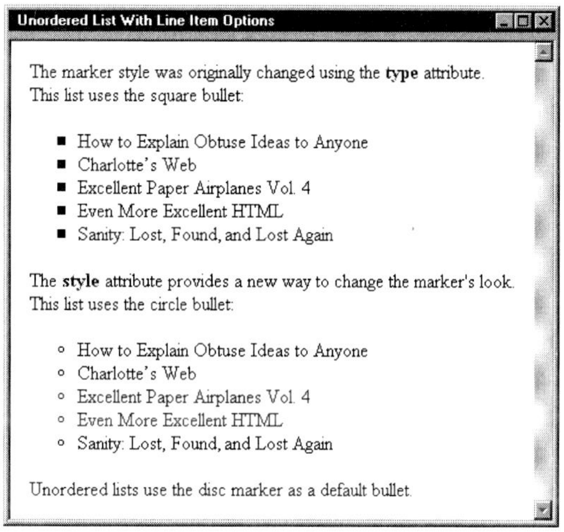

Figure 4.10 HTML code using the **type** and **style** attributes to change the markers in an unordered list.

The HTML code for changing the bullet to a circle using the **style** attribute is as follows: <UL style="list-style-type: circle">. The **style** attribute's list-style-type property is utilized in both ordered and unordered lists to change the look of the item label.

Note that some browsers don't recognize the type attribute used within the <LI> tag. For example, although Navigator will recognize the disc property within the <LI> tag, Internet Explorer will not. Consequently, it is best to avoid using the **type** attribute within the <LI> tag.

Lists of Lists (Nesting)

Sometimes it is necessary to build lists of lists. In both ordered and unordered lists, it is possible to put another list (a sublist) inside a list element. This procedure of *nesting lists* allows you to build structures that convey complex relationships.

Combining Ordered and Unordered Lists

Figure 4.11 shows an ordered list that has two small unordered lists within it. As you can see from this example, the browser indents the list within a list to in-

```
<HTML>
<HEAD>
<TITLE> Nested Lists </TITLE>
</HEAD>
<BODY bgcolor="#FFFFFF">
<!-- Background color = white -->

When packing a briefcase to go to school, be sure to:
<OL>
<LI>Pack Yoda, the laptop.</LI>
  <UL>
  <LI> Get the power cord and transformer.</LI>
  <LI> Find the box of disks.</LI>
  <LI> Check on the PCMCIA cards.</LI>
  </UL>
<LI> Check that the Day-Timer is there.</LI>
  <UL>
  <LI> Check that it is the right month.</LI>
  <LI> Check that it is the right year.</LI>
  </UL>
<LI> Take correct textbooks.</LI>
<LI> Make sure LUNCH is packed!</LI>
</OL>

</BODY>
</HTML>
```

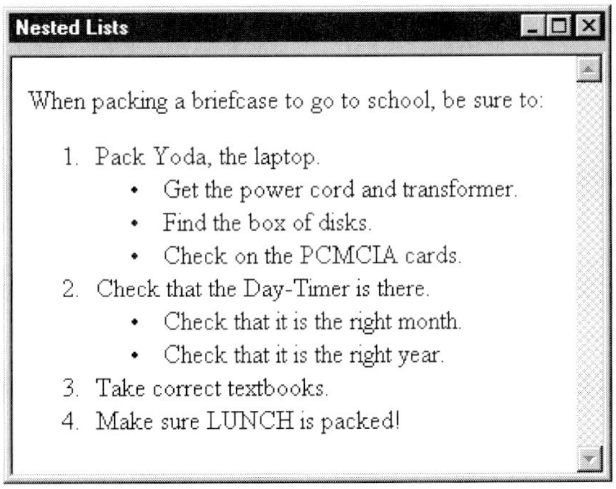

Nested Lists

When packing a briefcase to go to school, be sure to:

1. Pack Yoda, the laptop.
   - Get the power cord and transformer.
   - Find the box of disks.
   - Check on the PCMCIA cards.
2. Check that the Day-Timer is there.
   - Check that it is the right month.
   - Check that it is the right year.
3. Take correct textbooks.
4. Make sure LUNCH is packed!

Figure 4.11 HTML code for unordered lists contained within an ordered list.

crease readability. The fact that the subordinate lists are indented in the HTML code has no bearing on how the browser displays them. This indention is only to make the code easier to read.

Nesting Unordered Lists

In nested unordered lists, most browsers use different bullet types to show that some elements are subordinate to others. The code at the top of Figure 4.12 has three levels of nested unordered lists. In Navigator this code would generate the display shown in Figure 4.12. Notice that the browser uses different bullets on each of the different levels generated.

```
<HTML>
<HEAD>
<TITLE> Nested Unordered Lists </TITLE>
</HEAD>
<BODY bgcolor="#FFFFFF">
<!-- Background color = white -->

When packing a briefcase to go to school, be sure to:
<UL>
<LI>Pack Yoda, the laptop.</LI>
  <UL>
  <LI> Get the power cord and transformer.</LI>
  <LI> Find the box of disks.</LI>
    <UL>
    <LI>  Get this semester's homework disk.</LI>
    <LI>  Get the grading software disk.</LI>
    <LI>  Make sure the games disk is packed!</LI>
    </UL>
  <LI> Check on the PCMCIA cards.</LI>
  </UL>
<LI> Check that the Day-Timer is there.</LI>
  <UL>
  <LI> Check that it is the right month.</LI>
  <LI> Check that it is the right year.</LI>
  </UL>
<LI> Take correct textbooks.</LI>
<LI> Make sure LUNCH is packed!</LI>
</UL>

</BODY>
</HTML>
```

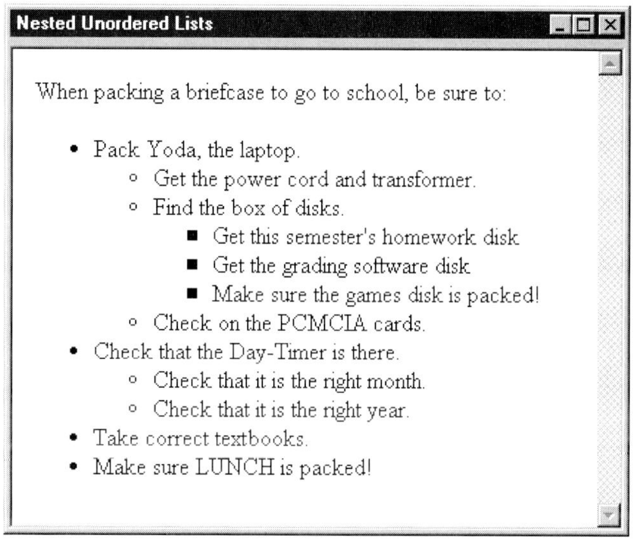

Figure 4.12 HTML code for nested unordered lists.

Nesting Ordered List

Nesting ordered lists allows the creation of outlines. For example, if we change the HTML code in Figure 4.12 to use ordered lists, the result would be as shown in Figure 4.13.

Hmmmm. Figure 4.13 is not quite what we had in mind. Although it does indeed show a nested list of ordered lists, it isn't all that readable. What we need to do is change the **style** attribute's `list-style-type` property to different list types to show subordination. It is best to use the standard outline order

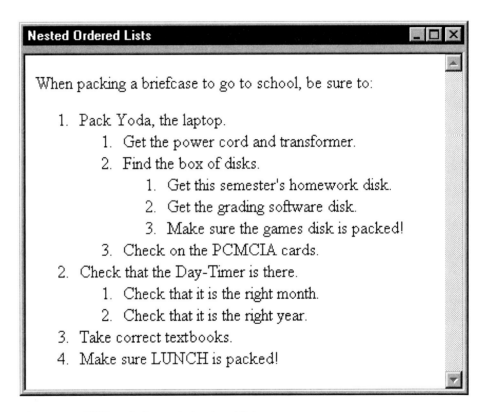

Figure 4.13 HTML code for nested ordered lists.

(I., A., 1., a.). Figure 4.14 presents the HTML code that will make the list more understandable. Notice that we need to specify the **style** attribute only for the opening of each list, not for each element.

Using ordered or unordered lists can make your page more understandable to your users. In later examples you will see why lists are becoming a standard feature of many of the pages on the Web. As you cruise the Net, look for examples of lists, both good and bad.

```
<HTML>
<HEAD>
<TITLE> Nested Ordered Lists </TITLE>
</HEAD>
<BODY bgcolor="#FFFFFF">
<!-- Background color = white -->

When packing a briefcase to go to school, be sure to:
<OL style="list-style-type: upper-roman">
<LI>Pack Yoda, the laptop.</LI>
  <OL style="list-style-type: upper-alpha">
  <LI> Get the power cord and transformer.</LI>
  <LI> Find the box of disks.</LI>
    <OL style="list-style-type: decimal">
    <LI>  Get this semester's homework disk.</LI>
    <LI>  Get the grading software disk.</LI>
    <LI>  Make sure the games disk is packed!</LI>
    </OL>
  <LI> Check on the PCMCIA cards.</LI>
  </OL>
<LI> Check that the Day-Timer is there.</LI>
  <OL style="list-style-type: upper-alpha">
  <LI> Check that it is the right month.</LI>
  <LI> Check that it is the right year.</LI>
  </OL>
<LI> Take correct textbooks.</LI>
<LI> Make sure LUNCH is packed!</LI>
</OL>

</BODY>
</HTML>
```

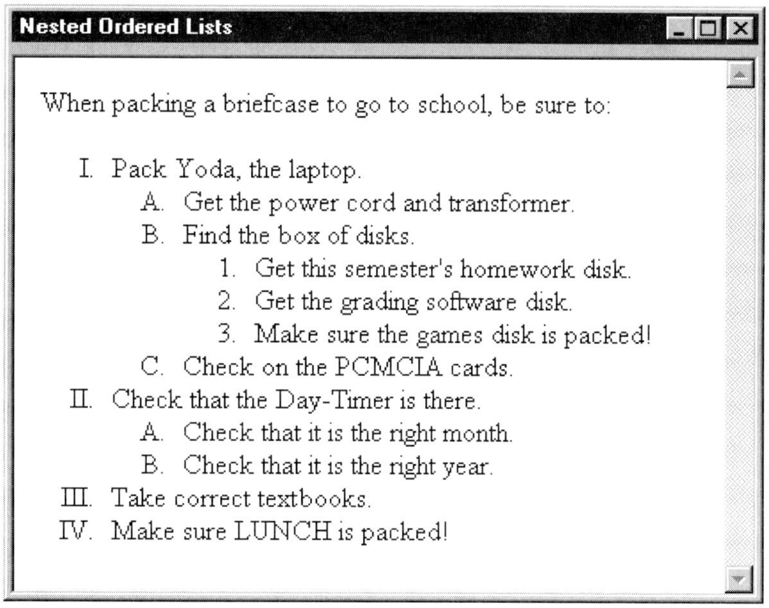

When packing a briefcase to go to school, be sure to:

I. Pack Yoda, the laptop.
   A. Get the power cord and transformer.
   B. Find the box of disks.
      1. Get this semester's homework disk.
      2. Get the grading software disk.
      3. Make sure the games disk is packed!
   C. Check on the PCMCIA cards.
II. Check that the Day-Timer is there.
   A. Check that it is the right month.
   B. Check that it is the right year.
III. Take correct textbooks.
IV. Make sure LUNCH is packed!

Figure 4.14 HTML code for nested ordered lists using different list styles.

Readability

This is a good time to bring up the issue of *readability.* As your HTML code gets longer and more complex, you will find that it saves you both time and effort if you take readability into account as you build the page.

A document with good readability uses white space to separate the page's design elements. These elements could be lists, paragraphs, tables, and so forth. Inserting a couple of blank lines around a particular structure, like a list, makes it just a little easier to find and yet requires little time and effort. Likewise, it is simple to insert a tab or a couple of spaces in front of subordinate items to show their relative relationship. Another good practice is to put each logical part of the HTML code on a separate line making the code easier to read and understand. The code in Figure 4.15 violates all of these readability rules. Although it is very short, you can see how much more difficult it is to read and maintain than the previous examples of HTML code.

If you look closely, you will find that this is the same HTML code that generated the ordered lists within lists of Figure 4.14. All the blank lines, tabs, and extra carriage returns have been removed. Both codes will generate exactly the same nested lists, but the code in Figure 4.15 is harder to read and understand than the code in Figure 4.14 and would be much more difficult to maintain.

```
<HTML><HEAD>,TITLE. Nested Ordered Lists</TITLE> Nested Ordered
Lists</TITLE></HEAD><BODY bgcolor="#FFFFFF">When packing a
briefcase to go to school, be sure to:<OL style="list-style-type: upper
roman"><LI>Pack Yoda, the laptop. <OL style="list-style-type: upper
alpha"><LI>Get the power cord and transformer.<LI>Find the box of
disks.<OL style="list-style-type: decimal"><LI>Get this semester's
homework disk.<LI>Get the grading software disk.<LI>Make sure the
games disk is packed!</OL><LI>Check on the PCMCIA
cards.</OL><LI>Check that the Day-Timer is there.<OL style="list-style-
type: upper alpha"><LI>Check that it is the right month.<LI>Check that it
is the right year.</OL><LI> Take correct textbooks.<LI>Make sure LUNCH
is packed!</OL></BODY></HTML>
```

Figure 4.15 HTML code written with minimal readability.

Good formatting will make it easier for you to find your way around in your own HTML code as well as making it easier for other people to see what you have done. Making longer and more complex pages readable will become ever more important as you begin to modify codes you have already written. You can puzzle out the code shown in Figure 4.15, but if you were faced with 20 pages of code all jammed together like that, it could be a daunting task. While this is an extreme example, some Web weavers build whole sites of pages like this, and they are for all intents and purposes unreadable. This example also brings home the point that while the Web weaver controls the content, the browser controls the format, because, remember, the jammed-together HTML code will generate exactly the same page in your browser as the more readable code.

<DL>definition list</DL>

Description: identifies terms and related definitions as part of a glossary-like list.
Type: container.
Attributes: dir, class, id, lang, onClick, onDblClick, onKeyDown, onKeyPress, onKeyUp, onMouseDown, onMouseMove, onMouseOut, onMouseOver, onMouseUp, style, and title.

Most browsers support this form of list, called a *definition list,* which presents a term and its definition formatted like a glossary or a dictionary. It is the ideal format to present lists of words or phrases with their meanings. Figure 4.16 presents the code for a definition list describing the various types of lists. As you can see, the browser does some nice formatting of the text.

```
<HTML>
<HEAD>
<TITLE> Definition List </TITLE>
</HEAD>
<BODY bgcolor="#FFFFFF">
<!-- Background color = white -->

<H2>The Three Common Types of HTML Lists:</H2>
<DL>
  <DT>Ordered Lists</DT>
  <DD>An ordered list contains several elements, each of them preceded
      by a number, letter, Roman numeral, or special symbol.
  </DD>

  <DT>Unordered Lists</DT>
  <DD>Unordered lists show a series of elements, preceded by some form
      of marker (bullet) character.  Most browsers show subordinate
      lists indented and preceded by a different marker.
  </DD>

  <DT>Definition Lists</DT>
  <DD>Definition list is used to display a word or phrase, followed by
      the definition or explanation of that word or phrase.  They are
      commonly used in dictionary or glossary lists.
  </DD>
</DL>

</BODY>
</HTML>
```

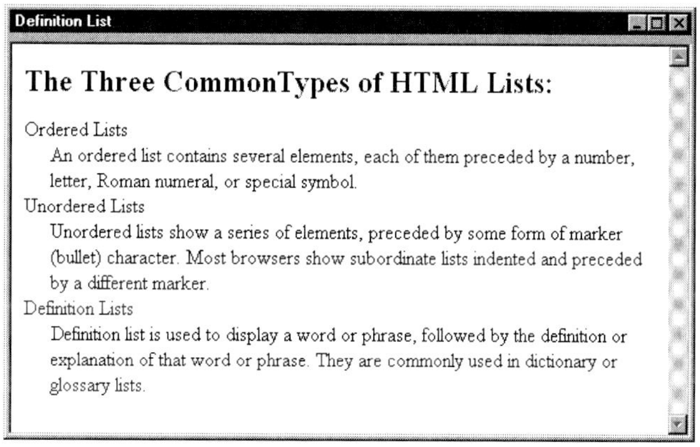

Figure 4.16 HTML code for a definition list.

Notice that the code for the definition list uses different elements (terms and definitions) than the list items employed by the other two types of lists we have studied. Our use of white space in the Figure 4.16 code is just to improve readability and has no bearing on the way the browser presents the lists.

Definition lists are enclosed within the <DL>definition list</DL> container. The </DL> ending tag is *never* omitted. Each element of a definition list is composed of two different parts, the word or phrase to be defined, followed by the definition. Each of the parts of an element has a particular HTML tag to define it. A definition list does not use the <LI>list element</LI> container unless the definition itself contains an ordered or unordered list.

<DT>definition term</DT>

Description: identifies a term in a definition list.
Type: container.
Attributes: dir, class, id, lang, onClick, onDblClick, onKeyDown, onKeyPress, onKeyUp, onMouseDown, onMouseMove, onMouseOut, onMouseOver, onMouseUp, style, and title.
Special note: This element is considered inline content.

The <DT>definition term</DT> container indicates the term that is to be defined as shown in Figure 4.16. It is valid only within a <DL> element. Although the <DT> element is formally considered a container, it can be used as an empty tag, like <LI>. It is technically possible to follow the <DT> tag with a long expression, but traditionally a single word or short phrase is used. There are no new attributes associated with the <DT> element.

<DD>definition definition</DD>

Description: identifies a definition in definition list.
Type: container.
Attributes: dir, class, id, lang, onClick, onDblClick, onKeyDown, onKeyPress, onKeyUp, onMouseDown, onMouseMove, onMouseOut, onMouseOver, onMouseUp, style, and title.
Special note: This element is considered block-level content.

The <DD> definition definition</DD> container is coded immediately following the word or phrase associated with the <DT> container. It marks the beginning of the definition segment of the <DL> list entry. You can code any HTML construct within the definition portion of the list. However, since your users generally expect this type of format to be used for definitions and the like, you should restrict your content to the succinct definition or explanation of the word or phrase shown by the <DT> tag. There are no unique attributes associated with the <DD> element.

Deprecated List Forms

As you cruise the Web, and look at code, you will see a couple of other types of lists, menus, and directories. These lists were used with older versions of HTML and are generally handled like unordered lists, so they have been deprecated. As with other lists that use the <LI> element, the **type** or **style** attribute, if recognized, specifies the marker design for the list.

<MENU>menu list</MENU>

Description: identifies a single-column list of no implied order.
Type: container.
Attributes: dir, class, id, lang, onClick, onDblClick, onKeyDown, onKeyPress, onKeyUp, onMouseDown, onMouseMove, onMouseOut, onMouseOver, onMouseUp, style, and title.
Special note: This element has been deprecated in favor of the unordered list.

The <MENU> element was designed to present single-column menu lists (Figure 4.17). In the past, <MENU> element was used to represent items in a pull-down menu format rather than in an unordered list. Some browsers eliminate the leading bullet when formatting this element. Each item is indicated by the <LI> tag, as in both ordered and unordered lists. Most browsers present this list just like an unordered list.

<DIR>directory list</DIR>

Description: identifies a multicolumn directory list of no implied order.
Type: container.
Attributes: dir, class, id, lang, onClick, onDblClick, onKeyDown, onKeyPress, onKeyUp, onMouseDown, onMouseMove, onMouseOut, onMouseOver, onMouseUp, style, and title.
Special note: This element has been deprecated in favor of an unordered list.

The <DIR> element was designed to be used for creating multicolumn direc-tory lists. Most browsers now treat it as an unordered list, but if they don't, the browser expects very short (20 characters or less) entries for each <LI> element in the list. In some of the older versions of the browsers, elements in a <DIR> list could be displayed in multiple columns. The graphical browser in Figure 4.17 presents this list the same way as an unordered list.

```
<HTML>
<HEAD>
<TITLE> Deprecated Lists </TITLE>
</HEAD>
<BODY bgcolor="#FFFFFF">
<!-- Background color = white -->

<H3>A MENU type list</H3>
<MENU>
  <LI>Breakfast Burrito</LI>
  <LI>Green Eggs and Ham</LI>
  <LI>Hash and Grits</LI>
</MENU>

<H3>A DIRECTORY type list</H3>
<DIR>
  <LI>HOMEPAGE.HTM</LI>
  <LI>INDEX.HTM</LI>
  <LI>README.TXT</LI>
</DIR>

</BODY>
</HTML>
```

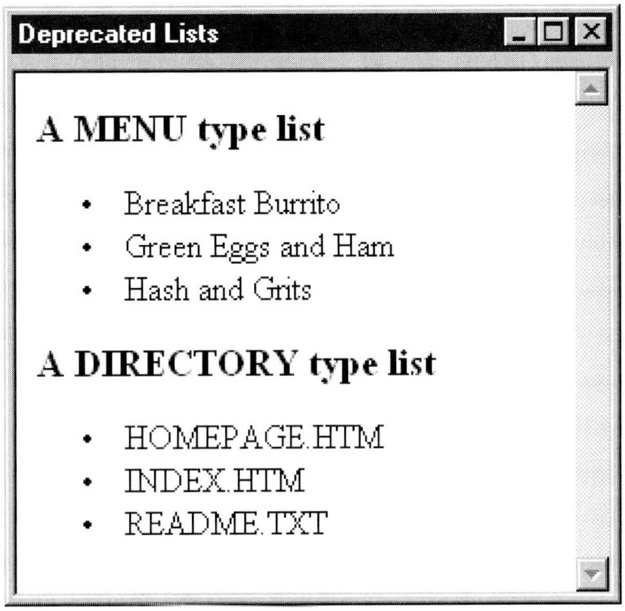

Figure 4.17 HTML code to create <MENU> and <DIR> lists.

Key Terms

Blocked element
Definition list
Inline element
Marker
Nesting lists
Ordered list
Readability
Unordered list

New Tags

```
<DD>
<DIR>
<DL>
<DT>
<LI>
<MENU>
<OL>
<UL>
```

Review Questions

1. What is the definition of each of the key terms?

2. How is each of the tags introduced in this chapter used?

3. What is an advantage to creating an ordered list using the <OL> element instead of manually numbering each item?

4. What are two ways you change the sequencing of an ordered list?

5. What are two ways you can change the style of the numbers or letters used in an ordered list?

6. Explain the rule for handling nonlist items in HTML-compliant code for lists.

7. What is the difference between an ordered and unordered list?

8. How do you change the shape of the marker used in an unordered list?

9. What can you do to make nested ordered lists easier to read?

10. Identify three ways you can make your HTML code more readable.

11. When would you use a definition list?

12. What are the two parts of a definition list?

13. What HTML element does the W^3C recommend using in place of a <MENU> or <DIR> list?

Exercises

4.1. Perform each step in order. Neither skip nor combine steps as you create an HTML document. This document should contain comments giving your name and the assignment due date after the <HTML> tag.

    a   List six of your favorite music CDs. Use only the <BR> tag, and number the items from 1 to 6. Print this code.
    b. Add an entry between items 4 and 5, then renumber the list.
    c. Change the list from Arabic numbers to lowercase letters (a–g). Print this code.

4.2. Duplicate the three steps from Exercise 4.1, but this time use the ordered list <OL> container. Perform all three steps in the same order.

4.3 Using multiple list containers, create an HTML document that displays the following outline. This document should contain comments with your name and the assignment due date after the <HTML> tag. Remember that nothing but <LI> items should occur within the <OL> and <UL> containers.

    I. Lists
       A.   Ordered
           1.   Type
               a.   Alpha
                    i.   Uppercase
                   ii.   Lowercase
               b.   Arabic numbers
               c.   Roman numerals
                    i.   Uppercase
                   ii.   Lowercase
           2.   Start
       B.   Unordered
           1.   Type
               a.   Square
               b.   Disk
               c.   Circle
    II. Examples

Note: The unordered list uses the **type** attribute to change the type of bullet. At the time of this writing, it works only in Netscape.

4.4. Retrieve the Homework home page you updated in Exercise 3.2. Every document should contain comments with your name and the assignment due date after the <HTML> tag.

    a. Place the links to your homework assignments in an ordered list.

    b. Create a new HTML document with the title of "My Favorite Teachers." Somewhere within the content of this document should be an ordered list that contains the names of at least four teachers you would recommend to others.

    c. Under each teacher's name place an unordered list that shows the school the teacher works in (or retired from) and the subject taught. This page should be linked to and from your Homework home page and contain a copy of the page footer.

4.5. Retrieve the Web page about your favorite movie that you updated in Exercise 3.4.

    a. Place the "What Others Think" links in an unordered list.

    b. Place the links to the biographical information in an unordered list. If possible, the markers in this list should be different from those used in part "a."

    c. Add a new "Quick Quiz" heading. Under the heading create a five-item ordered list. Each list item should be a trivia question about the movie.

    d. After each question, add the word "ANSWER" to activate a link to an HTML document with the answer.

    e. Create five new HTML documents that contain the following:
- The answer to one of the preceding questions in parts "a" through "e"
- A repeat of the question
- The name of the movie
- A link back to the next question under the "Quick Quiz" heading
- A copy of the footer used in the home page
- Comments with your name and the assignment due date

4.6. Retrieve your school's home page that you updated in Exercise 3.6.

    a. Place the links to school information in an unordered list.

    b. Convert the list of names and telephone numbers to a definition list. Use the names as terms and the telephone numbers as definitions. Add 10 new names and numbers to the list.

4.7. Cruise the Net to find and capture at least two examples of excellent uses for lists. Document where you captured them, and create a separate page for those two lists. They should WOW your classmates and your instructor! Be sure to leave a note telling the Web weavers of those sites that you are borrowing their lists for this purpose.

## CHAPTER five

FORMATTING—IS WHAT YOU SEE WHAT YOU GET?

Although the cardinal rule of HTML is that the author controls the content and the browser controls the format, there are some things you can do to control how your text appears on the screen. Actually, there are a few things you can do that will make your text look *very* different. In this chapter you will learn how to ask the browser to make your text look different and how to format the text in special ways.

Glyphs and Fonts

Every browser recognizes a variety of symbols, letters, and numbers generically referred to as **glyphs.** Arabic numbers (1, 2, 3, 4, . . .) and lowercase letters (a, b, c, . . .) are popular glyphs. When formatting different glyphs, you will change their **font** properties. These properties determine the typeface, weight, style, size, and other features used to display a glyph, which is usually text. *Typeface* describes the design of the characters in a font. The font-family is the name given to different typefaces, like **Arial** or **Times New Roman.** Text defaults to a normal (standard) weight in a browser, with bold considered a "heavy" weight. Text is displayed in italics when the font-style is set equal to *italic.* HTML lets you manipulate the following font properties when formatting text:

- font-family: serif | sans-serif | cursive | fantasy | monospace | others
- font-size: pt | 1-100% | larger | smaller | xx-small thru xx-large |
- font-size-adjust: <number> | none
- font-stretch: normal | wider | narrower | ultra-condensed thru ultra-expanded
- font-style: normal | italic | oblique
- font-variant: normal | small-caps
- font-weight: normal | bold | bolder | lighter | 100-900

Professional printers measure type size in *points,* which is abbreviated to *pt* when writing HTML code. One point equals $\frac{1}{72}$ inch when printed on paper. Figure 5.1 illustrates how different font sizes appear on popular graphical browsers. The default font size is usually 12 points; on an absolute scale from 1 to 7, the default would be 3, or on a scale from xx-small to xx-large, the default would be medium. But don't forget that each browser ultimately controls these default values.

As you would expect, type size affects the number of characters displayed per inch. The smaller the type size, the more words fit on a line. Another way of increasing the number of characters on a line is through **proportional spacing.** Proportional spacing is a way of naturally fitting letters together. Letters and symbols have different spacing depending on their widths instead of equal space for each character as on a typewriter. For example, the letters *M* and *W* require more space than the letters *i* and *l.* When each letter in a font is given equal space, it is known as a **monospace font.**

Professional printers were the first to use the terms *serif* and *sans serif* to describe typefaces. A typeface with *serifs* has short line segments or extensions projecting from upper or lower ends of the strokes of a character, for example, the leg of an uppercase *L* or *R.* As shown in Figure 5.1, *sans serif* (without serif) fonts do not include these short lines. A *cursive* typeface looks like the perfect handwritten script of the elementary schoolteacher who taught you handwriting.

It is generally acknowledged that serif fonts are easier to read because the serifs draw the reader's eye across a line of text. These typefaces are also more traditional. Reports and books written in the United States often use serif fonts for standard text, reserving sans serif type for titles, headings, and captions. Screen designs for Web pages are more liberal in their application of sans serif fonts, using them in a wider range of situations. Stay away from cursive fonts because they are hard to read unless displayed in very large font sizes.

Serif 8 point

Serif 10 point

Serif 12 point

Serif 14 point

Sans-Serif 9 point

Sans-Serif 11 point

Sans-Serif 13 point

Sans-Serif 15 point

Serif 28 point
Sans-Serif 36 point
Serif 48 point

Figure 5.1 Examples of different font typefaces and point sizes.

Document-Wide Style Changes

The need of Web weavers to have more control over the formatting of their Web pages and the W³C's desire to promote international and handicap-sensitive designs has led to an increased emphasis on *style sheets.* A style sheet is a set of design rules that apply to an HTML document.

Style sheets are not a new idea. Word-processing programs often make style sheets available to users to support the uniform development of related documents. Newsletters and books, for instance, use style sheets to maintain the same design elements, like the color of the headings or the font used as paragraph text, throughout the document.

There are basically two types of style sheets: document-level and external. A *document-level style sheet* establishes formatting rules that affect all of the elements found within the related document's <BODY> container. The <STYLE> container found as part of the <HEAD> element identifies these formatting rules, or style changes. *External style sheets,* which are independently written ASCII files, can be used by more than one HTML document to provide continuity between document designs. They will be discussed in more detail in Chapter 8.

<STYLE>document style changes</STYLE>

Description: identifies formatting changes to elements that appear in the document's <BODY> container.
Type: container.
Attributes: dir, lang, media, title, and type.

The <STYLE> container, shown in Figure 5.3, can only be placed within the <HEAD> element. Figure 5.3 is a modification of Figure 5.2. It shows how the page should be coded using style sheets rather than the older, inline formatting of page content. The idea is to identify all of the document-wide formatting changes within the <STYLE> container. Tags that have properties changed are

```
<HTML>
<HEAD>
<TITLE>Document-Level Style Sheets</TITLE>
<!-- No style sheet -->
</HEAD>

<BODY>
<H1>Week 1</H1>
<H2>Class Topics</H2>
<OL>
  <LI>Syllabus and class format</LI>
  <LI>Lab login procedures</LI>
  <LI>Discussion of browsers</LI>
</OL>
<H2>Homework (due next week)</H2>
<H3>Read</H3>
<P>Chapter 1 </P>
<H3>Turn In</H3>
<OL>
  <LI>Turn in the URL for a favorite Web site and be prepared to say a few
      words about what you like about this site in class.</LI>
  <LI>Turn in the URL for a Web site you think is poorly designed and be
      prepared to say a few words about what you don't like about this site
      in class.</LI>
</OL>
<H3>Key Terms</H3>
<UL>
  <LI>ASCII editor </LI>
  <LI>Uniform Resource Locator (URL) </LI>
</UL>

<HR noshade width="50%">
<P align="center">
<A HREF="#top">Top of Page</A><BR>
<A HREF="../index.htm">Back to Homework Home Page</A><BR>
Please send comments regarding this web page to:
<A HREF="mailto:TrainorT@Muskegon.cc.mi.us">TrainorT@Muskegon.cc.mi.us</A>
</P>
<H4>MUSKEGON COMMUNITY COLLEGE<BR>
221 South Quarterline Road<BR>
Muskegon, MI 49442<BR>
616.773.9131<BR>
</H4>
</BODY>
</HTML>
```

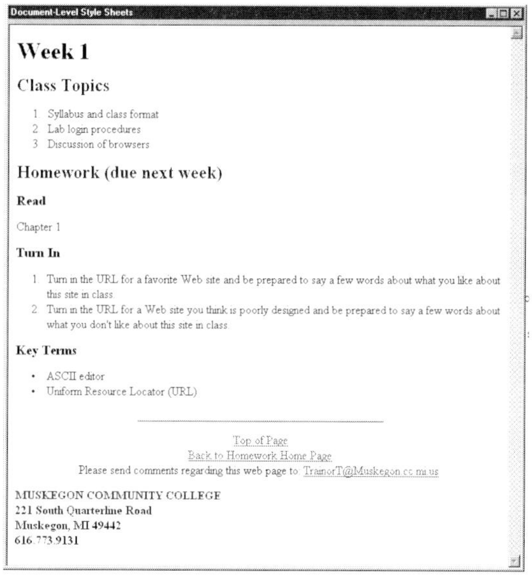

Figure 5.2 Original HTML code and browser display before style sheet was added.

listed on separate lines. We like to use the following rules when using the <STYLE> element to change tag properties:

1. Place each tag for which you are going to define properties on a separate line.
2. Put a left curly brace ({) after the tag name. Usually it is best to place this curly brace on the line following the tag name so you can line all the braces up; this alignment helps the readability of your code.
3. List each property name, like `font-family` or `font-weight`, followed by a colon. The colon tells the browser that a value for that property comes next.
4. Type in the property value, like **sans-serif** or **bold**.
5. Place a semicolon to mark the end of the value.
6. Close the property list with a right curly brace, again on a line by itself.

Look at the following example, then study Figure 5.3. You will notice how nicely the tags and their properties line up. This makes the code easier to read and maintain.

```
H1
    {
    font-family: sans-serif;
    font-size: 30pt;
    font-weight: bold;
    }
```

However, all of this information could be presented on a single line like this:

```
H1 {font-family: sans-serif; font-size: 30pt; font-weight: bold;}
```

It is not by accident that this syntax is the same used by the **style** attribute. The properties you previously used with **style** are also acceptable within the <SCRIPT> container. In Chapter 4 we introduced you to the `list-style-type` **style** property that changed the sequencing scheme of an ordered list and the marker in an unordered list. These tags are formatted by identifying the main and subordinate elements. In the following code the first-level items in an ordered list are sequenced using uppercase letters of the alphabet (A, B, C, etc.):

```
OL LI {list-style-type: upper-alpha}.
```

If you want the second-level items of an unordered list to use square markers, the code would look like this:

```
UL UL LI {list-style-type: square}
```

More than one tag can be assigned new properties at the same time. List them together, and separate each tag from the other by commas. For example, all of the heading tags in Figure 5.3 are set to a bold sans-serif font using this code:

```
H1, H2, H3, H4, H5, H6
    {
    font-weight: bold;
    font-family: sans-serif;
    }
```

```
<HTML>
<HEAD>
<TITLE>Document-Level Style Sheets</TITLE>
<STYLE>
<!--
H1, H2, H3, H4, H5, H6
  {
  font-weight: bold;
  font-family: sans-serif;
  }
H1
  {
  font-size: 30pt;
  text-align: center;
  }
H2
  {
  font-style: italic;
  font-size: 16pt;
  }
H3
  {
  font-size: 14pt;
  }
H4
  {
  font-size: x-small;
  text-align: center;
  }
OL LI
  {
  font-family: serif;
  font-size: 12pt;
  list-style-type: upper-roman;
  }
UL LI
  {
  font-family: serif;
  font-size: 12pt;
  list-style-type: square;
  }
-->
</STYLE>
</HEAD>
```

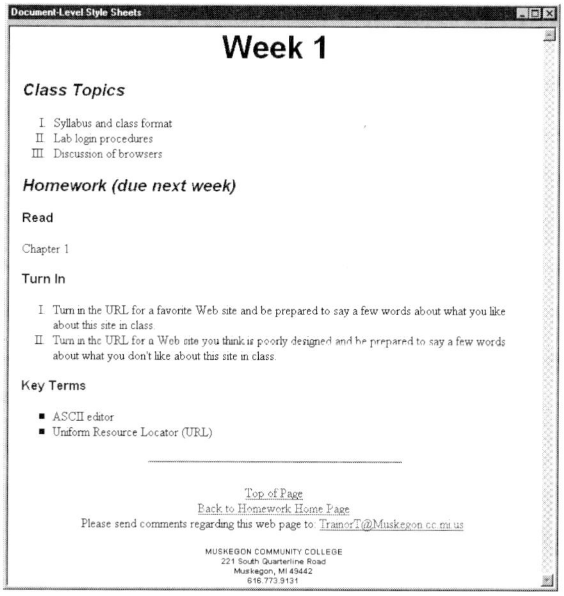

Figure 5.3 HTML code from Figure 5.2 with style sheet added.

The Web weaver can then fine-tune each heading by making specific changes. In Figure 5.3, the level-1 heading is set to a bold sans-serif font with the code just shown. When displayed by the browser, it is also centered and is shown in a 30-point font size because of this code:

H1 {font-size: 30pt; text-align: center;}

text-align: left | center | right | justify

The values assigned the text-align property should be familiar: left, center, right, and justify. The default value is dependent on whether the writing direction is set to left-to-right (default = left) or right-to-left (default = right).

The idea behind document-level style sheets is to take the time to establish your design before beginning to code. Then HTML coding within the <BODY> container becomes straightforward and easy, because you just use the tags without any attributes. The <STYLE> element has already established the attributes you want to use.

<!-- comment lines -->

In Figure 5.3 a comment line follows the beginning <STYLE> tag and precedes the ending </STYLE> tag; thus the style changes are enclosed within a comment container. This is done to prevent older browsers from accidentally displaying the format changes as text (see Figure 5.4). Since these browsers are not equipped to utilize document-level style changes, handling the related code in this way enables them to treat this code as comments. You will see comment containers used this way later in the book when handling scripts.

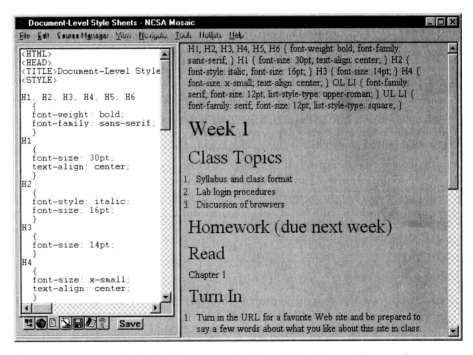

Figure 5.4 Results of code in Figure 5.3 when Mosaic (version 3.0) browser is used. It displays the contents of the uncommented <STYLE> container instead of using its contents for document-level formatting.

Font Changes

Before going crazy with the various font options provided by style sheets, remember that too many fonts within the same page will distract the reader. If the objective is to provide easy-to-read information to our readers, then you would be wise to follow the age-old KISS principle (Keep It Simple, Sweetie). Usually three typefaces per document are sufficient. Assign one typeface to the headings, another to the principal text used in paragraphs and list items, and a third to emphasize specific words. For example, we have been using a different typeface for style properties like `font-family`.

Bold and italics when used for emphasis must follow similar constraints. One or two bold words in a page adds emphasis to a point. A page full of bold and italic text neutralizes the impact these font values have for adding emphasis. The following is an overview of the more commonly used font properties available in HTML. We strongly suggest that you look over the current HTML and CSS (Cascading Style Sheets) recommendations for a comprehensive review of all the font properties at `http://www.w3.org/MarkUp/` and `http://www.w3.org/Style/` respectively.

`font-family:` serif | sans-serif | cursive | fantasy | monospace | [Arial, Courier, . . .]

The typeface used by the browser is controlled by the `font-family` property. You can use a specific family name (Arial or Times New Roman) or a generic name (serif or sans-serif). Family names that contain spaces need to be enclosed in quotes. Setting the `font-family` for a paragraph to **Times New Roman**, for instance, would appear in an HTML document as follows:

P {font-family: "Times New Roman"}.

Using a specific font name is practical only when the Web weaver knows that the font specified is available on all the computers accessing the page. The only time you can be sure that a specific font is available on every computer is when the page is being designed for use on an *intranet* within a company, where all of the machines are set up the same way.

Because the browser assigns representative typefaces to each generic family, it is always best to include a generic family name, rather than just specific fonts, in the list of typefaces. An example would be

P {font-family: "Times New Roman", serif}.

Five generic family names are currently identified in the W^{3}C recommendations:
1. cursive
2. fantasy
3. monospace
4. sans-serif
5. serif

Generic family names are keywords in HTML and therefore *must not be enclosed in quotes.*

`font-size:` pt | 1-100% | larger | smaller | xx-small thru xx-large

As you saw in Figure 5.1, the size of the font is measured and referenced in points ($1/72$ inch). However, there are other ways to change the size of the font, either absolutely or relatively. Popular browsers maintain a table of absolute font sizes that correspond to the following values:
- xx-small
- x-small

- small
- medium
- large
- x-large
- xx-large

These absolute sizes are shown in a typical graphical browser in Figure 5.5. Take note that these keywords are new as of 1998, and many browsers do not now and may never recognize them.

Absolute Font Sizes

xx-small

x-small

small

medium

large

x-large

xx-large

Font Stretches

ultra condensed

extra-condensed

condensed

semi-condensed

normal

semi-expanded

expanded

extra-expanded

ultra-expanded

Font Weights

bold

weight = 100

weight = 200

weight = 300

weight = 400 (normal)

weight = 500

weight = 600

weight = 700 (bold)

weight = 800

weight = 900

Font Variant

SMALL-CAPS

Font Styles

italic

oblique

Figure 5.5 Examples of common font properties.

You can also change the font size relative to the current setting. A relative size change can take place using the property value of **larger** or **smaller**. This would indicate a 20% relative change in size one way or the other. For example, if the default paragraph font size is 12 pt, the following code would set the point size to approximately 20% larger, or 14.4 pt:

```
P {font-size: larger}
```

Another way to change the relative size is to indicate a percentage increase or decrease in size. This code would set the font size of the paragraph to 40 percent of the current size, making the text very small.

```
P {font-size: 40%}
```

Font-Style

The font-style can be either **normal, italic,** or **oblique.**

font style: normal | italic | oblique

The difference in font styles between *italic* and *oblique* is a bit esoteric. Generally any text that is slanted when printed is considered oblique. Sometimes the family name will contain the word "slanted" or "incline" when it is considered oblique. Whereas the italic style is also considered slanted, it is a matter of degree that separates it from oblique. For all intents and purposes, both fonts have the same visual impact. The following code will set the paragraph to oblique if the browser supports this property:

P {font-style: oblique}

Font-Weight

The font-weight is what makes text look lighter or darker:

font-weight: normal | bold | bolder | lighter | 100-900

If you use a word processor, you know that bold is a popular way to emphasize text. The font-weight property actually provides the Web weaver with the tools to change the weight on an absolute or relative basis. The second cascading style sheet (CSS2) recommendations have assigned absolute values from 100 to 900 for quantifying the "boldness" of text. These numbers are incremented by hundreds, with 100 being the lightest and 900 being the darkest. Normal text has a bold value of 400, while bold text has a value of 700.

To make the text of an unordered list item as dark as the browser will make it, use this code:

UL LI {font-weight: 900}.

To change the relative boldness of that list item, you can reassign the weight value to 800, and thus make the text somewhat lighter:

UL LI {font-weight: lighter}.

font-variant: normal | small-caps

Basically the font-variant property is used to format text in small capital letters, called **small-caps:** The May 12, 1998 CSS2 specifications have this to say about **small-caps:**

> If a genuine small-caps font is not available, user agents (browsers) should simulate a small-caps font, for example by taking a normal font and replacing the lowercase letters by scaled uppercase characters. As a last resort, unscaled uppercase letter glyphs in a normal font may replace glyphs in a small-caps font so that the text appears in all uppercase letters. (Section 15.2.3)

The HTML code to change the level-4 heading to small capital letters looks like this:

H4 {font-variant: small-caps}.

`font-stretch:` normal | wider | narrower | ultra-condensed thru ultra-expanded

For a special effect, text can be squashed or stretched horizontally. The `font-stretch` property can be set to make this change absolutely or relatively:

The absolute options are as follows, from narrowest to widest:

- ultra-condensed
- extra-condensed
- condensed
- semi-condensed
- normal
- semi-expanded
- expanded
- extra-expanded
- ultra-expanded

To stretch a level-2 heading as far across a line as the browser permits, you would use this code:

H2 {font-stretch: ultra-expanded}.

The keywords **wider** and **narrower** are used to change the relative length of the text. We should also remind you that, like the keywords **xx-small** through **xx-large**, these stretch properties are new and not yet recognized by the popular browsers as shown in Figure 5.5.

`font:` font-style | font-variant | font-weight | font-size | font-family.

All of the example style changes we have shown you up until now have been delineated property by property as shown in Figure 5.3. The CSS2 specifications also allow for a shorthand notation to change a font's properties using the keyword `font`. You could, for example, set the level-1 heading to a 30-point, bold, italic, sans-serif typeface using this code:

H1 {font: italic bold 30pt sans-serif}.

Use a blank space (no commas) to separate the list of properties.

Deprecated Font Handling Techniques

In the past, document-level font changes were handled by the <BASEFONT> and <FONT> containers. These elements were deprecated in the HTML 4.0 specifications. They both support a set of font sizes that start at size 1 and run all the way through size 7. Font size 3 is the default size. You can both increase and decrease the size of the font displayed. According to the W³C specifications, the relationship between the different virtual font sizes is about 20 percent for each change. For example, font size 4 is supposed to be 20 percent larger than font size 3 (the default size), and font size 1 is supposed to be 40 percent smaller than font size 3.

<BASEFONT>basefont</BASEFONT>

Description: originally designed to change the size of the font used within a document.
Type: container.
Attributes: class, color, face, id, lang, size, style, and title.
Special note: deprecated in favor of the <STYLE> element and **style** attribute.

The <BASEFONT> element changes the size of the font in a page. Some Web weavers mistakenly code it as an empty tag; it is really a container. To use the <BASEFONT> tag for document-level style changes, place it in the head of the document. It can also be placed anywhere else in the document, and it can be used several times. As mentioned earlier, this tag uses the **size** attribute in a novel way. The size can be set to any integer value between 1 and 7. Figure 5.6 shows how the size of the basefont can be coded to change the way the text looks.

```
<H2>BASEFONT Size Changes</H2>
This line is shown in the normal font<BR>
<BASEFONT size=2> Change the basefont size to 2. <BR>
<BASEFONT size=5> Up to size 5, now we add the close tag
</BASEFONT> and the text drops back to 3 or 2 depending on the browser.<BR>
```

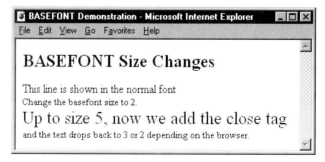

Figure 5.6 The </BASEFONT> container as handled by two popular graphical browsers.

The <BASEFONT> tag applies to all the text that follows it until the browser encounters another <BASEFONT> element, a closing </BASEFONT> tag, a <FONT> element, or the end of the document. When a browser encounters the </BASEFONT> tag, it resets the font size. Here is where things get a little dicey, as shown in Figure 5.6. When Internet Explorer encounters the </BASEFONT> in Figure 5.6, it changes back to the previous font size of 2. Now notice how the size of the font drops back to 3, the default value, when the </BASEFONT> tag is reached using Navigator. As the French would say, "Vive la différence!"

The **size** property of the <BASEFONT> tag also allows relative rather than absolute size specification. For example, you can code a **size** of +1 rather than changing the absolute value. Figure 5.7 shows a series of single-step size increases from the default to the maximum, and then back down to the minimum.

```
<HTML>
<HEAD>
<TITLE>BASEFONT Relative Size Changes</TITLE>
</HEAD>
<BODY bgcolor="#FFFFFF">
<!-- Background color = white -->

<BASEFONT size="3">This line is shown in the normal font<BR>
<BASEFONT size="+1"> Change the basefont size to 4 <BR>
<BASEFONT size="+1"> Up a size <BR>
<BASEFONT size="+1"> Up a size <BR>
<BASEFONT size="+1"> Up a size to the maximum<BR>
<BASEFONT size="-1"> Down a size <BR>
<BASEFONT size="-1"> Down a size <BR>
<BASEFONT size="-1"> Down a size <BR>
<BASEFONT size="-1"> Down a size <BR>
<BASEFONT size="-1"> Down a size <BR>
<BASEFONT size="-1"> Down a size now at the minimum 1<BR>

</BODY>
</HTML>
```

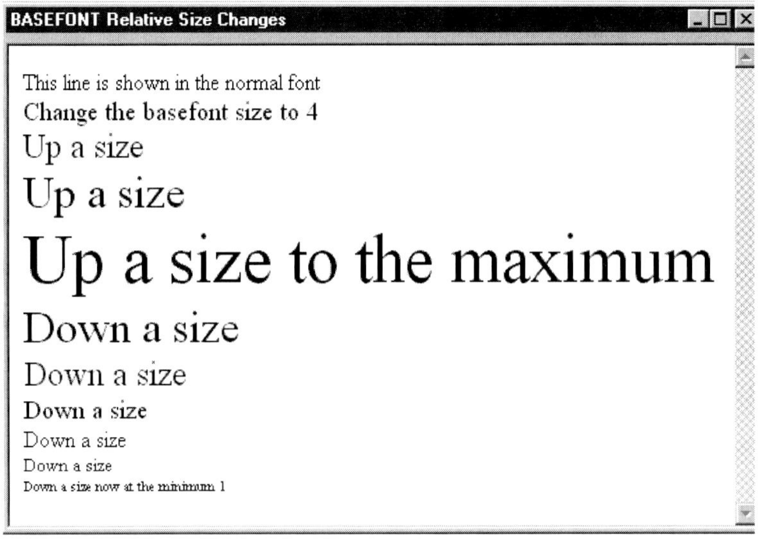

Figure 5.7 HTML code in which the BASEFONT size is incremented up or down by 1.

As you can see from Figure 5.7, changing the base font up and down with relative values has the same result as using absolute values. What is important to notice is that the effect is cumulative, or additive. Each time you use +1 or −1, the font changes from the *preceding value.* You can, of course, make relative steps larger than 1. For example, you could increase the size of the text from 3 to 5 by coding **size** = +2.

\<FONT\>font of text\</FONT\>

Description: changes the color, typeface, or size of the font.
Type: container.
Attributes: class, color, face, id, lang, size, style, and title.
Special note: deprecated in favor of **style** attribute.

The \<BASEFONT\> tag is useful for changing the size of the font for the whole page, or at least a substantial portion of it. But what should you do when you want to change the size—or the color or typeface—of the font for a small part of the page, perhaps even just a character or two? One way, but no longer the recommended way, would be to use the \<FONT\>\</FONT\> element. Because this is a container, you should always code the closing container tag, \</FONT\>. There are three common attributes for this tag: **color, size,** and **face.**

color

The color of the text enclosed in the container is set by the **color** attribute, just as you learned to set text color in the \<BODY\> tag. The recommended way is to use an octothorp followed by a six-digit (hexadecimal) number, with each successive pair of numbers representing the red, green, and blue (RGB) components of the desired color as shown on the color insert in the back of this book. While we don't recommend it, you can also use the "standard" color words. The HTML code to change the font color to blue looks like this:

```
<FONT color="#0000FF">This code changes the text to blue</FONT>
```

or

```
<FONT color="blue">This code changes the text to blue.</FONT>
```

size

The \<FONT\> container allows you to change the size of the contained text. You can code this **size** attribute just as you coded the **size** attribute for the \<BASEFONT\> tag. There is one critical difference, however, if you use relative size values. As you can see in Figure 5.7, with the \<BASEFONT\> tag, the relative size values are incremental up to a maximum of size 7. With the \<FONT\>

container, each relative calculation is based on the default, or the value set by the preceding <BASEFONT> tag.

Figure 5.8 illustrates this difference. This code tries to increase the font size two times, intending to move it from size 3 to size 5. The code then tries to decrease the font size two times. As you can see, the size increases from the base size of 3 to a size 4 the first time the code tries to increase it, but subsequent +1 size increases have no further impact. Attempts to decrease the font size meet with the same results; that is, the increase occurs only the first time. This is a significant difference between the way the <BASEFONT> and the <FONT> tags use relative size values. The reason this happens is that each time the <FONT> element is closed, it resets the size of the text to the default set by the <BASEFONT> element. If you don't explicitly close the <FONT> container, it will infer a closing tag before the next <FONT> container is opened. Because of the possible confusion generated, wise Web weavers specify the <FONT> **size** value as an absolute number rather than a relative one.

```
<HTML>
<HEAD>
<TITLE>FONT Changes</TITLE>
</HEAD>
<BODY bgcolor="#FFFFFF">
<!-- Background color = white -->

<FONT size="3">This line is shown in the normal font. </FONT><BR>
<FONT size="+1"> Up 1 to change the basefont size to 4. </FONT><BR>
<FONT size="+1"> Up another size does not work. </FONT><BR>
<FONT size="-1"> Down a size works the first time. </FONT><BR>
<FONT size="-1"> Down another size does not work. </FONT><BR>
<FONT size="3" face="sans-serif"> Generic family names like sans-serif work. </FONT><BR>
<FONT face="Forte">Family names like Forte are recognized if found. </FONT><BR>
<FONT color="gray">Text color changes to gray. </FONT><BR>
Line of text outside of the &lt;FONT&gt; container. <BR>

</BODY>
</HTML>
```

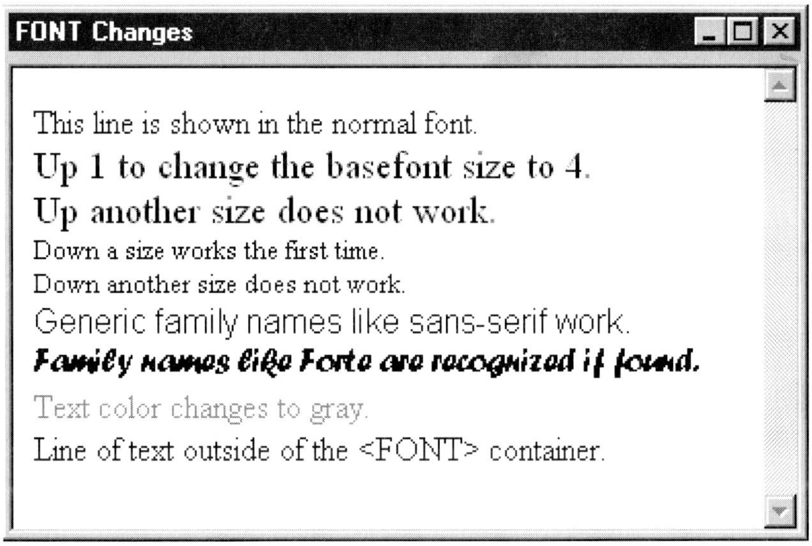

Figure 5.8 HTML code in which the <FONT> container changes font size, color, and typeface.

face

The **face** attribute of the <FONT> tag allows for the specification of a series of different typefaces for the text contained within the container. Usually the Web weaver will specify a series of different typefaces, hoping that the target machine contains one of them. If none of the specified typefaces are available on the target machine, the browser will use the default typeface. A browser using the following code would first try to use the Arial typeface; if Arial was not recognized, the default sans-serif typeface would be used:

```
<FONT face="Arial, sans-serif">This text is a sans-serif face.</FONT>
```

Inline Styles

The use of style sheets helps a Web author maintain related Web site pages. This does not mean that inline style changes are unnecessary or undesirable. They are used for special emphasis and for one-time style changes. There are two general forms of inline styles: logical style and physical style. For the purposes of this book, we will define them like this: *physical styles* describe the way the text is to look in a browser; *logical styles* describe the way the text within the container is used.

Physical Styles

All the style sheet properties we have been discussing, like `font-family` and `list-style-type`, are physical styles. Some of these physical styles relate back to a Teletype era when output was printed on paper by *dumb terminals*. These machines used a monospace font few oldtimers will ever forget. The <B>bold</B> and <I>italic</I> containers date back to the HTML 2.0 recommendations. These inline elements represent some of the earliest attempts by Web weavers to wrest control of the display from the browser.

Physical styles can play off each other, and it is acceptable to nest inline style containers. <B><I>bold italics</I></B> is popular. You nest the <BIG> or <SMALL> containers to increase or decrease the font size in steps of 1, in a fashion similar to **size** = +1 or −1 (see Figure 5.14). For example, <BIG><BIG>real big</BIG></BIG> is bigger than <BIG>big</BIG>. Table 5.1 shows the complete list of physical styles. The related HTML code and browser renditions are shown in Figure 5.9.

Logical Styles

Logical styles, also called *content-based styles,* require the Web weaver to consider not what the page should look like, but rather how the particular text sequence is supposed to be used as part of the information provided to the user. The logical styles shown in Table 5.2 can convey more information than the physical tags in Table 5.1 because they not only change the appearance of the text, but also explain why the text was set off from the body of the page. Use logical styles whenever you can, marking text according to how it is to be used rather than how you expect it to look.

Tag	Description	Special Note
<B>bold</B>	Darker typeface	
<I>italic</I>	Slanted typeface	
^{superscript}	Half line above text bottom	Used in scientific and mathematical notations.
_{subscript}	Half line below text bottom	Used in scientific and mathematical notations.
<TT>teletype</TT>	Monospaced typeface	
<CODE>computer code</CODE>	Monospaced typeface	
<KBD>keyboard</KBD>	Monospaced typeface	
<BIG>big text</BIG>	Default = 3; range from 1 to 7	Small (1) to large (7)
<SMALL>small text</SMALL>	Default = 3; range from 1 to 7	Small (1) to large (7)
<BLINK>blinking text</BLINK>	Text blinks on and off	Navigator only
<U>underlined text</U>	Line drawn under text	Deprecated
<S>strikethrough</S>	Line drawn through text	Deprecated
<STRIKE>strikethrough</STRIKE>	Line drawn through text	Deprecated

Description: physical inline tags.

Type: container.

Attributes: class, dir, id, lang, onClick, onDblClick, onKeyDown, onKeyPress, onKeyUp, onMouseDown, onMouseMove, onMouseOut, onMouseOver, OnMouseUp, style, and title.

Table 5.1 Common physical styles.

```
<HTML>
<HEAD>
<TITLE>Common Phyical Styles</TITLE>
</HEAD>
<BODY bgcolor="#FFFFFF">
<!-- Background color = white -->

<B>bold</B><BR>
<I>italic</I><BR>
super<SUP>script</SUP><BR>
sub<SUB>script</SUB><BR>
<TT>teletype</TT><BR>
<CODE>computer code</CODE><BR>
<KBD>keyboard</KBD><BR>
<BIG>big</BIG><BR>
<SMALL>small</SMALL><BR>
<BLINK>blink</BLINK><BR>
<U>underline</U><BR>
<STRIKE>strike</STRIKE><BR>
<BR>
Inline styles can be nested,<BR>
for example, <B><I>bold italic</I></B>.

</BODY>
</HTML>
```

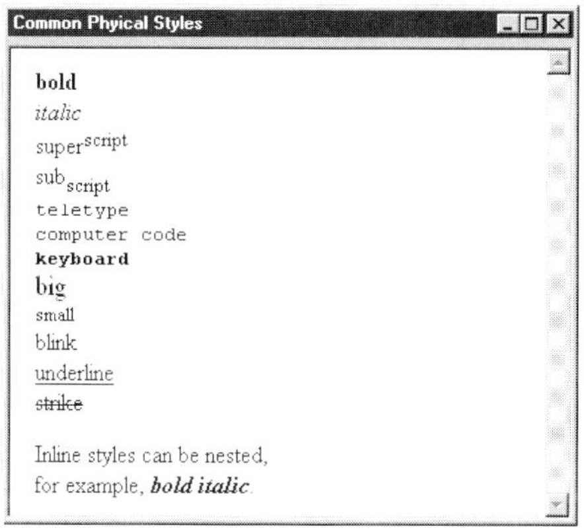

Figure 5.9 Common physical tags.

TAG	EXAMPLES	ATTRIBUTE
<ABBR><abbreviation</ABBR>	WWW, URL or W3C	
<ACRONYM>acronym</ACRONYM>	NASA BASIC	
<ADDRESS>address</ADDRESS>	4604 Briarwood Ave.	Adds at end
<BLOCKQUOTE>long quote</BLOCKQUOTE>	Longer than 40 words	**cite**
<CITE>citation</CITE>	1937 by Robert Frost	
<DEL>deleted text</DEL>	Removed from page	**cite** and **datetime**
<DFN>definition</DFN>	Large block object	
<EM>emphasized text</EM>	*Enroll by June 30th*	
<INS>inserted text</INS>	Added to page	**cite** and **datetime**
<Q>quote</Q>	Less than 40 words	**cite**
<SAMP>sample output</SAMP>	Printer output	
<STRONG>strongly emphasized text</STRONG>	**Warning!**	
<VAR>variablNe values</VAR>	Last_name = "Smith"	
Description: logical inline tags.		
Type: container.		
Attributes: class, dir, id, lang, onClick, onDblClick, onKeyDown, onKeyPress, onKeyUp, onMouseDown, onMouseMove, onMouseOut, onMouseOver, onMouseUp, style, and title.		

Table 5.2 Common logical styles.

The fact that a particular group of characters is enclosed within a specific logical container is what is important, not how the browser chooses to display those contents. For example, a scholar may search through many Web pages, pulling out the examples of character strings that are enclosed within <CITE> containers. That the Web weaver chose to enclose the text within that particular tag conveys the information that the text in the container is a citation. That information is far more important than how the text appears on the page. With this idea of conveying information in mind, you need to choose your logical styles carefully and consistently.

**<ADDRESS>
address
</ADDRESS>**

Any Web document you create should have your address, or at least the address of a responsible party, located somewhere on the page, usually in a footer. You may wish to use the <ADDRESS> . . . </ADDRESS> container to put your own name and address into a page so people can use both the regular postal service and e-mail to contact you. Figure 5.10 presents the code and typical display format for the <ADDRESS> container.

```
<HTML>
<HEAD>
<TITLE>Common Logical Styles</TITLE>
</HEAD>
<BODY bgcolor="#FFFFFF">
<!-- Background color = white -->

<ABBR>abbreviation</ABBR><BR>
<ACRONYM>acronym</ACRONYM>
<ADDRESS>address</ADDRESS>
<BLOCKQUOTE>blockquote</BLOCKQUOTE>
<CITE>citation</CITE><BR>
<DEL>delete</DEL><BR>
<DFN>definitions</DFN><BR>
<EM>emphasis</EM><BR>
<INS>insert</INS><BR>
<Q>quote</Q><BR>
<SAMP>sample</SAMP><BR>
<STRONG>strong</STRONG><BR>
<VAR>variable</VAR><BR>

</BODY>
</HTML>
```

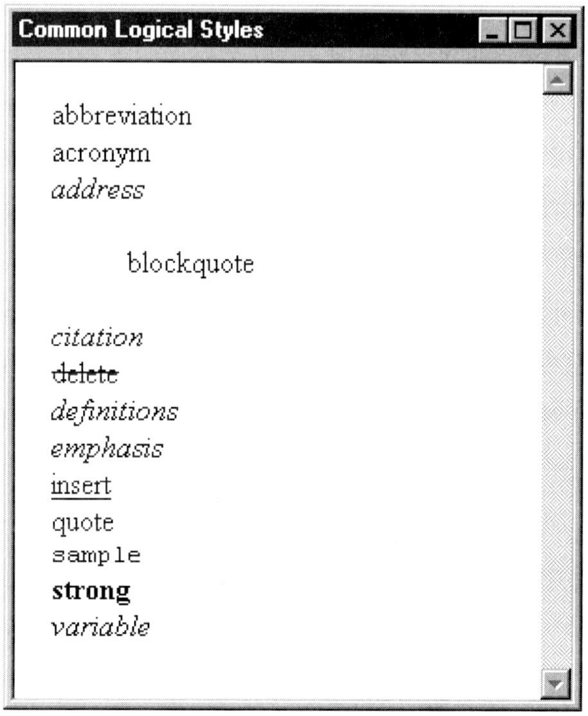

Figure 5.10 Common logical tags.

<STRONG>strongly emphasized text</STRONG>

The <STRONG> . . . </STRONG> container is used to bring strong emphasis to the enclosed text. Many browsers will bold the contents (see Figure 5.10), but that is not the required change. This tag calls for more emphasis than the <EM> tag, discussed next.

<EM>emphasized text</EM>

Text enclosed in the <EM> . . .</EM> container is supposed to be emphasized, but this tag indicates a milder form of emphasis than the <STRONG> tag. Currently most browsers will render this text in italics. Figure 5.10 presents code for both the <STRONG> and <EM> containers.

You can also nest one logical container inside another to achieve combined effects. Remember that all combinations are not necessarily supported, and you may not see exactly what you expect.

<CITE>citation</CITE>

When you put a bibliographical citation in your document, you can enclose it in the <CITE> . . . </CITE> container. This will help your user find the documents you are referencing. Figure 5.10 presents the code for a citation. As you can see, citation tags usually display text in an italic font. But the importance of the citation is to identify your references, not to change text to italics.

<ABBR>abbreviation </ABBR>

Our world is so full of abbreviations for words that the HTML 4.0 specifications added the <ABBR> element to identify them. The W^{3}C points out that abbreviations are not an Indo-European phenomenon—both the Chinese and the Japanese use analogous abbreviation mechanisms. Identifying abbreviations can assist spell checkers, speech synthesizers, translation systems, and search site indexing.

<ACRONYM>acronym</ACRONYM>

In addition to abbreviations, our world is also full of acronyms, like RADAR (RAdio Detecting And Ranging) or BASIC (Beginners All-Purpose Symbolic Code). As a result, the HTML 4.0 specifications added the <ACRONYM> element to identify these words. This feature can help spell checkers, speech synthesizers, translation systems, and search site indexing. Currently both the <ABBR> and <ACRONYM> elements are so new that none of the browsers are recognizing them.

<DFN>definition</DFN>

The <DFN>. . . </DFN> container sets apart a definition. Figure 5.10 illustrates how the popular browsers italicize text in the <DFN> container.

<VAR>Variable Values</VAR>

The <VAR> . . . </VAR> container is most frequently used with a tag like <PRE> (discussed later in this chapter) to identify a program variable or to show something that the user is supposed to input. Like the <CODE> tag, this one is usually used when showing computer input or a computer program. Figure 5.10 presents the code for the <VAR> container and the display by a popular browser.

<SAMP>output</SAMP>

The <SAMP> element also dates back to a time and place when the Internet was used to display computer programs and the resulting output. In these situations the <SAMP> . . . </SAMP> container is used to highlight sample computer output. Figure 5.10 illustrates the code and resulting screen display. This element is not used much anymore. The <CODE> tag is generally used to represent input, output, and code generated by a computer.

<BLOCKQUOTE> block quote </BLOCKQUOTE>

In a formal paper or article, a long quotation, usually more than 40 words, is set off in a separate paragraph that is usually indented on both sides. Sometimes it also appears in a different font from the rest of the text. You can create a similar effect with some of the browsers using the <BLOCKQUOTE> . . . </BLOCKQUOTE> container. Although the exact rendering will vary among the different browsers, the <BLOCKQUOTE> container indicates that the text contained within it is a quotation. Figure 5.11 presents the code for a block

```
<HTML>
<HEAD>
<TITLE>Long and Short Quotes</TITLE>
</HEAD>
<BODY bgcolor="#FFFFFF">
<!-- Background color = white -->

<H3>Block Quote</H3>
<BLOCKQUOTE cite="http://www.w3.org/TR/1998/REC-html40-19980424">
We recommend that style sheet implementations provide a mechanism
for inserting quotation marks before and after a quotation
delimited by BLOCKQUOTE in a manner appropriate to the current
language context and the degree of nesting of quotations.<BR>
<BR>
However, as some authors have used BLOCKQUOTE merely as a mechanism
to indent text, in order to preserve the intention of the authors,
user agents (browsers) should not insert quotation marks in the
default style.
</BLOCKQUOTE>

<H3>Inline Quote</H3>
Tim responded, <Q lang="en">I asked Diane for directions to the
Eiffel Tower, and she said,
<Q lang="fr">Tu es marteau! Nous sommes à Marseille</Q>
I just wanted to crawl into a hole and cover myself up after
that.</Q>

</BODY>
</HTML>
```

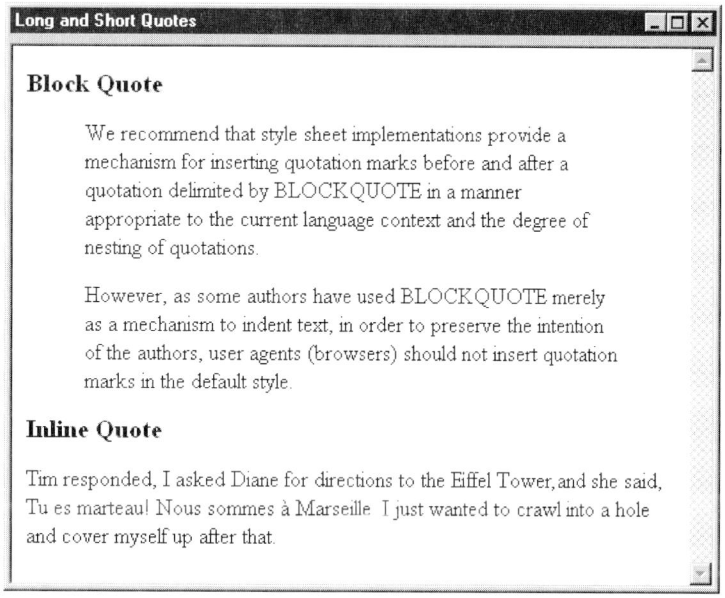

Figure 5.11 Applications for <BLOCKQUOTE> and <Q> container tags.

quote and shows how popular browsers will render this coding. Notice that the paragraph is indeed indented on both margins, and line breaks have been inserted before and after the text.

Both the <BLOCKQUOTE> and <Q> containers recognize the **cite** attribute. As shown in Figure 5.11, this attribute allows the Web author to reference the Web site the quotation comes from. However, instead of a URL, the **cite** attribute could contain text that provides a traditional citation for the quotation.

<Q>quote</Q>

The <Q> element was added to the list of logical styles as part of the HTML 4.0 specifications. Its addition reinforces our position that even with the trend toward style sheet formatting, it is appropriate for Web weavers to build their pages using logical styles. This element was added to provide support for short, inline quotation, leaving the <BLOCKQUOTE> element for long quotes that need to be visually separated from the body of the document.

Figure 5.11 demonstrates how the <Q> container can be nested inside another <Q> container. The handling of embedded quotes is language-dependent, but English-oriented text should enclose the embedded quotation in single quotes (') and enclose the outside quotation in double quotes ("). However, the example in Figure 5.11 does not contain either set of quotes, because at the time of this writing none of the popular browsers recognize this element.

<INS>insert</INS> and <DEL> delete</DEL>

We must not forget that HTML is a markup language. In keeping with this fact, the HTML 4.0 specifications added the <INS>insert</INS> and <DEL>delete</DEL> containers to help Web weavers maintain and update documents. For example, let's say that an online public safety document needs to be updated to take into account a speed limit change. Currently the online document reads, "A speed limit of 45 miles per hour has been posted for Woodward Avenue." To mark up this change we want to delete 45 and replace it with 55. With these new insert and delete tags, the HTML code would look like this:

```
<P>A speed limit of <DEL>45</DEL><INS>55</INS> miles per hour has
been posted for Woodward Avenue.<P>
```

As you know by now, how the changes are displayed is dependent on the browser. Internet Explorer and Navigator strike through text contained within the <DEL> element and underline text within the <INS> element (see Figure 5.10).

Both of these elements can be used for either inline changes or block-level (blocked) changes that incorporate text in several tags—like paragraphs, lists, and tables. However, they cannot represent both inline and block-level changes at the same time.

Both the <DEL> and <INS> beginning tags recognize the **cite** and **date-time** attributes. As mentioned earlier in regard to quotations, the **cite** attribute can contain a URL that references comments about the change or a traditional text citation for an article or book that provides more information. The **date-time** attribute lets you document a date and time that the change takes place. Using our earlier example of the speed limit change, we could use these attributes to document that the change occurs on January 1, 1999, and to inform the user that more information is available in the comments.html page at the highway Web site under limits:

```
<INS datetime="1999-01-01TO:00"
cite="http://www.highway/limits/comments.html">55</INS>
```

Special Characters

One drawback with powerful browsing agents like Netscape and Internet Explorer is that they try to interpret every recognizable character sequence as if it were a set of tags. For example, were we to convert this document into HTML and try to show it on a browser, a line that said, "The format of a standard tag is <tag> with the < starting the tag and the > closing it," wouldn't look like that when displayed, because the browser would try to resolve the <s and the >s. Being unable to do so, it would ignore them. Let's see how that would actually look. Figure 5.12 shows the HTML code and browser display for the previous

```
<HTML>
<HEAD>
<TITLE>Special Characters I</TITLE>
</HEAD>
<BODY bgcolor="#FFFFFF">
<!-- Background color = white -->

<B>Without Special Characters</B><BR>
For example, were we to convert this document into HTML and try
to show it on a browser, a line that said:<BR>
<BR>
'The format of a standard tag is <tag> with the < starting the
tag and the > closing it."<BR>
<BR>
wouldn't look like that when displayed, because the browser
would try to resolve the <s and the >s. Being unable to do so,
it would ignore them. Let's see how that would actually look.
</S>
<BR>
<BR>
<B>With Special Characters</B><BR>
'The format of a standard tag is &lt;tag&gt; with the &lt;
starting the tag and the &gt; closing it."<BR>
<BR>
</BODY>
</HTML>
```

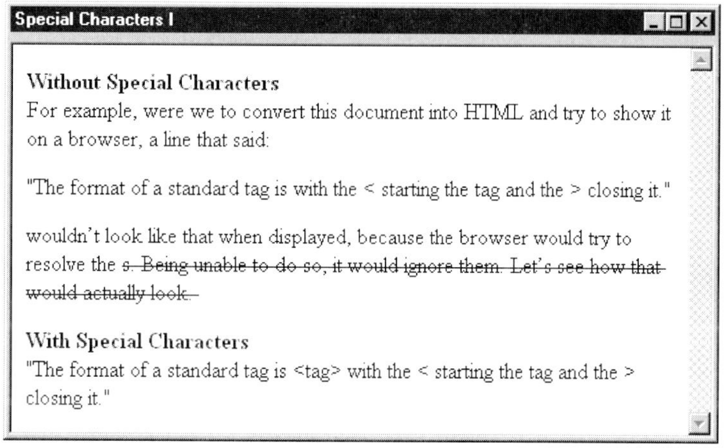

Figure 5.12 HTML code showing that special characters are needed to stand in for symbols.

several lines of text. All that is changed in the code is the addition of several line breaks to set the quoted statement off from the rest of the text.

This is even more interesting than we might have expected. Not surprisingly, "<tag>" is not shown because the browser can't figure it out and so ignores it. But the string "<s and the >" has been interpreted as an <S> (strikethrough) tag, with some unknown attributes, so the rest of the text is shown in strikethrough font. Obviously, we shouldn't use spurious special characters.

There are times when special characters are needed. For instance, we wanted to refer to the <FONT> tag in Figure 5.8. In that case we needed to illustrate how to code something in HTML. In other situations we might want to use special characters like © (copyright), ™ (Trade Mark), ® (Registered Trade Mark), & (ampersand), or even -D (the Icelandic eth). The designers of HTML anticipated this need and created a whole set of glyphs ranging from currency symbols like ¥ (the yen) to simple typographical symbols like . . . (the ellipsis).

Most of the common symbols can be coded two ways—either as a named entity or as that character's numeric position in the *Latin-1 standard character set* (Figure 5.13). The Latin-1 character set, designed by the International Standards Organization (ISO), is a list of common letters, numbers, symbols, and punctuation marks used in Western languages. Each symbol has a numeric value, and some also have names. The common ASCII character set is a subset of Latin-1.

```
<HTML>
<HEAD>
<TITLE>Special Characters II</TITLE>
</HEAD>
<BODY bgcolor="#FFFFFF">
<!-- Background color = white -->

<H3>Special Characters</H3>
&#38; or &amp; - ampersand <BR>
&#169; or &copy; - copyright <BR>
&#60; or &lt; - less than <BR>
&#62; or &gt; - greater than <BR>
&#174; or &reg; - registration <BR>
&#34; or &quot; - double-quote <BR>

<H3>Foreign Language</H3>
&#192; or &Agrave; - uppercase A + grave accent <BR>
&#193; or &Aacute; - uppercase A + acute accent <BR>
&#194; or &Acirc; - uppercase A + circumflex accent <BR>
&#195; or &Atilde; - uppercase A + tilde <BR>
&#196; or &Auml; - uppercase A + umlaut <BR>
&#197; or &Aring; - uppercase A + ring <BR>
&#198; or &AElig; - uppercase A + dipthong <BR>
&#199; or &Ccedil; - uppercase C + cedilla <BR>
&#208; or &ETH; - uppercase Eth (Icelandic) <BR>
&#216; or &Oslash; - uppercase O + slash <BR>
&#222; or &THORN; - uppercase THORN (Icelandic) <BR>

</BODY>
</HTML>
```

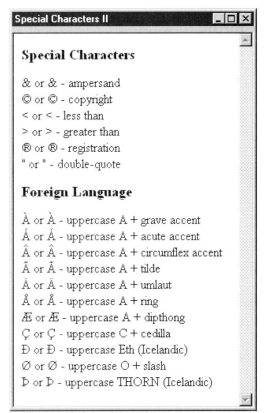

Figure 5.13 HTML code showing how special characters begin with an ampersand (&) and end with a semicolon (;).

For example, the ampersand (&) has a numeric value of 38 and the standard name of &amp. Appendix C presents a list of commonly used special characters currently recognized by the standard browsers. As the international flavor of HTML permeates the browsers, more and more characters will be added. Check the specifications at regular intervals to see if any new glyphs are available.

The Latin-1 character set has 236 different characters. This coding system adequately covers all the written characters traditionally used in English, French, German, and other Indo-European languages; however, it does not take into consideration other languages, such as Chinese and Japanese, that employ thousands of characters. A new coding system called *Unicode* supports 65,536 different possible binary combinations. According to the W^{3}C, Unicode is a *coded character set* that assigns unique numbers to (currently) about 30,000 of the possible characters in the world's languages. It is a superset of all standard character repertoires, including Latin-1. Unicode is designed as a way for computers to process and store text in every known written language. Appendix C includes a few commonly used Unicode codes.

When you code any symbol, you start with an ampersand (&) and end with a semicolon (;). After the ampersand, you put the standard name or an octothorp (#) followed by the numeric value for that character. That sounds confusing, but it is simple when you look at some examples. Figure 5.12 shows how a sentence would look using the < and > characters instead of <> in the HTML code. Figure 5.13 shows how the characters could be coded using their names and their numeric designations.

Turning Off Formatting

Sometimes it is necessary to prevent the browser from taking control of the way a portion of the screen looks. In the past, one way to achieve this outcome was to use the <PLAINTEXT> tag, which converted everything into plain text. Inexperienced Web weavers would get into trouble coding it, because after it was used in a document, no other HTML tags were recognized. It turned its own ending tag into text! The <PLAINTEXT> became obsolete with the HTML 4.0 specifications, which recommend the use of the <PRE> container instead.

<PRE>pre-formatted text</PRE>

Description: identifies preformatted text that the browser is instructed not to alter.
Type: container.
Attributes: class, dir, id, lang, onClick, onDblClick, onKeyDown, onKeyPress, onKeyUp, onMouseDown, onMouseMove, onMouseOut, onMouseOver, onMouseUp, style, title, and width.
Special note: replaces obsolete <PLAINTEXT>, <LISTING>, and <XMP> containers.

The <PRE>pre-formatted text</PRE> container is designed to present a block of text without enforcing additional formatting by the browser. In a <PRE> container, supernumerary (extra) blanks are not removed. This container has one optional attribute, **width,** which determines how many characters fit on a single line. This is a request to the browser, not an absolute demand. Lines that are longer than the width of the browser *pane* will extend outside the browser pane, requiring the user to scroll right in order to read all of the text. The browser pane is the part of the screen that is normally visible to the user without scrolling. The common browsers will support lines longer than their normal pane if they are required to by the HTML code. Usually it is a bad idea to force text beyond the browser pane, because the user may overlook it. Also, it places an additional burden on users because they have to scroll to access all the information you are providing.

You should not use tags that cause a paragraph break, like <BLOCK-QUOTE>, within the <PRE> container, because they may cause inconsistent behavior across browsers. Some browsers may interpret these tags as simple line breaks, whereas others may infer a </PRE> tag before the break and end the container. Style tags are allowed within a <PRE> block, so if the text within the block contains characters like the ampersand (&) or the greater-than (>) and lesser-than (<) signs, you will need to use the special symbols we just discussed to avoid having the browser simply ignore them (Figure 5.14).

Usually a <PRE> element is used to protect and illustrate tabs or other formatting for computer programs and the like. Don't use the <PRE> container simply to avoid having the browser format your text.

Figure 5.14 presents the code for a <PRE> block. This text was created to show how the DOS DIR command displays a disk directory. Sometimes you can get unexpected results, because the browser will use a much larger tab value than the HTML editor did. If you are going to use the <PRE> container, it is a good idea to use spaces rather than tabs to perform your alignment.

Final Comment

Formatting the text in your pages has become in one way much easier and in another way much more complex since the release of the HTML 4.0 specifications. Formatting is easier because by using document-level formatting with style sheets, you can, in one place, create the styles for all of the elements you wish to control. It is more complex because there are so many more features you can consider when making decisions on how the text should look. Be careful not to lose your message among the formatting codes! In Chapter 8 you will learn how to incorporate all of these refinements into cascading style sheets and external style sheets. Now it is time to practice what you have learned.

Key Terms

Document-level style sheet
Font
Glyph
Logical style
Monospace font
Physical style
Proportional spacing
Style sheet

```
<HTML>
<HEAD>
<TITLE>Using Pre-Formatted Text</TITLE>
</HEAD>
<BODY bgcolor="#FFFFFF">
<!-- Background color = white -->

<BIG><BIG><TT><B>DOS DIR Command</B></TT></BIG></BIG><BR>
After the DOS prompt type: <TT>dir a:</TT><BR>
The computer will display: <BR>
<PRE>
 Volume in drive A has no label.
 Volume Serial Number is 0000-0000

 Directory of A:\

08/24/98  01:33p                67,584 Case Study Prospectus.doc
08/18/98  02:34p                37,888 hwk102f.doc
08/18/98  02:20p                59,904 PSY102f.DOC
08/24/97  10:29a                78,848 100SYL.DOC
08/10/98  12:23p                 7,061 hwk110df.htm
08/10/98  12:31p                 6,891 hwk110nf.htm
08/10/98  11:15a                 4,317 cis110sy.htm
08/19/98  01:55p                72,727 cis110sg.jpg
08/19/98  01:59p                73,144 cis110tx.jpg
08/19/98  02:03p                71,025 cis110lb.jpg
08/19/98  02:06p                65,909 cis100tx.jpg
08/24/98  07:36p                29,184 CIS100HW.DOC
08/30/98  12:52p        &lt;DIR&gt;         work
09/28/98  12:33a                   808 nletter.css
09/28/98  12:33a                 3,327 newsletter.htm
10/05/98  12:39a                   962 e05-11.htm
10/05/98  12:39a                   491 e05-10.htm
10/04/98  09:59p                 2,351 e05-05.htm
09/09/98  05:57p               623,392 css2.txt
               19 File(s)    1,205,813 bytes
                                75,776 bytes free
</PRE>
<BR>
To clear the screen type: <TT>cls</TT>

</BODY>
</HTML>
```

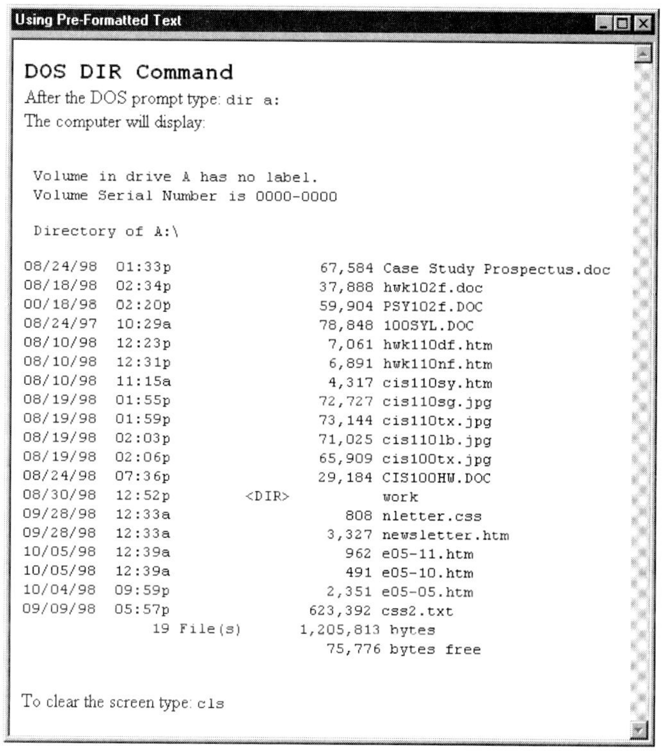

Using Pre-Formatted Text

DOS DIR Command

After the DOS prompt type: `dir a:`
The computer will display:

```
 Volume in drive A has no label.
 Volume Serial Number is 0000-0000

 Directory of A:\

08/24/98  01:33p                67,584 Case Study Prospectus.doc
08/18/98  02:34p                37,888 hwk102f.doc
00/18/98  02:20p                59,904 PSY102f.DOC
08/24/97  10:29a                78,848 100SYL.DOC
08/10/98  12:23p                 7,061 hwk110df.htm
08/10/98  12:31p                 6,891 hwk110nf.htm
08/10/98  11:15a                 4,317 cis110sy.htm
08/19/98  01:55p                72,727 cis110sg.jpg
08/19/98  01:59p                73,144 cis110tx.jpg
08/19/98  02:03p                71,025 cis110lb.jpg
08/19/98  02:06p                65,909 cis100tx.jpg
08/24/98  07:36p                29,184 CIS100HW.DOC
08/30/98  12:52p        <DIR>         work
09/28/98  12:33a                   808 nletter.css
09/28/98  12:33a                 3,327 newsletter.htm
10/05/98  12:39a                   962 e05-11.htm
10/05/98  12:39a                   491 e05-10.htm
10/04/98  09:59p                 2,351 e05-05.htm
09/09/98  05:57p               623,392 css2.txt
               19 File(s)    1,205,813 bytes
                                75,776 bytes free
```

To clear the screen type: `cls`

Figure 5.14 HTML code showing how the <PRE> tag is used to display screen lines exactly as originally formatted.

New Tags

```
<ABBR>
<ACRONYM>
<ADDRESS>
<B>
<BASEFONT>
<BIG>
<BLINK>
<BLOCKQUOTE>
<CITE>
<CODE>
<DEL>
<DFN>
<EM>
<FONT>
<I>
<INS>
<KBD>
<PRE>
<Q>
<S>
<SAMP>
<SMALL>
<STRIKE>
<STRONG>
<STYLE>
<SUB>
<SUP>
<TT>
<U>
<VAR>
```

Review Questions

1. What is the definition of each of the key terms?

2. How is each of the tags introduced in this chapter used?

3. What are four font properties?

4. What are two ways in which you can increase the number of characters per line of text?

5. In what situations is a sans-serif typeface used?

6. How can several tags be assigned new properties at the same time?

7. What is the default value for the `text-align` property dependent on?

8. Why should style changes within the <STYLE> element be embedded within a comment?

9. How does the KISS principle apply to style sheet design?

10. What are five properties that the font attribute can change?

11. How is the handling of relative size values different between the <BASEFONT> and <FONT> elements?

12. How are the situations using the <BLOCKQUOTE> and <Q> elements different?

13. What special syntax identifies a special character within HTML code?

14. What are the two different ways you can code a special character for the greater-than symbol (>)?

Exercises

5.1. Create a page that demonstrates the ten physical-style tags. Yes, you can use the <BLINK> tag—just this once! The title bar should display "Physical Style Demonstration" with your name and the assignment due date included within comment lines.

5.2. Create a separate page that demonstrates and explains the 13 logical-style tags. The title bar should display "Logical Style Demonstration" with your name and the assignment due date included within comment lines.

5.3 Use the <STYLE> container in a new HTML document to create a document-level style sheet that outlines the formatting rules shown here and establishes unique properties for all six heading levels. Provide copies of the HTML code and sample screen display using data of your own choosing. The title bar should display "Internal Style Sheet Demonstration" with your name and the assignment due date included within comment lines.

```
Ordered List
    I.  Uppercase Roman Numerals
        A.  Uppercase Alphabet
            1.  Decimal
                a.  Lowercase Alphabet
                    i.  Lowercase Roman Numerals
Unordered List
    ■  Square Marker
        •  Solid Disc Marker
            ○  Open Disc Marker
```

5.4 Create a document-level style sheet for the Homework home page used in earlier exercises, including Exercise 4.4. Establish unique properties for all heading levels, paragraphs, and list items used within the document.

5.5. Create a new HTML document with a short list, eight to ten items long, set off above and below by a nice pair of centered horizontal rules. The list should show special characters (different from those in Figure 5.13) and how they are coded. The title bar should display "Special Character Demonstration" with your name and the assignment due date included within comment lines.

5.6. Create a document-level style sheet for your school's home page or the one you created for the school in earlier exercises, including Exercise 4.6. Establish unique properties for all heading levels, paragraphs, and list items used within the document.

5.7. Create a 10-row by 3-column table of data using your ASCII editor, with tabs separating each column. The data could be a list of teams and their respective win-and-lose record or an inventory of items with quantity and unit cost. Copy the table into a new HTML document, and enclose it using the <PRE> container. The title bar should display "<PRE> Tag Demonstration" with your name and the assignment due date included within comment lines.

## CHAPTER SIX

INCLUSIONS—IMAGES AND MULTIMEDIA

"A picture is worth a thousand words" is certainly an understatement in the world of the Web. Here a picture is worth many thousands of words, at least in terms of how much space a picture takes. It is not unusual for a picture to take up thousands and thousands of bytes. For example, Figure 6.4 has a 12,000-byte file size. A text file takes up one byte per character. If we were to pick an arbitrary size for the "average" word, let's say a word of five characters, then any image that is larger than 5000 bytes (5 kilobytes) would be bigger than a thousand words!

Pictures and multimedia are what some people feel the Web is all about. They feel that without pictures, a Web site becomes just a collection of text files. Properly used, images and multimedia will enhance your Web pages, make them look more professional, draw users into the page, and make it easier for them to navigate through the information you provide. Of course, if the media you choose are overly large, or if you use too many, they can clutter up your page and significantly increase the download time for your users. Images and other multimedia elements are a critical part of the Web, and it is important for you to learn how to use them, when to use them, and when to avoid them.

Multimedia

Multimedia is the use of images, sound, video, and other special effects. According to the 1990 edition of *The New Lexicon Webster's Dictionary of the English Language,* multimedia refers to "a means of communication involving several media, e.g., film and sculpture, print matter, and voices." That's not quite the definition we use when talking about multimedia on the Net. Rather, we take the spirit of the *Webster's* definition and add what could be called a multisensory aspect. When Web weavers speak of multimedia, they are usually referring to sounds, video, animation, or other elements of a page besides images and text. We will examine each of these different features in this chapter, starting with images.

Image Formats

When HTML authors speak of images, they are referring to a whole range of picture-like elements, including such diverse things as scanned photographs, icons, illustrations, drawings, and simple animation. Let's take a closer look at the common image formats you encounter when cruising the Web.

GIF

Created by CompuServe, *GIF* stands for *Graphics Interchange Format*. It supports 8-bit color and is the most common image format. All graphical Web browsers recognize the .gif filename extension used by GIF images. There are three forms of the GIF format:

1. Plain GIF, in which the picture looks like a snapshot.
2. Transparent GIF, in which the background is invisible, so the image seems to be painted directly on the Web page.
3. **Animated GIF,** in which a series of still GIF images are quickly changed to create simple animation.

Figure 6.1 shows the difference between a plain GIF and a GIF with a transparent background. The page's background color shows through a transparent GIF file, whereas a plain GIF file supplies its own background color.

GIF compression is considered "lossless" because the quality of the image does not change (or suffer a "loss") through many conversions to GIF format. *Lossless compression* accounts for all the data bits in the image when the image is compressed. This results in a somewhat larger file, but the image quality does not degrade when it is compressed and then uncompressed many times. This type of compression is best suited for line art that contains large areas of the same color.

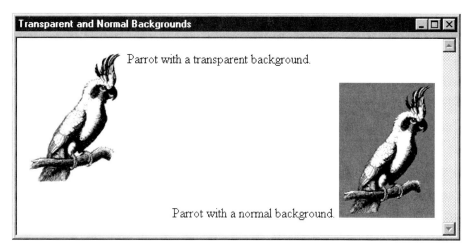

Figure 6.1 GIF images with transparent and normal backgrounds.

JPEG

JPEG stands for *Joint Photographers Experts Group* and is a better choice for photographic-quality color than GIF, because it can support either 8-bit or 24-bit color. A JPEG file is also smaller than a GIF file of the same image, because JPEG uses a higher compression ratio. However, you must be careful when repeatedly saving a JPEG file because of the **lossy compression** used to store the image. Each time an image is compressed into the JPEG format, some of the pixels are discarded. The first few times this happens, it doesn't really detract from the image, because the human eye cannot distinguish such a small loss of data. But when an image is repeatedly compressed into JPEG format, the image quality will discernibly degrade. All the graphical browsers support JPEG and recognize these files by the .jpeg or .jpg filename extensions.

When saving an image as a JPEG file, many image editors offer to save it in a "progressive" format. A **progressive image** file is saved as layers. You usually have a choice of saving three to seven layers. Graphical browsers will load and display the JPEG image one layer at a time, which has the visual effect of building the image. This is considered by some authors to be a visually appealing effect that catches the eye of interested users. Unfortunately, a progressive image file is slower to load.

PNG

PNG stands for *Portable Network Graphics* and is a newer format that supports both 8-bit and 24-bit color. It uses a lossless compression algorithm. PNG is currently an **open standard,** which means that anyone is free to use it, and no single body or organization has fixed all the parameters of the standard. In other words, an open standard is a standard that is still developing. PNG is supported by some of the most up-to-date browsers but not by all, the way GIF and JPEG are. A PNG file is recognized by the .png filename extension. There is a large and growing group that is trying to establish PNG as the Web standard.

PDF

PDF stands for *Portable Data Format.* These images are created with a special software package from Adobe called Acrobat. PDF images cannot be read by any current browser without an additional software package called Acrobat Reader that must be independently installed. An additional software package that works with a browser is called a *plug-in.* Currently the Acrobat Reader plug-in is available for free download. PDF documents can look like a magazine page, with multiple columns. The PDF files support "on page" searching and use the .pdf filename extension. This format is not yet widely used.

TIFF

TIFF stands for *Tagged Image File Format,* which is commonly used to exchange documents between different computer platforms. There are six different "flavors" of TIFF files, so any one TIFF image may not be correctly displayed if the user's viewing software expects one of the other "flavors." TIFF supports 1, 4, 8, and 24 bits per pixel. It is an older formatting scheme, but because of all its variations it is not considered a standard. TIFF files usually have the file extensions of .tif on Intel platforms and .tiff on systems that support longer file names.

BMP

BMP is a *Bit Mapped Picture.* It is a standard Microsoft Windows image format that uses a .bmp filename extension. It can support 1, 4, 8, and 24 bits per pixel. It is not compressed as a rule. These files are usually created using Microsoft's Paint or Paintbrush programs and are used for the wallpaper in Windows. The standard browsers do not currently support this file type without invoking a program like Microsoft Paint.

PCX

PCX is an older image format that was developed by Zsoft for the PC Paintbrush program. In the early days, since there were no standards, this became a de facto standard. It will support 1, 4, 8, and 24 bits per pixel. It does not seem to support compression and uses a .pcx filename extension. If you encounter a PCX-formatted file, your browser will need to start an external application like Paint to view it.

For now it may be best to use only GIF and JPEG image formats for your pages. They are the two standard formats that are supported by all the graphical browsers. Don't shy away from the new PNG image format, because both Navigator and Internet Explorer recognize it. Exotic formats (anything that is not GIF, JPEG, or PNG) may require installing a plug-in before viewing. Try to resist the temptation of using exotic images. If your user cannot display them, they have no value. Image editors and drawing packages allow a file to be saved in any of several formats, so the aspiring artist can usually save a file in either GIF, JPEG or PNG formats. In addition, you can use an image editor to convert exotic image types into something more recognizable.

If you are serious about building and maintaining Web pages, it would be a good idea to acquire a good *image editor.* Editors like Adobe's Photoshop or the shareware Paint Shop Pro allow you to modify images, add special effects like polarization or texturing, and convert from one form of file format to another. Many of the more interesting images available on the Web were created on paper and then scanned into machine-readable form. The most serious Web weavers have a good color scanner to create images this way.

Image Sizes

It is important to understand how quickly an image can become a large, slow, troublesome impediment to your users. Let's do some simple math to see how large an image can become. We will use an image size of 500 by 300, or 150,000, pixels. The image in Figure 6.2, including the 1-pixel black border, is this size. It is a rather large image, but not a full-screen picture. If we were to use the GIF file format, with 8 bits per pixel, we would have a file of 1,200,000 bits. If the user is using a 56.6-kilobits-per-second modem connection, and if the modem actually connects at 56.6, it would take about 21 seconds to download that one image. That's not too bad if that is the only image we have; most users will wait 21 seconds to see it. But remember, this is at 56.6 kilobits per second! Many modems actually operate at a speed of only 28.8 kilobits per second (*kbps*) during the day, regardless of their speed capacity. The same image that took 21 seconds to download at 56.6 kilobits per second will take 42 seconds to download at 28.8 kbps. That is a little long for our user to sit staring at the screen! And remember, that is just one image. If we have 10 or 12 images of the same large size on our page, we need to multiply the wait by the number of images. Then, too, this example is for an 8-bit (8 bits per pixel) image. Suppose instead we were to use a 24-bit image. You can see how images can really add to the download time for pages.

Bits per Pixel (bpp)

In the preceding discussion of file format types, you saw that each file format supports a specific range of bits per pixel (*bpp*). This count determines how many colors an image can contain, as follows:

- 1 bpp allows an image to have two colors, usually black and white, with no gray scale (see Figure 6.2).
- 4 bpp allows an image to have up to 16 colors. This is the old Windows palette. It is good enough for icons but not usually sufficient for pictures.

Figure 6.2 An image 500 by 300 pixels in size, stored in a monochrome format, or 1 bpp.

- 8 bpp allows an image to have up to 256 colors. This is the way GIF files are stored. This is an acceptable number of colors for most applications but does not provide the richness necessary for good rendering of photographs or scanned images.
- 16 bpp allows an image to have up to 32,768 colors. This is an older ratio and is not often supported, since the next level is so much richer. Many applications skip this level.
- 24 bpp allows an image to have more than 16 million colors! Specifically, it allows 16,777,216 different colors. This is sufficient for a good rendering of photographs and other scanned images. The downside of the 24 bpp range is that our example image of 150,000 pixels in Figure 6.2 would take more than 2 minutes to download at 28.8 kilobits per second.

Graphics Tips

Following are some techniques for reducing download time for users while still providing the visually rich environment you wish to create.
- *Simplify your graphics.* If you are building an image using a graphics package, keep the image simple. Use the fewest colors you can get away with, and save your image in either GIF or JPEG format. Avoid colors on the palette that are created using ***dithering*** (blending two colors among adjacent pixels to achieve a third color), because that can reduce the compressibility of the image. Another reason not to use dithered colors is that all systems don't dither the same way. Examples of dithering are illustrated in Figure 6.3. Large areas of a single color are best for compression.

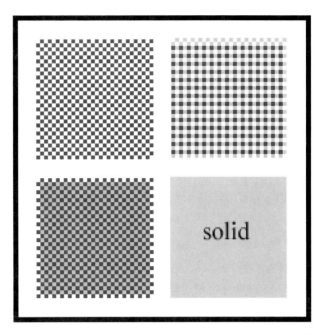

Figure 6.3 Examples of dithering in which new color blends are created by placing different colored pixels next to each other.

- *Divide up large pages.* This is a general rule for Web pages, but it is especially important when dealing with pages that have many graphics. Users would rather flip from one quickly loading page to another than wait for one slowly loading, large page. A good rule of thumb is to keep pages under a 50-kilobyte maximum size, including all the graphics. That way the pages will load fairly quickly, even with very slow connection speeds. An absolute rule of thumb is to keep the page, and all the graphics associated with the page, at a size less than 720 kilobytes. An easy way to accomplish this is to store all the data for one page, both text and the associated graphics, on a single, low-density 3.5 inch floppy disk. If the data won't fit on the disk, the page is too large.
- *Keep large graphics on their own page.* If you must have a large image, put it on a page by itself and provide a link to it from the current page. This type of image is referred to as an ***external image.*** We use a familiar tool, the <A>anchor</A> container, to reference external images. The following code displays the image shown in Figure 6.4 as an independent external image:

```
<A href="maddoc.gif">Full size Mad Dr. G's Home Page (110K GIF)</A>
```

You can either use a text link like, "I have enclosed a detailed picture of the part for you to examine; it is a 1.2 Meg image," or you can use a thumbnail image as the link. A ***thumbnail image*** is a very small version of the actual image. Figure 6.4 provides an example of a large graphic used on a home page. This single image is 110,000 bytes. It is a large image. Figure 6.4 also shows how it would look as a thumbnail 8000 bytes in size.

Figure 6.4 Home page image and associated thumbnail images used as a link.

In this example, the thumbnail is much smaller than the full GIF. That is a great savings for the user. Set up the page so that the user can click on the thumbnail image in order to see the full-size picture. It is also a good idea to tell the user how large that full size file will be. Then the user can decide if he wants to wait for it. If the "big picture" is an 18-megabyte file ($1024 \times 768 \times 24$ bpp), it could take several minutes to download!

- *Reuse the images on your page.* This is an especially important rule for icons; however, it is important for other images as well. Most browsers will *cache,* or store, images locally. That way, if you reuse the same image several times, the browser can take it from the local cache and not have to move it over the Net. While it might be nice, visually, to have a different icon for each item in a list, reusing the same icon could provide substantial savings in download time for your users.

> ## <IMG>
>
> ***Description:*** inserts graphs, photographs, line art, or other images into screen display.
> ***Type:*** empty.
> ***Attributes:*** align, alt, border, class, dir, height, hspace, id, ismap, lang, longdesc, onClick, onDblClick, onKeyDown, onKeyPress, onKeyUp, onMouseDown, onMouseMove, onMouseOut, onMouseOver, onMouseUp, src, style, title, usemap, vspace, and width.

Images are inserted into a document using the <IMG> tag. This is an empty tag. There are several attributes available for this tag, some of them specific to one or the other of the two main graphical browsers, Navigator and Internet Explorer. We will focus on <IMG> attributes identified in the W^3C HTML specifications. Because the <IMG> tag doesn't force a line break, you can insert an image into the text line (*inline*), and it will simply appear along with the text.

The rendering of images is very browser-dependent. Nongraphical browsers will ignore image tags or just display the alt value. Some browsers will force the images into specific size and color limitations. Some users will turn off automatic image loading, causing the browser to omit all the images unless the user specifically asks for one. So the pages you create must make sense even without their images. They must convey the same basic information whether the user uses a graphical browser or not.

Also, the browser will control the colors in the image. The actual hardware at the user site is involved here, too. If you have a wonderful image with 16,000,000 colors, and the user is displaying it on a monochrome monitor, it will appear as a black-and-white image. This is another example of the Web weaver supplying the *content* while the browser handles the *format*.

src

The **src** (source) attribute is the only required attribute of the <IMG> tag. This attribute tells the browser where to find the image that is to be inserted into your page. There are three schools of thought about where to keep your images:

- The first school of thought could be called the "minimize the home server's load" school. The idea here is that all the images should be on re-mote machines, and the **src** attribute should provide a link across the Net to the remote site. That way the load on the local server that is hosting the page is minimized. Generally, this is the *very worst thing* a Web weaver can do, because it causes the greatest load on the Net. In this model, each time a new image is requested, the browser must establish a link to another server where the picture is located and then download the picture before it can be displayed. Many Web sites that have pictures available for use will request that the images be copied rather than having a link pointing to their site. Following is an example of a link across the Net:

<IMG src="http://fred.dc3d.edu/images/parrot.gif">

- The second school of thought could be summed up as the "put everything in the same directory" approach. These folks like to be able to minimize the paths coded in the **src** attribute. They want to make it as easy as possible to move a page from one site to another. This school has merit for small Web sites or for people who intend to move their pages from site to site. It is very easy to upload and maintain a page when all the links and all the images are local to the home directory. But when the site is large, this may not be practical. Now look at a line of code that shows the minimal <IMG> tag (also shown in Figure 6.5): <IMG src="parrot.gif">. Here all the files, both HTML and images, have been grouped into a single directory.
- The third school could be described as the "a place for everything and everything in its place" approach. Here each type of file is kept in its own directory. Thus, the Web pages will be in a directory called "HTML" or "web-pages," the pictures in a directory called "images," the sound files in

```
<HTML>
<HEAD>
<TITLE>Images</TITLE>
</HEAD>
<BODY bgcolor="#FFFFFF">
<!-- Background color = white -->

Here is a picture of a nice parrot: <BR>
<IMG src="parrot.gif"> <BR>
Actually, this is a Cockatoo from Australia. <BR>

</BODY>
</HTML>
```

Figure 6.5 HTML code to display an image.

a directory called "sounds," and so forth. This approach can be taken to extremes, though, and become cumbersome for everybody involved. At some sites, for example, the "images" subdirectory is divided into "small-gif," "mediumgif," "biggif," "smalljpg," "mediumjpg," and "bigjpg." In the next example, the image is located in the "images" subdirectory, possibly because the site has many images, and several of them are used across many different pages: `<IMG src="images/parrot.gif">`.

Notice that in all three cases, the actual filename is enclosed in quotation marks. Those quotation marks are usually required for the image to work correctly. Sometimes they can be omitted and the image will appear correctly anyway, but at a later time, the image may stop appearing. It is best, therefore, to always code the image, or the image and path, inside quotation marks. Then it will always work as long as the path is correct. This may be the place for a word of caution. In the authors' vast experience helping students learn how to build Web pages, the most common problems with images are path problems. If you have an image that fails to load, the first thing you should check is that the path to that image is correct. The second thing you need to check is that the image name is spelled and capitalized correctly.

It is usually necessary to create a directory structure when building a commercial site, because that type of site will have hundreds of files, and many times several different pages will use the same images. If images are put in common areas, then everybody can use them. Also, updating them is easy. For example, if 15 different pages all use an image of the corporate logo, and they are stored in 15 different locations, the Web weaver would have to update 15 different files in 15 different directories if a new version of the logo were created. On the other hand, if a single copy of the logo is kept in a single directory, and all the pages use that one image, then it is easy to update the image.

For new users, it is usually easier to keep all the images, pages, and other files in one directory (the second school of thought in our previous discussion). As you become more sophisticated and as your Web site grows, you will find it easier to collect related files into directories. This will make uploading a little more complex, as you may need to change the paths in the **src** attributes, but it is a small price to pay for organization and easy update. Do not fall into the trap of linking across the Web to an image on a remote machine—that is the worst option available.

Figure 6.5 presented the code for adding `parrot.gif` to a Web page. Each line ends in a line break, `<BR>`, to force the image onto a line of its own. Later we will see how the **align** attribute allows some control over where the image is placed on the screen. We can see that the default alignment of the image is on the left margin. Figure 6.6 presents the same code, but without the line breaks. In this situation the browser treats the image just like any other text element. Images used this way are called ***inline images.*** Since there are no forced line breaks, an inline image appears like any other page element, in line with the text, and after the word "parrot," as we might expect. The first line of text is pushed down far enough to accommodate the image as well as the text. Notice how the bottom of the image is aligned with the bottom of the actual text. Soon we will see how to modify this vertical alignment as well as the horizontal alignment of an image.

```
<HTML>
<HEAD>
<TITLE>Images</TITLE>
</HEAD>
<BODY bgcolor="#FFFFFF">
<!-- Background color = white -->

Here is a picture of a nice parrot:
<IMG src="parrot.gif" alt="Cockatoo woodcut">
Actually, this is a Cockatoo from Australia.

</BODY>
</HTML>
```

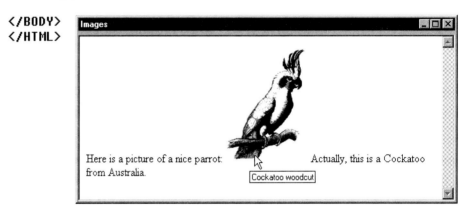

Figure 6.6 HTML code to display an inline image, with **alt** attribute describing the image.

alt

The **alt** attribute provides a text-based description of the image. Conscientious Web weavers always include the **alt** attribute to allow for text-based browsers and, in the future, aural (sound)-based browsers. This attribute contains a text string that is displayed when graphical browser users move the screen pointer over the image (see Figure 6.6). The text provided by the **alt** attribute is also displayed (as shown in Figure 6.7) when the browser can't display the actual image, either because it is not a graphical browser or because the user has turned off image loading. This text string must be enclosed in quotation marks if it contains any punctuation or spaces. The string can be up to 1024 bytes long.

As mentioned earlier in this chapter, the careful Web weaver never places information in an image that is not available somewhere else on the page. The **alt** attribute is one good way to present that information to users who cannot see the images. In addition to providing content support for nongraphical users, the **alt** attribute can serve as a substitute for icons. For example, you could include the following code in your page to indicate a new feature:

<H2>See the birdie <IMG src="hotnew.gif" alt="**NEW**"> </H2>

Users with graphical browsers see the "hotnew.gif" image, but those with text-only browsers or those who have turned off automatic image loading will see the string "**NEW**" after the text.

Figure 6.6 presents the code for the parrot page in Figure 6.5 with the **alt** attribute coded. In Figure 6.7 the alternative text is displayed because we temporarily removed `parrot.gif` from the local directory. Using the **alt** attribute should be standard procedure for any image you choose to add to your page.

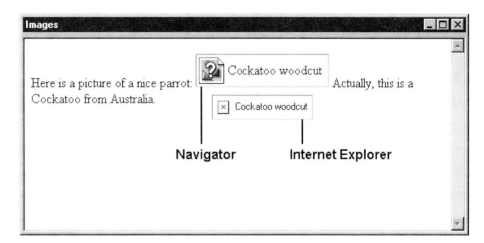

Figure 6.7 Display of the text provided by the **alt** attribute when the browser cannot find the related image.

longdesc

The **longdesc** attribute takes the logic behind the **alt** attribute one step further. It specifies a long description of the image that is stored as an independent file. The HTML code would look like this:

```
<IMG src="parrot.gif" alt="Cockatoo woodcut" longdesc="cockatoo.txt">
```

This attribute is especially useful when server-side images maps are found on the Web page. Both client-side and server-side image maps are discussed in Chapter 14.

height and width

One way to reduce the download time for the user is to tell the browser exactly how much screen real estate to reserve for the image. The **height** and **width** attributes do this. They eliminate the need for the browser to spend time calculating how much space to allow for the image before it continues downloading and presenting the page. In some instances—for example, in JavaScript—image height and width are required. The image dimensions are given in the number of pixels that compose a horizontal line (width) and a vertical line (height). The following code, also shown in Figure 6.8, would create an image 150 pixels high and 200 pixels wide:

```
<IMG src="bfly.gif" height="150" width="200">
```

It is a good coding habit to enclose the pixel count in double quotes as shown here.

Since you can control the actual size of the image using **height** and **width,** these attributes provide an easy way to create a thumbnail image (Figure 6.8). Be careful with this—even though the image appears small on the screen, the browser must still download the whole image. It is also important to keep the same proportions when you change the size of an image. If you don't retain the ratio of height to width, you can really distort an image. For example, if the **width** of the butterfly image were decreased without decreasing the **height** proportionally, the image would be distorted.

```
<HTML>
<HEAD>
<TITLE>Image Height and Width Attributes</TITLE>
</HEAD>
<BODY bgcolor="#FFFFFF">
<!-- Background color = white -->

At the <EM>Fly Away Home</EM> Web site you can experience <BR>
many of nature's pretty little creatures <BR>
as they frolic about the flowers of the pasture. <BR>
<IMG src="bfly.gif" alt="Painted Lady Butterfly" height="15" width="20">
<IMG src="bfly.gif" alt="Painted Lady Butterfly" height="150" width="200">
<IMG src="bfly.gif" alt="Painted Lady Butterfly" height="300" width="400">

</BODY>
</HTML>
```

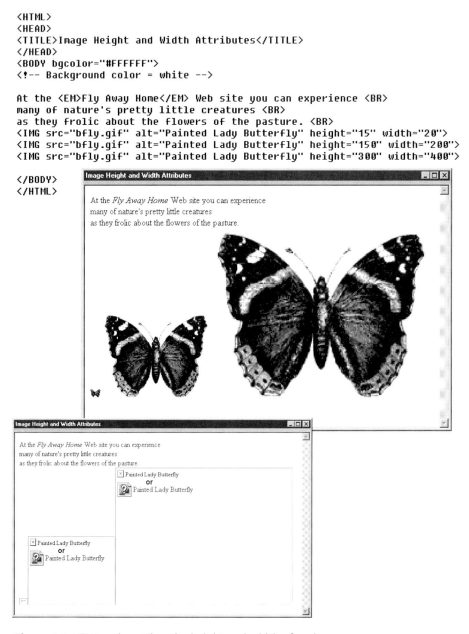

Figure 6.8 HTML code setting the height and width of an image.

Besides creating thumbnail versions of images, you can use this feature to enlarge small images as shown in Figure 6.8. Usually the larger version doesn't look as good as the original, but if you enlarge it only a small amount, the image quality doesn't suffer too much.

Another potential problem with coding image sizes is the effect created when the user has disabled the automatic image download. The browser still reserves space for the images, so the screen is filled with nearly empty frames containing only the **alt** text and meaningless place-holder icons. The page looks very unfinished and may be of little use. In Figure 6.8 you can see how such a page would appear. If the Web weaver had not coded the **height** and **width,** then the browser would have rendered all of the place-holders the same small size.

Furthermore, if you don't set the **height** and **width** attributes, and the user has the automatic download option turned off, the browser will also display these small place-holder icons inside the text block instead of reserving the large blocks of empty space shown in Figure 6.8.

Note that you must code the **height** and **width** attributes in pixels. Although it is not usually a good idea to code anything in pixels, as the number of pixels on your user's screen may differ from the number on your screen, in this case you have no choice. Just remember that there are variations in users' screens, and take this into account as you set the number of pixels. Suppose you build an image that takes up the right third of your screen, but you have a 1024 × 1080 screen whereas your user has a 600 × 400 screen. Your image will be a lot larger on the user's screen. The difference in size can cause problems in presenting information and maintaining a reasonable screen layout.

A final trick you can use with images is called *flood filling,* or extreme image expansion. Here you create a large colored area by using the **height** and **width** attributes to expand a very small image across the screen. For example, the code in Figure 6.9 creates a large line across the screen. The line is 450 pixels wide and

```
<HTML>
<HEAD>
<TITLE>Flood Filling</TITLE>
</HEAD>
<BODY bgcolor="#FFFFFF">
<!-- Background color = white -->

The following image is really only one pixel on size, <BR>
but by using <B>height</B> and <B>width</B> attributes, you can make it <BR>
look like a large bar across the screen! <BR>
<IMG src="onepixel.jpg" height="12" width="450"> <BR>
Pretty neat, huh! <BR>

</BODY>
</HTML>
```

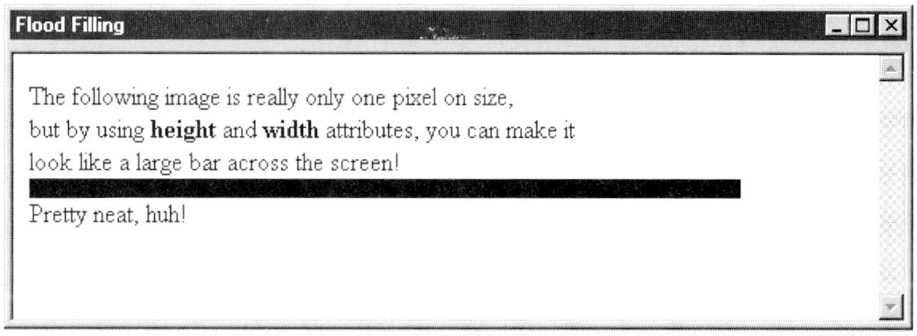

Flood Filling

The following image is really only one pixel on size,
but by using **height** and **width** attributes, you can make it
look like a large bar across the screen!

Pretty neat, huh!

Figure 6.9 HTML code using the **height** and **width** attributes to flood-fill an image of a single pixel.

12 pixels tall. This single-pixel black GIF is used to fill all 5400 points. Figure 6.9 also shows how the code looks in a graphical browser.

There are a couple of caveats about flood-fill imaging. First, browsers like Mosaic don't use the **height** and **width** browser extensions, so in Mosaic all the user would see is a single black pixel. Second, there is always a risk when using absolute pixel counts. If the user has a very high-resolution screen, this line might extend across only a small part of the screen. On the other hand, if the user has a low-resolution screen, the line might extend nearly the width of the whole screen. In either case, the user's browser and hardware will determine how the screen appears.

align

The browsers don't specify a default alignment across the page for images, because images are treated like any other text object. As you have seen, if you insert an image in the middle of a text block, it will simply appear there, with the line of text on either side of it. In most cases the browser will align the bottom of the image with the bottom of the text line. However, browsers vary, so a wise Web weaver will always specify where the image is to align if it makes a difference in the presentation of the information.

There are five different values to control the placement of the image on the page, and within the text line. The three standard **align** values are top, middle, and bottom, which control how the image lines up with the text line in which it is embedded.

TOP

The **align** value of TOP aligns the top of the image with the top of the tallest item in the current text line. If the tallest item is an image, TOP will align its image with the preceding one. If there are no other images in the current line, TOP will align its image with the top of the text. Figure 6.10 gives an example of a top alignment when there are no other images in the current text line.

MIDDLE

The **align** value of MIDDLE aligns the middle of the image with the bottom, or *baseline,* of the text (not the middle of the text). The baseline of the text is the imaginary line that runs across the bottom of the letters, like the point of the v and the bottom of the x, not counting the descenders, like the tails of y or g. Figure 6.10 also shows an example of a middle alignment.

BOTTOM

The **align** value of BOTTOM aligns the bottom of the image with the bottom, or baseline, of the text. Although BOTTOM is usually the default value, the wise Web weaver never counts on a browser's default value. It is better to code a value if it is important. This alignment is useful for putting special symbols (like dingbats) into the text line. Figure 6.10 gives an example of bottom alignment.

```
<HTML>
<HEAD>
<TITLE>Image Alignment</TITLE>
</HEAD>
<BODY bgcolor="#CCCCCC">
<!-- Background color = light gray -->

Align equals top
<IMG src="toad.gif" align="TOP" height="70" width="80">
when displaying the toad. <BR><BR>

Align equals middle
<IMG src="toad.gif" align="MIDDLE" height="70" width="80">
when displaying the toad. <BR><BR>

Align equals bottom
<IMG src="toad.gif" align="BOTTOM" height="70" width="80">
when displaying the toad. <BR>
<BR>

<BR>
<IMG src="toad.gif" align="LEFT" height="70" width="80">
Align equals left when displaying the toad. When enough text follows
the image it floats to the right and will eventually wrap underneath
the image. The point where the text wraps underneath the image depends
on the browser's screen dimensions. <BR>
<BR>

<BR>
<IMG src="toad.gif" align="RIGHT" height="70" width="80">
Align equals right when displaying the toad. When enough text follows
the image it floats to the left and will eventually wrap underneath the
image. The point where the text wraps underneath the image depends on
the browser's screen dimensions and possibly the user's screen size.
<BR>

</BODY>
</HTML>
```

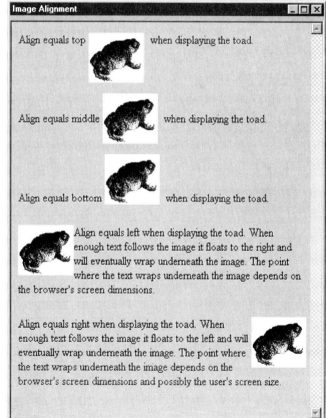

Figure 6.10 HTML code for common text alignment options.

LEFT

In addition to positioning the image vertically in the line, the extended browsers will also recognize codes to place images at either margin. Some Web weavers refer to these as *floating images.* It is often handy to be able to place an image at the margin and then flow the text next to the image, rather than imbedding the image in a single line. Figure 6.10 presents the code for a typical inline image with text aligned to the top, middle, and bottom. Underneath these examples, Figure 6.10 shows how the browser will render a left (and right) aligned image. By simply adding the **align** value, we have changed the whole look of the screen. Now the text flows along the right side of the image, so the information takes up much less space on the page. This is a nice option for images that are folded into the text stream.

The **style** attribute's `float` property can accomplish the same result. The following code would left-align the toad image:

```
<IMG src="toad.gif" style="float: left" height="70" width="80">
```

The preceding code would produce exactly the same results you see in Figure 6.10 when the **align** attribute is set equal to LEFT with this HTML code:

```
<IMG src="toad.gif" align="LEFT" height="70" width="80">
```

The `float` property is discussed in greater detail in Chapter 8 along with external style sheets.

RIGHT

The `align="RIGHT"` and `style="float: right"` options work just like the left alignments except that they place the image next to the right margin, with the text flowing around its left side. The choice of left or right image placement is determined by the aesthetic taste of the Web weaver.

Image placement at the margin is often the best choice for layouts with larger images. However, sometimes it is necessary, especially with small images or icons, to imbed the images inside the line. The use to which the image is put will usually dictate where it should be placed on the page.

Centering Text

Right and left alignments are nice, but what about centering an image? Ideally we should be able to place an image in the center of the screen and flow text on both sides of it. Unfortunately, this option has not yet been created. It no doubt will be in the future. For now, although there are two ways to get an image centered on the page, the text cannot be made to flow around it. The image will be isolated from the text. Let's look at these two ways of centering an image.

<CENTER>center text</CENTER>

Description: centers element within screen display.
Type: container.
Attributes: none.
Special note: deprecated in HTML 4.0 specifications.

One way of centering an image is to place it within a <CENTER> container. The image will be separate from the text, but it will be centered on the page. In Figure 6.11 the <CENTER> option is coded for the first image. To the surprise of some, this element was deprecated in the HTML 4.0 specifications in favor of setting a tag's **align** attribute equal to center. However, there is no "align='center'" attribute value for the <IMG> element.

```
<HEAD>
<TITLE>Centering Images</TITLE>
</HEAD>
<BODY bgcolor="#FFFFFF">
<!-- Background color = white -->

The toads are  very valuable helpers in most gardens. <BR>

<CENTER>
<IMG src="toad.gif" alt="toad" height="70" width="80">
</CENTER>

They eat many harmful insects including mosquitos, grubs, ants, and
flies. There are at least 11 species of toad that live in North
America. <BR>

<P align="CENTER">
<IMG src="toad.gif" alt="toad" height="70" width="80">
</P>

Almost all toads are nocturnal, so you will have to wait until late
evening or nightfall to see them out and about.  Although they are
usually covered with wart-like bumps, you cannot catch warts from a
toad. <BR>

</BODY>
</HTML>
```

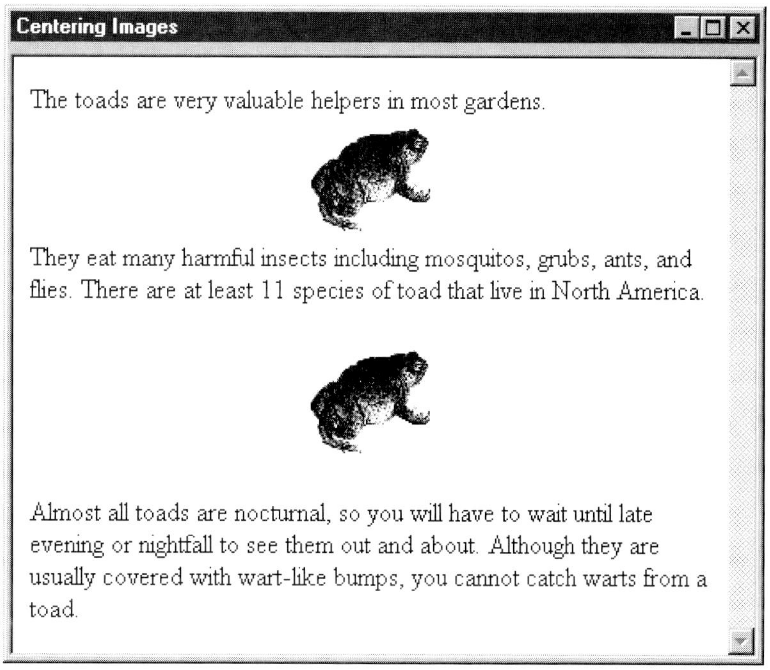

Figure 6.11 HTML code for two methods of centering an image within a page.

<P align= "CENTER">

Notice, in Figure 6.11, how the text is closer to the top and bottom of the first image than to the second. Although the <CENTER> container was used for the first image, a different method was used for the second. When you want more space above and below the image, you can isolate the image in a <P>paragraph</P> container that has an alignment of CENTER. This technique looks like this:

```
<P align="CENTER">
<IMG src="toad.gif" alt="toad" height="70" width="80">
</P>
```

From the code in Figure 6.11, you can see that the two techniques are easy to use. Notice again how the first image is very close to the text above and below it, whereas the second image is separated from the text by a blank line. Although it is not currently possible to imbed an image into a paragraph of text and have the text flow on both sides of the image, these two options for centering an image can be used to achieve the desired effect. Along with the two floating options (left and right), they give the Web weaver sufficient control over the placement of images on a page.

Image Links

Normally a browser will indicate text that is a link by making it a different color and underlining it, as you have seen in previous examples. It has become chic to replace textual links with icons or images. If the image is included within an anchor container, the image becomes a link to the URL specified in the anchor. For example, today it is common to have the link to the home page appear as a little house. The HTML code to make the image house.png a link to the home page looks like this: <A href="index.htm"><IMG src="house.png"></A>.

It is easy to fill a page with images, each a link somewhere, but try to resist the mountain-climber mindset: don't put images on your page just because they can be there. As we discussed at the beginning of the chapter, each image you place on your page should have a definite purpose. Its purpose should justify the space it is taking up on the page and the time it takes to download. The four images in Figure 6.12 are image links to the document test.htm.

border

If an image defines a link, the browsers usually surround the image with a 2-pixel border that is the same color as has been set for link text. The default color is blue for unvisited links and purple for links that have been visited. Some images don't look good when surrounded by a colored border. The **border** attribute within an <IMG> tag controls the width of the border on link-images.

Figure 6.12 presents the code for changing the size of the border on four images. Notice that the border can become large enough to be distracting. Also

```
<HEAD>
<TITLE>Image Borders</TITLE>
</HEAD>
<BODY bgcolor="#CCCCCC">
<!-- Background color = light gray -->

The following four images have the border set to 0, 2, 4, and 8 pixels respectively:<BR>
 
<A href="test.html"><IMG src="goldfish.gif" alt="carp" height="70" width="90" border="0"></A>
 
<A href="test.html"><IMG src="goldfish.gif" alt="carp" height="70" width="90" border="2"></A>
 
<A href="test.html"><IMG src="goldfish.gif" alt="carp" height="70" width="90" border="4"></A>
 
<A href="test.html"><IMG src="goldfish.gif" alt="carp" height="70" width="90" border="8"></A>

</BODY>
</HTML>
```

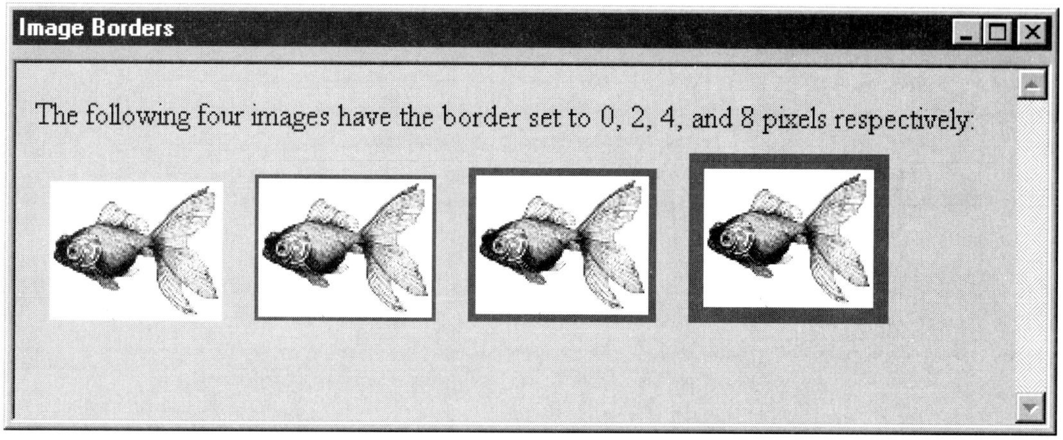

Figure 6.12 HTML code for image borders of varying widths.

notice the first image. It is actually a link, but there is no border around it to clue the user that it is a link.

All four of these images are the same size, and they align on the bottom edge, but the border actually controls the vertical placement on the line. The wide border image is much closer to the preceding line than the borderless image.

As pointed out, a too-large border around an image can be distracting. Figure 6.13 shows another example of how a border can be distracting. Here the border around the image with a transparent background defeats the purpose of the transparent background by defining a rectangle on the screen. Both images in this figure are links. The difference between the two is that the one on the left has the **border** attribute set to zero.

The image on the left is clearly floating on the background. If you choose to use a borderless image like this as a link, you must tell your user that the image is a link. Without a border, the only way users can tell that an image is a link is if they happen to pass the screen pointer over it and notice the way the pointer changes when it passes over the link. Since you can't count on this, you should tell the users that the image is a link by means of simple text instructions.

```
<HEAD>
<TITLE>Transparent Backgrounds with Image Borders</TITLE>
</HEAD>
<BODY bgcolor="#FFFFFF">
<!-- Background color = white -->

The following image links have transparent backgrounds.
They are presented here so you can see how a border looks when turned off and turned on:
<A href="test.htm"><IMG src="parrot.gif" align="LEFT" border="0"></A>
<A href="test.htm"><IMG src="parrot.gif" align="RIGHT" border="2"></A>

</BODY>
</HTML>
```

Figure 6.13 HTML code for a border around an image link that can be turned off or on.

vspace and hspace

Many Web weavers find that browsers leave too little room between the images and the text, as shown in Figure 6.14. Such close quarters are even more obvious when the image is a link, with a border around it. Graphical browsers have two attributes that control the horizontal and vertical space around images: **vspace** and **hspace.** The code in Figure 6.14 shows how the space around images can be manipulated. The three images in this code have different values for **vspace** and **hspace.** The double line breaks are necessary to push the text line down below the image to provide a consistent look.

Figure 6.14 shows how the popular browsers render the code. The vertical and horizontal spaces set the image off from the text more and more as the values for **vspace** and **hspace** increase. Since these values are measured in pixels, monitors of different resolutions will either increase the distance between the text and the image or decrease it. The higher the resolution of the monitor, the smaller will be the distance between the image and the text. For that reason, larger values for **vspace** and **hspace**—say, over 10 or 12—usually should be avoided.

```
<HTML>
<HEAD>
<TITLE>Vertical and Horizontal Spacing</TITLE>
</HEAD>
<BODY bgcolor="#FFFFFF">
<!-- Background color = white -->

The image below has no VSPACE and HSPACE attributes coded.
<IMG src="grayfish.png" height="70" width="90" align="LEFT">
Notice how close the text lies to the image. The goldfish has a long and interesting
past as a pet. Ancient Oriental civilizations kept goldfish in ponds, and valued
them for their color and graceful movements. Modern people find that a couple of
goldfish add a necessary touch of life to an otherwise dull and drab existence. <BR>
<BR>
<BR>
The image below has both VSPACE and HSPACE attributes set to 10.
<IMG src="grayfish.png" height="70" width="90" align="LEFT" vspace="10" hspace="10">
Notice how close the text lies to the image. The goldfish has a long and interesting
past as a pet. Ancient Oriental civilizations kept goldfish in ponds, and valued
them for their color and graceful movements. Modern people find that a couple of
goldfish add a necessary touch of life to an otherwise dull and drab existence. <BR>
<BR>
<BR>
The image below has both VSPACE and HSPACE attributes set to 20.
<IMG src="grayfish.png" height="70" width="90" align="LEFT" vspace="20" hspace="20">
Notice how close the text lies to the image. The goldfish has a long and interesting
past as a pet. Ancient Oriental civilizations kept goldfish in ponds, and valued
them for their color and graceful movements. Modern people find that a couple of
goldfish add a necessary touch of life to an otherwise dull and drab existence. <BR>
</BODY>
</HTML>
```

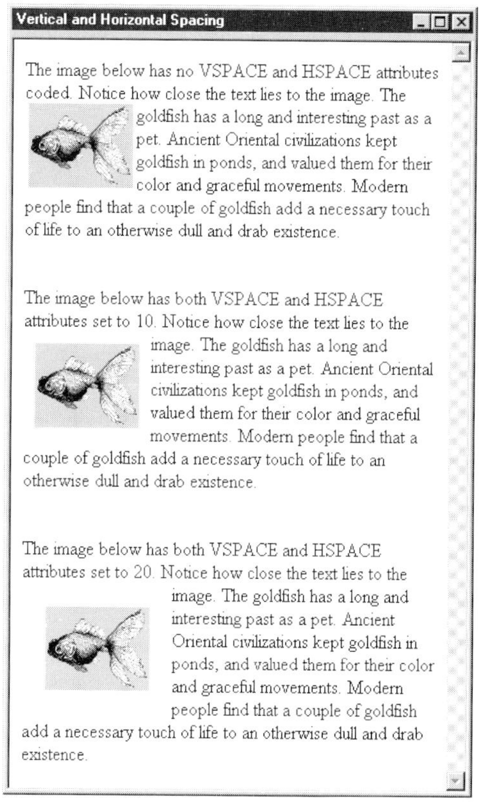

Figure 6.14 HTML code that controls both the vertical and horizontal white space padding an image.

Line Breaks

Back in Chapter 2 you learned how to insert new-line characters into your document with the <BR> tag. Now we need to explore that tag in a little more detail. In addition, there is a tag that prevents the browser from breaking a line of text (<NOBR>) and another tag that allows a line break at specific places if the text has extended past the margin of the browser window (<WBR>).

clear

Normally you will use the <BR> tag simply to insert a line break into a Web page. Figure 6.14, for example, contains <BR> tags where we wanted to end a line or create a blank line. However, we can now combine images with our text and need a way to use line breaks to stop the flow of text around an image. The **clear** attribute can be set to LEFT, RIGHT, or BOTH in order to do just that. In Figure 6.15 the <BR> tag uses a **clear** attribute set equal to LEFT to cause the browser to force a line break and then resume printing under the goldfish. In this way it looks like the caption to the photograph.

If you want to be sure to clear out all the previous alignments, you can use the following code: <BR clear="ALL">. This option is handy to prevent subsequent paragraphs from running up against an image and confusing the reader.

```
<HTML>
<HEAD>
<TITLE>Clear Text and Image Alignment</TITLE>
</HEAD>
<BODY bgcolor="#FFFFFF">
<!-- Background color = white -->

<IMG src="goldfish.gif" align="RIGHT" height="90" width="105" vspace="10" hspace="10">
The goldfish has a long and interesting past as a pet. Ancient Oriental civilizations
kept goldfish in ponds and valued them for their color and graceful movements.
<BR clear="RIGHT">
Modern people find that a couple of goldfish in a bowl adds a comforting touch of life
to offices and homes.
<BR>

</BODY>
</HTML>
```

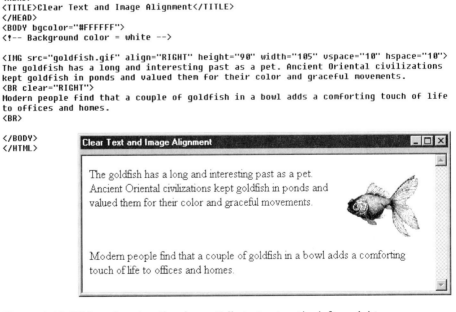

Figure 6.15 HTML code using the **clear** attribute to stop the left or right alignment of text around an image.

<NOBR>no line break</NOBR>

Description: overrides the browser's ability to wrap text to the next line.

Type: container.

Attributes: none.

Special note: not found in the HTML 4.0 specifications.

Sometimes it is necessary to display a long line—for example, a line the user should input into the computer. To create a single, unbroken line, you can code the <NOBR>text</NOBR> container. Text within the container will not be wrapped at the right edge of the browser window but instead will continue off the right side of the screen, requiring the user to scroll to the right to see the end of the line. The <NOBR> tag is most often used to display the following:

1. A line of computer code.
2. A computer input prompt and the associated command as it ought to be typed.
3. Some line of text that would be confusing if it were broken over a line boundary.

Figure 6.16 presents the code for instructions on inputting a long line of computer code. Don't worry about understanding this Unix code; just look at the first paragraph of the HTML document, and find the text that is surrounded by the <NOBR> tag. We want to stop the browser from arbitrarily breaking this line of text. Now notice that the first display is wide enough to display the whole line. In the second display the text runs off the screen, and you need to use the horizontal scroll bar to bring it into view because of the <NOBR> tag.

The <NOBR> also causes a line break before the line if it is longer than the browser window. It is a very intelligent little tag. In the No Break example in Figure 6.16, users needn't wonder how to code the line. However, they must use the scroll bar or scroll arrows to see the right side of the line. If they don't notice the scroll bar, they might miss the right end of the line. That is the trade-off you need to make: reducing confusion but possibly pushing data beyond the right margin of the browser window.

To make matters more complex, you can code a <BR> inside a <NOBR> container, and most browsers will honor it. If you need to code line breaks into your <NOBR> container, consider the <WBR> tag, discussed next.

<WBR>within no line break</WBR>

Description: inserts a conditional break in text contained within a <NOBR> container.

Type: container.

Attributes: none.

Special note: not found in the HTML 4.0 specifications.

```
<HTML>
<HEAD>
<TITLE>To Break or Not To Break</TITLE>
</HEAD>
<BODY bgcolor="#FFFFFF">
<!-- Background color = white -->

<H3>No Break</H3>
In some cases, especially when you need to present a long line for the user to
duplicate, it can be confusing if the line is broken. The user may not know whether
to use the multi-line format, or enter it as just one long line. For example, if
this were a UNIX tutorial, the user might be instructed to type the following line:
<BR>
<NOBR>
<TT>prompt% find /home/machine/user_list/mydir -name "sample_program*.html" -print
&gt; /tmp/list_of_HTML_files
</TT>
</NOBR>

<H3>Overriding No Break</H3>
In some cases, especially when you need to present a long line for the user to
duplicate, it can be confusing if the line is broken. The user may not know whether
to use the multi-line format, or enter it as just one long line. For example, if
this were a UNIX tutorial, the user might be instructed to type the following line:
<BR>
<NOBR>
<TT>prompt% find /home/machine/user_list/mydir -name "sample_program*.html"
<WBR>-print &gt; /tmp/list_of_HTML_files
</WBR>
</TT>
</NOBR>

</BODY>
</HTML>
```

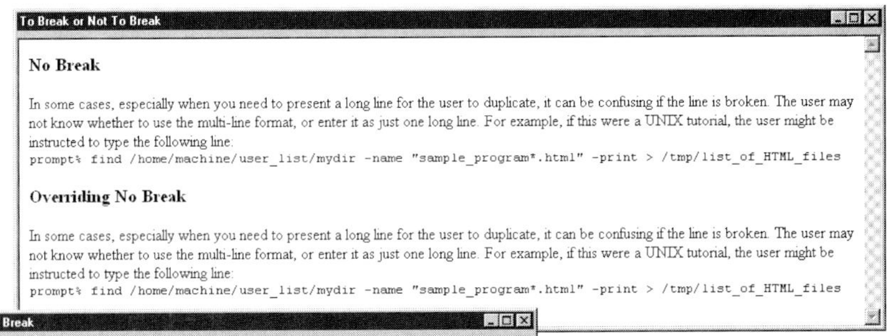

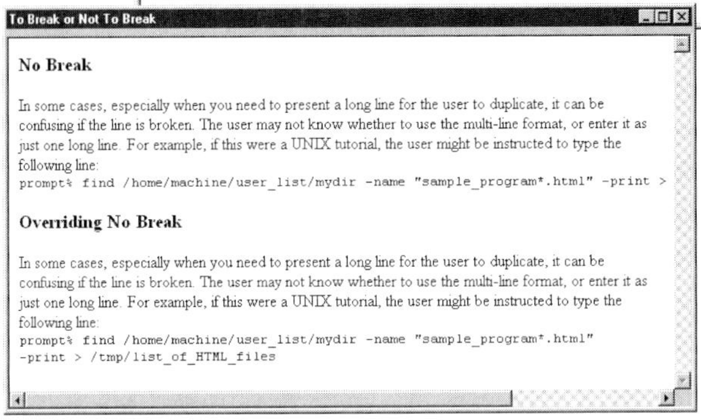

Figure 6.16 HTML code that forces the browser not to break a line of text and code that overrides this no-break condition.

The <WBR> tag is probably the most sophisticated style element we have encountered so far. It allows you to insert a conditional break in lines contained within a <NOBR> container. The <WBR> tag will cause a break (carriage return/line feed) in a line contained within a <NOBR> container if the line would extend beyond the right margin of the browser window. You won't use this tag every day, but you can use it to control when the browser breaks a long line of text.

Figure 6.16 also presents the code for using the <WBR> tag. As mentioned earlier, no line break is necessary in the first display. The second screen display, under Overriding No Break, shows a line break after .html, because otherwise the text would have scrolled off the right margin as shown earlier. Although this break makes the Unix code look a little odd, the browser follows the rule of breaking before extending the line beyond the right margin.

Even though the <NOBR> and <WBR> tags fall outside the HTML 4.0 guidelines, both Navigator and Internet Explorer recognize these tags. You won't use them often, but they are handy to know about.

To Image or Not to Image

When you use images on your pages, you must bear in mind that a portion of the Net population will not or cannot use the information contained in images. These are the people who choose to use text-only browsers like Lynx to cruise the Web and those who turn off automatic image download on graphical browsers. They usually fall into one of three categories:

1. Users with slow modems who don't want to spend lots of time and/or money downloading images.
2. Users with a visual impairment. Many of these users employ text-to-speech software to gather information from the Net. They are candidates for using the aural style sheets discussed in Chapter 8.
3. Users who want to access lots of information quickly and don't care about "pretty pictures," so they turn off the automatic image download function of their browser.

To accommodate these users, the wise Web weaver never includes important information only in an image. It is really tempting to scan in a complex table, store the data as an image, and simply place the image of the table on the page. Unfortunately, the information from that table is available only to those who use graphical browsers.

An additional problem with placing information only in images is that most search engines ignore images. If you want the search engines to find the information you are providing to the world, that information must be presented as text, not as an image.

However, the best argument for a judicious use of images on your pages is the time it takes to download images. Each image you include causes the browser to establish another download session with your page. Users must wait until all the images are downloaded before they have the complete content of your page. Many times the page will not begin to paint up until the majority, or all, of the images are downloaded. Serious users do not want to wait for the pictures to show up. You, too, may have had the experience of waiting and waiting for a page to download, then finally clicking on the "Stop" button and moving on to another page rather than waiting further. Wise Web authors will not force their users to wait to see pictures.

Considerations When Using Multimedia

Multimedia is currently the "rage" on the Web. That has an unfortunate effect on the load on the Net. Multimedia files are HUGE! They download slowly because of the great amount of information that must be transferred. To give you some idea, consider sound files on the Net. The most common are the WAV files, discussed under "RIFF WAVE" in this chapter. These files require about 10 megabytes of storage for each *minute* of sound. That's 10 million bytes of storage per minute! So a sound is worth a whole lot of words—660 times more words than a picture. Considering the expense of multimedia files in terms of download time and Net traffic, they have to be of great significance before you can justify using them.

Like images, multimedia objects are not available to all users of a site. Unlike images, most multimedia objects require the user to have additional hardware, some sort of sound card, and speakers. Besides the audio-related hardware, the user must have loaded and configured any additional plug-ins specifically needed by the multimedia object. If the user hasn't installed the plug-in, or if the browser doesn't support such a plug-in, the information available in the multimedia object is lost. If the multimedia object contains essential information, or information that is only available in that format, then those data on the page are not available to the widest audience.

Currently multimedia objects are inserted into HTML documents using an <A>anchor</A> container with an **href** attribute identifying the object. When the object is an image we call it an *external image,* because a graphical browser displays it on a new page (Figure 6.17). A sound file is accessible to the user when this HTML code is added to a document: <A href="taps.wav"> Goodnight! (WAV file @ 39K) </A>.

<APPLET>java applet</APPLET>

Description: initiates the execution of a Java applet.
Type: container.
Attributes: align, alt, archive, class, code, codebase, height, hspace, id, name, object, style, title, vspace, and width.
Special note: deprecated in the HTML 4.0 specifications in favor of <OBJECT> element.

In the past the only way to handle multimedia objects was as an image, or *applet*—a small program that runs within a window inside the browser. The <APPLET> tag was designed specifically to handle applets written using the Java programming language. These *Java applets* provide users with audio, video, and animation as well as allowing them to interact with the Web page. For example, an applet can let you order a product you see on the screen. The user is asked to input her name, address, and credit card information. In return she receives an order confirmation number. Other applets elicit information

```
<HTML>
<HEAD>
<TITLE>Image Objects</TITLE>
</HEAD>
<BODY bgcolor="#FFFFFF">
<!-- Background color = white -->

<H3>Inline Image Using Image Tag</H3>
<IMG src="bug.png" alt="Ladybug">

<H3>External Image Using Anchor Tag</H3>
<A href="bug.png">Ladybug</A>

<H3>Inserting Image Using Object Tag</H3>
<OBJECT data="bug.png" type="image/png">
Ladybug
</OBJECT>

</BODY>
</HTML>
```

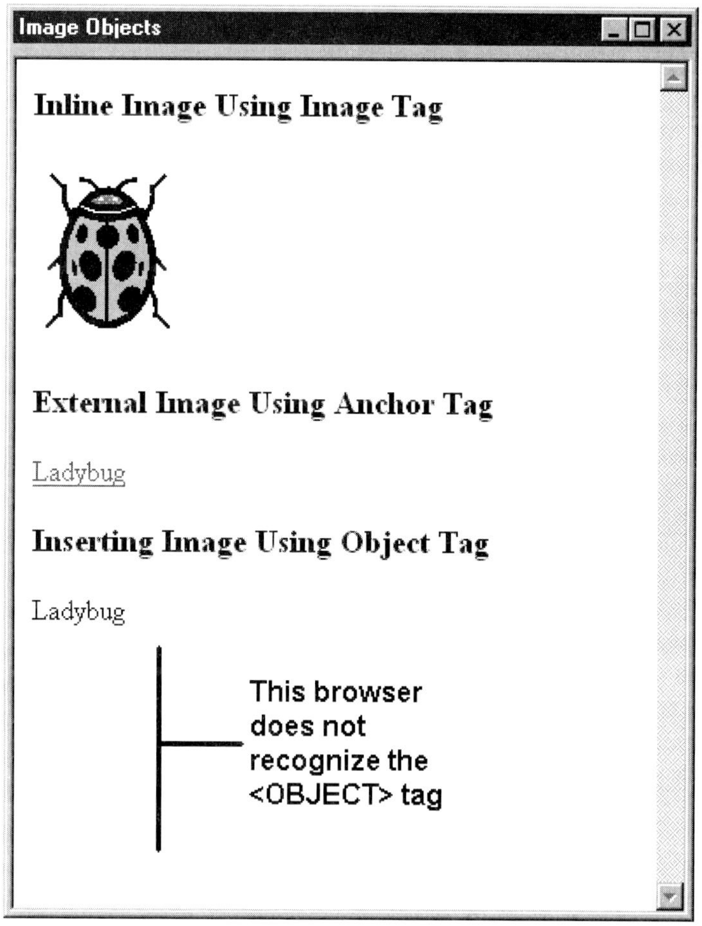

Figure 6.17 HTML code for three different ways to insert an image.

from the user and produce changes on the screen based on the input information. The code to execute the orderitem applet looks like this:

```
<APPLET code="orderitem" height="500" width="300">
~~~parameters go here~~~
Java applet to take customer orders.
</APPLET>
```

The <APPLET> tag was deprecated in the HTML 4.0 specifications because W^3C decided that it was too limiting. The reasoning was that Web-based multimedia needed to support not only Java applets but also the flexibility to incorporate a variety of other multimedia objects and their related plug-ins. The specifications say this:

> To address these issues, HTML 4.0 introduces the OBJECT element, which offers an all-purpose solution to generic object inclusion. The OBJECT element allows HTML authors to specify everything required by an object for its presentation by a user agent [browser]: source code, initial values, and run-time data. In this specification, the term "object" is used to describe the things that people want to place in HTML documents; other commonly used terms for these things are: applets, plug-ins, media handlers, etc. (HTML 4.0 specifications, Section 13.1)

<OBJECT>insert object</OBJECT>

Description: identifies image, html text, sound, video, or other external element for inclusion within the page.
Type: container.
Attributes: align, archive, border, class, classid, codebase, codetype, data, declare, dir, height, hspace, id, lang, name, onClick, onDblClick, onKeyDown, onKeyPress, onKeyUp, onMouseDown, onMouseMove, onMouseOut, onMouseOver, onMouseUp, standby, style, tabindex, title, type, usemap, vspace, and width.

Web designers face a dilemma when it comes to using <OBJECT> elements to replace <IMG> and <APPLET> tags. The former works only on the latest graphical browsers. The latter are tried and true methods for inserting multimedia objects into a Web page. But <APPLET> has been deprecated and appears to be on its way to obsolescence. Time is on the side of the new <OBJECT> tag. The closer you are to or beyond the new millenium when you read this, the more we would recommend using <OBJECT> tags to insert multimedia objects into your Web pages. At the time we are writing this, neither Navigator nor Internet Explorer recognizes the <OBJECT> element.

The <OBJECT> element can insert images and run Java applets. The HTML code to run the orderitem Java applet using <OBJECT> is written as follows:

```
<OBJECT codetype="application/java" classid="orderitem" height="500"
  width="300">
~~~parameters go here~~~
Java applet to take customer orders.
</OBJECT>
```

Figure 6.17 illustrates how an image is inserted using the <OBJECT> tag. The **height** and **width** attributes define the screen area used to display the object. We have used several new attributes in these examples that need further explanation.

classid and data

The **classid** and **data** attributes identify the object. It is our understanding that **classid** is used to identify executable objects—like applets and scripts. The **data** attribute identifies data—like images and sounds. The value of these attributes tells the browser the name of the object and where to find it (URL, path, etc.). For example, the **data** attribute in Figure 6.17 identifies the image bug.png.

codetype and type

The object identified by the **classid** attribute supports the **codetype** attribute. Likewise, the object assigned to the **data** attribute is reinforced by the **type** attribute. If the **classid** is assigned to a Java applet, then the **codetype** is set equal to application/java. In Figure 6.17, when bug.png is inserted, **type** is set equal to image/png. While the **codetype** and **type** attributes are optional, their use helps the browser to identify the object it is being asked to insert into the Web page. This information can only help make your HTML documents more robust when working with a variety of browsers.

Adding Sound

Next to images, sound is the most common type of multimedia data added to Web pages. The sound you normally hear is a continuous series of different tones and noises. These types of data are called *analog data* because the values flow from one to another continuously. Computers don't handle analog data well; they want their input as *digital data.* Digital data are *discrete,* meaning the values are represented by numbers, not by a continuous energy fluctuation. For analog data to be converted to digital data, the data must be captured and encoded as numbers, usually represented as binary 1s (ones) and 0s (zeroes). In the case of sound, the more samples taken, the better the sound reproduction is. As you might expect, the files are also bigger for sound. By the same token, the larger the space used to encode the sound value, the better the sound representation is. In other words, bigger sound files produce more lifelike sounds.

Usually sound files are recorded at sampling rates of either 11 kHz, 22 kHz, or 44 kHz. A *kilohertz (kHz)* is 1000 cycles per second, or roughly 1000 samples per second. As mentioned earlier, the more samplings per second, the better the sound quality will be. Sound can also be stored as either an 8-bit or 16-bit number. A 16-bit sound file will be much more accurate than an 8-bit sound file.

The price we pay for quality sound is measured in an audio file's size. An 8-bit, 8-kHz sample is about the quality of a standard telephone call—not very good for audio on a Web page. A 16-bit, 44-kHz sample is nearly the audio quality of a compact disc (CD) player. A minute of 8-bit, 8 kHz sound takes about 1.5 megabytes of file space. A minute of 16-bit, 44-kHz sound takes 10 megabytes. If you want to add stereo, you have to double these numbers! Let's take a look at the different types of sound files.

Types of Sound Files

Audio files can be found in several different formats. Usually each format requires a different plug-in, so it is a good idea to limit the format of the sound files on your page to one of the common types. That way the user needs only one plug-in to play all of the sounds you present.

Software packages exist that can convert one type or format of sound file to another. For example, a program called SOX, for PC-compatible machines and Unix boxes (written by Lance Norskog), can convert between most of the common formats and do some simple processing like filtering as well. WAVany, also a PC package (written by Bill Neisius) can also convert most formats to the WAV format. SoundApp (written by Norman Franke) is a similar program for the Macintosh. These products or others like them are often available for downloading from the Internet.

μ-law (mu-law)

The most widely supported, most commonly used type of sound file on the Net is the μ-*law* file. Originally developed for the Unix operating system, it uses a 2:1 compression ratio and is an international standard for compressing voice-quality audio. These files are supported by almost all operating systems. Figure 6.18 shows the audio playback plug-ins used by Navigator and Internet Explorer. A μ-law file usually ends with the extension .au. This type of file supports only *monaural* (single-channel) sound, not *stereo* (multiple-channel) sound. There is a library of sounds in .au format located at http://sunsite.unc.edu/pub/multimedia/sun-sounds/.

RIFF WAVE

Resource Interchange File Format Waveform (RIFF WAVE) audio format, or *WAVE,* is a proprietary format sponsored jointly by Microsoft and IBM. It is the audio file format most commonly used on Microsoft Windows products. This audio format is also supported by most operating systems. The RIFF WAVE file usually has a file extension of .wav.

Normally this sound format takes about 10 megabytes of file data to produce a single minute of audio. It is an uncompressed format, so a given WAVE sound file is roughly twice the size of the same sound encoded in μ-law format. There are other encoding methods—for example, using 8 bits rather than 16 bits to store the sounds—that can be employed in WAVE files to reduce the amount of storage required. But these methods degrade the quality of the sound. The RIFF WAVE format can support both monaural (single-channel) and stereo (multichannel) audio. There is a large collection of sounds in this format at http://sunsite.unc.edu/pub/multimedia/pc-sounds/.

AIFF and AIFC

Audio Interchange File Format (*AIFF*) is used to store high-end audio data. It is uncompressed and takes about the same amount of space as WAVE files, 10 megabytes per minute of audio. This recording format can support both

```
<HTML>
<HEAD>
<TITLE>Sound Objects</TITLE>
</HEAD>
<BODY bgcolor="#FFFFFF">
<!-- Background color = white -->

<H3>Directions to Our Store</H3>
<P>We are easy to find.</P>

<IMG src="storemap.jpg" height="200" width="300"> <BR>

<A href="directions.au">Audio directions to our store (AU file @ 862K)</A> <BR>

</BODY>
</HTML>
```

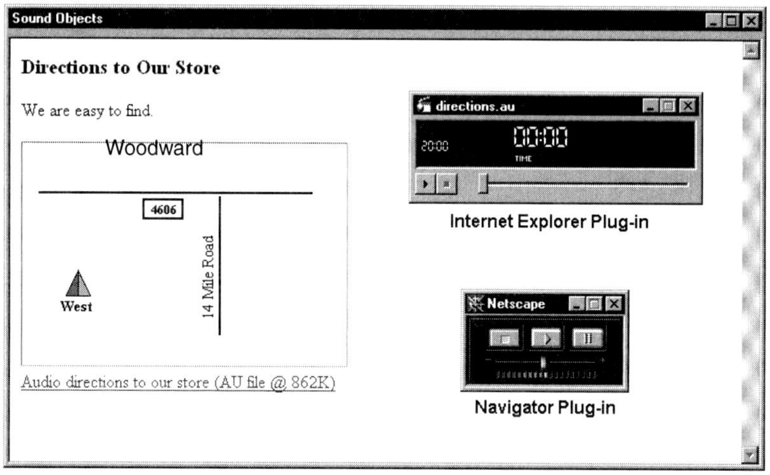

Figure 6.18 HTML code that uses a sound file.

monaural and stereo recordings and uses the .aiff filename extension. It was developed by Apple and is most often used by Macintosh and Silicon Graphics software. Because it takes so much space to store audio data in AIFF, Apple developed AIFF-C, better known as *AIFC* for *AIFF Compressed Format*. This compression algorithm can compress sounds up to 6:1, but it is a *lossy* form of compression. As in the lossy JPEG image compression, some of the data bits are removed from the sound file as it is compressed in the AIFC format. The result is a deterioration of the sound. Nevertheless, usually the reduction in quality is not sufficient to outweigh the benefit of the saving of space.

MPEG Audio

From the International Standard Organization (ISO) comes the *Moving Picture Experts Group (MPEG)*, which has defined a standard for audio that has the best compression algorithms. These algorithms can compress to a ratio of 4:1 with almost no loss of signal quality. MPEG-compressed audio is the best format for distributing high-quality sound files online. MPEG files are usually designated with an extension of .mp2. Since MPEG is also used to store, transmit, and display video, make sure the files you collect for audio are just audio files, not small videos with audio.

MPEG3 audio compression is now available and has a lot of people excited about the ability to deliver CD-quality sound files at much smaller file sizes. It takes less than 1 megabyte of storage space to store one minute of music when using MPEG3. It uses a 12:1 compression ratio with very little degradation of sound quality to achieve this storage capacity. Compare these numbers to those of a WAVE file, where one minute of music requires 10 megabytes of storage space. Computers using MPEG3 need a 16-bit sound card. These files have a .mp3 filename extension.

MIDI

A standard has been developed within the music industry for connecting electric instruments to each other and to computers. The standard is called *MIDI,* which stands for *Musical Instrument Digital Interface.* A MIDI recording is not a digital representation of an analog sound, but a description of how to create the sound. The 8-bit code identifies events like note on, note off, pitch blend changes, control changes, and so on, along with identifying in which of the 16 channels to apply the event. Therefore, the actual sound or music is not stored in a MIDI file. Instead, the 8-bit codes indicate which sound (voice) to play, when a sound is to be switched on or off, the code for the sound (such as "3C" for middle C), and a velocity code for volume control. A 10-kilobyte MIDI file could easily hold more than a minute of music.

To play a MIDI file, the computer must have access to a WAVE table, synthesizer, or some means of generating the sounds the MIDI data turns on, adjusts the volume of, and turns off. In most cases a sound card contains at least a WAVE table. Selected MIDI codes identify key pressure and after-touch that allow the composer to bend sounds and warble a note. These files have a .mid or .midi filename extension.

Other Formats

Many other formats can be used to move sound files across the Internet; however, the ones just discussed are by far the most common. One of the other formats is Creative Voice (.voc) files, used by Creative Lab's Sound Blaster audio cards. Another format, used by Sun/NeXT computers, usually with an extension of .snd, is far less common, but it does show up occasionally.

Which Format to Use?

With all these choices, how does the wise Web weaver decide on one? Sometimes the choice is easy. If you find a sound you like, and it is in one of the common formats, or if it is in a format that has an available plug-in for your browser, you will probably decide to use that format. Problems result only if your users don't have the same software you choose to use.

Most Web weavers will agree that .au and .wav are the two most useful types of sound files. If you keep all your sounds in one of these two formats, you can be assured that the majority of the graphical browsers will have plug-ins able to use them. Remember to do your best to limit all the sounds to a single format on a Web site. That reduces the work the browser has to do, and it could speed up your users' work as well.

Regardless of the format, you should describe the sounds you have included so your user will know what he is downloading. It would be a shame to have a user spend several minutes downloading a sound file in a format he cannot listen to. As with large images, you should give your user an idea about the size of the file. That way he can decide if he wants to spend the time necessary to download it.

If you have audio processing and editing software available, you may consider creating a very short sound bite that can serve as a lead-in to the larger sound file you have available for download. Then the user can download the smaller sound byte first and, based on that, decide if she wants to spend the time necessary to download the actual, large file. It is also common courtesy to use a special, easily recognizable icon to indicate sound files. Politeness is always in fashion, and describing the file a user can download in terms of content, format, and size is indeed polite.

Ethical Questions

It is very easy to collect sound files from sites all across the Net. All you need to do is look at the URL of the sound site and *ftp* the sound to your own computer. In addition, many people have built pages that contain a large number of links to sound files that enable you to quickly download the sounds. But sounds and music are often copyrighted, just like images, so before you download sounds to use on your page, make sure they are free or get permission from the owner of the sound you wish to use.

Be careful, because the fact that a sound appears on XYZ page does not necessarily mean that the owner of XYZ page has the authority to give you permission to use it. For example, if you were to go to the Oldies Web page, and download a three-minute cut of a Beatles song with the permission of the Web weaver of that page, you could well be in violation of the copyright on the song. You probably need to obtain permission from Michael Jackson, who owns the rights to many of the Beatles' songs!

Show tunes, theme songs, and popular music are all available on the Web, but most of them are copyrighted works. You can get into trouble for using them without permission. Another common mistake Web weavers make is downloading and using short audio snippets from television-program dialog. These, too, are usually copyrighted works.

If you are going to use sound that you have not created yourself, make sure that the sounds you use are in the *public domain,* meaning you can use them without permission. If they are not in the public domain, you will need to obtain permission for their use from the copyright holder, who may or may not be the Web weaver of the site where you find the sounds.

Adding Video

Video playback is another new tool that is being incorporated into some Web sites to add interest and provide an additional medium for transferring information. As we saw in the previous section, adding audio to a Web page increases the download time because audio objects are large compared with text or even pictures. Video files are a collection of images usually with a related sound file, so they are larger then either pictures or audio! The following code would make a sample movie available to the Web user: `<A href="sample.mov:>Movie (MOV file @ 862K)</A>`.

Capturing analog video at regular intervals and saving each capture as a distinct image, called a *frame,* creates digital video clips. Frames are played back at a particular *frame rate,* which is the number of frames displayed per second. As the frame rate approaches 30 frames per second, the video becomes smooth and looks like a videotape playback or television broadcast. A digital video file may also have an audio track associated with the frames. One job of the video display software is to synchronize displaying the images and playing the related sounds to keep the two together.

MPEG Video

The *MPEG* format, devised by the *Motion Picture Experts Group,* is the most common format for digital video files, or movies, because all the graphical browsers support it, and viewers exist for all the platforms. Unlike the case with AVI, which we will discuss later, anyone with a graphical browser can either download a plug-in or use a browser to play MPEG movies. Although this is the most common type of movie on the Net, it has three disadvantages:

1. MPEG files are very slow to decompress. Often this decompression is handled by a special, separate expansion card that assists in preparing the file for viewing. If the user's machine cannot decode the frames quickly enough, the MPEG player will drop some frames from the playback. The result is a jerky or choppy motion.
2. MPEG files require a fast processor for software decompression. Again, the user needs a powerful, fast computer to keep up a pleasing frame rate in decompression. If the processor is too slow, the resulting video is choppy. Normally MPEG video does not have an associated sound track, because just the video takes most of the processor's capability.
3. MPEG files are very expensive to create. MPEG encoders are expensive, requiring equipment costing several thousand dollars. That is beyond the range of most users. Creating MPEG files is not usually an option for the casual Web weaver, but using these files is easy, and all the graphical browsers support an MPEG viewer.

MPEG files usually have the file extensions of .mpg on Intel platforms and .mpeg on systems that support longer file names.

QuickTime

QuickTime was developed for the Apple Macintosh. It is nearly as common as MPEG (some of the Macintosh folks say it is more common), and is another Net standard. QuickTime movies can be played on PCs using the QuickTime for Windows (QTfW) software. They can be played using the Xanim program on Unix machines. Usually QuickTime movies have an extension of .qt or .mov on all platforms.

AVI

Microsoft developed *Video for Windows* (*VfW*) for the PC. It is the nominal standard for PC video, and a large number of files exist on related platforms. However, there are few players outside the PC platform, so it is far less suitable for use across the Net. It is not, nor is it expected to become, a Net standard. Video for Windows files usually have a file extension of .avi, which stands for *Audio/Video Interleave*. Internet Explorer allows the Web weaver to incorporate AVI video files as an inline movie without adding a new plug-in. Those of you using Navigator will need to install an AVI plug-in.

Streaming Audio/Video

Web-oriented companies like Macromedia and RealAudio are marketing new multimedia formats. Usually they will make a very basic version of the software's browser plug-in available for free downloading from their corporate Web site. If the user likes the product, she can purchase editing software, more sophisticated plug-ins, and related products. Movies created with Macromedia's Director program and the company's Flash 3 animation use what they call the *Shockwave* multimedia format. These multimedia presentations feature **streaming** audio and video, which means that the movie or audio clip starts as soon as the browser plug-in begins to receive the file. As the frames are downloaded from the Net, they are displayed. Ideally, the frames are downloading more quickly than they are being displayed, so the download stays ahead of the presentation. Consequently, the multimedia event begins more quickly, because the user doesn't have to wait for the whole file to download.

The drawback to streaming presentations is that a slow Net connection can produce a choppy presentation in which the audio seems to fade in and out. Some streaming audio presentations, like RealAudio, provide a live Net radio broadcast site. On slower computers and/or modems these broadcasts have the characteristics of old AM radio transmission. The signals sometimes wax and wane, with interference and garbled sound occurring. On faster computers these Net radio broadcasts provide good-quality production of live music and up-to-the-minute news.

Although streaming audio and video is exciting, it places a huge demand on the Net. Other forms of multimedia that require the user to download and store the presentation before it is played affect the Net only while the file is being downloaded. In contrast, streaming technology places a high demand on the Net all through the presentation. As modems become faster and compression becomes better, more and more streaming audio and video will probably appear on the Net. Its presence may have a serious impact on Internet traffic.

To Link or to Copy?

When using multimedia, there is a temptation to simply link to a large file on another server rather than store that file on your own server. Indeed, some authors of multimedia ask that you link to their site rather than copying the files to your own server. The advantages of saving space as well as having a current copy of an event make the idea of linking to another server appealing. Yet, this practice increases congestion on the Net. When users make a connection to your Web page, they are putting a certain load on the Net. If you require another connection, to another machine, that increases the load. In addition, making your users wait to retrieve data from another machine adds to the delay. So the idea of linking to resources on another machine is not as good as it first appears. It is best to copy a resource from a remote site and store it on the same server that hosts your page, unless, of course, the resource is copyrighted and you cannot obtain permission to use it. In any case, it is considered proper to put a small credit line on your page indicating where the resource came from, even if it is in the public domain.

Key Terms

Analog data
Animated GIF
Applet
Baseline
bpp
Digital data
Dithering
External image
Floating image
Flood filling
Frame
Frame rate
Image editor
Inline image
Lossless compression
Lossy compression
Multimedia
Open standard
Progressive image
Streaming
Thumbnail image

New Tags

<APPLET>
<CENTER>
<IMG>
<OBJECT>
<NOBR>
<WBR>

1. What is the definition for each of the key terms?

2. How are each of the tags introduced in this chapter used?

3. What is the file name extension and media type (image, sound, or video) associated with each of the following?

   a. Audio Interchange File Format
   b. Bit Mapped Picture
   c. Creative Voice Format
   d. Graphics Interchange Format
   e. Joint Photographers Experts Group Format
   f. Moving Picture Experts Group Audio Format
   g. Moving Picture Experts Group Video Format
   h. Musical Instrument Digital Interface Format
   i. PC Paintbrush Format
   j. Portable Data Format
   k. Portable Network Graphics
   l. QuickTime Format
   m. Resource Interchange File Format Waveform
   n. Tagged Image File Format
   o. μ-law File Format
   p. Video for Windows

4. What is the difference between a plain and transparent GIF image?

5. What type of image is best saved as a GIF file, and what type is best saved as a JPEG file?

6. Describe a situation where using a lossy compression format could get you into trouble.

7. How many colors are associated with 1 bpp, 4 bpp, 8 bpp, 16 bpp, and 24 bpp?

8. What are four ways you can reduce the download time of an HTML document?

9. What are the three schools of thought regarding where you should store images?

10. What are two situations where a browser will not display an image?

11. What are nine different ways you can align an image?

12. What are two different ways to center a paragraph within the screen display?

13. How do you break a line of text that is floating next to an image?

14. What is the major consideration when using images or multimedia?

15. What should a Web weaver do when using other people's work within a Web page?

16. What is considered a broadcast-quality frame rate for a video?

Exercises

6.1. Using a nontransparent image and text of your own choosing, create a Web page that demonstrates each of the possible alignments: TOP, MIDDLE, BOTTOM, LEFT, and RIGHT. Make sure the text allows you to demonstrate the alignments correctly. The title bar should display "Image Alignment Options" with your name and the assignment due date included within comment lines.

6.2. Surf the Web to find at least five nice, small (1–3 kilobytes), public domain images. Download them and insert them into a new HTML document. Include **alt** descriptions for each object you insert. The title bar should display "My Favorite Images" with your name and the assignment due date included within comment lines. Turn off auto-loading of images on your browser, or use a text-only browser to verify that your **alt** description works. Print two copies of the page: one with the images turned on and one without the images.

6.3. Create a new HTML document with a sound and video object you have found on the Net. Put text on the page explaining where you found the image. The title bar should display "Sounds and Video by Your Name" with the assignment due date included within comment lines. Create a link to the sites where the objects were found so that your user can go harvest other objects from these sites.

6.4. Retrieve the Homework home page you updated in Exercise 5.4. Use a digital camera, scanner, or free-drawing software to create an image of yourself, and insert it into the page. Make sure you include an **alt** description that your mother would approve.

6.5. Retrieve the Web page about your favorite movie you updated in Exercise 4.5. Surf the Internet to find and download an image, video clip, or sound file that relates to the movie or one of the actors. Insert the object into the page. Include **alt** descriptions for each object you insert.

6.6. Retrieve your school's home page that you updated in Exercise 5.6. Use a digital camera or scanner to obtain an image of the school that you think reflects positively on you and your fellow classmates, and insert the image into the page. Make sure you have an **alt** description that does the image justice.

6.7. Create a new HTML document with an image you have found on the Net. The title bar should display "My Favorite Objects" with your name and the assignment due date included within comment lines. Put text on the page explaining where you found the image. Create an image link to the site where the image was found so that your user can go harvest other images from that site. Demonstrate (a) how the object can be centered by itself with no text around it and (b) how it can be aligned with text on either the right or left.

6.8. Create a personal animated GIF you can use as your signature on Web pages you design. The file should not exceed 15 kilobytes in size. A popular image editor like Corel Draw or shareware like Animagic can be used to create an animated GIF.

## CHAPTER seven

TABLES—DATA IN ROWS AND COLUMNS

W e saw in Chapter 4 how lists could help our user collect information efficiently. Now let's look at the way tables can also help us in our task of presenting information in the most efficient manner possible. Before tables were built into HTML, the only reasonable way to create tabular data (rows and columns) was to use a <PRE> container or to capture the data in an image. The <PRE> tag could not provide the power or the flexibility gained with the table tags.

What's in a Table?

The *table* is one of the most concise, direct, and efficient tools for presenting certain types of data. Numeric data, data that show a relationship, any data that are usually displayed in a spreadsheet—all are excellent candidates for an HTML table. In addition, tables are a great way to present related data like pictures with their descriptions. Because of its utility, the table feature was one of the first features extended into HTML 2.0. It became standard in release 3.0 of HTML.

Tables are composed of *rows* of data running across the screen, and *columns* that run up and down:

```
        C
   R    O    W
        L
        U
        M
        N
```

The intersection of a row and a column is called a *cell.* Most browsers consider each cell a unique entity, and they arrange the data to fit within the space allowed by that cell. Some special formatting provisions and extensions exist that we will discuss later in this chapter, but for the most part, you can think of each cell as a unique, albeit small, page unto itself. Every table must have at least one row and at least one cell. Everything in a table is contained within a cell except the caption.

Tables are referred to by row first and by column second. A "2 by 3" or "2 × 3" table has two rows and three columns (Figure 7.1). As you begin to code tables, you will see why this convention is followed. To build a table, you must first declare a row and then declare the elements of each column in that row. Each cell in a table has a row and column address, with the row address preceding the column address.

Nearly anything you can put into an HTML document can be put into the cell of a table, including other tables. You can put in images, rules, headings, lists, and even forms. The original world of tables included five relatively sophisticated tags:

1. <TABLE> . . . </TABLE> encloses the table.
2. <TH> . . . </TH> defines the table headers.
3. <TR> . . . </TR> defines the table rows.
4. <TD> . . . </TD> surrounds the actual table data.
5. <CAPTION> . . . </CAPTION> allows you to place a caption either above or below the table.

The latest HTML specifications added five new table tags that let you either format table columns or format and scroll portions of long tables.

1. <TBODY> . . . </TBODY> identifies a scrollable area of a table.
2. <TFOOT> . . . </TFOOT> appears below the scrolling body.
3. <THEAD> . . . </THEAD> appears above the scrolling body.
4. <COLGROUP> . . . </COLGROUP> provides means for combining a group of columns in a table.
5. <COL> . . . </COL> allows you to control the appearance or attribute specifications for one or more table columns.

Figure 7.1 presents the code for a simple table so that you can see how all the parts fit together. We will discuss each of the table tags in detail, but it's worth-

```
<HTML>
<HEAD>
<TITLE>2 by 3 Table</TITLE>
</HEAD>
<BODY bgcolor="#FFFFFF">
<!-- Background color = white -->

The table following is just a simple 2 x 3 table.  It has very few fancy
attributes, but it does show how the parts of the table fit together.
<TABLE border="5">
<CAPTION align="BOTTOM"> This caption is aligned to the bottom.
</CAPTION>
<TR>
  <TD>Row1/Column1 </TD>
  <TD> R1/C2 </TD>
  <TD> R1/C3 </TD>
</TR>
<TR>
  <TD>R2/C1</TD>
  <TD>R2/C2</TD>
  <TD>R2/C3</TD>
</TR>
</TABLE>
The table in this example has 6 cells and this text starts below the
table.
</BODY>
</HTML>
```

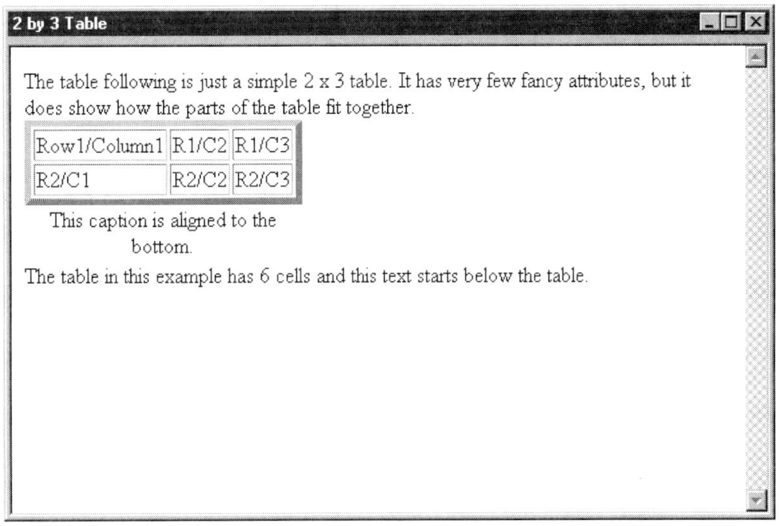

Figure 7.1 HTML code for a 2 by 3 table.

while to look at a simple table first. As you can see, the coding for a table is just a little more complicated than anything we have considered so far.

It is a good idea to draw your table on paper before you start coding it so that you know how many rows and columns you need and what headings you want to use. As your tables get more complex, this design step will be more and more important. Drawing the table on paper may end up saving you a great deal of time.

The only special attribute used in this example is **border,** which makes the outer frame around the table a little larger. (This attribute will be discussed in detail later.) The caption appears beneath the table as a result of using the **align** attribute. Otherwise, this is a plain-vanilla table meant to give you the basic idea of how a table is built.

> # <TABLE>table</TABLE>
>
> ***Description:*** defines the rows, columns, and caption that make up a table.
> ***Type:*** container.
> ***Attributes:*** align, bgcolor, border, cellspacing, cellpadding, class, frame, dir, id, lang, onClick, onDblClick, onKeyDown, onKeyPress, onKeyUp, onMouseDown, onMouseMove, onMouseOut, onMouseOver, onMouseUp, rules, style, summary, title, and width.

The <TABLE> </TABLE> container surrounds the whole table. The browser will stop the current text flow, break the line, insert the table at the beginning of a new line, then restart the text flow on another new line following the table. Normally the table picks up the alignment of the current paragraph, so most tables are aligned left. If the paragraph containing the table is centered, <P align="CENTER">, or if the <CENTER> tag precedes the table, then the table could be aligned in the center of the page.

Although a *cell* in a table can contain almost any other HTML structure that can appear on a page (obviously tags like <HTML> or <BODY> won't work in a table), only the <TR> and the <CAPTION> containers are allowed and recognized within the <TABLE> container. A 3 by 2 demonstration table is shown in Figure 7.2. This table has no attributes coded.

```
<HTML>
<HEAD>
<TITLE>3 by 2 Table</TITLE>
</HEAD>
<BODY bgcolor="#FFFFFF">
<!-- Background color = white -->
<H3>The Team's Home Schedule</H3>

<TABLE>
<TR>
  <TD>Dallas </TD>
  <TD>November 5th </TD>
</TR>
<TR>
  <TD>Detroit </TD>
  <TD>November 11th </TD>
</TR>
<TR>
  <TD>Toronto </TD>
  <TD>November 17th</TD>
</TR>
</TABLE>

</BODY>
</HTML>
```

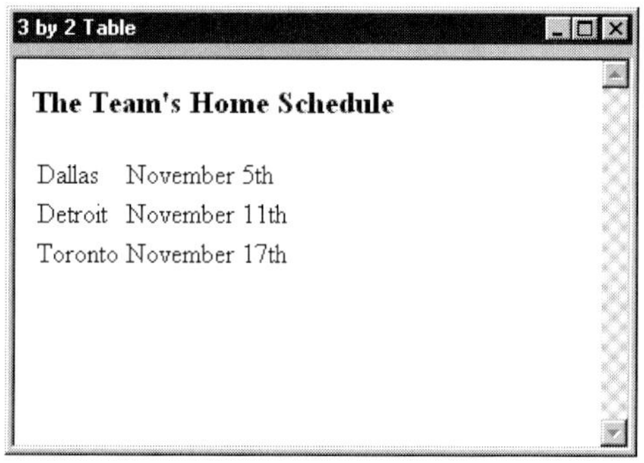

Figure 7.2 HTML code for a 3 by 2 table without attributes.

<TABLE>table</TABLE>   **185**

border

The *border* is the line around the table and between each cell. The table in Figure 7.1 has a border defined; the table in Figure 7.2 does not. The **border** attribute allows you to tell the browser whether or not to put a border around the table and how wide to make the border. A border can be subdivided into frames and rules. The *frame* is the line that surrounds a single cell or the whole table. A *rule* is the horizontal or vertical line that separates the rows and columns of cells.

The **border** attribute's default value is 1, meaning there will be a 1-pixel border around the table and around each of the cells in the table. The table in the top left corner of Figure 7.3 has a 1-pixel border. If you code a number larger than 1, the browsers will make a wider border around the table, but the division between cells will still be a 1-pixel border (unless you code a **cellspacing** attribute, discussed later). For example, the table in Figure 7.1 has a border of 5 pixels because of this code: <TABLE border="5">.

If you code a zero or omit the **border** attribute, there will be no border around the table, but there will still be some space between the cell contents that is referred to as *padding.* In other words, the padding is the space between the cell's content and the border. It appears as the cell's background, which is white in Figure 7.2.

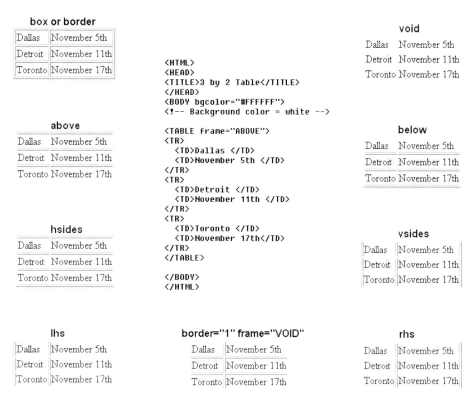

Figure 7.3 HTML code for the **frame** attribute, controlling which sides of a border are displayed with a table.

frame

The **frame** attribute specifies which sides of a table's border—that is, the frame—are visible. Whereas the **border** attribute determines a border's thickness (in pixels), the **frame** attribute turns different border combinations on and off, as shown in Figure 7.3. This attribute is new with the HTML 4.0 specifications and currently recognized only by Internet Explorer. The following values are identified by the specifications:

- border: all four sides
- box: all four sides
- void: no sides (default)
- above: top sides only
- below: bottom sides only
- hsides: top and bottom sides only—horizontal sides
- vsides: right and left sides only—vertical sides
- lhs: left-hand side only
- rhs: right-hand side only

Setting frame="VOID", like setting border="0", produces the same result as just omitting the attribute. This is illustrated in Figure 7.2 and the table in the top right corner of Figure 7.3. Also illustrated in Figure 7.3 is what happens when you turn on the border and then void the frame. What is left are the internal borders that separate the cells.

HTML code to turn on a 1-pixel border could use the **frame** attribute like this:<TABLE frame="BORDER">. The same results, as shown in the top left corner of Figure 7.3, would occur by setting the border equal to a width of 1 pixel with this code: <TABLE border="1">.

The **frame** attribute gives you quite a bit of control of the frame around the table and the frame around individual cells within a table row or column.

rules

On closer examination of Figure 7.3, you will notice that the frame lines are broken when displaying the frames above, below, horizontal, vertical, left, and right. If you want to maintain continuous lines around the table, but not within or between the table rows or columns, you need to use the **rules** attribute. This attribute specifies which rules appear between cells within a table as shown in Figure 7.4. These rules are also new with the HTML 4.0 specifications and currently recognized only by Internet Explorer. The following values are identified by the specifications:

- none: no rules, just the outside frame (default)
- rows: rules will appear between rows only.
- cols: rules will appear between columns only
- all: rules will appear between all rows and columns
- groups: rules will appear between row groups (see <THEAD>, <TFOOT>, and <TBODY>) and column groups (see <COLGROUP> and <COL>) only.

Between the **frames** and **rules** attributes there are enough combinations to keep any table junkie happy.

The basic code for turning on the horizontal rules for the table's rows looks like this: <TABLE rules="ROWS">. The results are shown in Figure 7.4.

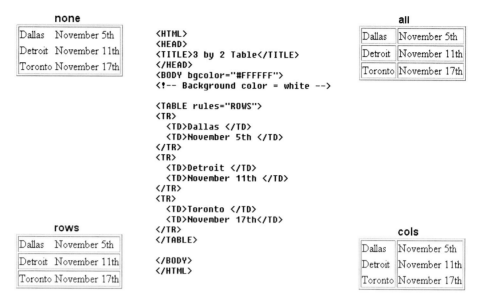

Figure 7.4 HTML code for the **rule** attribute, controlling which lines separating table cells are displayed in a table.

width

The **width** attribute controls how wide a table is—that is, how much of the horizontal browser-window real estate is covered by the table. Normally the browser will make the table wide enough to present the data you have put into the table, with a little padding. You cannot make the table smaller than the minimum necessary to present the information you have coded. You can, however, make the table wider than necessary.

As with the horizontal rule (<HR>), there are two ways to code the **width** attribute for a table: either as a fixed number of pixels or as a percentage of the screen width. Good practice is to always code in percentages, because different monitors have different resolutions (pixels per inch), so some pixels are bigger than others. Coding a width in pixels can also lead to problems if you are expecting to put a particular amount of text next to a table and have coded in pixels. On a low-resolution screen (big pixels), there will not be as much room next to the table as on a high-resolution screen. Coding your table width as a percentage of the screen will often eliminate this problem. Figure 7.5 shows a version of our table coded so it takes up roughly 10 percent of the screen. The following code is used: <TABLE width="10%">.

Notice that a table's cell becomes only as small as the largest word in a column. Cells with two words will wrap one word under the other when the table is displayed in a small window, like the one in Figure 7.5. You cannot use the **width** attribute to make the table smaller than is necessary to display the data. For example, if we coded a **width** of "5%", the first column of the table would still be as wide as it is in Figure 7.5. The **width** attribute cannot be used to compress the table.

```
<HTML>
<HEAD>
<TITLE>3 by 2 Table With Border</TITLE>
</HEAD>
<BODY bgcolor="#FFFFFF">
<!-- Background color = white -->

<TABLE border="10" width="10%">
<TR>
  <TD>Dallas </TD>
  <TD>November 5th </TD>
</TR>
<TR>
  <TD>Detroit </TD>
  <TD>November 11th </TD>
</TR>
<TR>
  <TD>Toronto </TD>
  <TD>November 17th</TD>
</TR>
</TABLE>

</BODY>
</HTML>
```

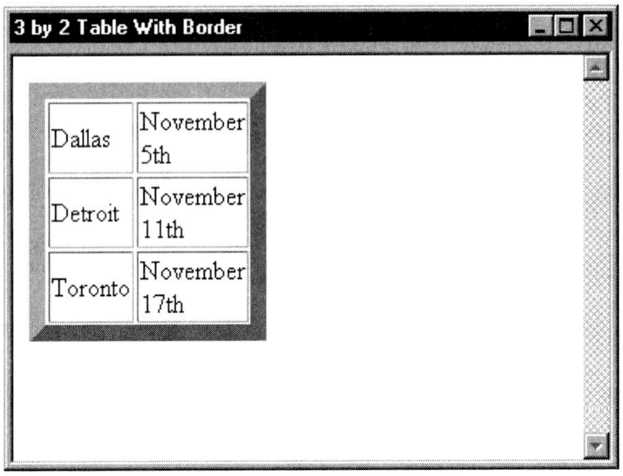

Figure 7.5 HTML code showing that a table's width can never be smaller than the length of the longest word in any cell in the column.

cellpadding

Both Navigator and Internet Explorer allow you to determine the amount of space (padding) between the data in a cell and the cell border. This value is set using the **cellpadding** attribute. The default padding is 1 pixel. You can set it higher to make the data appear to float in the middle of the cell, or you can set it to zero to make the cells as small as possible. On previous figures showing the demonstration table, notice how the "N" of "November" seems to touch the left border of the cell. The space between the "N" and the border is 1 pixel, the default value for the space around the data. Let's see what happens when we add an attribute of cellpadding="10" to the table. The code looks like this: <TABLE border="10" cellpadding="10">.

In the top left table in Figure 7.6, notice how the size of the table has increased compared with the table in Figure 7.5 that was created with default settings. This padding of 10 pixels makes the data seem to float in the center of the cells, and it increases the space on all sides of the data.

cellspacing

Another area you can control in tables is the distance between cells. The **cellspacing** attribute allows the Web weaver to set the distance between the cell borders and also between the cell border and the table's border. This attribute can make each cell in a table stand out. Setting the **cellspacing** to zero

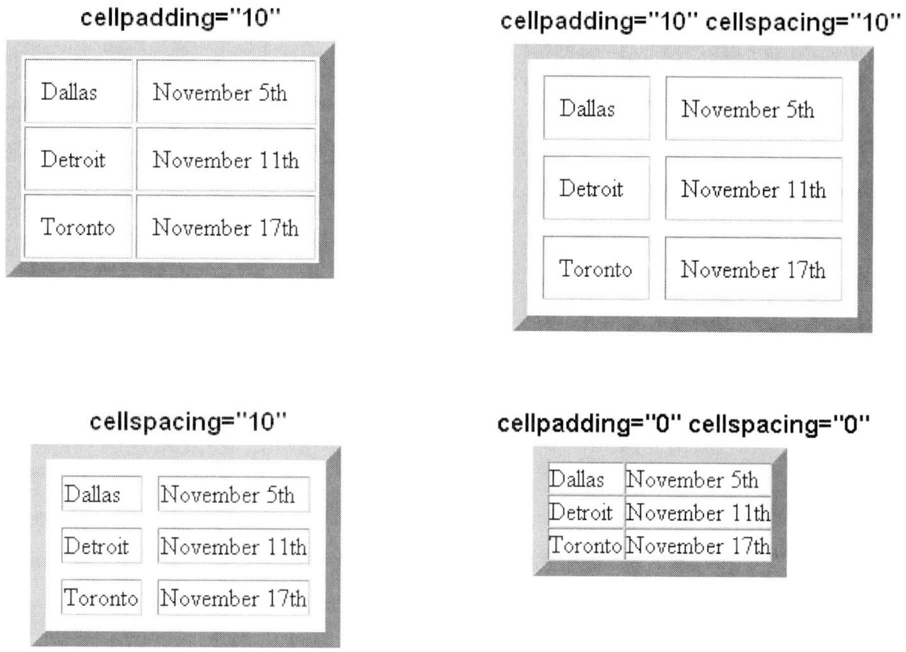

Figure 7.6 Examples of **cellpadding** and **cellspacing.**

will create the narrowest possible interior cell borders. The code for setting **cellspacing** looks like this: <TABLE border="10" cellspacing="10">.

Figure 7.6 shows the result of cellspacing="10". Notice how the white space between the cells has increased in width and definition. Now let's take away the **cellspacing** altogether by setting cellspacing="0" as illustrated in the bottom right corner of Figure 7.6. With the border coded, cell rules become a single combined line. This is the smallest **cellspacing** available.

bgcolor

It is possible, at least with Internet Explorer and Navigator, to change the color of the background for the text inside the table using the **bgcolor** attribute. Like other places where you can code color, you can use either the standard color names (a practice we discourage) or the hexadecimal codes for the table background (see color insert in back of book). As with the background color on your page, you should make sure that the background color of your table will work with the color of the font used for the text. The text should strongly contrast with the background color to be easily readable. As you can see in Figure 7.7, Internet Explorer continues the background color into the cell spacing as well; Navigator does not.

Figure 7.7 shows a simple border; all that was coded here was the **border** attribute, set equal to 5 pixels and a background color. The border defaults to two different shades of gray, creating a three-dimensional effect, as if the border were raised up from the plane of the document. Be careful when choosing a background color, because if the wrong background color is used, you can lose

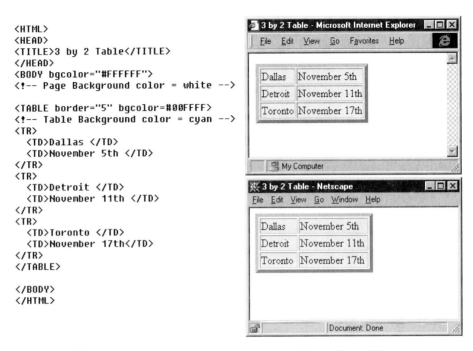

```
<HTML>
<HEAD>
<TITLE>3 by 2 Table</TITLE>
</HEAD>
<BODY bgcolor="#FFFFFF">
<!-- Page Background color = white -->

<TABLE border="5" bgcolor=#00FFFF>
<!-- Table Background color = cyan -->
<TR>
   <TD>Dallas </TD>
   <TD>November 5th </TD>
</TR>
<TR>
   <TD>Detroit </TD>
   <TD>November 11th </TD>
</TR>
<TR>
   <TD>Toronto </TD>
   <TD>November 17th</TD>
</TR>
</TABLE>

</BODY>
</HTML>
```

Figure 7.7 HTML code for changing background color within cells and the two different ways the code is handled by the popular graphical browsers.

part of the border. If your background is too dark, you will lose the bottom and right sides of the border. If your background is too light, you will usually lose the upper and left sides of the border.

It is important to realize that each new release of either of the two major graphical browsers, Navigator or Internet Explorer, incorporates some of the tags and attributes that were formerly unique to the other browser. In this way the "standard" is increased even without official sanction. For example, before release 3 of Navigator, the **bgcolor** attribute was an option only for Internet Explorer. Now it is supported by both browsers. Before release 3 of Internet Explorer, only Navigator supported the **cellpadding** attribute. Now both browsers support it. In this way more and more features are available to the Web weaver as the browsers continue to evolve.

As a case in point, the HTML 4.0 specifications address changing the border color only in terms of using the **style** attribute's property of border-color. However, Internet Explorer allows you to code different border colors using the **bordercolor, bordercolorlight,** and **bordercolordark** attributes. When it uses **bordercolor,** all four sides of the border are changed to the same color. Navigator supports only the **bordercolor** attribute, and it maintains the 3-D look, with the top and left sides lighter in color than the bottom and right sides.

summary

The **summary** attribute is specifically intended for users relying on aural presentations of a Web page. It provides a brief description of the table that is heard but not displayed on the screen. The HTML code looks like this:

<TABLE summary="This year's Home games include Dallas on November 5th, Detroit on November 11th and Toronto on November 17th.">

It should go without saying that the conscientious Web weaver will always include a brief descriptive summary of the content and structure of each table.

align

Tables are objects, like images, that are placed within the browser window. Yet, unlike images, tables are not part of the normal text flow. Instead, they signal a break in the flow. Normally text flows above or below a table but not next to it. The original way of changing that was with the **align** attribute, which specifies the margin to which the table is justified, with the text flowing around the table if there is room. For example, the following code would right-align the table and allow text to flow to the left: <TABLE border="5" align="RIGHT">. This HTML code would produce results similar to those shown in Figure 7.8. Notice how the text now flows to the left of the table.

The **align** attribute was deprecated in the HTML 4.0 specifications in favor of the **style** attribute's float property, discussed next.

style

The introduction of the **style** attribute as part of the HTML 4.0 specifications has had a broad impact on coding practices for style sheets and inline formatting. The new emphasis on style as part of more dynamic HTML code has given rise to several **style** properties that affect a table's format. Three properties control the different table characteristics we have just discussed: border-color, float, and padding.

As covered in Chapter 5, the basic syntax for the **style** property is to assign a property to a recognized value: <TABLE style="property1: value1; property2: value2">. A semicolon separates two or more property/value pairs. As shown in Figure 7.8, all of the property/value pairs are enclosed in a single pair of quotation marks.

border-color

Although the popular graphical browsers recognize the **bordercolor** attribute, the "official" way to change the color is with the **style** attribute's border-color property as shown in Figure 7.8. As mentioned before, you can use either the standard color names or the hexadecimal codes as property values. We recommend using the hexadecimal codes because older browsers recognize them. In our examples we use browser-safe color names (see color insert in back of book) when illustrating new 4.0 codes, like the **style** attribute, that are not recognized by older browsers. For instance, this code sets the border color to red (#FF0000): <TABLE border="5" style="border-color: red">. Other border properties, discussed in Chapter 8, let you change the width and appearance of the border.

```
<HTML>
<HEAD>
<TITLE>3 by 2 Table Using Styles</TITLE>
</HEAD>
<BODY style="background-color: white">
<H3>The Team's Home Schedule</H3>

<TABLE border="5" style="border-color: Fuchsia; float: right; padding:
5px">

<CAPTION align="bottom">Games start at 8:00 p.m.</CAPTION>

<TR>
  <TD>Dallas </TD>
  <TD>November 5th </TD>
</TR>
<TR>
  <TD>Detroit </TD>
  <TD>November 11th </TD>
</TR>
<TR>
  <TD>Toronto </TD>
  <TD>November 17th</TD>
</TR>
</TABLE>

Show the home team your support by attending one of the remaining home
games. Our guys need to hear from you as they battle for the
championship. It's a lot of fun, so bring the whole family!

</BODY>
</HTML>
```

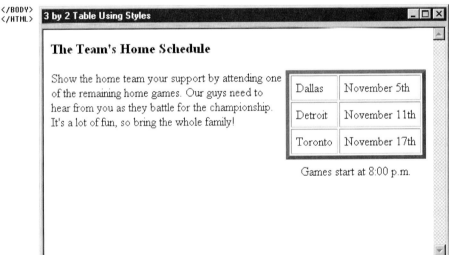

Figure 7.8 HTML code showing how the **style** attribute provides a Web author with a great deal of control over a table's format.

float

As mentioned earlier, the **align** attribute recommended in the HTML 3.2 specifications has been deprecated in favor of the **style** attribute's float property in which a table is floated to the left or right of the text. The following HTML code would align a table along the left margin and float text to the right: <TABLE border="5" style="float: left">.

When the **style** attribute's float property is set right, as shown in Figure 7.8, text is floated to the left of the table. You can also set float to "none", in which case the text flow is broken above the table and resumes below it.

padding

The style attribute's `padding` property replaces the **cellpadding** attribute. Either can set the number of pixels between the cell's content and the border. When using the `padding` property you must specify whether you are providing the measurement in pixels (px) as shown in Figure 7.8, metric (mm or cm), or English (in). If you were going to set the cell padding to a half inch, the following code could be used: `<TABLE border="5" style="padding: 0.5in">`. You can adjust the padding for just one side or a combination of sides. These options are discussed in Chapter 8.

<TR>table cells</TR>

Description: defines a table row.
Type: container.
Attributes: align, class, char, charoff, dir, id, lang, onClick, onDblClick, onKeyDown, onKeyPress, onKeyUp, onMouseDown, onMouseMove, onMouseOut, onMouseOver, onMouseUp, style, title, and valign.

In HTML, tables are built row-first. Each row defines and contains the cells within it that make up the columns. The <TR>table row</TR> container surrounds the data tags that contain the content of a table. Some Web professionals feel you need not code the </TR> closing tag, because the browser can infer one when it reaches another <TR> or an end-of-table, </TABLE>, tag. But skipping the closing tag is not a good idea, because it may cause a compatibility problem with later versions of the browsers. Also, the lack of a closing tag makes finding the end of a particular row just a little harder.

Some of the attributes for the <TR> tag look suspiciously like attributes for the <TABLE> tag, but they have different meanings when used with the <TR> tag. As an example, let's look at the **align** attribute.

align

When used within the <TABLE> tag, the **align** attribute determines the justification of the table and whether text will flow next to the table. When used within the <TR> tag, **align** specifies the horizontal alignment of the data within the cells composing this row. An alignment specified for a particular row affects only the cells in that row, not the cells in other rows. In addition, you can use the **align** attribute to set the common alignment for the row, then change the alignment of one or more particular cells on a cell-by-cell basis.

You will need to set the alignment of the data within cells only if you don't want to use the defaults. Navigator and Internet Explorer use a default *center* alignment for headers and a *left* alignment for data. So, for example, if you want all the data in a particular row centered rather than left-justified, you can code the **align** attribute in the <TR> tag to set center alignment for all of the cells in that row. Figure 7.9 shows a table with the three different alignments. This table is coded with width="50%" to give enough space in the cells to really see the alignment.

You can also align cell values based on a character found in one of the table cells. For example, you might want to align a group of numbers on their decimal points or a list of names after a colon. This is accomplished by setting align="CHAR". The character the browser aligns with is specified by the **char** attribute, discussed shortly.

```
<TABLE border="5" width="50%">
<TR align="LEFT">
  <TD>Left</TD>
  <TD>Align Left</TD>
</TR>

<TR align="CENTER">
  <TD>Center</TD>
  <TD>Align Center</TD>
</TR>

<TR align="RIGHT">
  <TD>Right</TD>
  <TD>Align Right</TD>
</TR>

<TR valign="TOP">
  <TD>Vertical Alignment Top</TD>
  <TD>Top</TD>
</TR>

<TR valign="CENTER">
  <TD>Vertical Alignment Center</TD>
  <TD>Center</TD>
</TR>

<TR valign="BOTTOM">
  <TD>Vertical Alignment Bottom</TD>
  <TD>Bottom</TD>
</TR>

<TR valign="BASELINE">
  <TD>Vertical Alignment Baseline</TD>
  <TD>Baseline</TD>
</TR>
</TABLE>
```

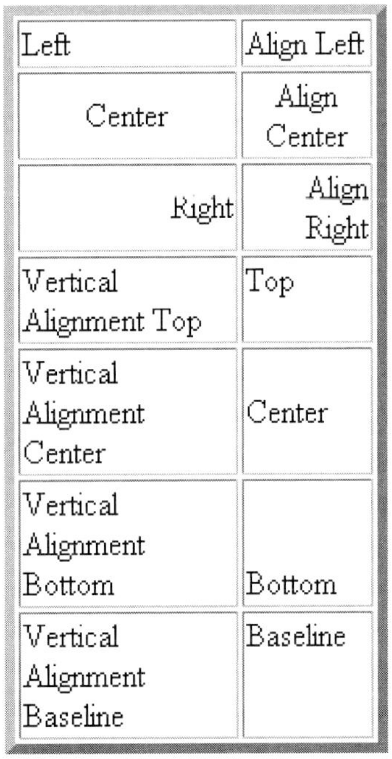

Left	Align Left
Center	Align Center
Right	Align Right
Vertical Alignment Top	Top
Vertical Alignment Center	Center
Vertical Alignment Bottom	Bottom
Vertical Alignment Baseline	Baseline

Figure 7.9 HTML code for horizontal and vertical text alignment within table cells.

valign

The **valign** attribute is an extension supported by the common browsers. This attribute instructs the browser regarding the vertical placement of the data within the cells in that row. Four different values are available for this attribute. The default is

CENTER. Then, in addition to TOP and BOTTOM, there is a BASELINE value that aligns the data with the bottom of the first row of text in any other cells.

Figure 7.9 shows a table with these different alignments. A different **valign** value was used for *each cell* to illustrate how they all look. Remember, the default for **valign** is centered, so you need to code it only if you want other than centered data.

char

The **char** attribute allows you to align text based on a specific character—like a period (.) or comma (,). The browser will use the decimal-point character for the current language as set by the **lang** attribute (e.g., the period (.) in English and the comma (,) in French) as the default. To align cell values with a colon, the following code would be used: <TR align="CHAR" char=":">. Interestingly, the W^{3}C does not require browsers to support this attribute.

charoff

Web weavers can offset the alignment of text within a cell by using the **charoff** attribute. When this attribute is employed, it specifies the offset for the first occurrence of the alignment character specified with the **char** attribute. The code to offset text two spaces after a colon looks like this: <TR align="CHAR" char=":" charoff="2">. The offset direction is determined by the **dir** attribute. In left-to-right text, like English, offset is from the left margin. In right-to-left texts, offset is from the right. If the designated alignment character is missing, the text is shifted horizontally to the end of the alignment position. As with the **char** attribute, the W^{3}C does not require browsers to support the **charoff** attribute.

Table Data and Table Headers: <TD>, <TH>

We have finally reached the containers that will hold the actual data in the table. The <TD>table data</TD> and <TH>table header</TH> tags surround the information for the table. Each instance of these containers describes one cell in the table. Any content for the table must appear within one of these containers, or the <CAPTION> container. Should you code content that is not enclosed within one of these containers, unexpected results will occur as shown in Figure 7.10.

<TD>table data</TD>

Description: defines table data (one cell).
Type: container.
Attributes: abbr, align, axis, bgcolor, class, char, charoff, colspan, dir, headers, height, id, lang, nowrap, onClick, onDblClick, onKeyDown, onKeyPress, onKeyUp, onMouseDown, onMouseMove, onMouscOut, onMouseOver, onMouseUp, rowspan, scope, style, title, valign, and width.

```
<HTML>
<HEAD>
<TITLE>3 by 2 Table</TITLE>
</HEAD>
<BODY bgcolor="#FFFFFF">
<!-- Background color = white -->

<TABLE border="5">
<TR>
  <TD>Dallas </TD>
  <TD>November 5th </TD>
</TR>

The Dallas game starts at 8:00 p.m.  ◄─── Misplaced Code

<TR>
  <TD>Detroit </TD>
  <TD>November 11th </TD>
</TR>
<TR>
  <TD>Toronto </TD>
  <TD>November 17th</TD>
</TR>
</TABLE>

</BODY>
</HTML>
```

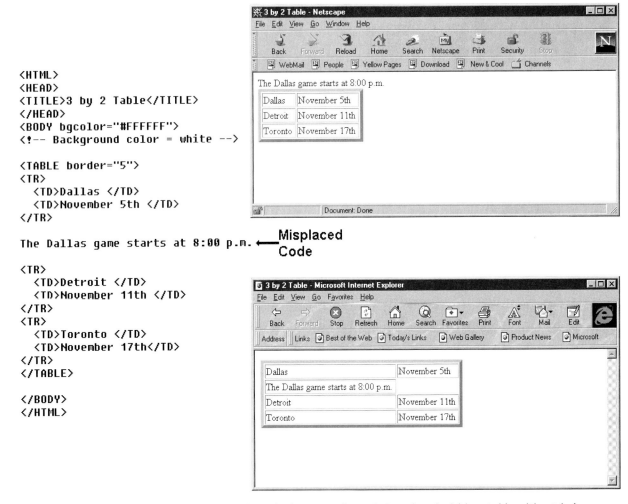

Figure 7.10 HTML code producing unexpected results because of text being placed within a table without being enclosed in an acceptable container.

<TH>table header</TH>

Description: defines a table header (one cell).
Type: container.
Attributes: abbr, align, axis, bgcolor, class, char, charoff, colspan, dir, headers, height, id, lang, nowrap, onClick, onDblClick, onKeyDown, onKeyPress, onKeyUp, onMouseDown, onMouseMove, onMouseOut, onMouseOver, onMouseUp, rowspan, scope, style, title, valign, and width.

The browser renders the <TH> headers in a bold font and centers them, whereas text within the <TD> container is left-aligned and displayed in a regular font. In the past some browsers treated data in the <TH> container the same as data in a <TD> container. This is no longer the case; all the popular graphical browsers handle data within the two tags as shown in Figure 7.11.

There is an order of precedence for the attributes of a table. Attributes coded at the cell level have precedence over those at the row level. Attributes coded at the row level have precedence over those coded at the table level. Consequently, you have quite a bit of control over the elements of a table. Some of the attributes available for the <TD> and <TH> tags are identical in name and function to those used with the <TR> tag. Others are unique to the <TD> and <TH> tags, giving you even more control over the appearance of the table. First let's look at the attributes that are common with other table tags.

```
<HTML>
<HEAD>
<TITLE>Tables With Headers</TITLE>
</HEAD>
<BODY bgcolor="#FFFFFF">
<!-- Background color = white -->

<H3>Vertical Table Layout</H3>
<TABLE border="5" width="100%">
<TR>
   <TH>Opponent </TH>
   <TH>Date </TH>
</TR>
<TR>
   <TD>Dallas </TD>
   <TD>November 5th </TD>
</TR>
<TR>
   <TD>Detroit </TD>
   <TD>November 11th </TD>
</TR>
<TR>
   <TD>Toronto </TD>
   <TD>November 17th</TD>
</TR>
</TABLE>

<H3>Horizontal Table Layout</H3>
<TABLE border="5" width="100%">
<TR>
   <TH>Opponent</TH> <TD>Dallas</TD> <TD>Detroit</TD> <TD>Toronto</TD>
</TR>
<TR>
   <TH>Date</TH> <TD>November 5th</TD> <TD>November 11th</TD> <TD>November 17th</TD>
</TR>
</TABLE>
```

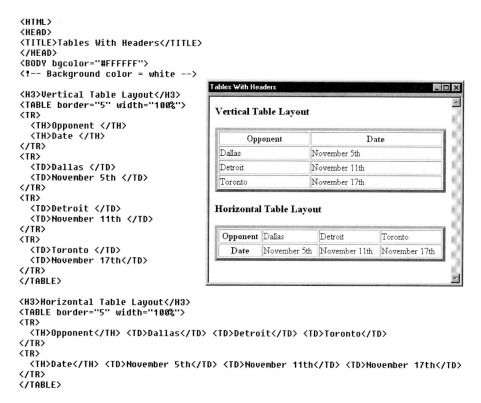

Figure 7.11 HTML code using the <TD> and <TH> tags to identify table data in two different tables.

align

The **align** attribute for <TD> and <TH> works exactly like the **align** attribute for <TR>, with the exception that the alignment is only for the cell for which it is coded. The alignment of the next cell reverts to the alignment specified by the row. If that alignment is not set, it reverts to the alignment set by the table itself. Like the **align** attribute of the <TR> container, this **align** attribute can be set to one of four values: LEFT, RIGHT, CENTER, or CHAR.

bgcolor

Like the **bgcolor** attribute for the <TABLE> tag, the **bgcolor** attribute for <TD> and <TH> allows you to set the background color for a particular cell. You can set the color with either a color name or a hexadecimal code as shown on the color insert in the back of this book. The color you code within this tag applies only to the cell described. The other cells of the row will be the color set in the <TABLE> tag. As always when using color, you need to be very careful not to create a visual unpleasantness. The **bgcolor** attribute may be of use in creating a table with one or two cells highlighted to bring attention to their contents.

valign

The **valign** attribute is functionally identical to its namesake associated with the <TR> tag. It allows for vertical alignment of the data within a single cell of the table. It is useful for altering the way the data in one specific cell are presented. The alignment of data or headings in subsequent cells is not affected.

How you lay out the actual HTML code for a table makes a big difference in how easy it is to understand—and, more importantly, how easy it is to change. Figure 7.11 illustrates two different ways to lay out HTML table code in a readable way. In the vertical table example at the top of Figure 7.11, the headings and each piece of the data for each table row is placed on its own line and indented. At the bottom of Figure 7.11 is a table with a horizontal layout. The related code is organized to mimic that table's screen appearance, with the heading and data for each row on the same line and indented within the <TR>table row</TR> container. However you lay out your tables, make sure they are easy to read, understand, and change.

colspan

There are times, usually with headings, that some cell information needs *column spanning* capabilities because it applies to more than one column. To arrange for that, you need to code the **colspan** attribute and tell the browser how many columns you want the particular cell to span. Figure 7.12 presents a small table with a header that spans all six columns at the top of the table. The HTML code to have a cell span across six cells looks like this: `<TH colspan="6">`.

The **colspan** attribute is also used twice in row 3 to span a single price across two different columns. Remember, either <TD> or <TH> cells can have this attribute. However, if the **colspan** attribute is applied to a situation where there are not enough columns in the table to span, it won't add columns to make the **colspan** work. It may cause an alignment problem.

```
<HTML>
<HEAD>
<TITLE>Column Spanning Cells</TITLE>
</HEAD>
<BODY>
<TABLE border="5" width="100%">
<TR>
  <TH colspan="6">Home Ticket Options</TH>
</TR>
<TR>
  <TH>Zone</TH>
  <TD>Red</TD>
  <TD>Blue</TD>
  <TD>Green</TD>
  <TD>Yellow</TD>
  <TD>Orange</TD>
</TR>
<TR>
  <TH>Price</TH>
  <TD>$101.00</TD>
  <TD colspan="2">$25.50</TD>
  <TD colspan="2">$9.00</TD>
</TR>
</TABLE>
</BODY>
</HTML>
```

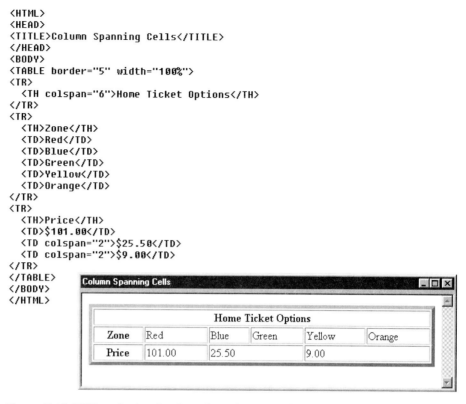

Figure 7.12 HTML code showing how the **colspan** attribute allows cell content to span more than one column.

rowspan

HTML allows the creation of a cell that has *row spanning* capabilities for use when information is the same for more than one row. The **rowspan** attribute creates a cell that spans two or more rows. This attribute is useful for creating headings and legends for the cells in a table. The **rowspan** attribute is set to an integer number equal to the number of rows the cell is to span. Figure 7.13 shows a simple table with the **rowspan** attribute set. Notice that these are the same data presented in Figure 7.12, but in a vertical layout instead of a horizontal layout. The first header spans all six rows because of this code: <TH rowspan="6">.

Since the browser renders the table from the top left to the bottom right, the **rowspan** attribute is placed in the <TH> or <TD> container that incorporates the first of the rows to be spanned. Therefore, when the ticket price of $25.50 needs to span both the Blue and Green rows, the attribute is set in the first <TD> definition like this:

```
<TR>
    <TD>Blue</TD>
    <TD rowspan="2">$25.50</TD>
</TR>
<TR>
    <TD>Green</TD>
</TR>
```

```
<HTML>
<HEAD>
<TITLE>Row Spanning Cells</TITLE>
</HEAD>
<BODY>
<TABLE border="5" width="100%">
<TR>
  <TH rowspan="6">Home Ticket Options</TH>
  <TH>Zone</TH>
  <TH>Price</TH>
</TR>
<TR>
  <TD>Red</TD>
  <TD>$101.00</TD>
</TR>
<TR>
  <TD>Blue</TD>
  <TD rowspan="2">$25.50</TD>
</TR>
<TR>
  <TD>Green</TD>
</TR>
<TR>
  <TD>Yellow</TD>
  <TD rowspan="2">$9.00</TD>
</TR>
<TR>
  <TD>Orange</TD>
</TR>
</TABLE>
</BODY>
</HTML>
```

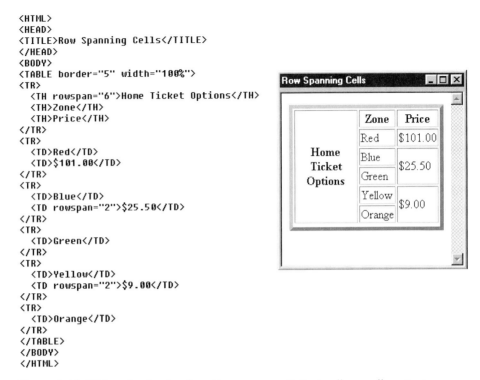

Figure 7.13 HTML code showing how the **rowspan** attribute allows cell content to span more than one row.

With **rowspan** established for the Blue row, the <TD> container for the next row contains only the data "Green." The browser then spans the cell with "$25.50" across both rows.

As with the **colspan** attribute, if we code **rowspan** greater than the number of rows remaining, the browser will not add rows to grant our request.

abbr

As we have seen, there are limits to how small a table can be rendered, because the browsers are unable to shrink cells smaller than the longest word. The **abbr** attribute allows Web weavers to assign abbreviations to cell contents that are used only in situations where the table needs to be as small as possible. For example, the following code would provide abbreviations for the cell values displayed in the second row of Figure 7.12:

```
<TH abbr="Z">Zone</TH>
<TD abbr="R">Red</TD>
<TD abbr="B">Blue</TD>
<TD abbr="G">Green</TD>
<TD abbr="Y">Yellow</TD>
<TD abbr="O">Orange</TD>
```

The W^{3}C also foresees these abbreviations being used by aural-oriented pages where speech synthesizers will output the abbreviated headers before rendering the cell's content. This attribute is not currently supported by either major browser.

headers

The **headers** attribute specifies the list of header cells that provide header information for specific table cells. This is another of the new HTML 4.0 attributes that is designed to support nonvisual browsers, especially those relying on speech synthesis. Values assigned to this attribute are a space-separated list of cell names that relate to cells with specific identifiers established by the **id** attribute. The W^{3}C states that this attribute will most likely be used in conjunction with style sheets, however, it is not currently supported by either major browser.

scope

Because tables are a great way to organize data, they are found on the Web in a variety of sizes and formats. The W^{3}C added the **scope** attribute in the 4.0 specifications to be used as an alternative to the **headers** attribute when designing simple tables. When specified, this attribute must have one of the following values:
- row: Header cell provides header information for the rest of the row.
- col: Header cell provides header information for the rest of the column.
- rowgroup: Header cell provides header information for the rest of the row group.
- colgroup: Header cell provides header information for the rest of the column group.

None of the browsers currently support this attribute.

axis

The **axis** attribute is also new with the HTML 4.0 specifications. Although none of the popular browsers currently recognize this attribute, the W^{3}C has this to say about its application within HTML documents:

> This attribute may be used to place a cell into conceptual categories that can be considered to form axes in an *n*-dimensional space. User agents [browsers] may give users access to these categories (e.g., the user may query the user agent for all cells that belong to certain categories, the user agent may present a table in the form of a table of contents, etc.). Please consult the section on categorizing cells for more information. The value of this attribute is a comma-separated list of category names. (HTML 4.0 specifications, section 11.2.6)

width

The **width** attribute is the first we will discuss that is different when used with the <TH> and <TR> tags, or the <TABLE> tag. As in the other uses of **width,** you can code it as an absolute number of pixels (Figure 7.14), which will change with the varying resolutions of the monitors, or you can code it as a percentage. But **width** coded for <TR> and <TH> differs from the **width** attribute for the <TABLE> tag in that when you code it as a percentage, that percentage is of the *width of the table,* not the width of the page. Figure 7.14 shows the three-column table in which the left column is set to a

```
<HTML>
<HEAD>
<TITLE>Width and Height Attributes</TITLE>
</HEAD>
<BODY bgcolor="#FFFFFF">
<!-- Background color = white -->
<TABLE border="5">
<TR>
  <TH width="75" rowspan="6">Home Ticket Options</TH>
  <TH width="100" height="50">Zone</TH>
  <TH width="100" >Price</TH>
</TR>
<TR align="CENTER">
  <TD height="50">Red</TD>
  <TD>$101.00</TD>
</TR>
<TR align="CENTER">
  <TD height="30">Blue</TD>
  <TD rowspan="2">$25.50</TD>
</TR>
<TR align="CENTER">
  <TD height="30">Green</TD>
</TR>
<TR align="CENTER">
  <TD height="30">Yellow</TD>
  <TD rowspan="2">$9.00</TD>
</TR>
<TR align="CENTER">
  <TD height="30">Orange</TD>
</TR>
</TABLE>
</BODY>
```

Figure 7.14 Setting table dimensions using the **width** and **height** attributes.

width of 75 pixels, with the remaining columns set to be 100 pixels wide. We used absolute cell width in the left column to ensure that "Home Ticket Options" would fall on three lines.

Remember that the width you set for a particular cell also sets the width for that column in the whole of the table. As is true for the table's width, you cannot set a width that is less than what the browser determines is the minimum necessary to display the existing contents of the cells in that column. If you happen to code more than one width in the same column, the browser will take the largest value for the whole column. If you code a width, it is best for maintenance and readability to code it on the first occurrence of that column in the table, as shown in Figure 7.14. The **width** attribute was deprecated in the HTML 4.0 specifications in favor of the **style** attribute's width property.

height

While the **width** attribute adjusts the horizontal size of a table column, the **height** attribute adjusts the vertical size of a table row. As shown in Figure 7.14, the height is given in pixels and affects only the row in which the attribute appears. The browser will not let you make the height of a row shorter than is necessary to display the contents.

In Figure 7.14 the height of the top two rows is set to 50 pixels. Notice that setting the height and width in effect sets the cell padding. Setting the height of the remaining cells in the middle column ("Blue," "Green," "Yellow," and "Orange"), automatically determines the height of the row-spanning cells in the right column. As with the **width** attribute, the **height** attribute was deprecated in the 4.0 specifications in favor of the **style** attribute's `height` property, discussed next.

```
<HTML>
<HEAD>
<TITLE>Cell Width and Height Using Styles</TITLE>
</HEAD>
<BODY style="background-color: white">
<TABLE border="5">
<TR>
  <TH style="width: 75px" rowspan="6">Home Ticket Options</TH>
  <TH style="width: 100px; height: 50px">Zone</TH>
  <TH style="width: 100px">Price</TH>
</TR>
<TR style="text-align: center">
  <TD style="height: 50px">Red</TD>
  <TD>$101.00</TD>
</TR>
<TR style="text-align: center">
  <TD style="height: 30px">Blue</TD>
  <TD rowspan="2">$25.50</TD>
</TR>
<TR style="text-align: center">
  <TD style="height: 30px">Green</TD>
</TR>
<TR style="text-align: center">
  <TD style="height: 30px">Yellow</TD>
  <TD rowspan="2">$9.00</TD>
</TR>
<TR style="text-align: center">
  <TD style="height: 30px">Orange</TD>
</TR>
</TABLE>
</BODY>
</HTML>
```

Home Ticket Options	Zone	Price
	Red	$101.00
	Blue	$25.50
	Green	
	Yellow	$9.00
	Orange	

Figure 7.15 HTML code showing how the **style** attribute can produce the same results as the code in Figure 7.14.

Setting Height and Width with Style

The HTML 4.0 specifications provide a number of alternatives for formatting Web pages using the **style** attribute. As you might expect, the Web author can use it to set a table's column width and row height, as shown in Figure 7.15. The table that results from the code in Figure 7.15 is exactly the same as the table in Figure 7.14. The difference in the HTML codes is representative of the changes brought about by the 4.0 specifications. For example, you could set the width of a table column to 50 pixels using this deprecated code: `<TH width="50">Text</TH>`. But the alternative—and more up-to-date—way to handle the same situation uses the **style** attribute like this: `<TH style="width: 50px">Text</TH>`.

Although deprecated attributes like **height** and **width** will be recognized by browsers for some time to come, you would be wise to add the **style** attribute to your HTML vocabulary.

nowrap

Normally the browsers will wrap the contents of a cell across multiple lines to make the data fit, visibly, in the requisite cell. However, there are times when it is necessary to prevent the browser from wrapping lines. As we saw with the <NOBR> container, there are situations in which a broken line could be confusing for the users. Originally this situation was handled in HTML code by adding the **nowrap** attribute to the table definition. The code would look like this:

```
<TD nowrap>This text would not be wrapped within the cell.</TD>
```

Once again the W^{3}C has decided to deprecate an attribute, in this case the **nowrap** attribute, in favor of the **style** attribute. To prevent the contents of a cell from wrapping using the **style** attribute, you would set the `white-space` property to `nowrap`. Here is an example of the related HTML code:

```
<TD style="white-space: nowrap">This text would not be wrapped within
the cell.</TD>
```

Other values for the `white-space` property are covered in Chapter 8.

<CAPTION>caption</CAPTION>

Description: defines a table caption.
Type: container.
Attributes: align, class, dir, id, lang, onClick, onDblClick, onKeyDown, onKeyPress, onKeyUp, onMouseDown, onMouseMove, onMouseOut, onMouseOver, onMouseUp, style, and title.
Special notes: only permitted immediately after the <TABLE> start tag.

Most tables need a *caption* to explain their contents. The popular browsers recognize the <CAPTION> tag and place the contents above the table. Like any of the cells in the table, the <CAPTION> can contain anything that can be placed in the <BODY> of an HTML document, but the wise Web weaver will constrain the contents of the <CAPTION> tag to a terse description of the table.

Note that the </CAPTION> closing tag is *never* omitted. Also note that there can only be one <CAPTION> container per table. The popular browsers center the caption with respect to the table edges, as shown in Figure 7.16. While the W^{3}C specifications state that the caption tag should immediately follow the starting <TABLE> tag, we have found that the browsers are a little more relaxed about the placement, allowing the Web weaver to place the <CAPTION> element elsewhere in the <TABLE> container. We recommend that you follow the W^{3}C recommendations as closely as possible, though, to ensure compliance with later versions of browsers that will conform more closely to the specifications.

```
<HTML>
<HEAD>
<TITLE>Table With Caption</TITLE>
</HEAD>
<BODY bgcolor="#FFFFFF">
<!-- Background color = white -->
<TABLE border="5">
<CAPTION align="BOTTOM">Multiplication Table</CAPTION>
<TR>
  <TH> </TH> <TH>1</TH> <TH>2</TH> <TH>3</TH> <TH>4</TH> <TH>5</TH>
</TR>
<TR>
  <TH>1</TH> <TD>1</TD> <TD>2</TD> <TD>3</TD> <TD>4</TD> <TD>5</TD>
</TR>
<TR>
  <TH>2</TH> <TD>2</TD> <TD>4</TD> <TD>6</TD> <TD>8</TD> <TD>10</TD>
</TR>
<TR>
  <TH>3</TH> <TD>3</TD> <TD>6</TD> <TD>9</TD> <TD>12</TD> <TD>15</TD>
</TR>
<TR>
  <TH>4</TH> <TD>4</TD> <TD>8</TD> <TD>12</TD> <TD>16</TD> <TD>20</TD>
</TR>
<TR>
  <TH>5</TH> <TD>5</TD> <TD>10</TD> <TD>15</TD> <TD>20</TD> <TD>25</TD>
</TR>
</TABLE>
</BODY>
</HTML>
```

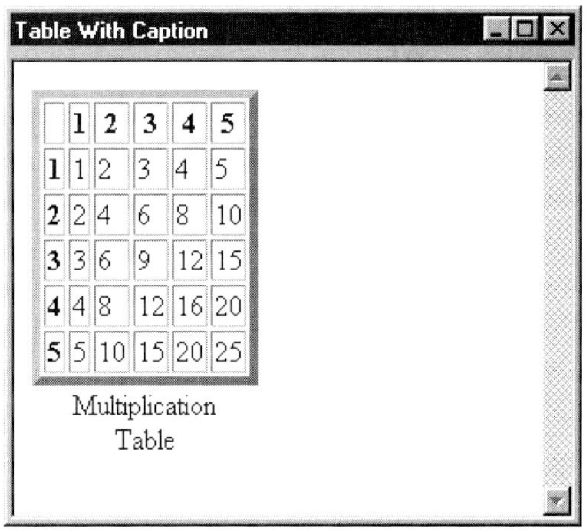

Figure 7.16 HTML code showing how a caption can be aligned on the table's top or bottom.

align

All of the browsers support placement of the caption either above or below the table, and they default to placing the caption above (TOP) the table. This is a major improvement over past practices, in which each browser had a different default setting and in some cases used a different attribute! Figure 7.16 illustrates a caption that is aligned at the bottom of the 5 by 5 (6-cell by 6-cell) multiplication table. When align="BOTTOM" is set, the browser takes the responsibility of displaying the caption's content below the table.

The HTML 4.0 specifications actually recognize alignment values set to TOP, BOTTOM, LEFT, or RIGHT. However, at the time of this writing, none of the browsers recognize RIGHT or LEFT values. Also, the specifications have deprecated the **align** attribute, but at this time we cannot determine what code is expected to be used in its place.

\<COLGROUP\>column group\</COLGROUP\>

Description: creates structural divisions within a table that can be independently formatted.
Type: container.
Attributes: align, char, charoff, class, dir, id, lang, onClick, onDblClick, onKeyDown, onKeyPress, onKeyUp, onMouseDown, onMouseMove, onMouseOut, onMouseOver, onMouseUp, span, style, title, valign, and width.

As tables are row-oriented, Web weavers have been limited in their ability to format across columns. Before the \<COLGROUP\> element was added to the specifications, Web weavers who wanted to change the background color of selected columns or needed to align a column of numbers on the decimal point could not easily do it. With \<COLGROUP\>, they can designate specific columns in a table for special treatment, that is, formatting. Figure 7.17 shows our multiplication table with the \<COLGROUP\> element applied to the first three columns.

A table can contain more than one column group, but if it does, you should be careful to end the first group's definition with a \</COLGROUP\> tag before defining the next group. You will find the \<COLGROUP\> tag is a very powerful HTML element that offers a variety of alternatives, especially when used with the **span** attribute, discussed next.

span

The **span** attribute allows the Web weaver to apply format changes across several columns in a group. In Figure 7.17 the **span** attribute is set equal to 3. As you can see, the other attributes included in the \<COLGROUP\> element, **width** and **style,** are then applied to the first three columns in the table. **Span** must always be an integer greater than 0.

To further explore the \<COLGROUP\> element, we need to introduce the \<COL\> empty tag before going on any further.

\<COL\>column\</COL\>

Description: allows authors to group together attribute specifications for table columns but does not group columns together structurally.
Type: empty.
Attributes: align, char, charoff, class, dir, id, lang, onClick, onDblClick, onKeyDown, onKeyPress, onKeyUp, onMouseDown, onMouseMove, onMouseOut, onMouseOver, onMouseUp, span, style, title, valign, and width.

```
<HTML>
<HEAD>
<TITLE>Multiplication Table</TITLE>
</HEAD>
<BODY bgcolor="#FFFFFF">
<!-- Background color = white -->
<TABLE border="5">
<CAPTION align="BOTTOM">Multiplication Table</CAPTION>
<COLGROUP span="3" width="50"
  style="
    font-family: sans-serif;
    font-style: italic;
    font-size: 16pt;
    text-align: center;
  ">
</COLGROUP>
<TR>
  <TH> </TH> <TH>1</TH> <TH>2</TH> <TH>3</TH> <TH>4</TH> <TH>5</TH>
</TR>
<TR>
  <TH>1</TH> <TD>1</TD> <TD>2</TD> <TD>3</TD> <TD>4</TD> <TD>5</TD>
</TR>
<TR>
  <TH>2</TH> <TD>2</TD> <TD>4</TD> <TD>6</TD> <TD>8</TD> <TD>10</TD>
</TR>
<TR>
  <TH>3</TH> <TD>3</TD> <TD>6</TD> <TD>9</TD> <TD>12</TD> <TD>15</TD>
</TR>
<TR>
  <TH>4</TH> <TD>4</TD> <TD>8</TD> <TD>12</TD> <TD>16</TD> <TD>20</TD>
</TR>
<TR>
  <TH>5</TH> <TD>5</TD> <TD>10</TD> <TD>15</TD> <TD>20</TD> <TD>25</TD>
</TR>
</TABLE>
</BODY>
</HTML>
```

	1	*2*	3	4	5
1	*1*	*2*	3	4	5
2	*2*	*4*	6	8	10
3	*3*	*6*	9	12	15
4	*4*	*8*	12	16	20
5	*5*	*10*	15	20	25

Multiplication Table

Figure 7.17 HTML code showing how the <COLGROUP> element formats groups of columns.

The <COL> element is an interesting addition to the 4.0 specifications and will probably go through more evolution as an HTML element before all of its capabilities are universally recognized. It is an empty tag that by design works inside the <COLGROUP> element as an alternative to the **span** attribute. However, the W[3]C tells us that the <COL> element can be used outside a column group as shown in Figure 7.18.

Up until now we have used the **span** attribute within a <COLGROUP> tab to format a group of columns. The <COL> element can also represent one or more columns in a column group. It recognizes the **span** attribute

```
<HTML>
<HEAD>
<TITLE>Multiplication Table</TITLE>
</HEAD>
<BODY bgcolor="#FFFFFF">
<!-- Background color = white -->
<TABLE border="5">
<CAPTION align="BOTTOM">Multiplication Table</CAPTION>
<COL width="10">
<COL width="20" style="font-style: italic">
<COL width="30" style="font-size: 8pt">
<COL width="60" span="2" style="text-align: center">
<COL width="30" style="font-family: sans-serif">
<TR>
  <TH> </TH> <TH>1</TH> <TH>2</TH> <TH>3</TH> <TH>4</TH> <TH>5</TH>
</TR>
<TR>
  <TH>1</TH> <TD>1</TD> <TD>2</TD> <TD>3</TD> <TD>4</TD> <TD>5</TD>
</TR>
<TR>
  <TH>2</TH> <TD>2</TD> <TD>4</TD> <TD>6</TD> <TD>8</TD> <TD>10</TD>
</TR>
<TR>
  <TH>3</TH> <TD>3</TD> <TD>6</TD> <TD>9</TD> <TD>12</TD> <TD>15</TD>
</TR>
<TR>
  <TH>4</TH> <TD>4</TD> <TD>8</TD> <TD>12</TD> <TD>16</TD> <TD>20</TD>
</TR>
<TR>
  <TH>5</TH> <TD>5</TD> <TD>10</TD> <TD>15</TD> <TD>20</TD> <TD>25</TD>
</TR>
</TABLE>
</BODY>
</HTML>
```

	1	2	3	4	5
1	1	2	3	4	5
2	2	4	6	8	10
3	3	6	9	12	15
4	4	8	12	16	20
5	5	10	15	20	25

Multiplication Table

Figure 7.18 HTML code for selected table columns formatted using the <COL> element.

(Figure 7.18). To show you how both of these <COLGROUP> options work, let's explore the use of the **width** attribute.

width

By this time the **width** attribute has become an old friend. It is particularly powerful when used within the <COLGROUP> element, because you can set the width of many or all the columns in a table with a single application. For example, the following code would set the width of each of 30 columns in a table to 60 pixels: <COLGROUP span="30" width="60">.

Web weavers can specify column widths in three ways:

1. Fixed—based on pixels (width="60")
2. *Percentage*—based on the percentage of the horizontal space available to the table (width="25%"). This is the preferred method.
3. *Proportional*—based on portions of the horizontal space required by a table (width="5*")

The proportional, or relative, specification needs a little more explanation. This **width** option must work in conjunction with a fixed table width provided by the <TABLE> element. For discussion's sake, let's suppose this HTML code was used to set a table's width to 600 pixels: <TABLE border="5" width="600">. With this fixed table width established, we could use the <COLGROUP> element to span six columns of our table and equally distribute the column widths: <COLGROUP span="6" width="6*">.

In this case the math is easy, and you probably figured out that all six columns would be 100 pixels wide. This logic would work just as well if the width were set to 500 pixels. The proportional **width** option also goes beyond this simple application, because you can vary the proportion of horizontal space allocated across columns.

Consider the following HTML code in respect to a three-column table with a fixed width of 600 pixels:

```
<COLGROUP style="font-style: italic">
<COL width="1*">
<COL width="3*">
<COL width="2*">
</COLGROUP>
```

In this situation the proportional widths assigned to each column are as follows:

- Column 1: assigned $\frac{1}{6}$ of the horizontal space assigned to the table, i.e., 100 pixels.
- Column 2: assigned $\frac{1}{2}$ of the table's horizontal space, i.e., 300 pixels.
- Column 3: assigned $\frac{1}{3}$ of the table's horizontal space, i.e., 200 pixels.

Notice how the <COL> element is used instead of the **span** attribute to format columns within the column group. The <COLGROUP> tag can still apply style changes across all three columns, in this case setting the font style to italics, while the <COL> tag specifics the horizontal space assigned to each column. You will find the <COL> element most useful when having to format noncontinuous columns within the column group. For example, when you want to alternate the column widths every other column or every third column.

Just remember our old caveat about the browser always having the final say regarding this type of formatting. The W^{3}C even reminds us of this fact when it writes, "User agents [browsers] may render the table incrementally even with proportional columns" (HTML 4.0 specifications, section 11.2.4).

Just to add a little spice to things, the W^{3}C has thrown in a special form of the proportional width attribute—"0*". The HTML code looks like this: <COLGROUP width="0*">. This code tells the browser to set each column's width to the minimum necessary to render the content. This means the column's content must be known before the width is computed and the table displayed. Using the option means your tables will require a minimum amount of screen real estate but will be slower to load, because the browser cannot render them incrementally.

valign

The **valign** attribute works the same way as it does within the <TR>, <TH>, and <TD> tags. It allows for vertical alignment of the data within all the cells in the specified column. You might remember that the popular browsers recognize four different values for this attribute: CENTER (the default), TOP, BOTTOM, and BASELINE. Figure 7.9 shows a table with these different alignments.

Scrolling Big Tables

In the past, displaying long tables was a problem, because the column headers scrolled off the screen as the table's body did. Users had to scroll back to them when they needed to refresh their memories concerning a column's content. Along the same line, printing these long tables caused a problem in that the column headers appeared only at the beginning of the table, which was often on another page. A running header (or footer) that would always stay on the screen and would appear on each printed page was desirable, but no such tags were identified in the HTML 3.2 specifications. The only way to accomplish this was to use frames; definitely a kluge.

Fortunately, the 4.0 specifications addressed this concern with the <TBODY>, <THEAD>, and <TFOOT> containers, although at the time of this writing, none of the browsers have implemented them. What follows is an overview of these elements and a short discussion of how they are supposed to work.

<THEAD>table header</THEAD>

Description: defines a table's header.
Type: container.
Attributes: align, char, charoff, class, dir, id, lang, onClick, onDblClick, onKeyDown, onKeyPress, onKeyUp, onMouseDown, onMouseMove, onMouseOut, onMouseOver, onMouseUp, style, title, and valign.

The <THEAD> element must precede the <TBODY> element, as shown in Figure 7.19. It defines a nonscrolling column heading, which is what distinguishes its contents from those used within a <TH> tag. In other words, the contents of a <TH> tag will scroll off the screen when a long table is displayed, but the contents of the <THEAD> tag will remain on the screen while the table body scrolls underneath it. The <THEAD> element must have the same number of columns as the table body.

<TFOOT>table footer</TFOOT>

Description: defines a table's footer.
Type: container.
Attributes: align, char, charoff, class, dir, id, lang, onclick, onDblClick, onMouseDown, onMouseUp, onMouseOver, onMouseMove, onMouseOut, onKeyPress, onKeyDown, onKeyUp, style, title, and valign.
Special notes: must precede the <TBODY> element.

The <TFOOT> element defines nonscrolling column labels that appear below the table body. You need to define the table footer before you define the table body (see Figure 7.19). Though it may seem a little strange to define the footer before the body, it is necessary because the browsers must be able to render both the header and footer before loading all the table rows that make up the table body. The <TFOOT> element must have the same number of columns as the <TBODY> element.

<TBODY>table body</TBODY>

Description: defines a table's body.
Type: container.
Attributes: align, char, charoff, class, dir, id, lang, onClick, onDblClick, onKeyDown, onKeyPress, onKeyUp, onMouseDown, onMouseMove, onMouseOut, onMouseOver, onMouseUp, style, title, and valign.

The <TBODY> container identifies the table's contents. The *table body* defines which rows in the table will scroll when the table is bigger than the browser's display area. There can be more than one <TBODY> element within the same table if more than one scrollable area is needed. Figure 7.19 illustrates the syntax for defining a table's body.

As you can see from this chapter, tables provide a new level of sophistication for our Web page designs. You will find that as your page designs increase in sophistication, so does the need to rough draft the design before you start coding. It is one thing to throw together a single, independent Web page; it is another thing entirely to start coding an integrated set of pages that will make up a corporate Web site. In the latter case, some preliminary design work is essential before the coding begins—if for no other reason than that the people paying you will want to approve the content and design first.

```
<HTML>
<HEAD>
<TITLE>Headers and Footers</TITLE>
</HEAD>
<BODY style="background-color: white">
<TABLE border="5" width="100%">
<CAPTION>Common Software Tools</CAPTION>

<THEAD>
  <TR>
    <TH>Icon</TH> <TH>Description</TH>
  </TR>
</THEAD>

<TFOOT>
  <TR>
    <TH>Icon</TH> <TH>Description</TH>
  </TR>
</TFOOT>

<TBODY style="text-align: center">
  <TR>
    <TD><IMG src="save.jpg"></TD> <TD>Save</TD>
  </TR>
.
. code was removed here to reduce figures's size
.
  <TR>
    <TD><IMG src="right.jpg"></TD> <TD>Right Align</TD>
  </TR>
</TBODY>

</TABLE>
</BODY>
</HTML>
```

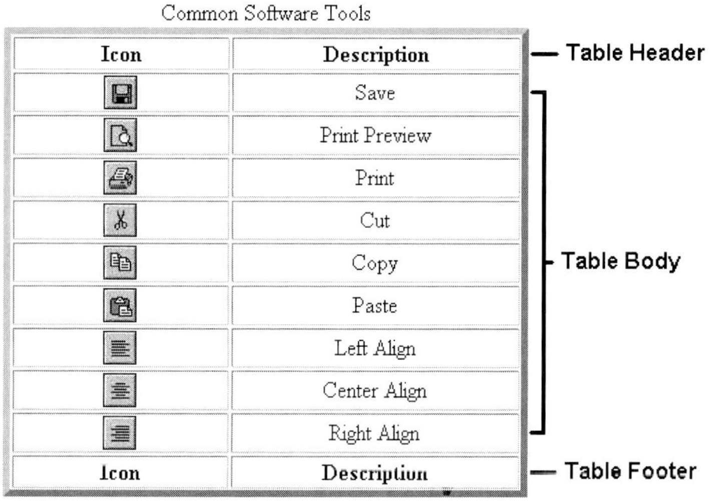

Figure 7.19 HTML code for table headers and footers that will not scroll off the screen when the body is scrolled.

Key Terms

Border
Caption
Cell
Column spanning
Frame
Padding
Row spanning
Rule
Table
Table body
<TABLE>
<TR>

New Tags

<TD>
<TH>
<CAPTION>
<COLGROUP>
<COL>
<TBODY>
<THEAD>
<TFOOT>

Review Questions

1. What is the definition of each of the key terms?

2. How is each of the tags introduced in this chapter used?

3. How do you build a table?

4. What is the default width of a table border?

5. What are three different HTML tags that can turn on a table's default border?

6. What is the recommended way to designate a table's width?

7. What is the difference between cell spacing and cell padding?

8. What can happen to a table if you make the background of the page too light or too dark?

9. What are two ways you can align a table within the browser' screen display?

10. What is the order of precedence for attributes within a table definition?

11. What are four attributes designed for use with speech synthesizers?

12. How is the **width** attribute's percentage option handled differently when used in a <TABLE> element versus a <TD> or <TH> element?

13. Which of the <CAPTION>'s **align** attribute values are recognized by the popular browsers?

14. What are two different ways the <COLGROUP> element can be used to format two or more columns?

15. How is the special form of the proportional width attribute "0*" interpreted by HTML-compliant browsers (4.0 specifications)?

16. How is the <COL> tag used to align numbers around the decimal point? Hint: "char" plays a big part in this answer.

17. What two problems associated with long tables do the <TBODY>, <THEAD>, and <TFOOT> elements address?

Exercises

7.1. Create a page that has three tables on it, each table measuring 2 by 3 and each having six elements. The page should be filled with "words" demonstrating how a table can be aligned on the left, right, or center of the page. Use a nice border and background color for the table. The title bar should display "Page Alignment" with your name and the assignment due date included within comment lines.

7.2. Modify the "My Favorite Images" Web page you created in Exercise 6.2 to display the five images within a table. The images should all be in the same column with a description and credit given in a parallel column. Don't forget to include the **alt** descriptions. Add the new due date to the comment line under your name.

7.3. Create a page that has six tables demonstrating the difference between cell spacing and cell padding. The **colspan** or **rowspan** attribute should be used in every table. The title bar should display "Comparison of Cell Spacing vs. Cell Padding" with your name and the assignment due date included within comment lines.

7.4. Retrieve the Homework home page you updated in Exercise 6.4. Add a new "Important Addresses" link to the home page. This link should take you to a new HTML document that contains a table of names and addresses (street and/or e-mail). At a minimum there should at least five names and table headers for Name and Address. The headers should have a different background color. Include your name and the assignment due date within comment lines.

7.5. Create a page that contains a table of sports statistics for four of your favorite athletes. It would be particularly cool if you could find royalty-free images of each player to include in the table. Include your name and the assignment due date within comment lines.

7.6. Retrieve your school's home page that you updated in Exercise 6.6. Add a new "Sports Schedule" or "Performances" link to it. This link should take the user to a new HTML document that contains a table listing the sports, theater, or music performance schedule of your choice. At a minimum there should be four events and table headers for Date and Time. The headers should have a different background color from the rest of the table. Include your name and the assignment due date within comment lines.

7.7. Create a table that demonstrates the four different valign attribute values for a table row. Use at least two different cell widths. The title bar should display "Comparison of Vertical Alignments" with your name and the assignment due date included within comment lines.

7.8. Create a 10 by 3 table of browser-safe screen colors using the color insert in the back of the book as a model. Use the <TBODY>, <THEAD>, and <TFOOT> elements with the table body, which should contain 10 rows. In the body, one column of cells should have the background color set to a specific browser-safe hexadecimal code. A parallel column should contain the related hexadecimal code as text, and a third column should contain the standard color name if there is one. Leave this cell blank if there is not a standard name. Use the following labels as the table header and table footer: "Color," "Color Code," and "Standard Name." Include your name and the assignment due date within comment lines.

## CHAPTER eight

S TYLES—SOME HAVE IT AND SOME DON'T

T he HTML 4.0 specifications reflect the new respect Web weavers have for the professional development of the Internet, specifically the World Wide Web. The maturation of the Web from infancy to what could be considered adolescence means acquiring more sophistication—maybe polish is a better word! The emphasis on style sheets as part of the new "dynamic" HTML is a prime example of this growing sophistication. We don't think in terms of developing a single page at a time, but collections of interrelated documents that require continuity among the pages.

Three types of style sheets

• linked style sheet
• embedded " "
• inline " "

217

What Is a Cascading Style Sheet?

Cascading style sheets (CSS) establish the precedence among style sheets and HTML containers that apply formatting changes to a given element within an HTML document. In this chapter we will focus on cascading style sheets that reflect the W³C CSS1 and CSS2 (May 1998) recommendations. Those recommendations specify that when more than one source tries to change an element's format, the cascading order of precedence is as follows:

1. Inline style changes, like <BOLD>, take first precedence (they are always used)
2. Then document-level changes specified within the <STYLE></STYLE> container (which is coded in the <HEAD> container) are implemented.
3. Next external files using the .css extensions identify changes.
4. Finally the default values established by the browser are used if no changes are identified in one of the preceding options.

For example, let's say that a browser's default font size is 12 points and it loads an HTML document that references an external style sheet that sets the font size to 14 points. Furthermore, this HTML document contains a <STYLE> element that sets the font size to 16. Finally, an inline **style** attribute sets a specific paragraph's font size to 18 points. When that document is displayed as a Web page, the paragraph in question is displayed using an 18-point font size. The remaining text in the page is displayed using a 16-point font size.

As you can see, cascading style sheets establish a means of determining which style to use when an HTML element is assigned conflicting style specifications. A general rule of thumb is that the style defined closest to the element takes precedence over any others.

Why Use External Style Sheets?

We introduced inline and document-level style sheets in earlier chapters. Both of these techniques are used to custom-design a single document. They take precedence over external rules and the default properties used by the browser. For home-brew Web designers, tinkering with their personal home pages, these design tools are sufficient.

The professional Web weaver, on the other hand, working with dozens, if not hundreds, of HTML documents, needs a way to easily maintain consistency among these large collections of pages. This is the main reason for integrating external style sheets with HTML documents. Professional authors need to keep their pages up to date and looking fresh. This often requires changing the format of documents within a site. Changing the font in a single heading is one thing; changing the level-1 heading's font in 28 related documents is something else—namely, a tremendous waste of time and effort! In addition, the possibility of mistakes creeping in increases proportionally with the number of pages that need updating. With external style sheets, you change the font once, in one place, and it is reflected in all the documents that use that external style sheet.

An external style sheet is downloaded separately from the HTML document and can be used by several Web pages. This reduces the size of all the related HTML documents, because they do not have to contain the code for inline and document-level styles. The smaller the document, the faster it is downloaded to the browser.

External Style Sheets

An external style sheet is a stand-alone ASCII file with a .css filename extension. Figure 8.1 shows the external style sheet we will use with a weekly Internet newsletter on travel tips. One of the newsletters is found in Figure 8.2. A close look at Figure 8.1 reveals familiar-looking HTML code. External style sheets use the same HTML syntax as the <STYLE> element. A left curly brace ({) follows the tag name. Properties appear after the brace and are separated from the desired values by a colon. Semicolons separate one property-value pair from another. A right curly brace (}) closes the style changes. The final semicolon after the last property-value pair is not required, but we strongly recommend that you include it. If it is there, it is easy to add another element to the style sheet entry, and it doesn't cause an error. Comments are added to the file between /* and */ symbols. This is a common convention for comments used in the C computer programming language.

```
/* External Style Sheet */
BODY {background-color: #FFFFCC}
        /* light yellow background */
H1, H2, H3, H4, H5, H6
    {
    font-weight: bold;
    font-family: sans-serif;
    color: #996666; /* rust  */
    }
H1
    {
    font-size: 30 pt;
    }
H2
    {
    color: #999999; /* dark gray */
    font-size: 16 pt;
    }
P
    {
    font-family: "Book Antiqua", serif;
    font-size: 12pt;
    }
UL LI
    {
    font-family: "Book Antiqua", serif;
    font-size: 12pt;
    list-style-type: square;
    }
```

Figure 8.1 HTML code for an external style sheet saved as an ASCII file with a .css filename extension.

```
<HTML>
<HEAD>
<TITLE>External Style Sheets</TITLE>
<LINK rel="stylesheet"
      href="nletter.css"
      type="text/css">
</HEAD>
<BODY>
<H1>Travelers Newsletter</H1>
<H2>For People In The Know and On The Go!</H2>

<P>In this issue we want to explore Australia. While half-a-world away, you can escape
the cold and damp of winter in the North and embrace summer again by traveling there.
The people are friendly. The exchange rates are favorable. And there are plenty of places
were you can get away from it all!
</P>

<H2>Postcards From Down Under</H2>
<P>One of the most pleasant ways to travel in Australia is by train. The rhythmic rumble of
the rails provides a soothing backdrop to the beautiful country as it rolls by. Riding the
rails gives you time to meet people, appreciate the country side, and to slow down the hectic
pace in which travelers may find themselves. AustRail passes are inexpensive and cover 8,
15, and 21 days of train travel.
</P>

<H2>Wine, Women and Song</H2>
<P>If you like fine, wonderfully priced wines, Australia is the place to visit. Many of the
metropolitan areas have wineries a short distance away. Ask your friends in the know about
wines if they have tried any of the Aussie wines. We'll bet they have only nice things to
says.
</P>
<H3 style="color: #999900">Austrialian Wine Growing Areas:</H3>
<!-- olive font color -->
<UL>
   <LI>Barossa Valley Wineries - north of Adelaide </LI>
   <LI>Hunter Valley Wineries - north of Sydney </LI>
   <LI>Margaret River Wineries - south of Perth </LI>
   <LI>Mt. Avoca Wineries - northwest of Melbourne </LI>
</UL>
```

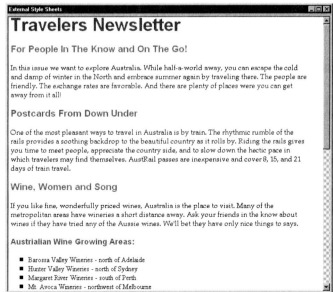

Figure 8.2 HTML code for a document formatted by an external style sheet.

More than one tag can be assigned new properties at the same time. For example, all of the heading tags are set to a bold, rust-colored, sans-serif font using this code:

```
H1, H2, H3, H4, H5, H6
    {
    font-weight: bold;
    font-family: sans-serif;
    color: #996666; /* rust */
    }
```

Tags that can be nested, for example, lists, are formatted by identifying the main and subordinate elements. In the following code the first-level items in an ordered list are set to be sequenced using Roman numerals (I, II, III, etc.): `OL LI {list-style-type: upper-roman}`.

If you want the second-level items of the ordered list to be sequenced using uppercase letters, the code would look like this: `OL LI LI {list-style-type: upper-alpha}`.

Be careful. If you make even a small mistake in coding your external style sheet, the processing of that sheet will simply stop at the error and not continue. We found this out the hard way when a hyphen between `font` and `family` was missing. None of the style changes that followed the line with the mistake were recognized, even though the syntax on these lines was correct. If your browser is having trouble applying the style sheet, check your syntax. Then check it again, and then have somebody else check it. The browser does not give any warning messages; it just ignores the rest of the style sheet!

Let's take a look at how you link an HTML document to this external style sheet file.

<LINK>

Description: identifies external files that relate to the document in various ways.
Type: empty.
Attributes: charset, class, dir, href, hreflang, id, lang, media, onClick, onDblClick, onKeyDown, onKeyPress, onKeyUp, onMouseDown, onMouseMove, onMouseOut, onMouseOver, onMouseUp, rel, rev, style, target, title, and type.
Special note: must be coded within the <HEAD> container.

The <LINK> tag specifies relationships between the current HTML document and external files. We will explore several variations of the <LINK> element in subsequent chapters. In this instance, we want to link the external style sheet nletter.css to our newsletter. To do so, we code the following in the document's <HEAD> element: `<LINK rel="stylesheet" href="nletter.css" type="text/css">`.

rel and type

The **rel** attribute of "stylesheet" establishes that the external file is related to the current document as a style sheet. The hyper-document reference (*href*) identifies the path to the style sheet file and the file's name. If the file is found at another Web site, then the complete URL needs to be included here. The **type** attribute specifies that the external file is text that follows the CSS conventions.

More than one <LINK> tag can appear in a document's <HEAD> element. These options are discussed in more detail in later chapters. For now, link your HTML document to a single external style sheet.

The external style sheet in Figure 8.1 was used to create the newsletter shown in Figure 8.2. The HTML code shown in Figure 8.2 is void of any attributes, except for a color change to the <H3> heading. This inline style change was included to reinforce the main point of this chapter: inline and document-level style changes are for custom, one-of-a-kind changes. Professional Web weavers use external style sheets to design their pages and make them easy to maintain.

Classes of Styles

As your page designs become more sophisticated, you may need to apply a set of style changes across multiple elements. For example, the masthead of the newsletter appears at the top of each newsletter document. It contains the name of the newsletter (Travelers Newsletter) and the newsletter's logo (For People In The Know and On The Go). Other mastheads might contain the publisher's and editor's name, year of publication, issue number, and so on. Our masthead incorporates centered level-1 and level-2 headings using a green italic Times New Roman font if possible. Otherwise, any serif font will do.

Instead of using inline styles to format each line, we can associate these style changes with the *class* name `masthead`. A class is a name given to a set of properties assigned to different HTML elements. The class name always begins with a period. The HTML code to create a class looks like this:

```
.masthead
    {
    color: #009900; /* green */
    font-style: italic;
    font-family: Times New Roman, serif;
    text-align: center;
    }
```

class

Once a class name has been assigned to a specific set of style changes, either in an external style sheet or by the <STYLE> element, it can be applied to elements within the associated HTML document. The code to assign the masthead to the first two headings in the newsletters follows:

```
<H1 class="masthead">Travelers Newsletter</H1>
<H2 class=masthead>For People In The Know and On The Go!</H2>
```

The relationship between the external style sheet, the document's HTML code, and the browser's handling of the page display is illustrated in Figure 8.3.

Inheritance

Notice that the masthead class says nothing about the font size, so the headings are displayed in the font sizes assigned to the H1 and H2 headings by the external style sheet. This is an example of *inheritance,* which means that an element

External Style Sheet

```
/* Classes used in the newsletter */

.masthead
    {
    color: #009900; /* green */
    font-style: italic;
    font-family: "Times New Roman", serif;
    text-align: center;
    }
```

HTML Code
Using
Class
Attribute

```
<HTML>
<HEAD>
<TITLE>External Style Sheets</TITLE>
<LINK rel="stylesheet"
      href="nletter.css"
      type="text/css">
</HEAD>
<BODY>
<H1 class="masthead">Travelers Newsletter</H1>
<H2 class="masthead">For People In The Know and On The Go!</H2>
```

Browser's
Rendering
of Code Above

Travelers Newsletter

For People In The Know and On The Go!

In this issue we want to explore Australia. While half-a-world away, you can escape the cold and damp of winter in the North and embrace summer again by traveling there. The people are friendly. The exchange rates are favorable. And there are plenty of places were you can get away from it all!

Figure 8.3 HTML code formatted by an external style sheet.

maintains (inherits) styles previously defined and will continue to have these styles unless overridden by an acceptable design element.

Every style property recognizes the inherit value. Web weavers use this value when they want the browser to pass on properties assigned to the element. But only computed values get inherited. Specified percentage values are not inherited.

Generic and Tag-Level Classes

The masthead example presented here is considered a **generic class** because it can be applied to a variety of tags. A **tag-level class** is assigned to a specific tag. In the following example, three special classes for the <P>paragraph</P> container are established:

```
P.left
    {
    font-family: Times New Roman, serif;
    left-margin: 3em;
    right-margin: 3em;
    }
```

What, you might ask, is an **em**? When we are using *proportional spacing,* an em is the measurement of the horizontal line space taken up by the letter *M. En* is the measurement of the space taken up by the letter *N.* As a result, a 3-em right indent would indent the paragraph the length of three *Ms*. In this typeface, 3 ems would be *MMM* long. Since screen sizes vary so much, we would recommend you set margins using relative sizes like ems or percentages.

```
P.right
    {
    font-style: italic;
    text-align: right;
    left-margin: 3em;
    right-margin: 3em;
    }
P.centered
    {
    font-weight: bold;
    text-align: center;
    }
```

These tag-level classes can be applied only to the <P> container. However, the HTML syntax is the same as that used with generic classes. The following code would right-align the text and display it in an italic font style by using the .right class just defined:

```
<P class="right">Publisher: McGraw-Hill</P>
```

<DIV>divide document<//DIV>

Description: identifies one or more blocks of text for the purpose of special formatting or identification.
Type: container.
Attributes: align, class, dir, id, lang, onClick, onDblClick, onKeyDown, onKeyPress, onKeyUp, onMouseDown, onMouseMove, onMouseOut, onMouseOver, onMouseUp, style, and title.

Once you understand how class attributes are used in page design and maintenance, then you will see uses for the <DIV> element and its smaller cousin <SPAN>. Consider the newsletter example we have been developing. Special travel advisories, or warnings, need special handling in our document. As a result, a new class, called advisories (Figure 8.4), is created to place a border around any advisories and print the text using a red italic font.

The <DIV> container works with block-level elements, while the <SPAN> container is limited to inline changes. In Figure 8.4, several elements, including a heading and ordered list, are enclosed within a <DIV> container set to use the advisories class for formatting.

The <DIV> element can be confusing to some people, because it does not produce any visible change in the browser window when used by itself. Enclosing several paragraphs of text within a <DIV> element wouldn't usually have any visual impact on the page. The <DIV> element is useful for marking off large sections of a page for purposes of identification. In other words, it can divide a large document into identifiable sections. If one of those large sections needs special formatting, the Web weaver can also use <DIV> to selectively apply style changes.

External Style Sheet

```
.advisories
   {
   border: #FF0000 solid 2px; /* red */
   color: #FF0000; /* red */
   font-style: italic;
   }
```

HTML Code
Using
Class
Attribute

```
<DIV class="advisories">
<H2>Travel Advisories</H2>
<P>The U.S. State Department has posted travel advisories for the
following countries until further notice:
</P>
<OL>
   <LI>Afghanistan</LI>
   <LI>Bosnia</LI>
   <LI>Congo</LI>
   <LI>Indonesia</LI>
   <LI>Sri Lanka</LI>
</OL>
</DIV>
```

Browser's
Rendering
of Code Above

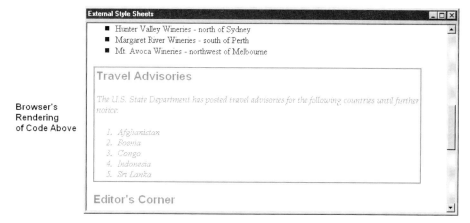

Figure 8.4 HTML code using the <DIV> container and class attributes for special formatting.

This container works best with the **id, class,** and **style** attributes. The **id** attribute assigns the block a name that can be used with intrapage links within a document and interpage links from outside the document. The **class** attribute allows the Web weaver to selectively change the format of any HTML elements that fall within the <DIV> container.

The **class** attribute is not the only way to make format changes using a <DIV> element. For example, the following code would right-align the elements within the <DIV> container:

```
<DIV align="RIGHT">
<H2>Editor's Corner</H2>
<P>For some of us the grass is always greener after a 4-hour flight to
   someplace else. However, your own backyard, the one you take for
   granted, may be someone else's exotic getaway.
</P>
</DIV>
```

In addition, the **style** attribute can be applied to the <DIV> container. In the following code, all the enclosed elements have a 1-inch left margin and are set to bold:

```
<DIV style="font-weight: bold; margin-left: 1in">
<H2>Editor's Corner</H2>
<P>For some of us the grass is always greener after a 4-hour flight to
    someplace else. However, your own backyard, the one you take for
    granted, may be someone else's exotic getaway.
</P>
</DIV>
```

Yet, the power of the <DIV> container still resides in the ability of the Web weaver to use it for assigning class-level formatting changes to groups of HTML elements.

<SPAN>span area</SPAN>

Description: identifies an arbitrary section of text for the purpose of special formatting.
Type: container.
Attributes: align, class, dir, id, lang, onClick, onDblClick, onKeyDown, onKeyPress, onKeyUp, onMouseDown, onMouseMove, onMouseOut, onMouseOver, onMouseUp, style, and title.

The <SPAN> container works something like the <DIV> container, but is usually used for inline text that needs to be handled in a special way. In the newsletter, a reader's comment is meant to be a travel advisory to others. Since the comment is within an ordered list, the <SPAN> container is coded to use the advisories class for formatting—see the highlighted section of Figure 8.5.

As mentioned earlier, the <SPAN> container makes no style changes by itself. It is only by using the class attribute that elements within the container take on new formats. The <SPAN> container can also work with the **id** attribute to identify areas within the document that can be linked together.

We use these parallel applications of the advisories class (see Figures 8.4 and 8.5) to illustrate how well-designed **class** designations can be used over and over. One factor that separates the professional Web weaver from the wannabe is the ability to create and use external style sheets with functional design elements and flexible classes.

Common Style Properties

In Chapter 4, we covered list item (<LI>) values associated with the list-style-type property. In Chapter 5, we covered font properties. What follows is an overview of other properties and associated values we feel are useful when designing Web pages. These properties can be used within the <STYLE> container and with tags that recognize the **style** attribute. All of these properties are part of the W³C's current specifications for HTML, and, as you have heard many times by now, they may not be recognized by older browsers.

External Style Sheet

```
.advisories
{
border: #FF0000 solid 2px; /* red */
color: #FF0000; /* red */
font-style: italic;
}
```

HTML
Code
Using
Class
Attribute

```
<H2>Reader's Comments</H2>
<UL>
   <LI>AJ from Hackley, Michigan liked our coverage of skiing in the French Alps, but
      thought we "shortchanged the cross-country skiing in Chamonix."</LI>
   <LI>PT from Boulder, Colorado thought we should have been stronger on
      <SPAN class="advisories"> "the warning to travelers in Thailand about people who try
      to befriend you in the marketplace. These people have ulterior motives that rarely
      dovetails with those of the traveler."</SPAN></LI>
   <LI>SY from Tacoma, Washington had several flashbacks when reading our piece on
      Guadeloupe. "Tell your readers to take a dip in the Cascade Aux Ecrevisses
      (Crayfish Falls).  They will never forget the experience." </LI>
</UL>
```

Browser's
Rendering
of Code
Above

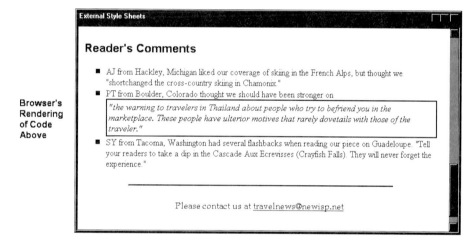

Figure 8.5 HTML code with <SPAN> container using advisories class to format text.

Text Manipulation and Alignment

The **style** attribute's properties shown in Table 8.1 include some of our old favorites. The color property allows you to change the typeface color using either the color keywords or hexadecimal RGB color codes we have discussed earlier (see the color insert in the back of this book).

The other properties manipulate the look or placement of text on the screen. For example, the text-declaration property runs a horizontal line over, under, or through the text as shown in Figure 8.6. When text-align is set equal to justify, the browser should align the words in a line with both the left and right sides of the screen.

Indenting the first line of every paragraph is common to many document designs. The following style code would indent the first line of the paragraph 3 ems to the right: P {text-indent: 3em;}.

The line-height and vertical-align properties play off each other. Adjustments to the vertical alignment move the text up and down within the vertical line space set aside to display a line of text, that is, the line height. You manipulate the vertical alignment when setting the text to subscript or superscript. The **base-line** is the horizontal plane on which text is normally displayed. You can see where that is by drawing a line connecting the bottoms of all the letters in the line of text. Note that some of the letters have *descenders*, portions (like the tails on the lowercase *g* or *y)* that hang below the baseline. Subscripted text appears below the baseline, and superscripted text is displayed above the baseline.

PROPERTY	DESCRIPTION	VALUES	SPECIAL NOTES
color	Changes typeface's color	Color keyword or associated hexadecimal number	See the insert in the back of this book for color options.
letter-spacing	Increases (+) or decreases (–) spacing between letters	normal | [length] | inherit	Length is measured in ems or centimeters (cm). Decimals are acceptable.
line-height	Determines the vertical space set aside for a line of text	normal | [number] | [length] | [percentage] | inherit	Number is the value to be multiplied by the text height.
text-align	Orients text left, right, or in the middle of a screen	left | right | center | justify | [string] | inherit	String applies to cell alignment in a table based on a string value.
text-decoration	Draws horizontal line through text area or turns area on and off	none | underline | overline | line-through | blink | inherit	Applies only to text and has no impact on images.
text-indent	Moves start of first line to the left or right of text area's default edge	[length] | [percentage] | inherit	Length is given in ems. Negative numbers move text left.
text-shadow	Overlays another character image left or right (x), up or down (y)	none | color | x y blur | inherit	Coordinates and blur are given in pixels (px): –x goes left and –y goes up.
text-transform	Standardizes the case of the text	none | capitalize | uppercase | lowercase | inherit	Capitalize converts the first character of each word to uppercase.
vertical-align	Orients text up and down within the vertical line space assigned to each line of text in the text area	baseline | sub | super | top | text-top | middle | bottom | text-bottom | [percentage] | [length] | inherit	Baseline = "0%" or "0cm". Positive values raise text above baseline, and negative values lower text below baseline.
word-spacing	Increases (+) or decreases (–) spacing between words	normal | [length] | inherit	Length is measured in ems or centimeters (cm).

Table 8.1 Text properties and values.

```
<STYLE>
H3 {font-family: sans-serif}
P.underline {text-decoration: underline}
P.overline {text-decoration: overline}
P.line-through {text-decoration: line-through}
P.gray {color: gray}
P.caps {text-transform: capitalize}
P.upper {text-transform: uppercase}
P.lower {text-transform: lowercase}
</STYLE>
```

Manipulations

underline

overline

~~line through~~

Capitalize TEXT

UPPERCASE TEXT

lowercase text

gray text

normal black text

```
<H3>Manipulations</H3>
<P class="underline">underline</P>
<P class="overline">overline</P>
<P class="line-through">line-through</P>
<P class="caps">capitalize TEXT</P>
<P class="upper">uppercase TEXT</P>
<P class="lower">lowercase TEXT</P>
<P class="gray">gray text</P>
<P>normal black text</P>
```

Figure 8.6 HTML code for text manipulations.

The line-height property is also used in conjunction with the font-size property. The standard way of figuring the line-height is to take the font-size (in ems) and multiply it by 1.2. This difference between the font size and the computed value of the line height is called the **leading** (pronounced "ledding"). When the line height is smaller than the font size, the tops of the letters on one line touch the bottom of the characters in the line above (called *bleeding*). The following code computes the line height by multiplying the ems of the current 12-point font by 1.2:

DIV {line-height: 1.2; font-size: 12pt} /* number */.

A Web author can also set the line height to a specific height. For example, this code sets the line height to a height of 1.1 em:

DIV {line-height: 1.1em; font-size: 12pt} /* length */.

In addition, the line height can be set as a percentage of the font size. This HTML code sets the line height at 120 percent of the 12- point font size:

DIV {line-height: 120%; font-size: 12pt} /* percentage */.

Background:color|image|repeat|attachment|position|inherit

The background property replaces the **background** and **bgcolor** attributes used within the <BODY> container. In Figure 8.1, we used the background-color property to set the body of the newsletter to light yellow. Background images are set using the background-image property as documented in Table 8.2.

The properties described in Table 8.2 provide the Web weaver with a greater level of control because they are used with a wide variety of elements. For example, the following HTML code would assign the image canvas.png as the background for a level-1 heading (see Figure 8.7):

H1 {background-image: url("canvas.png")}

```
H1
{
background-image: url("canvas.png");
font-size: 30pt;
}
```

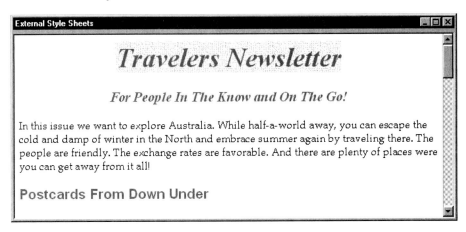

Figure 8.7 HTML code for setting a background image for a specific element.

Notice the different syntax of this assignment: rather than setting the URL equal to an address, we used the form url(path/imagename). Background colors are assigned to specific elements in the same way. For example, if you wanted to set a level-2 heading to appear as if it were highlighted, (black text on a yellow background), you could code the following:

H2 {background-color: #FFFF00;} /* yellow */

Top Left 0% 0%	Top or Top Center 50% 0%	Top Right 100% 0%
Left or Center Left 0% 50%	Center or Center Center 50% 50%	Right or Center Right 100% 50%
Bottom Left 0% 100%	Bottom or Bottom Center 50% 100%	Bottom Right 100% 100%

Figure 8.8 Examples of horizontal and vertical positioning.

PROPERTY	DESCRIPTION	VALUES	SPECIAL NOTES
background-attachment	Determines whether background moves when window scrolls	scroll | fixed | inherit	
background-color	Sets background color	[color] | transparent | inherit	Color is 6-digit hexadecimal code or color keyword found on the color insert at the back of this book.
background-image	Loads background graphic from designated URL	[url] (path/filename) | none | inherit	A background image takes precedence over the color.
background-position	Provides xy coordinates for positioning image within page	% | [length] | top, center or bottom | left, center or right | inherit	Length measurements can be in either inches (in) or centimeters (cm).
background-repeat	Determines if small background images repeat horizontally (x) or vertically (y)	repeat | repeat-x | repeat-y | no-repeat | inherit	Repeat makes the image repeat vertically or horizontally.

Table 8.2 Background properties and values.

The background-position property is used when the Web author wants to control the horizontal and vertical location of an image within the Web page. The horizontal coordinates are presented using the following percentages or words:

- 0% (left)
- 50% (center)
- 100% (right)

The vertical coordinates are presented using these percentages or words:

- 0% (top)
- 50% (center)
- 100% (bottom)

Therefore, the horizontal (x) and vertical (y) coordinates together should be interpreted like this (Figure 8.8):

- Top left or left top: same as "0% 0%"
- Top, top center, or center top: same as "50% 0%"
- Top right or right top: same as "100% 0%"
- Left, center left, or left center: same as "0% 50%"
- Center or center center: same as "50% 50%"
- Right, center right, or right center: same as "100% 50%"
- Bottom left or left bottom: same as "0% 100%"
- Bottom, bottom center, or center bottom: same as "50% 100%"
- Bottom right or right bottom: same as "100% 100%"

The following HTML code would center the image horizontally and vertically within the page:

```
BODY
   {
   background-image: url("map.png");
   background-position: center; /* 50% 50% */
   }
```

You can also use inches (in) or centimeters (cm) to identify the xy positioning. However, as with all the other opportunities for coding either an absolute number or percentage, we strongly recommend you use percentages (shown in Figure 8.8).

The CSS2 recommendations also allow for the keyword background to be used as a shortcut when assigning two or more background properties to a document. The acceptable syntax is to include the **color, image, repeat, attachment,** and **position** values within the curly braces and separated by spaces. The following code (1) would set the background color to light yellow if the image is not present, (2) use the image paper.png if the image is present, and (3) freeze the image when the screen is scrolled: BODY {background: light-yellow url("paper.png") fixed}. Fixing, or *freezing,* the background image is a technique that allows the Web weaver to make sure that the background image does not scroll off the first page.

Changing Link Colors

The colors used to identify links can be changed when the background color or image conflicts. The following code is used in place of the **link, alink,** and **vlink** attributes associated with the <BODY> element:

```
BODY {background: #FFFFCC; color:#0000FF}
   A:link {color: #FF0000}
   A:visited {color: #00FFFF}
   A:active {color: black}
```

Although it is possible to change the colors of the link, visited link, and active link, we urge you not to change them unless you are absolutely forced to. Changing these values can cause a great deal of confusion for your users. Users expect the unvisited links on a page to be blue, the visited links to be that funky purple color, and the active link to show up as red. Changing the colors is a very bad idea unless your background requires it. If that is the case, first consider changing your page design to accommodate the default colors.

Box Definitions

Each HTML element is actually enclosed within a virtual "box" that can be used to define the properties of that area of the screen that surrounds the element. That is, the properties that define the screen real estate occupied by an element apply to an area of a page generally referred to as a "box." The white space set aside for margins, together with any borders and padding that surround the HTML element, is known as the ***CSS box model*** (Figure 8.9). This model provides the framework for placing empty space around the element, called padding, just like similar white space within a table. The model allows for an optional border around the padding as well. It also gives the HTML author

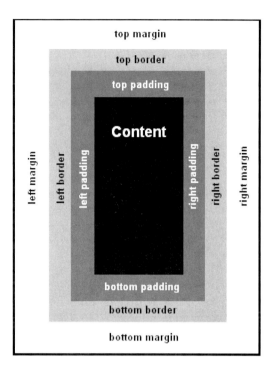

Figure 8.9 CSS box model.

control of the box's margins, always set to transparent, which define the outside edge of the box. A Web weaver uses the margin properties to specify where the border, if there is one, and the HTML element are positioned within the box. The box could contain a heading, text, image, or list. When this book was written, the major browsers only supported a fraction of these properties. It may take some time before they are fully supported.

width: [absolute] | [percentage] | auto | inherit

You can establish the horizontal space taken up by a CSS box using the width property. The width is given in a fixed length using ems, pixels (px), English measurements in inches (in), or metric measurements in millimeters (mm) or centimeters (cm). When a percentage is used, the width of the box is computed using the width of the element contained inside the box. When the **auto** value is used, the width of the box is determined by the values of other properties, for instance, margins, padding, and borders. This sample code sets a paragraph's width to 80 percent of the browser's display width: P {width: 80%}.

height: [absolute] | [percentage] | auto | inherit

You set how tall a CSS box is by using the height property. Like the width property, the height property is given in a fixed length, a percentage, or is set to **auto.** The following code establishes a paragraph height of 3 centimeters: P (height: 3cm}.

margin: top | right | bottom | left

Table 8.3 identifies all four margin properties. The only reason to individually identify each property would if the width of each margin is different.

PROPERTY	DESCRIPTION	VALUES	SPECIAL NOTES
margin-bottom	Defines transparent area at the bottom of the CSS box	[length] | [percentage] | auto | inherit	Length is measured in ems, centimeters or inches.
margin-left	Defines transparent area at the left side of the CSS box	[length] | [percentage] | auto | inherit	Length is measured in ems, centimeters (cm), or inches (in).
margin-top	Defines transparent area at the top of the CSS box	[length] | [percentage] | auto | inherit	Length is measured in ems, centimeters (cm), or inches (in).
margin-right	Defines transparent area at the right side of the CSS box	[length] | [percentage] | auto | inherit	Length is measured in ems, centimeters (cm), or inches (in).
white-space	Determines how tabs and repeated spaces are handled	normal | pre | nowrap | inherit	Both pre and nowrap recognize "\A" as a line break symbol.

Table 8.3 Properties and values that affect a CSS box.

The following code would set the top margin to 0.5 ems, the right margin to 2 ems, the bottom margin to 1 em, and the left margin to 2.5 ems:

```
BODY
    {
    margin-top: 0.5em;
    margin-right: 2em;
    margin-bottom: 1em;
    margin-left: 2.5em;
    }
```

The shortcut to this code is to use the `margin` property:

```
/* top right bottom left */
BODY {margin: 0.5em 2em 1em 2.5em}
```

The assumed order when four values are used is **top, right, bottom,** and **left.** The newsletter would look like Figure 8.10 if these margins were used.

When fewer than four values are used with the `margin` property, the following rules apply:

- One value: all margins are the same.
- Two values: top and bottom margins are the same, and left and right margins are the same.
- Three values: the first value is for the top, the second value is for the right and left, and the third value is for the bottom margin.

Here is the example from the CSS2 specifications:

```
BODY {margin: 2em} /* all margins set to 2em */
BODY {margin: 1em 2em} /* top & bottom = 1em, right & left = 2em */
BODY {margin: 1em 2em 3em} /* top=1em, right=2em, bottom=3em,
    left=2em */
```

Figure 8.10 Display of margins as follows: left, 2.5 ems; right, 2 ems; top, 0.5 ems, and bottom, 1 em.

white-space: normal | pre | nowrap | inherit

The white-space property determines just how the browser handles extra spaces and tabs. Normally additional spaces and tabs are skipped over, or, in other words, compressed into a single space. When the white-space value is set to **nowrap,** the browser also ignores all line breaks. On the other hand, when the white-space value is set to **pre,** the browser displays every space and tab in the associated container. With **nowrap** and **pre text,** line breaks occur only when the <BR> tag is encountered. Some browsers also recognize \A as a page break symbol.

border: width | style| color

The border box surrounds an element or elements with a line of various styles, colors, and thickness. The distance between the element and the border is determined by the padding, as illustrated in Figure 8.9. You can change the color, line style, and thickness (see Table 8.4) on one, two, three, or all of the sides of a CSS box.

The border-style, border-color, and border-width properties set values for all four borders. When a single value is given, every side is displayed the same way. For example, in the following code, the border's color, style, and thickness are set to blue, solid, and thin, respectively, for all four sides:

```
H3
    {
    border-color: #0000FF; /* blue */
    border-style: solid;
    border-width: thin;
    }
```

The following code using the border property provides a convenient shortcut to produce the same border property changes as the preceding code.

```
H3 {border: thin solid #0000FF} /* blue */
```

All of the CSS box properties have this type of shortcut.

PROPERTY	DESCRIPTION	VALUES	SPECIAL NOTES
border-color	Changes the color of the border	[color] | transparent | inherit	Alternatives: `border-top-color, border-right-color, border-bottom-color, border-left-color`
border-style	Changes the look of the border line	none | hidden | dotted | dashed | solid | double | groove | ridge | inset | outset	Alternatives: `border-top-style, border-right-style, border-bottom-style, border-left-style`
border-width	Changes thickness, style, and color of border line	thin | medium | thick | absolute value	Alternatives: `border-top-width, border-right-width, border-bottom-width, border-left-width`
border-bottom	Changes thickness, style, and color of bottom border	thin | medium | thick | [length] | hidden | dotted | dashed | solid | double | groove | ridge | inset | outset | [color] | transparent	
border-left	Changes thickness, style, and color of left border	thin | medium | thick | [length] | hidden | dotted | dashed | solid | double | groove | ridge | inset | outset | [color] | transparent	
border-top	Changes thickness, style, and color of top border	thin | medium | thick | [length] | hidden | dotted | dashed | solid | double | groove | ridge | inset | outset | [color] | transparent	
border-right	Changes thickness, style, and color of right border	thin | medium | thick | [length] | hidden | dotted | dashed | solid | double | groove | ridge | inset | outset | [color] | transparent	

Table 8.4 Border properties and values.

The border width can be described in pixels (px), millimeters (mm), inches (in), or with the keywords thin, medium, and thick. Figure 8.11 illustrates the different border styles. You can also designate none or hidden as border styles; in both cases the border width is set equal to zero, with the hidden property taking precedence when table borders conflict. The color property value is set using either the color keywords or hexadecimal RGB color codes (see the insert in the back of this book).

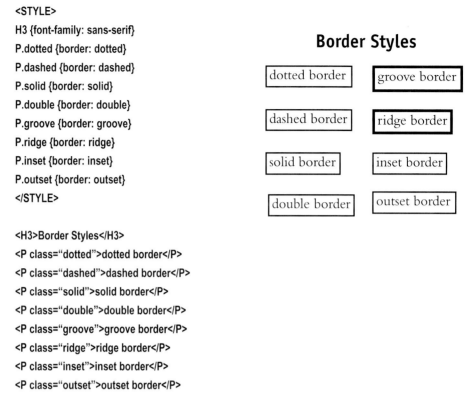

```
<STYLE>
H3 {font-family: sans-serif}
P.dotted {border: dotted}
P.dashed {border: dashed}
P.solid {border: solid}
P.double {border: double}
P.groove {border: groove}
P.ridge {border: ridge}
P.inset {border: inset}
P.outset {border: outset}
</STYLE>

<H3>Border Styles</H3>
<P class="dotted">dotted border</P>
<P class="dashed">dashed border</P>
<P class="solid">solid border</P>
<P class="double">double border</P>
<P class="groove">groove border</P>
<P class="ridge">ridge border</P>
<P class="inset">inset border</P>
<P class="outset">outset border</P>
```

Figure 8.11 HTML code for different border styles.

The ability to independently alter any side of the border creates a wide variety of coding alternatives. Shortcuts like border-style, border-color, and border-width allow the Web weaver to change any of the sides, the top and bottom, left and right, and each side independent of the other. When all four sides are changed, the presentation order of the values is as follows:

1. Top
2. Right
3. Bottom
4. Left

A sample of code that would make each border side a different color follows: H1 {border-color: red yellow blue green}. In this case the top border is red, the right border is yellow, the bottom border is blue, and the left border is green.

When two values are given, the top and bottom borders are the same, and this value is listed first. Then the value for the left and right borders is given. In the following code, the top and bottom borders are dashed and the left and right borders are dotted: H4 {border-style: dashed dotted}.

Three values after the property name would result in the first value setting the top border, the second value setting the right and left borders, and the third value setting the bottom border. To set the top border to a thin width, the left and right borders to a medium width, and the bottom border to a thick width, you could use this code: H5 {border-width: thin medium thick}.

Each of the borders can have the color, width, and style independently changed using the specific border property keywords shown in the "Special Notes" area of Table 8.4 as alternatives. Another way to approach changing the properties of a specific border is to use the border-top, border-right, border-bottom, and border-left properties. Acceptable values would include **thin, medium, thick, [absolute value], hidden, dotted, dashed, solid, double, groove, ridge, inset, outset, [color]** or **transparent** as outlined in Table 8.4.

padding: top | right | bottom | left

You can adjust the padding within a CSS box just as you can in a table. This and other table properties are discussed in Chapter 7. In both cases the padding is the white space between the content and the border. As shown in Figure 8.12, padding values are given in ems, inches (in), centimeters (cm), or even millimeters (mm), but they cannot be negative. Like margin properties, percentage values for padding properties are acceptable, and we encourage you to use either percentages or ems.

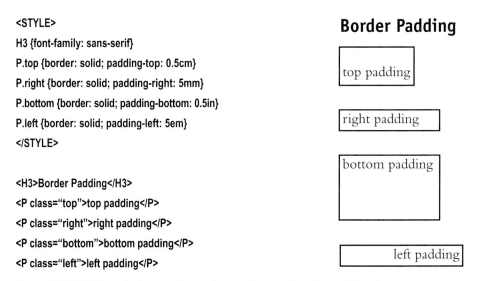

```
<STYLE>

H3 {font-family: sans-serif}

P.top {border: solid; padding-top: 0.5cm}

P.right {border: solid; padding-right: 5mm}

P.bottom {border: solid; padding-bottom: 0.5in}

P.left {border: solid; padding-left: 5em}

</STYLE>


<H3>Border Padding</H3>

<P class="top">top padding</P>

<P class="right">right padding</P>

<P class="bottom">bottom padding</P>

<P class="left">left padding</P>
```

Figure 8.12 HTML code for padding values set to centimeters, millimeters, inches, or ems.

The padding values can be individually set, as documented in Table 8.5, or set using the padding shortcut. When independently changing all four sides to different values, you could use this code:

```
BLOCKQUOTE
    {
    padding-top: 1em;
    padding-right: 3em;
    padding-bottom: 4em;
    padding-left: 5em;
    }
```

The shortcut for the same code would look like this:

```
BLOCKQUOTE {1em 3em 4em 5em}
```

As you can see, the same precedence rules apply, with top, right, bottom, and left being the designated order when four values are given. When fewer than four values are used with the `padding` property, the standard precedence rules also apply:

- One value: all padding is the same.
- Two values: top and bottom padding is the same, and left and right padding is the same.
- Three values: the first value is for the top padding, the second value is for the right and left padding, and the third value is for the bottom padding.

The color of the padding area is set by the `background` property.

PROPERTY	DESCRIPTION	VALUES	SPECIAL NOTES
padding-top	Changes thickness of white space between the top of the contents and border line	[padding-width] | inherit	Padding width is measured in %, em, cm, mm, or in.
padding-right	Changes thickness of white space between the right of the contents and border line	[padding-width] | inherit	Padding width is measured in %, em, cm, mm, or in.
padding-bottom	Changes thickness of white space between the bottom of the contents and border line	[padding-width] | inherit	Padding width is measured in %, em, cm, mm, or in.
padding-left	Changes thickness of white space between the left of the contents and border line	[padding-width] | inherit	Padding width is measured in %, em, cm, mm, or in.

Table 8.5 Padding properties and values.

float: left | right | none | inherit

The `float` property allows you to align elements side by side. For instance, notice how the text at the bottom of Figure 8.13 starts next to the image, not after it. The `float` property works this way with text, images, and tables. Content flows down the right side of a left-floated box and down the left side of a right-floated box.

The following code was used to display the image and line of text shown at the top example in Figure 8.13.

```
<IMG src="flamingo.gif">
Birds of a feather flock together and in some cases just buddy around.
```

To float the text as shown at the bottom of Figure 8.13 you would need to add this code to the <STYLE> container or the active external style sheets: IMG {float: left}.

no float Birds of a feather flock together and in some cases just buddy around.

IMG {float: left} Birds of a feather flock together and in some cases just buddy around.

Figure 8.13 Image set for no float and for left float.

clear: none | left | right | both | inherit

Sometimes you want a paragraph of text to flow to the left or right of an image or table, but you want headings or some other element to start underneath. The clear attribute ends the float property's control of the text flow. If you float text next to images as part of a page's design, then the following code would ensure that the headings would not accidentally flow to the right or left of an image: H1, H2, H3, H4, H5, H6 {clear: both}.

The values **left** and **right** would work just like <BR clear="LEFT"> or <BR clear="RIGHT">, discussed in Chapter 6, in that the respective float properties would be turned off at the time the **clear** property value was encountered.

Aural Style Sheets

The W³C and CSS2 recommendations opened a new design dimension for our Web pages—sound. Although using music, voices, and other sounds was not new to Web weavers, these recommendations outlined a level of control that made it possible to design the content to be read aloud.

An *aural style sheet* combines auditory icons and speech synthesis. ***Auditory icons*** are distinctive semantic elements that "bing" and "ping" before or after specific words are spoken. Applications for aural style sheets go beyond the needs of visually impaired users. In Chapter 15 we will explore some of these applications, but first you need know how the different aural properties work.

media

An aural style sheet is intended for computers with speakers, sound card, and a speech synthesizer. You designate style sheets as aural by setting the **media** attribute. The default value is screen, and other acceptable **media** values include braille, embossed, handheld, print, projection, tty, and tv.

Both the <STYLE> and <LINK> tags recognize aural as a value for this attribute. When you designate a document-level style sheet as aural, the following code works:

```
<STYLE type="text/css" media="aural">.
```

When you use external style sheets, your code looks like this:

```
<LINK rel="stylesheet" media="aural" href="nletter-aural.css"
  type="text/css">
```

Aural Properties

These properties present a new way of thinking about the content of a Web page. Instead of font families, aural style sheets use voice families. Do you want the text on the page spoken in a smooth female voice that spells out each word? Or would a rich male voice that pronounces each word work better? Would you like a bell to sound before a level-1 heading is read? Would you like the browser to say "goodbye" when closing a document?

The following code could be used to present a screenplay in which all level-1 headings are spoken in a male voice, preferably one designated as the "announcer." Walter Cronkite's voice would be good here. The voices of Norton and Trixie have several properties set.

```
H1 {voice-family: announcer, male}
P.part.norton
   {
   voice-family: norton, male;
   richness: 70; /* max 100 */
   pitch: low;
   pitch-rate: 80; /* max 100 */
   speech-rate: fast;
   stress: 90; /* max 100 */
   volume: loud;
   }
P.part.trixie
   {
   voice-family: trixie, female;
   richness: 40; /* max 100 */
   pitch: x-high;
   pitch-rate: 90; /* max 100 */
   speech-rate: x-fast;
   stress: 90; /* max 100 */
   volume: medium;
   }
```

A complete list of aural properties is found in Table 8.6.

volume: [number] | [percentage] | silent | x-soft thru x-loud | inherit

The volume property is representative of many of the aural properties in that you can set it with either a keyword like soft or a relative value from 0 through 100. A volume value of zero does not mean the same as silent. No sound is created with silent, whereas a value of zero means something can be heard, you just have to have really good ears.

Property	Description	Values	Special notes
azimuth	Changes the left/right orientation of the sound within a 360-degree surround-sound environment	[angle] | left-side | far-left | left | center-left | center | center-right | right | far-right | right-side | behind | leftwards | rightwards | inherit	Angle is set from –360 to 360 degrees (deg) with center=0deg, right=90deg, behind=180deg, and left=270deg or –90deg. Rightwards=+20deg and leftwards=–20deg.
cue-after	Provides sound after event as auditory icon	[url] | none | inherit	
cue-before	Provides sound before event as auditory icon	[url] | none | inherit	
elevation	Changes up/down orientation of sound	[angle] | below | level | above | higher | lower | inherit	Angle is set from –90 to +90 degrees (deg) with level=0deg, above=90deg, and below=–90deg. Higher=+10deg and lower=–10deg.
pause-after	Time after speaking an element's content and before starting next text	[time] | [percentage] | inherit	Time is measured in milliseconds (ms) and seconds (s).
pause-before	Time before speaking an element's content	[time] | [percentage] | inherit	Time is measured in milliseconds (ms) and seconds (s).
pitch	Adjusts frequency (pitch) of speaking voice	[frequency] | x-low | low | medium | high | x-high | inherit	Frequency is given in Hertz (Hz), with low being a lower frequency than medium.
pitch-range	Specifies variation in average pitch	[number] | inherit	Number ranges from 0 to 100, with 0 being flat and 100 being animated.
play-during	Specifies sound to play as a background while element's content is spoken	[url] mix | repeat | auto | none | inherit	When mix is used, the url sound is played along with background sound.
richness	Identifies how a voice will carry in a large room; rich carries well while smooth does not	[number] | inherit	Number ranges from 0 to 100, with 0 being smooth and 100 being rich.
speak	Determines how text is rendered aurally	normal | none | spell-out | inherit	Normal means language-dependent pronunciation rules are used. Spell-out means each letter is spoken.
speak-numeral	Controls how numerals are spoken; pronunciation is language-dependent	digits | continuous | inherit	With digits, 123 would be spoken as "one, two, three." With continuous, 123 would be spoken as "one hundred twenty-three."
speak-punctuation	Determines if punctuation is spoken	code | none | inherit	Code means punctuation is spoken.
speech-rate	Adjusts speed at which words are read	[number] | x-slow | slow | medium | fast | x-fast | faster | slower | inherit	Number is given in words per minute, with x-slow=80, medium=180, and x-fast=300. Faster=+40 and slower=–40.
stress	Specifies intonation peaks within voice inflection	[number] | inherit	Number ranges from 0 to 100, and what "number" means depends on language.
voice-family	Sets tenor of speaking voice; you could even use your own voice	[specific-voice] | [generic-voice] | inherit	Generic voices include male, female, and child.
volume	Adjusts a sound's dynamic range	[number] | [percentage] | silent | x-soft | soft | medium | loud | x-loud | inherit	Number ranges from 0 to 100, with x-soft=0, medium=50, and x-loud=100.

Table 8.6 Aural properties and values.

Furthermore, there is a difference between the `volume` property set to **silent** and the `speak` property with a value of **none**. The former takes up the same time as if the actual text had been spoken, but no sound is generated. The latter takes no time, and nothing is done. The values for volume are designed to allow the specific browser to accommodate differences in the environment as well. For example, a volume of 50 would produce a very different sound level in a browser used in a library than it would in a browser used in an automobile.

`cue`: cue-before | cue-after | inherit

Two of the aural properties include shorthand properties. The `cue` property is used to create auditory icons. It can set both the **cue-before** and **cue-after** values. If two values are given, the first value is **cue-before** and the second is **cue-after**. If only one value is given, it applies to both properties. For example, the following code initiates the playing of zing.wav before and after a level-1 heading is read:

```
H1 {cue-before: url("zing.wav"); cue-after: url("zing.wav")}
```

This code does the same thing:

```
H1 {cue: url("zing.wav")}
```

`pause`: [time] | [percentage] | inherit

Just as white space is a valuable design tool for visual designs, the use of pauses is important to aural designs. A pause is inserted between the element's content and any **cue-before** or **cue-after** content using the pause property. If two values are given, the first value is **pause-before** and the second is **pause-after**. If only one value is given, it applies to both properties. The following code pauses the speaking for 20 milliseconds after the cue has sounded and waits 30 milliseconds after the words are spoken before sounding the next cue:

```
H1 {pause: 20ms 30ms} /* pause: before 20ms & after 30ms */
```

This code sets both pauses to 10 milliseconds:

```
H1 {pause: 10ms} /* pause: before 10ms & after 10ms */
```

Sound Orientation

The aural properties even let you control which speakers will broadcast different voice families. You actually have control of sound reproduction all around the listener using the `azimuth` property if a surround-sound audio system is available. Speaker locations above or below the listener can be manipulated using the `elevation` property.

All of the properties listed in Table 8.6 are new in the HTML 4.0 specifications, and we will have to wait for a new generation of browsers before we can use many of them.

Frames were officially anointed in the HTML 4.0 specifications. Popular browsers began to recognize frames before these specifications were released, but older browsers (before Netscape 2.0 and Internet Explorer 3.0) will not support them. For that reason, you should use the <NOFRAMES> container to accommodate browsers that don't support frames.

To make matters more "interesting," you can build a framed document that appears *within the frame* of another framed document! This brings to mind the ancient Oriental curse, "May you live in interesting times." Although frames within frames—and, by extension, frames within frames contained in frames—can show the logical prowess of the Web weaver, they are of little use in most circumstances and can leave the user totally confused.

By the same token, the proper application of frames can create a user-friendly interface that integrates a set of Web pages. When using frames, special consideration should be given to the users' navigation needs. For example, you can build a narrow frame along one of the margins, top, bottom, right, or left (Figure 9.1), that contains a table of contents to your site. The user selects different choices from the table of contents, and the text and graphics for the chosen pages appear in the main frame. That way the user always has her navigation tools available, and she doesn't have to link forward and backward to peruse your site.

```
<HTML>
<HEAD>
<TITLE>Music Hall of Frames</TITLE>
</HEAD>
<FRAMESET rows="15%,*">
    <FRAME src="toc.htm" >
    <FRAME src="opener.htm" name="body">
</FRAMESET>
</HTML>
```

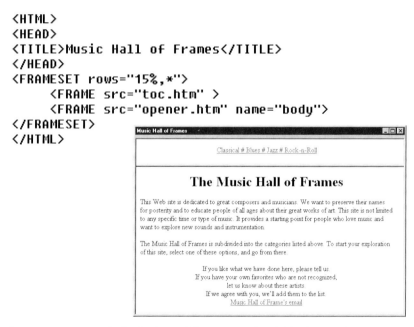

Figure 9.1 HTML code for horizontal frame rows in which the top frame acts as the table of contents.

Another factor you need to consider is the way the "Back" and Forward" buttons on the browser work, or, rather, in the case of frames, don't work. Instead of moving the user from page to page as usual, "Back" and "Forward" have a different effect in a framed document. Sometimes they will change the contents of the most recent active frame. Using these buttons may cause results that are very upsetting to your users.

Another major difference for Web weavers is the way "view source" works in a framed document. If you ask to "view source," you will see the source of the main frame document, with the <FRAMESET> tag, and so on. To view the source of the document displayed within the frame, you must right-click on the frame and choose from the shortcut menu either View Frame Source when using Navigator or View Source when using Internet Explorer. This, too, can be confusing.

To add even more interest to the life of your users, the URL of the framed document doesn't change, regardless of how many pages you load. That defeats the bookmarking tools most users have come to depend upon. Consequently, they may have difficulty finding their way back to a specific part of your site. To help them, you could put the URL of each page that is displayed in a frame somewhere on that page. Then they could at least copy and paste the URL into another document.

In addition, you need to ensure that each page presented in a frame has a way to link to the main page. That way your user always has a good navigation tool available. Let's look at a simple framed document to see exactly what we are talking about.

Frame Navigation

The print medium forces us to show you a series of "still" frames instead of the dynamic document. Figure 9.1 shows the first screen, called opener.htm. Notice the two frames, one with four navigation links (Classical, Blues, etc.) and the second, larger frame taking up the lower 85 percent of the screen.

Figure 9.2, shows what happens when the user activates the first link, "Classical." The larger "text" window now displays a second document, called classical.htm. Even though the larger window changed, the smaller navigation window did not. That is one feature of frames that makes them useful. The user can change the text in one frame without losing the control given by the navigation frame.

```
<HTML>
<HEAD>
<TITLE>Classical</TITLE>
</HEAD>
<BODY style="background-color: white">

<H1>Classical</H1>
<UL>
<LI>Bach, Johann Sebastian (1685-1750) </LI>
<LI>Beethoven, Ludwig Van (1770-1827) </LI>
<LI>Chopin, Frederic (1810-1849) </LI>
<LI>Debussy, Claude (1862-1918) </LI>
<LI>Gershwin, George (1898-1937) </LI>
<LI>Haydn, Franz Joseph (1732-1809) </LI>
<LI>Mozart, Wolfgang Amadeus (1756-1791) </LI>
<LI>Schubert, Franz (1797-1828) </LI>
<LI>Tchaikovsky, Piotr Ilyich (1840-1893) </LI>
</UL>

</BODY>
</HTML>
```

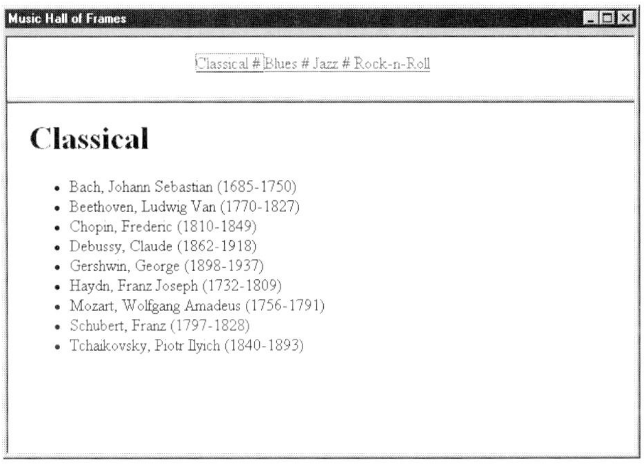

Figure 9.2 HTML code for the "Classical" link.

Now let's see what happens when the user activates the "Blues" link. As Figure 9.3 shows, the contents of the "text" window changed again. It now displays the contents of the document blues.htm. The HTML documents displayed in the frame can be any HTML document or any graphic that the browser can display. Using this type of "table of contents" (the code is shown in Figure 9.3) and a large display window can be very effective for a series of pictures. Use the small frame to allow the user to choose among the images and the larger window to display them.

```
<HTML>
<HEAD>
<TITLE>Table of Contents</TITLE>
</HEAD>
<BODY style="background-color: white">

<P align="center">
<A href="classical.htm" target="body">Classical # </A>
<A href="blues.htm" target="body">Blues # </A>
<A href="jazz.htm" target="body">Jazz # </A>
<A href="rock.htm" target="body">Rock-n-Roll </A>
</P>

</BODY>
</HTML>
```

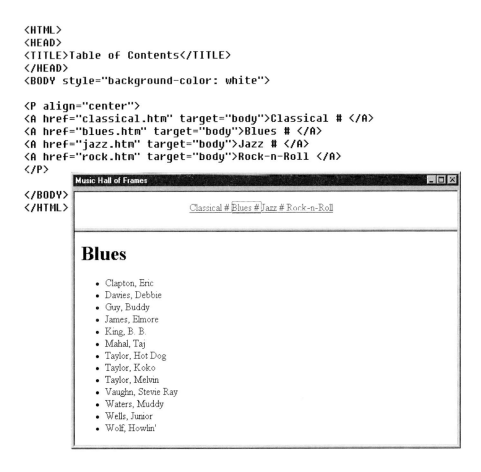

Figure 9.3 HTML code for the table of contents.

Figure 9.4 also shows what happens when the user activates the "Rock-n-Roll" link. Notice the scroll bar that suddenly appeared on the right side of the frame. That is another feature you can choose to control or allow the browser to control for you. In this case, the browser detected that the contents of the document were larger than could be displayed in the frame window, so it added the scroll bar to allow the user to see the complete contents of the document.

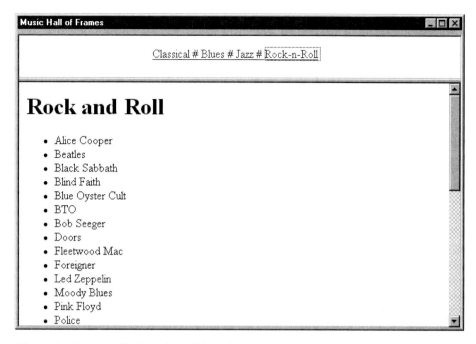

Figure 9.4 Browser display of scroll bar that appears when an HTML document does not fit in a frame.

Figure 9.1 presents the code that generates the frames that display these four documents. Notice that there is no <BODY> container. The <FRAMESET> container replaces the <BODY> container. This is the *driver,* or master document, that builds the frames, which are then filled by various other documents. This is also what the user sees if he activates "view source." We will explore each of the tags and attributes in detail, but for now, just look at the overall structure of the frame document.

Figure 9.3 presents the code for the menu in our frames example. Figure 9.2 presents the code for the classical screen. The other HTML documents are basically the same design as the classical screen but with different data. One of the important things to note is that the pages that are placed into the frames look like the documents we have seen all through our experience with HTML. That is an important concept. The documents that fill frames are simply HTML documents that are placed within frames. They need no special formatting to appear in a frame.

Formatting Frames

Although the documents that *fill* frames are just like any other HTML document, the document that *has* frames must be constructed differently from any HTML document we have seen so far. In a framed document, there is no <BODY> container. As you may have noticed in our example in Figure 9.1, the <FRAMESET> container replaces the <BODY> container for a framed document. This distinction is important, because if a browser encounters a <BODY>

tag before the <FRAMESET> tag, it will ignore the <FRAMESET> altogether. Thus, you can have a traditional HTML document with a <BODY>, or you can have a framed document with a <FRAMESET>, but not both.

<FRAMESET>framed document</FRAMESET>

Description: describes how the browser window is subdivided into frames.
Type: container.
Attributes: id, class, cols, title, style, onload, onunload, and rows.
Special note: cannot appear within an HTML document's <BODY> element.

The <FRAMESET> container defines a page that contains one or more frames. Although it is possible to have a page with a single frame, most of the time a Web weaver will have at least two different frames within the same page. It is also possible to have a nearly unlimited number of frames defined, but with more than four or five, the user could get lost, and the contents would be difficult to find. The <FRAMESET> container defines the physical layout of the page, determining how much of the real estate of the screen is given to each of the different frames.

The </FRAMESET> ending tag must never be omitted. Some browsers will not even build the page if this closing tag is left out. All you will see is an empty screen. There are four new attributes used within the <FRAMESET> container, **rows, cols, onload,** and **onunload.**

rows and cols

Together **rows** and/or **cols** define how many frames are on the screen. You can use either attribute alone, or you can use both attributes together to define a more complex layout. At least one of these attributes must be coded in the <FRAMESET> open tag. Both have values expressed either in absolute pixels or as a percentage of the screen. As you might expect, it is considered better to define sections of the screen as percentage values than to use absolute pixel sizes, because all screens are not of the same resolution as the one you use to build the document.

To make it easier for you to figure out the relative percentages, you can use the asterisk (*) for one of the values, as shown in Figure 9.1. The browser will fill in the asterisk with whatever is left over when your exact percentages are subtracted from 100. For this figure, given the code `rows="15%,*"`, the browser will replace the * with `85%`. This feature is also available if you choose to code your **rows** and **cols** in pixels.

The browser can help you further with your math: If you were to code `cols="25%,60%,25"`, the browser would actually build three columns that added up to 100 percent, with roughly the proportions you asked for.

Bear in mind that the browsers will also allow the user to resize the frames by dragging the frame dividers, unless you specifically prevent it. That means that a savvy user can undo all your careful frame size calculations.

onload and onunload

Usually the intrinsic events we see as attributes deal with mouse events like clicking on or moving over a place on the screen. The **onload** and **onunload** attributes are a variation of these events, which are discussed in detail in Chapter 13. In either case the attribute is used to activate a script or applet. For example, the **onload** attribute is activated when an HTML document finishes loading into a frame. The following code could be used to run the add-one( ) function:

```
<FRAMESET rows="15%,*" onload="add-one( )">
      <FRAME src="toc.htm">
      <FRAME src="opener.htm" name="body">
</FRAMESET>
```

This script counts the number of visits to a site. The **onunload** attribute works in similar fashion. It is activated just before the document is removed from the frame. These attributes are also recognized by the <BODY> element. They activate scripts or applets when the contents of a page are loaded into or unloaded from the browser's window.

Nested <FRAMESET> Containers

"Like a circle in a spiral, like a wheel within a wheel," you can include one or more <FRAMESET> containers within an outer <FRAMESET> container. This allows the creation of some fancy formatting, with different numbers of rows or columns across the page. For an example, examine the code and resulting screen in Figure 9.5. The left column (of size 40 percent), contains only one frame. It displays the document called frame1.htm. The second column contains the nested <FRAMESET> with three rows, occupying 33 percent, 40 percent, and 27 percent, respectively. The three documents—frame2.htm, frame3.htm, and frame4.htm—are displayed from the top to the bottom of that column. You need to be very careful as you construct your nested <FRAMESET>s, because skipping something as simple as a closing angle bracket may produce very strange results.

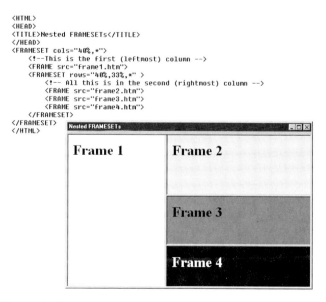

Figure 9.5 HTML code for nested <FRAMESET> containers that create complex screen layouts.

Now let's consider a slightly more complex nesting situation. Figure 9.6 presents the code for two nested <FRAMESET>s, the left one with two rows, and the right one with three. The placement of the </FRAMESET> tag in this example is critical. Although one frameset can be enclosed within another, the end of one frameset cannot occur after the beginning of another. In other words, you cannot overlap framesets as shown in Figure 9.6.

```
<HTML>
<HEAD>
<TITLE>Incorrect Nesting of FRAMESETs</TITLE>
</HEAD>
<FRAMESET cols="40%,*">
    <!-- This is the first (leftmost) column -->
    <FRAMESET rows="50%,*">
        <FRAME src="frame1.htm">
        <FRAME src="frame2.htm">
        <FRAMESET rows="20%,40%,*">
        <!-- This is the second (rightmost) column -->
    </FRAMESET>
            <FRAME src="frame3.htm">
            <FRAME src="frame4.htm">
            <FRAME src="frame5.htm">
        </FRAMESET>
</FRAMESET>
</HTML>
```

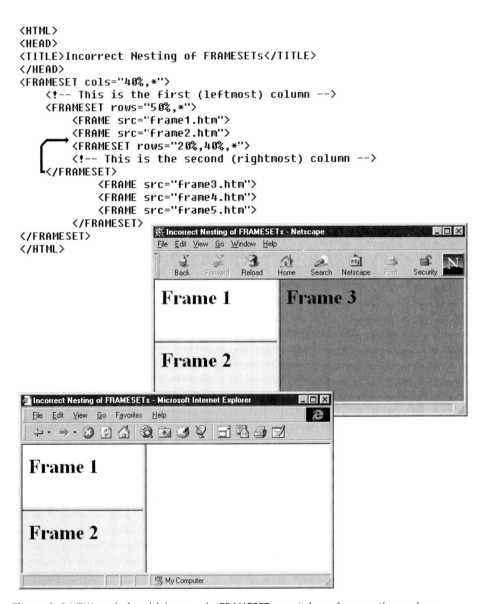

Figure 9.6 HTML code in which nested <FRAMESET> containers incorrectly overlap.

Note that the third frameset is started before the second is closed, causing an overlapping of framesets. The frameset that has two rows, each 50 percent, is still open when the frameset that has three rows, 20 percent, 40 percent, and 40 percent, is opened. The very next line of code closes the second frameset.

In Figure 9.6, both of the popular browsers become confused and take different courses of action. The Navigator browser knows that there are two columns of data to fill. It starts off the right column frame with frame 3, but gets confused by the overlapping <FRAMESET> containers and skips over frames 4 and 5.

The Internet Explorer browser, also shown in Figure 9.6, cannot infer a close to the frameset, so it ignores the new open <FRAMESET> tag. When it finds the closing tag, since it doesn't understand how <FRAME> tags can exist within a <FRAMESET> tag, it ignores the closing tag as well. The result is the large empty column on the right.

Figure 9.7 presents the corrected code and the proper screen display. The frames now appear as intended. Be aware that this example may have too many frames to be functional. It was designed only to illustrate nested framesets, not to show proper coding or good page layout.

```
<HTML>
<HEAD>
<TITLE>Correct Nested FRAMESETs</TITLE>
</HEAD>
<FRAMESET cols="40%,*">
    <!-- This is the first (leftmost) column -->
    <FRAMESET rows="50%,*">
        <FRAME src="frame1.htm">
        <FRAME src="frame2.htm">
    </FRAMESET>
        <FRAMESET rows="20%,40%,*">
        <!-- This is the second (rightmost) column -->
            <FRAME src="frame3.htm">
            <FRAME src="frame4.htm">
            <FRAME src="frame5.htm">
        </FRAMESET>
</FRAMESET>
</HTML>
```

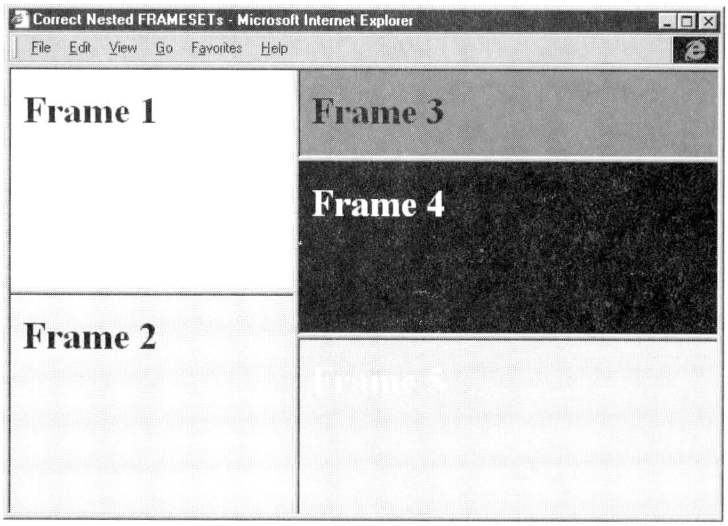

Figure 9.7 HTML code showing the correction to the nested <FRAMESET> container in Figure 9.6.

\<FRAME\>

Description: identifies the contents of a frame.
Type: empty.
Attributes: class, frameborder, id, longdesc, marginheight, marginwidth, name, noresize, scrolling, src, style, target, and title.
Special note: new with HTML 4.0 specifications.

The \<FRAMESET\> container is not designed to display any information, just to format, or structure, a page with frames. Only containers coded within the \<FRAMESET\> can present data. There are two types of containers in this class, \<FRAME\> and \<NOFRAMES\>. The latter will be discussed later in this chapter.

The \<FRAME\> tag allows presentation of one or more HTML documents within a specific frame on the page. Each \<FRAME\> container is controlled by a series of attributes defining the properties of the frame as well as specifying its initial content. You will find that early implementation of the \<FRAME\> element includes the \</FRAME\> closing tag. However, \<FRAME\> was introduced in the HTML 4.0 specifications as an empty tag. This is logical because the \<FRAME\> container can exist only within the confines of a \<FRAMESET\>. As any other tag within the \<FRAMESET\> will cause the browser to infer a close to the \<FRAME\>, the \<FRAME\> can be safely treated as an empty tag.

src

The value coded for the **src** attribute is the URL of the document, image, multimedia presentation, or any other displayable object that initially appears in the frame. If you want to create a very complex page, you can even use the URL of another framed document in one of the frames. This **src** attribute may well be the most important attribute for the \<FRAME\> tag, because with some browsers, if there is no **src** and associated value coded in any particular \<FRAME\>, that frame can *never* have any content.

Figure 9.8 provides an example of how the **name** attribute works. Notice that the \<FRAME\> descriptor for the second frame has no **src** attribute, but it does have a **name** attribute. In the screen display in Figure 9.8, Frame 2 seems to be missing its content. The link in Frame III would supply content to the area where Frame 2 is missing because it has a **name**—in this case, "area2".

If you are using Navigator and a frame has no initial content, trying to push another document into the frame is impossible. For example, Frame III contains this code: `<A href="Frame2.htm" target="area2"><B>Link to Frame 2</B></A>`. Navigator ignores the reference to "area2". It starts another browser with Frame 2 when the link is selected instead of inserting it into the frame named "area2". The moral of this story is that frame *must* have an initial **src** document declared when it is defined.

```
<HTML>
<HEAD>
<TITLE>Area 2 Missing src</TITLE>
</HEAD>
<FRAMESET cols="40%,*">
    <!-- This is the first (leftmost) column -->
    <FRAMESET rows="50%,*">
    <FRAME src="frame1.htm" >
    <FRAME name="area2"> ──────── Missing src
    </FRAMESET>
        <FRAMESET rows="40%,30%,*" >
        <!-- This is the second (rightmost) column -->
            <FRAME src="frameIII.htm">
            <FRAME src="frame4.htm">
            <FRAME src="frame5.htm">
        </FRAMESET>
</FRAMESET>
</HTML>
```

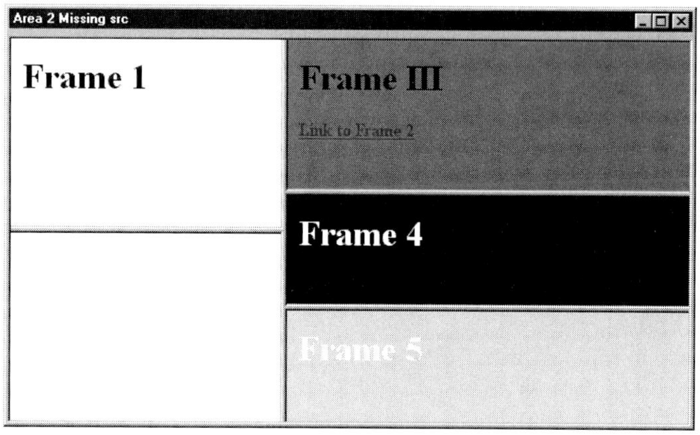

Figure 9.8 HTML code without a source (src) for frame 2.

name

The **name** attribute allows the named frame to be the target of other links, so other frames and scripts can change the content of a specific frame. You saw this in Figure 9.1 when we used a framed document to create a table of contents and a text page. In Figure 9.3, the horizontal links (Classical, Blues, etc.) in the table of contents page identified (targeted) the text page by the name "body". When the user selects one of the links, the related HTML document is opened in the other frame.

Figure 9.9 shows a simple modification of the HTML code in Figure 9.1, where **rows** is replaced by **cols.** The narrow column on the left is now the vertical table of contents (the related HTML code is also shown in Figure 9.9), and the larger frame on the right is the text area of the selected HTML document. As the user activates the various options from the menu on the left, the text that corresponds to that option appears in the frame on the right. If the user clicks on the "Classical" choice, the screen looks like the display in Figure 9.9. As with the earlier example, the navigation links do not change when new contents appear in the text area. This is an excellent example of the navigational power of frames.

Now that you see what the browser can provide, let's take a closer look at the code. The first page, coded in Figure 9.9, is the actual frame document. It has only two frames defined. The first is for the table of contents, since the frames are built left to right, top to bottom. This frame takes up 15 percent of the whole area of the frames. The second frame gets what is left (roughly 85 percent), and it is named "body". It is initially assigned the document opener.htm. The contents are shown in the screen display in Figure 9.1.

Figure 9.9 also shows the code for the table of contents document. This *menu* is nothing more than a list containing the links to the different HTML files that present the data. In each anchor tag, the **target** attribute is defined. That attribute directs the browser to place the contents of the HTML file listed in the anchor—for example, "jazz.htm"—into the frame or window with the name of "body". This is how one frame, in this case the table of contents, can affect another frame, the "body" frame. We will examine the **target** attribute in detail later in the chapter.

```
<HTML>
<HEAD>
<TITLE>Music Hall of Frames</TITLE>
</HEAD>
<FRAMESET cols="15%,*">
    <FRAME src="vtoc.htm" >
    <FRAME src="opener.htm" name="body">
</FRAMESET>
</HTML>
```

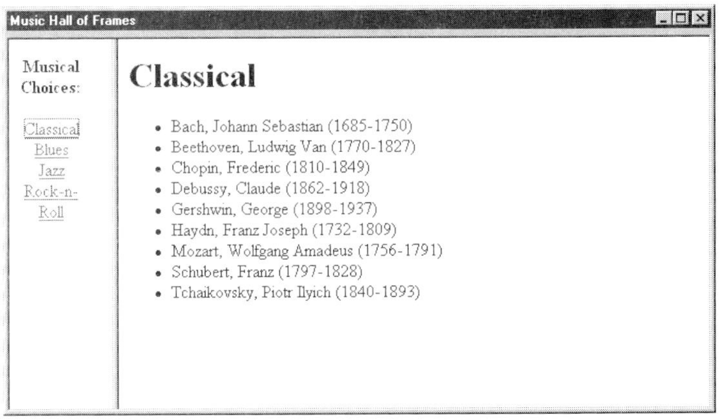

```
<HTML>
<HEAD>
<TITLE>Vertical Table of Contents</TITLE>
</HEAD>
<BODY style="background-color: white">

<P align="center">
<B>Musical Choices:</B> <BR>
<A href="classical.htm" target="body">Classical</A> <BR>
<A href="blues.htm" target="body">Blues</A> <BR>
<A href="jazz.htm" target="body">Jazz</A> <BR>
<A href="rock.htm" target="body">Rock-n-Roll</A> <BR>
</P>

</BODY>
</HTML>
```

Figure 9.9 HTML code for vertical frame layout with the table of contents in the left frame.

The code for an actual content page is shown in Figure 9.12. As we said be-fore, an HTML document that appears as the content of a frame requires no special formatting or special attributes. It is simply a regular HTML document placed within a subdivision (frame) of the screen.

id

All throughout this book we have been saying that the **name** and **id** attributes work in the same way. This is not the case with frames. Suppose you replaced the **name** attribute with the **id** attribute so the <FRAME> code from Figure 9.9 looked like this: <FRAME src="opener.htm" id="body">. The result would be dramatically different. Currently both Internet Explorer and Navigator would open a new browser window and display the linked files in this new window. Since the HTML 4.0 specifications do not address the issue of targeting frames using the **id** attribute, we do not expect this difference to be resolved in the near future.

scrolling

If the user selects the "Rock-n-Roll" option, the screen will look similar to Fig-ure 9.4, with the appearance of a scroll bar. Unless you force a scroll bar on every frame or prevent scroll bars from being created, the browser will create a scroll bar only when the contents of the document to be displayed extend beyond the boundaries of the window. You can prevent the generation of scroll bars by using the scrolling="NO" option with the <FRAME> tag. Figure 9.10 shows how the "Rock and Roll" page looks with the scrolling="NO" option set.

```
<HTML>
<HEAD>
<TITLE>Music Hall of Frames</TITLE>
</HEAD>
<FRAMESET cols="15%,*">
     <FRAME src="vtoc.htm" >
     <FRAME src="opener.htm" name="body" scrolling="NO">
</FRAMESET>
</HTML>
```

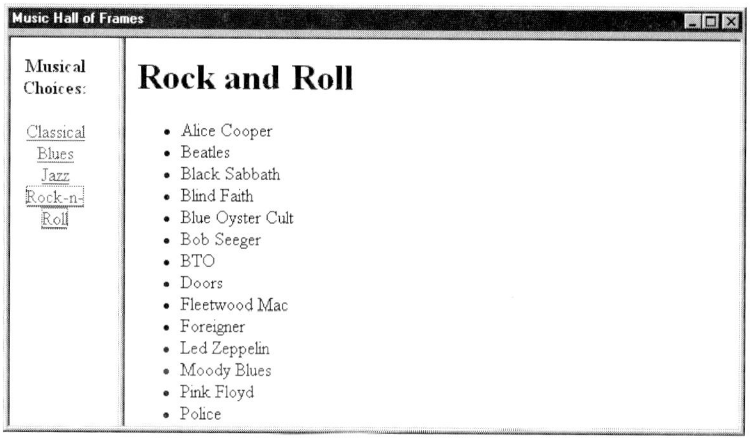

Figure 9.10 HTML code showing how the Web weaver can prevent the browser from displaying a scroll bar.

As shown in the "Rock and Roll" example, you can control whether the browser puts scroll bars on the frames you build. If you don't code this **scrolling** option, the browser defaults to scrolling="AUTO", which allows the browser to add scroll bars if the document's content is larger than the frame space allowed to display it. If the entire content of the document can be displayed, then no scroll bar is created. If scrolling="YES" is coded, however, the browser will always create a scroll bar on the frame, whether the contents extend beyond the boundaries of the frame or not.

In the previous example, the frame was created with a scrolling ="No" option. That prevented the browser from adding scroll bars, even though the content of the document was larger than the frame space. As you can see in the example, some of that content was unavailable. Text outside the frame will always be unavailable if there is no scroll bar to bring it into the visible part of the frame.

Usually it is best to allow the browser to use the default mode of "AUTO" and place scroll bars on the frame only when necessary. There appears to be no good reason to turn off scrolling.

noresize

In most cases, the user can control the size of the windows on his screen simply by dragging the frame dividers. Thus, he can compensate for any errors in your "guess" as to the best fit. This ability of the user to adjust a frame is usually the browser's default option. But if you have an image that must fit exactly in a specific size space, and you have placed it in a frame of that exact size, you may wish to restrict the user from playing with the size of that frame. You can do so by coding the **noresize** attribute to the <FRAME> tag. For instance, we could lock in the size of the left frame with this code:

```
<FRAMESET cols="15%,*">
      <FRAME src="vtoc.htm" noresize="YES">
      <FRAME src="opener.htm" name="body">
</FRAMESET>
```

Bear in mind, the **noresize** option is set for the whole frame, and for the life of the frame. Like the **scrolling** option, this attribute sets the characteristics of the frame, not of a specific document shown in the frame. If you code the **noresize** attribute, the frame will *never* be resizable.

If you have only a few frames on your document, let's say three columns, and you code **noresize** on the center frame, you have effectively locked in the horizontal size of all three frames. The two center dividers cannot be moved, so the size of all three frames is fixed. Use this option very judiciously. It is occasionally necessary, but most of the time the user can benefit from being able to resize the frame.

marginheight and marginwidth

The browsers usually place a minimum amount of space between the frame edges and the text within the frame. In some cases this space is so small that parts of the letters may be lost along the margins. To create a better visual effect, especially in a tight frame, use the **marginheight** and **marginwidth** attributes to add spacing along the edges of the frame.

Figure 9.11 presents the code for setting margins in our frame document. The margins are excessively large, chosen to illustrate how the presentation of the document can differ based on these attributes. Normally a margin of 5 to 10 pixels is sufficient to visually separate the contents from the frame. Here the margin height is coded for 25 pixels and the margin width for 50 pixels. To see the difference, compare the screen display in Figure 9.11 with Figure 9.1. The default margins are used in Figure 9.1.

```
<HTML>
<HEAD>
<TITLE>Music Hall of Frames</TITLE>
</HEAD>
<FRAMESET cols="15%,*" title="Music Hall of Frames">
     <FRAME src="vtoc.htm">
     <FRAME src="opener.htm"
          name="body"
          frameborder="0"
          marginheight="25"
          marginwidth="50">
</FRAMESET>
</HTML>
```

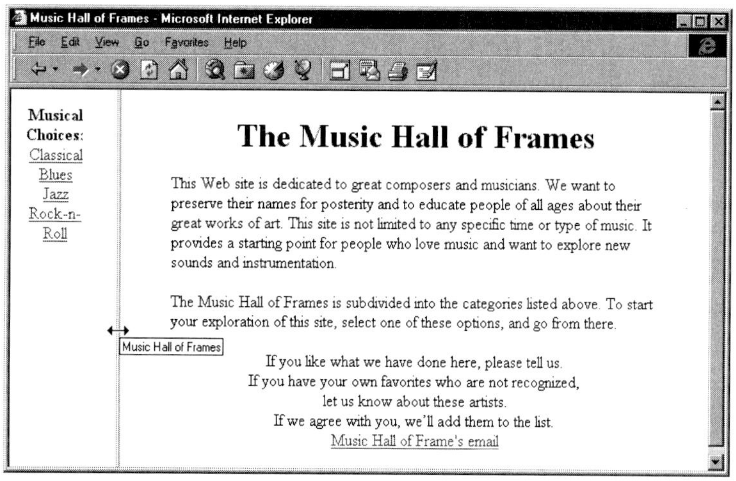

Figure 9.11 HTML code for a "body" frame with a margin height of 25 pixels and a margin width of 50 pixels.

title and longdesc

Both the **title** and **longdesc** attributes are used to describe the related object. The **title** attribute provides a short two- or three-word description. The description provided by the **title** attribute can be used as the text for a *tool tip message,* the popup text box that appears when the screen pointer moves over an object on the screen. Internet Explorer displays the "Music Hall of Frames" tool tip shown in Figure 9.11 using the **title** attribute found in the <FRAMESET> element. The code looks like this: <FRAMESET cols="15%,*" title="Music Hall of Frames">.

The **longdesc** attribute specifies a longer description of the contents, one that goes beyond the **title** attribute's description. The text that makes up the long description is stored as an independent file. You set the **longdesc** attribute equal to the text file's URL, path, and filename. With respect to frames, both of these attributes could be useful for nonvisual users cruising the Web.

frameborder

The **frameborder** attribute is used to turn the frame border on (1) or off (0). The browser recognizes only the values 1 or 0. A frame's border is turned off with the following code: <FRAME src="vtoc.htm" frameborder="0">. Similar code is used in Figure 9.11.

Both the popular browsers also recognize **frameborder** as part of the <FRAMESET> element as shown in Figure 9.12. All of the borders are turned off with this code: <FRAMESET cols="40%,*" frameborder="0">. Navigator will completely eliminate any borders between frames when the **frameborder** attribute is set equal to "0". Some versions of Internet Explorer still display part of the border, as shown in Figure 9.11.

```
<HTML>
<HEAD>
<TITLE>No Frame Borders</TITLE>
</HEAD>
<FRAMESET cols="40%,*" frameborder="0">
    <!-- This is the first (leftmost) column -->
    <FRAMESET rows="50%,*">
        <FRAME src="frame1.htm">
        <FRAME src="frame2.htm">
    </FRAMESET>
        <FRAMESET rows="20%,40%,*">
        <!-- This is the second (rightmost) column -->
            <FRAME src="frame3.htm">
            <FRAME src="frame4.htm">
            <FRAME src="frame5.htm">
        </FRAMESET>
</FRAMESET>
</HTML>
```

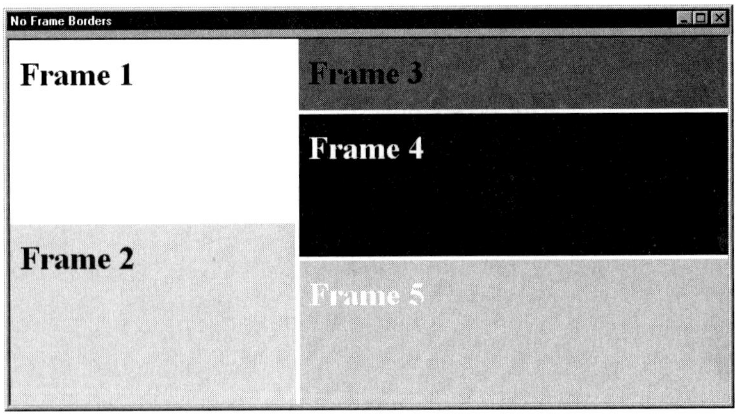

Figure 9.12 HTML code for turning off the frame borders.

<NOFRAMES>no frames</NOFRAMES>

Description: provides content for browsers that do not recognize
the <FRAMESET> element.
Type: container.
Attributes: none.
Special note: introduced in HTML 4.0 specifications.

Not all browsers support frames. Mosaic and early versions of Netscape and
Internet Explorer do not support this extension to the HTML language.
Browsers that do not recognize HTML codes recommended by the W^{3}C specifications are referred to as ***noncompliant browsers.*** For users with noncompliant frame browsers, HTML has the <NOFRAMES>. . .</NOFRAMES>
container. Although the use of this tag is not required by the syntax of HTML,
you should always code it within your framed document. Otherwise your page
will be worthless for users with browsers that don't support frames. Whenever
you design a set of documents, always make the contents available to the
widest audience.

You can code any HTML tag set within the <NOFRAMES> container,
even a <BODY> tag. A frame-compliant browser will ignore the contents of
the <NOFRAMES> container, while a browser that doesn't support frames
will usually display them.

The way <NOFRAMES> works takes advantage of the flexibility of the
browsers. When a browser encounters a tag it doesn't know, it ignores that tag.
Because a noncompliant browser ignores all the frame tags, including the
<NOFRAMES> tag, all it finds to display are the contents of the
<NOFRAMES> container. There are a few very strict browsers that will not
even display the contents of a <NOFRAMES> container and will generate an
error message instead, but they are in the distinct minority.

Figure 9.13 shows how a <NOFRAMES> container would be coded and
displayed in a noncompliant browser. In this case the browser is Mosaic 3.0.
The message within the <NOFRAMES> element explains to users with noncompliant browsers that they need to either upgrade their browser or link to
<u>index</u>. The link will take them to a table of contents document called
nftoc.htm specifically written for noncompliant browsers. When invoked this
way, the table of contents page takes up the whole browser window, as shown
in the figure.

```
<HTML>
<HEAD>
<TITLE>Music Hall of Frames</TITLE>
</HEAD>
<FRAMESET cols="15%,*">
    <FRAME src="vtoc.htm" >
    <FRAME src="opener.htm" name="body">

<NOFRAMES>
<H2>Non-Frame-Compliant Browser</H2>
I am sorry, but this document is designed to be read by a frame compliant browser.<BR>
If you see this message, your browser doesn't support frames.<BR>
You can either update your current browser to one that supports framing, or you can see
the same content, page by page, using the <A HREF="nftoc.htm">index</A> and the "BACK"
button. Sorry for the inconvenience.<BR>
The Management<BR>
</NOFRAMES>

</FRAMESET>
</HTML>
```

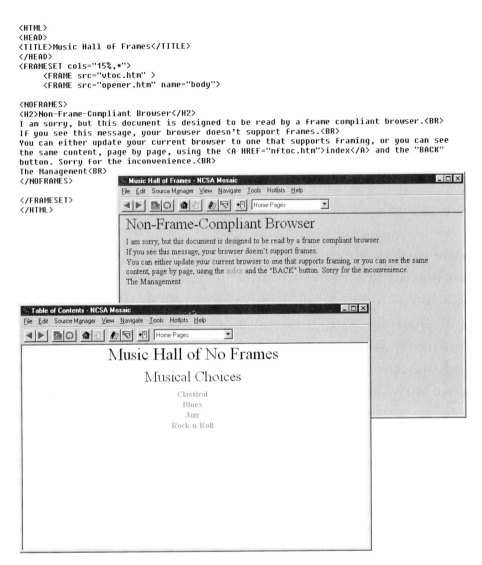

Figure 9.13 Adding the <NOFRAMES> element for non-frame-compliant browsers.

When the user activates one of the links, the browser ignores the **target** attribute. Why? Because there is no frame with that name, the target doesn't exist; therefore, the browser loads the image onto the current screen, replacing the table of contents. To get back to the table of contents, the user merely activates the "Back" button. However, there should also be a link back to the opening page from each of the informational documents. A strategy for handling this situation is discussed in the next section in regard to the special "_parent" target. This is one of several special applications of the **target** attribute you need to know about.

target

As we saw throughout the examples of framed windows, you can specify a label, or **target** attribute, in an anchor (<A>) tag and thus direct the browser to load the document referenced in the **href** into the window or frame specified. For example, the line, `<A href="blues.htm" target="body">Blues</A>`, loads the HTML document `blues.htm` into the window or frame labeled "body" when the user activates the <u>Blues</u> link. If there is no frame with the **name** attribute of "body", the browser will create a new window and call it "body".

Let's suppose the Web weaver makes a mistake coding the anchor and calls the target "boddy". When the <u>Blues</u> link is selected, the browser cannot put the document into the frame specified in the anchor, because the name "boddy" doesn't match the known **target** name of "body". Therefore, the browser opens a new window and places the document there. In some cases a mistake like this may even cause the operating system to create a second browser session. It is very important that you code accurate tags when you choose to use targets from a link.

Another common mistake is to forget to include the target with the link. If the user chooses the instructions link from this menu, the framed document will be overlaid by a standard window containing only the data found in the `blues.htm` document. As just mentioned, when the browser encounters a document that has no target, it will create a new window for that new document. That sounds almost like a rule, so there must be an exception to it. Our next subject, the <BASE> tag, provides that exception.

<BASE>

Description: specifies a document's base URL explicitly. Relative path references then use the base URL as a reference point.
Type: empty.
Attributes: href and target.
Special note: Must be placed within the <HEAD></HEAD> container.

You can set a default target for each link that uses a specified target by coding the <BASE> tag. Thus, we could change the code in the table of contents page as shown in Figure 9.14. This HTML code would produce exactly the same results as the code in Figure 9.9. Notice that the individual links no longer specify a target, yet the page behaves exactly the same as when they did. The <BASE> tag with the **target** attribute sets the target for any link that is not explicitly specified. This default **target** works only on the page that has the <BASE> tag, but it will save us some keyboard time and ensure that we have a consistent presentation.

```
<HTML>
<HEAD>
<TITLE>Vertical Table of Contents</TITLE>
<BASE target="body">
</HEAD>
<BODY style="background-color: white">


<P align="center">
<B>Musical Choices:</B> <BR>
<A href="classical.htm">Classical</A> <BR>
<A href="blues.htm">Blues</A> <BR>
<A href="jazz.htm">Jazz</A> <BR>
<A href="rock.htm">Rock-n-Roll</A> <BR>
</P>


</BODY>
</HTML>
```

Figure 9.14 HTML code using the <BASE> tag to identify "body" as the default target.

Special Targets

The browsers support four special targets that serve particular needs. These special target names are called *reserve names* because their spellings have been set aside by the W^{3}C to have a specific meaning that cannot be changed. All of these reserve names start with an underscore. The browser will ignore any other target coded with an underscore.

_blank

To initiate a newly opened window, the browser uses the _blank target. It is usually used for unnamed windows. There is no real use for this target by most Web weavers; it is included here for completeness.

_self

If an anchor tag (<A>) does not specify a target value, the _self target is the default target. This target points to the current frame or window, that is, the one containing the document that is the source for the anchor, <A>. The _self tag is useful when the Web weaver wants to place a particular document into the frame or window that called it but has a <BASE> target defined. Otherwise this tag is redundant and unnecessary.

_parent

The _parent target causes the document to be loaded into the *parent window,* which is the window containing the frameset that has the actual hypertext reference. If there is only one level of frame structure, then this is the same as the target of _top.

In our discussion of the <NOFRAMES> element, we mentioned that a good Web weaver provides links back to the opening page. However, this becomes a little tricky when trying to write HTML code that supports both frame-compliant and noncompliant browsers. One workable solution is to include the following code at the bottom of all the information windows: `<A href="mhf.htm" target="_parent">Back to Opening Page</A>`.

Non-frame-compliant browsers ignore the target attribute and return to the opening page (`mhf.htm`) shown in Figure 9.13. Frame-compliant browsers also return back to the opening page and maintain the original frame layout of the parent page. As shown in Figure 9.11, the original layout contained two vertical frames: the left 15 percent of the screen area and the right 85 percent of the screen area.

Interesting results occur in frame-compliant browsers when you do not set `target="_parent"`. Suppose the following code is used as a backward link to the opening page: `<A href="mhf.htm">Back to Opening Page</A>`. A frame-compliant browser would place the opening page inside the left frame as shown in Figure 9.15.

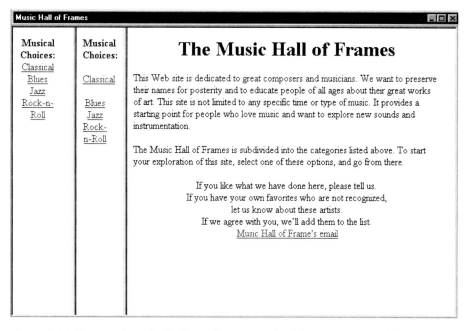

Figure 9.15 Error that resulted when a frame-compliant browser reopened the <FRAMESET> page without returning to the parent window.

_top

The most important special target is _top. It causes the browser to load the document into a window without any frames, that is, the top, or initial, window. If you are going to send your user off your Web site to a remote page (one that is not part of your Web site), you probably won't want to keep your menu on the screen. It would make little sense to your user. As a general rule, when using frames or special formatting, you should always code a target of _top for a link to a remote document. That way, the new document will be loaded into the entire contents of the browser window, not just the portion allocated by your formatting. The code would look like this:

```
<A href="http://www.masters.org/masters.htm" target="_top">Masters of
Music</A>
```

<IFRAME>inline frame</IFRAME>

Description: inserts a frame in the same line with text and other objects.
Type: container.
Attributes: align, class, frameborder, height, id, longdesc, marginheight, marginwidth, name, scrolling, src, style, target, title, and width.
Special note: new with HTML 4.0 specifications.

Inline frames are a new wrinkle the W^{3}C inserted into the world of frames with the HTML 4.0 specifications. The <IFRAME> element allows a Web weaver to insert a frame within a line of text. It is no different than inserting any inline element within a section of text. The **align, height,** and **width** attributes allow the author some control over the size and placement of the frame. The information to be inserted inline is identified by the **src** attribute. The HTML code to create a 200-pixel by 500-pixel inline frame looks like this:

```
<IFRAME src="document.htm" height="200" width="500">
Text displayed by non-compliant browsers.
</IFRAME>
```

Any text included within the <IFRAME> container is displayed only by non-compliant browsers. As you can see in Figure 9.16, this text is ignored by compliant browsers.

The final variation of the Music Hall of Frames, now called the Music Hall of Inline Frames, is shown in Figure 9.16. As you can see, we have employed an *indexed sequential* design with *intrapage* links to each of the inline frames. The frames are all 100 pixels tall and 400 pixels wide. The **name** attribute assigns each frame a unique target name that is used as the hypertext reference (**href**) in the anchors at the top of the page.

```
<P>
The Music Hall of Frames is subdivided into the categories listed below. to start your
exploration of this site, select one of these options, and go from there.
</P>
<DIV align="center">
<A href="#classical">Classical # </A>
<A href="#blues">Blues # </A>
<A href="#jazz">Jazz # </A>
<A href="#rock">Rock-n-Roll</A>
</DIV>
<BR>
<IFRAME src="classical.htm"
    name="classical.htm"
    height="100"
    width="400">
Text in Classical frame can be viewed at
<A href="classical.hmt">http://mhfdemo.com/classical.htm</A>
<IFRAME>
<BR>
<BR>
<IFRAME src="blues.htm"
    name="blues"
    height="100"
    width="400">
Text in Blues frame can be viewed at
<A href="blues.htm">http://mhfdemo.com/blues.htm</A>
<IFRAME>
<BR>
<BR>
<IFRAME src="jazz.htm"
    name="jazz"
    height="100"
    width="400">
Text in Jazz frame can be viewed at
<A href="jazz.htm">http://mhfdemo.com/jazz.htm</A>
<IFRAME>
<BR>
<BR>
<IFRAME src="rock.htm"
    name="rock"
    height="100"
    width="400">
Text in Rock-n-Roll frame can be viewed at
<A href="rock.htm">http://mhfdemo.com/rock.htm</A>
</IFRAME>
```

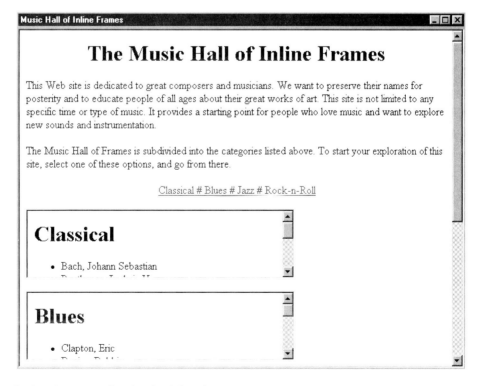

Figure 9.16 HTML code showing an application for inline frames.

Final Comments

Now that the W^{3}C has endorsed frames as an HTML element, it is easier for us to advocate using them in your HTML code. Nevertheless, as we have said throughout this chapter, professional Web weavers still need to account for non-frame-compliant browsers. Furthermore, although frames provide some nice navigation features and a certain amount of consistency in Web page design, they can also cause navigation problems, especially when bookmarks and favorites are employed. To design an easy-to-navigate frame-based Web site takes a lot of work. Use frames only if you must.

Key Terms

Noncompliant browser
Reserve name
Tool tip message

New Tags

<FRAME>
<FRAMESET>
<IFRAME>
<NOFRAMES>

Review Questions

1. What is the definition for each of the key terms?

2. How is each of the tags introduced in this chapter used? (Provide examples.)

3. What are three disadvantages and one advantage to using frames in designing a Web page?

4. What special HTML tags are needed for a document to appear within a frame?

5. What attributes must be coded with the <FRAMESET> tag?

6. How is an asterisk (*) used within the <FRAMESET> beginning tag?

7. What is one important rule for nesting one <FRAMESET> element within another <FRAMESET> element?

8. What are the only containers that can present data within a <FRAMESET> element?

9. What happens when a <FRAME> element does not contain a **src** attribute?

10. Describe how the **name** attribute works with the **target** attribute to allow a specific document to appear in a specific frame.

11. What type of user is most likely to need a descriptive title, or **longdesc** attribute?

12. What do **frameborder** attribute values of 1 and 0 indicate?

13. When should you use the <NOFRAMES> container?

14. What happens when you accidentally use a target name that does not exist?

15. How would you set a frame named "**text-area**" as the default target value?

16. Identify and describe four special target names.

17. When do users see the text contained within an <IFRAME> container?

Exercises

9.1. Build a framed document that looks like the accompanying figure. It should have four frames: two vertical frames that are each divided into two horizontal frames. Frame 1 should display text that tells about an image in frame 2. The text in frame 3 should describe the image in frame 4. The title bar should display "Interesting Images" and your name and the assignment due date should be included within comment lines.

Frame 1 text	Frame 2 image
Frame 3 text	Frame 4 image

9.2. Build a framed document that looks like the accompanying figure. The left frame should be a table of contents for five HTML tags: <OL>, <UL>, <HR>, and two of your own choice. The right frame should open with a page that identifies the document as an HTML reference site. The remaining five HTML documents should correspond to options from the table of contents. Each page should identify the tag, all attributes, and at least one example of the tag. The title bar in the <FRAMESET> document should display "HTML Reference Page," and all the HTML documents you create should have your name and the assignment due date included within comment lines.

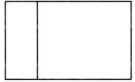

9.3. Build a framed document that looks like the accompanying figure. The top frame should be a table of contents for four of your favorite sports teams or musical groups. The bottom frame should open with a page that identifies the document as a quick reference to when and where you can next see these teams/musicians. The remaining four HTML documents should correspond to options from the table of contents. Each page should identify the group's name, Web site if there is one, and the locations and days for where and when you can see them. If the group is a sports team, provide its schedule. If it is a musical group, provide the next tour dates and locations. The title bar in the <FRAME-SET> document should display "Your Name's Guide To ____." All the HTML documents you create should have your name and the assignment due date included within comment lines.

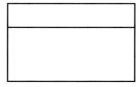

9.4. Redesign the Homework home page used in earlier exercises, including Exercise 8.4, utilizing the accompanying figure as a model. In frame 1 place your name, an image of yourself if you have one, and links to Web sites you commonly use, like your favorite search engine, your instructor's site, and McGraw-Hill's site for this book. Place links to your homework assignments in frame 2. Frame 3 should contain a personalized footer that includes your e-mail address and your favorite animated GIF file.

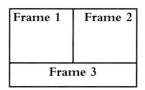

9.5. Create an HTML document that can serve as a takeout menu for a local restaurant. This document must use inline frames for each of the major areas of the menu as shown in the accompanying figure. At least six options should be available for each area of the menu. The inline frames should be 200 pixels high and 400 pixels wide. The name of the restaurant should appear at the top of the page and in the title bar. All the HTML documents you create should have your name and the assignment due date included within comment lines.

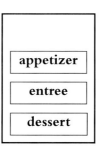

9.6. Redesign your school's home page or the one you created for the school in earlier exercises, including Exercise 8.6, utilizing the accompanying figure as a model. In frame 1, center the school's name in large letters, and place the school's address and telephone number in smaller letters under its name. Place a calendar of current school events, like sporting events or concerts, in frame 2. Frame 3 should contain a map to the school or a photograph of the school or of some school event.

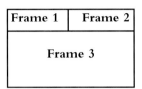

FORMS—HANDLING USER INPUT

I n this chapter, we will explore ways the Web weaver can design interactive pages that allow the user to input information, and in some cases get a response back. This is usually done by the user interacting with all or part of a form. The user either touches the Enter key (on a very simple form) or activates some sort of "Submit" button that sends the data that the user has filled in on the form to the server that hosts the page. That server processes the information using a *script.* A script is a program, often written by the Web weaver, that processes the data from the form and creates a response that is sent back to the user via the browser.

This response could be an HTML document that either requests more information, provides the user with some information requested, or simply thanks the user for providing information.

Not all pages need this capability, but well-designed forms with good scripts for processing data can give the Web weaver a tool for collecting and distributing information from users. In addition, the author can use buttons, text areas, and other *input controls* to trigger scripts.

Form controls are one of the few ways that a script can accept input from a user. In later chapters you will learn how the input features of a form can invoke and control scripts. In this chapter, we will focus on the role forms play in initiating data processing.

Form and Function

Before we get into the nitty-gritty details of building forms, you need to have an idea of how the forms and their data are actually processed. The form shown in Figure 10.1 is an independent HTML document, but it could also be part of an existing document that allows users to provide input by performing any of several actions:

- Selecting one of a set of radio buttons
- Choosing one or more checkboxes
- Using a list box to select an element from a predefined list
- Entering free-flowing text into a text field

After entering all their data, users activate a submission button (such as "Submit Query" or "Order Catalog") to send the data to the server hosting the Web page or to the specified e-mail address. We will use the e-mail approach throughout this chapter and save the subject of server based scripts for the next chapter.

Figure 10.1 presents a simple form designed to allow users to input three fields: their name, their favorite buggy pastime, and an e-mail address for the electronic catalog. After typing in their name, users select one of the two *radio buttons* indicating what they like to do with bugs and then enter their e-mail address. Finally, they activate the "Request Catalog" button to send the data to the server for processing. Obviously, this is a simple form, but it will serve as an example to start our exploration of forms. Figure 10.2 shows an example of this form filled out by a user.

```
<BODY>
<SPAN style="font-family: sans-serif; color: #0000FF;
        text-align: center">
<H1>Bugs Bee Wee</H1> </SPAN>
<H2>Online Catalog Order Form</H2>
We would love to send you our newest online catalog.<BR>
To do that we need to have you supply a little
information so we can better serve you.
Please supply the following data:
<FORM
        action="mailto:scarab@bugsbeewee.com"
        method="POST"
>
Your name:
        <INPUT type="TEXT" name="name" size="30" MAXsize="80">
<BR><BR>
What do you like to do with your bugs?<BR>
        <INPUT type=RADIO name="gender" value="W"> Watch 'em
        <INPUT type=RADIO name="gender" value="E"> Eat 'em <BR><BR>
E-Mail address:<BR>
        <INPUT type="TEXT" name="email" size="30" MAXsize=80> <BR><BR>
<INPUT  type="SUBMIT" value="Request Catalog"><BR>
</FORM>
</BODY>
```

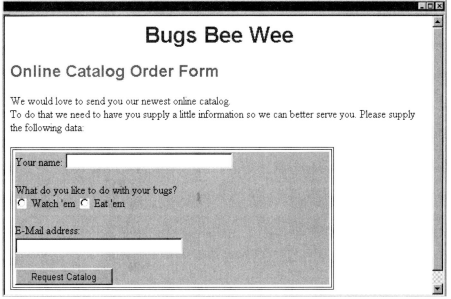

Figure 10.1 HTML code for a simple form.

When the user activates the "Request Catalog" control, the Web weaver receives the following e-mail: name=Patti+Toad&use=E&email=pattit%40toad-hall.com. Since we are looking at e-mail submission of data, let's consider what the Web weaver will need to do with these data.

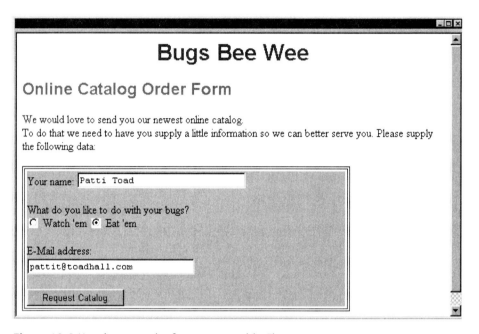

Figure 10.2 User input on the form presented in Figure 10.1.

Handling Electronic Mail

To collect a small amount of data from a few users, you may not need to go through the exercise of building a program to handle those data. In our "Bugs" example, the form sends an e-mail containing the data that were collected. The <FORM> beginning tag looks like this (notice the **action** attribute):

<FORM action="mailto:scarab@bugsbeewee.com" method="POST">

In this example, the data will be sent to scarab, (actually, Jon Scarab), at the e-mail address of bugsbeewee.com rather than being sent to a program running on the server. Note: You must always use the POST method instead of the GET method to send data using e-mail.

The first thing Jon will need to do is to *parse* the data—that is, divide the data into fields. Since he expects only a few catalog requests, this e-mail method is probably a good choice. However, if the Bugs Bee Wee page becomes popular, and many users are sending information, the e-mail method could pose some problems:

- It takes a significant amount of time to process the data, as each form requires several processing steps. Consequently, if there are a lot of responses, the mail server could get bogged down or overloaded. As a result, the user may not get a timely acknowledgement. Jon would have to write back to the user, and that could take a couple of days.
- In order to submit a response, the user must have an e-mail account and must have that portion of his browser correctly configured. Some users are therefore excluded from responding to the form.

- The user must be willing to send data that are not *encrypted*. Many users prefer to keep their personal information private. So, again, some users will be excluded from responding to the form.

The following data string would show up as part of an e-mail message in Jon's mailbox shortly after the user touches the "Request Catalog" button:

name=Patti+Toad&use=E&email=pattit%40toadhall.com

Notice that there are no spaces in the data string. The space between Patti and Toad is replaced by the plus sign (+). The form established values for three *variable names,* (name, use, and email) chosen by the Web weaver when the form was built. A variable name is a generic way of referring to a location in the computer's memory. The computer stores data at specific addresses in memory, like F7DA42. It is much easier to remember a variable name like *"email"* or *"name"* than one like F7DA42 or DD8F31. Using variable names makes the program more usable and readable by people. The computer always translates the variable name back into an actual memory address before it is used.

These form data were processed by sending them to the browser's mail utility, which then passed them on to the address specified in the action, in this case scarab@bugsbeewee.com. Jon Scarab will need to decide what to do with these data now, since there will be no automatic processing. Probably he will do the following:

1. Parse the message, changing the plus signs to spaces, removing the leading ampersands (&), and converting the special characters from their encoded values to the normal ASCII characters. If the user uses special characters, like the exclamation point (!), the browsers will usually code it as its hexadecimal value. For example, the string "Froggie the Third!" would look like this: Froggie+the+Third%21. The spaces between the three words are replaced by the plus sign, and the exclamation point is coded as hexadecimal 21 (%21). In the previous example, @ shows up as %40.
2. Store the name, the use, and the e-mail address in a database for later use.
3. Send a copy of the online catalog to the user.

Remember that the user must have a working mail program available on her computer system. Since the mailto: action generates one or more additional screens for users, you should warn them about what will happen before they submit their data. Figure 10.3 shows the warning screen generated by the two major browsers.

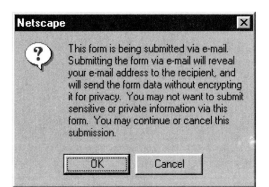

Figure 10.3 E-mail warning messages as presented by Navigator (left) and Explorer (right).

> ### <FORM>contents of the form</FORM>
>
> *Description:* indicates that the contained data are part of a form.
> *Type:* container.
> *Attributes:* accept-charset, action, class, dir, encytpe, id, lang, method, name, onClick, onDblClick, onKeyDown, onKeyPress, onKeyUp, onMouseDown, onMouseMove, onMouseOut, onMouseOver, onMouseUp, onReset, onSubmit, Style, target, and title.

The <FORM> container holds the contents of the form. The ending tag of </FORM> is never omitted. Although this container currently has 24 attributes, only the **action** and **method** attributes are required. Browsers treat the <FORM> as if it were an image embedded in the text, flowing the rest of the text around it.

There are no special layout rules for forms, other than that they should be easy to read and use. You can use most of the standard HTML elements within a form, so you can control the placement of the fields and text within the body of the form as you would in the rest of the document. The only real restriction on forms is that you cannot embed one form within another. While it is indeed possible to code more than one form on a page, this is not considered a good practice. Limit the use of multiple forms per page to cases where the user will fill out only one of the forms.

action

The **action** attribute points to the application that will process the data captured by the form. You can have the data sent to the server and processed by a CGI script, or you can have the data e-mailed directly to your mailbox.

Common Gateway Interface (CGI) Action

If you choose to use the *CGI script* method, described in detail in Chapter 11, the URL of the CGI script should specify not only the path but also the filename of the receiving program. Usually the program is in a directory called cgi-bin because that is the place most Web site administrators would put a CGI script. An example of an **action** attribute specifying a CGI script follows:

```
<FORM action="http://www.bugsbeewee.com/cgi-bin/bugorder.cgi">
```

In this example, the data entered by the user would be sent to server www.bugsbeewee.com. The server would then run the script called bugorder.cgi, located in the cgi-bin directory, and pass the data to it. Most Web site administrators keep all the CGI programs and scripts in a common directory called something like cgi-bin or cgibin. That way, the Web server software, as well as all the Web weavers, will know where the scripts reside.

Electronic Mail Action

As you have seen from the Bugs Bee Wee examples earlier in the chapter (see Figure 10.1), a form can be used to send data via electronic mail. This action uses the mailto: protocol and looks like this:

```
<FORM action="mailto:scarab@bugsbeewee.com" method="POST">.
```

When the user activates the submit button, the data from the form are formatted and sent to the e-mail address listed. In this case scarab@bugsbeewee.com will receive the data.

method

The **method** attribute tells the browser how to send the data to the server. There are two ways to do this: GET or POST. These two methods place very different demands on both the server and the Net. GET and POST are named after the http commands that the browser uses to communicate with the server. The mailto: action always requires the POST method (see Figure 10.1) used throughout this chapter. We will explore these two methods in detail in the next chapter.

enctype

The **enctype** attribute allows you to specify a different encoding format for the data sent from the form to the CGI script. It is very unlikely that you will ever need to use this attribute, and it is of value only when you are sending binary data or non-ASCII data, usually as part of a file. You would specify an encoding format in this manner:

```
<FORM enctype="text/plain"
      action="mailto:scarab@bugsbeewee.com"
      method="POST">
```

The standard encoding type, specified by the "text/plain" value for the **enctype** attribute, is called *application/x-www-form-urlencoded*. This coding is necessary to prevent the data from becoming corrupted during transmission from the browser to the server. We saw an example of this standard encoding when we looked at the data Jon received via e-mail from the browser. Although it is called an "encoding" method, application/x-www-form-urlencoding does *not* protect the user data; the data are quite readable. Application/x-www-form-urlencoded data use the following conventions:

1. All spaces are converted to plus signs (+).
2. Non-alphanumeric characters are represented by their ASCII code, that is, as a two-digit hexadecimal number preceded by a percent sign (%).
3. Each field name except the first is preceded by an ampersand (&).

These conventions are important to remember if you choose to use the mailto action rather than the CGI script action. They are also important to remember when *debugging* scripts.

A second type of encoding, called *multipart/form-data encoding,* encloses the data in a form as several parts of a single document. Each field's data are preceded by a line of 30 minus signs (−) followed by a large random number. The minus signs and the random number serve as dividers between the different data fields. Each field is represented by at least one line of header information, then the actual data. The actual data are not encoded, so there is less possibility of corrupting binary data when transmitted.

Multipart/form-data encoding is normally used to send binary file data, so your forms processing will most likely not need to handle them. If you choose to specify multipart/form-data encoding, you must use the POST method. With this encoding method, each variable ends up as a separate file in the mail message. Figure 10.4 shows what Jon Scarab would see if he had specified "form-data" rather than "text/plain". As you can see, each variable is sent as its own plain-text file. If the responses were long, this might be useful, but in this case it makes Jon's job more difficult, because he has to open three files rather than one.

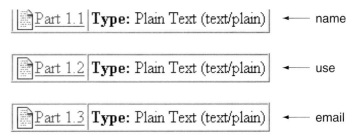

Figure 10.4 E-mail showing multipart/form-data-encoding output. Each variable is a file.

target

The **target** attribute allows the Web weaver to direct the return data from a script to a different window or frame than the one that originally contained the form. This attribute serves the same purpose here as it did for frames, which you saw in Chapter 9. That is, the **target** attribute can specify a different frame or page than the one containing the form. In addition, a new window can be specified. This attribute is important if your CGI script is used to fill in one frame while the form is in another frame. We won't use it with mailto:, but you could encode it like this when using a CGI script that returned a page:

```
<FORM target="buggyframe"
     action="http://www.bugsbeewee.com/cgi-bin/catalog.cgi"
     method="POST">
```

The results would be sent to the frame called "buggyframe" in the current document.

accept-charset

The **accept-charset** attribute is an example of a feature that the W[3]C added to promote internationalism on the Web. This attribute allows the author to specify a collection of character sets that the server must support to correctly present the page. Suppose you want your page to print in a Korean character set. If you wanted to accept the version of the Korean character set used in UseNet News, you could code this:

```
<FORM accept-charset="EUC-KR"
     action="mailto:scarab@bugsbeewee.com"
     method="POST">
```

On the other hand, you would use

```
<FORM accept-charset="ISO-2022-KR"
     action="mailto:scarab@bugsbeewee.com."
     method="POST">
```

if you wanted to support the 7-bit ISO (International Standards Organization) code used for Korean e-mail.

style

As you know by now, the **style** attribute was added in the HTML 4.0 specifications. It is used to create an inline style for the form, overriding any previous style rules. There is a caveat to using **style** within a form. If you code a background color and a special font face in the **style** attribute of the form, those values will apply to the form itself, but not necessarily to the contents of button labels, nor to the text areas in which the user will type. Figure 10.5 shows the same form as represented by the two popular graphical browsers.

```
<STYLE>
                FORM { border: #0000CC double 4px;
                    width: 80%;
            }
        H1 {color: #CC00FF;
                font-family: sans-serif;
                }
</STYLE>
</HEAD>
<BODY>
<H1>Online Catalog Order Form</H1>
We would love to send you our newest online catalog.<BR>
To do that we need to have you supply a little
information so we can better serve you.
Please supply the following data:
<FORM
        action="mailto:scarab@bugsbeewee.com"
        method="POST"
        style="font-style: italic; background-color: #CCFFFF;"
>
```

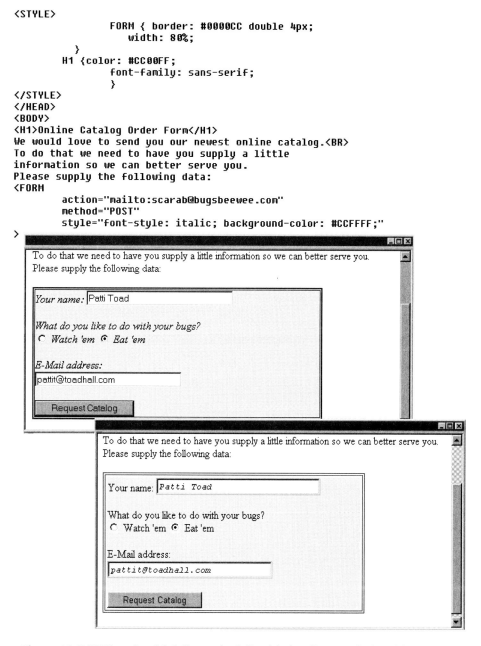

Figure 10.5 HTML code with inline style defined in heading, as displayed by Explorer (top) and Navigator (bottom).

As you can see, the two browsers handle the form style somewhat differently. Be aware of this if you choose to employ inline style elements in your form. What is even more interesting is that without the style defined in the heading, the two browsers' handling of the inline style has even more variation, as shown in Figure 10.6.

```
<STYLE>
        H1 {color: #CC00FF;
                font-family: sans-serif;
                }
</STYLE>
</HEAD>
<BODY>
<H1>Online Catalog Order Form</H1>
We would love to send you our newest online catalog.<BR>
To do that we need to have you supply a little
information so we can better serve you.
Please supply the following data:
<FORM
        action="mailto:scarab@bugsbeewee.com"
        method="POST"
        style="font-style: italic; background-color: #CCFFFF;"
>
```

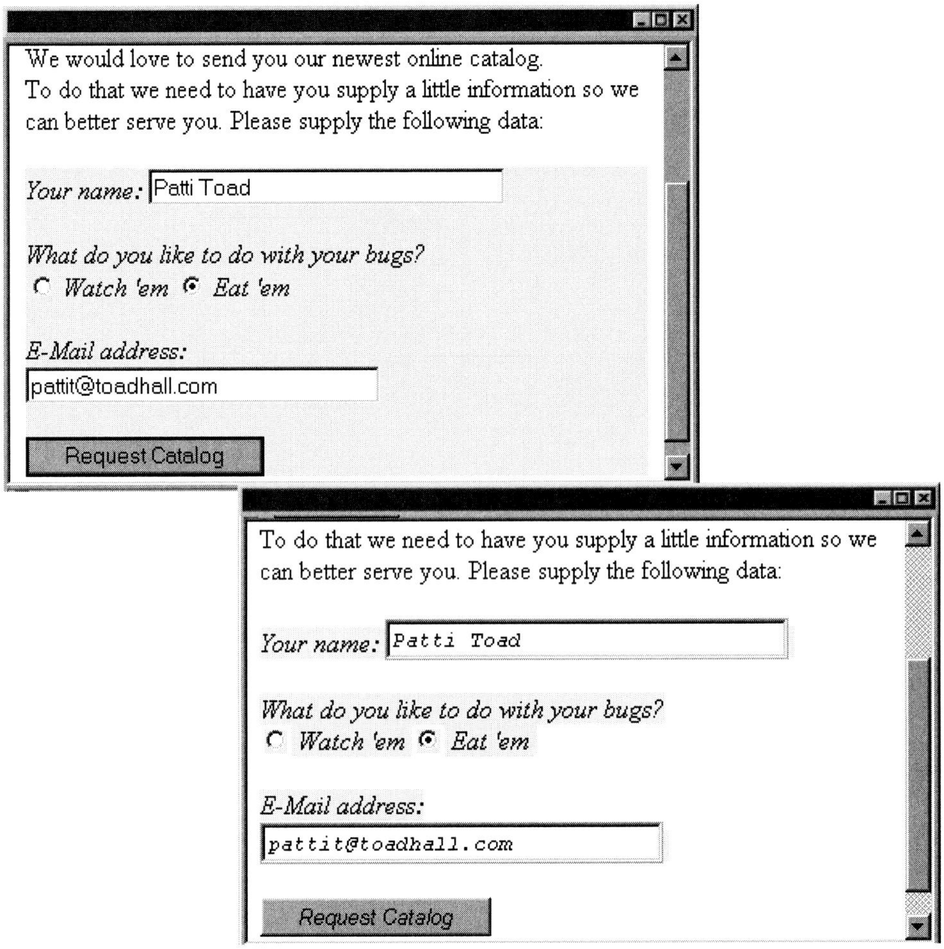

Figure 10.6 HTML code without inline style defined in heading, as displayed by Explorer (top) and Navigator (bottom).

Notice that in the upper screen capture (Explorer), the user input in the text box and the button text are not italic, but the text in the body of the form is italic. In the lower screen capture (Navigator), the text in the form and all of the input areas is the same style, as we would expect. However, looking at the background color we see that in Internet Explorer, a large area of the page is colored, while in Navigator the background color applies only to the text lines. Neither browser honors the background color for the text box. All in all, using inline styles with forms can cause varying output.

class

Like **style,** the **class** attribute allows the Web weaver to apply a predefined class to the form. The same caveats apply to **class** as to **style.** The two browsers treat **class** differently, as shown in Figures 10.5 and 10.6. One sets the same values to the attributes as to the class; the other does not.

name

The name attribute is used to specify an identity for the form. This name can be used by hyperlinks, JavaScript, and applets to identify the form, and to establish an order of hierarchy for specific fields within the form. We will make extensive use of this attribute in later chapters, when we build JavaScript scripts to accept data from, or place data into specific fields within a specific form.

title

Currently, the **title** attribute is used only within the form. It is ignored by the popular browsers, but it may have some significance for nongraphical browsers. The wise Web weaver will keep checking with W^{3}C to see if this attribute has taken on any additional significance. Its intended use is to provide an identification for the form that is spoken when used by nonvisual browsers. It cannot be used as identification by hyperlinks, applets, or JavaScript, use **name** instead.

Intrinsic Events

The standard intrinsic events, onClick, onDblClick, onKeyDown, onKeyPress, onKeyUp, onMouseDown, onMouseMove, onMouseOut, onMouseOver, onMouseUp, also apply to the <FORM> tag. In addition, there are two new intrinsic events as well: onSubmit and onReset. All 12 of these intrinsic events can be used to trigger JavaScript methods, expressions, or functions. We will explore how this is accomplished in the JavaScript chapter.

There are two important reasons to use the onSubmit event. The first is to trigger a JavaScript to perform value checking and input validation on the various data fields that the user submitted. That way the server script doesn't have to check each value and send back error screens if the data are incorrect. The second use is to verify for the user that the form has actually been sent. Some authors also blank the fields in the form to further reassure the user that the data have been processed. This is especially important when using the mailto: action.

<INPUT>

Description: creates an input element (control) within a form.
Type: empty tag.
Attributes: accept, accessKey, align, alt, border, checked, class, dir, disabled, id, lang, maxlength, name, onBlur, onChange, onClick, onDblClick, onFocus, onKeyDown, onKeyPress, onKeyUp, onMouseDown, onMouseMove, onMouseOut, onMouseOver, onMouseUp, onSelect, readonly, size, src, style, tabindex, title, type, usemap, and value.

The <INPUT> tag is the tool used to create the actual, user-manipulated areas of a form. Each type of input area is called an *input control* in the HTML 4.0 specifications. Actually, the specifications speak of two different types of control: *successful controls,* which must be coded within the body of a <FORM> container, and *unsuccessful controls,* which are <INPUT> elements coded within the body of an improperly coded <FORM> container. Remember that a <FORM> container must have an associated action. If you fail to code an action or method for your <FORM>, any input control within that form will be unsuccessful. Unsuccessful controls are often created as triggers for JavaScript events, as we will see in a later chapter.

Using <INPUT> controls allows the Web weaver to create text-input fields, multiple-choice lists, selectable images, submission and reset controls, and radio buttons. In addition, the 4.0 specifications created a new control called simply a button.

With the exception of submission, reset, and button controls, all the different forms of input require the use of the **name** attribute, and every <INPUT> control requires the **type** attribute. Each input control requires a particular collection of attributes. Table 10.1 shows all of the controls with their required attributes. After looking at some guidelines for forming names, we will explore all these different types of input control, along with the applicable attributes for each.

CONTROL	REQUIRED ATTRIBUTE(S)
Button	**name, value**
Checkbox	**name, value**
File	**name**
Hidden	**name, value**
Image	**src**
Password	**name, value**
Radio	**name, value**
Reset	*None*
Submit	*None*
Text	**name**

Table 10.1 Form controls and their required attributes.

name

The **name** attribute is required by nearly every <FORM> control. It specifies the *label,* or variable name, that makes up the left half of the **name=value** pair. The **name,** then, is the identifier, variable name, or label, with which the data will be associated when passed back to the server. The other half of the pair is the **value** of the variable, the actual data stored at the memory location specified by the name.

The selection of a good, useful name is very important. The rules for forming a name are very flexible, but common practice in programming has provided a few guidelines that will make your work with **name=value** pairs less confusing.

1. Make the name meaningful. While it is acceptable to the browser and script to use names like "a," "n," and "e," they usually make little sense to anyone but the author. Names like "age," "name," and "email" tell you and anyone else who is reading your form or script what data you are processing. The few extra keystrokes are more than justified by the ease of understanding that meaningful names provide. Remember that someone else may have to change your code later.

2. Use lowercase letters for the name. Some operating systems, like DOS, don't recognize uppercase and lowercase letters as being different, but other operating systems, like Unix and Windows NT, do. That means that the variable name "Email" is different from the variable name "email." Try to always use lowercase variable names. Unix programmers usually use lowercase for their variable names because

    a. Lowercase text is slightly easier to read (it has more cues like descenders).

    b. Lowercase text usually won't conflict with system variables, which are usually all uppercase.

    c. It is easier to type all lowercase text, since there is no need to use the shift key.

3. Start the name with an alphabetic character. Although you can start the name with nearly any character, if you limit your names to alphabetic characters, there is less chance of either browser or CGI script problems. Avoid special characters like the ampersand and asterisk, since they can cause problems.

4. Make the name continuous (no intervening spa ces). With some systems, it is possible to embed blanks in variable names. This may work on your computer, but it is generally considered poor programming practice and may well cause problems if you need to move your pages to another computer. To create multi-word names, use an underscore rather than an embedded blank. For example, the variable name of "first name" describes the content, starts with an alphabetic character, and is lowercase. It is a good variable name except that it contains a space between "first" and "name." Some operating systems may try to make it into two different variable names, "first" and "name." It would be better to use "first_name," in which the underscore holds the place between the two words.

A properly formed name will make life easier for you and anyone else who chooses to use your form or your script. Take a few minutes to select variable names that make sense and are well formed.

type

The **type** attribute defines which type of control the form will provide for the user. Each control has different required attributes associated with it. Let's examine each of the values for the type attribute.

TEXT

Text-entry fields, **type**="TEXT", are probably the most common type of <INPUT> field. They require little from the Web weaver other than assigning a **name.** However, some of the other attributes can provide additional features. Figure 10.7 presents a very simple form with a text-entry control that uses only default values. This control takes in any length of text the user wants to enter, scrolling the window to the left as the user keeps typing. The figure shows that the default text window is 20 characters wide, but as the maximum possible size of the field was not specified, the user can just keep typing, and the most recent 20 characters will show. Figure 10.7 also shows the code for this simple form. Note that the only attributes for the <INPUT> tag in this code are **type, name,** and **style.** The **style** attribute is there to center the text. The other **style** information is coded in the header. All the rest of the layout of the control is the default set by the browser.

```
<HTML>
<HEAD>
<TITLE> Bugs Bee Wee </TITLE>
<STYLE>
    FORM { background:#CCCCCC;
                    border: #0000CC double 4px;
            }
</STYLE>
</HEAD>
<BODY>
<H1>Customer Questionnaire</H1>
As part of a continuing effort to better serve our
 customers, we at
<SPAN style="font-family: sans-serif; color: #0000FF">
Bugs Bee Wee </SPAN> request that you consider the following
question:<BR>
<FORM
        action="mailto:scarab@bugsbeewee.com"
        method="POST"
>
What are we missing?<BR>
Is there an insect you especially like, that you would
like us to carry?  If so, please enter its name below.<BR>
 <INPUT
        type="TEXT"
        name="question1"
        style="text-align: center"
 >
</FORM>
</BODY>
```

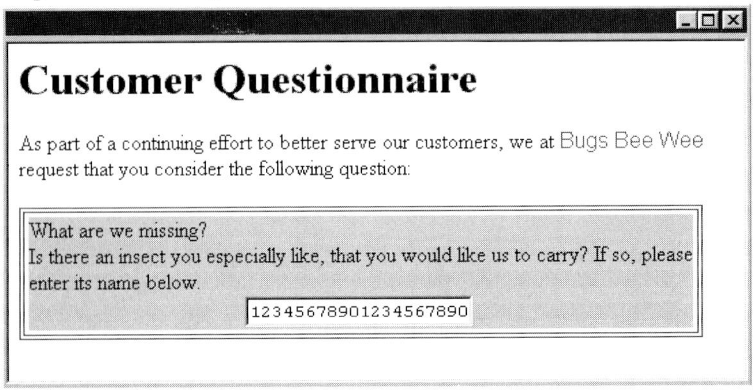

Figure 10.7 HTML code including a text-entry field.

Careful examination of the code in Figure 10.7 shows that there is no control for submission of the form data. This page represents a special case in forms processing. If the form has only one field, and it is a text-entry field, then the browser will submit the data when the user touches the Enter key. While this is a special case, it is well worth noting, as there are many forms with only one text-input field, and users expect to be able to press the Enter key to submit the form.

Using all default values is often not a good idea, because the layout will vary among the various browsers. Let's look at some other attributes that should be specified.

size

The **size** attribute specifies the length of the text-entry field. Figure 10.8 shows the same form shown in Figure 10.7 but with a **size="15"** attribute added. Now the text-entry area is only 15 characters wide. The user can enter as many characters as the browser will allow (normally a very large number), but only the rightmost 15 will show in the window. Note: In this and subsequent screen captures, we will show only the code segment that has changed; the rest of the page is identical to that shown in Figure 10.7.

```
What are we missing?<BR>
Is there an insect you especially like, that you would
like us to carry?  If so, please enter its name below.<BR>
 <INPUT
        type="TEXT"
        name="question1"
        style="text-align: center"
        size="15"
 >
```

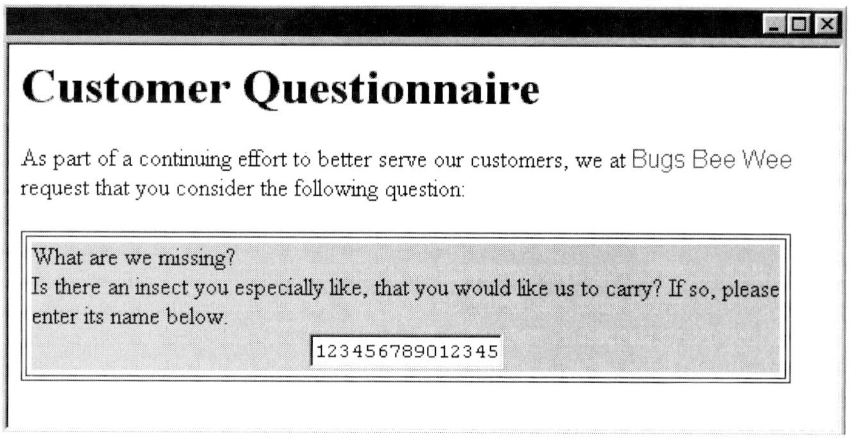

Figure 10.8 HTML code for a text-entry field with a size specified.

maxlength

The **maxlength** attribute limits the actual number of characters the user can enter. Figure 10.9 shows how the form looks with a **maxlength="10"** coded for the text-input control. Only 10 characters can be typed in the space, although it has a size of 15. This is because the **maxlength** value was set to 10. Setting a **maxlength** that is smaller than the length coded in the **size** attribute can be confusing for the user. The browser will sometimes issue a warning sound each time the user tries to type beyond the **maxlength,** so it can be distracting as well. Usually it is best to have the **size** of the text-input field smaller or, ideally, equal to the **maxlength** of that field.

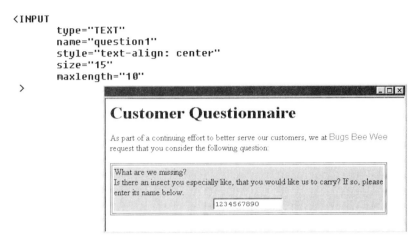

```
<INPUT
      type="TEXT"
      name="question1"
      style="text-align: center"
      size="15"
      maxlength="10"
>
```

Figure 10.9 HTML code for a text-entry control with a maxlength attribute.

value

The Web weaver can assign a default **value** to the field so that if the user wishes to use the default value, the only action he needs to take is to submit the form. Figure 10.10 shows the simple form we have been building with a **value**="Default" coded. If the user types anything in the field, it is *appended* (added) to whatever was specified by the **value** attribute. The user must delete the data placed in the field before he can enter his own. Use the **value** attribute sparingly, and only when you feel quite sure that the user will most likely take the default value you have provided. It takes significantly more work for the user to replace your **value** than to simply type in her own data.

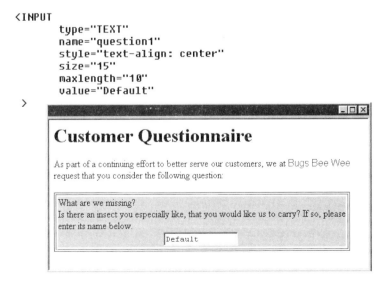

```
<INPUT
      type="TEXT"
      name="question1"
      style="text-align: center"
      size="15"
      maxlength="10"
      value="Default"
>
```

Figure 10.10 HTML code for the standard text-input control showing a default value of "Default".

Regardless of what type of prompt you use, the user can type anything that fits into a text line. If, for example, you want to have the user type a number, she could as well type any combination of letters or characters. There is no way to *validate* the user's input in the <FORM> container. Your CGI script or a JavaScript must do the validation. Validation can be a long, complex process, so the best bet is to give your user specific instructions as to your expectations for her input.

type="PASSWORD"

There are times when you want to help users protect the data they are typing from prying eyes at their site. If you set the **type** to "PASSWORD," anything the user types will appear as special characters, usually asterisks. Obviously, this is most often used to hide passwords, hence the name, but it can also be used to hide other selection data. Figure 10.11 shows our simple input form with the **type** changed to "PASSWORD". As you can see, even the default value was changed to asterisks.

Although the data in a field of **type**="PASSWORD" are protected from people looking at the browser screen, data are not protected when sent to the server. When the data are sent across to the server, the data can be intercepted and read.

```
<INPUT
       type="Password"
       name="question1"
       style="text-align: center"
       size="15"
       maxlength="10"
       value="So Secret"
>
```

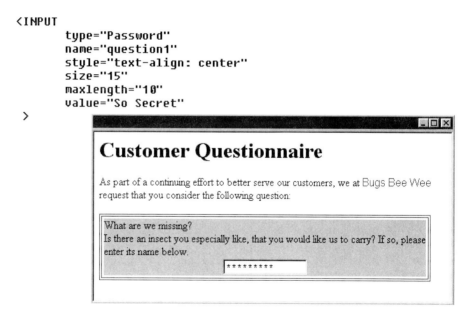

Figure 10.11 HTML code for **type**="PASSWORD" control, showing a default value of "So Secret" in protected format.

type="FILE"

Sometimes the user needs to send a file back along with the form data. For example, if you had a site that would store pages for the users, they could submit some form data and a page for the CGI script to post to the server. It would be possible for them to enter the file's URL in a text field and have the CGI script find and retrieve the file, but that would be cumbersome. Fortunately, the developers of HTML have taken that need into account, and the **type="FILE"** control has a special feature to help users find the name of the file they want to send. Figure 10.12 shows a simple form that takes a file as one of the input controls. Look carefully at the screen generated in this figure and compare it to the code. One feature should become obvious quite quickly: there is *no code* that generates the "Browse" control! That's right, when the browser sees a **type="FILE"**, it automatically generates a working "Browse" button. If the user activates the browse control, he sees a pop-up window generated with the name of the input control at the top.

```
<H2>Culinary Bug Data</H2>
<FORM
        action="mailto:scarab@bugsbeewee.com"
        method="POST"
        enctype="multipart/form-data"
>
Please be so kind as to give us the name of your
special bug recipe:<BR>
<INPUT
        type="TEXT"
        name="dish"
        size="30"><BR>
Next please type in the file containing your recipe:<BR>
 <INPUT
        type="FILE"
        name="infile"
        size="25"><BR>
<INPUT
        type="SUBMIT"
        value="Send the File">
</FORM>
```

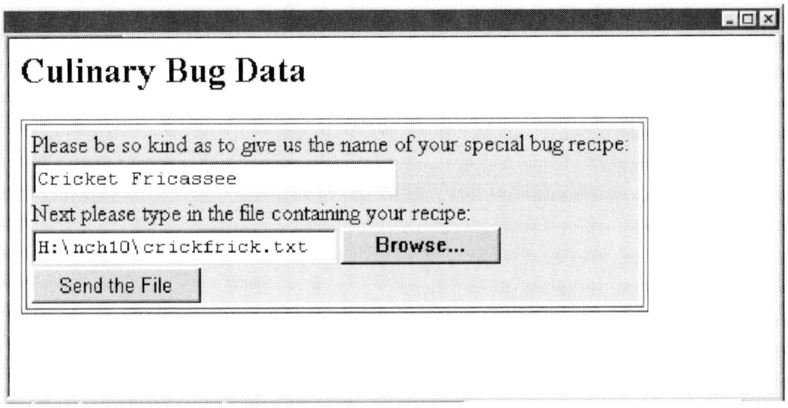

Figure 10.12 HTML code for **type ="FILE"** control, showing the automatically generated "Browse" control.

Figure 10.13 shows this feature using the data directory for this chapter on Tim G's machine. As you can see, the user merely chooses one of the selections, then activates the "Open" button (or double-clicks on the filename), and the File Upload screen will put the selected name into the control area. Of course, the user could always simply type in the filename, just as if it were a text-input control.

There is one important caveat for using this method; the **enctype** attribute must be set to "multipart/form-data" rather than the default, "text/plain". Should the Web weaver forget this step, the browser would send back the *name* of the file rather than the *contents* of the file!

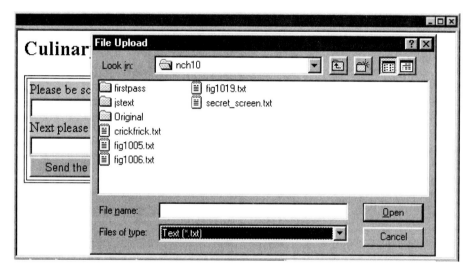

Figure 10.13 HTML code for **type** ="FILE" control, showing the File Upload window.

type="CHECKBOX"

Using a set of checkboxes is an easy, fast way for your user to enter data. Checkboxes also minimize data-entry errors! All the user needs to do is select and/or deselect different items from the control to indicate preferences. If you design your form efficiently, setting **type** to "CHECKBOX" will allow your users to quickly enter the data you are requesting. Furthermore, you will be able to accurately retrieve those data with less need for data validation, because the possible input data is known and limited. Unlike *radio buttons,* several checkboxes from a series can be selected.

Figure 10.14 shows a form with a set of checkboxes allowing the user to select bugs he wants more information about. The code shown in this figure is only the snippet that contains the <FORM> container, as the rest of the page is not essential to your understanding of the form. The code for the entire page is available on the CD that accompanies this text, as well as on the Web page.

```
<FORM
        action="mailto:scarab@bugsbeewee.com"
        method="POST"
>
Please tellus about your favorite insects by selecting
 those you would like to know more about.<BR>
  Choose all that apply.<BR>
  <INPUT
        type="CHECKBOX" name="favbug" value="jbug">June Bug<BR>
  <INPUT
        type="CHECKBOX" name="favbug" value="dbtl">Darkling Beetle<BR>
  <INPUT
        type="CHECKBOX" name="favbug" value="hbee">Honey Bee<BR>
  <INPUT
        type="CHECKBOX" name="favbug" value="lbug">Lady Bug<BR>
  <INPUT
        type="CHECKBOX" name="favbug" value="ewig">Ear Wig<BR>
  <INPUT
        type="CHECKBOX" name="favbug" value="vant">Velvet Ant<BR>
<INPUT type="SUBMIT" value="Tell Us">
</FORM>
```

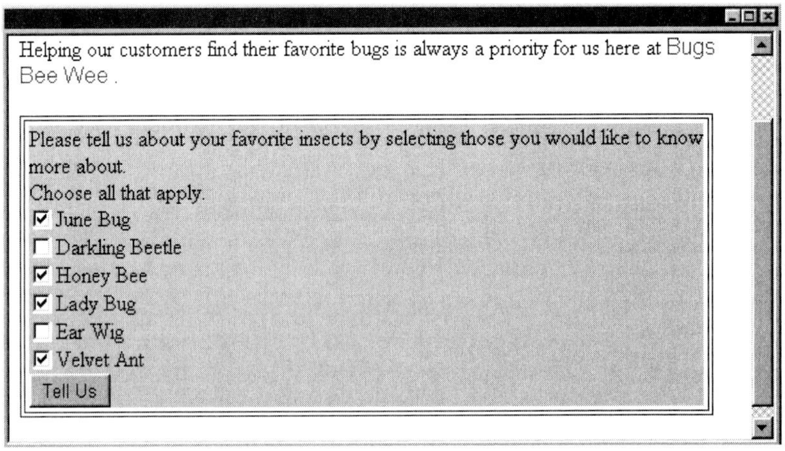

Figure 10.14 HTML code for **type** ="CHECKBOX" control, showing the code and the generated screen.

Notice that each line of code ends in a break (<BR>) to force the different selections to appear on individual lines. Leaving out the breaks would cause the checkboxes to appear in a line across the browser window. Careful layout of the form is the job of the Web weaver. The idea is to make the form easier to understand. Notice that the values for the different checkboxes are short, and all are coded in lowercase letters. These features make the code easier to process on the server and result in shorter e-mail messages as well.

The form in Figure 10.14 has been filled out by a user. When the user clicked on a box (checkbox) in front of an insect, the browser marked the selected box with a checkmark (✔). Some older browsers may use an X rather than a checkmark, but all mark the box. Here the user selected four different insects. When the user activates the "Tell Us" control, the browser will send the following data stream back to the server:

favbug=jbug&favbug=hbee&favbug=lbug&favbug=vant.

Checkboxes are a very efficient way to transmit data, both for the Web weaver and the user. On the other hand, using this example, if the user really likes an insect that is not listed, like the dung beetle, the form will not represent his choice. You run the risk of alienating your users if you don't give them enough choices. Probably a text field called "Other" should be added. Be careful, too, to provide some order to your choices when possible, and lay out the form in a way that makes it easy for your user to use.

checked

As with the text field, you can set a default value, or values, for a checkbox form. When the user opens the page, one or more of the checkboxes can show as already chosen, or checked. Figure 10.15 shows how this works. The **checked** attribute is added to the <INPUT> tag. The user must activate the checkbox that is marked in order to turn the mark off. This may cause the user extra work, and it may give you invalid data if the user doesn't bother to turn off your preselected choice(s).

```
<FORM
      action="mailto:scarab@bugsbeewee.com"
      method="POST"
>
Please tell us about your favorite insects by selecting
  those you would like to know more about.<BR>
  Choose all that apply.<BR>
  <INPUT
      type="CHECKBOX" name="favbug" value="jbug">June Bug<BR>
  <INPUT
      type="CHECKBOX" name="favbug" value="dbtl">Darkling Beetle<BR>
  <INPUT
      type="CHECKBOX" name="favbug" value="hbee" checked>Honey Bee<BR>
  <INPUT
      type="CHECKBOX" name="favbug" value="lbug">Lady Bug<BR>
  <INPUT
      type="CHECKBOX" name="favbug" value="ewig">Ear Wig<BR>
  <INPUT
      type="CHECKBOX" name="favbug" value="vant">Velvet Ant<BR>
<INPUT type="SUBMIT" value="Tell Us">
</FORM>
```

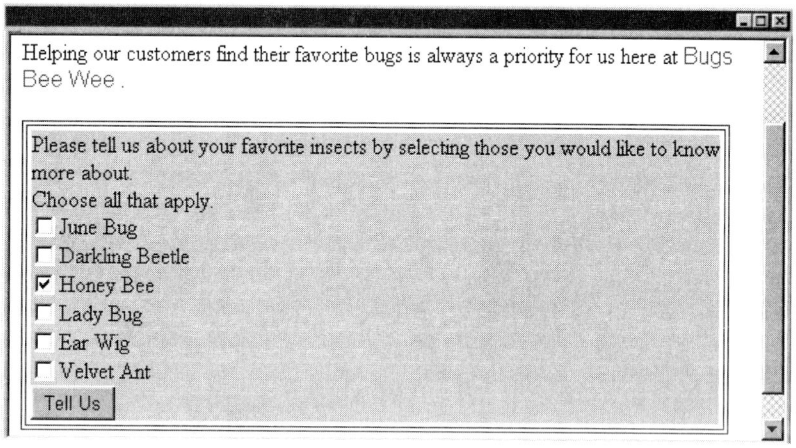

Helping our customers find their favorite bugs is always a priority for us here at Bugs Bee Wee .

Please tell us about your favorite insects by selecting those you would like to know more about.
Choose all that apply.
☐ June Bug
☐ Darkling Beetle
☑ Honey Bee
☐ Lady Bug
☐ Ear Wig
☐ Velvet Ant
Tell Us

Figure 10.15 HTML code for the **checked** attribute.

type="RADIO"

As we just explained, checkboxes are good when you want the user to be able to select more than one option from the form. But *radio buttons* are best when you want to ensure that the user selects only one option from a list.

The term "radio button" needs a little explanation. Not all *that* long ago, car and console radios had a series of mechanical buttons for selecting the radio station. Pushing one button would cause the previously pressed button to pop out. In that way, only one selection could be made at a time. It was a somewhat complex, mechanical way of ensuring that only a single button was depressed at any one time. Likewise, the radio-button type of input item in HTML code ensures that only one of a series of choices can be selected.

There are many uses for the radio type of input form: salary ranges, age, and gender, to name a few. As with checkboxes, you can group a set of radio buttons by giving all of them the same **name** attribute. Also like checkboxes, each radio button must have a **value** assigned. The **value** assigned should be different for each button, so that the recipient of the e-mail, or the CGI script, can figure out which one the user selected.

Figure 10.16 shows a set of radio buttons that allow the user to select her entomological snack. Unlike the checkboxes in the previous examples, the user can select only one from this series. When he clicks on one of the selections, the "button" changes from a plain circle to one with a dot inside it. If he selects another button, the browser deselects the first choice. That button goes back to the simple circle, and the button for the new selection is changed.

```
<FORM
    action="mailto:scarab@bugsbeewee.com"
    method="POST"
>
What is your favorite insect snack?<BR>
<INPUT
    type="RADIO" name="snack" value="mwm">Meal Worm Meal <BR>
<INPUT
    type="RADIO" name="snack" value="cc">Crispy Crickets<BR>
<INPUT
    type="RADIO" name="snack" value="gf">Grasshopper Fritters<BR>
<INPUT
    type="RADIO" name="snack" value="cca">Chocolate Covered Ants <BR>
<INPUT
    type="RADIO" name="snack" value="rgs">Roast Grub Worm Surprise <BR>
<INPUT type="SUBMIT" value="Tell Us">
</FORM>
```

Figure 10.16 HTML code for radio buttons.

checked

As with checkboxes, you can preselect one of the radio buttons for your user with the **checked** attribute. Indeed, some browsers will preselect one of the buttons for you, usually the first button in the series. Others don't preselect. It is always a good idea to preselect one of the radio buttons so you are assured of having a value sent to the server. Unlike the case with preset values in checkboxes, the user can deselect your choice in radio buttons simply by selecting another button. As a result, preselection creates no more work for the user.

Since one of the radio-button controls should always be preselected, always have more than one radio button on a form. But, remember, radio buttons should be used only when the user is making a selection that is exclusive of the others in the list.

One easy way to cause problems for the script parsing the form data—and to confuse your user as well—is to misspell one of the values used for the **name** attribute. For example, in the code in Figure 10.17, the value for the **name** ("snak") in the grasshopper line is misspelled. Therefore, as the figure shows, when the user has activated the "Chocolate Covered Ants" control, the "Grasshopper Fritters" button is also still selected. It is critical that you check your code for this kind of sneaky error.

```
<FORM
        action="mailto:scarab@bugsbeewee.com"
        method="POST"
>
What is your favorite insect snack?<BR>
 <INPUT
        type="RADIO" name="snack" value="mwm">Meal Worm Meal<BR>
 <INPUT
        type="RADIO" name="snack" value="cc">Crispy Crickets<BR>
 <INPUT
        type="RADIO" name="snak" value="gf" >Grasshopper Fritters<BR>
 <INPUT
        type="RADIO" name="snack" value="cca">Chocolate Covered Ants<BR>
 <INPUT
        type="RADIO" name="snack" value="rgs">Roast Grub Worm Surprise<BR>

<INPUT type="SUBMIT" value="Tell Us">
</FORM>
```

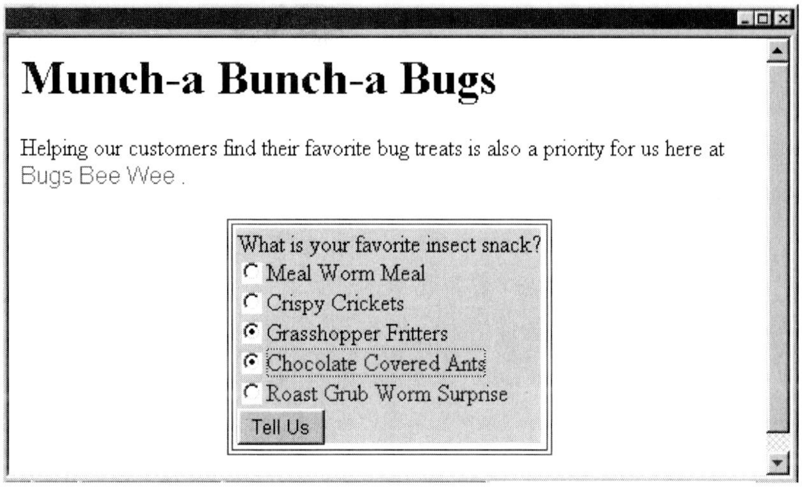

Figure 10.17 HTML code for radio buttons with the **name** attribute misspelled.

Local Action Controls

All of the input fields we have examined so far set up data to be sent to Jon Scarab via e-mail. The next three controls cause the *browser* to perform specific actions and so are called *local action controls*. You are already familiar with the "SUBMIT" control, used to send data to the server or to initiate an e-mail. Now let's look at another type of local action control.

type="RESET"

A **type** of "RESET" provides a control that causes the browser to reset, or change, all the input areas back to the way they were when the user entered the page. Any **checked** controls will again be set, and anything that the user had entered or selected will be reset to the original values, or deselected. Always include a reset button on any form you create. It will enable a user to quickly undo errors she has made or to easily change her mind.

Figure 10.18 shows the code for our simple form, now including a reset button. The reset button is labeled "Clear Selections" to give the user an idea of

Figure 10.18 HTML code for a page with the "RESET" control.

its function. If you assign a **value** to the <INPUT> field of a reset button, that **value** will replace the default name of "Reset." Sophisticated users will understand the function of "Reset," but for less Web-wise users, a more explicit label, such as "Clear Selections," may help to let the user know that he can put the screen back to the way it was before any selections were made. In other words, by activating just one button, the user can undo everything selected. The Web weaver has no control over what is reset when this button is clicked. It is not currently possible to undo only part of a form. A "RESET" control resets all the fields on the form.

type="SUBMIT"

The **type="SUBMIT"** control does just what it implies—it starts the process of the browser encoding and sending the information to the server or invokes the browser's associated e-mail program. Like the "RESET" control, if you just use a **type="SUBMIT"**, the browser creates a small button for the user, in this case labeled "Submit Query." As you have seen in the previous examples, if you want to change the label on this submission button, you need to supply a **value** attribute to the input element.

Figure 10.18 shows our simple form, but with both the reset ("Clear Selections") and submit ("Tell Us") buttons on the bottom of the form. Notice how one is on the left and the other on the right to help the user avoid activating the wrong one by mistake. One clever way to handle layout of the submit and reset controls is to use a table. The two <INPUT> fields are put into a table to control their placement on the form. The **width** attributes are used to force the size of the table elements. The **align** attributes are set to "RIGHT" and "LEFT" to justify the input fields.

Multiple Submit Controls

You can also supply a **name** attribute to the "SUBMIT" control, and the browser will add the name=value pair to the information sent to the server. This allows you to set up multiple submit buttons, each with a different **name** and **value,** and the browser will add the value from the activated control to the input stream. Each submit element can, in that way, signal a different processing step within the CGI script or a different response through e-mail.

For example, you could create a form that allows the user to learn about your product line by requesting information about any of several different catalogs. Alternatively, you could create a form that allows the user to order one of several different products by choosing different submit controls. Figure 10.19 shows a form that lets the user choose which of the four different catalogs she wants by using different submit controls. When she clicks on any one of these selections, the data are sent to Jon. These are all submit controls.

Figure 10.19 provides a simple example of using a submit button to send additional information. Notice that all four controls have a **type** value of "SUBMIT", all have the same **name,** and each has a different **value,** reflected in its name on the form, signifying its relative contents, or value. Using multiple submit controls can simplify processing for your user. In addition, multiple submit buttons provide an easy way to create an additional variable that can give direction to your CGI scripting or, if you are using e-mail, provide more data in the mail sent to you. In this example, simply by activating one submit control, the user sends information to Jon Scarab, telling him which type of catalog to send.

```
<H1>Get our Catalog</H1>
We have four different catalogs here at
<SPAN style="font-family: sans-serif; color: #0000FF">
Bugs Bee Wee</SPAN>.   Please select which of them you
would like to receive:<BR>
<SPAN style="text-align:center">
<FORM
       action="mailto:scarab@bugsbeewee.com"
       method="POST"
>
Which catalog would you like to have us send you?<BR>
  <INPUT
       type="SUBMIT" name="cat" value="Bugs for Eat'en"><BR>
  <INPUT
       type="SUBMIT" name="cat" value="Cuddle Bugs"><BR>
  <INPUT
       type="SUBMIT" name="cat" value="Pretty Bugs"><BR>
  <INPUT
       type="SUBMIT" name="cat" value="Working Bugs"><BR>

</FORM>
```

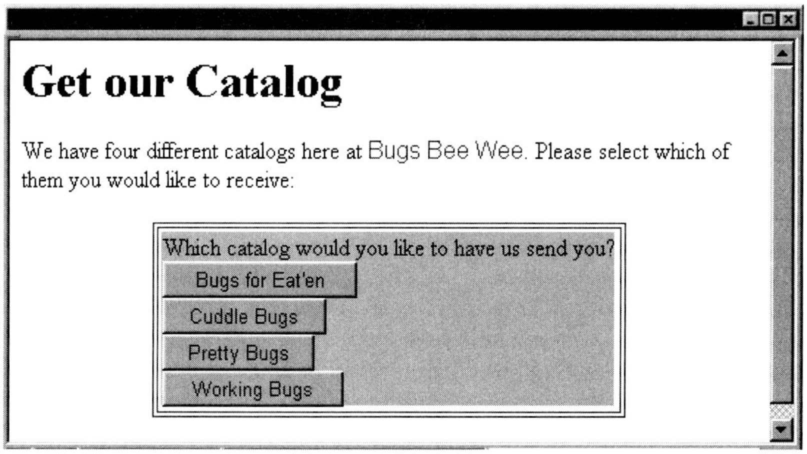

Figure 10.19 HTML code for a form using multiple submit controls, each with a different value.

type="BUTTON"

The HTML 4.0 specifications give Web weavers a new control feature called the *button*. With **type="BUTTON"**, an author can create a control that has no predefined function. Currently the only use for this control is as a trigger for JavaScript.

Graphical Buttons

You will recall from Chapter 6 that when you built anchors that were links, it was possible to include a graphic or image that served as part of the link. It is also possible to do that with the <INPUT> tag. However, the processing done by the browser is very different in these two cases. In the case of the anchor link, when the user activates the image, the browser loads the file pointed to by the associated address. If the Web weaver adds an image to an <INPUT> tag, a graphical browser treats it like a mouse-sensitive image map rather than a simple glyph.

type="IMAGE"

When the Web weaver has coded an <INPUT> tag with **type**="IMAGE", the user sees a picture that she can click on. However, rather than simply sending the preset value for the name of the input field, the browser sends an X,Y coordinate pair representing the location of the mouse pointer, associated with the **name** attribute. The *script,* or recipient of the e-mail, needs to process the X,Y pair to determine just where in the image the user clicked. Figure 10.20 shows a simple example of an image used as a button to send in an order.

```
<H1>Free Butterfly Raising Instructions </H1>
At <SPAN style="font-family: sans-serif; color: #0000FF">
Bugs Bee Wee</SPAN>,we are always trying to find ways to bring the
beauty of insects into our customers' worlds. <BR>
<SPAN style="text-align:center">
<FORM
        action="mailto:ttg@flash.net"
        method="POST"
>
Our most recent publication will show you how to
raise beautiful butterflies in your very own garden.  <BR>
Click on the image of our friendly caterpillar below to receive your
catalog.<BR>
 <INPUT
        type="IMAGE"
        name="bfly"
        src=cat1.gif
        style="text-align: center"><BR>
</FORM>
```

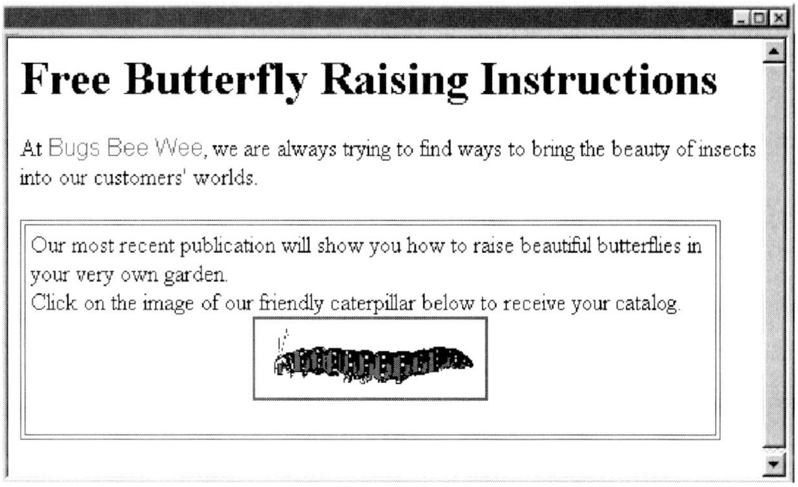

Free Butterfly Raising Instructions

At Bugs Bee Wee, we are always trying to find ways to bring the beauty of insects into our customers' worlds.

Our most recent publication will show you how to raise beautiful butterflies in your very own garden.
Click on the image of our friendly caterpillar below to receive your catalog.

Figure 10.20 HTML code for a form with a graphical button, created with **type** ="IMAGE".

A naive Web weaver might think that the browser will simply submit the order when the user activates the "caterpillar" button, but that is not so. The browser will also send the X,Y coordinates of the actual mouse position within the graphic in the following form: bfly.x=84&bfly.y=27. Here **84** represents the number of pixels in from the left edge of the image, and **27** represents the number of pixels down from the top edge of the image. The coordinates bfly.x=0 and bfly.y=0 would be the upper left corner of the image.

Notice that the image, "catl.gif", is in the same directory as the page, so it is not necessary to code the path to that image. Since the graphic functions like a link, most of the browsers will put a frame around the image, as we saw earlier with images used as links. As you can see from the example, it is possible to control the alignment of the image using the **style** attribute. There may be some specialized need to create a graphical button, but in most cases, it simply increases the load time of the page and the load on the Net, so we don't advise using them.

In Chapter 14 we will look at the way image maps are used, and how the actual X and Y position of the pointer can contain important data. It is generally not a good idea to use an image as a submit button, unless the design of the page demands it.

An important principle is to use only the HTML tools you need to do the job, avoiding the trap of creating fancy code just because you can. A text-only browser can do no more than submit the form, as there is no mouse pointer from which to return the coordinates.

Hidden Data Fields

Sometimes you will want to send CGI script data that you don't want the user to be able to manipulate or even see. For example, if part of the processing involves sending you an e-mail message about some of the contents of the data stream, you would want to send the script to your e-mail address in a way that the user could not modify the address. Another example of using hidden data fields would be special coding that tells the server exactly which form was used to send the information. Those data, too, should be coded in a hidden field and sent to the server so as to prevent any interference by the user. Finally, one of the more common uses of hidden data fields is to send data that was captured with a previous form. Those data need to be sent, but the user has no need to see them.

type="HIDDEN"

An <INPUT> field with data that users need not see requires only three attributes: **name, value,** and **type="HIDDEN"**. Here is a sample line from a form that sends some hidden data to the server:

<INPUT type="HIDDEN" name="mailto" value="Adephaga@bugsbeewee.com">

Neither the user nor the browser sees this field. It is passed exactly as coded to the server for processing at that end. Hidden fields are not a common feature of Web pages, but they provide a very useful way to handle some specialized situations.

<BUTTON>button text and/or images</BUTTON>

Description: indicates that the contained data should be formatted and should function as a button control.
Type: container.
Attributes: class, dir, disabled, id, lang, name, onBlur, onClick, onDblClick, onFocus, onKeyDown, onKeyPress, onKeyUp, onMouseDown, onMouseMove, onMouseOut, onMouseOver, onMouseUp, onReset, onSubmit, style, tabindex, title, type, and value.

The <BUTTON> element is new in the HTML 4.0 specifications. It provides a button within a form. Currently only Internet Explorer provides support for this element, but we expect that to change. The difference between the <BUTTON> element and the <INPUT type="BUTTON"> control is that the former provides for a more sophisticated set of contents. Images and text can both appear within the container, allowing the Web weaver to create a very attractive button. This element introduces a couple of new attributes.

disabled

The button element can be set as inactive by including the **disabled** attribute inside the <BUTTON> tag. Disabled elements will not be sent to the server, nor will they perform their designated actions if the user attempts to activate them. Generally this is used only for testing purposes; users should never see disabled buttons.

tabindex

Each element within a form can be selected by using the Tab key. As the user tabs through the form, each different control is successively given *focus.* In the world of HTML, focus means that the control is the currently active control and able to receive input. Normally the order in which the controls will be accessed matches the order they appear in the <FORM> container. The Web weaver can alter this order with the **tabindex** attribute. Thus, setting the value of the **tabindex** attribute determines the order of access of the elements. If the author wants a particular element to be skipped when the user is tabbing around the form, she can set the **tabindex** to zero.

Intrinsic Events

The standard intrinsic events as discussed in Chapter 2 also apply to the <BUTTON> element. Each of these can be used to trigger JavaScript methods, expressions, or functions. We will explore how this is accomplished in Chapter 13.

<TEXTAREA>optional text string
</TEXTAREA>

Description: creates an area for multi-line text input box.
Type: container.
Attributes: class, cols, dir, disabled, id, lang, name, onBlur, onChange, onClick, onDblClick, onFocus, onKeyDown, onKeyPress, onKeyUp, onMouseDown, onMouseMove, onMouseOut, onMouseOver, onMouseUp, onselect, readonly, rows, style, tabIndex, title, and wrap.

All of the input tools discussed thus far limit the user to a single line of input. Even the **type="TEXT"** input tool shows the user only a single line of input. Users can type an unlimited number of characters if the Web weaver has not set a **maxlength** attribute, but the input appears on only one line, with only part of a large input string visible at a time. The <TEXTAREA> container sets the user free from the single-line restriction by creating an area in the browser pane for textual input; </TEXTAREA> is never omitted.

It is possible, and even advisable, to include default text in a <TEXTAREA> field to give the user instructions. When the form is submitted to the server, the browser takes all the lines of text that have been entered. Each line is separated by a *carriage-return line feed* (CrLf), called a *newline* in Unix. That long text stream is sent to the CGI script or e-mail address in the value of the variable specified by the **name** attribute.

Figure 10.21 shows a form that provides the user with a text area for input. What is shown here is the standard, or default, text-area box. It has scroll bars, but it shows only one line of text. Browsers don't seem to understand the need

```
<FORM
       action="mailto:scarab@bugsbeewee.com"
       method="POST"
>
Please use the space below to tell us all about your
adventures with the insects in your world.  We may even
share your story with our other friends who visit the
Web page!<BR>
<TEXTAREA
       name="story">
</TEXTAREA><BR>
 <INPUT
       type="SUBMIT"
       value="Tell Us"><BR>
</FORM>
```

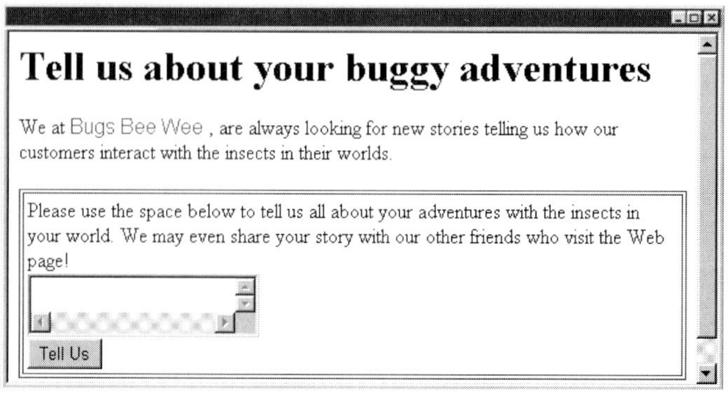

Tell us about your buggy adventures

We at Bugs Bee Wee , are always looking for new stories telling us how our customers interact with the insects in their worlds.

Please use the space below to tell us all about your adventures with the insects in your world. We may even share your story with our other friends who visit the Web page!

Tell Us

Figure 10.21 HTML code for the default <TEXTAREA> control.

for size that prompts us to use a <TEXTAREA>, so they build a minimal area for text input. Fortunately, there are a couple of attributes that allow us to build a better looking, more useful text area.

rows and cols

The **rows** and **cols** attributes define the initial size of the text-input area. Not surprisingly, **rows** specifies the number of lines (rows) in the input block, and **cols** is a count of the number of characters (columns) across each line. Together they define a rectangular region on the screen that is set aside for user input. It is good HTML practice to always code **rows** and **cols** in text areas. Figure 10.22 shows a new version of our form, with **rows="7"** and **cols="60"**. As you can see, this is a much more appealing area into which to enter text.

```
<FORM
        action="mailto:scarab@bugsbeewee.com"
        method="POST"
>
Please use the space below to tell us all about your
adventures with the insects in your world.  We may even
share your story with our other friends who visit the
Web page!<BR>
<TEXTAREA
        name="story"
        rows="7"
        cols="60">
</TEXTAREA><BR>
 <INPUT
        type="SUBMIT"
        value="Tell Us"><BR>
</FORM>
```

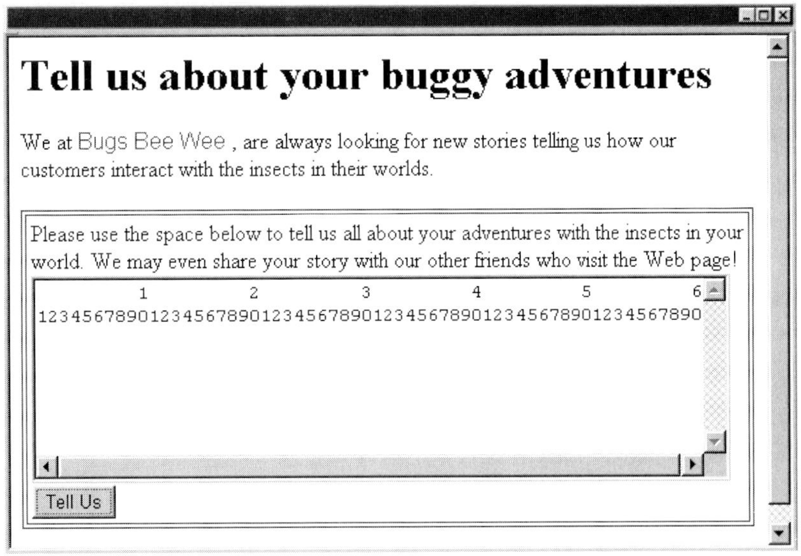

Figure 10.22 HTML code for the <TEXTAREA> control with **rows="7"** and cols="60".

Notice that the text-input area in Figure 10.22 is exactly 60 characters wide (the numbers were entered after the form was generated, as input, to show a count of the columns). There are still scroll bars, because the user can enter more than seven lines, and each line can be as long as the user wants. Remember that the browser and the form merely supply a place for the user to enter text. At this point they do not restrict or control how the text looks. Users who type long lines can still lose sight of part of what they have typed. Because users have become used to the word-wrap feature of most word-processing packages, they may find it annoying to have to keep touching the Return or Enter key to move down to the next line. Again, the designers of HTML have taken that into account by providing the **wrap** attribute, discussed next.

wrap

The **wrap** attribute causes the browser to break lines on word boundaries as close to the right margin as possible and continue the text on the following line. This is like the word-wrap feature of most word processors. Coding **wrap** will make your <TEXTAREA> a friendlier place for your users. And, indeed, they will expect this feature from a sophisticated Web page. We recommend that you always code the **wrap** attribute. It has three different values, as follows.

wrap="VIRTUAL"

When the **wrap** attribute is set to "VIRTUAL", it causes the browser to break the input lines at word boundaries on the user's screen. When the text is transmitted to the server, only those *carriage-return line feeds* (*CrLfs*) that the user actually entered will be in the text stream. Most of the time the text will be passed as a continuous stream with no CrLfs. Usually this is not the ideal choice for most applications.

wrap="PHYSICAL"

With the **wrap** option set to "PHYSICAL", the line breaks happen at the browser just as they do with a "VIRTUAL" wrap, but the actual CrLfs are added to the text the user enters as if the user had actually coded them. This is the preferred option on the **wrap** attribute, because it creates a more readable copy. However, it must be noted that using this attribute option will cause the browser to add data, albeit just CrLfs, to the data the user enters.

wrap="OFF"

The **wrap**="OFF" option sets the browser to the standard default processing, where the only CrLfs either shown or sent are those actually entered by the user, and the text can scroll to the right indefinitely. For almost all applications, **wrap**="PHYSICAL" is a better option than **wrap**="OFF". Figure 10.23 shows two <TEXTAREA> controls. The first has the default **wrap** attribute, "OFF", the second is coded with **wrap**="PHYSICAL".

```
<TEXTAREA
        name="place"
        rows="3"
        cols="60">
</TEXTAREA><BR>
In the space below, please let us know the different types
of creatures you have seen.
<TEXTAREA
        name="types"
        rows="3"
        cols="60"
        wrap="PHYSICAL">
</TEXTAREA><BR>
 <INPUT
        type="SUBMIT"
        value="Tell Us"><BR>
```

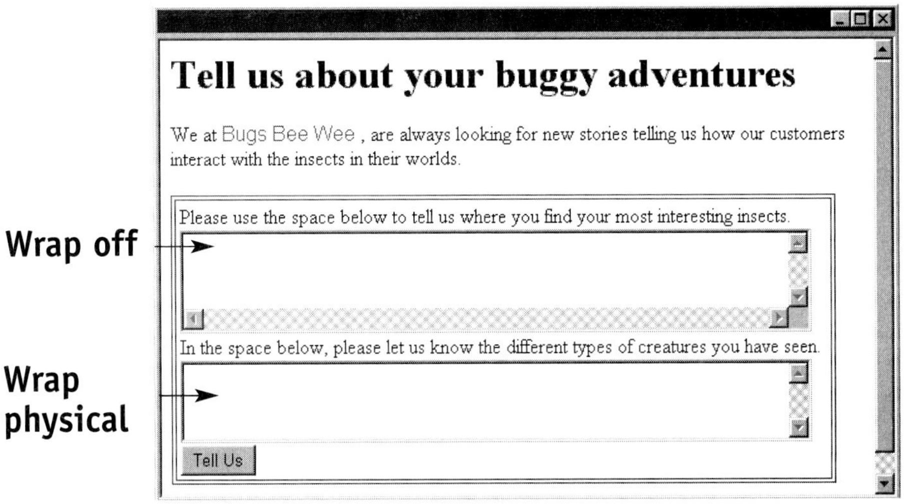

Figure 10.23 HTML code for two <TEXTAREA> controls, one with wrap="OFF" and one with wrap ="PHYSICAL".

Notice how only part of the text shows in the first <TEXTAREA>, while all of it is present in the second. Where the lines break is determined by the **width** of the <TEXTAREA>, so the actual layout of the text in the second example is governed by the width of the text area. Notice that the second area doesn't have a horizontal scroll bar. It isn't needed!

Using the techniques you have learned in this chapter, you can create forms that will enable your users to send you all sorts of interesting and useful data. However, as we mentioned earlier, when your site becomes more popular, and/or as the volume of your data increases, using e-mail becomes cumbersome. In the next chapter we will look at ways to automatically process data sent by forms and see some additional controls you can use to enhance your forms.

Key Terms

Button
Focus
Input controls
Parse
Radio button
Script
Variable name

New Tags

<BUTTON>
<FORM>
<INPUT>
<TEXTAREA>

Review Questions

1. What is the definition for each of the key terms?

2. How is each of the tags introduced in this chapter used? (Provide examples.)

3. What is the easiest way to distribute data collected with a form?

4. What are five disadvantages to using the distribution method identified in Question 3?

5. What attributes are required with every <FORM> element?

6. How are data encoded using the application/x-www-form-urlencoded encryption altered?

7. What are the two intrinsic events that are unique to forms?

8. What are six types of input controls?

9. What information is contained within a name=value pair?

10. What are the authors' guidelines for creating variable names?

11. How is a checkbox control different from a radio button control?

12. Which control starts the process of the browser encoding and sending information to the server?

13. What is the easiest way to clear a user's form entries?

14. How is a text box different from a text area?

Exercises

10.1. Create a new HTML document containing a form. The title bar should display "Operating System Survey by Your Name" with your name and the assignment due date included within comment lines. Form results should be sent to your e-mail account or an e-mail account given to you by the instructor. At a minimum the form should contain the following:

    a. Text boxes to accept the person's name and e-mail address
    b. Checkboxes with **name** and **value** attributes for these operating systems:
        (1) CP/M
        (2) Macintosh OS
        (3) PC/MS-DOS
        (4) Unix
        (5) Windows
    c. Radio buttons with **name** and **value** attributes that correspond to the operating systems listed in Exercise 10.1. These buttons need to allow the user to rate the systems as follows:
        (1) Good
        (2) Bad
        (3) Never used it
    d. Submit control
    e. Reset control

10.2. Create a new HTML document containing a form. The title bar should display "Bugs Bee Wee Order Form" with your name and the assignment due date included within comment lines. Form results should be sent to your e-mail account or an e-mail account given to you by the instructor. At a minimum the form should contain the following:

    a. Text boxes to accept the person's name and e-mail address
    b. Checkboxes with **name** and **value** attributes for these bugs:
        (1) Ladybug
        (2) Praying mantis
        (3) Cricket
        (4) Honey bee
    c. Text box for the credit card number
    d. Radio buttons for these credit card companies:
        (1) American Express
        (2) Discover
        (3) Master Card
        (4) Visa
    e. Submit control
    f. Reset control

10.3. Create a new HTML document containing a form. The title bar should display "Complaint Form" with your name and the assignment due date included within comment lines. Form results should be sent to your e-mail account or an e-mail account given to you by the instructor. At a minimum the form should contain the following:

- a. Text boxes to accept the person's name and e-mail address
- b. Text area for complaint
- c. Radio buttons with **name** and value attributes for these options:
    - (1) I just wanted you to know.
    - (2) Please respond to the e-mail address given.
    - (3) Contact my lawyer.
    - (4) Go to #!$#★.
- d. Text boxes to accept the lawyer's name and address
- e. Submit control
- f. Reset control

10.4. Retrieve the Homework home page you updated in previous exercises. Create a new HTML document containing a form and a link to this page on your home page. The title bar on the page with the form should display "Personal Survey by Your Name." Also include your name and the assignment due date within comment lines on the form page. The form should collect information from the user that is sent to your e-mail account or an e-mail account given to you by the instructor. It needs to contain submit and reset controls. The information collected must include the user's name and his or her e-mail address, along with any or all of the following:

- a. Favorite musicians and related songs
- b. Favorite athletes and related teams
- c. Favorite actors and actresses
- d. Favorite television shows
- e. Favorite movies

10.5. Create a new HTML document containing a form. The title bar should display "Voting Form" with your name and the assignment due date included within comment lines. Form results should be sent to your e-mail account or an e-mail account given to you by the instructor. At a minimum the form should contain the following:

- a. Text boxes to accept the person's name and e-mail address
- b. At least five radio buttons the user can use to vote for a candidate for some office.
- c. Text box for write-in alternative
- d. Checkboxes with name and value attributes for these options:
    - (1) This is the first time I have voted online.
    - (2) I have periodically voted online.
    - (3) I always vote online.
    - (4) Online voting is not patriotic.
- e. Submit control
- f. Reset control

10.6. Retrieve your school's home page updated in previous exercises. Create a new HTML document containing a form and a link to this page on the home page. The title bar on the page with the form should display "Course Request Form." Also include your name and the assignment due date within comment lines on the form page. The form should collect information from the user that is sent to your e-mail account or an e-mail account given to you by the instructor. It needs to contain submit and reset controls. The information collected must include the user's name and his or her e-mail address, along with all of the following:

    a. Course prefix and number
    b. Course name
    c. Radio buttons identifying the semester/term and the year the user wants to take the class
    d. Reason the user needs that class

## CHAPTER eleven

CGI—LET THE MACHINE DO IT FOR YOU

In Chapter 10 we discussed the <FORM> element attributes and the <TEXTAREA> container. In all of those examples, we had the form send the data to the Web weaver using electronic mail (e-mail). That is fine for small amounts of data that are infrequently sent, but this procedure causes some problems when there is a large volume of data or a high message count.

In addition, there are many times when the user would like an immediate response rather than an e-mail message at some later time. Certainly with *e-commerce,* purchasing products online, users expect a Web site to fill their order while they are still online, not later. These cases require the server to handle the user request, not

313

ship the data off via e-mail. In this chapter we will first look at some additional control elements that can be included in advanced forms, then explore the **Common Gateway Interface (CGI),** a way to enable the server to process forms data directly. CGI is a set of procedures that the server uses to invoke a user-written program called a *script* and pass data collected from a Web page to that program.

All of the controls we saw in Chapter 10 occupied consistent screen real estate. They allowed the user to select from a list that was always shown in the browser window (radio buttons or checkboxes) or to enter data into either a text line or text area. The only exception was the file input control, which automatically provided the user with a browse capability. The <SELECT> element allows the form's designer to easily create a pull-down menu of choices for the user.

<SELECT>Set of <OPTION>elements</SELECT>

Description: creates a list box made up of the enclosed <OPTION> elements.

Type: container.

Attributes: class, cols, dir, disabled, id, lang, multiple, name, onBlur, onChange, onClick, onDblClick, onFocus, onKeyDown, onKeyPress, onKeyUp, onMouseDown, onMouseMove, onMouseOut, onMouseOver, onMouseUp, onSelect, size, style, tabindex, and title.

Special note: The <SELECT> container must contain at least one <OPTION> element.

The <SELECT> container is a very powerful yet easy-to-use tool. Use it to create a list box of selections. Normally <SELECT> acts like a radio button in that only one of the options in the list can be selected. However, using the **multiple** attribute, you can cause <SELECT> to act like checkboxes instead, allowing the selection of multiple data elements.

Figure 11.1 shows a screen created with code that includes a <SELECT> container. When the user looks at this screen, the arrow on the selection window tells him that there are more options available. If he activates the down arrow, the list expands as shown in Figure 11.2.

When the user activates one of the selections, that option is highlighted and the value sent back to the CGI script. The code shows a nearly generic <SELECT> list box. When the user selects one of the options, the form sends the actual option as the value in the goodbug=**value** string. For example, if the user selects "Lace Wing", then the form sends goodbug=Lace+Wing back to the CGI script. (Remember from Chapter 10 that spaces are changed to plus signs (+) before the data are sent to the server.) Unlike the case with the other elements we have discussed, if the user does not select an option here, the value of the **name**

```
<FORM
        action="http://www.bugsbeewee.com/cgi-bin/vote.cgi"
        method="POST"
>
Which of these insects do you feel is most beneficial
in YOUR garden?
<BR>
<SELECT
        name="goodbug">
<OPTION>Lady Bug</OPTION>
<OPTION>Assassin Bug</OPTION>
<OPTION>Lace Wing</OPTION>
<OPTION>Praying Mantis</OPTION>
<OPTION>Orchard Bee</OPTION>
<OPTION>Dung Beetle</OPTION>
</SELECT>
 <INPUT
        type="SUBMIT"
        value="Send"><BR>
</FORM>
```

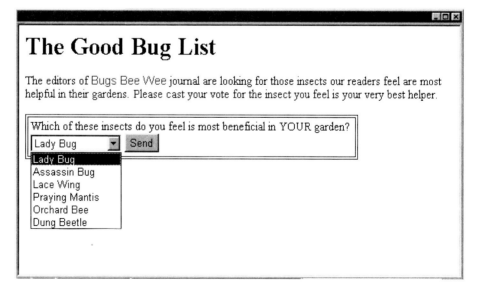

Figure 11.1 HTML code for <SELECT> container.

Figure 11.2 Expanded version of the <SELECT> list, showing all of the <OPTION>s.

attribute is *null*. A null value is a variable that has no value—not blank, not zero, but absolutely no value. Usually null is represented by binary zeros.

Look back at our previous examples of selection sets, checkboxes, and radio buttons. The value returned in those elements could be different from the value in the prompt. Like the other controls, if the Web weaver doesn't want to use the whole prompt, for example, "Praying Mantis," she can code a **value** attribute to specify a string other than the prompt. This attribute is discussed later. There are two unique attributes for the <SELECT> container: **size** and **multiple.**

size

The **size** attribute, which should be a positive integer, determines how many of the choices are shown in the initial list box. The default is a single entry with a downward scroll arrow next to it. Figure 11.1 shows how this looks on the screen. Only one element, the first in the list, appears. However, when the user clicks on the down arrow next to the selection, the whole list of options appears as a drop-down list, shown in Figure 11.2. This is a very handy option. When the user activates her choice, the list contracts back to a single entry, with the choice highlighted and shown in the window. If you want your user to see a fixed number of options and be able to scroll among them, set the **size** to that number. However, the default for the **size** attribute is often the most effective choice.

Figure 11.3 shows the same <SELECT> container with a **size** attribute of 4. The only difference between the code in Figure 11.3 and the code in Figure 11.2 is this **size** attribute on the <SELECT> container. Now the user must scroll down the list, only seeing four choices at a time. This is less desirable than the default value in most cases, because it takes up more screen area without providing all the list options. The user still must scroll to see all the options.

multiple

The **multiple** option allows the <SELECT> element to accept multiple inputs. This is the "check all that apply" rather than "check only one" option. Used this way, the <SELECT> option works like checkboxes rather than like radio buttons. The **multiple** attribute is a *toggle* and takes no value; it is just coded as an attribute. There are three ways for the user to select multiple entries:

1. She can hold down the Shift key and click on two different values, in which case *all the values* between the first and second are highlighted and chosen.
2. She can hold down the right mouse button and move the pointer, covering several different contiguous values, *all of which* are chosen when she lifts the mouse button.
3. She can hold down the Control key and then click on any of the selections. Each one that has been clicked will appear highlighted.

If the user simply clicks on one selection, then another, only the most recent selection is chosen.

```
<FORM
        action="http://www.bugsbeewee.com/cgi-bin/vote.cgi"
        method="POST"
>
Which of these insects do you feel is most beneficial
in YOUR garden?
<BR>
<SELECT
        name="goodbug"
        size="4">
<OPTION>Lady Bug</OPTION>
<OPTION>Assassin Bug</OPTION>
<OPTION>Lace Wing</OPTION>
<OPTION>Praying Mantis</OPTION>
<OPTION>Orchard Bee</OPTION>
<OPTION>Dung Beetle</OPTION>
</SELECT>
 <INPUT
        type="SUBMIT"
        value="Send"><BR>
</FORM>
```

The Good Bug List

The editors of Bugs Bee Wee journal are looking for those insects our readers feel are most helpful in their gardens. Please cast your vote for the insect you feel is your very best helper.

Which of these insects do you feel is most beneficial in YOUR garden?

Lady Bug
Assassin Bug
Lace Wing
Praying Mantis   Send

Figure 11.3 A screen capture showing a <SELECT> list with a size="4" attribute coded.

<OPTION>option text</OPTION>

Description: defines one element of a menu list created with a <SELECT> element.

Type: container.

Attributes: class, dir, disabled, id, label, lang, onClick, onDblClick, onKeyDown, onKeyPress, onKeyUp, onMouseDown, onMouseMove, onMouseOut, onMouseOver, onMouseUp, onSelect, selected, style, title, and value.

Special note: The <OPTION> container is coded only within a <SELECT> element.

The <OPTION> container has a closing tag, and although it is considered optional, we still recommend that you use it. Remember that wise Web weavers always close their containers. The text contained within the <OPTION> container is displayed in the pull-down selection box. In almost all cases, the text should be short, only a word or two rather than a phrase. The choices should be distinct from one another so that the user clearly knows what he is choosing.

value

Normally the <SELECT> tag returns the text string contained within the selected <OPTION> element as a value. For example, if the user selects the fifth <OPTION> from the set shown in Figure 11.3, the browser will return the string "bestbug=Orchard+Bee" to the CGI script. Notice that the blank between Orchard and Bee has been replaced by a plus sign, as per normal encoding. Figure 11.1 shows how a set of <OPTION> elements without values is coded. Look at Figure 11.4, where we have added values to make the script a little easier to code. The HTML page is identical to the one shown in Figure 11.1.

If the CGI script is to understand the input data from the form, it must be programmed to match the input data string with an expected value. Generally speaking, it takes more work to check for long strings made up of multiple words. When there are spaces in the input string (converted to plus signs), they must either be removed or matched. Establishing a value that is a short string of letters makes it easier to check for expected values. Should the user choose the "Orchard Bee" when using the form in Figure 11.4, the browser will return the string "goodbug=ob" to the selected script. It is almost always worth the small effort required to set the **value** attributes, because they make the CGI or JavaScript script much easier to code.

```
<FORM
        action="http://www.bugsbeewee.com/cgi-bin/vote.cgi"
        method="POST"
>
Which of these insects do you feel is most beneficial
in YOUR garden?
<BR>
<SELECT
        name="goodbug">
<OPTION value="lb">Lady Bug</OPTION>
<OPTION value="ab">Assassin Bug</OPTION>
<OPTION value="lw">Lace Wing</OPTION>
<OPTION value="pm">Praying Mantis</OPTION>
<OPTION value="ob" selected>Orchard Bee</OPTION>
<OPTION value="db">Dung Beetle</OPTION>
</SELECT>
 <INPUT
        type="SUBMIT"
        value="Send"><BR>
</FORM>
```

Figure 11.4 HTML code for a <SELECT> list showing value attributes. The page on screen will be identical to the one in Figure 11.1.

selected

Just like the **checked** attribute for radio buttons and checkboxes, the **selected** attribute causes the <OPTION> in which it is coded to be preselected. The **selected** attribute has no value associated with it. You can preselect only one option with **selected,** unless the **multiple** attribute is coded within the <SELECT> element. If you try to preselect more than one option without the **multiple** attribute specified, none of them will be preselected.

If you don't specify a **size** attribute, and do preselect one of the options, then that option will appear in the selection box regardless of its position in the list. When the user opens the list, that selection will be highlighted. If the **multiple** attribute has been coded, then you can use **selected** to preselect several of the options, and each will appear highlighted. Generally, it is considered a good idea to preselect at least one <OPTION>, because if the user doesn't select one, the browser will return a null value for that control. The code in Figure 11.5 shows the result of preselecting "Orchard Bee" without specifying a **size** attribute.

Notice that even though the "Orchard Bee" <OPTION> is next to the last in the list, it appears in the selection box because it was **selected.** Figure 11.5 also shows the results page sent back from the server. We will examine the script that creates that page during our discussion of CGI later in the chapter (see Figure 11.11).

<OPTGROUP>collection of related options</OPTGROUP>

Description: defines a related group of <OPTIONS> elements within a <SELECT> container.
Type: container.
Attributes: class, dir, disabled, id, label, lang, onClick, onDblClick, onKeyDown, onKeyPress, onKeyUp, onMouseDown, onMouseMove, onMouseOut, onMouseOver, onMouseUp, onSelect, style, and title.

The <OPTGROUP> container is new in the HTML 4.0 specifications and is supposed to serve as a submenu element to break up long lists of options. For example, rather than putting up a list of all 50 states (which would be a pain to use), you could subdivide the country into four regions. States in each region would then be coded in an <OPTGROUP>. You would have 12 or 13 states in each <OPTGROUP>, making the list much more manageable. There is, however, one small fly in the ointment. The <OPTGROUP> element isn't currently supported by either of the popular browsers.

```
<FORM
        action="http://www.bugsbeewee.com/cgi-bin/vote.cgi"
        method="POST"
>
Which of these insects do you feel is most beneficial
in YOUR garden?
<BR>
<SELECT
        name="goodbug">
<OPTION value="lb">Lady Bug</OPTION>
<OPTION value="ab">Assassin Bug</OPTION>
<OPTION value="lw">Lace Wing</OPTION>
<OPTION value="pm">Praying Mantis</OPTION>
<OPTION value="ob" selected>Orchard Bee</OPTION>
<OPTION value="db">Dung Beetle</OPTION>
</SELECT>
 <INPUT
        type="SUBMIT"
        value="Send"><BR>
</FORM>
```

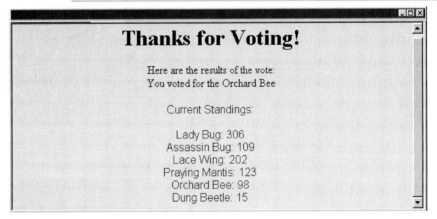

Figure 11.5 HTML code for the **selected** attribute with no **size** attribute coded and the results page returned.

Common Gateway Interface (CGI)

Up until now, we have looked at forms only from the perspective of the browser, but the real work with forms occurs at the server. Remember that the form is a tool for collecting and/or delivering data from the user. In most cases, after the data are collected, the browser packages them up, then ships them to the server for processing. The server runs a set of programs that takes these data from the browser, processes them, and passes them to a script that does *something* with the data. This process can be confusing, so let's look at the terms for a minute.

The set of programs that handles the data formatting and passing is called the *Common Gateway Interface (CGI)*. The user-written program that processes the user data and sends the results back to the user is usually called a **script**. A script is the name we give to programs, usually written by the Web weaver, that do the actual data processing.

Exactly what that *something* is that a script does with the data can vary greatly. It may simply thank users for their input. Or it may run a sophisticated search program, retrieve some collection of data from a database, and create an HTML document to present those data back to the users. Actually, the only limitations on what a script can do are those imposed by the imagination of the scriptors! The Web-based package-tracking program used by Federal Express is an example of how complex this type of program can become. Figure 11.6 shows the Federal Express home page.

Figure 11.6 Federal Express home page, a site that uses powerful CGI scripting (www.fedex.com).

CGI provides the standards and format that browsers use to send data to the server, as well as the format the server uses to hand the data off to a script. That program, usually called the *CGI script,* does whatever is necessary to process the data and send something back to the user.

There are three ways to obtain a CGI script:

1. You can write your own, usually in either the Perl or C programming languages or as a *shell script* (discussed later) on your Unix machine. Although Perl and C are the most common high-level languages used for CGI scripting, theoretically any high-level language can be used for this purpose.
2. If you are not a programmer, you can have a programmer write the script for you.
3. You can search across the Net, find a script that will work for you, download it to your server, and use it.

If you choose this last course, respect the *intellectual property* of others. Copy only *public domain* software, or *freeware.* The problem with this third method of obtaining a CGI script is that you must use the tools available from some source on the Net rather than having a tool crafted to your exact needs. Using "off the Net" scripts is fine for simple applications and for testing, but if you are contemplating a complex response to the user, you will usually need to find a way to create your own specialized CGI script.

Teaching programming is beyond the scope of this text. Instead, we will present some simple scripts and show you how to modify them. If you already know how to program in a high-level language, you can use the introduction to CGI in this chapter to help you create your own CGI scripts on your server. Even if you are not a programmer, you can use these simple scripts to get started, then have a programmer build a specialized script for you. CGI is becoming very popular as a forms-processing tool.

How CGI Works

CGI is a collection of programs the Web server uses to communicate with scripts on the server. The most common use of CGI is processing forms, but there are other, more sophisticated ways to use CGI to pass data. However, we will direct our attention to the use of CGI to process data from forms. Following are the steps for using a CGI script on a server to process a form:

1. The browser requests a form from the server.
2. The user fills out the form and activates the submit control.
3. The browser sends the form to the server.
4. The server recognizes the CGI *call* and passes the script name and the associated data to the set of programs called CGI.
5. The CGI application massages the data and creates a set of environmental variables, then starts the requested script.
6. The CGI script runs, usually generating a response to the user along with the other processing.
7. The CGI software passes the response created by the script back to the server.
8. The server passes the processed data and response back to the browser.
9. The browser displays the processed data and response to the user.

The only parts of this process that concern the Web weaver are the form the user fills out and the CGI script that processes the data and sends them back, along with a proper response, to the user. The rest can be considered part of the "magic of http." When a server gets a request for a CGI script, the server handles it differently than the request for just another Web page. Rather than posting the requested document back to the browser, the server looks for the script, or program, specified in the request, or *call,* and tries to run that CGI script. For example, the following line

```
http://www.bugsbeewee.com/cgi-bin/vote.cgi?goodbug=lb
```

asks the server, www.bugsbeewee.com, to invoke the script called vote.cgi that resides in the /cgi-bin directory.

Part of preparing the CGI script to run is passing the data from the client to the script. In our example here, the data are a single variable (goodbug=lb). This format for sending data illustrates the **method="GET"** process. If the **method** were "POST", the data would not be sent as part of the URL. Different platforms and different operating systems dictate different ways that the CGI scripts get their data.

On Unix systems, a CGI script will get data from one of two sources. If the data are sent via the POST method, it will appear in standard input, the input file given to all processes created on a Unix system. If the data are sent via the GET method, they will be placed in a special environmental variable, $QUERY_STRING. Because this is a Unix example, the fact that the variable name is uppercase is critical.

Figure 11.7 is an example of a simple Perl script, either.pl, that will process a single data element sent with either method, (GET or POST) and create a small HTML page to be sent back to the user.

```perl
#!/usr/bin/perl
#               This perl script will take a single variable, in either
#               GET or POST how, and report back to the users a small
#               HTML page showing the data they sent. To actually process
#                the data would require the further processing that appears at the end of
#               this script.
#
$how = $ENV{'REQUEST_METHOD'};
if ($how eq "GET")        {
      $form_data = $ENV{'QUERY_STRING'}
#               with a GET, all data are in QUERY_STRING
                        }
else                    {
      $form_size = $ENV{'CONTENT_LENGTH'};
      read (STDIN,$form_data,$form_size);
#               with POST I need to read from standard input
                        }
#               the data are now collected into the variable $form_data
#               let's parse it apart into name and value.
#
($nameis,$valueis)=split (/=/,  $form_data);
#
#               the data are now stored in the variables $nameis and
$valueis
#
#               Let's create the HTML code
print   "Content-type: text/html\n\n";
#
#       Now set up different background colors depending on method:
#
if ($how eq "GET")   {print  "<BODY style=\ "background-color: #FFFFCC\">\n";}
else {print "<BODY style=\"background-color: #FFCC99\">\n";}
print  "<H1>Your data </H1>\n";
print  "<H2>Submitted via the <SPAN style=\"color: #009900\">$how</SPAN> method</H2>\n\n";
print  "<H2>Variable name      $nameis </H2>\n\n";
print  "<H2>Variable value      $valueis </H2>\n\n";
print  "Isn\'t that nifty";
exit (0);
```

Figure 11.7 A Perl script that does simple CGI processing, echoing the data back to the browser (either.pl).

The page returned from this script will list a single data element sent from the form (see Figure 11.8). This script has little value for users except as a testing and *debugging* tool. It illustrates the necessary input and output processing for either method. We have included this script on the CD and stored it at the Web site so you can use it as a testing tool. It is rather handy to have this sort of tool available when developing forms.

```
<FORM
      action="http://www.bugsbeewee.com/cgi-bin/either.pl"
      method="Post"
>
Which of the following
<SPAN STYLE="font-style: italic; font-weight: bold;">Lepidoptera</SPAN>
is your favorite?<BR>
Choose only one.
<BR>
<INPUT TYPE="radio" name="fav" value="mb">Monarch <BR>
<INPUT TYPE="radio" name="fav" value="lm">Luna Moth <BR>
<INPUT TYPE="radio" name="fav" value="st">Black Swallow Tail <BR>
<INPUT TYPE="radio" name="fav" value="cs">Common Sulphur <BR>
<INPUT TYPE="radio" name="fav" value="mk">Milkweed Butterfly <BR>
<INPUT TYPE="radio" name="fav" value="tm">Tiger Moth <BR>
<INPUT
      type="SUBMIT"
      value="Send via POST"><BR>
</FORM>
```

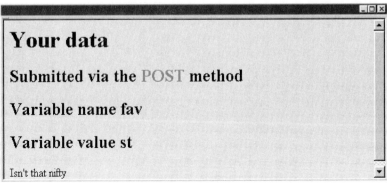

Figure 11.8 HTML code for the POST version of a form and the response page.

Figures 11.8 and 11.9 show two different versions of the same page, one sending data using the POST method and the other sending data using the GET method (look at the submit button). The code is identical for the two pages except for the submission method.

The script that does the processing, shown in Figure 11.7, is written in the Perl scripting language. If you are serious about building scripts, learning Perl is almost a must. Perl was written by Larry Wall, initially as a program to hang together various Unix tools. It has grown and been ported to all of the various Windows platforms, Macintosh, MS-DOS, VMS, Plan 9, and even OS/2. It is a very powerful language that is an excellent choice for CGI scripting. There are several good books designed to help you learn Perl, the most important being those written by Larry Wall.

When the code in Figure 11.7 is run, it creates one of two Web pages, shown in Figures 11.8 and 11.9. These pages simply show the method used to send the data, and the name and value of the variable sent to it—nothing fancy, but they do illustrate the concept. The script is available on the CD that accompanies this textbook. It is ready to run, and you might want to have your Web administrator install it so you can play with it. Since this isn't a book on

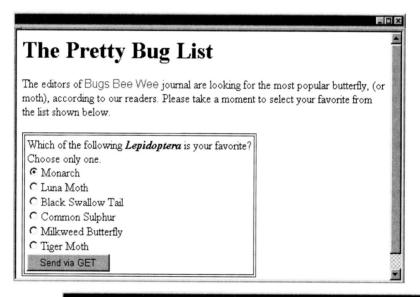

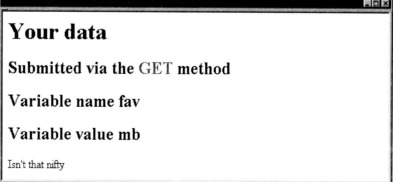

Figure 11.9 GET version of the form and the response page in Figure 11.8. HTML code is identical to that in Figure 11.8 except for submission method.

Perl, we will not discuss the script in Figure 11.7 in any detail. However, there is a detailed breakdown of that script available on the Web page for the text, as well as on the CD. The name of that file is either1.pl. It is a version of the same Perl script, and it contains extensive documentation explaining each step.

Building CGI Scripts

Now that you have seen what a CGI script can do, let's look at how scripts are constructed. We aren't going to cover all the possible things you could do in a CGI script; that would take a HUGE book. Rather, we are going to look at some of the more common features of CGI scripts.

Heading Information

When the CGI script prepares the data to return to the browser through the server, it must conform to some rules.

1. The return data must begin with either
   a. Some http header data telling the receiving system what type of file is being passed.
   b. The URL of another HTML document.
2. The header information *must* end with a blank line. That is how the browser and the server know where the end of the header is, by the blank line.
3. Everything following the blank line is considered part of the body of the returned document, unless you code a <HEAD> container. If you code a <HEAD> container, the actual content-type: line (discussed next) and a blank line should precede the <HEAD> container.

There are several other header data you can code, but we will let the server handle most of those for us. If you return a partial header to the server, it will fill in the missing information before sending it on to the browser. For now we will allow the server to help us out like that. If you want to explore creating your own complete http headers, read one of the several books on the market that deal exclusively with CGI (such as *CGI Programming on the World Wide Web* by Shishir Gundavaram, published by O'Reilly & Associates, Inc.). For purposes of this overview, we will focus on the least complex header information. The two most common lines in a simple header are discussed next.

content-type:

The content-type: header specifies the MIME content type of the data being sent back to the browser. ***MIME*** stands for ***Multipurpose Internet Mail Extensions.*** It was originally developed to send different types of files through the Net using electronic mail. The browser needs to know what type of information it is receiving so that it will be able to decipher it. Some of the more common content types are

- text/plain
- text/html
- image/gif
- image/jpeg

A complete description of the different MIME types is available on the Net at `http://www.w3.org/`. The `content-type:` line must be followed by a blank line to tell the server that the heading information is completed.

location:

Instead of sending back a dynamically created HTML document, the `location:` header line specifies the URL of a different HTML page that is to be sent in response to the user's request. This header line allows you to build dynamic pages on your site. This option is a very powerful tool for certain applications. When the user submits some form data for example, the browser will display one of many different pages depending on the choices specified in the form.

Let's suppose Bugs Bee Wee had a series of different bug data sheets for different areas of the country and for different uses for the bugs. One way of presenting this information would be to create a large table with links to each of the different pages as shown in Table 11.1.

REGION	PRETTY BUGS	TASTY BUGS	USEFUL BUGS
North West	Nwpb	Nwtb	Nwub
West	Wpb	Wtb	Wub
South West	Swpb	Swtb	Swub
North Central	Ncpb	Nctb	Ncub
South Central	Scpb	Sctb	Scub
North East	Nepb	Netb	Neub
East	Epb	Etb	Eub
South East	Sepb	Setb	Seub

Table 11.1 A representation of possible data sheets for different regions.

But a table like this could be very confusing for the user. It would be better to create a simple form asking users to select a data sheet by picking a region and a type of bug, using, for example, radio buttons. The CGI script would look at the user's selections and return the correct page. Figure 11.10 shows what that kind of form might look like.

The simple form in Figure 11.10 (on page 328), requiring the user to simply activate two radio buttons and then submit his choices, replaces a complex 24-element table (8 regions times 3 uses). When the user activates the "Send Data" control, the browser submits the form to the server, and the server runs the CGI script to select the correct page to return to the user. Figure 11.10 also presents the code for the page. The code will pass two parameters to the CGI script, the geographic region ("`region`") and the use to which the user wishes to put the insects ("`use`").

```
<BODY style="background-color: #CCFFCC;">
Many of the wonderful users of the
<SPAN style="font-family: sans-serif; color: #0000FF">
Bugs Bee Wee </SPAN>
Web pages have sent us data on some of their favorite
insects.  To receive these data sheets, please select
your geographic region, and the type of data sheets
you wish to read from the list below.  Activate the
"Send Data" button to see your choices.<BR>
<SPAN style="text-align: center">

<FORM method="POST" action="http://www.bugsbewee.com/cgi-bin/bugc
<H1>Bug Data Sheets</H1>
<H3>Please select your region of the country:</H3>
<INPUT type="RADIO" name="region" value="nw"> North West
<INPUT type="RADIO" name="region" value="w"> West
<INPUT type="RADIO" name="region" value="sw">South West <BR><BR>
<INPUT type="RADIO" name="region" value="nc"> North Central
<INPUT type="RADIO" name="region" value="sc"> South Central <BR><
<INPUT type="RADIO" name="region" value="ne"> North East
<INPUT type="RADIO" name="region" value="e"> East
<INPUT type="RADIO" name="region" value="se"> South East <BR>
<H3>Please select the type of data you would like:</H3>
<INPUT type="RADIO" name="use" value="p"> Pretty bugs
<INPUT type="RADIO" name="use" value="t"> Tasty bugs
<INPUT type="RADIO" name="use" value="u"> Useful bugs <BR><BR>
<INPUT type="SUBMIT" value="Send Data">
</FORM>
</SPAN>
```

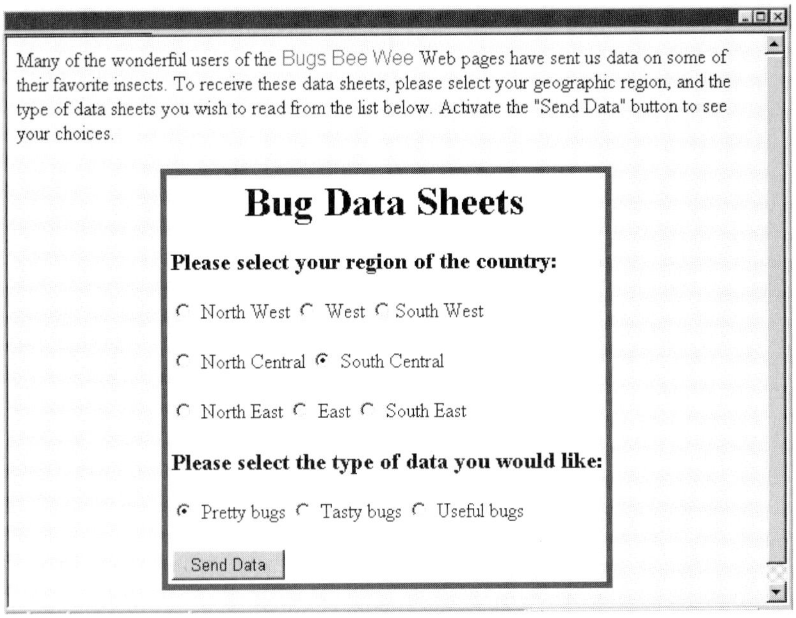

Figure 11.10 HTML code for the form used to select data sheets by server relocation.

Figure 11.11 (on page 329) presents part of a Unix shell script to process the data and return one of 24 different pages to the user. A ***shell script*** is a type of program that is built from a collection of Unix commands that the server runs, like a program written in a high-level language. In Figure 11.11, the command test is used to evaluate the relational expression that follows it, returning either "true" or "false."

This script is a little long, but the general idea is that first we select a region, then a test for the use within the specified region. Each of the 24 choices actually

```
#!/bin/bash
read line
data=`echo $line | sed -f datafix.sed`
where=`echo $data | awk '{print $1}'`
what=`echo $data | awk '{print $2}'`
case $where
    in
    sc)
            if test $what = "t"
            then
            echo location: http://www.bugsbeewee.com/bugdata/sct.html
            echo
            fi
            if test $what = "u"
            then
            echo location: http://www.bugsbeewee.com/bugdata/scu.html
            echo
            fi
            if test $what = "p"
            then
            echo location: http://www.bugsbeewee.com/bugdata/scp.html
            echo
            fi
            ;;
    nw)
            if test $what = "t"
            then
            echo location: http://www.bugsbeewee.com/bugdata/nwt.html
            echo
            fi
            if test $what = "u"
            then
            echo location: http://www.bugsbeewee.com/bugdata/nwu.html
            echo
            fi
            if test $what = "p"
            then
            echo location: http://www.bugsbeewee.com/bugdata/nwp.html
            echo
            fi
            ;;
    *)
            echo location: http://www.bugsbeewee.com/bugdata/nodata.html
            echo
            ;;
esac
#
```

Figure 11.11 A partial CGI script (bugdata.cgi) to select one of 24 pages.

specifies the location of a small HTML screen. For purposes of this example, only the North West and South Central selections actually resolve to new pages; all of the rest get the "no data" screen. If you are faced with this type of selection situation, you can expand the example in Figure 11.11 to create a much bigger page.

This technique is called ***server redirection,*** because rather than using a content-type: assignment in the header, the script returns the URL of a preset Web page for the browser to display. The code looks like this:

Location: URL-to-transfer-to.

The page designated by new URL would be loaded into the browser. It is critical that a blank line follow the Location: line. This is a very powerful technique to let the user see different pages based on her choice.

Basic Programming Structures

Before we get into the actual CGI coding, we need to consider the basic programming structures:

1. Sequence block
2. Selection block
3. Iteration block

Sequences

A *sequence* is simply a set of statements that are executed one after the other, in the order they appear in the program. The following snippet of a shell script shows a set of instructions that form a sequence. Don't worry about understanding all of the code—just look at the way the lines of code are arranged.

```
read line
data=`echo $line | sed -f datafix.sed`
where=`echo $data | awk '{print $1}'`
what=`echo $data | awk '{print $2}'`
```

Each of these lines of code is executed, one after the other, in a sequence. The data are read into the variable line, then a sed script is run on the data. Next, the first awk is executed, and then the second awk is executed. The statements are executed in sequential order, hence the name, *coding sequence* or sequence block.

Selection

The next type of construct used to create programs is the *selection* block. In most programming languages, the selection block allows the execution of one of two different sets of code based on some condition. It is also called an IF block. Selection is the heart of most programs. The ability of a section of code to actually make decisions is very important. Selection allows us to create code that can respond to a variety of conditions. You can see a simple selection example in the following code fragment, where the script checks to see if the user wants an "Edible" bug catalog or a "Watchable" one. Based on whether or not the variable use is set equal to "Edible," the script mails one of two catalogs.

```
if test $use = "Edible"
     then
     mail -s "Edible Insect Catalog" $addr < $pth/ecat.txt
     else
     mail -s "Pretty Insect Catalog" $addr < $pth/pcat.txt
fi
```

Looking at the code, we see that one of two different mail messages, either ecat.txt or pcat.txt, will be sent based on whether the variable $use was equal to "Edible" or not. The way to read this code is as follows:

- IF the value stored at location $use is equal to "Edible", then send the user the catalog of edible bugs, ecat.txt.
- ELSE (the value stored at $use is not equal to "Edible"), so send the user the catalog of pretty bugs, pcat.txt.

In some books on programming this is called an IF/THEN/ELSE block. When the selection statement uses these words, it implies the following:

- IF will start the selection block.
- THEN will indicate what is to be done if the condition that IF is testing is true.
- ELSE will indicate what is to be done if the condition that IF is testing is false.

Of course, in the Unix code presented here, you will notice that IF, THEN, and ELSE are in lowercase letters.

The "fi" is used to mark the end of the if block.

Iteration

Iteration means to repeat a set of code, and it is often referred to as a *program loop*. Iteration usually requires two lines of code, one to mark the first line that is to be repeated, and another to mark the last line in the loop. Although we do not need to iterate any code right now, keep this structure in mind. It will come in handy later.

Script Dissection

Now that we understand the basic programming structures involved, let's look at the steps in the following script in detail:

```
#!/bin/bash
read line
data=`echo $line | sed -f datafix.sed`
where=`echo $data | awk '{print $1}'`
what=`echo $data | awk '{print $2}'`
```

This set of lines finds the values associated with the two variables of region and use. The second line reads in the variable line, which contains both name=value pairs passed to the script from the browser. The variable line looks like this:

```
region=sc&use=p.
```

The region sc is "South Central" and the use, p indicates "pretty bugs." The next line runs the stream editor (sed) against the "name=value" pairs, removing the variable names, the ampersand, and the equal signs, and leaving the two values separated by a single space. In this case the result of executing sed would be to assign the variable data the value of "sc p". The next two lines use the awk utility to peel out the two different values and assign them to two script variables—where and what. At this point we have assigned the values to variables that we can use in the script itself. The next step is to decide which page the user really wants. To do that, the script combines a *case structure* (discussed next) with a set of three if blocks:

```
case $where
    in
    sc)
                if test $what = "t"
                then
                echo location: http://www.bugsbeewee.com/bugdata/sct.html
                echo
                fi
                if test $what = "u"
                then
                echo location: http://www.bugsbeewee.com/bugdata/scu.html
                echo
                fi
                if test $what = "p"
                then
                echo location: http://www.bugsbeewee.com/bugdata/scp.html
                echo
                fi
                ;;
```

Case Structures

The case structure is a sophisticated tool that selects among more than two different values based on a condition. In contrast, the if structure is limited to two choices. Suppose we ask case to look at the variable where (we ask for the contents by prepending a $ to the front of the variable name) and see if it matches any of several different possible values, each of which is followed by a closing parenthesis. If the value stored at $where matches the string listed, in this example sc, then the case structure executes the instructions following the parenthesis.

In this example, there are three if statements following the case selector. Each of the if statements corresponds to one of the three uses the user could request—t for tasty, u for useful, and p for pretty. Depending on which of the three options the user chooses, a different page location is returned to the browser. Thus, if the user chooses pretty bugs, ($what = "p"), the script would return Location: http://www.bugsbeewee.com/bugdata/scp.html.

This page should contain the data the user requested, a newsletter on pretty insects found in the South Central region of the country. The blank line, produced by *echo* with nothing after it, is critically important. Just as the Content-type: line must be followed by a blank line, so must the location: line.

When creating these CGI scripts, it is often useful to enlist the assistance of the Web administrator in order to gain access to the CGI error logs on the server. Those logs are not usually available to the casual user but can be helpful when debugging a CGI script.

This script is actually very simple. It does not do any error checking. If for some reason the browser sends data that don't fit the pattern, the script simply generates a "There were no files found, try again" page. This is not very helpful, but you could add additional code if you feel so inclined. Using this shell script as a model, you can create more complex and useful scripts.

A very valuable though infrequently used pair of header tags are `Pragma:` and `Expires:`. This pair of tags can be used as follows:

1. `Pragma:` prevents the browser from caching the page.
2. `Expires:` forces the browser to reload the page after a specified date.

Pragma:

Suppose you are creating a page that supplies different information but of the same type over and over. Some examples might be the current temperature, the results of different mathematical operations, or even a page that returns the results of a poll. In these cases, you don't want the browser to reload a previous version of the page from cache memory; rather, you want it to download the new page from the server.

An example of such an operation is the first script we discussed in this chapter, the "favorite insect" counter (Figure 11.5). The first couple of times we tested the script, it seemed to work just fine. However, every once in a while it failed to update the counter for our insect, especially if we chose the same insect twice or more in a row. Finally, we tried reloading the page each time, and found that the problem was the browser, not the script. Sometimes the browser would reload the page from the server; other times it would just present the page already cached in memory. To prevent the browser from using a cached page, we can include the following line in the header information: `Pragma: no-cache`.

Pragma, according to the *Princeton Online Dictionary,* stands for pragmatic, or useful, information. This is a standardized form of comment that has special meaning to a program, usually a compiler. A *compiler* is a utility program that translates a human-readable language like C or COBOL into machine-readable language, that is, binary code. A pragma usually conveys information that is nonessential but helps optimize the program. The only value currently defined for `Pragma:` in HTML is `no-cache`.

The code in Figure 11.12 (on page 334) shows the script that processes the data sent by the form you last saw in Figure 11.5, the "favorite bug" report. You might want to page back and take a little peek at that form so that you know what data this script will be receiving.

Let's take a close look at the script in Figure 11.12. The second line sets the variable `pth` to the path for all of the files. It is generally considered a good idea to explicitly code the path to each file. That way there are no assumptions or surprises when the files are created or stored.

The next set of lines creates the beginnings of the response document. Notice the use of the `Pragma:` statement to prevent the browser from caching the page. Because of this statement, the user should always see the correct and current count. Since `Pragma:` is part of the heading data, there is the requisite blank line following the `Pragma:` line.

The next line invokes the `sed` utility to process the input data, cleaning it up. This is very similar to the `sed` we saw in the server redirection script (see Figure 11.11). The line following the `sed` makes a copy of the current file so that the `awk` utility can create a new version of the file with the updated count.

There are three calls to `awk` in the script. The first one creates the line that informs the user of her choice—for example, "You chose the Orchard Bee." The next `awk` is the one that performs the actual vote tabulation. The third `awk`, a few

```
#!/bin/bash
pth= '/etc/httpd/cgi-bin/public'
echo Content-type: text/html
echo Pragma: no-cache
echo
echo '<HEAD>'
echo '<STYLE>'
echo '        BODY { background-color: #FFCCCC }'
echo '</STYLE>'
echo '</HEAD>'
echo '<BODY>'
echo '<CENTER>'
echo '<H1>Thanks for Voting!</H1>'
echo 'Here are the results of the vote:<BR>'
read line
vote=`echo $line | sed -f votefix.sed`
cp $pth/votes $pth/vote2
awk -f votewho.awk $pth/vote2 $vote
awk -f votecnt.awk $pth/vote2 $vote > $pth/votes

echo '<BR>'
echo '<SPAN style="font-family: sans-serif; color: #000099; font-size: medium">'
awk -f voterpt.awk $pth/votes
echo '</SPAN>'
echo '</BODY>'
#
```

Figure 11.12 The CGI script that processes "favorite bug" votes (vote.cgi).

lines later in the script, prints the updated totals, including the user's choice. The awk program is the real workhorse in this and many CGI scripts. The echo statements simply output the text string that follows them, in this case HTML code.

All of the scripts in this example are included on the CD and on the Web site for the book. If you have a Unix machine available to you, feel free to put those scripts on your server and play with them. The examples from the book should also work on the McGraw-Hill Web site for the text.

Expires:

Expires: defines a date after which the page should be considered outdated and so must be reloaded from the server. You can use this header information to force the browser to always reload a page from the server. Just specify the expiration date as being before the current date. For example, you could code the following in a heading:

Expires: Monday, 01-Jan-90 00:00:00 GMT

This code would cause the browser to reload the page each time it was referenced, because the existing page, in cache, would be marked as expired.

Putting It All Together

Now let's look at a little more complex problem. The folks at Bugs Bee Wee aim to build a small database of customers who want their catalog. That way they can both send the customer the current catalog and have a file of e-mail addresses to send further catalogs as they are created. Remember the situation back in the beginning of Chapter 10? Jon Scarab was getting e-mails requesting catalogs, manually e-mailing out the catalogs, and updating the company database so he could send other data later. Once the company became popular, Jon was spending several hours each day just handling the e-mail. Well, now it's time to free Jon from that labor, so he can go outside and look at all the pretty butterflies. Figure 11.13 shows the new form. From the user's perspective, it looks just like the old one, but notice that there is one slight difference in the <FORM> tag. Compare the code in Figure 11.13 with that in Figure 10.1. Notice that instead of sending the data to Jon via e-mail, this script sends the data to a CGI script.

```
<FORM
        action="http://www.bugsbeewee.com/cgi-bin/bugorder.cgi"
        method="POST"
        style="font-family: fantasy; background-color: #CCFFFF;"
>
Your name:
        <INPUT type="TEXT" name="name" size="30" maxsize="80">
<BR><BR>
What do you like to do with your bugs?<BR>
        <INPUT type=RADIO name="use" value="W"> Watch 'em
        <INPUT type=RADIO name="use" value="E"> Eat 'em <BR><BR>
E-Mail address:<BR>
        <INPUT type="TEXT" name="email" size="30" maxsize=80> <BR><BR>
<INPUT   type="SUBMIT" value="Request Catalog"><BR>
</FORM>
```

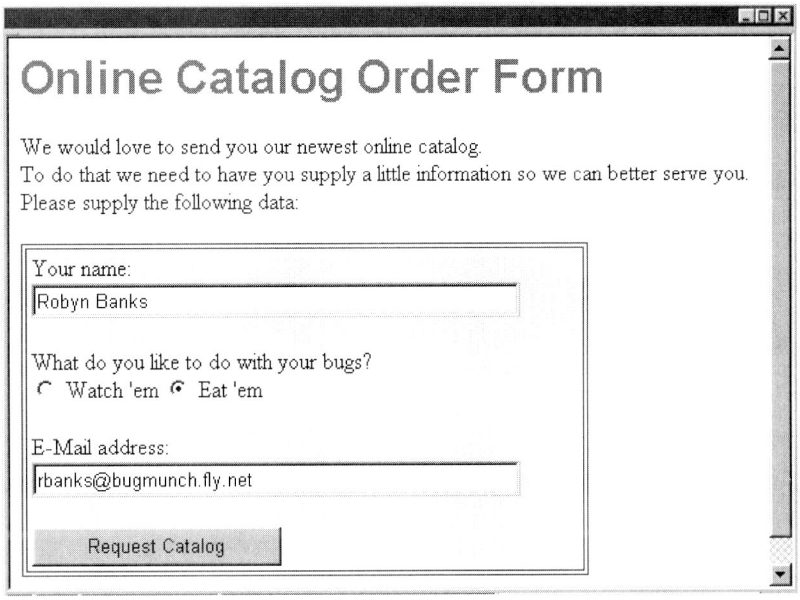

Online Catalog Order Form

We would love to send you our newest online catalog.
To do that we need to have you supply a little information so we can better serve you.
Please supply the following data:

Your name:

Robyn Banks

What do you like to do with your bugs?
○ Watch 'em ● Eat 'em

E-Mail address:

rbanks@bugmunch.fly.net

[Request Catalog]

Figure 11.13 HTML code for updated catalog request form, now using a CGI script.

The script, bugorder.cgi, is a much more complex script than those we have examined so far, as it should be, for it is a real production script. Let's look at the whole script, and then break it down. Some of the code will look familiar; good code deserves to be repeated. Figure 11.14 shows all of the CGI script.

```bash
#!/bin/bash
pth='/etc/httpd/cgi-bin/public'
echo Content-type: text/html
echo
echo '<HEAD>'
echo '<STYLE>'
echo '        BODY { background-color: #FFCC99 }'
echo '</STYLE>'
echo '</HEAD>'
echo '<BODY>'
echo '<CENTER>'
echo '<H1>Thanks for Your Order!</H1>'
read line
order=`echo $line | sed -f orderfix.sed`
#               Now we have three elements in the order string:
#                    whom, use, e-mail address
#               Let's parse them out.
whom=`echo $order | awk -F: '{print $1}'`
#               Grab the first field, delimited by colons, and
#               stuff it into the variable "whom"
use=`echo $order | awk -F: '{print $2}'`
#               Now grab the use, E or W
#
addr=`echo $order | awk -F: '{print $3}'`
#               And the e-mail address
#
#               Now that we have the data, let's change the
#               use to be correct, Edible or Watchable
if test $use = "E"
    then
    use="Edible"
    else
    use="Watchable"
fi
echo "Here are the data that we are entering into our database for:"
echo '<SPAN style="font-family: sans-serif; color: #9933FF; font-size: medium">'
echo " $whom <BR>"
echo '</SPAN>'
echo "You are interested in our"
```

Figure 11.14 The CGI script that processes catalog orders for Bugs Bee Wee.

```
echo '<SPAN style="font-family: sans-serif; color: #9933FF; font-size: medium">'
echo "$use Insect"
echo '</SPAN> catalog.<BR>'
echo "We will send your catalog to"
echo '<SPAN style="font-family: sans-serif; color: #9933FF; font-size: medium">'
echo "$addr </SPAN>"
echo ", your e-mail address.<BR>"
echo "<BR>"
echo '</SPAN>'
echo "<H2>Thanks again for your order, your catalog is on the way!</H2>"
echo '</BODY>'
echo '</HTML>'
#          Now do the database
echo "$order" >> $pth/catorder.data
sort -u $pth/catorder.data -o $pth/catorder.data
#          Got the datafile, let's send 'em the catalog of choice!
#
if test $use = "Edible"
    then
    mail -s "Edible Insect Catalog" $addr < $pth/ecat.txt
    else
    mail -s "Pretty Insect Catalog" $addr< $pth/pcat.txt
fi
```

Figure 11.14 continued

The first part of the script duplicates code we have seen before, simply building a Web page to return information to the user. The interesting change in the sed script is the addition of the restoration of the "at" sign, @, in the e-mail address. The browser encodes this sign as %40, so the sed script must convert that value back to @.

The series of three calls to the awk utility will parse the three data elements out of the data stream so that the script can generate a pretty report to send back to the user. Following the awk calls is a little if block that changes the value of the use variable from a single letter, as sent by the form, to either the string "Edible" or the string "Watchable" for later use in the reporting page.

The next sequence block of code simply builds the variable portion of the reporting page. It doesn't perform any real magic. The power of the script is housed in the last few lines. Let's look at those lines one at a time. First:

```
echo "$order" >> $pth/catorder.data
```

This line adds a new entry to the catalog data file, (catorder.data), by concatenating (cat) the new input line $order to the existing file. *Concatenation* means to add to or extend, in this case to extend the data file. It puts the new order data (name, type, and e-mail address) at the end of the existing set of data. Figure 11.15 shows a segment of that data file.

12. How is a case structure different from an if structure?

13. How can the Web administrator help you in writing CGI scripts?

14. What does the echo statement do within a CGI script?

15. What does a browser do when a Web page's expiration date has passed?

Exercises

11.1. Create a new HTML document with a form. The title bar should display "What Are Your Favorite Things?" with your name and the assignment due date included within comment lines. Form results should be sent to your e-mail account or an e-mail account given to you by the instructor. At a minimum the form should contain the following:

    a. Text boxes to accept the person's name and e-mail address
    b. List boxes with value attributes that provide the user with three or more options corresponding to these preferences:
       (1) Favorite color
       (2) Favorite day of the week
       (3) Favorite season
       (4) Favorite holiday
    c. Submit control
    d. Reset control

11.2. This exercise requires the modification of a CGI script bugorder.cgi that is found on the attached CD or the text's associated Web site. Make a copy of bugorder.cgi and call it ex11-2.cgi. The new CGI script must be loaded onto your Web server before you can complete this exercise. Retrieve the Bugs Bee Wee Order Form you created in Exercise 10.2 and modify it to use the CGI script ex11-2.cgi instead of posting the results using e-mail. The CGI script should be modified to send an order confirmation back to the user with the bug selection and credit card company he or she submits.

11.3. This exercise requires the modification of a CGI script bugdata.cgi that is found on the attached CD or the text's associated Web site. Make a copy of bugdata.cgi and call it ex11-3.cgi. The new CGI script must be loaded onto your Web server before you can complete this exercise. Retrieve the Complaint Form you created in Exercise 10.3 and modify it to use the CGI script ex11-3.cgi instead of posting the results using e-mail. Create four independent HTML documents that respond to the user when he or she chooses one of the following:

    a. I just wanted you to know.
    b. Please respond to the e-mail address given.
    c. Contact my lawyer.
    d. Go to #!$#*.

The CGI script should be modified to send one of the response documents back to the user when a valid selection has been submitted.

11.4. This exercise requires the creation of a new CGI script called `ex11-4.cgi`. It uses program logic from `bugdata.cgi` and `bugorder.cgi`, which are found on the attached CD or the text's associated Web site. The new CGI script must be loaded onto your Web server before you can complete this exercise.

Retrieve the Homework home page you updated in Exercise 10.4. Create a new HTML document containing a form and a link to this page on your home page. The title bar on the page with the new form should display "What Do You Think?" Also include your name and the assignment due date within comment lines on the new form page. The form should collect information from the user and use the CGI script `ex11-4.cgi` to process the data. The form needs to contain submit and reset controls. The information collected must include the user's name and his or her e-mail address along with an evaluation of your page that offers the following radio-button options:

    a. Great site, keep up the good work.
    b. Good content, but design needs some work.
    c. I like the design, but you didn't say much with it.
    d. You need to start over with this site.

Each option should include a **name** and **value** attribute.

The CGI script should send a confirmation back to the user thanking him or her for the time and effort. The confirmation should use the name the user submits along with an appropriate response to the radio-button selection.

11.5. This exercise uses the Perl script `either.pl` that must be loaded onto your Web server before you can begin. Retrieve the Voting Form you created in Exercise 10.5 and modify it to use the Perl script `either.pl` instead of posting the results using e-mail. This script is provided on the attached CD or the text's associated Web site. Two different HTML documents, one that uses the GET method and another that uses the POST method, need to be created. Print a copy of both the HTML documents and the resulting screen display.

11.6. This exercise requires the modification of a CGI script `bugorder.cgi` that is found on the attached CD or the text's associated Web site. Make a copy of `bugorder.cgi` and call it `ex11-6.cgi`. The new CGI script must be loaded onto your Web server before you can complete this exercise. Retrieve your school's home page updated in Exercise 10.6 and modify it to use the CGI script `ex11-6.cgi` instead of posting the results using e-mail. The CGI script should be modified to send a Course Request confirmation back to the user with the course prefix, number, and description he or she submitted.

## CHAPTER twelve

FEATURES TO HELP THE USERS

S everal HTML techniques that can bring added life to your pages—and make life much easier for your users—are a bit outside the mainstream of "standard" HTML. Some, like searchable documents or server-based dynamic documents, may require close work with your Web administrator.

Searchable
Documents

A document that runs a search on your Web site, called a *searchable document,* can be a great feature for your users. It enables them to run a keyword search on your site, or on a subset of the files on your site, to find specific information. However, it can present a security concern for your Web server administrator. As mentioned in the chapter on CGI scripting, you need to be very aware of the presence of unethical users. Just as you should carefully review your CGI scripts with your Web server administrator, likewise you should consult with your Web server administrator when you are going to set up a searchable document.

Here's the reason for the security concerns. The server normally expects to return an HTML document to the browser and then go on to something else. When a search is involved, the server has to run a search program and send the results back to the browser. As with a document that executes a CGI script, a searchable document invokes a user-written search script that could access any file on the Web server. This is dangerous, because sensitive files could be accidentally exposed within the search domain. In this chapter we will consider how to prevent problems with the server.

<ISINDEX>

Description: indicates that the document contains a tool to perform searches.
Type: empty tag.
Attributes: Action, class, dir, id, lang, prompt, style, and title.
Special notes: The <ISINDEX> tag was deprecated in the HTML 4.0 specifications in favor of the <INPUT> element. The specifications require that the tag be coded in the <HEAD> container, but most browsers support its inclusion in the <BODY> element as well. In the latter case, the browser will place the search field where the <ISINDEX> element is positioned.

The <ISINDEX> element is another way to link to the browser. This tag is much like the <A>anchor</A> and <SUBMIT> tags. The difference is that <ISINDEX> passes only one or more keywords to the server as a string to be matched by the search script. The HTML 4.0 specifications have deprecated the <ISINDEX> element in favor of the <INPUT> element we discussed in Chapter 10. We will use the recommended method in our examples, but be aware that older pages may use the <ISINDEX> element.

Using the <INPUT> method requires additional code, and a little more work to create the CGI script that does the work; but, hey, we want to be HTML 4.0 compliant, right? A sample script is shown in Figure 12.5. The *search script* may look at the contents of a single file or database, or it may search across one or more directories. It may even search every file on the server to locate specific data requested by the user. If you are designing the script to search more than a single file, *be sure* to check with your Web site administrator to ensure that any sensitive files are protected from the script.

The Calling Document

You can include a search element on one of your Web pages, but it is often more useful for your users, and easier to code, if you create a separate page to serve as the search-form page. A ***calling document*** is then needed to bring the search page up. Figure 12.1 shows an example of a calling document. Notice that the link invokes a CGI script on the server. The user can activate the link that acts as a request for information, and a new screen will pop up to allow him to perform the search. When the user activates search, the link invokes a CGI script on the server called search1.cgi. He can enter the data he wants on the search page, touch the Enter key, and see another screen that gives him the results of his search. There is a single CGI script that either sends the user the search form or sends back the results of the search. This is a more sophisticated script than those we have seen so far, but it is not beyond understanding with a little careful study.

```
<HTML>
<HEAD>
<TITLE> Interesting Trivia </TITLE>
</HEAD>
<BODY >
<CENTER><H1>Interesting Trivia</H1></CENTER>
One of the things everybody needs to know is the gestation period of
various animals.  I mean, after all, you never know when somebody,
somewhere is going to come up and ask you the gestation period
of a camel.  So if you want to learn the gestation period for
different animals, you can
<A HREF="http://searchable.school.edu/cgi-bin/search1.cgi">search</A>
for that gestation period using a nifty search page.<BR>
Have fun!
</BODY>
</HTML>
```

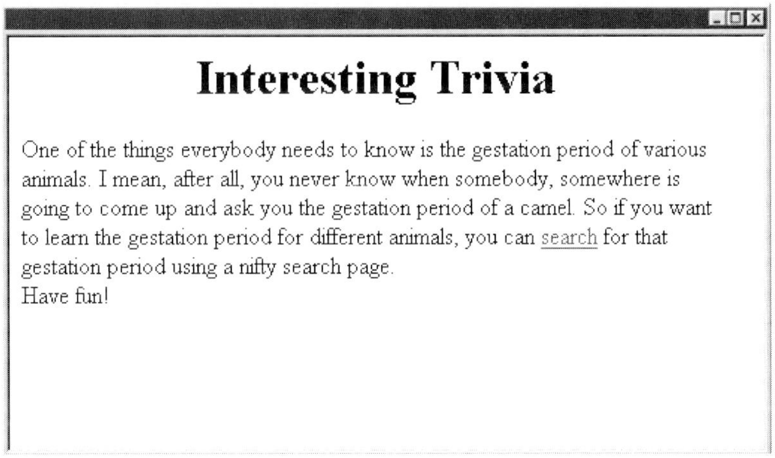

Interesting Trivia

One of the things everybody needs to know is the gestation period of various animals. I mean, after all, you never know when somebody, somewhere is going to come up and ask you the gestation period of a camel. So if you want to learn the gestation period for different animals, you can search for that gestation period using a nifty search page.
Have fun!

Figure 12.1 HTML page code that invokes the CGI script to do server searching.

The Search-Request Page

In Figure 12.1, no data are passed to the script. Therefore, the script assumes the user wants to see the search-request page, that is, the form for entering data, as shown in Figure 12.2. (We will see the entire source code for this page and for the result pages in Figure 12.5.) The browser displays the Web page that was generated by the search script and waits for the user to type in an animal name and touch the Enter key. In our example here, the user has asked for the gestation period of a camel. Smart user! She will be ready when asked! The browser sends the requested word, "Camel," back to the address specified in the **action** attribute of the form that contains the <INPUT> element. (This is the same URL that was requested with the link to the search itself.) This step works like the CGI examples you saw in the previous chapter. The difference is that there is no <SUBMIT> control.

One of the less than obvious features of a form with a single text <INPUT> control is that the user can submit it simply by touching the Enter key. This is a handy bit of knowledge to tuck away. That is the case here as well. The address to which the browser sends the data is the address of the search script, so this works just fine.

Beware, however, if you choose to use the <INPUT> tag from within a regular HTML document rather than using the technique presented here. There could be a problem with your document handling the return data. The <INPUT> tag will send the data back to the URL of the page that contains it. That means that the URL of the page that contains the <INPUT> must be able to process the data returned to it. The <BASE> tag, discussed later in this chapter, is very useful, as it modifies the URL of the document to the one specified in the tag.

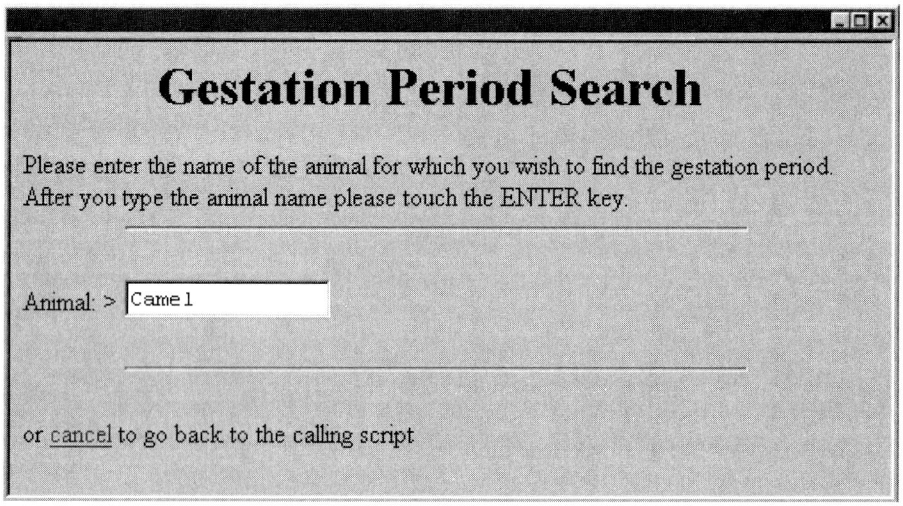

Figure 12.2 The first HTML page returned by the CGI search script (the search request page).

The "Success" Page

After the user sends a request to the server, the script that created the page for the user to enter the choice builds another, different HTML page, (a "success" page), containing the requested data and sends it back to the user. Notice that the user has the option of canceling the search by activating cancel on the search page (Figure 12.2). Figure 12.3 shows the document generated by the search1.cgi script that is returned when the browser finds one or more matches in the database.

Besides presenting the user with the results of the search, this document also provides some additional navigation tools. If the user wants to search for a different animal, she can activate the search link and go back to the search page. If the user is finished searching, she can activate the calling page link and go back to the document that originally offered the search link.

If the user chooses the "Back" button on the browser, it will go back to the search page as well. Additional navigation tools are essential, because the page may have been bookmarked and the user may want to return to it. In that case, the browser would be sent to the search engine with the word requested, and the search script would return the same results page. The URL stored in the bookmark file would be http://a.server.somewhere/cgi-bin/search1.cgi. Notice that this looks suspiciously like the CGI calls we saw before, because the <INPUT> element is part of the CGI we have already studied!

If the user had only this screen bookmarked, and if there were no navigation links on the screen, the browser would only be able to return to the search itself, not the page that called the search. The URL of the calling page would not be available in the computer's *cache,* that is, in the memory accessible to the browser. Navigation links are essential on *all* the pages you create!

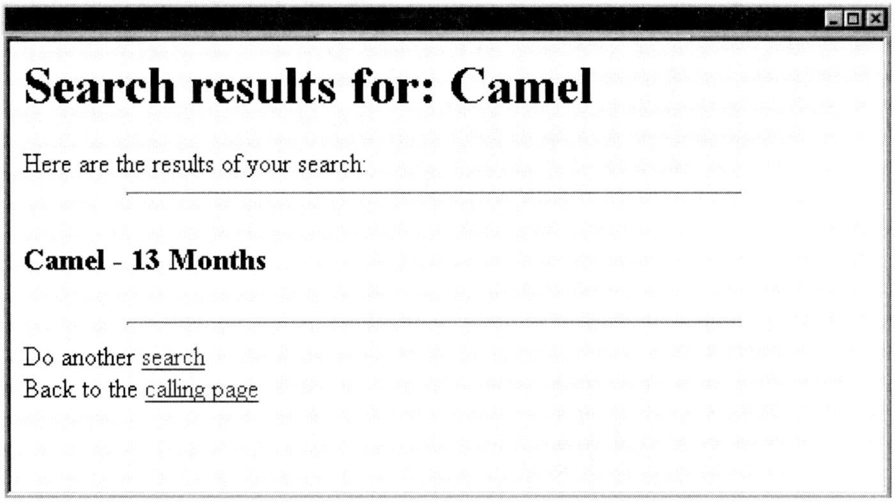

Search results for: Camel

Here are the results of your search:

Camel - 13 Months

Do another search
Back to the calling page

Figure 12.3 The HTML page generated by the CGI script when there is a match in the database, (the "success" page).

The "Miss" Page

Now let's look at the case when the search script doesn't find a match—that is, when the search was unsuccessful and generated a "miss." If the user requests data about an animal that is not in the database, he is politely told that there is no entry for that animal. The user is then allowed to either start a new search or go back to the page that sent the browser to the search in the first place. This kind of navigation tool is also critical.

Figure 12.4 shows the screen the user sees (the "miss" page) when the gestation period of a toad is requested. (Note: Toads are amphibians, so they lay eggs. The time it takes an egg to hatch is usually called the incubation period not the gestation period.) The user is given the same navigation tools as those presented in the case of a match. The screen looks similar to the screen that gives the results if the search is successful. It is important to keep some consistency of style, or similarity of layout, across related screens in a series.

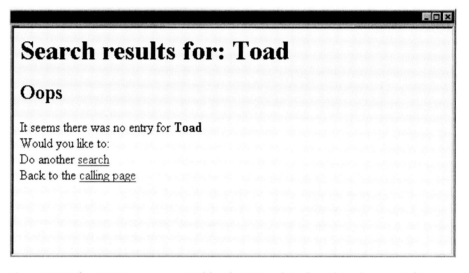

Figure 12.4 The HTML page generated by the CGI script when there is no match in the database (the "miss" page).

The Search Script

Now, without further ado, we present for your amusement and edification, Figure 12.5, the CGI shell script that does all these wonderful things. The script is a Bourne shell script, which should run on most Unix machines with little or no modification. The following discussion is not intended to teach you Unix scripting, but is only an overview. This script can be used "as is" or modified to generate many different HTML pages. It can be logically divided into three different areas:

1. The code to generate the search page
2. The page to report a miss
3. The code to report on successful matches

```sh
#!/bin/sh
# This shell script will do a simple search of a document to demonstrate
# how the <INPUT type="text"> tool can be used. It allows the user to submit
# a request for the search form by calling this script w/ no
# arguments, or to cause a search by calling the document w/
# an argument. The script will check first and generate different
# HTML documents depending upon the presence or absence of command
# line parameters.
#
echo "Content-type: text/html"
echo
echo "<HTML>"
echo "<HEAD>"
#       Put out the standard header info. . .
#
if test $REQUEST_METHOD = "POST"
      then read QUERY_STRING
fi
if test -z $QUERY_STRING
then
#              Ok, so they didn't give us any parameters. . .give-em
#              the form so they will do it right! :)
    echo "<TITLE>Gestation Period Search </TITLE> "
    echo "</HEAD> "
    echo "<BODY style=\"background-color: #CCFFFF\"> "
    echo " <CENTER><H1>Gestation Period Search </H1></CENTER>"
    echo " Please enter the name of the animal for which you"
    echo " wish to find the gestation period. <BR>"
    echo " After you type the animal name "
    echo " please touch the ENTER key. <BR>"
    echo "<HR width='75%'>"
    #                  Set up the form to get the request
    echo "<FORM action='search1.cgi' method='POST'>"
    echo "Animal: &gt;"
    echo " <INPUT type='TEXT' size='15' name='lookfor'>"
    echo "</FORM>"
    echo "<HR width='75%'>"
    echo "<BR>"
    echo "or"
    echo "<A href=\"/test-search.html\">cancel</A>"
    echo "to go back to the calling script"
else
#              Great, they gave us a word to look for. . .build the
#              basis for the results page. . .
    echo " <TITLE> Search results for: $VALUE </TITLE>"
    echo " </HEAD>"
    echo " <BODY style=\"background-color: #DDFFFF\">"
```

Figure 12.5 The CGI code that generates the three pages seen in Figures 12.2, 12.3, and 12.4.

```
     VALUE=`echo $QUERY_STRING | awk -F"=" '{print $2}'`
     echo " <H1>Search results for: $VALUE </H1>"
     lost=`grep -i "$VALUE" /etc/httpd/cgi-bin/Gestlist.txt 2>&1 /dev/null`
#          do the grep, to see if it gets a hit. . .
     if test $? -ne 0
     then
#                   OK, if the previous command (grep) returned non-zero
#                   then we got no hit. . .so the search failed, tell user.
          echo " <H2>Oops </H2>"
          echo " It seems there was no entry for <B>$VALUE </B> <BR>"
          echo " Would you like to: <BR>"
     else
#                   The previous grep worked, do it again but
#                   let the output happen
          echo " Here are the results of your search: <BR>"
          echo " <HR width=\"75%\" ALIGN=\"CENTER\">"

          grep -i "$VALUE" /etc/httpd/cgi-bin/Gestlist.txt

          echo " <HR width =\"75%\" ALIGN=\"CENTER\">"
     fi
     echo " Do another <A href=\"/cgi-bin/search1.cgi\">search</A> <BR>"
     echo " Back to the <A href=\"/test-search.html\">calling page</A> <BR>"
fi
#  Now put in the standard ending lines, closing the body and HTML.
#
echo " </BODY>"
echo "</HTML>"
```

Figure 12.5 continued

The script follows this basic program logic:

- IF the input data is less than one character (in other words, if it is empty), then send the browser the code for the "search" page.
- ELSE check to see if the word exists in the data file.
- IF it does not, display the "miss" page.
- ELSE display the "success" page.

Areas that are common to one or more pages are coded only once to increase efficiency and reduce maintenance time and effort.

In the Beginning

Before the initial search page is generated, the code starts with the four echo lines that output the content-type:, a trailing blank line, and the <HTML> and <HEAD> lines. These lines are generated first, as they are standard for any page this script will create. It is more efficient to put them in this script once, rather than doing the same thing over again for each of the three scripts that may be created.

There must be a blank line after the required header line to tell the browser where the header information ends. The echo command causes the information following it to be sent to standard output, and the server will send that output back to the browser.

Initial Search Page

Next, the script checks to see how the user sent the data. The system variable $REQUEST_METHOD contains the <FORM> method used to send data. If the method was POST, the script needs to load the variable $QUERY_STRING. If the method was GET, then that variable, $QUERY_STRING, is already loaded. After this check, the script looks to see if the user has included any data.

The Bourne shell variable $QUERY_STRING now contains the data sent by the form. The if test -z (minus z) selection statement checks the length of the string. If that length is less than 1 (i.e., zero), then the user didn't send any word to search for. In our program logic this means the user did not make a valid entry, so the script generates the lines of code to build a <TITLE> and the rest of the HTML code needed to make up the search page shown in Figure 12.2.

The syntax of a Bourne shell if statement is if test condition. The test part of the statement actually calls a program named "test" to evaluate the condition that follows it. This condition can be many different things: testing the status of a file, comparing the contents of two variables, or, as in this case, checking the size of the contents of a variable.

Figure 12.6 presents the actual code generated by this option of the script. The first two lines of the code are generated before the initial if statement. They are the common lines across all of the scripts. (The content-type: line and the blank line don't show in this screen capture of "view source" selection, but they are there. If they weren't, the screen wouldn't build. The browser reads those two lines and processes them but doesn't display them in a "view source" screen.) The rest of the lines up to the </BODY> tag are also generated by this part of the script. The last two lines of the script are likewise common across all the scripts that will be generated, so the script will create them in only one place, after all the other processing has been done. This kind of efficiency makes the script short and sweet and easy to understand and maintain. Well, okay, *easier* to understand.

```
echo "Content-type: text/html"
echo
echo "<HTML>"
echo "<HEAD>"
#       Put out the standard header info. . .
#
if test $REQUEST_METHOD = "POST"
        then read QUERY_STRING
fi
if test -z $QUERY_STRING
then
#       Ok, so they didn't give us any parameters. . .give-em
#       the form so they will do it right! :)
        echo "<TITLE>Gestation Period Search </TITLE>"
        echo "</HEAD>"
        echo "<BODY style=\"background-color: #CCFFFF\">"
        echo " <CENTER><H1>Gestation Period Search </H1></CENTER>"
        echo " Please enter the name of the animal for which you"
        echo " wish to find the gestation period. <BR>"
        echo " After you type the animal name"
        echo " please touch the ENTER key. <BR>"
        echo "<HR width ='75%'>"
        #               Set up the form to get the request
        echo "<FORM action='search1.cgi' method='POST'>"
        echo "Animal: &gt;"
        echo " <INPUT type='TEXT' size='15' name='lookfor'>"
        echo "</FORM>"
        echo "<HR width ='75%'>"
        echo "<BR>"
        echo "or"
        echo "<A href=\"/test-search.html\">cancel</A>" echo "to go back to the calling script"
```

```
<HTML>
<HEAD>
<TITLE>Gestation Period Search </TITLE>
</HEAD>
<BODY BGCOLOR=lightblue>
 <CENTER><H1>Gestation Period Search </H1></CENTER>
 Please enter the name of the animal for which you
 wish to find the gestation period.  <BR>
 After you type the animal name
 please touch the ENTER key. <BR>
<HR WIDTH='75%'>
<FORM action='search1.cgi' method='POST'>
Animal: &gt;
 <INPUT type='TEXT' size='15' name='lookfor'>
</FORM>
<HR WIDTH='75%'>
<BR>
or
<A HREF="/test-search.html">cancel</A>
to go back to the calling script
 </BODY>
</HTML>
```

Figure 12.6 The CGI code that generates the initial search page, along with the generated HTML code.

Searching

If the script detects a value stored in the variable $QUERY_STRING, it must first *parse* the search term from the name=value pair (Figure 12.7). Remember that the form sends data in name=value pairs, for example lookfor=Camel. The line that starts with the VALUE variable causes another neat Unix program, awk, to split apart the name=value pair, on the equal sign, and save the second part. For example in the lookfor=Camel pair, Camel would be saved. Once the script has the value, it creates the code for the header, then searches for the string in the file Gestlist.txt. It performs the search on the file specified in the grep line. *Grep* is one of those wonderful cryptic Unix commands. It stands for *Global Regular Expression Print*. What that means is the command looks in the file or files specified to see if the word or words, the *target,* requested are there. If they are, it returns the line or lines containing that word or phrase. In this script, grep is used twice. The first time, shown in Figure 12.7, the results are used to see if a match to the user's entry was found.

```
VALUE=`echo $QUERY_STRING | awk -F"=" '{print $2}'`
echo " <H1>Search results for: $VALUE </H1>"
    lost=`grep -i "$VALUE" /etc/httpd/cgi-bin/Gestlist.txt 2>&1 /dev/null`
#        do the grep, to see if it gets a hit. . .
    if test $? -ne 0
```

Figure 12.7 The CGI code that actually performs the search.

When grep searches the specified file for the target string specified by the user, stored in $VALUE in this case, it sets the variable $? to zero if it finds the target, and to a nonzero value if it doesn't. In other words, if the results from the grep are zero, then the word occurs at least once in the file, and we have success. If the grep returns any other value, we know the word does not exist in the file, so we have a miss. Following the order of the script, we will first look at the code the program logic uses when no match was found, i.e., a miss.

The "Miss" Page

If the first grep failed, there is no reason to go on with the searching. The word the user specified does not exist in the data file. All we have to do is report the miss to the user and ask him what to do next, as illustrated in Figure 12.4. The code generated to do that, shown in Figure 12.8, is very simple. The header and first two lines of the HTML code have already been generated, so all we need to do is add the code to tell the user about the miss. After telling the user that the word isn't on the list, the generated code will give him two choices: either to do another search, going back to the search script, or to go back to the calling program. The URL of the calling program must be hard-coded into the document. In this case, it is the test-search. html document.

In Figure 12.8, notice the search term "Toad" has been inserted into the actual code in the generated HTML. Each time the script misses, it will generate a different page based on the user's input. In this case, the user correctly tried to find information for a "Toad." Unfortunately, there are no toads in the file.

```
echo " <H2>Oops </H2>"
echo " It seems there was no entry for <B>$VALUE </B> <BR>"
    echo " Would you like to: <BR>"
echo " Do another <A HREF=\"/cgi-bin/search1.cgi\">search</A> <BR>"
echo " Back to the <A HREF=\"/test-search.html\">calling page</A> <BR>"
```

```
<HTML>
<HEAD>
 <TITLE> Search results for:    </TITLE>
 </HEAD>
 <BODY BGCOLOR="#DDFFFF">
 <H1>Search results for: Toad </H1>
 <H2>Oops </H2>
 It seems there was no entry for <B>Toad </B> <BR>
 Would you like to: <BR>
 Do another <A HREF="/cgi-bin/search1.cgi">search</A> <BR>
 Back to the <A HREF="/test-search.html">calling page</A> <BR>
 </BODY>
</HTML>
```

Figure 12.8 The CGI code that generates the "miss" page and a screen capture of the HTML source code for that page.

The "Success" Page

If the initial grep returns a zero, then the word or words the user specified occur at least once in the file. In this case, we will have good data to return to the user, so instead of the "miss" page, we will return a "success" page. Figure 12.9 shows the code that generates the success page. In this example, the user looked for the gestation period of a camel. The initial part of the success page looks just like the preceding pages, so we won't bother to show them. In Figure 12.9 you can see there is an <H1> header, a horizontal rule, and then the results of the actual grep command. The <H3> header is the actual line from the file. It contains the word "Camel," so grep returns it. (The -i option on grep tells it to ignore the case of the word, so "Camel," "CAMEL," and "camel" would all match.) This illustrates the importance of the design of the data file. As you can see in Figure 12.10, the data file actually contains the <H3> heading lines that appear in the HTML document.

```
echo " Here are the results of your search: <BR>"
echo " <HR width=\"75%\" align=\"CENTER\">"

grep -i "$VALUE" /etc/httpd/cgi-bin/Gestlist.txt

echo " <HR width =\"75%\" align=\"CENTER\">"
fi
echo " Do another <A href=\"/cgi-bin/search1.cgi\">search</A> <BR>"
echo " Back to the <A href=\"/test-search.html\">calling page</A> <BR>"
```

```
<HTML>
<HEAD>
  <TITLE> Search results for:   </TITLE>
  </HEAD>
  <BODY BGCOLOR="#DDFFFF">
  <H1>Search results for: Camel </H1>
  Here are the results of your search: <BR>
  <HR WIDTH="75%" ALIGN="CENTER">
<H3>  Camel - 13 Months</H3>
  <HR WIDTH="75%" ALIGN="CENTER">
  Do another <A HREF="/cgi-bin/search1.cgi">search</A> <BR>
  Back to the <A HREF="/test-search.html">calling page</A> <BR>
  </BODY>
</HTML>
```

Figure 12.9 The CGI code that generates the "success" page and a screen capture of the HTML source code for that page.

Following the line or lines drawn from the data file by grep is another horizontal rule to act as a visual bottom for the data section. The closing lines of the generated document are the same that were on the miss document, so they were added outside the IF/THEN/ELSE structure.

The Data File

It was easy to write the code for this search because the data file, shown in part in Figure 12.10, was correctly designed. Each entry in the file was created as an HTML heading (<H3>) element, so when the grep retrieved the line or lines from the file, they were already formatted for use in the document. In an alternate form of this code, the data file could be composed of list <LI> entries, and the list structure could be generated to surround the elements and make them into a list. Each line in Figure 12.10 is an <H3> level heading, so no matter how many are retrieved, they stand out one from another and produce an attractive screen. Correctly designing the data file is a very important part of setting up for almost any searchable structure or set of files. If your user is going to select data from several different files, it may be necessary to add code to your script to format the data. That kind of additional formatting was not necessary in our example, because the data file was designed to work with the script.

```
<H3> Anteater - 6 months</H3>
<H3> Ardwolf - 3 months</H3>
<H3> Aardvark - 7 months</H3>
<H3> Bear - 7-9 months</H3>
<H3> Bison - 9 months</H3>
<H3> Bobcat - 2 months</H3>
<H3> Bow Head Whale - 12 months</H3>
<H3> Bush Baby - 4 months</H3>
<H3> California Sea Lion - 12 months</H3>
<H3> Camel - 13 Months</H3>

<H3> Walrus - 12 months</H3>
<H3> Wolf - 2 months</H3>
<H3> Zebra - 13 months</H3>
```

Figure 12.10 The contents of a portion of the data file used for the search page.

\<BASE\>

There are two ways to refer to an address (URL) within a page. An *absolute* URL has all the parts of the address coded, as follows:

http://www.myserver.edu/mydir/neatpage.html.

Alternatively, a *relative* URL is not a complete address and might look like this:

pagetwo.html.

With the relative URL, the browser would supply all the additional necessary data to the left of the data we supplied. In this example, the browser would fill in the address of the server hosting the current document. Suppose neatpage.html is the current page, and we are using a relative link to pagetwo.html. The browser would complete the address for the link as follows:

http://www.myserver.edu/mydir/pagetwo.html.

We are able to use relative—that is, partial—addresses because the browser will fill in the missing pieces. Normally, the browser simply uses the URL of the current page as the basis for this completion. Sometimes, however, it would be handy to be able to tell the browser to use a different path than the one to the current page. For example, suppose we wanted to access a series of 19 documents in a subdirectory different from the one housing the current page. We would have to code the absolute address for each of the 19 documents—what a pain!

Fortunately, the authors of HTML have anticipated this need. The \<BASE\> tag allows the Web weaver to specify a different base address for the browser to use when completing relative addresses. The browser uses the address specified in the \<BASE\> tag when completing relative URLs instead of using the address of the current page.

The \<BASE\> element is an empty tag and must be coded inside the \<HEAD\> container. It changes the way relative addresses are specified for all the \<A\>, \<IMG\>, \<LINK\>, and \<FORM\> elements in the whole document.

<BASE> is a very powerful and useful tag. Be careful with it, though. If you insert it into an existing document that is already using relative addressing, the additional data necessary to complete the relative URL will be taken from the tag instead of from the actual URL of the page. Therefore, you need to either (1) change all relative addresses to absolute URL or (2) move the items being relatively addressed.

href

The **href** attribute is the only required attribute for the <BASE> tag. It is used to specify the address of the URL that is to become the new base for relative addressing. The specified URL can be an absolute address or a relative address. For example, we can code

```
<BASE href="/docs/">
```

for the previous example, and the browser will then complete the relative URL, making it the completed URL where the documents would be stored:

```
http://www.myserver.edu/docs/.
```

target

The progressive browsers also support **target** as a second attribute to the <BASE> tag. As we saw in Chapter 9 on frames, the **target** attribute can specify a particular named frame as the default frame where the browser will display redirected documents. In addition, if the Web weaver sets a **target="_top"** in the <BASE> tag, any framed document will be forced out of frames and displayed in a full browser window. You will not need to code <BASE> in most of the documents you build, but when you need it, it is a most handy tag.

Document Relationships

Up until now we have not been concerned with the relationships among different documents or pages except for supplying a direct link to send users to the URL of the page they need. However, in addition to this, several tags can establish relationships among different pages. For example, suppose you had a document with several pages that the user could read in any order but that had a logical order, like the chapters in a book. You could use document-relationship tags to establish a "next" and "previous" page for the user.

These relationships might seem to provide more documentation than an actual change in the document, but they are important in working with a set of pages that compose one large, related document. Some pundits envision changes to the browsers that use these types of data to create browser-generated buttons that will go forward and back using the data coded in the document-relationship tags. The specifications even talk of browsers creating pull-down menus of several destination pages based on these types of tags. There are two places to code the relationship among several documents: the <A> tag and the <LINK> tag.

\<A\>

We have already explored most of the attributes for the anchor, \<A\>, element in Chapter 3. Now we will look at the two that define document relationships: **rel** and **rev.** Both specify the relationship between the source document and the target of the link. These attributes are not widely used as yet, often only by specialized browsers, but they are expected to gain importance with new releases of the standard browsers.

rel and rev

The **rel** attribute points forward, from source to target. The **rev** attribute goes backward, from target to source. Both describe the relationship between the URL and the **href** attribute. The set of possible valid values is open-ended. More are being defined, and as the browsers begin to support them, some standardization should evolve. Here are four of the more common values for **rel** and **rev:**

- next—indicates that the URL referenced in the **href** is the next in the series. This is usually used only with the **rel** attribute. Here is an sample of a link to the next page in a series:

```
<A rel="next" href="http://nifty.bug.site.com/p2.html">More Bugs</A>
```

- index—shows that the document pointed to by the **href** is the index or table of contents for the series. Here is how an index looks when coded:

```
<A rel="index" href="http://fleas.beetles.flies.com/index.html">Index</A>
```

- previous—shows that document pointed to by the **href** is the previous element in a series. That is, the element is the one that precedes the URL in the **href.** Normally this is used with the **rev** attribute. The anchor shown here illustrates the use of this value.

```
<A rev="previous" href="http://nifty.bug.site.com/p1.html">Sum Bugs</A>
```

- parent—indicates that the document listed as the URL for the **href** is the original source, or parent, of the file that points to it.

```
<A rev="parent" href="http://major.bug.site.com/index.html">Original
Page</A>
```

\<LINK\>

Description: defines a link to another document.
Type: empty tag.
Attributes: charset, class, dir, href, hreflang, id, lang, media, onClick, onDblClick, onMouseDown, onMouseUp, onMouseOver, onMouseMove, onMouseOut, onKeyPress, onKeyDown, onKeyUp, rel, rev, style, title, and type.
Special note: The \<LINK\> element may appear only within the \<HEAD\> container.

The <LINK> tag occurs inside the <HEAD> container because it links an entire document to another object, rather than linking some part of a document to an external object. Users do not see this element (unless they view the source, of course), so its only purpose is to provide additional data to the browser—or to some other Web tool that can search the header. Some search engines and some indexing programs are smart enough to read the header data and parse out information like <LINK>.

A number of different attributes are associated with <LINK>. Some of the more common are discussed next. At this time, it seems that the <LINK> tags are usually ignored, but they will most likely become very important in future releases of the HTML standard.

class

The **class** attribute usually indicates either style information or, more commonly, subdivides a common **rel** or **rev** attribute. For example, if a user could go three different places with a **rel**="NEXT" attribute, depending on her level of expertise, the following set of links might appear in a document head:

```
<LINK rel="NEXT" class="BEGINNER" href="http://somewhere.edu/txt/ begin.html">
<LINK rel="NEXT" class="EXPERT" href="http://somewhere.edu/txt/ expr.html">
<LINK rel="NEXT" class="WIZARD" href="http://somewhere.edu/txt/ wiz.html">
```

Depending on the expertise of the user, she can take different paths through the document. At present, the acceptable list of **class** values is very open-ended; some set of standard values still needs to be devised.

href

The **href** (Hypertext Reference) is a required attribute of the <LINK> tag. There can be only one **href** attribute per <LINK>. It should point to some valid http address, either internal or external to the document that contains it. When **href** is used with the <A> container, some browsers may display its value when the user moves the pointer over the associated link.

title

The **title** attribute usually describes the object pointed to by the **href** attribute. A browser may choose to display the value of the **title** attribute rather than the **href** when the user moves the mouse pointer over an <A> tag, or it may use the **title** attribute in an e-mail SUBJECT: field when the mailto: option is selected.

rel and rev

The list of possible values for the **rel** and **rev** attributes is still growing. Some specialized HTML agents use these relationship attributes already. SCO (Santa Cruz Operation) has a browser that uses a subset of these tags in its online documentation project. Various groups are building specialized browsers to handle large online document projects. After all, HTML is an offshoot of SGML, which was designed to enable people with different machines to see documents formatted for their screens. This sort of project suggests a trend toward returning to the roots of HTML.

Some of the values supported by most of these specialized browsers follow:

- MADE—indicates the author, or "maker," of an HTML page. Usually the **href** associated with this attribute is the mailto: address of the author of the page. Most often, this value is used with the **rev** attribute.
- NEXT—indicates an author-defined relationship, like the pages or chapters of a book. Thus, **rel**="NEXT" indicates that the document pointed to by the **href** is the next document or page in the series, and **rev**="NEXT" indicates that the current page should follow the page specified in the **href**. NEXT is the inverse of PREVIOUS.
- PREVIOUS—indicates an author-defined relationship that is the inverse of NEXT. Thus, **rel**="PREVIOUS" indicates that the target document or page should precede the current page, and **rev**="PREVIOUS" indicates that the current document should precede the target document.
- CONTENTS—indicates a table of contents and can also be coded TOC. Thus, **rel**="CONTENTS" identifies a document pointed to by the link as the table of contents for the current document or for the collection of documents, and **rev**="CONTENTS" identifies the current document as the table of contents.
- INDEX—indicates an index to either the current document or to the collection of documents. Thus, **rel**="INDEX" identifies the document pointed to by the link as an index, and **rev**="INDEX" identifies the current document as the index.
- NAVIGATE—the least well defined of this set of values. Anything that helps the user navigate around the document or document set is considered a navigation tool. For example, the **href** may be part of a table of contents, a list of documents, or a page that describes the current set of documents.

Some of the possible values for the **rel** and **rev** attributes are specifically disallowed. For example, HOME, BACK, and FORWARD are never allowed, because these are always to be defined by the browser itself and not reset by the code. The **rel** and **rev** attributes are among the more dynamic ones in the current release of HTML. Many other values are proposed for these two attributes that will define other, more complex relationships.

charset

The **charset** attribute enables a Web weaver to specify the character set of the document indicated by the **href** value. It is useful when a document contains special characters or symbols.

hreflang

The **hreflang** attribute specifies the actual language of the document pointed to by the **href** attribute. While **charset** indicates the character set or character encoding, **hreflang** indicates the actual language. This is most often useful when dealing with translations of a page. Some **hreflang** values are shown in Table 12.1.

fr	French
ar	Arabic
pt	Portuguese
nl	Dutch
en	English
de	German
it	Italian
el	Greek
es	Spanish
he	Hebrew
ru	Russian
zh	Chinese
ja	Japanese
hi	Hindu
sa	Sanscrit
en-US	English (U.S. version)
en-cockney	English (Cockney version)
i-Navajo	Navajo (Spoken by some Native Americans)
x-klingon	The primary tag "x" indicates experimental language.

Table 12.1 Sample hreflang values and their meanings.

media

The **media** attribute is one of the very powerful new additions that the HTML 4.0 specifications provide. It allows the Web author to specify alternative URLs for different media types (in this context, media types are really output device types.) One instance where this becomes important is when large, multipage documents are created for the HTML environment. In many cases, trying to print one of the pages results in a less than ideal document. Some more responsible Web weavers create different versions of their documents to account for different uses. It is not at all uncommon to find links to "printable versions" of documents. Creating documents that are best viewed with a tactile output device, like a Braille printer, or documents that are designed to be played (aural documents) rather than read are also critical for some members of the online community. In the near future, with the profusion of new devices and the W^{3}C's focus on accessibility, this attribute will take on more and more importance. A partial list of the different values for media follows:

screen—general computer screens

tty—teletype devices and limited-display devices as well

tv—television-type devices that are low-resolution and color (did somebody say Web-TV???)

projection—overhead projectors

handheld—handheld devices (small screen, monochrome, bitmapped graphics, limited bandwidth)

print—good old-fashioned paper-output devices, and other members of their family

braille—tactile feedback devices or Braille printers

aural—speech synthesizer output

all—usable for any output devices

Notice that even handheld devices are addressed in this list of values. Someday it may be possible to access the Net, reasonably, from a handheld device, if wise Web weavers create versions of pages designed for those devices. With this profusion of output devices, we, as Web authors, must begin to look at our pages in a different light.

<META>

Description: supplies additional information about the document.
Type: empty tag.
Attributes: content, dir, http-equiv, lang, name, and scheme.
Special note: The <META> element can appear only as part of the contents of the <HEAD> container.

As if there weren't enough HTML tags to learn about already, we will now look at one that allows the Web weaver to create new tags, the <META> tag. In everyday parlance, the term meta means "about," or "information about some topic." *Meta-language* is information about language, and so forth. The choice of the word *meta* in this instance allows the user to add information about the HTML page. The use and importance of the <META> header element is growing and it will become more important in the future.

This empty tag is always located in the <HEAD>. . .</HEAD> container. It provides some interesting options to Web weavers. Many of the <META> attribute values are still under discussion, and not all browsers and search or indexing engines use the same ones, nor do they all use them the same way. Much debate exists at the present time, about their use, but they will become standardized in the future, and then they will become even more important and valuable.

Some of the <META> attribute values are already useful. One of the emerging standards is called the *Dublin Metadata Core Element Set* (or *Dublin Core*) proposed by the March 1995 Meta Data Workshop in Dublin, Ohio, and updated for the HTML 4.0 specifications. It specifically addresses information stored in documents as opposed to other forms of data, like image or sound files. You can find a great deal of information on these values by searching the Web for "Dublin Core" or "OCLC/NCSA Meta Data Workshop Report."

The <META> tag is an empty tag with up to six different attributes: **http-equiv, content, name, lang, dir,** and **scheme.** The two language attributes, **lang** and **dir,** have been discussed elsewhere. Two of these attributes, **http-equiv** and **name,** are mutually exclusive; you can use one or the other, but not both. Each <META> tag has one of these two forms:

```
<META http_equiv="name" content="value">
```

or

```
<META name="name" content="value">
```

The "name" in this code is the name of one of the special attributes, and the "value" is the content, or value, assigned to that name. Following is a discussion of the attributes for the <META> tag.

http-equiv

Coding an **http-equiv="name"** is the same as including that "name" in the http header. We saw a simple http header when we looked at the procedure for returning generated Web pages from CGI scripts. These values are often used by browsers, search engines, and *spiders* to perform specialized actions. Let's look at the more commonly used **http-equiv** names. This list is not exhaustive, and it will change and grow over time.

expires

The expires value for the **http-equiv** attribute sets a date and time after which a document is said to have expired. When some of the browsers pull a document from cache rather than requesting the document from the Net, they will check to see if there is an expires value. If the document has "expired," then the browser will generate a Net request and download a new copy of the document. This is something like the "sell by" date on dairy products.

An example of this <META> attribute follows:

```
<META http-equiv="expires" content="Wed, 29 Mar 2000 00:00:00 GMT">
```

This code will mark the page that contains it to expire at midnight on March 29, 2000. The format of the date field must be coded exactly correctly, or the browser will consider it an invalid date. When the browser encounters an invalid expiration date, it considers the date to be *now* and reloads the page. If the expires value is zero, the browser will never use the page in cache and will always consider the page expired and reload it from the source.

content-type

A value of content-type can be used to direct the browser to load a specific character set before it displays the page. This is a little used value, but it can be important if the page contains special text characters or is designed to be displayed in a nonstandard character set. This value will probably take on greater significance as the browsers begin to better support the HTML 4.0 standard, using scripting language and the style-sheet language for the document.

content-language

If you are designing a page to be read in a specific language, like British English rather than whatever the browser defaults to, you can use the content-language value. The language must be specified as a "language-dialect" paired value, for example, content="en-GB", which signifies that the language to be used is en (English) with the GB (Great Britain) dialect.

window-target

The most common use for the window-target value is to stop a document from appearing in a frame. Specifying the following <META> tag, attribute, and value will normally cause the document to appear in a full window rather than being displayed inside a frame:

<META http-equiv="WINDOW-TARGET" content="_TOP">

This value works much like the **name** attribute we have already discussed in relationship to the <FORM> and <FRAME> tags. Window-target works with some browsers but not all, so don't depend upon it.

pics-label

The **http-equiv** attribute's value of pics-label stands for Platform for Internet Content Selection. This value is a way to specify the type of content for the document or page. Some legislators want to require ratings on all Web pages as a way to get around the Supreme Court's rejection of the Exxon amendment or the "Digital Decency Act," as unconstitutional. The scheme of pics-label use is flexible and intended for other purposes as well as censorship, but some are concerned that this rating scale might eventually be imposed on Web weavers by an outside agency. As a Web professional, you need to become aware of the ways pics-label can be used or abused. Then you should educate others about your findings.

refresh

The refresh value provides one of the most dynamic and exciting uses currently available for the <META> tag. Using refresh allows the Web weaver to specify when a page should be reloaded from the server ("refreshed"). This is very handy when the contents of a page change at regular intervals. For example, if you have the ultimate "watch me work in my cube" or the greatest "fish tank" page, and the digital camera puts out a new picture every 30 seconds, you can have your Web page refresh each 30 seconds as well. If you code an **expires** value and a **refresh**, the user will always get the newest picture.

Refresh enables Web-potatoes to watch the scene on the screen change without even having to click their mouse to update the page: the ultimate in convenience. **Refresh** is also handy if your page is driven from a CGI script that updates data on a regular basis. You can force your page to reload at regular intervals to capture the new, updated information.

Refresh allows the skillful Web weaver to mimic ***push technologies*** as well. To the users, this reload attribute is invisible. All the users know is that at specific intervals the page refreshes itself with new data. It is really a ***pull technology,*** but it looks like push. A pull technology is one where the browser requests data from the server, "pulling" the data from the source. A push technology is one where the server sends data to the browser, "pushing" it, without the browser requesting it.

The most exciting way this attribute can be used, though, is to display a series of pages without the user having to do anything. This is very handy if you are creating a kiosk or other Web-driven attention-getting display. It is also handy to cycle among a set of pages in one small frame on a page. For example, if you have a business selling fruit, you can create a framed Web page with one of the frames containing a set of "refresh"ing documents, each of which presents a picture of your orchards at different seasons. Thus, one corner of your Web page will have a pretty, attractive frame of small pictures to attract your customers. Subsequent pages will produce a loop of pages, each pointing to the next in the series. Assume you have four pages, the first of which is shown in Figure 12.11. The fourth page points back to the first page to start the cycle over again.

```
<HTML>
<HEAD>
<TITLE> A refresh series page 1 </TITLE>
<META http-equiv="REFRESH" content="3;
URL=FILE:///H|/nch12/refrsh2.htm" >
<!--This screen will wait for 3 seconds, then refresh with the
second screen in the set...-->
</HEAD>
<BODY style="background-color: #FFFFCC">
<H1>First screen in a refresh series</H1>
This screen will display for 3 seconds<BR>
then it will be replaced by the second screen in the series.<BR>
The background color will change too, to make it obvious that the<BR>
screens are changing.
</BODY>
```

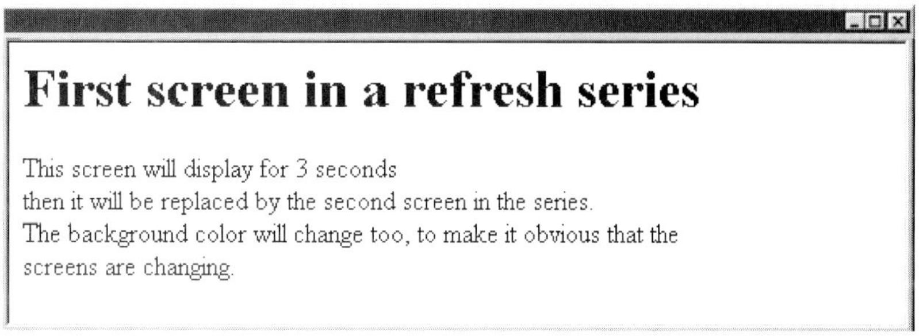

First screen in a refresh series

This screen will display for 3 seconds
then it will be replaced by the second screen in the series.
The background color will change too, to make it obvious that the
screens are changing.

Figure 12.11 HTML code for the first of four refreshing pages.

These pages have a very short refresh, so it is easy to see them work. They are available on the CD that comes with this book and on the Web site for this book. Notice the <META> line. It is the only new code in this page; you have seen the rest many times before. The **http-equiv** is assigned the value of REFRESH, and the content is allocated both (1) the time to wait before the screen is refreshed (3 seconds), and (2) the address of the new file to refresh from after that time interval. Look closely at the syntax for the content attribute. The time and the URL are both contained within the same set of quotation marks, and the URL is separated from the time by a semicolon. In addition, the URL must always be specified as an absolute path; this element *cannot* use relative path names.

If you make a mistake in coding this tag, the results can be very interesting. For example, if you use two sets of quotation marks at the beginning of the **content** attribute's value, the screen will begin to refresh at once, reloading the same page that contains the <META> tag with an interval of close to zero. If there are any mistakes in coding the URL, such as using a relative path, the browser will simply ignore the URL and refresh the *current page* at the interval specified. Correctly coding the value for the **content** is critical, but REFRESH is well worth the effort, for when it works, it is really a neat effect. In the code in Figure 12.12, the only changes involve the URL of the new target (now it points to the next page), the duration (which changes to 5 seconds), and the color of the background.

```
<HTML>
<HEAD>
<TITLE> A refresh series page 2 </TITLE>
<META http-equiv="REFRESH" content="5;
url=FILE:///H|/nch12/refrsh3.htm" >
<!--This screen will wait for 5 seconds, then refresh
with the third screen in the set...-->
</HEAD>
<BODY style="background-color: #CCFF99">
<H1>Second screen in a refresh series</H1>
This screen will display for 5 seconds<BR>
then it will be replaced by the third screen in the series.<BR>
The background color will change too, to make it obvious that the<BR>
screens are changing.
</BODY>
```

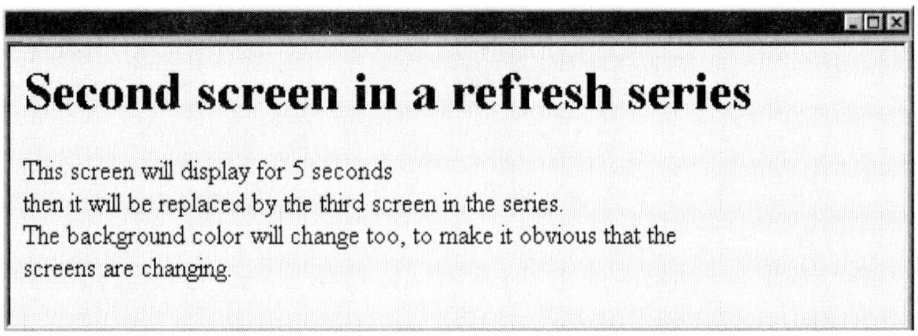

Second screen in a refresh series

This screen will display for 5 seconds
then it will be replaced by the third screen in the series.
The background color will change too, to make it obvious that the
screens are changing.

Figure 12.12 HTML code for the second screen in the refresh series.

If you use a stopwatch to time the screens, you will see that the REFRESH values are not exact measures of time. Rather, the intervals specified are guidelines, or "relative" time intervals. A window that refreshes after 10 seconds will change more slowly than one that refreshes after 8 seconds. Don't try to create a time-sensitive series with this sort of REFRESH. With timing, as with formatting, you are a bit at the mercy of the browser.

The third screen in the series changes only the URL, the delay time, and the background color. If you go to the Web site for the book and look at this series, or if you code them yourself, you will notice that the delay is getting progressively longer on each screen—3, 5, and then 7 seconds. Like the other screens of the series, the fourth screen in the series has a different duration, color, and URL. This page sends the user back to the first screen to start the whole process over again. It has a short duration of only 3 seconds. This set of four screens is designed to illustrate the *looping* that can be accomplished with the **refresh** value.

Notification When Web Site Moves

Another interesting and user-friendly way to use this feature is to automatically redirect the user to a new URL when a page or Web site moves. Code a page at the old URL that says something like the message in Figure 12.13 to automatically send the user to the new page. You should always give users the option of activating the new URL rather than waiting for your code, and give them enough time to read the screen before you send them off.

```
<HTML>
<HEAD>
<TITLE> OOPS, we moved </TITLE>
<META http-equiv="REFRESH"
content="20; URL=HTTP://www.somewhare.else.com/~waybig">
</HEAD>
<BODY bgcolor="#99CCCC">
<CENTER>
<H1>OOPS! </H1>
<H3>Sorry, this site got soooo big we just HAD <BR>
to move to a bigger server.  Please point your browser to:
<A href="http://www.somewhare.else.com/~waybig/">
http://www.somewhare.else.com/~waybig/ </A><BR>
and you will find us there. <BR> OR!<BR>
Wait a few more seconds, and we will take you there<BR>
through the magic of HTML!  <BR>
See you there!</H3>
</CENTER>
</BODY>
</HTML>
```

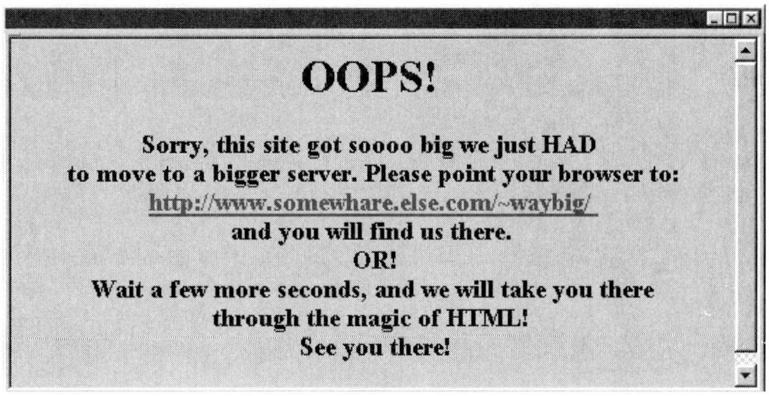

OOPS!

Sorry, this site got soooo big we just HAD
to move to a bigger server. Please point your browser to:
http://www.somewhare.else.com/~waybig/
and you will find us there.
OR!
Wait a few more seconds, and we will take you there
through the magic of HTML!
See you there!

Figure 12.13 HTML code to send the user to a new server.

If the user activates a link within the page, the browser will interrupt the REFRESH timer and go to the link the user chose. User input always has precedence over automatic REFRESH. For that reason, you should give your users a link to activate, rather than forcing them to endure the series you have created. The code in the four-screen refreshing loop in our previous example has no such links, so it locks the user into the series. That is an error of design.

Notice that the screen in Figure 12.13 allows the user to go to the new site manually as well. This is a nice, polite, "I'm sorry to inconvenience you" one, telling the users that you have moved your site. The new address is shown so that they can write it down, cut and paste it, or activate it and then bookmark the site. After about 20 seconds, the browser will refresh the screen with the data from the new URL. The first screen the users see at the new location should remind them to bookmark the new site and edit their list of bookmarks to remove the old URL.

Look at the code in Figure 12.13, and notice that in the <META> tag, the absolute URL is typed out and the refresh time is a reasonable one for allowing the user to read the screen. Remember, however, that the older browsers don't recognize this <META> tag. Therefore, you should always give your users the option of clicking to go to the address REFRESH will send them to. This is true even if you are simply refreshing the current screen to update the information.

Guidelines for Using Refresh

Like all the other neat tools we have discovered, refresh too can be abused. There are a few rules of thumb that should be followed so as not to abuse refresh and thus abuse your user.

First, give the user enough time to read the contents of the screen before you refresh it. As the Web weaver, you probably wrote the page you are refreshing, so you know the content. When you read the page, you are really just skimming it because you already know what it says. You are reading it *much* faster than the average reader will. Give your reader ample time to read the wonderful content you have provided before you send her to a new page.

Second rule of thumb: use pages that paint up quickly. The whole purpose of this technique is to provide some action or activity for the user. Don't have pages in your set that contain lots of graphics or that are many screens long, as that will violate the first guideline and this one as well. The pages you set up in this sort of series should be small and contain few graphics that are also small, so the pages will paint up quickly.

Third rule of thumb: provide a way for your user to stop the series. As was noted earlier, the browser will always take user input over a refresh. If the user activates any link in the page, the browser will take him there rather than loading the new page or reloading the existing page. Usually this type of automatic sequence is used to provide some dynamics to an otherwise static Web kiosk or unattended browser. Give the user a way out of the series, or at least allow him to go to the new page without waiting.

URL

The **URL** value is used, as we have seen, with the **refresh** value. It specifies the URL of the page to which control is passed when the **refresh** time expires. The syntax for this context requires the URL to be a complete, or *absolute,* URL. The browser will not supply any portion of the URL, so *relative* URLs will not work. The URL itself should be enclosed in quotation marks and be separated from the time value by a semicolon. The syntax of the **content** for **refresh** is very critical; any mistake may cause the **refresh** to fail, possibly refreshing only the current screen.

name

The **name** attribute is used for other data that do not correspond to the standard http header tags. You can declare additional data for use by your own software using the different values of the **name** attribute. Some of the **name** values will move into **http-equiv** as the browsers become more sophisticated. For example, the **KEYWORDS** value is almost universally recognized and will most likely move into **http-equiv** in the near future. Keywords will be discussed in more detail shortly.

DESCRIPTION

The **DESCRIPTION** value will allow some search engines to capture a description of your page. Normally the search engine takes the first few lines from the page content as the description, but if you have a framed document, or one with extensive formatting, those lines may not tell what your page is about. You can code the following to give the search engines a better idea of the content of your site:

```
<META name="DESCRIPTION" content="A collection of great. . .">
```

KEYWORDS

Just as the **DESCRIPTION** content value helps the search engines display the true content of your site, the **KEYWORDS** value allows the index-based search engines to have a better idea of the topics available on your site. Usually the index-based search engines take the keywords from the title of the document. Using this <META> tag attribute value of **KEYWORDS** will give those search engines a better set of words for referencing the content of your site. Code the tag like this:

```
<META name="keywords" content="Unix, Ferengi, HTML">
```

Notice that the **content** is a list of keywords, separated by commas and enclosed in quotation marks. This is one of the more important tags if you want the index-based search engines to accurately represent the content of your site.

AUTHOR

The **content** of the AUTHOR value should be self-explanatory . . . but if not, it is the name of that wonderful individual who wove the page. This is a nice feature to include.

Other Common Name Values

Many other values exist for the **name** attribute, most of them specific to a particular application or browser. New values will be incorporated into the standard, and the <META> tag will take on additional importance in future versions of the HTML standard. Table 12.2 lists the current 15 elements in the Dublin Core set. The contents associated with most of these are pretty self-evident. They are used to provide additional information to the browser or other user-agent that reads the page.

TITLE	RESOURCE TYPE	AUTHOR
Format	Keywords	Resource identifier
Description	Source	Publisher
Language	Other contributor	Relation
Coverage	Date	Rights management

Table 12.2 Dublin Core set.

scheme

The **scheme** attribute allows the Web weaver to provide browsers with additional information about the context of the data. The following two examples are discussed in the HTML 4.0 specifications.

```
<META name="date" scheme="Mo-Day-Year" content="06/05/02">
<META name="identifier" scheme="ISBN" content="024772-2">
```

In the first case, the **scheme** explains that the date is June 5th, not May 6th, as some Europeans may interpret the date, because they traditionally use a day-month-year format. In the second example, the **scheme** indicates that the identifier is actually the ISBN number. The **scheme** attribute is a valuable addition to the HTML 4.0 specifications.

Custom Bullets

As we learned long ago—gee, it sure seems a long time ago—there are usually three different bullet types in an unordered list. Sometimes it is necessary, or at least pretty, to have a list that contains special images rather than circles, discs, or squares. Figure 12.14 shows an example.

```
<BODY style="background-color: #CCCCCC" >
<H1>The following shows the use of special bullets</H1>
The following elements are necessary to create really GREAT Chili:
<DL>
<DT>
  <DD><IMG src="chili.gif"
       width=35 height=28> Lean, Range fed Texas beef</DD></DT>
<DT>
  <DD><IMG src="chili.gif"
       width=35 height=28> Home grown Pinto beans (lots of'em)</DD></DT>
<DT>
  <DD><IMG src="chili.gif"
       width=35 height=28> One Red chili pepper (use tongs)</DD></DT>
<DT>
  <DD><IMG src="chili.gif"
       width=35 height=28> Two cups Jalapeno peppers</DD></DT>
<DT>
  <DD><IMG src="chili.gif"
       width=35 height=28> One teaspoon Mesquite honey</DD></DT>
</DL>
<FONT  size=-1><B>Chili pepper bullets...No Whar But Texas!  :-)</B>
</FONT>
</BODY>
```

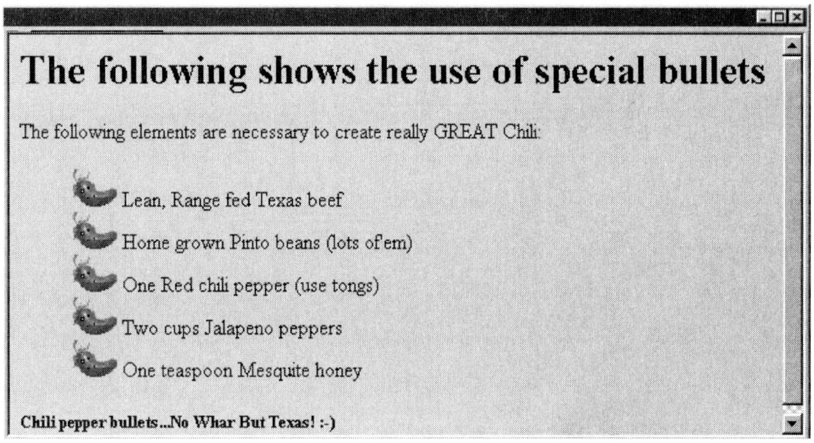

Figure 12.14 HTML code for custom bullets.

The custom bullets are a nice little addition, as long as the images aren't too big. Remember, pictures take time to download. In this case, however, the little pepper is only a 1.22 K file, and it needs to be downloaded only once, because the browser will reuse the cached version on each of the five lines of the page.

Figure 12.14 also presents the code for the page with the fancy bullets. As you can see, we used the definition list (<DL>) and inserted an image into each line of the definition. It isn't a real bulleted list, but it looks like one. This is a way to bend the rules, just a little, to create some interest without loading up the page with big graphics. The technique works fine for very short lines. When the lines are long enough to wrap, the text will align with the left edge of the graphic, not the left edge of the previous text line as you might want.

Figure 12.15 shows what happens when we add a line that is a bit too long. Because the image is embedded within the actual definition, the text wraps to the edge of the image, not to the edge of the text. You could put the image in the <DT> container, but then the image wouldn't align with the text. Figure 12.16 shows how that would look. The placement of the bullets is not as attractive, although the text will be aligned. This technique of creating fancy bullets is

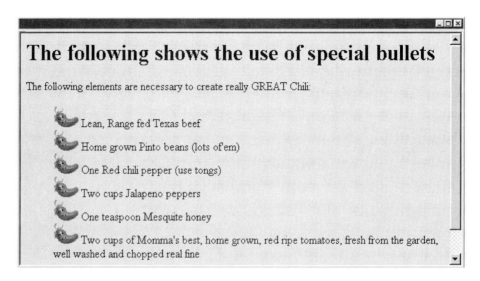

Figure 12.15 Example of custom bullets with over-long text—oops.

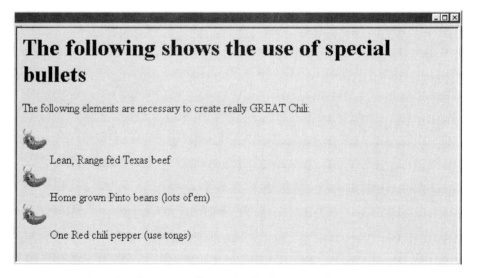

Figure 12.16 Example of custom bullets using both <DT> and <DD>.

not one to use with impunity, but it will serve in those special occasions when you need to make your list look outstanding. It may be a good technique for your home page, but probably not for all the pages on your site. On the other hand, used carefully, this technique can provide a consistent look across several pages. Remember, the browser will need to download the image file only once. Later pages will not be affected, as the GIF will be cached.

Multicolumn Pages

If you want your page to look like a magazine or newspaper, you will need to construct multicolumn pages. Currently there is no HTML code designed specifically to create the multicolumn layout, but as we saw in the last example, we can use an existing container to perform tasks other than that for which it was specifically designed. We will use a table to create our multicolumn page. Figure 12.17 shows how it looks in the browser.

Although Figure 12.17 looks like a simple columnar text, the source code shows what was done to force the text into this format. HTML code works differently than a word processor, which simply creates columns and then flows the text into them. In HTML code, the text needs to be manually placed into the columns. If one of the columns contains more text than the other, the results look most strange, as we can see in Figure 12.18.

```
<HTML>
<HEAD>
<TITLE> Showing off a three column page </TITLE>
</HEAD>
<BODY>
<TABLE border="0" cellspacing="10" >
        <TR>
                <TD width="48%"> This is the text that will appear
in the first column of the table.  You could use this format to
display text that looks like a newspaper or magazine layout.
It is interesting to note that the data in this column appears without
borders, as it should, because the Web weaver set the BORDER attribute
to zero, which did away with the borders.
                </TD>
                <TD> <BR><BR>
                <TD width="48%">This is the second column.  You could
control the width of the different columns by setting the WIDTH
attribute.
   In this instance, the width of the two columns is set to 48%.  That
means that  the middle column has all of 4% left.  The middle column
contains a pair of line breaks, &lt;BR&gt;, and that is all.
The line breaks are necessary to hold space.
                </TD>
        </TR>
</TABLE>
</BODY>
</HTML>
```

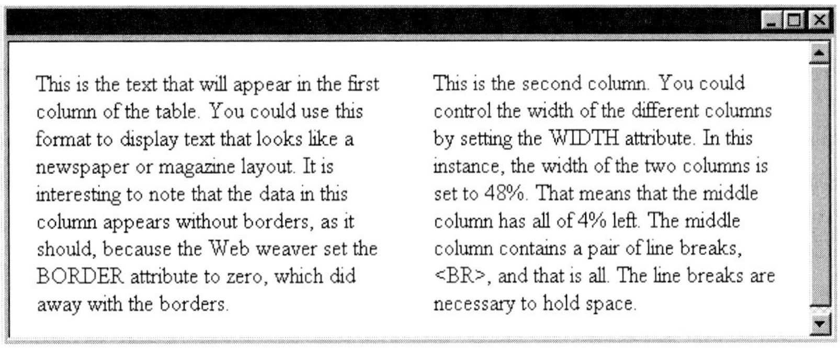

This is the text that will appear in the first column of the table. You could use this format to display text that looks like a newspaper or magazine layout. It is interesting to note that the data in this column appears without borders, as it should, because the Web weaver set the BORDER attribute to zero, which did away with the borders.

This is the second column. You could control the width of the different columns by setting the WIDTH attribute. In this instance, the width of the two columns is set to 48%. That means that the middle column has all of 4% left. The middle column contains a pair of line breaks, <BR>, and that is all. The line breaks are necessary to hold space.

Figure 12.17 HTML code for a multicolumn page.

The text in the left column in Figure 12.18 seems to float, somewhat suspended, whereas text fills the right column. If you are going to present text using this technique, it is best done after all the text has been written, so you can balance the two columns, keeping approximately the same number of lines in each. Obviously, the task becomes more difficult as the number of columns grows. This technique is valuable, but it is somewhat more difficult to apply than other text presentations.

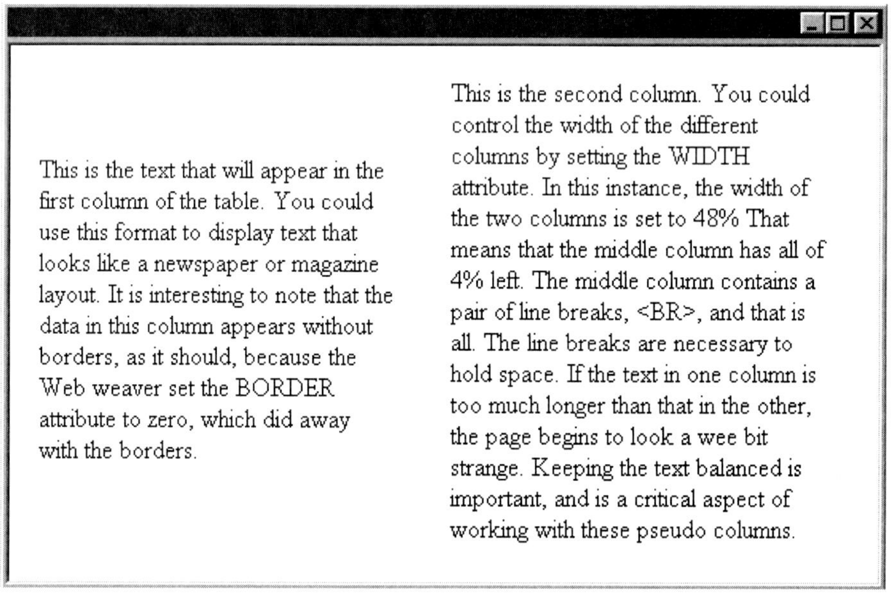

Figure 12.18 An example of columns with uneven amounts of text.

Headlines

Of course, by using the **colspan** attribute and changing the font, you can create headline-like text. Figure 12.19 provides an example. Several tags were used to create this headline-like text. Notice that we added a new row of code to handle the headline, and we forced alignment, increased the font size, and bolded the text. The result looks like a headline, and that is what we were shooting for.

If you find your code causes you to use a lot of tags, like the code in Figure 12.19, you might consider better utilizing the HTML you know. The following line will produce the same output as the code for the headline in Figure 12.19, but with fewer tags:

```
<TH colspan="3" ><FONT size="+3">EXTRA !!! NEAT HEADLINES </FONT>
```

Using the table header <TH> tag instead of <TD> took care of the bolding and the centering. This code is more efficient and much more readable as well. It represents better HTML!

```
<HTML>
<HEAD>
<TITLE> Showing off a three column page </TITLE>
</HEAD>
<BODY>
<TABLE border=0 cellspacing=10 >
        <TR>
                <TD colspan="3" align="CENTER"><FONT size="+3">
                <B>EXTRA !!! NEAT HEADLINES</B> </FONT></TD>
        </TR>
        <TR>
                <TD width="48%"> This is the text that will appear in
the first column of the table. You could use this format to
display text that looks like a newspaper or magazine layout.  It is
interesting to note that the data in this column appears without
borders, as it should, because the Web weaver set the BORDER attribute
to zero, which did away with the borders.
                </TD><TD> <BR><BR></TD>
                <TD width="48%">This is the second column.  You could
control the width of the different columns by setting the WIDTH
attribute.  In this instance, the width of the two columns is set to
48%.  That means that
 the middle column has all of 4% left.  The middle column contains a
pair
of line breaks, &lt;BR&gt;, and that is all.  The line breaks are
necessary
 to hold space.
                </TD></TR>
</TABLE>
</BODY>
</HTML>
```

Figure 12.19 HTML code for a headline layout.

Sidebars

Sometimes it is handy to have a *sidebar,* or side head, to set the heading off from the rest of the text of the document. Figure 12.20 shows what sidebars look like. They take up a lot of space but make a nice visual division of the page. In addition, they can help your user find things more easily on your page. While they are not a good idea for long pages, because you need to put all the text into a table, they are a very powerful tool for smaller pages where the content is divided into specific thoughts.

Figure 12.21 presents the code for the sidebars in Figure 12.20. As you can see, the way the text is coded, the sidebar takes up 10 percent of the width of the screen. That is a significant amount of space in a long document. This technique is best used for shorter pages, and only when it is needed to draw the reader's attention. Now that you have all of these great techniques in your repertoire, it is time to put them to use.

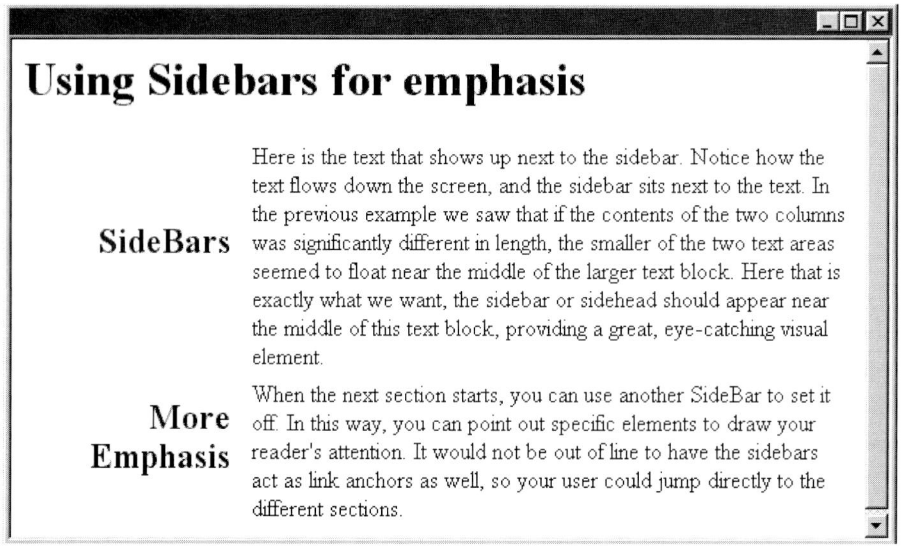

Figure 12.20 Example of sidebars.

```
<BODY>
<H1>Using Sidebars for emphasis</H1>
<TABLE>
<TR>
 <TH width="10%" align="RIGHT"> <H2> Sidebars</H2></TH>
  <TD> <BR></TD>
  <TD>
    Here is the text that shows up next to the sidebar. Notice how
    the text flows down the screen, and the sidebar sits next to the
    text. In the previous example we saw that if the contents of the
    two columns was significantly different in length, the smaller
    of the two text areas seemed to float near the middle of the
    larger text block. Here that is exactly what we want: the sidebar,
    or side head, should appear near the middle of this text block,
    providing a great, eye-catching visual element.
  </TD>
</TR>
<TR>
 <TH width="10%" align="RIGHT"> <H2>More Emphasis</H2></TH>
  <TD> <BR> </TD>
  <TD>
    When the next section starts, you can use another Sidebar
    to set it off. In this way, you can point out specific elements
     to draw your reader's attention. It would not be out of line
    to have the sidebars act as link anchors as well, so your user
    could jump directly to the different sections.
  </TD>
</TR>
</TABLE>
</BODY>
```

Figure 12.21 HTML code for sidebars.

Key Terms

Calling document
Pull technology
Push technology
Search script
Searchable document

New Tags

<BASE>
<ISINDEX>
<LINK>
<META>

Review Questions

1. What is the definition for each of the key terms?

2. How is each of the tags discussed in this chapter used? (Provide examples.)

3. What is the security concern associated with searchable documents?

4. How could the use of an <ISINDEX> tag within a regular HTML document cause a problem?

5. When using searchable documents, why should you make sure the page showing the results also contains navigation buttons back to the calling document?

6. What does the Unix grep utility do?

7. When would you use the <BASE> tag?

8. How are the **rel** and **rev** attributes used to define document relationships?

9. What are some other media that an HTML document can be designed to support?

10. What type of information is identified by a <META> tag?

11. How could you use the <META> element's **http-equiv** attribute to redirect users when your Web site has moved to a new URL?

12. What are the authors' guidelines for using <META> elements to refresh a screen?

13. How can <META> tags be used to help register your Web page with a search site?

14. Why should you try to reuse custom bullets?

15. How can you create a multicolumn page layout?

Exercises

12.1. Create a Web page to present a two-column online newsletter. The HTML document should include comments containing your name and the assignment due date. Use a table that contains no borders and 10-pixel cell spacing. If you are not feeling creative, you can use the Traveler's Newsletter we developed in Chapter 8.

12.2. This exercise requires the modification of the CGI script `search1.cgi` that is found on the attached CD or the text's associated Web site. Make a copy of `search1.cgi` and call it `ex12-2.cgi`. The new CGI script must be loaded onto your Web server before you can complete this exercise. Create a set of HTML documents that can be used with the Bugs Bee Wee Web site to search for bugs the customer can order. Included in the development of this search site are the following:
- Search-request page that accepts search condition
- "Miss" page to display when no match is found
- "Hit" (or "success") page to display related information when match is found

The database should include the following information:

a. Assassin bug, 1-ounce bag, $15.00
b. Crickets, 1-pound bag, $4.00
c. Dung beetle, 1 dung ball, $3.00
d. Honey bees, 2-pound box, with queen, $50.00
e. Lace wing, 1-ounce container, $12.50
f. Lady bugs, 1-ounce bag, $5.00
g. Orchard beetle, 1 wood block, $10.00
h. Praying mantis, 1 egg case, $9.00

12.3. Build a framed document with three sections as shown in the accompanying figure. In the top left frame (Frame 1), use a set of three HTML documents that each display one image or graphic from a series of three. Your name and the assignment due date must be included as comment lines within each document. The document that appears in Frame 1 should contain a <META> tag with a **refresh** attribute that waits 5 seconds and then has the browser display the next page in the sequence. The last page should reference the first page.

Frame 2 contains text that describes the images or graphics in Frame 1. Frame 3 should contain your name, e-mail address, the page's creation date, and any other information you would like to include in a page footer.

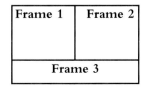

12.4. Retrieve the Homework home page you previously updated in Exercise 11.4. Use custom bullets for one or more of the lists contained within the related pages associated with this site.

12.5. Create three HTML documents, each containing a table of the same size. The tables should have two columns in one row and another row that spans across the two columns as shown in the accompanying figure. The bottom right cell (Cell 3) of each page should display a different image or graphic from a series of three. All the title bars should display "Another Application for the META Tag." Your name and the assignment due date must be included as comment lines within each document. Each document should contain a <META> tag with a **refresh** attribute that waits 2 seconds and then has the browser display the next page in the sequence. The last page should reference the first page. Cells 1 and 2 are the same in all three documents. Cell 2 contains text that describes the images or graphics in Cell 3. Cell 1 contains a brief title that corresponds with the table's contents.

Cell 1	
Cell 2	Cell 3

12.6. Your school's home page is going to move to a different Web site. In preparation for this move, create a new HTML document that supersedes the home page. Change the filename for the school's current home page to index2.htm or index2.html. Create a new HTML document, and save it using the school's old home page filename, most likely index.htm or index.html. The title bar should display your school's name like this: "School's Name Is Moving." Add your name and the assignment due date to comment lines within the HTML document. The page should contain the following:

a. School's name and address
b. School-related image or graphic
c. Link to index2.htm or index2.html
d. Footer with your name and the date the page was created

Add a <META> tag with a **refresh** attribute that waits 5 seconds and then has the browser display the old home page (index2.htm or index2.html).

## CHAPTER thirteen

JAVASCRIPT PROGRAMS FOR HTML

J avaScript was added to Netscape way back in 1995. It is an example of ancient technology that is still useful today. Actually, JavaScript started life as an addition to Navigator 2.0. Back in those days, it was called LiveScript, as it was part of the Netscape LiveWire server product. It was initially designed as a scripting language, used to write queries to the server and handle the daily administration tasks of server management. When the folks at Netscape Communications Corporation started a collaboration with Sun Microsystems, which developed the computer programming language Java, they renamed the product JavaScript. Browsers, starting with Navigator 2.0

381

and Internet Explorer 3.0+ to support it. Today JavaScript is recognized as a powerful programming tool that can enhance your Web pages in wonderful ways. In this chapter, we overview the JavaScript language and related syntax; but it would take another book like this to explain everything you need to know to become a JavaScript programmer.

Although this chapter focuses on the scripting language JavaScript, you can substitute any other scripting language, like Tcl, Visual Basic, or the like, in using the principles explained here.

Misconceptions About JavaScript

Before we look at JavaScript, this extension to HTML, there are a couple of serious misunderstandings about it that we need to dispel. So let's do that right off the bat.

JavaScript Is Not Java 'Lite'

JavaScript is *not* Java. It is a ***scripting language,*** a somewhat simplified programming language that provides only some of the features of a full-blown programming language like COBOL (or Java!). For example, it cannot read from files on the hard drive, write files to the hard drive, create temporary files, or perform other file-related activities.

JavaScript has no stand-alone output functions; it can only use the output features of the browser. Short, single-purpose programs, especially those written in the Unix environment, are often called *scripts.* JavaScripts, in keeping with the "script" portion of the name, are usually short and are designed to perform a specific task.

Java had already made an impact on the Net when JavaScript was developed. Some say it is unfortunate that the Netscape folks, in collaboration with Sun Microsystems, decided to use the Java moniker, but it was a popular programming language, and JavaScript does look something like Java ... if you don't look too closely, that is.

JavaScript Is Not a Wimpy Language

While JavaScript may not have the incredible programming power of Java, it is not a "wimpy li'l thang" (in Texas parlance), either. It is a very useful language that will enable you to build and maintain sophisticated code that will add functionality and *verve* to your pages. Some of the applications of JavaScript are quite powerful; and, as is true with most programming languages, the limitations of what you can create are mostly the limitations of your own imagination, not of the language.

There are many very powerful applications for JavaScript already in use across the Net, and many more are being developed. JavaScript will enable you to create Web applications that are dynamic. It will enable you to build powerful, client-based applications. However, there are a few things that JavaScript can't do for you.

**Things
JavaScript
Can't Do**

There are four major areas where JavaScript lacks power; all are related to either personal computer security concerns or the browser environment:

1. JavaScript doesn't have any graphical abilities.
2. It can't read or write files on the client machine. This is a very serious security matter. To maintain personal computer security, you wouldn't want a strange piece of software to be able to read from or write to your hard disk. There is a small exception here, in the area of *cookies,* but the script won't write the cookie to a file, although the browser may do that at the request of the script.
3. JavaScript supports networking only as it is involved in downloading the contents of specified HTML pages from URLs.
4. No ***multithreading*** capabilities are built into JavaScript, meaning the CPU cannot be shared among multiple tasks, or threads.

While we are talking about things that JavaScript cannot do, we need to address *JScript,* Microsoft's version of JavaScript. According to Microsoft, on its Web page,

> JScript is Microsoft® implementation of the JavaScript scripting language. It is a full implementation, plus some enhancements that take advantage of capabilities of Microsoft Internet Explorer.

What that means to us is that whereas JavaScript is understood by both major browsers, JScript is understood, in its entirety, only by Internet Explorer. Therefore, as we want to be as browser-neutral as possible, we will not explore the special features of JScript in this text.

**Things
JavaScript
Can Do**

JavaScript is an object-oriented language designed to interface with HTML. It recognizes objects like **document, browser,** and **date** that make our job of page design easier and a lot more fun! Table 13.1 lists some of the more common things you can find JavaScripts doing on progressive Web pages.

As you can see from the table, JavaScript provides the Web weaver with a wide assortment of tools to help present information to users. However, this isn't a book about writing JavaScript. We are devoting this chapter to its use. Thus, we will present a couple of JavaScript examples that are handy to examine, but we will write only one simple JavaScript program from scratch. Our focus is not on writing JavaScript, but on how to show you how to incorporate it into your HTML pages.

CONCEPT	EXPLANATION
Control browser features	Using JavaScript, the author can control various features and elements of the browser. Some of the more common are to display simple messages, open new windows, and even generate HTML code on the fly.
Modify document appearance	JavaScript allows the author to set up controls on the page that enable the user to change the appearance of the page. Background color and text color can be altered.
Modify document content	Up until now, using CGI scripts on the server was your only way to generate dynamic content. JavaScript allows the author to create code that runs only on the client, changing the page content on the fly.
Store and use information about user	One of the more controversial uses for JavaScript is the creation and use of *cookies*. These small data elements are actually stored by the browser and then read by JavaScript. They allow the author to keep track of information about users.
Interact with applets	Java applets can extend the functions of your pages. JavaScript can control aspects of an applet, even deciding whether to run an applet or not.
Manipulate images	JavaScript can allow the user to select one from a set of images on the page.
React to state of browser and client system	JavaScript enables the author to create pages specifically tailored to the browser and user accessing that page. It can pick up local information and respond to those data by creating additional content or modifying the content of the page.

Table 13.1 Features of JavaScript.

Introducing JavaScript

Before we get into actually writing JavaScript, we need to look at a few programming concepts. Figure 13.1 shows a simple JavaScript *function* that puts the phrase "Hello World" on the screen. A function is small piece of code that performs a single well-defined task that may accept a value to be processed. While this isn't exactly computing the trajectory to the moon, the "Hello World" function will serve as a good introduction to JavaScript.

Compare the screen capture with the code in Figure 13.1. Notice that the function itself is coded within a <SCRIPT> container placed inside the <HEAD> container. The function here simply puts the words "Hello World" on the screen.

We write functions for two reasons:

1. They allow us to reuse the same code more than once in the same page.
2. They allow us to move the code from page to page easily.

Let's look at how we built the script. The first new feature is the <SCRIPT> container.

```
<HTML>
<HEAD>
<SCRIPT type="text/javascript">
// <!-- Protection from older browsers
// This function will display the famous phrase "Hello World"
//
function Hello() {
var OutputString = "<CENTER><BIG><I><B>Hello World
</B></I></BIG></CENTER>"
document.writeln(OutputString)
}
// -->
</SCRIPT>
<TITLE>My First Function</TITLE>
</HEAD>
<BODY style="background-color: #FFFFCC">
<H1>The Output from the Hello() function</H1>
<SCRIPT type="text/javascript">
//<!-- Protection starts
Hello()
//-->
</SCRIPT>
<H3>That's all she wrote, folks</H3>
Wowsers, wasn't that exciting!
</BODY>
</HTML>
```

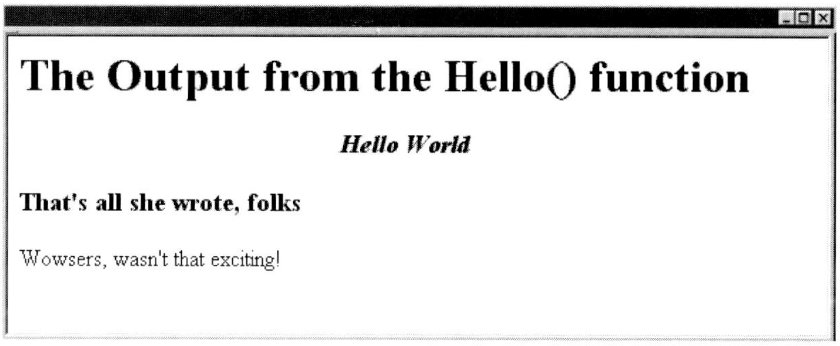

The Output from the Hello() function

Hello World

That's all she wrote, folks

Wowsers, wasn't that exciting!

Figure 13.1 HTML code for the "Hello World" function.

> ## <SCRIPT>script(s)</SCRIPT>
>
> *Description:* encloses the actual elements of the scripting language—JavaScript, Vbscript, etc.
> *Type:* container.
> *Attributes:* src, type, language, defer, and charset.
> *Special note:* Although the nominal contents of this container are JavaScript commands, Web weavers often include commands that generate HTML code as well.

The <SCRIPT> container contains all the JavaScript (or other scripting language) code within an HTML page. Any scripting code must be enclosed within this container, or the browser won't be able to recognize it as a script and will most often simply display it as text.

src

The **src** attribute can be used to specify the URL of an external script in the same way you link external style sheets or images into your document. This is a really nice way to standardize a set of functions across several pages and keep the updating to a minimum. For example, if all the pages in a site need to use the same function, linking each page to the function with the **src** attribute would allow all of them to use the same code. Moreover, the Web administrator can make a change in one place (the script file), and that change will be reflected across all the pages at once.

If you don't link the function, each page will have a copy of the function, and the Web administrator will need to change the code in each HTML document. Having to maintain the same code on many pages is a cumbersome and error-prone task.

If you want to use a function or script from an external file, you need to specify the URL of the JavaScript file as the argument to the **src.** The external Javascript file must use a .js filename extension, as shown in the following code:

```
<SCRIPT src="neatscript.js" >
```

This source file should contain no HTML code, only JavaScript.

type

The **type** attribute should always be used with <SCRIPT>. It specifies the scripting language used for that particular script. Some of the possible values are "text/javascript", "text/tcl", and "text/vbscript". The HTML code would look like this:

```
<SCRIPT type="text/javascript">
    some great JavaScript commands
</SCRIPT>
```

If you don't code a **type** the browser may pick a default value for your scripts. Currently JavaScript is the default used by the popular browsers, but it is much better to explicitly code the value so there is no mistake. The W^{3}C is very clear on this point. It explains that this attribute must be coded, and that you should not expect a default value for it. Even if a browser currently defaults to a specific language, there is no guarantee that it will continue to do so in the future. By coding a **type** attribute for each <SCRIPT> element, your code will work even if the browser creators decide to use a different default.

You can also use a <META> tag to set the default for the whole page. Two examples of the format are as follows:

```
<META http-equiv="Content-Script-Type" content="text/javascript">
<META http-equiv="Content-Script-Type" content="text/tcl">
```

Using one of these <META> tags in the <HEAD> container will set the default scripting language for the whole page. If you code the **type** attribute in a <SCRIPT> element, it will override the value set in the <META> tag.

defer

The **defer** attribute tells the browser whether the code in the script is necessary to build the page. The value set for **defer** is a toggle. If **defer="true"**, then the browser doesn't have to wait for the execution of the script as it builds the page.

language

In previous versions of HTML, the **language** attribute was used to identify the script's language to the browser—for example, "vbscript" or "JavaScript". In the HTML 4.0 specifications, the W^{3}C has deprecated this tag in favor of the **type** attribute. However, wise Web weavers will code both.

A Simple Script

Now that we know about the <SCRIPT> element, let's look at the script coded in Figure 13.1. The first collection of three lines constitute the *comments*. Comments start with a double right slash (//). Here are the first three comment lines:

```
// <!-- Protection from older browsers
// This function will display the famous phrase "Hello World"
//
```

The first line of the comments also shows a second type of comment code that you already know all about. It is the HTML comment you have come to know, love, and use. We need to hide our script from older browsers that don't understand JavaScript, just as you hid the document-level style sheets. The second comment line explains what the function does. The next section of the code is the actual "Hello World" function, taken from Figure 13.1.

In this case, it tells us that the function will display the famous phrase of "Hello World" within the page. The reason "Hello World" is famous is that many wise programming instructors require their noble students to build their first program to display those words. This tradition has a long and honorable history. It started with a paper called "The Programming Language B," written in 1973 by Johnson and Kernighan. (The B language was the precursor to the C programming language, still in use today.) In this paper, which was formatted partly as a technical report by Johnson and partly as a tutorial by Kernighan, the first instance of a "Hello World" program is presented. And you thought history was boring!

```
function Hello( ) {
var OutputString = "<CENTER><BIG><I><B>Hello
World</B></I></BIG></CENTER>"
document.writeln(OutputString)
}
```

Note that the first line tells the browser that what follows is a function. It also gives the function a name and tells the browser that there are no ***parameters*** for the function. A parameter is a value passed to the function. The function then uses the parameter to perform some action. For example, if we built a function that adds two numbers and outputs the total, we could pass two numbers as parameters. The code would look like this: `function sum(num1, num2)`, where `num1` and `num2` are the parameters to the function `sum`.

In the "Hello World" function shown in Figure 13.1, the curly brace following the parentheses marks the actual beginning of the function code. This looks a lot like setting up a document-wide style sheet.

The next line creates the variable name `OutputString` and stores the text string "Hello World" at the memory location assigned to `OutputString`. In the world of programming, a *variable name* is a handy way to reference a place in the computer's memory. It is a name we give to a location in the memory of the computer. It is much handier to ask the computer to store a value at a place called `OutputString` than it is to use the actual memory address `F9DB742A`.

Once we have defined a variable name, we can assign a value to that location. Since this value can change, we call it a variable. The **value** (variable) assigned to a variable name is the information that appears on the right side of the equal sign (=) in an assignment statement. For example, in

`OutputString = "<CENTER><BIG><I><B>Hello World</B></I></BIG></CENTER>"`

the value is the ***string,***

`"<CENTER><BIG><I><B>Hello World</B></I></BIG></CENTER>"`

A string is a series of characters enclosed in either single or double quotation marks that are displayed as ASCII text.

The third line of the function actually displays the string in the browser. For this simple function, we didn't need to create the variable `OutputString` to display "Hello World." We could have simply coded

`document.writeln("<CENTER><BIG><I><B>Hello World</B></I></BIG></CENTER>")`

which would have produced the same results as those shown in Figure 13.1. However, this style of coding is considered poor practice, because it is often more difficult to modify. Therefore, it is preferable to use the variable Output-String as presented earlier, which represents the professional way to write maintainable code.

Just as a left curly brace opened the function, a right curly brace is required to mark the end of the function code. It is possible to code several functions within the <SCRIPT> container. You will see an example of that when we look at the date last modified function later in this chapter. But since there is only one function in this page, we can close the <SCRIPT> container after we close the function. Notice that just before we close the <SCRIPT>, we close the HTML comment block.

One rule of defensive coding that we try to promote is to always put the open and close curly braces on a line by themselves. That way they are easy to find. It also helps if you align them horizontally on the line so that they are visually in the same column.

This is the actual code to invoke the function:

```
<SCRIPT type="text/javascript">
//<!--Protection starts
Hello()
//-->
</SCRIPT>
```

The first thing we notice here is a return of the <SCRIPT> container. Each time we declare or use a script, we need to use the <SCRIPT> container. That way the browser knows that the element(s) enclosed within the container are to be executed as scripts rather than simply output to the screen as text. Figure 13.2 shows what would happen if we forgot to enclose the *function call* in a <SCRIPT> container. The function call is the place in the code where we request the results returned from the function. In this case, the function call shows where we want the string "Hello World" to appear.

```
<BODY style="background-color: #FFFFCC">
<H1>The Output from the Hello() function</H1>

Hello()

<H3>That's all she wrote, folks</H3>
Wowsers, wasn't that exciting!
</BODY>
```

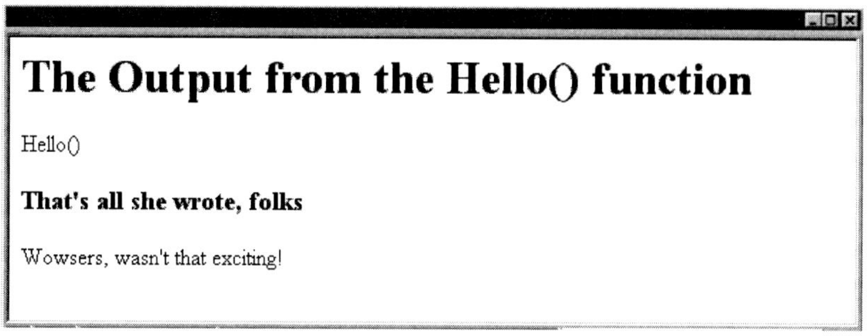

The Output from the Hello() function

Hello()

That's all she wrote, folks

Wowsers, wasn't that exciting!

Figure 13.2 HTML code with the <SCRIPT> element removed from the body of the page.

Obviously, the browser doesn't have any way of knowing that the string "Hello()" is supposed to call a function rather than be output as text. Inside the <SCRIPT> container, we need to protect the function call from older browsers, just as we did in the previous <SCRIPT> element. The actual invocation (call) of the function, "Hello()", tells the browser to find a function called hello and pass no parameters to the function. Here is where some function magic happens! Figure 13.3 shows the generated code for the function call.

```
<BODY style="background-color: #FFFFCC">
<H1>The Output from the Hello () function</H1>
<SCRIPT type="text/javascript">

//<!C- <CENTER><BIG><I><B>Hello World </B></I></BIG></CENTER>

<H3>That's all she wrote, folks</H3>
Wowsers, wasn't that exciting!
</BODY>
```

Figure 13.3 HTML code generated by the "Hello()" function.

Note: The leading comment "//<!C " is a navigator artifact.

Look closely at the function call. That's right, it isn't there anymore. One rule of functions says that when the function is executed, the function call is replaced by the results of that call—the output from the function. The "Hello()" line has been replaced by the centered, bold, italic, big words **Hello World.** That is one reason why it is so difficult to know what the functions look like. "View source" can only show us the result. The result is called the *generated code.*

Now that we know what a function looks like and a little about how to use one, we need to examine some programming concepts that will help us better understand how to use, modify, and finally write JavaScript.

Basic Programming Structures

Every program or script is composed of statements that are rendered in the language of that particular programming language. Each language has a syntax that dictates how any specific verb is used within the language. You are already used to dealing with the syntax of HTML, where attributes must be coded within the angle brackets of the beginning tag and the like. We overviewed CGI syntax in Chapter 11. Now we need to learn something about JavaScript syntax.

We know from Chapter 11 that the three standard building blocks for most programs are sequences of statements, selection statements, and groups of statements that are iterated. Let's take another look at these basic programming structures using JavaScript syntax.

Sequences

A *sequence* is simply a set of statements that are executed one after the other, in the order they appear in the program. The following snippet of JavaScript shows a set of instructions that form a sequence.

This sequence of code establishes the variable **myWindow** and sends to the browsers the first four elements of an HTML document: <HEAD>,

<TITLE>, <BODY>, and <FORM>. As you can see from Figure 13.4, each of the lines of code is executed, one after the other, in a sequence.

```
myWindow = window.open("", "Preview", "toolbar=0, location=0,directories=0,status=0,menubar=0,scrollbars=0,
resizable=0,copyhistory=0,width=275,height=275");
        myWindow.document.open();
        myWindow.document.write("<HTML><HEAD>");
        myWindow.document.write("<TITLE>Little Horse Pictures</TITLE>");
        myWindow.document.write("</HEAD><BODY BGCOLOR='#FFFFFF' TEXT='#000000'>");
        myWindow.document.write("<FORM><CENTER><B><FONT SIZE=+1>");
```

Figure 13.4 Snippet of JavaScript showing a coding sequence.

Selection

Selection is the heart of most programs. This structure allows us to create code that can respond to a variety of conditions. Figure 13.5 shows a script that checks to see if the browser is actually Java-enabled. Based on that decision, the script presents one of two messages. Notice that first the code puts out a <CENTER> tag. Then it decides whether or not the browser supports Java. Based on that decision, the code outputs the correct message. The code here simply demonstrates the IF/ELSE block. The way to read this code is as follows:

- IF the result of the `navigator.JavaEnabled` function is true, then write the lines that indicate that the browser is Java-enabled.
- ELSE (i.e., the result of the `navigator.JavaEnabled` function is not true), then write the lines that indicate that the browser is not Java-enabled.

In some books on programming, this is called an IF/THEN/ELSE statement. Since JavaScript doesn't use the word THEN, it is just an IF/ELSE statement for us.

```
document.writeln("<CENTER>")
document.writeln("<H1>This Browser Is")
if (navigator.javaEnabled()) {
                document.writeln( "Java Enabled </H1>")
                document.writeln("</CENTER>")
                document.writeln("Way to Go! <BR>")
                }
        else {
                document.writeln(" NOT Java Enabled </H1>")
                document.writeln("</CENTER>")
                document.writeln("What a pity")
                }
```

Figure 13.5 Snippet of JavaScript showing an IF/ELSE block.

Iteration

To *iterate* is to repeat a sequence of instructions. (To irritate, on the other hand, is to annoy!) In programming parlance, an iteration construct is characterized as an initial condition, an iterative step, and a termination condition. Another name for an iteration is a ***loop.*** Here is an example of a very simple loop. The code counts down from 10 to one, by ones.

```
for (var count=10; count >=1; count--)
{
document.writeln("Value of count = "+count+"<BR>")
}
document.writeln("We have ignition...We have liftoff!")
```

If this code were imbedded in an HTML document, the results would look something like Figure 13.6. This figure shows the output of the loop. Notice that using an iteration construct, a programmer can get ten lines of output with just four lines of code.

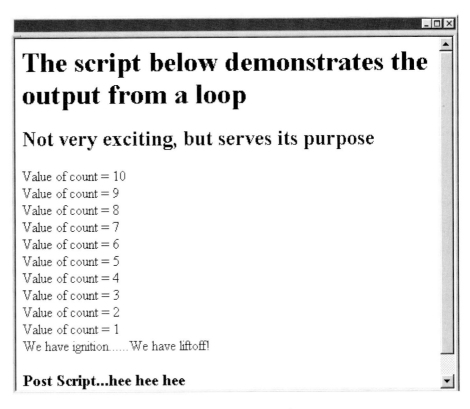

Figure 13.6 Execution of a FOR loop within an HTML document.

Usually iterative code can be replaced by a fairly large block of sequential code. For example, the code in Figure 13.7 will accomplish the same result as the loop in Figure 13.6.

```
var count=10
document.writeln("Value of count = "+count+"<BR>")
count--
document.writeln("Value of count = "+count+"<BR>")
count--
document.writeln("Value of count = "+count+"<BR>")
count--
document.writeln("Value of count = "+count+"<BR>")
count--
document.writeln("Value of count = "+count+"<BR>")
count--
document.writeln("Value of count = "+count+"<BR>")
count--
document.writeln("Value of count = "+count+"<BR>")
count--
document.writeln("Value of count = "+count+"<BR>")
count--
document.writeln("Value of count = "+count+"<BR>")
count--
document.writeln("Value of count = "+count+"<BR>")
document.writeln("We have Ignition...We have liftoff!")
```

Figure 13.7 The JavaScript sequence to replace the loop.

It becomes fairly obvious that it is much simpler and more efficient to code the little loop of four lines than to code twenty lines to achieve the same result. In this way, loops allow us to reuse instructions, making our programs far more efficient.

You now know how three building blocks look using JavaScript. Every script you build will be composed of some or all of these three building blocks.

Object-Oriented Concepts in JavaScript

JavaScript is an *object-oriented language,* meaning that it is based on a set of specialized entities called **objects.** Although the whole of the JavaScript language is far beyond the scope of this text, we will examine four different objects that are very handy for Web weavers: **date, document, window,** and **navigator.** Although many other objects are available in JavaScript, these four provide some particularly useful tools. If you want to learn more, you will need to consult one of the many books devoted solely to JavaScript or visit one of the many Web-based tutorials on the subject.

Object-oriented programmers use the term *object* to mean an entity like a document, a button, or a form. There can be more than one example of each object, as there is more than one example, called an **instance,** of the "student" object in a classroom. Some JavaScriptors call objects by their numbers, like form[1] or button[0]. This is rather like calling two students Student0 and Student1. We would prefer to see you use the **name** attribute to call each object something that reflects its use or function.

Every object has **properties**, which are attributes of the object, like the color of the text, links, and background of a document. It also has **methods,** which are predefined functions that manipulate data, like the `navigator.javaenabled()` method we saw in Figure 13.5, and the `writeln()` method for the **document** object we used to display variables. Table 13.2 shows the four objects that will be discussed here with their associated properties and methods. This table does not list all of the properties and methods for each of the objects, only some of the more common ones. We won't address all these properties and methods in this text. Instead, we will examine some of the more commonly used ones.

OBJECT	PROPERTIES	METHOD(S)
Date	Prototype	getDate, getDay, getHours, getMinutes, getSeconds, getMonth, getTime, getYear, getMilliseconds-(JavaScript 1.3)
Document	alinkColor, anchors, applets, bgColor, cookie, fgColor, images, lastModified, linkColor, links, referrer, title, URL, vlinkColor	close, open, write, writeln
Window	closed, defaultStatus, document, frames, history, location, locationbar, menubar, name, opener, parent, self, status, statusbar, toolbar, top, window	alert, back, close, confirm, find, forward, home, open, print, prompt, scroll, stop
Navigator	appCodeName, appName, AppVersion, language, mimeTypes, platform, plugins, userAgent	javaEnabled, plugins.refresh, preference

Table 13.2 Some properties and methods of four common objects.

The Date Object

The **date** object returns the current time and date. If you have spent any time surfing the Net, you have seen many pages that show you the time. However, most of those pages use a CGI script to display the time and date. Remember, using a CGI script means at least one call to the server and one return from the server. If the clock updates each second, there is a call to the server at least 60 times every minute! This is not a good way to reduce Internet traffic.

To make our point, we are going to introduce you to Valerie, owner of Valerie's Venerable Volume Vault, a used-book store in Little Horse, Texas. Valerie wants to incorporate a clock on one of her Web pages. The page shown in Figure 13.8 shows a JavaScript that does its magic at the client side, and so does not require any extra data to be passed across the Net.

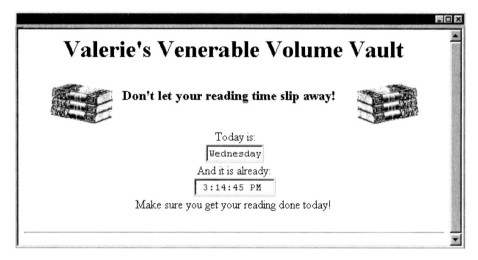

Figure 13.8 A screen that shows the output of a JavaScript that works with the date() object.

The screen in Figure 13.8 just gives the day of the week and the time. Figure 13.9 presents the code for that screen. Don't let all that code bother you; we will look at it in detail later, but for now we are interested in the part of the code that uses the **date** object.

The user created functions of whatTime() and whatDay() to create a new object that contains the current date. In the first case, the line now = new Date(); creates a new object called now in the whatTime() function. That object inherits its properties from the **date** object, and we use it to collect all of the date information we need in order to determine the time. We will reuse this function about once a second to keep the display current. The second call creates the new object when that we use to determine the day of the week in the whatDay() function.

There is a small function called driver() whose only purpose is to invoke the two date functions. Using this driver function makes it easier to start the programs running when the page is first loaded. Look at the first line of the code including this function:

```
<BODY style="background-color: #FFFFCC" onLoad="driver();">
```

We have a new attribute coded here, the **onLoad** attribute. This is an example of an intrinsic event. These events can be used to trigger JavaScript code. In this

```html
<HTML>
<HEAD>
<TITLE>A cool clock example</TITLE>
<SCRIPT>
function driver() {
//          This function will call the two day and
//          time functions. This just makes it easier
//          to run them both "on page load".
    whatTime();
    whatDay();
        }
function whatTime() {
//          Get the current date, and stuff
//          it into the variable
//          now
    now = new Date();
//          Using the current time,
//          parse out the hours data
    hours = now.getHours();
//          Parse out the minutes
    minutes = now.getMinutes();
//          Parse the seconds
    seconds = now.getSeconds();
//          Now for some magical stuff:
//
//          Add the hours to a string called timeVal
    timeVal = " " + ((hours > 12) ? hours - 12 : hours);
//          What this does: If the hours are greater
//          than 12 (it is afternoon), subtract 12 from
//          the hours number because we will put an AM/PM
//          indicator on the time block.
    timeVal += ((minutes < 10) ? ":0" : ":") + minutes;
//          In this case, if the minutes are less than
//          ten, put in the leading zero. This is a very
//          nice example of using this structure.
    timeVal += ((seconds < 10) ? ":0" : ":") + seconds;
    timeVal += (hours >= 12) ? " PM" : " AM";
    document.time.timer.value=timeVal;
    setTimeout("whatTime()",1000);
}
function whatDay() {
        when= new Date();
    day = when.getDay();
    if (day == 0) day=" Sunday";
    if (day == 1) day=" Monday";
    if (day == 2) day=" Tuesday";
    if (day == 3) day="Wednesday";
    if (day == 4) day="Thursday";
    if (day == 5) day=" Friday";
    if (day == 6) day="Saturday";
        document.time.day.value=day;
}
</SCRIPT>
</HEAD>

<BODY style="background-color: #FFFFCC" onLoad="driver();">
<!--    color #FFFFCC is a very pale yellow-->
<H1 style="text-align: center">Valerie's Venerable Volume Vault</H1>
<DIV style="text-align: center">
<P>
<FORM name="time">
<TABLE width="90%">
<TR>
<TD align="left"><IMG src="3booksl.gif" height="60" width="90"></TD>
<TD><H3>Don't let your reading time slip away!</H3></TD>
<TD align="right"><IMG src="3booksr.gif" height="60" width="90"></TD>
</TR>
</TABLE>
Today is:<BR>
        <INPUT type="text" name="day" size="9"><BR>
And it is already: <BR>
        <INPUT type="text" name="timer" size="13"><BR>
Make sure you get your reading done today!
</FORM>
</DIV>
<HR>
</BODY>
</HTML>
```

Figure 13.9 JavaScript that includes the date() object.

case, when the **onLoad** event happens, the script driver() is executed to call the time and day functions.

Table 13.3 shows some of the event names and what they mean. Notice the strange capitalization. It is important to key these events with this capitalization because some of the browsers are case-sensitive.

Event	What Triggers It	Associated Tags
onBlur	The user moves off the object by moving the mouse pointer or tabbing.	<BUTTON>, <INPUT>, <LABEL>, <SELECT>, <TEXTAREA>
onChange	The user alters the contents of the object.	<INPUT>, <SELECT>, <TEXTAREA>
onClick	The user clicks the mouse button on the object.	*Most tags.*
onDblClick	The user double-clicks the mouse on the object.	*Most tags.*
onFocus	The user moves to the object either by mouse movement or tabbing.	<BUTTON>, <INPUT>, <LABEL>, <SELECT>, <TEXTAREA>
onKeyDown	The user presses a key over the object.	*Most tags.*
onKeyPress	The user presses and releases a key over the object.	*Most tags.*
onKeyUp	The user releases a key over the object.	*Most tags.*
onLoad	The browser finishes loading a window or all the frames within a <FRAMESET>.	<BODY>, <FRAMESET>
onMouseDown	The user presses the button on the mouse while the pointer is over the object.	*Most tags.*
onMouseMove	The user moves the pointer while it is positioned over the object (different from onMouseOver).	*Most tags.*
onMouseOut	The user moves the pointer off, or away from, the object.	*Most tags.*
onMouseOver	The user moves the pointer onto the object.	*Most tags.*
onMouseUp	The user releases the mouse button over the object.	*Most tags*
onReset	The user activates the reset control.	<FORM>
onSelect	The user selects some text in a text field.	<INPUT>, <TEXTAREA>
onSubmit	The user activates the submit control.	<FORM>
onUnload	The browser removes the element from the window or frame.	<BODY> <FRAMESET>

Table 13.3 Intrinsic events.

Although you can't see it, the time value in Figure 13.8 updates roughly each second. (JavaScript counts time in thousandths of a second, that is, in milliseconds.) It is a handy and very workable dynamic addition to a Web page.

Although Valerie's "Reading Time" page isn't all that much to look at, it was designed to show you how the **date** object works. To learn JavaScript, you should build small pages like this that allow you to experiment with a single concept or a set of related tools, as did this page. There are many more uses for the **date** object. We will examine one of them in Chapter 14 on Dynamic HTML.

The Document Object

The **document** object is one of the most common objects JavaScript programmers use. Some of the methods, like document.write() or document.writeln(), are used to display lines on the page. The example in Figure 13.10 uses document.writeln to output the data. This object helps you change the colors of some of the features of the page. Values like bgColor, fgColor, linkColor, alinkColor, and vlinkColor are grouped under the title "display properties." Here are some additional properties of the **document** object:

- You have probably opened a page on the Web that set a *cookie*. That is done using the document.cookie property. Cookies allow the browser to store data that the script can access to keep information about things like user preferences. We will explore cookies in more depth in Chapter 14.
- JavaScript can access the URL of the document that contains the link that sent the browser to your document. This value is contained in the document.referrer property.
- JavaScript maintains lists of the anchors (document.anchors), the links (document.links), the images on the page (document.images), and the applets used with a page (document.applets). It even keeps track of the different forms on your page in the document.forms property.
- There are also some interesting methods associated with the **document** object. For example, document.open() and document.close() control moving data into an existing window. In addition, the document.clear() method is supposed to clear the contents of the browser window. In practice, document.clear() doesn't usually work. The ***workaround*** is either to issue a document.open() or just do a document.write() with no contents in the document.write(). A workaround is a way to achieve the results of a command that doesn't work by using other commands that were not designed for that effect but can nevertheless produce the desired result.
- The document.lastModified property takes the last changed date from the file information stored on disk, so the browser always displays the correct date last updated. Figure 13.10 provides an example of the use of the document.lastModified property.

As you can see from Figure 13.10, the date the document was last modified appears at the bottom of the screen. Look closely at the date and time. What do you notice? Yes, that is correct, it is in a format that could cause confusion for some surfers that visit your site. We will upgrade this function in Chapter 14 to make the date more "internationally correct." Notice, too, that the <SCRIPT> at the bottom of the page uses the document.writeln() function to output the document.lastModified property.

```
<STYLE>
.logo {font-family: sans-serif; font-size: 12pt;
 font-weight: bold}
</STYLE>
</HEAD>
<BODY style="background-color: #FFCCFF" >
<!--         The color #FFCCFF is a rather nice purple -->
<DIV style="text-align: center">
<IMG src="books.gif">
<H1>The New Books Page</H1>
Here at
<SPAN class="logo">Valerie's Venerable Volume Vault</SPAN>, we get
new (well...new to us at least) books nearly every day.  Each
time we get new tomes in, we will update this page.  You should
check this page regularly!<BR>
<HR width="75%">
<H2>New to our shelves!</H2>
<SPAN style="font-family: sans-serif; font-size: 12pt">
"The Adolescence of P1" by Ryan<BR>
"Neuromancer" by Gibson<BR>
"Withdrawls Without Deposits" by Robyn Banks<BR>
</SPAN>
<HR width="75%">
</DIV>
<P style="text-align: right; font-size: 9pt; font-family: sans-serif">
<SCRIPT>
document.writeln("We last added new books: "+ document.lastModified)
</SCRIPT>
</P>
```

Figure 13.10 HTML code demonstrating the document.lastModified property in JavaScript.

The Window Object

The **window** object sits at the top of the hierarchy of JavaScript objects. Because of that, it has some properties that are different from those of any other object. The control of an existing window is very limited, but by generating a new window, your script can control many of its properties.

One of the unique attributes of the **window** object is that you don't need to reference it; it is assumed. Earlier we used the document.writeln( )method. Actually, the correct reference to that method is window.document.writeln( ), but because everything takes place in a window, the window part is assumed. That in and of itself is very special among object-oriented programming languages.

Status Bar

Among the things you can control in an existing window is the status bar. Now, whether or not you *should* change or control the status bar is another question. Some Web weavers think the status bar should never be altered, as Web surfers have come to expect certain predictable things there. Other Web weavers believe that their users never even think to look at the status bar, so putting information there is a waste of time. Nevertheless, there is a cadre of Web weavers who believe that if status bar is there, they should put content in it. Figure 13.11 shows an example where the status bar changes when the user moves the screen pointer over a link. Figure 13.12 shows the same page as viewed with the Internet Explorer browser. Figure 13.13 shows the code for the page.

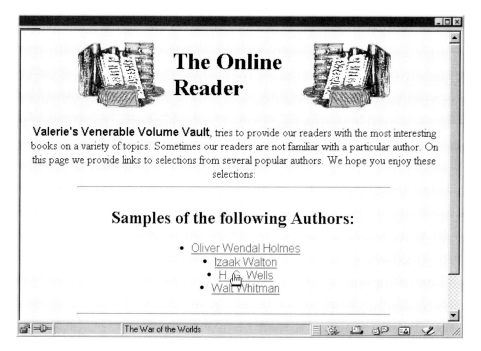

Figure 13.11 The altered status bar message when the user moves the pointer over the link (Navigator).

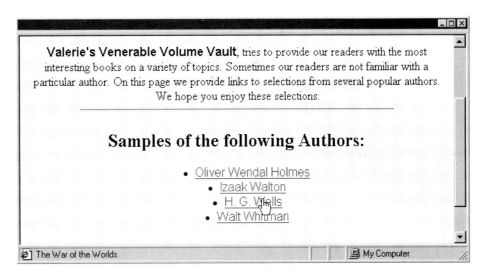

Figure 13.12 A partial screen, showing the altered status bar message when the user moves the pointer over the link (Explorer).

```
<DIV style="text-align: center">
<HR width="75%">
<H2>Samples of the following Authors:</H2>
<UL>
<LI style="font-family: sans-serif; font-size: 12pt">
<A HREF="holmes. htm"
onMouseOver="window.status = 'Autocrat of the Breakfast Table';
          return(true)">Oliver Wendal Holmes</A>
<LI style="font-family: sans-serif; font-size: 12pt">
<A HREF="walton.htm"
onMouseOver="window.status = 'The Compleat Angler';
          return (true)">Izaak Walton</A>
<LI style="font-family: sans-serif; font-size: 12pt">
<A HREF="wells.htm"
onMouseOver="window.status = 'The War of the Worlds';
          return (true)">H.G. Wells</A>
<LI style="font-family: sans-serif; font-size: 12pt">
<A HREF="whitman.htm"
onMouseOver="window.status = 'Leaves of Grass';
          return (true)">Walt Whitman</A>
</UL>
<HR width="75%">
</DIV>
```

Figure 13.13 HTML code using the onMouseOver event to change the status bar.

Notice how in using the JavaScript event **onMouseOver,** we reset the status bar message by giving the property window.status a new value. This tool is a simple way to alter the status bar. The code following the semicolon, return(true), is required to tell the browser to preform the update of the status bar.

One difference we have noticed is that with the default status message, the message changes when the pointer is moved off the link. The updated version doesn't recognize the **onMouseOut** event, so the message doesn't change when the mouse moves away.

Figure 13.14 is a partial screen capture showing the default status message when the user moves over a link. Notice the status bar in this figure. It shows the default message that tells the user the target of the link. That is not as informative a message as the ones shown in Figures 13.11 and 13.12. Sometimes it is useful to tell users where they are going. Careful use of this field can be considerate of your users. However, as with all the other neat features we have learned, resist the temptation to overuse it.

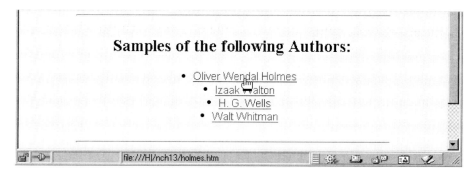

Figure 13.14 The standard status bar message when the user moves the pointer over the link (Navigator).

It is also possible to set up a scrolling status bar message. There is but one word of discussion necessary about creating a scrolling status bar message— DON'T! They are annoying and distracting, so don't build them.

Dialog Boxes

There are three methods associated with the **window** object that deserve careful attention. Each produces a dialog box that requires the user's input: window.alert(), window.confirm(), and window.prompt(). Figure 13.15 shows samples of each of the different dialog boxes. (It is a composite screen; in real life each of the dialog boxes would appear on its own screen.)

```
<CENTER>
This page demonstrates an alert box, confirmation dialog box,
prompting dialog box<BR>
<BR>
<SCRIPT>
alert("That book is not in stock")

confirm("Do you really want to quit?")

passwd=prompt("Please enter your password:","")
</SCRIPT>
</CENTER>
```

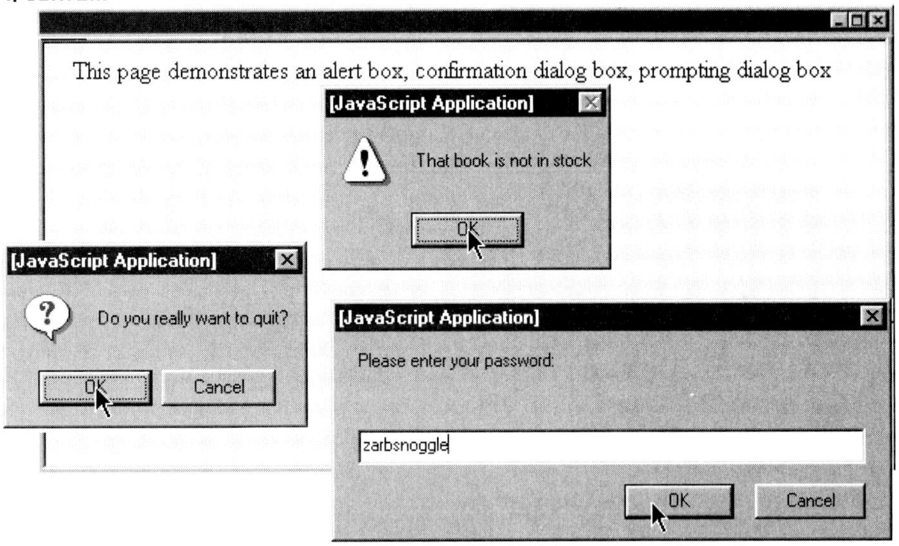

Figure 13.15 HTML code using JavaScript for alert, confirm, and prompt dialog boxes.

These dialog boxes are said to be **modal,** which means they will stay on the screen and prevent the user from doing anything else until she responds to them. Alert boxes, in particular, are very useful when you debug your JavaScript scripts. However, in day-to-day use, having to constantly respond to a modal dialog box is very annoying.

Each of the dialog boxes has different requirements. The alert box simply requires the user to activate the "OK" button. The confirm dialog box asks the user to activate either "OK" or "Cancel." Usually the confirm dialog box is used with an IF/ELSE statement, because it returns a value of "true" or "false." The prompt dialog box asks the user for input. In this case, it asks for a password. Notice how the password is *not* protected from casual view.

The Web weaver can set a default value for the input string, and the user can simply activate the "OK" button to accept it. If there is a default value, it shows up as a highlighted string so the user doesn't have to delete it before entering his own value. All he needs to do is start typing. To send his response to the prompt, the user needs to activate the "OK" button. To abandon the response, he can activate the "Cancel" button.

Dialog boxes can be very useful tools if they are not overused. One of the worst offenders in overuse is the alert box. Some unwise Web weavers use them far too often. Use them only when absolutely necessary.

New Windows

Another useful tool is the ability to open a completely new window. Unlike frames, new windows give the user a separate entity with which to interact. The new window is under the Web weaver's control as far as size and features go.

Writing the content to the new window is a little more complex than building the HTML code in an editor, because it all needs to be packaged in one large *character string variable* that is written with one document.write( ) call. In Chapter 14, we will examine more of the options, but for now, let's look at a sample page in Figure 13.16 that creates a new, small window. Figure 13.17 illustrates what happens when the "The Attic View" button is activated.

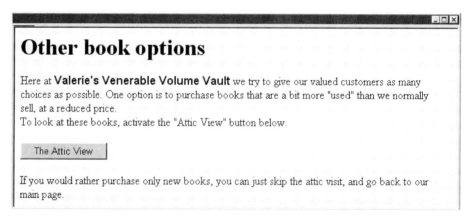

Figure 13.16 A page that creates a new window.

The Web weaver can control the following window features:
• Size
• Use of a tool bar, status bar, or scroll bars
• Whether or not the window is resizable
• Contents

One thing that is outside the author's control is where the window appears. It will always be in the upper left quadrant of the existing browser window. For now, at least where the window is generated is not an option.

Figure 13.17 shows the new window, superimposed over the old window. It is possible to have the new window actually open another HTML document, which is very handy for applications where the primary use of the windows is viewing documents. Each newly created window could contain a different document.

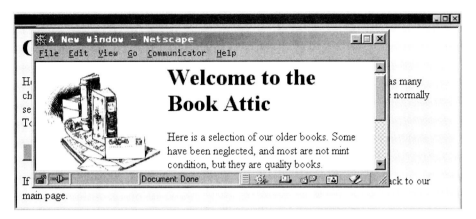

Figure 13.17 A page showing a newly created window.

In addition to creating new windows, you can allow the user to close them. Figure 13.18 shows the new window with a button added to close the window. This way the user won't have to activate the "X" button in the top right corner of the window to close it.

Figure 13.18 A page showing a button that will close the new window.

Note that closing the window doesn't necessarily mean deleting it. A closed window may simply be minimized, not removed. Figure 13.19 shows the code for the page presented in Figure 13.18.

Let's look at some selected lines from the code in Figure 13.19. The function `newwin()` creates and populates the window using the JavaScript (see code at top of Figure 13.19). It is called when the "The Attic View" button is activated. The other button, created in the second form, closes the window.

The new window is created with the call to the `window.open` method, which creates a new window of a particular size that also has a menu bar, scroll bars, and a status line. This instance of the `window.open` method is assigned to the variable `NewWindow` that is the name of the newly created window. The variable `Content` stores one very large text string that is the content of the newly created window. The operator `+=` is used to concatenate additional pieces to the original contents

```
<HTML>
<HEAD>
<TITLE>New Window Creation</TITLE>

<SCRIPT>
<!--
/*===================================================================
=
            new_win()

            Description:
                    This function creates a new window, and writes
                    a single line to it.
===================================================================
*/
function new_win() {
var NewWindow = window.open("","Newbie","height=150,width=500,status,menubar,scrollbars, resizable")
if (NewWindow != null) {
//                      Test to make sure the window actually opened.
//                      If it did, build the content for it.
            var Content="<HTML><HEAD><TITLE>A New Window</TITLE> </HEAD>"
            Content += "<BODY style='background-color: #FFFFCC'>"
            Content += "<IMG src='atticbk.gif' align='left'>"
            Content += "<H1> Welcome to the Book Attic </H1>"
            Content += "Here is a selection of our older books."
            Content += "Some have been neglected, and most are not"
            Content += "mint condition, but they are quality books."
            Content += "<HR width='70%'>><UL>"
            Content += "<LI>First old book</LI>"
            Content += "<LI>Second old book</LI></UL>"
            Content += "</BODY></HTML>"
//          Notice that the whole content for the page is put
//          in one long string. However, if you build a complex
//          page, you can use the technique shown above to keep
//          the individual parts of the page separated just a
//          bit for readability
//
//          Now we build the new page
            NewWindow.document.write(Content);
            NewWindow.document.close()
// close the input stream for the
//
            new window.
                                } // End of if block
                    }           // End of function

//-->
</SCRIPT>
<STYLE>
.logo {font-family: sans-serif; font-size: 12pt;
font-weight: bold}
</STYLE>
</HEAD>
<BODY style="background-color: #CCFFFF">
<!--            color #CCFFFF is a soft blue -->
<H1>Other book options</H1>
Here at
<SPAN class="logo">Valerie's Venerable Volume Vault</SPAN>
we try to give our valued customers as many choices as possible. One option is to purchase books that are a bit
more "used" than we normally sell, at a reduced price.<BR>
To look at these books, activate the "Attic View" button below.<BR>
<FORM>
<INPUT type="button" name="MakeNew" value="The Attic View" OnClick="new_win()">
</FORM>
Once you have explored the attic, activate the "Close the Attic" button below to close the attic window.
<FORM>
<INPUT type="button" name="Clunk" value="Close the Attic"
        OnClick="if (NewWindow != null) NewWindow.close()">
</FORM>
</BODY>
</HTML>
```

Figure 13.19 HTML using JavaScript code for a new window.

of the variable. This is a reasonable technique for creating the contents of the new page. A foolish Web weaver could also code the whole page like this:

```
var Content="<HTML><HEAD><TITLE>A New Window</TITLE></HEAD>
<BODY style='background-color: #FFFFCC'><IMG src='atticbk.gif'
align='left'><H1> Welcome to the Book Attic </H1>Here is a selection of
our older books. Some have been neglected, and most are not mint
condition, but they are quality books. <HR width='70%'><UL> <LI>First
old book</LI><LI>Second old book</LI></UL></BODY></HTML>"
```

But we think that is a bit harder to understand. Spacing it out makes the page easier to code, and easier to understand if we need to fix it later.

The next two lines output the value associated with Content into the window, then close the data stream for the new window. This last step is important, because if the input stream is not closed, the browser doesn't know that the document is complete and may wait for it to complete. The delay can cause some browsers to hang up. Also, results may be unpredictable. Always close the input stream with the code

```
NewWindow.document.close().
```

The code for the *calling page* doesn't contain many new features until you get down to the two <FORM> containers. A calling page is simply the page that calls, or invokes, the function in question. The first <FORM> contains the button that, when activated, invokes the JavaScript that creates the new window. The second <FORM> contains the button that closes the newly created window:

```
<INPUT TYPE="button" NAME="Clunk" VALUE="Close the Attic"
        OnClick="if (NewWindow != null) NewWindow.close()">
```

Notice that the **onClick** only invokes the NewWindow.close() if the NewWindow variable is not null: if (NewWindow != null) NewWindow.close(). This prevents the code from trying to close a window that isn't open.

Opening windows is a very handy way to add functionality to your pages. Rather than writing all of the code for the page, as in our example, you can also specify the URL of a different page to be opened in the new window. Your user can see a new page, and you can control many of the features of the window. If you want to open an existing document in a new window, simply code the URL as the first argument. If the first argument is null, the browser won't load any document into the new window, and you must supply the content. For example:

```
window.open("newt.htm","newt","height=100,width=200,scrollbars")
```

This line would open a new window named "newt", 100 by 200 pixels, with scroll bars, containing the content of the HTML document "newt.htm". This is a very useful technique.

onLoad and onUnload

In addition to the methods and properties we have already discussed, two event handlers can be very important when designing pages. The **onLoad** and **onUnload** event handlers can be used to trigger JavaScript functions. The **onLoad** event occurs when the page has completed the loading process. The loading process includes moving images from the server, loading and starting Java applets, and loading and starting all of the plug-ins. The following line, found in Figure 13.9, invokes the script function called driver() when the page finished loading.

<BODY style="background-color: #FFFFCC" onLoad="driver();">

The **onUnload** event or events occur just before the document is cleared from the browser window. Obviously, you wouldn't want to run user-interactive scripts just as the window closed. Usually **onUnload** events are used for housekeeping or statistical purposes.

The **window** object has many other features beyond those discussed here. As you begin to use the **window** object, you will discover the features most important to you.

The Navigator Object

One point that could be confusing about the **navigator** object is its name. Navigator is, of course, the name of a popular browser, yet the **navigator** object speaks to any browser and to the platform on which the browser is running. The major browser manufacturers all recognize and support the **navigator** object.

The **navigator** object is often called an "advanced object" because it doesn't really fall within the normal JavaScript hierarchy. It isn't a large object. It has only five methods (Table 13.4) and ten properties (Table 13.5).

METHOD	EXPLANATION
navigator.javaEnabled()	Returns true if the browser supports Java applets and false if it doesn't
navigator.plugins.refresh	Creates an array, plug-ins[], that lists all the installed plug-ins
navigator.preference()	Checks or sets user preferences
navigator.savePreferences)	Saves user preferences
navigator.taintEnabled)	Returns true if the data-tainting security model is supported and enabled (deprecated in Navigator version 4)

Table 13.4 Methods for the **navigator** object.

Property	Meaning/Use
navigator.appCodeName	The coded name of the browser
navigator.appName	The name of the browser
navigator.appVersion	The version of the browser
navigator.language	The language supported by the browser; currently supported only by Navigator 4+
navigator.mimeTypes[]	An array of all the MIME types recognized by the browser; currently supported only by Navigator 4+
navigator.platform	The platform on which the browser is running
navigator.plugins[]	An array of all the plug-ins that are installed in the browser; currently supported only by Navigator 4+
navigator.systemLanguage	The system-level language code; currently supported only by Explorer 4+
navigator.userAgent	The string passed to the browser as the http user agent in the request
navigator.userLanguage	Like navigator.language, but this is the Explorer 4+ version

Table 13.5 Properties for the **navigator** object.

The **navigator** object is most often used to gather information about the client platform, such as to see if the platform running the browser supports the Java language. You may wish to check whether a user has the latest and greatest browser, capable of utilizing your fancy page. If you wish to use browser-dependent features, you may create different versions of your pages, specifically tailored to each version of each of the browsers. Most Web weavers are too busy to build that many versions of the same page . . . but it can be done.

An amusing use for the **navigator** object is to tell your user about the computer system she is using, as shown in Figure 13.20. Figure 13.21 illustrates how the JavaScript works after the user activates the "Tell Me!" control. Figure 13.22 shows the same screen in a different browser. Notice that even though the source code is identical, Explorer doesn't seem to recognize the <SPAN style="text-align: center"> container, so it doesn't center the image. This is a good example of the compatibility problems across browsers, even in a simple example.

Figure 13.20 The initial page that invokes a script to display **navigator** object properties.

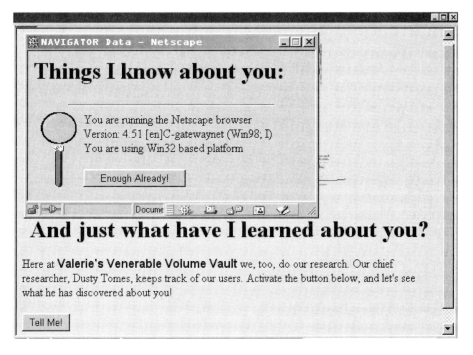

Figure 13.21 A page showing the window with client information generated after "Tell Me!" is activated (Navigator).

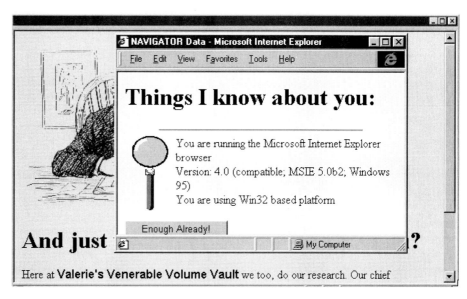

Figure 13.22 A page showing the window generated with client information after "Tell Me!" is activated (Explorer).

The **navigator** object will most likely take on more features in each release of the browsers. For now it is useful if you want to capture information about the browser your user is employing. With those data, you could build different versions of the page based on the browser in use. Figure 13.23 shows the code for the page in Figure 13.22.

You should notice that much of the code in Figure 13.23 looks like that in Figure 13.19. Reusing code that works is called *code leveraging*. Why invent a new way to do the same thing every time you need to redo it? Using code leveraging has three advantages:

1. Coding is faster, because you don't need to "reinvent the wheel" each time.
2. Debugging is minimized, because presumably the existing code works, so you won't need to debug it.
3. The code is faster to maintain. Once you learn how one JavaScript works, you also know about any others that employ the same code.

```
<HTML>
<HEAD>
<TITLE>New Window Creation</TITLE>

<SCRIPT>

<!--
var NewWindow = null;
//                      This variable, NewWindow, must be global so both the
//                              function and the onClick can reference it.
//
/*================================================================
=
        NavStuff()

Description:
        This function creates a new window, and loads in the
                NAVIGATOR data. It includes a close button too.
================================================================
*/
function NavStuff() {
NewWindow = window.open("","Smilie","height=200,width=400,status, menubar")
if (NewWindow != null) {
//                      Test to make sure the window actually opened.
//                      If it did, build the content for it.
        var Stuff="<HTML><HEAD><TITLE>NAVIGATOR Data</TITLE></HEAD>"
        Stuff +="<BODY BGCOLOR='#CCFFFF'>"
        Stuff += "<H1>Things I know about you:</H1>"
        Stuff += "<HR width='75%'>"
        Stuff += "<IMG src='magglas1.gif' height='100' width='50'
                align='left' alt='Magnifying Glass' hspace='10'>"
        Stuff += "You are running the "+ navigator.appName+" browser<BR>"
        Stuff += "Version: "+ navigator.appVersion + "<BR>"
        Stuff += "You are using "+ navigator.platform +" based
                platform<BR>"
        Stuff += "<FORM> <INPUT type='button' name='s'
                value='Enough Already!'"
        Stuff += " OnClick='window.close()'>"
        Stuff += "</FORM>"
        Stuff +="</BODY></HTML>"
//                      Notice that the whole content for the page is put
//                      in one long string. However, if you build a complex
//                      page, you can use the technique shown above to keep
//                      the individual parts of the page separated just a
//                      bit for readability.
//
//                      Now we build the new page.
        NewWindow.document.write(Stuff);
        NewWindow.document.close()
//                              close the input stream for the
//                              new window
                        }  // End of if block
}       // End of function
-->
</SCRIPT>
<STYLE>
.logo {font-family: sans-serif; font-size: 12pt;
font-weight: bold}
</STYLE>
</HEAD>
<BODY style="background-color: #FFCCFF;">
<!--            color #FFCCFF is a light purple -->
<SPAN style="text-align: center">
<IMG src="smiley.gif" alt="A woodcut of a smiley fellow">
<H1>And just what have I learned about you?</H1>
</SPAN>
Here at
<SPAN class="logo">Valerie's Venerable Volume Vault</SPAN>
we, too, do our research. Our chief researcher, Dusty Tomes, keeps track of our users. Activate the button below, and
let's see what he has discovered about you!
<FORM>
<INPUT type="button" name="TellAll" value="Tell Me!"
        OnClick="NavStuff()"><BR><BR>
</FORM>
</BODY>
</HTML>
```

Figure 13.23 HTML code using JavaScript and showing some of the properties of the **navigator** object, as seen in Figure 13.22.

All in all, code leveraging makes good sense, provided the first time you write the code you do a good, careful, maintainable job.

The new objects in this example are shown in the following code snippet:

```
var Content="<HTML><HEAD><TITLE>NAVIGATOR Data</TITLE></HEAD>"
      Content +="<BODY BGCOLOR='#CCFFFF'>"
      Content += "<H1>Things I know about you:</H1>"
      Content += "<HR width='75%'>"
      Content += "<IMG src='magglas1.gif' height='100' width='50'
            align='left' alt='Magnifying Glass' hspace='10'>"
      Content += "You are running the"+ navigator.appName+"
            browser<BR>"
      Content += "Version:"+ navigator.appVersion + "<BR>"
      Content += "You are using" + navigator.platform + " based
            platform<BR>"
      Content += "<FORM> <INPUT type='button' name='s'
            value='Enough Already!'"
      Content += "OnClick='window.close()'>"
```

The three **navigator** objects capture the application name and version and the platform that is running the browser. The other new object is shown in the last line of the snippet. Notice that the window.close() method is coded inside the new window. Look back at Figure 13.21 or 13.22. The button marked "Enough Already!" activates this method and closes the window from inside! Using this technique, the window is actually closed, not just minimized. Play with these screens either on the Web site for the book or copy them from the CD. You really need to see them in action.

JavaScript and the Browsers

More than once in the preceding sections we have seen cases where the browsers don't all handle the same code the same way. These problems to a great extent are caused by the different browser creators not all working for the same goals. Figure 13.24 shows a screen capture of our **navigator**-driven page in the Mosaic browser. Quite a difference! First, notice the code that forms the first line of the image. It seems that the Web weaver forgot to protect the style from the browser, and Mosaic doesn't recognize the <STYLE> container, so the contents of that container are displayed. Oops! Second, look at the pointer as it sits over the "button"; it isn't a clickable field but rather a text area (the pointer is the I-beam)! Using this page in Mosaic is not all that useful.

This is a case where a kind, conscientious, careful Web weaver would put code into the page to display browser-appropriate information. You should experiment with the Mosaic browser. It is free to download, and wise Web weavers will test their code with at least four browsers, Navigator, Explorer, Mosaic, and Lynx. Although the Mosaic browser is not being upgraded anymore, it still provides a valuable platform to test how your page may look in one of the dozens of specialty browsers that populate the Web. Sources for the browsers are listed in Table 13.6.

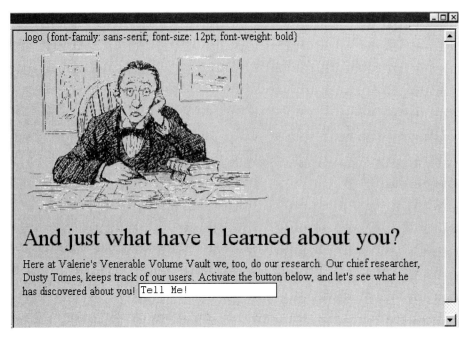

.logo {font-family: sans-serif; font-size: 12pt; font-weight: bold}

And just what have I learned about you?

Here at Valerie's Venerable Volume Vault we, too, do our research. Our chief researcher, Dusty Tomes, keeps track of our users. Activate the button below, and let's see what he has discovered about you! `Tell Me!`

Figure 13.24 How the Mosaic browser shows our page, not expanding the button.

We have included the most recent version of each browser on the CD with this book, but newer, improved versions may have been released. Check on new versions, and test your code with them. In addition, testing engines are available within ScriptBuilder™ and other JavaScript validation tools on the Net. A copy of ScriptBuilder is on the CD that accompanies this text. You should find a validation tool you like. When you do, use it!

Chapter 14 will address some exciting uses for JavaScript, creating truly dynamic HTML pages with the techniques you have learned here.

BROWSER	URL OF SOURCE
Internet Explorer	www.microsoft.com
Lynx	www.crl.com/%7Esubir/lynx/binaries.html
Mosaic	www.ncsa.uiuc.edu/SDG/Software/WinMosaic/HomePage.html
Navigator	home.netscape.com

Table 13.6 The "big four" browsers and where to find them.

Things JavaScript Shouldn't Do

Sometimes a language makes it easy to become really obnoxious with your Web pages. For example, HTML has the *nefarious* <BLINK> tag that can be used to create visually distracting pages. JavaScript has some of these unrecommended uses, too. Here are some general guidelines to follow to keep from misusing this tool.

- Don't use the alert, confirm, and prompt windows just to display text. These functions should be reserved for their intended purposes, not used just because they are available. In your experience with JavaScript, you will probably see more than you please of these boxes. Don't be among those who abuse them!
- Don't scroll messages on the status bar. The status bar can be an important tool. When you really need to put information there, do so, but don't scroll it. A scrolling status bar is distracting; it pulls your user's eyes away from the content of the page, and it also becomes annoying in very short order.
- Actually, it is best not to scroll anything. It used to be interesting to use JavaScript to create scrolling lines of text. And some Java applications use scrolling to good effect if they have text scrolling from more than one direction. However, with most JavaScript scripts the scrolling will move in only one direction. That is boring, distracting, and should be considered passé.

Keywords

Calling page
Code leveraging
Function
Function call
Generated code
Instance
Loop
Methods
Modal
Multithreading
Object
Parameter
Properties
Scripting language
String
Workaround

New Tag

<SCRIPT>

Review Questions

1. What is the definition for each of the key terms?

2. How is the <SCRIPT> tag used? (Provide an example.)

3. What was JavaScript, a.k.a. LiveScript, originally designed to do?

4. What are four things that JavaScript does not do?

5. What two places can you find JavaScript code?

6. Why are two different types of comment lines used within a JavaScript?

7. What special characters are used to identify the beginning and ending of the function code?

8. What happens to a function call when the function is executed?

9. What are four JavaScript objects that are useful to Web authors?

10. How is running JavaScript different from running a CGI script in regard to Net traffic?

11. How does JavaScript count time?

12. What is a unique feature of the window object?

13. Identify three different kinds of modal dialog boxes and describe the differences between them.

14. When opening a new window, what are four things the author can control through JavaScript and one thing the author cannot control?

15. Why should you always close the input stream with JavaScript code?

16. How is the **navigator** object most often used?

17. What are three advantages to code leveraging?

18. What are three things JavaScript should not do?

Exercises

13.1. Create a new HTML document that includes JavaScript code displaying the following:

    a. Your name
    b. The course prefix, number, and name of your HTML class
    c. The instructor's name for this class

The document's title bar should display "Sample JavaScript Code" with your name and the assignment due date included within comment lines.

13.2. Create a new HTML document that includes JavaScript code modifying the count-down loop shown in Figure 13.6. The modification should count up from 1 to 15. The document's title bar should display "Count Up From 1 to 15" with your name and the assignment due date included within comment lines.

13.3. Create a new HTML document that includes JavaScript code displaying a modal dialog box prompting the user to enter his or her mother's maiden name. The document's title bar should display "Internet Privacy Concerns" with your name and the assignment due date included within comment lines. The content of this new page should discuss privacy concerns as they relate to Internet applications. In addition, somewhere within the page, display a button that calls the JavaScript shown in Figure 13.23. This code opens a new window that displays information about the user's computer platform.

13.4. Retrieve the Homework home page you updated in previous exercises. Add to the page footer the call to a JavaScript that displays the last date the page was modified.

13.5. Create a new HTML document that includes a button that calls a JavaScript to open a new window. The new document's title bar should display "Used Computer Equipment" with your name and the assignment due date included within comment lines. The page content should look like a want ad advertising at least one used computer for sale. Under the description of the sale item(s), place a button labeled "Warranty." When this button is activated, it should open a new window that displays the company name, address, telephone number, e-mail address, and cost for a one-year warranty.

13.6. Retrieve your school's home page that you updated in previous exercises. When the user moves the screen pointer over the school's name, a JavaScript should be called that displays a team cheer in the status bar. For example, if your school colors are black and blue, and the team name is the "Banana Slugs," you could display "Go Black and Blue!" or "Slime-em Slugs!"

DYNAMIC HTML— CHARISMATIC PAGES

I n this chapter, we will explore a set of dynamic ways to present information. Chapter 13 set the stage by introducing the fundamentals of JavaScript. We can now expand on these skills and put JavaScript to work enhancing our page designs. We have used the word **dynamic** to mean having action, motion, or responding to the user. Most of the dynamic features that we will explore in this chapter are centered in JavaScript, but some, like **image maps,** are enhancements to good old HTML. We have included these particular examples because we think they represent a good cross section of the different types of dynamic possibilities available to the wise Web weaver. Feel free to copy these examples, modify them to meet your needs, and incorporate them into your own documents.

Image Maps

The first dynamic feature we can add to our pages allows the user to select different parts of an image to cause an event to happen. These areas, called *hot spots,* can act as links to other pages or can invoke JavaScript programs. Each hot spot is associated with some event, usually a link to a new page or to a target within the current page. There are two ways to implement image maps in HTML: on the client side or on the server side.

Server-Side Image Maps

Server-side mapping sends data to the server to be processed by a CGI script. We mentioned this method when we looked at using images as submit buttons in Chapter 10. Server-side image mapping has fallen from favor in the Net community. It is expensive in terms of Net resources because it requires the browser to send data along with related X and Y image coordinates to the server. Then the server must process those data and send the results back to the browser. We have found the following disadvantages to server side mapping:

- **Increased Net traffic.** Each time the user activates any part of a server-side image map, the browser must send the coordinates of the screen pointer to the server. This process increases the traffic on the Net, because the browser doesn't know if the coordinates selected will map to an actual URL or not, and each activation causes another transaction over the Net.
- **Confusion for the user.** Normally, when the user moves the mouse pointer over a link, the URL is displayed on the screen. In a server-side model, the browser has no idea what URL, if any, is associated with any part of the image. Therefore, the browser displays either the URL of the image-map program or the X and Y coordinates of the screen pointer location. Neither is very helpful for the user.
- **Much slower response for the user.** In a server-side model, each response for the user must be generated by the server. That means that the browser has to send a signal to the server requesting that the server process the information about a mouse click. Then the client has to wait until the server returns the information before it can continue processing. If there is much congestion on the Net, that response can take significant time to reach the client. The user has to wait for the request from the client to reach the server, then for the server to process the request and reply to the client.
- **Local testing is impossible.** To test a server-side image map, the Web server must run a special image-mapping program and process the X and Y coordinates sent from the client. Thus, it is impossible to test the functionality of a server-side image map without being connected to a Web server. This is a big hindrance for many Web weavers who work "off-line" at home or in the office.

- **There are several different server-side mapping packages.** If the Web weaver chooses to use server-side image mapping, he must decide which type of image mapping software is run on the Web server. Two of the most common are the W^3C (CERN) httpd server and the NCSA (National Center for Supercomputing Applications) httpd server. Each requires different, incompatible coding from the browser.
- **Often a system administrator must set up the server code.** Although it is possible in some circumstances for the Web weaver to also maintain the Web server, in most cases the Web weaver doesn't control the server. Consequently, the system administrator must load the software necessary to receive, process, and reply to the image. Loading the software adds another step in implementing new Web pages.

For all these reasons, server-side image mapping is not used much as it once was. Client-side image mapping (discussed next) poses none of the problems of server-side mapping. If you are forced to use server-side mapping, you will need to do some research into the **ismap** attribute for the <IMG> container.

Client-Side Image Maps

Client-side mapping means that the client (user's computer) does all the work. The browser processes any reaction to the image activation locally. This is a newer methodology, and most Web weavers prefer it because it has the following advantages:

- It is usable by people browsing with nongraphical browsers.
- It provides immediate feedback as to whether the pointer is over an active region of the image (*hot spot*).
- It decreases loading on the Net and generally allows faster response to the user.
- It can be tested and modified without having a connection to the server already up and running.
- It can be accomplished by the Web weaver with no outside help from the Web server administrator.

A minor drawback to client-side mapping is that it is supported only by relatively newer browsers, like Netscape 2.0+ and Internet Explorer 3.0+. Nevertheless, with most of the industry moving to new browsers as soon as they are released, this is a small price to pay for all the benefits that client-side mapping provides.

Identifying the coordinates of all the map's hot spots can be a time-consuming task. Software like Mapedit or Mapthis makes the creation of client-side maps very simple by allowing the Web weaver to outline the proposed hot spot on the map using the screen pointer. The mapping software then converts the outline into the proper XY coordinates. Figure 14.1 shows a simple page containing an image that is set up as a client-side image map. There are just a few differences between the page shown in Figure 14.1 and those you have been building thus far. Following is a discussion of these differences, including the additions to the HTML code necessary to create an image map: <IMG>, <MAP>, and <AREA>.

```
<HTML>
<HEAD>
<TITLE>Search our bookshelves</TITLE>
<STYLE>
.logo {font-family: sans-serif; font-size: 12pt;
  font-weight: bold}
</STYLE>
</HEAD>
<BODY style="background-color: #FFFFCC">
<H1>Browsing the shelves</H1>
One of the great adventures you could have in a conventional
  bookstore is searching the shelves for books that interest
  you. Since that is a little difficult to accomplish over the net,
<SPAN class="logo">Valerie's Venerable Volume Vault</SPAN>
  has tried to recreate that experience for you. Move your mouse
pointer over the bookshelf below, and watch the
status bar to see titles that may interest you. If you run into one
you would like to examine, click your mouse button to "take it off the shelf." <BR>
  Go ahead, poke through our shelves, and have fun!<BR><BR>
<SPAN style="text-align: center">
<IMG src="bookshlf.gif" usemap="#bookshlf" border="0">
</SPAN>
<map name="bookshlf">
<area shape="rect" alt="Great books by Isaac Asimov"
        coords="34,26,78,57" href="asimov.htm">
<area shape="rect" alt="Some Edgar Rice Burroughs stories"
        coords="66,28,125,58" href="burroughs.htm">
<area shape="rect" alt="Excellent HTML texts"
        coords="133,24,212,55" href="html.htm">
<area shape="rect" alt="Scary stories by Stephen King"
        coords="35,66,124,98" href="king.htm">
<area shape="rect" alt="Cyberpunk adventures by Bruce Sterling"
        coords="134,66,213,98" href="sterling.htm">
<area shape="rect" alt="Titillating titles by the master himself, Tim Trainor."
        coords="39,108,125,132" href="trainor.htm">
<area shape="rect" alt="New and old reference texts"
        coords="130,106,213,132" href="reference.htm">
<area shape="rect" alt="Famous catalogs"
        coords="39,138,124,169" href="catalogs.htm">
<area shape="rect" alt="Unix like it ought to be"
        coords="133,138,142,169" href="unix.htm">
<area shape="rect" alt="Selected cyberpunk, especially William Gibson!"
        coords="143,141,214,170" href="cyberpunk.htm">
<area shape="rect" href="#bookcase" coords="0,0,260,201">
</map>
<A name="bookcase">
<H2>Sorry</H2>
We can't sell our bookcase. Where would we display our books?
</BODY>
</HTML>
```

Figure 14.1 HTML code for a simple but useful image.

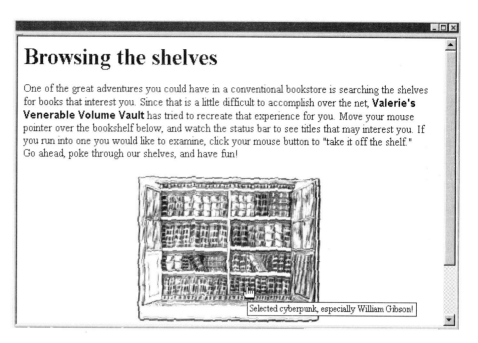

Browsing the shelves

One of the great adventures you could have in a conventional bookstore is searching the shelves for books that interest you. Since that is a little difficult to accomplish over the net, **Valerie's Venerable Volume Vault** has tried to recreate that experience for you. Move your mouse pointer over the bookshelf below, and watch the status bar to see titles that may interest you. If you run into one you would like to examine, click your mouse button to "take it off the shelf." Go ahead, poke through our shelves, and have fun!

Selected cyberpunk, especially William Gibson!

Figure 14.1 continued

<IMG>

The first difference comes in the <IMG> container:

```
<IMG src="bookshlf.gif" usemap="#bookshlf" border="0">
```

The **usemap** attribute specifies a client-side image map as opposed to the **ismap** attribute, which indicates server-side mapping. This attribute is assigned the name of the URL that identifies the actual mapping information. Mapping information is designated by the <MAP> container and the related <AREA> tags (both will be discussed in turn). In most cases, as with Figure 14.1, the URL is within the current HTML document, so the URL is simply the internal target name preceded by an octothorp—#bookshlf.

In Figure 14.1, our <MAP> tag is located by the target name bookshlf in the body of the HTML document. Notice that all the code necessary to process the image map is contained within this page.

Here is the way the image map works: When the user activates any part of the image, the X and Y coordinates of the position of the screen pointer are captured. Then they are processed by the browser on the client computer using the coordinates provided by the <MAP> container. When the browser receives the coordinates, it compares them with each of the different <AREA> coordinates.

In this example, the screen pointer appears within a rectangle that has a top left corner of 143,141 and a bottom right corner of 214,170, the <AREA> associated with cyberpunk books. When the user clicks anywhere within the image, the browser simply transfers control to the hypertext reference (**href**) associated with that area of the image map.

If the user clicks anywhere within the image that has not been defined by any of the book-related rectangles, control is transferred to the bookcase target.

Notice that the last hot spot is a rectangle that encloses the whole image and references bookcase. You can overlap the <AREA> definitions, but the first one the browser encounters, working from top to bottom, will take precedence. As a result, we need to arrange our <AREA>s from most precise to most general, or from smallest to largest. In Figure 14.1, the rectangle identifying cyberpunk books takes up a small area of the image map and references a specific topic. It is listed before bookcase, which identifies a bigger area—the whole image map — and is used to catch selections not covered by specific books (topics).

<MAP>Contents of image map processing data</MAP>

Description: encloses client-side image map data specified by the **usemap** attribute.
Type: container.
Attribute: class, del, dir, id, name, onBlur, onClick, onDblClick, onFocus, onKeyDown, onKeyPress, onKeyUp, onMouseDown, onMouseMove, onMouseOut, onMouseOver, onMouseUp, rev, style, tabindex, target, title, and type.
Special note: The **name** attribute is required.

The <MAP> container encloses all the HTML code that defines a client-side image map. There is one required attribute, **name,** that is used to identify the container as a target for the **usemap** attribute, just like anchor (<A>) elements use an anchor name as a target. The browser associates the value assigned to the **name** attribute with a particular set of mapping instructions. The following HTML code is used in Figure 14.1 to identify the coordinates of the image map named bookshlf:

```
<MAP name="bookshlf">
```

This **name** attribute value is then assigned to the **usemap** attribute in the <IMG> tag to identify the source image to be used as the image map. There-fore, the name must be unique from any other map name on that page. Like anchor elements, the leading octothorp (#) in the **usemap** attribute value sig-nifies that the source URL (name) is local to the document. This code identi-fies bookshlf.gif as the image and #bookshlf as the local source for the image coordinates:

```
<IMG src="bookshlf.gif" usemap="#bookshlf">
```

The octothorp is omitted from the **name** attribute of the <MAP> container be-cause it identifies where the image map coordinates are located—that is, the target.

In addition to the **name** attribute, the <MAP> container holds a set of <AREA> tags, one for each hot spot in the image.

> ## <AREA>
>
> *Description:* defines the coordinates and link for one region of a client-side image map.
> *Type:* empty tag.
> *Attributes:* accesskey, alt, class, coords, href, id, lang, nohref, onBlur, onClick, onDblClick, onFocus, onKeyDown, onKeyPress, onKeyUp, onMouseDown, onMouseMove, onMouseOut, onMouseOver, onMouseUp, shape, style, tabindex, target, and title.
> *Special note:* The **coords,** and either the **href** or **nohref** attribute, are required.

The real work of a client-side image is described by the <AREA> tag. This empty tag defines each hot spot in the image map and tells the browser what to do if the user activates it. When the user moves the screen pointer over any area that has been defined by an <AREA> tag, the pointer changes to a pointing finger, and the browser displays the URL of the related link in the status bar.

alt

In addition, as shown in Figure 14.1, the value for the **alt** attribute is displayed. You should always use the **alt** attribute with each <AREA> to help your users understand where they are going. Four other commonly used attributes for this tag are **shape, coords, href,** and **nohref.** Let's consider each in turn.

shape

The **shape** attribute works with the **coords** attribute (discussed next) to define the hot spots on the page. **Shape** tells the browser how to process the coordinates. It also, as its name implies, describes the general shape of the hot spot. There are four valid shapes:

1. circle
2. rectangle or rect
3. polygon or poly
4. default

Browsers are not consistent in their treatment of these values. Navigator doesn't recognize the word "rectangle," but both browsers recognize "rect," so the abbreviated name is the preferred usage. On the other hand, Internet Explorer doesn't understand the "default" shape, so defining a polygon for the whole image is a better way to handle the "default" option.

coords

The **coords** attribute is required. It describes the boundaries of a hot spot. Each entry in this list is an XY coordinate pair. All coordinates are measured in *pixels.* The **coords** attribute can be the vertices of polygons, or the X and Y coordinates of the center of a circle and the radius of the circle. Following are the three types of shapes with the required **coords** values for each:

- circle="x,y,r" requires the X and Y coordinates of the center of the circle and the length of the radius.
- poly="x1,y1,x2,y2,x3,y3..." requires the X and Y coordinates for each vertex, or corner.
- Rect="x1,y1,x2,y2" requires two sets of coordinates. The first is the X and Y coordinates for the top left corner, and the second is the X and Y coordinates for the lower right corner of the rectangle. The rectangle is a specialized form of polygon. You need specify only two points to define it.

href

Each <AREA> must have an associated **href** or have the **nohref** attribute coded. Usually the **href** attribute describes the URL of the HTML document to be displayed when the user clicks within the defined area of that <AREA>. If you are using the identified area to link to a local HTML document, or to a target within the existing document, simply code the URL of the document or target as the value for this attribute. The code in Figure 14.1 shows both types of **href.** The first 10 references link to external documents, and the last one links to an internal target.

nohref

The **nohref** attribute defines an area that the user can activate but that contains no link. Thus, the user can activate the hot spot described by the <AREA>, but *nothing will happen.* There are only two reasons for using this attribute. If you are building a large image map and want to define all the areas in the beginning but don't have URLs created for some of the hot spots, you could bring up the page and fill in the **href**s later. The other reason for using this attribute would be if you want to annoy your users. This attribute creates hot spots that the user can click with no response. That could be very frustrating.

HTML 4.0 Considerations

In the HTML 4.0 specifications, the W[3]C recommends using an <OBJECT> container rather than the <IMG> tag to identify a client-side image map. It also recommends using <A> tags within the <MAP> element rather than <AREA> tags to identify the actual mapped areas within the image. At the time this book was written, the popular browsers supported neither of these techniques, so we will show no example.

Making It Easy

It is fairly simple to use an image mapping software package, like Mapedit by Boutell.Com, Inc., to create the <MAP> container for you. These software packages are usually WYSIWYG packages that take as input an HTML file with the image(s) to be mapped already coded in one or more <IMG> tags. The software asks which image you wish to map. It then displays that image. You simply outline each region you want to be a hot spot. The software next prompts you for the URL to be associated with that hot spot, and it creates the <MAP> container for you, right in the HTML document specified.

If you don't have access to an image mapping program, you could probably use a drawing package (Figure 14.2) to determine the required points of reference on any figure. Most drawing packages provide the option of having all the corners and points labeled with their X and Y coordinates. In that case, you will need to record those coordinates and create your own <MAP> container. For example, Figure 14.2 shows one of the corners in the cyberpunk area of the image. Recording each corner would give us the coordinates necessary to specify that rectangle in the <AREA> element.

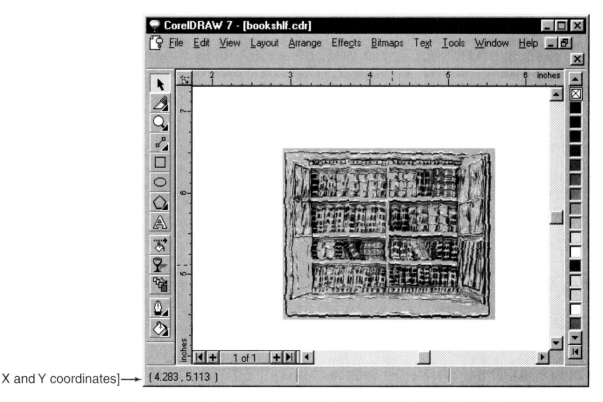

X and Y coordinates] → (4.283 , 5.113)

Figure 14.2 Sample of a drawing tool showing coordinates in lower left corner.

Other Considerations

Not all browsers support client-side images. In fact, not all browsers support image mapping. To make your pages as friendly as possible for the whole range of potential users, you could include your image map within an anchor tag. That way if the user cannot use image maps, she at least has the option of linking to a page that provides her with more useful options. If the user doesn't have a browser that supports client-side image mapping, she can click anywhere on the image and see the document you defined, which should contain a set of links to all of the documents available from the image map. Hence, a majority of users will be able to access your information.

If you choose to build a graphics-dependent page using image maps, you should also build a parallel page designed for the text-only browser. Many professionally designed sites allow the user the choice of seeing a graphical rendering or a text-only page right from the home page. This technique will win you the gratitude of the text-only users on the Net.

Floating Definitions

Another useful and very dynamic feature you can add to your pages is a pop-up window that provides additional content for the user. We saw how to use JavaScript to create new windows in Chapter 13. Now we will examine a useful application of that feature.

The Page

Figure 14.3 shows part of a screen from an online data communications course. Notice that two of the words, "data" and "communications," look like links. When you look at the code in Figure 14.4, you will see that they are indeed links. The dynamic feature of the page happens when the user moves the mouse pointer over the underlined words. Rather than having to go to a separate file to

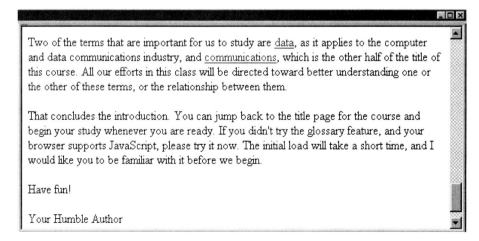

Two of the terms that are important for us to study are data, as it applies to the computer and data communications industry, and communications, which is the other half of the title of this course. All our efforts in this class will be directed toward better understanding one or the other of these terms, or the relationship between them.

That concludes the introduction. You can jump back to the title page for the course and begin your study whenever you are ready. If you didn't try the glossary feature, and your browser supports JavaScript, please try it now. The initial load will take a short time, and I would like you to be familiar with it before we begin.

Have fun!

Your Humble Author

Figure 14.3 The first screen, before the inclusion of a definition window.

```
<HTML>
<HEAD>
<TITLE>General Introduction </TITLE>
<SCRIPT language="JavaScript">
<!--- Hide from Non-JavaScript browsers. . .
var gloswin = null;
//          Put gloswin outside the function so it will be global!
//          This lets us use it in the Closer function too.
// *  *  *  *  *  *  *  *  *  *  *  *  *  *  *  *  *  *  *  *  *  *  *
function Datadef(term) {
//      The "term" above is the URL of the term to be defined
//
gloswin = window.open("','gloswinnav','width=600,height=100,
          scrollbars=1');
    if (gloswin != null) {
        if (gloswin.opener == null)  {
          gloswin.opener = self;
                                         }
        gloswin.location.href = term;
                          }
}   //End of function Datadef
// *  *  *  *  *  *  *  *  *  *  *  *  *  *  *  *  *  *  *  *  *  *  *
*  *
function Closer( )
{
//      All this function does is close the glossary window.
//      It is called from the OnMouseOut event.
//
          done = gloswin.close( )
}  // End of function Closer
// End of the hidden section -->
</SCRIPT>
</HEAD>
<BODY style="background-color=#FFFFCC">
.

.
Plain, old-fashioned HTML code removed for clarity
.

.
<P><A name="data"></A>Two of the terms that are important for us to
study are
<A href="gintro.html#Data" onMouseOver="Datadef('gintro.html#Data')"
  OnMouseOut="Closer( )">data</A>,
as it applies to the computer and data communications
industry, and <A NAME="comm"></A>
<A HREF="gintro.html#Comm" ONMOUSEOVER="Datadef('gintro.html#Comm')"
  OnMouseOut="Closer( )"> communications</A>,
which is the other half of the title of this course.
All our efforts in this class will be directed toward better
understanding one or the other of these terms, or the relationship
between them. </P>
<P>That concludes the introduction. You can jump back to the title page for the course and
begin your study whenever you are ready. If you didn't try the glossary feature, and your
browser supports JavaScript, please try it now. The initial load will take a short time,
and I would like you to be familiar with it before we begin. <BR>
<BR>
Have fun! </P>
<P>Your Humble Author </P>
```

Figure 14.4 HTML code for the definition/glossary screen.

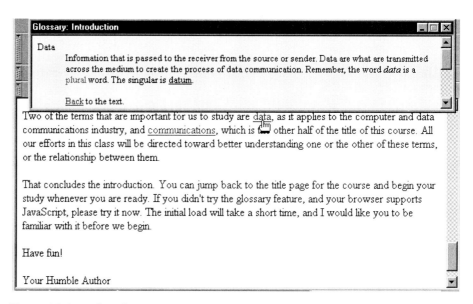

Figure 14.4 continued

see the definition of the word in question, the user will see the definition appear in a new, small browser window. Figure 14.3 shows what the window looks like.

When the user moves the pointer off the word, the definition window disappears. The two event attributes of **onMouseOver** and **onMouseOut** trigger the appearance and disappearance of the definition window. Here are a couple of code segments we need to look at.

The Functions

First, let's look at the data definition function that retrieves the data when the user moves the screen pointer over the link.

```
function Datadef(term) {
//      The "term" above is the URL of the term to be defined
//
gloswin = window.open('','gloswinnav','width=600,height=100,
          scrollbars=1');
if (gloswin != null) {
          if (gloswin.opener == null)    {
          gloswin.opener = self;
                                            }
gloswin.location.href = term;
                    }
}    //End of function Datadef
```

This example illustrates the concept of passing parameters to the function. In this case, the parameter "term" is passed to the function. That parameter is actually the URL of the definition of the word. For example, in the case of the word "data," the term passed to the function in the first instance is

'gintro.html#Data'

which is the URL of the term "data" in the file gintro.html. The actual processing of the function works as we saw in Chapter 13. It creates a window, 600 by 100, and uses the **location** attribute to load the content from the glossary file (gintro.html) into the window.

The glossary file contains the definition of the term and has a back link after each word so that users with nongraphical browsers can return to the main page after they select the link. Here is a snippet of code from the glossary file:

```
<DL>name
<A ="Data">
<DT>Data</DT>
<DD>
Information that is passed to the receiver from the source or
sender. Data are what are transmitted across the medium to
create the process of data communication. Remember, the word<I>
data</I> is a <FONT color="FF0033">plural</FONT> word. The singular
is <U>datum</U>.<BR><BR>
<A href="dcintro.html#data">Back</A> to the text.
</DD>
```

The return link sends users back to the link they left, because the return link uses a target that is defined just before the link, in the body of the page.

The closer() function just closes the newly opened window. It is very simple; the only trick is that it must specify the glossary window. For this reason, we made it a *global variable* (discussed later). Otherwise, it could accidentally close the main window.

The Events

The functions are invoked by two different mouse events, **onMouseOver** and **onMouseOut.** The code to activate the glossary windows follows:

```
    <A href="gintro.html#Data"
onMouseOver="Datadef('gintro.html#Data')"
  OnMouseOut="Closer()">data</A>
```

Notice that the element that serves as the base for the invocation is an anchor tag, which sends the user to gintro.html at the Data anchor name. If the user is using a nongraphical browser or a browser that does not recognize scripts, he can simply activate the link and go to the glossary document.

The second function call invokes the closer() function that closes the glossary window if it is open. That function is called when the screen pointer moves off the anchor.

The first time the glossary page is loaded, it takes a second or two to download the page from the server. From then on, when the user moves her pointer over one of the words, the glossary window appears almost at once. The actual code and the simple glossary are included on the CD that accompanies this book. The code is slightly different in the example in this chapter because we removed the majority of the text and shortened some of the names.

Simple Rollovers

The term *rollover* is used to describe a feature of the page that changes as the screen pointer moves over it. Usually rollover applications involve images and even image maps. The screen capture in Figure 14.5 shows a very simple image rollover before the screen pointer "rolls over" the image. You know how to make a page look like this by simply inserting an image and setting the **align** attribute or the **style** attribute's **float** property to **left**. However, look at Figure 14.6, and see what happens when the user puts the screen pointer on the book image. Notice that the image of the closed book is replaced by one of an open book. Simply by moving the screen pointer, the user causes the page to, dare we say, dynamically change the image on the screen. Figure 14.7 shows the code for the page. Pay attention to the <A> container; this is where the enhancement happens.

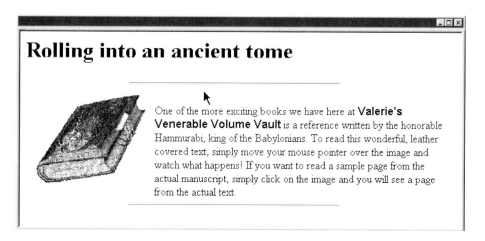

Figure 14.5 A simple rollover example before the "rollover."

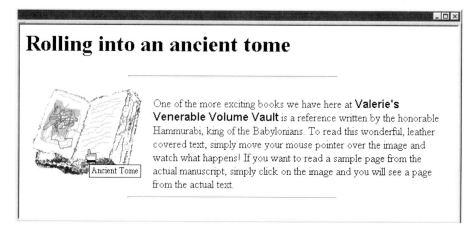

Figure 14.6 A simple rollover example after the user rolls the screen pointer over the image.

```
<HTML>
<HEAD>
<TITLE>Looking into a text</TITLE>
<STYLE>
.logo {font-family: sans-serif; font-size: 12pt;
font-weight: bold}
</STYLE>
</HEAD>
<BODY>
<H1>Rolling into an ancient tome</H1>
<HR width="50%">

<A href="ancient.html"
  onMouseOver="document.pic.src='obook.gif' "
onMouseOut="document.pic.src='cbookl.gif' ">
<IMG src="cbookl.gif" border="0" name="pic"
align="left" hspace="10" alt="Ancient Tome"
height="169" width="135"></A>

One of the more exciting books we have here at
<SPAN class="logo">Valerie's Venerable Volume Vault</SPAN>
is a reference written by the honorable Hammurabi, king of the Babylonians. To read
this wonderful, leather covered
text, simply move your mouse pointer over the image
and watch what happens! If you want to read a sample
page from the actual manuscript, simply click on the image
and you will see a page from the actual text.
<BR clear="all">
<HR width="50%">
</BODY>
</HTML>
```

Figure 14.7 HTML code for a simple rollover example.

Look at the code for the anchor tag in Figure 14.7. Here we are using the **onMouseOver** and **onMouseOut** events to trigger changes in the **src** for the object named pic in the current document. Back in Chapter 13 we talked about how naming objects was the preferred way to address them. When the user moves the screen pointer over the image, the **onMouseOver** event is triggered, and the source for the image is changed from "cbookl.gif" to "obook.gif". When the user moves the screen pointer off the image, the **onMouseOut** event is invoked, and the "cbookl.gif" image is put back as the image in the space named pic. This is a very nice way to add a dynamic element to your pages.

The only attribute necessary to address the space on the page is name="pic", which gives the image object a name we can reference as we change the content. Of course, the image that changes can be a button that goes from dark to light, or a word that starts out normal and becomes outlined in color when the screen pointer moves over it. One of the more sophisticated uses for rollover images is loading an image map as the second image. That presents a little more of a coding and design challenge, but it can be very effective.

Remember that in all of our discussions of images, they are available only to users with graphical browsers, so it isn't wise to become too dependent upon this technique. One of the problems with images in general, and specifically rollovers, is that a second image increases the download time for the user. We will address this problem in the next section.

Professional Rollovers

Actually, this section should be called "no-wait rollovers" because the technique we will demonstrate reduces the "wait time" for the user by pre-loading the images while the page is building. This code also takes into account the older-browser problem and the "non-JavaScript" browser problem. With this code, the page will look and work the same as it does in Figures 14.5 and 14.6. The difference is that the images will already be in cache when the rollover calls for them, so they will load very quickly.

Figure 14.8 shows a code snippet for this new version. The only difference is the code in the <SCRIPT> element in the <HEAD> container. There is a script at the beginning of the page that does two things. First, it checks to see if the browser can identify images. If it can't, then it simply sets the images to blanks. Only browsers that support JavaScript 1.1, like Navigator 3.0+ and Internet Explorer 4+, have the document.images object. If the browser can sup-

```
<SCRIPT>
<!-- Cache images during initial download
if (document.images) {
        openbook = new Image();
        closbook = new Image();
        closbook.src='cbookl.gif' ;
        openbook.src='obook.gif' ;
            }
else    {
        document.pic=" ";
        closbook=" ";
        openbook="";
        }
// end of caching code-->
</SCRIPT>
</HEAD>
<BODY>
<H1>Rolling into an ancient tome</H1>
<HR width= "50%">
<A href= "ancient.html"
  onMouseOut= "document.pic.src=closbook.src"
onMouseOver= "document.pic.src=openbook.src">
<IMG src= "cbookl.gif" border= "0" name= "pic" align= "left" hspace= "10" alt= "Ancient Tome"
height= "135" width= "169">
</A>
```

Figure 14.8 The changed HTML code for the "no wait" rollover example.

port images, then the script creates two new image objects, openbook and closbook. Once these objects are created, the browser uses the **.src** property to begin loading the images into the objects. This image-loading takes place while the rest of the screen is building and while the user is reading the screen. When the user moves the mouse over the image, the alternate image has already been loaded into cache and so is available to quickly load into the page. This technique makes the image rollover much smoother; it looks more professional.

You would not notice a change if you took the images from the CD that comes with this book, but you should see a difference if you load the pages from the Web site for this book. If you are using the Web site, be sure to flush your cache before you download the page, because it uses the same images as those in Figures 14.5 and 14.6.

Color Changing on the Fly

One of the least complex changes you can make is to allow the user to alter the background color of the page while he is looking at it. Although we are always at the mercy of the browser when it comes to the final appearance of our documents, JavaScript allows us to make some changes on the fly. One common change is to allow the user the choice of background colors. It is fairly easy to give the user a set of radio buttons, or even a simple text field, and allow her to alter the color of the background. Altering the color of the foreground is a tad more complex; we will see a JavaScript that allows the user to play with both foreground and background colors in a bit. It is also possible to change the colors of the links—like the **alink, vlink** and **link** options on the <BODY> tag. All in all, JavaScript allows you to build an environment that gives the user some control over the way the page looks. This can be a nice touch.

Figures 14.9 and 14.10 show a little page created just to demonstrate the user's ability to change the background color. Figure 14.9 shows the default version of the screen just as the user encounters it. Figure 14.10 shows the screen after the user chose the "Blue" background. This screen is not particularly dynamic, but it gives the users some control over their screen displays, which many users appreciate.

Research into color preferences among users has revealed that a majority of them prefer to read dark text on a light background. Since that combination has been around for thousands of years, building a site with dark text and a light background is generally the best bet.

Using JavaScript to change the way a document looks is one of the easier tasks. However, there are definite limits as to what you can control. The only unique and exciting code in Figure 14.9 is the **<INPUT>** part of the form, used to invoke the JavaScript. Notice that the form container has no associated action or method. It is used only to contain the elements used to activate the JavaScript. The following line shows the scripting:

```
<INPUT type= "RADIO" name="BGCOLOR"
onClick="document.bgColor= '#FFFFFF';">White
```

Notice that the JavaScript simply reacts to the event of the mouse click by changing the bgColor property of the document, which changes the background color. This is a simple, yet elegant use of one of the object properties.

```
<SPAN class="logo">Valerie's Venerable Volume Vault</SPAN>
are always trying to make our site as friendly as possible.
To help you enjoy our page more, please use the
buttons below to set the background of the page to a
color with which your are comfortable.
<BR clear="right">
<FORM>
<P>
I would like the background color to be:<BR>
<INPUT type="RADIO" name="BGCOLOR" onClick="document.bgColor= '#FFFFFF';">White
<INPUT type="RADIO" name="BGCOLOR" onClick="document.bgColor='#FFCCCC';">Cream
<INPUT type="RADIO" name="BGCOLOR" onClick="document.bgColor='#FFCCFF';">Lilac
<INPUT type="RADIO" name="BGCOLOR" onClick="document.bgColor='#FFFF33';">Yellow
<INPUT type="RADIO" name="BGCOLOR" onClick="document.bgColor='#OOCCOO';">Green
<INPUT type="RADIO" name="BGCOLOR" onClick="document.bgColor='#66CCFF';">Blue
<INPUT type="RADIO" name="BGCOLOR" onClick="document.bgColor='#66OOFF';">Indigo
<INPUT type="RADIO" name="BGCOLOR" onClick="document.bgColor='#9900F9';">Violet
<INPUT type="RADIO" name="BGCOLOR" onClick="document.bgColor='#OOOOOO';">Black
</FORM>
</P>
</BODY>
</HTML>
```

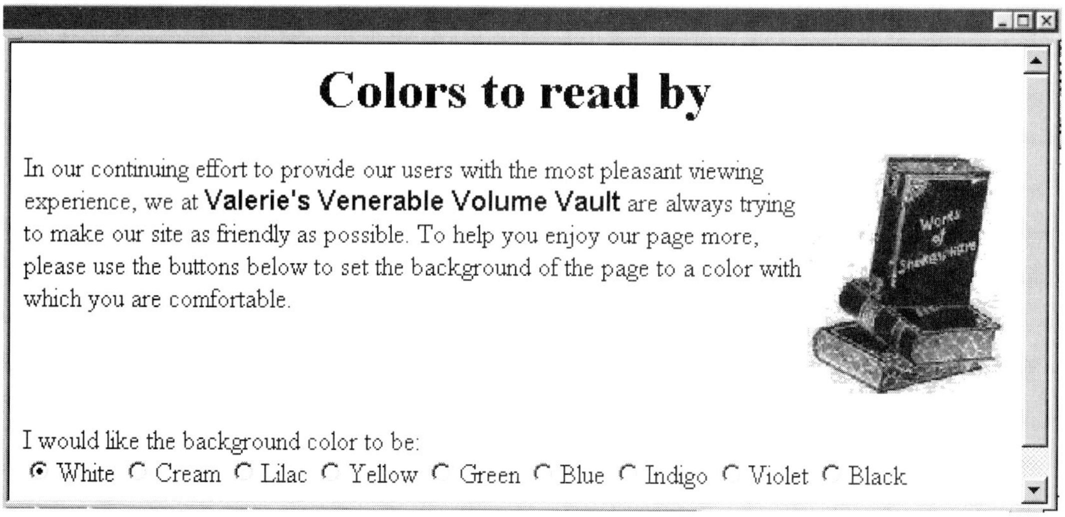

Figure 14.9 HTML code for screen allowing the user to change the initial background color.

Changing the foreground color is a little more complex, as it is normally set when the <BODY> tag is parsed. That means that the browser needs to get the foreground color while the page is loading but before executing the <BODY> tag. Figure 14.11 shows the modifications we made to the previous color changer to allow the user control over the foreground color.

The obvious difference between Figure 14.10 and Figure 14.11 is the prompt box that asks the user for her choice of text color (foreground). After the user enters a text color, either as a word or as a hexadecimal number, the form allows her to click on a radio button and change the background color. If she enters an unknown color or nonsense word, the browser simply guesses, not too well in most cases. You could create a page like this to test various background/foreground color combinations. This page gets very interesting for the

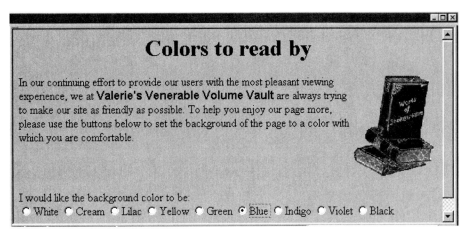

Figure 14.10 Screen showing the background color changer after a user selection.

```
<HEAD>
<TITLE>First color changer page</TITLE>
<SCRIPT language="javascript">
<!-- Hide me Hide me
var textcol = window.prompt("Please enter your choice of\
text colors", "black");
document.fgColor = textcol ;
// no more hiding -->
</SCRIPT>
<STYLE>
.logo {font-family: sans-serif; font-size: 12pt;
 font-weight: bold}
</STYLE>
</HEAD>
<BODY >
```

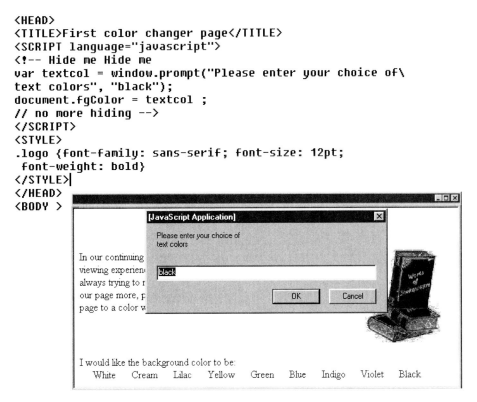

Figure 14.11 HTML code for screen allowing the user to change the foreground color.

user if she selects something like black text and a black background. Makes reading the text a bit challenging!

Looking at the code snippet shown in Figure 14.11, you can see that the changes are the inclusion of the <SCRIPT> container and the change in the <BODY> tag. The script is very short, using a prompt box to request the color from the user. Notice that it simply sets the document property document.fgColor to whatever value the user entered. This makes the browser do all the work of trying to figure out what the user wanted. One interesting anomaly surfaced while we were working on this example. Notice the backslash before the *carriage-return line feed* in the script:

⇓

```
var textcol = window.prompt("Please enter your choice of \
```

If that carriage return is not protected by the backslash, the script will not work. For some reason, this script doesn't like unprotected carriage returns. Little idiosyncrasies like this make working with any programming language, well, um, er, interesting.

The prompting dialog box function takes two values: the prompt string and a default value to place in the input area. In this case, we chose "black" as the input color. We could have left the input area blank by coding an empty string, "", for the second value. If we had left off the second value, the browser would have filled in a value of "default"—not too pretty.

How the Cookie Crumbles

Now that we can allow the user to select a color, maybe it would be nice to keep track of that color for him so that he can see it the next time he visits our site. To do that we need to store a **cookie** on his browser. A cookie, or more precisely, a *persistent cookie,* is a small data set stored by the user's browser on the user's machine. If you are using cookies, you need to be aware of some limitations of this methodology:

- There can be a maximum of 300 cookies in the cookie file.
- A cookie can contain only 4 kilobytes (4000 characters) of data. That total is the sum of both the cookie's name and value.
- The browser will store a maximum of 20 cookies per server or domain.

Since JavaScript cannot access the hard drive, it must depend on the browser to write and later read the cookie. A cookie is stored in a file called cookies.txt somewhere on your hard drive. We found cookies stored in the following places, depending on the platform being used:

- On a Windows 95 computer using Navigator, the cookies.txt file is located in Program Files\Netscape\Users\ttg.
- Internet Explorer tosses its cookies in Windows\Profiles\ttg\cookies when using Windows 95.
- On Macintosh computers, Navigator has a file called MagicCookie stored in the Netscape folder within the Preferences folder inside the System folder.
- Internet Explorer on the Mac stores its cookies in a file called Internet Preferences in the Preferences folder within the System folder.

You must *not* edit this file. It is created by the browsers and must be preserved *exactly* as it is, or you risk breaking a link.

JavaScripts cannot actually modify the contents of the hard drive of the client machine, nor can they read from the hard drive of the client machine.

However, they can ask the browser to store and retrieve small amounts of data for them. In the "old days" these data were shipped across the Net to a CGI script, which then processed them. Now JavaScript can use the data locally as well, often eliminating the need for the slower CGI scripts.

Cookies allow the Web page to act as if it has a little bit of memory. For example, let's look at the page designed to allow the user to select her favorite background color. A cookie-enabled page will save that color, and the next time the user comes to that page, a little JavaScript will look at the cookie data and set the background to the color of choice. Saving information like this is also called *maintaining state.* In some circumstances it is useful to allow the browser to save information about the state of a particular page. Users may appreciate feeling that they are important enough for you to ask for and remember their preferences.

One of the most significant advantages of cookies is their persistence. Once set, they can remain on the client machine for days or months or even years. The cookie in our example will remain, or persist, for two years from the date it was created. If the user comes back to the site any time in the next two years, the page will be able to set the environment to his liking.

Figure 14.12 shows the modified code for our page that stores and reads the cookie data. On the first visit, the page looks much like the one shown in Figure 14.11. We will make a repeat visit in just a bit. Of course, the user will always be allowed to set a foreground color; that is independent of the process of setting the background color. Although it is possible that a page could also remember the user's foreground preference, the user wouldn't be able to change it once the page was loaded, so we will allow her to alter that color when she enters the page. Figure 14.12 shows the code that allows the page to "remember" the background color. It looks somewhat complex, but it makes sense if you break it down into manageable hunks. We will dissect it one function at a time.

To parse this page, let's first look at the functions that were added. This code segment starts with the <SCRIPT> element. The first thing that was coded was a pair of variable names, bc, for background color, and Hits, a counter used to determine how many times the user has opened this page. These two *variable names* are declared here so they can be used as **global variables.** A global variable is a value stored at a location that is known to all of the functions in this page. A **local variable** is known only to the function in which it is created. We will see an example of each in the first function. Had we declared the variables inside one of the functions, only that function would know about these local variable names and the values (variables) stored there. But instead, with our global variable, all of the functions can read and modify the same storage location, or variable name.

The first function, Changebg(hexadecimal), shown in Figure 14.12, takes as input some hexadecimal value, passed in the parameter and stored in the local variable name hexadecimal. The function then changes the background color using the bgColor property of the document, and stores the color value in the global variable name bc. This function is invoked when the user elects to change the background color using one of the form controls.

```
<INPUT type="RADIO" name="BGCOLOR"
onClick="Changebg('#FFFFFF');">White
```

When the user activates one of the form controls, the **onClick** event calls the Changebg( ) function and passes it the hexadecimal code for the chosen color. With a value for bc set, the code to store the cookie can save the value stored in bc.

```
<TITLE>Colors to read by, I'll Remember</TITLE>
<SCRIPT language="javascript">
<!-- Hide me Hide me
var bc='#FFFFFF';
var Hits=0;
//var textcol = window.prompt("Please enter your choice of\
//text colors", "black");
//document.fgColor = textcol ;


//****************************************************
function Changebg(hexadecimal) {
document.bgColor=hexadecimal;
bc=hexadecimal;
}
//****************************************************
function BakeCookie(Cname,value)
{
var zap = new Date();
zap.setTime (zap.getTime() + (730 *86400000));
//              730 = 2 years, 86400000 = milliseconds in a day
//              This sets the expire time 2 years ahead
document.cookie=Cname+"="+value+";expires="+zap.toGMTString();
}
//****************************************************
function CheckCookie()
//              This function is called on page load to check and
//              see if the user has been there before, and what
//              their background color choice is if they have.
//
{               // Start of function
//                      bc and Hits are global.
if (document.cookie != "") {
//                      Ok, there is a cookie set. Let's parse it.
        CookieBatch=document.cookie.split(";");
//              Parse the whole cookie into individual cookies
//                      giving name=value pairs.
//
//                      Now, let's look at the first one. . .should be
//                      visits.
if (CookieBatch[0] != ""){
//                      Look at the first cookie. If not null. . .cool.
        bc=CookieBatch[0].split("=")[1];
//                      The value, bc, is equal to the second piece
//                      of the first element of the CookieBatch array.
//                      Remember, each element is a name=value pair.
//                      This code splits off the value, removes the
//                      escaped code, and stores it in the variable
//                      bc (bc is a global variable, used other
//                      places).
        }
if (CookieBatch[1] != ""){
//                      Ok, it is redundant, but we now check that there
//                      is a second value available.
        Hits=eval(CookieBatch[1].split("=")[1]);
//                      Now let's do the background if they have been
//                      here before. Then we will give them a little welcome
```

Figure 14.12 HTML code for a cookie that remembers a background color.

```
//              message too.
        }
if (Hits > 0)  {
        document.bgColor=bc;
        document.writeln('<H4>Welcome back My Friend, to the show that never ends!</H4>');}
}
}              // end function
//*****************************************************
function Cook()
{
//              This function calls BakeCookie twice, setting
//              Visit count and background color
//
        BakeCookie("bc",bc);
        BakeCookie("Hits",Hits+1);
}
//*****************************************************
//*****************************************************
// no more hiding -->
</SCRIPT>
<STYLE>
.logo {font-family: sans-serif; font-size: 12pt;
font-weight: bold}
</STYLE>
</HEAD>
<BODY onUnLoad='Cook()'>
<SCRIPT type="text/javascript">
<!--
CheckCookie()
//-->
</SCRIPT>
<H1 ALIGN="CENTER">Colors to read by</H1>
<IMG src="sbooks.gif" align="right" alt="Three old books" width="118" height="140"></IMG>
In our continuing effort to provide our users with the
most pleasant viewing experience, we at
<SPAN class="logo">Valerie's Venerable Volume Vault</SPAN>
are always trying to make our site as friendly as possible.
To help you enjoy our page more, please use the
buttons below to set the background of the page to a
color with which you are comfortable.
<BR clear="right">
<FORM>
<P>
I would like the background color to be:<BR>
<INPUT type="RADIO" name="BGCOLOR" onClick="Changebg('#FFFFFF');">White
<INPUT type="RADIO" name="BGCOLOR" onClick="Changebg('#FFCCCC');">Cream
<INPUT type="RADIO" name="BGCOLOR" onCLick="Changebg('#FFCCFF');">Lilac
<INPUT type="RADIO" name="BGCOLOR" onCLick="Changebg('#FFFF33');">Yellow
<INPUT type="RADIO" name="BGCOLOR" onCLick="Changebg('#00CC00');">Green
<INPUT type="RADIO" name="BGCOLOR" onCLick="Changebg('#66CCFF');">Blue
<INPUT type="RADIO" name="BGCOLOR" onCLick="Changebg('#6600FF');">Indigo
<INPUT type="RADIO" name="BGCOLOR" onCLick="Changebg('#9900F9');">Violet
<INPUT type="RADIO" name="BGCOLOR" onCLick="Changebg('#000000');">Black
</FORM>
</P>
</BODY>
</HTML>
```

Figure 14.12 continued

The second function, `BakeCookie(Cname,value)`, actually sets the cookie value. The term "cookie" leads to all kinds of wonderful word plays, and someone must have had that in mind when the feature was named. This function takes two parameters: the name of the cookie and the value assigned to that name. In addition to the variable name and value, which looks a lot like the name=value pairs we saw in the chapter on CGI, a cookie must have an expiration date. This expiration date determines how long the cookie will persist on the user's machine before it becomes inactive. The default expiration date is "today," so that the cookie disappears when the browser closes. The expiration date is calculated in milliseconds. In our example, the cookie is supposed to stay active on the user's machine for two years from the time it was set. Looking at the code, we see the expiration time is calculated as follows:

```
var zap = new Date();
zap.setTime (zap.getTime() + (730 *86400000));
```

First a local variable name of `zap` is created as an instance of the `Date()` object. Next the `getTime` method is used to find the current time. Finally, 730, the number of days in two years is multiplied by 86,400,000, the number of milliseconds in a day. (The number of milliseconds in a day is obtained as follows: 24 hours × 60 minutes/hour × 60 seconds/minute × 100,000 milliseconds/second.) The result is added to the current time to get the date that we store as the variable `expires`. Whew! Now we use the `cookie` property of the `document` object to ask the browser to store the name=value pair with the expiration date in the cookie file:

```
document.cookie=Cname+"="+value+";expires="+zap.toGMTString();
```

This last little bit of code tells the browser to convert the time to Greenwich Mean Time format. This is the date format that the browser expects.

If we make even a little mistake in coding the expiration date, the browser will replace our time with "now," and the cookie won't be stored. This seems a lot of work just to store some data, but the effect is certainly worthwhile.

The `bakeCookie()` function is called twice, to set the value of the background color and to increment the number of times the user has been to this page. The function `Cook()` calls `bakeCookie()`. `Cook()` is invoked when the browser *exits* this page. This way the user can change the background color several times, but only the last change is stored.

The next function, `CheckCookie()`, asks the browser to see if there is a cookie named `Hits` set on the user's machine. If `Hits` exists and has a value greater than zero, the user has been to the page before. Note: One of the features of cookies is that only the server that created the cookie may read that cookie. Therefore, we don't have to worry about naming our cookie a unique name, as our version of "Hits" belongs to the server. In that case, we welcome her back and set the background color to the one she used during her last visit. The code is a little complex, so it is heavily documented. What it does is parse out the possible parts of the cookie, then divide the parts of the cookie into their name and value pairs. Then it picks out the values and assigns them to the global variable names used in the JavaScript. The last IF structure does the real work on the current page, setting the background color and putting out a welcome message if the user has returned.

We made an interesting discovery when we were working with this code. It seemed natural to use the **onLoad** event to trigger the `CheckCookie` function. However, when we did that, the only content for the page was either a blank screen the first time the page was invoked, or the welcome message on subsequent loads. This seems to mean that the browser considers the code generated by the function as the only content for the page if it encounters it before the rest of the content start to build. It is a surprising "feature" of the browser.

A Better "Date Last Modified" JavaScript

In Chapter 13 we examined a useful script that automatically read the date the Web page file had last been modified and reported it on the bottom of the page. Figure 14.13 shows a screen capture of the time-stamp output of that date function. Looking at this screen capture with a critical eye, we see that there are a couple of problems with the format of the date last modified. First of all, the date does not comply with the internationalization we have come to expect. It isn't clear if the date is January 12th or December 1st. Second, does our user really want to know that the page was updated at the 44th second of the 19th minute of the 21st hour? Hardly. Let's build some functions to display the last date modified in a more readable and user-friendly format.

We last added new books: 01/12/01 21:19:44

Figure 14.13 The first version of the "date last modified" JavaScript.

Figure 14.14 shows an example of the same page we saw in Chapter 13 but with a more useful and internationally correct date. This page has a much more understandable date and time format. The day of the week is included to help the user decide if the content is new to him. The time is in 12-hour format, with the AM/PM designator provided so the user doesn't have to do the math to convert the 24-hour format. All in all, it is a much nicer layout. Figure 14.15 shows the code for this new page. The functions are a little long, but upon examination they are fairly easy to understand.

Figure 14.14 A better "date last modified" page.

```html
<HTML>
<HEAD>
<TITLE>New books today?</TITLE>
<SCRIPT>
<!-- I'm Hiding, I'm Hiding, and no one knows where!
function MTime() {

//              Get the date last modified, and stuff
//              in into the variable now.
//              Notice that it is different than the
//              previous incarnation of this function!
        now = new Date(document.lastModified);
//              Using the current time,
//              parse out the hours data.
        hours = now.getHours();
//              Parse out the minutes.
        minutes = now.getMinutes();

//
//              Add the hours to a string called timeVal.
//
        timeVal = " " + ((hours > 12) ? hours - 12 : hours);

//
//              What this does: If the hours are greater
//              than 12 (it is afternoon), subtract 12 from
//              the hours number because we will put an
//              AM/PM indicator on the time block.
        timeVal += ((minutes < 10) ? ":0" : ":") + minutes;
//              In this case, if the minutes are less than
//              ten, put in the leading zero. This is a very
//              nice example of using this structure. It is
//              read "If the minutes are less than 10, then
//              add :0 to timeVal, otherwise just add : to
//              timeVal. Then append the value for minutes
//              to timeVal.
        timeVal += (hours >= 12) ? " PM" : " AM";
//              This piece sets the AM/PM indicator by checking
//              whether the number of hours shows it to be
//              noon or later. (Time is returned in 24 hour,
//              or military, format.)
//              The statement below returns the value of
//              the string timeVal created by this function.
//              That allows us to use the function call
//              directly as if it were this value.
        return(timeVal);
}
function MDay() {
        when= new Date(document.lastModified);
    day = when.getDay();
//              This is one way to select a value based on
//              the number (0-7) returned by the getDay
//              method. In each case, the value returned and
//              stored in day is checked against one of the
//              possible values, and if it matches, a string
//              value is assigned to the variable day. Not
//              terribly elegant. A cleaner solution is
//              shown in the next function.
        if (day == 0) day=" Sunday";
        if (day == 1) day=" Monday";
        if (day == 2) day=" Tuesday";
        if (day == 3) day="Wednesday";
        if (day == 4) day="Thursday";
        if (day == 5) day=" Friday";
        if (day == 6) day="Saturday";
          return(day);
}
```

Figure 14.15 HTML code for a better "date last modified" JavaScript.

```
function MDate() {
dlm=new Date(document.lastModified);
mMonth=dlm.getMonth();
dDate=dlm.getDate();
yYear=dlm.getYear();
        if (yYear < 70) {yYear += 2000}
        else {yYear += 1900};
//          The year returns years since 1900. . .add 1900 to
//                  get the correct year. . .No Y2K problems w/ this
//                  script! :-)
var MonthName = new Array(12);
MonthName[0]="January";
MonthName[1]="February";
MonthName[2]="March";
MonthName[3]="April";
MonthName[4]="May";
MonthName[5]="June";
MonthName[6]="July";
MonthName[7]="August";
MonthName[8]="September";
MonthName[9]="October";
MonthName[10]="November";
MonthName[11]="December";
//                  The code below will set the variable mMonth to
//                  the correct string by using the numerical value
//                  as an index into the array MonthName created just
//                  above. A more elegant way to select a string, but
//                  it does require more memory. There are always
//                  tradeoffs.
mMonth=MonthName[mMonth];
//                  Since the getMonth function returns the numerical
//                  value for the month (0-11), we need to translate
//                  that to a character string to make it friendly.
dater_str= " "+mMonth + " " + dDate + ", " + yYear;
return(dater_str);
}
// -->
</SCRIPT>
<STYLE>
.logo {font-family: sans-serif; font-size: 12pt;
font-weight: bold}
</STYLE>
</HEAD>
<BODY style="background-color: #FFCCFF" >

NOTE: snip. . .removed the plain old HTML to make the illustration smaller

<HR width="75%">
</DIV>
<P style="text-align: right; font-size: 9pt; font-family: sans-serif">
<SCRIPT>
<!--
//     Here we build a string for output. We could do it with
//     a set of calls to the functions right in
//  the writeln, but
//     this lays out better, and is more readable.
var ModStr="This page was last modified on " + MDay();
ModStr+= "," + MDate() + " at " + MTime();
document.writeln(ModStr);
//-->
</SCRIPT>
</P>
</BODY>
</HTML>
```

Figure 14.15 continued

The real interesting parts of this page are the three functions that parse and massage the value stored in the `document.lastModified` property. The three scripts were written using two different methods to find the date values we want to use. The actual code is fairly well documented. We will look only at the overall functioning and point out some of the "interesting" features. The details are in the actual code.

The first function, `MTime()`, handles the parsing and reformatting of the time that the page was modified. The first thing it does is use the `Date()` object to create a value for the date the page was last modified by collecting those data from the `document.lastModified` property. It stores those data in the variable `now`. Next it parses out the hour and minute that the page was modified by using, respectively, the `gethours()` and the `getminutes()` methods. With the individual parts of the time separated, the function builds a character string that contains three components: the hour, the minute, and the AM/PM indicator.

Building these strings is an interesting exercise, because we can use the same addition operator to concatenate the various components together, forming a longer string. For example, the line

```
timeVal += ((minutes < 10) ? ":0" : ":") + minutes;
```

takes the current value stored at `timeVal` (the hour value) and adds the colon and then the minute value to the string. This construct is a shortcut to an IF/ELSE block. It says: *If* the value stored at "minutes" is less than ten, then add a colon and a zero. *Else* (if the value stored at minutes is ten or more), just add a colon, and then append the minute value.

The last line of the function is also worth our attention. This line tells the function to return the value it stored in `timeVal` to the script that called the function. Remember, back when we discussed functions, we noted that one of the features of functions was that the call to the function is replaced by the value returned. This is how the actual time is inserted into the page.

The second function, `Mday()`, takes the value for the day from the `lastModified` property and converts it to a string containing the day of the week. This function shows how a series of IF statements is used to select a value from a range (Sunday through Saturday). The `lastModified` value keeps the day as a digit in the range 0–6, where 0 is Sunday, and 6 is Saturday. This script also illustrates how JavaScript can use the same variable name, in this case `day`, to store either a number or a character string. Notice that this function, too, returns the actual day in place of the function call.

The last function is actually the most complex. It creates the month, day, and year portion of the date. The month is stored as a number in the range 0–11, where 0 is January and 11 is December. The day of the month is simply stored as a number in the range 1–31. The year presents an intriguing problem. It is stored as a one- or two-digit value representing the last one or two digits of the year. For example, the year 1999 would be stored as `99`, but the year 2002 would be stored as `2`. And thus the "year 2000" problem is created. If we only had to deal with the twentieth century, all we would have to do is add 1900 to the value returned. However, in 2000, adding 1900 will result in our being a hundred years off.

To solve this problem, and the solution is not perfect, we will use a feature of the browsers that will be helpful until the year 2070. It just so happens that the browsers won't return a date earlier than 1970. That is their base date.

Therefore, if the value returned from the getYear( ) function is less than 70, it must be in the twenty-first century, but if the value is 70 or more, the value must indicate a year in the twentieth century. Like we said, it's not a refined solution, but it does seem to work.

The second feature of this function determines the month name from the month number. In this instance, we are using an *array,* or subscripted variable, to hold all of the month names. An array is a contiguous segment of memory that is addressed using one variable name to access a series of different values. In this case we tell JavaScript to reserve storage for 12 different values at the location specified by the variable name month. We then assign each location, starting with location zero, the appropriate value. Finally, we use the value of the month number, returned from lastModified property, to select one of the entries. Using the array takes less processing power but requires that we store all of the month names in memory.

The last part of this code presents these data on the page. The final function in the page combines text strings with the values returned from the functions and creates a long string that tells the user when the page was modified.

There are two ways to use this script. You could duplicate this code in all of your pages, or you could simply store the code in a file and then include that file in each page where you wish to use that function. Rather than all of the code shown in Figure 14.14, you could code:

```
<SCRIPT src="dlm.js">
</SCRIPT>
```

That will load a file called dlm.js (*date last modified. JavaScript*) into the document. The file dlm.js is on the CD that comes with the text as well as on the Web page for the text. Feel free to download it and use it in your pages. Putting a set of functions in an external file has four advantages:

1. It makes your page much simpler, because there isn't a whole lot of JavaScript cluttering up the beginning of the document.
2. It saves space, because the code is stored only in one location on the server, not in each file that uses it.
3. It saves maintenance, because the code can be fixed in one place, and the fix will be propagated to all the files that use that code.
4. If the code is used in several pages, the browser can cache the functions and then not have to download them for each page. This makes it faster to download subsequent pages, and reduces Net traffic as well.

Creating a library of JavaScript tools is a handy way to add functionality to a whole collection of pages across a Web site. We recommend you start your JavaScript tool library with this file and add to it as you identify new needs for your pages.

Validating User Input

In Chapter 11 we learned about CGI and about using forms to collect and then transmit data to the server for processing. One of the tasks involved in processing data in this fashion is verifying that the user has entered the correct data. This task is simplified by using predefined controls like checkboxes and radio buttons. Problems most often arise when we allow the user free input in text fields. In those cases we may need to validate just what the user typed, ensuring the data at least *seem* to be what we are asking for.

In the following example, the folks at Valerie's are inviting their users to subscribe to their monthly e-mail newsletter. To do that, the users need to submit their e-mail addresses to the Web master. Since Valerie's isn't a large site, the Web master will collect the addresses via e-mail. A problem is posed by the fact that Valerie can't use a program running on the server to make sure the users have entered their e-mail addresses on the form. JavaScript comes to the rescue. Figure 14.16 shows the page that allows the user to subscribe to the newsletter, and Figure 14.17 shows the code for that page.

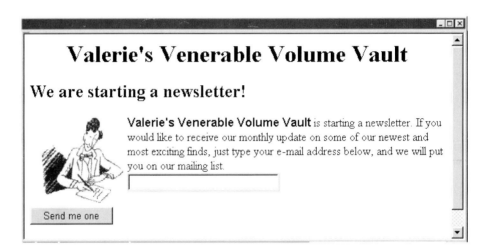

Figure 14.16 A page that requests user input and validates that input.

There are a number of mistakes a user could make when entering an e-mail address. This form checks for several of the more common errors. If the user makes an error, the form will pop up an alert box telling the user what is wrong, then highlight the e-mail field and let the user fix the error. Only if the e-mail address entered passes all of the tests will the JavaScript let the `mailto:` action occur.

Look at the code in Figure 14.17. There are only two functions here. One acts as the driver function by calling the checking function and setting up the user to correct the e-mail address if it contains an error. The second function makes a series of tests on the data the user entered. Let's examine the testing function, `CheckEmail`, first.

`CheckEmail` performs a series of tests on the string the user entered in the field named `email` in the form called `newsltr`. The first step is to create a variable that contains the most commonly used illegal characters for e-mail addresses. That list could be updated with some nonprinting characters too.

The second step is to check that there is, in fact, something coded in the field. If the field is empty, it does no good to do the other checks.

If there is something in the field, then we need to see if there are any bad characters in the data. Users often accidentally include a blank space in their e-mail address. Other common inclusions are the backward slash, the colon and semicolons, and a comma rather than a period. The second block of code loops through each of the bad characters and checks to see if that character appears anywhere in the input data.

```
<HTML>
<HEAD>
<TITLE>All the News that's fit to print</TITLE>
<SCRIPT>
<!-- Camo works!
function CheckEmail(addr) {
// This function will check for some of the common errors
// in an e-mail address. It is not foolproof, but it will
// weed out some of the problems.
var badChars="/ ;,:";
//              E-mail addresses cannot contain slash, blank,
//              semicolon or colon.
//
//              The first test is to see that there is, indeed, an
//              address (or something) in the control.
if (addr == "") {
       alert("E-mail address missing");
       return(false);
                    }
//         Ok, so we have something, let's see if it has any
//         bad characters in it.
for (indx=0; indx<badChars.length; indx++) {
              badun = badChars.charAt(indx);
       if (addr.indexOf(badun,0) != -1) {
       alert("E-mail address contains an invalid character");
       return(false);
                                   }
                                        }
//         Good so far. Now let's make sure it has an @ sign.
WheresAt = addr.indexOf("@",0);
       if (WheresAt == -1) {
       alert("E-mail address must contain an at sign '@'.");
       return(false);
                         }
//         Great, we are making progress. Now let's see if
//         it has any extra @ signs.
if (addr.indexOf("@",WheresAt+1) != -1) {
       alert("E-mail address contains multiple at signs '@'.");
       return(false);
                                      }
//         The address looks good to me. . .let it go.
return(true);
}      // End of CheckEmail function
function SendIt(newsltr) {
       if (!CheckEmail(newsltr.email.value)) {
//         If the address is broken, point back to the field
           newsltr.email.focus();
//         Then highlight that field and let them re-enter
           newsltr.email.select();
//         Send back a "false" so the mailto: won't work
           return(false);                          }
else
       return(true)
}      // End of SendIt function
//-->
</SCRIPT>
<STYLE>
.logo {font-family: sans-serif; font-size: 12pt;
font-weight: bold}
</STYLE>
</HEAD>
<BODY style="background-color: #FFFFCC" >
<H1 style="text-align: center">Valerie's Venerable Volume Vault</H1>
```

Figure 14.17 JavaScript code for validating an e-mail address.

```
<H2>We are starting a newsletter!</H2>
<P>
<FORM
          name="newsltr"
          action="mailto:dusty@vvvvault.com"
          method="POST"
          onSubmit ="return SendIt(this)">
<IMG src="newsltr.gif" width="129" height="118" align="left"
          alt="Dusty writing the news - 8755 Bytes">
<SPAN class="logo">Valerie's Venerable Volume Vault</SPAN>
is starting a newsletter. If you would like to receive
our monthly update on some of our newest and most
exciting finds, just type your e-mail address below, and
we will put you on our mailing list.<BR>
<INPUT type=text size="25" name="email"> <BR><BR>
<INPUT type="submit" value="Send me one">
</FORM>
<HR>
</BODY>
</HTML>
```

Figure 14.17 continued

Look closely at the following code, which is an excellent example of using the features of the language to make the program simple, yet elegant.

```
for (indx=0; indx<badChars.length; indx++) {
    badun = badChars.charAt(indx);
    if (addr.indexOf(badun,0) != -1)
```

The code sets up a loop to step through the five bad characters, one at a time. It assigns to the variable `badun` the value of each of the bad characters and then uses the `indexOf` method to find the index (or placement) of that character within the data string. If the `indexOf` method finds the character, it returns the location of the character in the input string. If it doesn't find the character, it returns a negative one. The IF statement checks the return value to see whether or not it is equal to negative one. If it is not (the value is not a negative one), then the `indexOf` has found an occurrence of the bad character. In this case the IF statement activates an alert box and sends back a return value of "false," indicating that the input data contains an error.

The third block of code checks to make sure that the user has an @ sign in his e-mail address. It uses the `indexOf` method as well, this time checking that the result is "positive," which means that an @ was found. If the result is a negative one, that means there is no @ sign, and the e-mail address is malformed.

The last block of code starts checking at the byte one greater than the location where the previous test quit after finding the first @ sign. It checks to see if there is another @ sign in the string. If it finds one, it signals an error, because an e-mail address can have only one @ sign.

If the e-mail address passes all of these tests, it is considered valid, and the `SendIt( )` function allows the script to send the message. If any of the previous steps return a value of "false," the `SendIt( )` function aborts the e-mail, highlights the contents of the field, and gives users a chance to reenter the data. When they reenter the data, the whole process starts over again.

The user's activation of the "Send Me One" button will trigger the **onSubmit** event. They could also activate the **onSubmit** event by pressing the Enter key. Recall from our discussion of forms that if there is only one control in a form, and if that control is a text-entry field, then the user can simply touch the Enter key to submit the form.

This validation is pretty simple. However, it does not check all of the possible errors with an e-mail address. For instance, it could check to make sure there is a period in the address, since there has to be at least one period in any valid e-mail address.

You can use this type of JavaScript validation to verify that radio buttons have been activated, that the user has checked at least one checkbox, and all sorts of other input criteria. Remember, all of this checking is done in the browser; only if the data pass the muster of the JavaScript will they be sent across the Net.

You have seen several different ways to make your pages more dynamic. In this chapter we have looked at image maps and various JavaScripts. These JavaScripts popped up definitions, altered images when the screen pointer moved over them, allowed the user to alter the background color, created cookies to help document these changes when the user came back to our page, updated the date last modified, and even validated input data. Obviously, JavaScript is a very useful tool for Web weavers. Feel free to incorporate these techniques into your pages, and be sure to continue to explore the wonderful world of JavaScript, for we have merely scratched its surface.

Key Terms

Array
Client-side mapping
Cookie
Dynamic
Global variable
Hot spot
Image map
Local variable
Maintaining state
Rollover
Server-side mapping

New Tags

<AREA>
<MAP>

Review Questions

1. What is the definition of each of the key terms?

2. How is each of the tags introduced in this chapter used? (Provide examples.)

3. What are the advantages to using client-side mapping?

4. What <IMG> attributes are used to create server-side and client-side image maps?

5. What is the order of precedence when <AREA> definitions overlap hot spots within an image map?

6. Identify three valid shapes that can define an image map's hot spot, and identify the format of the associated coordinates for each.

7. What would be an application for floating definitions and rollovers?

8. What is the conclusion of research into users' screen color preferences?

9. What are the limits to the size and number of cookies the browser can maintain?

10. What unit of time is used in cookie expiration date calculation?

11. How is the "year 2000" problem handled when using JavaScript to process the last date updated?

12. What are four advantages to using an external script?

13. During validation of an e-mail address, what conditions would indicate an error?

Exercises

14.1. Create a new HTML document with text that uses at least three different examples of jargon or slang with which you are familiar. The title bar should display "Jargon Revealed" with your name and the assignment due date included within comment lines. Create a floating definition for each jargon example. A window with the definition should open when the user moves the screen pointer over the term.

14.2. Create a new HTML document that is designed to display a single work of visual art. The title bar should display the artwork's title and the artist's name. Your name and the assignment due date must be included within the document as comment lines. The page should include the image, the artist's name, and creation date if it is known. The document should also incorporate the code introduced in this chapter that lets the user select radio buttons to change the screen's background color.

14.3. Retrieve the "Internet Privacy Concerns" page you created in Exercise 13.3. Add the code to create a cookie that stores the browser name and computer platform used by the person reading the Web page.

14.4. Update the Homework home page's "last date modified" JavaScript you added in Exercise 13.4. When the date is displayed, the month and day of the week should be spelled out. The time should be presented using AM/PM instead of a 24-hour time designation.

14.5. Create four new HTML documents. One document should contain a client-side image map. The map needs at least three hot spots. Activating a hot spot should open one of the three HTML documents. Each hot spot should open a different document. Your name and the assignment due date must be included within each document as comment lines.

14.6. Update the school's home page to include a rollover with an image or graphic already used on one of the related pages. The choice is up to you. Here are some ideas for the image:

- Your school in summer with rollover of same view in winter
- Basketball player dribbling with rollover of same player shooting
- Drummer hitting drum with rollover of drummer with sticks in the air
- Student in library reading with rollover of same student sleeping on book

## CHAPTER fifteen

PRAGMATIC HTML—IT AIN'T ALL PICTURES!

T o the novice HTML author, Web weaving means building home pages, or maybe creating an e-commerce site replete with graphics, dynamic content, and lots of artistic effort. However, in today's world of intranets there is a growing corporate and private use of the browser interface to provide access to information. In this environment, many professional Web weavers find themselves creating extremely large documents using only the linking and display features of the browser. These documents don't use graphics, sound, or dynamic features; they simply supply massive amounts of text, often with hyperlinks to other documents.

455

Many of these documents are sent to the browser as `Content-Type: text/plain`, which means that they won't even be recognized as HTML files. They are usually displayed in a monospaced font like Courier. Figure 15.1 shows an example of this type of file. As you can see from the figure, plain text is really plain, and really just text. It is useful for moving lots of text data—not as pretty to read as a proportional font, but very functional and extremely quick to code.

Several classes of documentation are beginning to appear on the Web. Among these are literature, corporate/government documentation, electronic books, Web-based instruction manuals, online help, and online education.

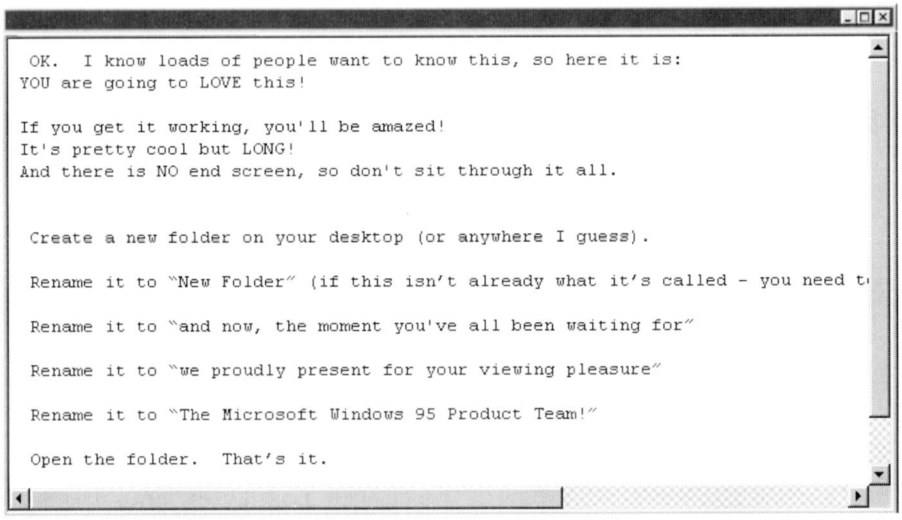

```
   OK.  I know loads of people want to know this, so here it is:
YOU are going to LOVE this!

If you get it working, you'll be amazed!
It's pretty cool but LONG!
And there is NO end screen, so don't sit through it all.


Create a new folder on your desktop (or anywhere I guess).

Rename it to "New Folder" (if this isn't already what it's called - you need t

Rename it to "and now, the moment you've all been waiting for"

Rename it to "we proudly present for your viewing pleasure"

Rename it to "The Microsoft Windows 95 Product Team!"

Open the folder.  That's it.
```

Figure 15.1 An example of Content-Type: text/plain.

Literature

Some interesting examples of great works of literature have been hosted on the Net by selfless groups. In Chapter 1 you saw some of the offerings from the University of Virginia's online library. A list of several collections of this type is included at the end of this chapter. Check them out and enjoy some classic reading. The usual caveat applies, however, that the addresses of some of these sites may have changed between our reading of them and your reading of this text. Figure 15.2 shows a partial list of the works available from the University of Michigan.

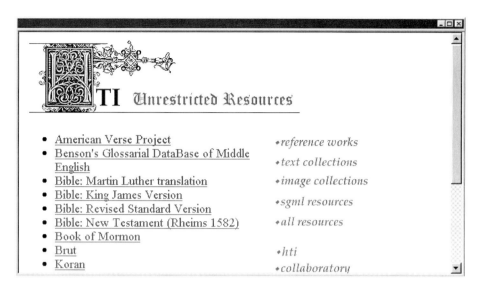

Figure 15.2 Partial listing of the main categories available at the University of Michigan's HTI site.

Text-Only

Many text-only documents are simply online versions of the paper originals. In some cases, they include translator's notes, but most are simply long, text-only documents. They don't involve many of the features of the browser and have no links to word definitions. All they do is present the text, either in the plain version as we saw in Figure 15.1 or in proportional fonts like the one used in this book. Such projects are a wonderful use for the Web. They allow anyone with Web access the opportunity to read a great variety of literature, often in the original language. For example, Figure 15.3 shows a screen capture from the Book of Merlin in Olde English. This particular work is 1549 Kb(!) of pure proportional text.

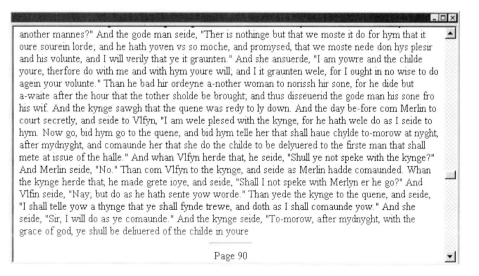

Figure 15.3 Part of a page from the Book of Merlin.

Text and Illustrations

Other literature collections provide their readers with some illustrations to accompany the text. For example, one of the versions of Alice's adventures has scans of some of the accompanying illustrations. Figure 15.4 shows a screen capture of one of the pages. Actually, it is in color and quite nice to see if you visit. The address is in the list at the end of this chapter.

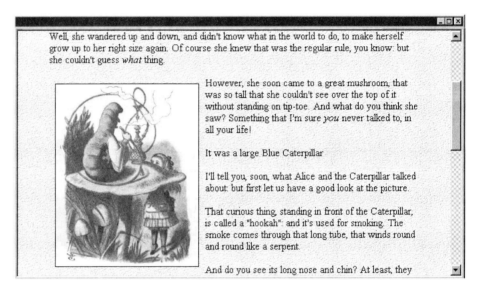

Figure 15.4 Screen capture illustrating the use of HTML code and illustrations in a large document.

Hyperlinked Text

The most powerful use of HTML in presenting text occurs when the Web weaver uses links to tie several documents together. In some cases these documents give the reader actual links to documents that are referenced, or they may provide an online glossary or dictionary that supplies the definitions of certain **hot words** when the user activates those links. Figure 15.5 shows a screen capture from *The Hacker's Dictionary*. The words that look like links are actually links to other words in the dictionary. (By the way, this is a great place to learn new jargon!)

Using hyperlinks to retrieve definitions or to branch the user to supplementary documents brings to bear the power of the Net. The previous examples in this chapter show how the Web can be used to emulate a paper-and-print text. The fourth example, from *The Hacker's Dictionary,* shows how a wise Web weaver can utilize the hyper part of HyperText Markup Language to create a document with features that were previously unheard of.

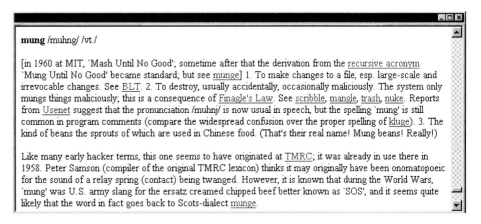

Figure 15.5 Screen capture showing hyperlinks within a document.

Corporate/ Government Documentation

Many applications exist in the government and the corporate world for producing large collections of HTML pages to replace hard-copy documentation. Some of these uses are policy and procedure manuals, employee manuals, current legislation, government reports, budgets, and the like. Figure 15.6 shows part of a page from an online personnel manual. It is a simple, unadorned text document, easy to read and well indexed. If anyone in the organization, or a prospective employee, wants to read part of the manual, he can do so any time of the day or night, provided the server is up.

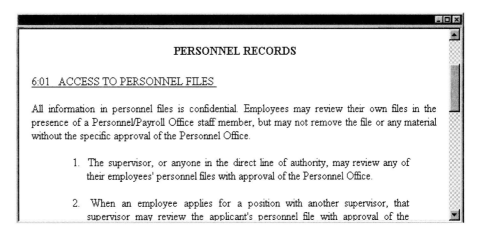

Figure 15.6 Part of an online personnel manual.

There are several good reasons to produce manuals and other documents online rather than in a paper version:

- Probably the most important benefit is that each user will always have access to the most recent data. Doctors, for instance, can have access to the latest government research without having to wait for it to be published in a medical journal.

- The expense of publishing online is usually much less than printing many paper copies. (In addition, it is supposed to save trees, although in practice most people go ahead and print copies of the pages.)
- Updates to existing online documents are available across the whole user community as soon as they are entered. This reduces the chances that some subset of an organization will not be informed of a change in policy.
- Online documents are available anywhere there is an Internet connection. A user at a remote location can have access to the whole set of corporate documentation in the field.
- In addition, other companies or government agencies can look at an organization's methods to help formulate their own.

Creating and maintaining a set of online corporate/government documents is a monumental task, because accuracy and availability are always essential issues.

Electronic Books

Someday in the not too distant future, texts that are loaded into an electronic book will supplement books like the one you are holding. Two companies that are pushing the envelope in this area are NuvoMedia Inc. and SoftBook Press. Both companies advertise that the reader can download electronic texts from the Net (from Web sites like Barnes and Noble) and then load the data into their electronic book for reading.

The books would have an internal dictionary so you could find the meanings of words you didn't know. In addition, each device would hold around 4000 pages of text and graphics, so you could have several texts in the book at the same time. Features would include adjustable fonts, multiple bookmarks, and even highlighting. The reader would buy the text online, download it to her PC, and then transfer the data to the electronic book through a serial port.

Once the book was downloaded, it would transfer only to your electronic book, because the text would be encrypted. The procedure would be something like scrambling on a cable TV channel. If you wanted to lend the text to a friend, you would have to loan him the whole electronic book. This procedure is currently used to download data to *personal digital assistants (PDAs)*. It could be a great boon to students, who would only have to carry one, electronic, book with them, having the equivalent of several textbooks in a three-pound package.

Web-Based Instruction or Reference Manuals

You can find out how to do almost anything on the Net these days, from making artificial reef balls at (http://reefball.com/) to programming the 65C02 integrated circuit (http://sls.mcs.usu.edu/~kurto/lynx/programming/6502ref.html). Figure 15.7 shows part of the online document for the reef ball project.

As with online corporate/government documentation, online instruction manuals have several benefits for both the author producing them and the user.

- The online reference can be as current as the author is willing to keep it. The company who owns the product can update the online manual to reflect problems, features, or even misunderstandings conveyed to them by their customers.
- Users can't lose an online reference. Unlike hard-copy manuals, they don't get lost behind the refrigerator, under the couch, or buried in a file drawer.

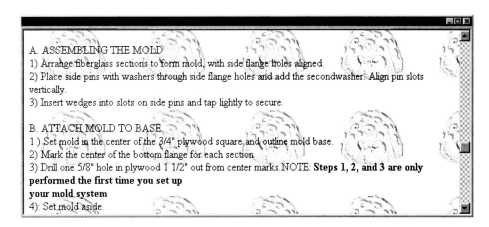

Figure 15.7 Part of an online instruction.

- If the customer buys a device second-hand, the requisite documentation is still available even if the original owner lost the paper version.
- Should the customer want to print the manual, she can do so, at her own expense.
- Using the full range of HTML, CSS, JavaScript, and multimedia tools, a careful Web weaver can create a multimedia user's guide that is far more comprehensive than a printed manual could ever be. In addition to written instructions, a Web site can supply actual MPEG video clips showing how the product is to be used, along with narration to help the user through more complex tasks, like software installation.

All in all, online manuals provide a superior way to supply many forms of user's guides, manuals, and reference works.

Online Help

Another area where Web weavers are increasingly involved is in the creation of help files for packages and programs. Microsoft has abandoned its traditional WinHelp format and gone to a new tool called HTML Help. That means that now Microsoft help files will be written using a variant of HTML rather than the previous format. Unfortunately, Microsoft has chosen to use Active-X controls in this package, so it isn't useful across all the browsers. However, when a major player in the computing field begins to use HTML-based help, it won't be long before there are other, more compatible packages available. If you want to explore this tool, or want to download the Microsoft HTML Help creation tool, you can visit the Microsoft site at

http://microsoft.com/workshop/author/htmlhelp/

for a description of the product, the process, and the actual software.

Of course, Netscape wasn't about to be left out in the cold, so it developed NetHelp, another HTML-based help tool. It uses Communicator, which isn't cross-platform compliant either. You can find out more about NetHelp by visiting

http://home.netscape.com/eng/help/

You can download the NetHelp SDK (Software Development Kit) from this site. Figure 15.8 is a screen capture from the Netscape site showing how NetHelp would look for an imaginary topic. Notice that the help screen looks much like a regular Web page . . . that is the whole idea!

Figure 15.8 A screen capture showing how a NetHelp screen might look.

Online Education

One arena where the Web has had a major impact is in training. Both in-house corporate training and distance learning in schools and colleges have jumped on the HTML bandwagon. While other forms of distance learning have slowed in growth or are even dwindling, Web-based education is becoming a hot topic. There are several reasons for this:

- Online education is available whenever and wherever the student can find a computer tied into the World Wide Web. Students can learn at their own pace, and on their own schedule. They don't have to wait for a professor, nor are they limited in how quickly they can complete a unit of instruction. By the same token, the student doesn't have to commit to a pre-specified block of time at a regularly scheduled interval.

- A college doesn't need the overhead of a physical plant to conduct online classes. All they need do is supply a host or server computer, the necessary software, and the content. There is no need for classrooms, desks, whiteboards or chalkboards, a cafeteria, or even a parking lot.

- All the students receive the same instruction. This can be good or bad. The quality of the experience depends, in part, upon the skills of the author building the course.

- Once instruction has been developed, it takes less effort to update and modify it. Of course, this advantage depends on the sponsoring organization recognizing and committing itself to the necessity of regular updates. As neophyte Web weavers, you already know the importance of checking and maintaining your pages on a regular basis. Unfortunately, not all the folks in management do.

- Finally, online courses can provide a web of learning that exceeds the scope of a single professor. A science course could be designed using the expertise of a dozen or more specialists, all writing Web pages about their own areas of study, or it could include the use of original sources available only via the Web. No single professor can duplicate that!

There is a fly in the ointment, however. Each of the points just listed has a counterpoint. The old saying that "those who refuse to learn from history are condemned to repeat it" applies here. *Computer-assisted instruction (CAI)* was going to revolutionize education in the early 1980s by replacing professors with terminals and classrooms with computers and cubicles. It didn't happen. The major reason was that educational designers didn't take into account the limitations and strengths of the new medium. Among the many problems with CAI was the impossibility of forcing traditional teaching methods into the new medium. CAI courses were often nothing more than automated page-turning tools. Students spent hours and hours reading text on eye-straining terminals, all alone. One of the biggest complaints voiced by students subjected to early CAI was that they were lonely. Overall, the CAI effort failed to yield even a fraction of the gains that were expected of it.

By the same token, those authors who begin developing Web-based education must look at the medium and study its inherent strengths and weaknesses. They can't treat it like a traditional delivery system with a screen. There are untold strengths available to the HTML author, who can tap into multimedia in a way never before possible in the history of education. Much research must be done in this new area of education, but the potential is staggering.

Figure 15.9 shows the beginnings of an online data communications course. This set of pages was designed to take the place of a student's lecture notes. It doesn't incorporate multimedia or extensive links.

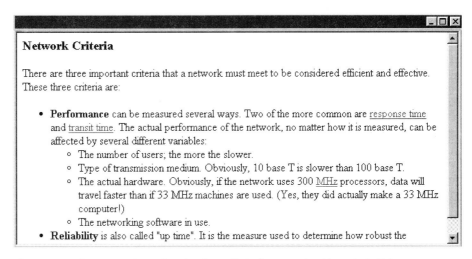

Figure 15.9 Screen capture showing hyperlinks in an early attempt at distance education.

Perhaps the very best instructional delivery system is a professor sitting on one end of a log and the student on the other. That kind of one-on-one teaching/learning is probably the ideal. However, in our widely scattered world, HTML-based teaching seems to be the very best method of distance learning we have ever had.

Web Site versus Web Page

In Chapter 3 you saw four different organizations of pages: sequential, indexed sequential, hierarchical, and custom. You saw that you could create a single page to serve as a table of contents and linkage point for a series of poems. That was just a tiny example of a Web site. In addition, Chapter 3 mentioned the importance of *storyboarding* your site so you could design both the flow of the pages and the way the user would interact with that flow. Now we will build on those ideas.

Consider for a moment what the design of an encyclopedia site would look like. The initial design would probably be sequential, simply flowing from one page to the next, just as users would read a book if they were reading it front to back. But that model doesn't work for an encyclopedia, because it is a reference work, and people don't usually read it from front to back for entertainment. (Mind you, if you haven't tried that, it is amazing what you can learn just by picking up a volume of a good encyclopedia and reading for a few dozen pages.) Besides that, a single page that contained the whole content of a good encyclopedia would take a LONG time to download.

This is the model used for the online version of a book or class: The first step is to make the material more useful by including a set of *intrapage* links. These links will allow the user to select any of the letters of the alphabet and jump to the first page that has entries starting with that letter. The next step might be to divide the page into 26 different pages, one for each letter of the alphabet as shown in Figure 15.10.

The online notes for each chapter from the book should be stored in a separate file, and the master table of contents, or index should contain links to each chapter. Each of those pages could have its own index to allow selection of entries from that page.

Finally, each letter of the alphabet could have its own page, with a large list of links to various topics, each of which has its own page. This model could easily involve hundreds or even thousands of pages. In such a model, the design would have to be carefully crafted to ensure that the pages all tied correctly forward and backward. Indeed, this type of design creates a set of links so complex it would justify the term Web weaving!

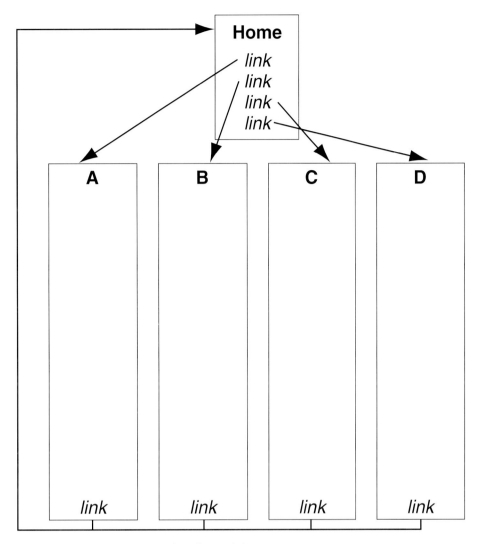

Figure 15.10 An online encyclopedia model.

Migrating from Text to Hyper

When an individual or an organization decides to migrate from a paper-based document system to an online document model, there is a lot of initial work that must be done. The first step is to design, or storyboard, the site, showing the linkages among all of the different documents and pages within those documents. This is a critical step, because navigation is often where online sites fail. Users must be allowed to find and retrieve the information they need with little or no hindrance. The relationships need to be carefully crafted to enable free-flowing movement across the whole of the content.

The second step, designing a page's "look and feel," is almost as critical as the first. This is another area where some companies fail to consider their users. On the one hand, a page layout that is too busy, too loud, or loads too slowly is a disservice to the user. On the other hand, plain vanilla pages using black text on stark white do little to make the user's experience pleasant.

You learned about page footers in Chapter 3. During the page layout stage, details such as footers will also need to be finalized. A small graphic of the company's logo in a "header" may help unify and define the documents. However, remember that headers and footers will appear on each page as it is printed. The way the documents will look when printed is an important consideration.

Finally, the most interesting question: How will the actual content be migrated from paper to Web-based format? We won't attempt to deal with a document that exists only in paper format. The operations of selecting **OCR** (optical character recognition) software, scanning, and proofreading for correctness and completeness are beyond the scope of this text.

We will assume that we are starting with a document that exists in some electronic form—for example, a document in a word processor format like Word 97. There are a plethora of packages that claim to take text in some form like ASCII, RTF (rich text format), MS Word, PostScript, WordPerfect, and so on, and convert that text form into HTML. Some of these packages perform better than the others do. On the W³C's Web site alone, more than 70 different converter packages are listed. Some are freeware, some are shareware, and others are commercial products. All of them claim to create HTML from some other application format. None that we tested did a perfect job. In every case, the output needed some tweaking to make it useful. We discussed HTML *text-file converters* in Chapter 1, so we have no need to go into detail about them here. Suffice it to say, we did some serious research on such converters using the various tools available and found that all of the conversion packages—using built-in word processor tools, external conversion tools, or importing the text into an HTML editing package—created documents that still needed additional work.

Most likely, the HTML documents produced by such converters require less work than a plain ASCII file would if you had to add all of the HTML features. Moreover, using external style sheets could ease the job of standardization and allow for quicker conversions.

If you are faced with the task of converting a set of text files to HTML, the best bet would be to get samples of several of the conversion programs. Run all of them against one example file that has the features found in the target files, and look at the resulting HTML files. Find the one that is most complete, or that requires the least manipulation, and then acquire that package. Over time, packages like Web Publisher and Microsoft Word will become increasingly complete, creating documents with a high degree of reliability.

Aural HTML

Not everyone in the Web community uses a visual browser. Some 3 percent of users (as per the W³C) have a visual condition that renders the traditional Web page less than ideal for them. An additional 4–5 percent don't use a graphical browser for reasons of connection speed, hardware limitations, or because they choose not to be bothered by distracting graphics. In addition, the wise Web weaver will take into consideration users who cannot appreciate graphical content because of the situation in which they find themselves. For example, in the relatively near future, our cars may well be equipped with HTML browsers. It would be great to be able to cruise the Web while cruising the Interstate, but not with graphics! In the auto-browser, the user would prefer an aural, meaning "relating to the ear" or "hearing," presentation rather than a graphical one.

One of the noteworthy features of the HTML 4.0 specifications, according to the W^{3}C, is a significant increase in the support for accessibility. Using an aural component on your page allows those Web cruisers who are not using graphical browsers to implement other possibilities.

The following code is supposed to add aural presentation to a page:

```
H1 { voice-family: heidi;
    volume: medium;
    richness: 30
      }
```

Please note that aural presentations are a combination of both audio cues, or *audio icons,* and synthesized speech. Audio icons are used much like graphical icons to delimit parts of the text, to highlight specific phrases, and to call attention to changes in the content. Unlike the current practice of converting the Web page to plain text and then passing it to a text-to-speech reader that simply reads all of the characters passed to it, the aural styles allow the rich environment of the Web page to be transferred to an aural modality.

Although the aural rendering of the page can be considered separate from the graphical, as images will be replaced by the values of their **alt** attributes and the various characteristics of the text, such as headings, will be represented by aural cues, the major content will still be intact. Aural characteristics include properties that control the volume, speech properties, pausing before or after, cue before or after, and playing an aural content during another type of activity. In addition, a rich set of voice properties is available, the most interesting being the voice family designated by names like paul, heidi, peter, and goat!

The aural presentation space is three-dimensional, so with proper audio gear, a Web weaver can design sounds that come from different directions and elevations. Of course, those users who have that sort of surround-sound stereo setup correspond to graphical users with 21-inch, 64-million color monitors. The wise Web weaver won't require that level of hardware commitment, but it does provide an interesting aural palette. Let's look at that code again. It will set level-1 headings to be played in a very smooth voice of heidi, at mid-level volume:

```
H1 { voice-family: heidi;
    volume: medium;
    richness: 30
      }
```

If this were coded as part of a document's style sheet, and if the user had a sound-equipped browser, level-1 headings would be presented in sound, and perhaps in text as well. Currently there is no way to test aural styles in the standard browsers, but new and better browsers are being created all the time.

International Considerations

The world seems to grow smaller every day, and the World Wide Web is one of the major forces that seem to be shrinking it. Content on a Web page is available to anyone, worldwide, who has a browser and access to the Net. In light of that fact, the W^{3}C added a significant number of features to the 4.0 specifications to take into account people who want to host pages in languages other than English.

As you have seen, there are attributes available on nearly every tag that allow the Web weaver to specify both the language for that element and the direction that the language is to be read. The direction is important for things like punctuation marks and the like. As you cruise the Web, you will see more and more sites that provide content in languages other than English. The internationalization of the HTML specifications is an important step to promote accessibility worldwide. As Web authors, we should strive to make our content available to as wide an audience as possible, both those folks who have preferences as to their chosen form of input and those who don't speak our language. Over time, the browsers will allow more and more people access to our content.

Online Text Sites

Here are some of the more interesting sites that have text documents available on the Web.

- http://www.hti.umich.edu/all/unrestrict.html—This is a list of links to famous and not so famous works. Several religious texts are included. (Notice that the site address looks like a hypertext link. If this were an online document, you could just click on the address and go to that site. Alas, you are reading this on paper and so must go elsewhere to link to the site.)
- http://home.earthlink.net/~lfdean/carroll/nursery/chapter01.html— The first chapter of *Alice's Adventures in Wonderland*. You can read many of Lewis Carroll's works at this site.
- http://www.tuxedo.org/~esr/jargon—Technically this is called the *Jargon File* and the paper version, published by MIT press, is *The New Hacker's Dictionary*. It is a wonderful site that can consume many a rainy afternoon, providing chuckles, chortles, and even a few guffaws. Check it out!
- http://www.promo.net/pg/—Project Gutenberg is attempting to make 10,000 electronic editions of books available on the Net before the year 2001. This project has the following philosophy:

  > The Project Gutenberg Philosophy is to make information, books and other materials available to the general public in forms a vast majority of the computers, programs and people can easily read, use, quote, and search.

- http://www.ipl.org/—The Internet Public Library is just what its name implies, a large collection of electronic documents available for your perusal.
- http://www.cs.cmu.edu/books.html—This is called the *online books page*. It boasts over 7000 titles, including a very interesting list of books that have been banned by one group or another.

Key Term

Hot word

Review Questions

1. What is the definition for the key term?

2. What is the most powerful use of HTML?

3. What are five benefits to maintaining documents online?

4. What features do the authors speculate would be available with electronic books?

5. How could you benefit from learning online?

6. How would a sighted person use an aural browser?

Exercises

15.1. Use the online references provided in this chapter to find out how many books are currently available from Project Gutenberg.

15.2. Send an e-mail to the software house of the browser you use. Ask it when the next release of its software will be available. Include in the e-mail at least one inquiry about an HTML- recommended feature you would like to see supported, for example, aural style sheets. If you use Internet Explorer, e-mail Microsoft. If you use Navigator, e-mail Netscape or America Online.

15.3. Use the HTML format of *The Hacker's Dictionary* to find the definition of "Hamster."

15.4. Create a link to *The Hacker's Dictionary* on your Homework homepage.

15.5. Use the online references provided in this chapter to find out the size of the biggest reef ball.

15.6. Create a new HTML document that provides links to at least three of the online resources provided in this chapter. Add a link to this page on the school's home page you updated in previous exercises. The title bar on the page with the online reference links should display "Online References." Also include your name and the assignment due date within comment lines on the new page.

style guides

Style—we all feel we have it when we are building our pages, and our pages always look good to us. But there are some guidelines that will make your Web pages more readable and more usable. Or, as Robert Burton (1576–1640) said,

"It is most true [that] 'stylus virum arguit,' our style bewrays us."

The following style guidelines—and they are just that, guidelines not rules—come to you from a number of different sources. First, they reflect the page-design experience of the authors of this textbook, plus the experiences of their students. Some of these endeavors worked, and some serve as good examples of what not to do.

Second, these guidelines come from many different style guides found across the Net. They are too numerous to mention, but a collection of some URLs that served as resources appears at the end of this section. Third, these guidelines were derived from the ranting and raving of many users who have written in mail groups, left messages, and generally made their feelings clear about what they like and don't like about different sites.

General Guidelines

- **Have a purpose for your page.** Don't create a Web page just because you can. Have a distinctive purpose for your pages, and let the reader know, up front, what that purpose is.
- **Be consistent.** Consistency is critical. Decide on things such as how you are going to use headings, what colors will mean, how site navigation will be accomplished, and then stick with that design across all your pages. In addition, use consistent images when you mean the same thing, and use a consistent background to tie all your pages together (or use a different but

consistent background to identify related collections of pages). Use the same navigation controls on all your pages, like "Back," "Forward," and "Home."

- **Always design for both graphical and nongraphical browsers.** Not everyone uses a graphical browser, so if you want your information to be accessible to all users, design your pages to be accessible to nongraphical browsers. In fact, in large areas of the world, most folks depend on fast, small, text-only browsers. Always look at your page in Lynx, a text-only browser, or turn off image loading in your graphical browser to see what it looks like. One site recently visited looked like this in Lynx:

[LINK]

[LINK]

[LINK] [LINK] [LINK]

[LINK]

That is not very helpful, now, is it?

- **Don't try to be "slick."** Fancy, powerful, animated images and applets are wonderful toys, but most users don't appreciate a page full of distracting elements that get in the way of finding what they need on your page. Creating pages that use the very latest Web technology will probably be of value only to a small minority of users who play on the cutting edge. For the majority of users, your innovations will either be invisible (at best) or render your page useless (at worst). Don't design pages to simply show off how complex you can make a page. Always remember that your primary goal is to create a page that enables users to efficiently and enjoyably find the information they seek.

- **Use big pages and images only when necessary.** Size *is* important! Big, slow-to-load pages do not reflect good design. If you need to display a large image, put it on a page by itself, and give the user a link to that page. One nice way to do that is to use a *thumbnail image* as the link. When using thumbnails, make sure you tell the user how big the image is or how long it may take to download. Your home page should download very quickly. A good rule of thumb is to keep your home page with all its images smaller than 1 megabyte of disk space. That way it will be relatively quick to download. A good test is to link to your page from a browser connected through a modem, and see if you can hold your breath until your page fully loads. If you can't, consider making the page smaller.

- **Maintain your page!** After you have spent the time to create a page, it's worth a little extra time to ensure that all the links on that page work and that the other elements of the page are correct. Plan to spend some time each week checking your page. It is always more fun to create new content for your pages, but your users deserve to find a good, useful, accurate page when they make the effort and take the time to come to your site. Make sure your links work and that the information you put on your page is accurate. If you choose to use the "date last modified" script we showed you in Chapters 13 and 14, it may encourage you to update your page frequently, because it reflects the date of the last change.

- **When you update your site, do it all at once.** Don't upgrade a site piecemeal. If you are changing the look of your site, plan the effort so that you bring all the pages with your new look online at the same time. It can be confusing for your users if they move from screen to screen of your site and find significant differences among the pages.
- **Don't change the colors of the linking text unless your design absolutely forces you to.** Should you feel forced by your design to change the colors of the linking text, it might be better to change your design. Coding colors for the **alink, link,** and **vlink** attributes that are different from the defaults can confuse your users. Even though the default colors are not necessarily the very best, and there may be good arguments for changing them, users still expect unvisited links to be blue and visited links to be purple. Stick with that color scheme whenever possible.
- **Use background images with care.** A background image will, *without a doubt,* interfere to some extent with the readability of your page. Use background images when necessary, but know that you will be reducing, albeit slightly in some cases, the readability of the text on your page.
- **Use light backgrounds with dark text when you can.** They are easier to read than dark backgrounds with light text. If you doubt this, ask yourself if it is easier to drive a car during the day or at night. Dark backgrounds make seeing more difficult. In addition, white text on a dark background will not usually print out if the user tries to print your page. White text doesn't show up well on a white page! We realize that there is some attraction to creating pages with very dark backgrounds. However, as your experience with the Web increases, you will find that style less and less attractive. Generally, those pages with dark backgrounds are built by Web newbies. Experienced Web weavers know that dark text on light background has been with us for a long time. It has been the style of choice for thousands of years—to be exact, 5000 years—ever since papyrus sheets were used in place of the later invented paper. Unless there is a very compelling reason for the opposite, use light backgrounds with dark text.
- **Use color sparingly.** Color is a powerful tool, but too much color on a page is worse than no color. Color can focus the attention of your user, or it can distract from the content. One of the glaring mistakes that novice Web weavers make is to create pages that are a veritable riot of colors. Bright colors for text and background, color images, initial caps in a contrasting color to the rest of the text—color, color, color everywhere. Those pages are visually brutal to view and downright difficult to read. Subtle use of color is always better than the assault on the senses employed by some Web weavers.
- **Choose browser-safe colors.** Several places throughout the text we have mentioned browser-safe colors. Those 216 colors that are browser-safe should provide as much of a palette as any designer needs. We have included them on the color insert in the back of this book to make your job easier. Remember, too, that all platforms will not render even the browser-safe colors *exactly* the same way.
- **Build your pages so any browser can use them.** It doesn't really make much sense to create pages that contain features that are supported by only one of the browsers. We have been careful to show you things that

will work in both of the major graphical browsers. Avoid the trap of building a page "best viewed with ExplorerScape." There is a campaign on the Net to encourage Web weavers to create browser-neutral pages. Visit the home page for this movement at **www.anybrowser.org/campaign/**.

Look for buttons like the one in Figure A.1 as you cruise the Web. The movement is growing!

Figure A.1 Best viewed with any browser.

- **Always provide a way for the user to get in touch with you.** You will want your users to be able to tell you of problems they found or give you kudos for things they liked. Your address should be on your home page or on the main page of a collection. This way, since all the other pages will have navigation links back to the home page or to the central link for a series of pages, the user can always get to the page with your address on it by means of the `mailto:` link. Make sure that the mailto link is documented as well. A cute, animated GIF is nice, but it is invisible in a text-only browser.

- **Cross-link all the pages in your site.** Avoid dead-end paths that force people to use the "Back" button on their browser. If you have a worthwhile page, someone will bookmark it. When she comes back to your page using a bookmark, she will need to be able to move back to the rest of your site. She must have a set of navigation tools to do that. One of the more useful tools is a small one-row table at the bottom (or top) of each page that contains links around your site. See the section on making a table of contents for an example of this structure.

- **Date your pages.** Always include the date on your pages so your user knows when the site was last updated. For example, it does him no good to have a site that lists all the important astronomical events for 1994. It might be interesting in a historical context, but it's not of much interest to the user who is trying to find out when to look for the next Perseid meteor shower.

    You owe it to your readers to date your page. Besides, it may encourage you to keep your page up to date if the time of your last update is noted there for everyone to see. Along this same line, when you put the date on your page, use the formal style of "Last updated March 4, 1998" rather than "Last updated 03/04/98." Why? Because in Europe that date means April third, not March fourth. (Europeans place the day number first, then the month number.) Using the "date last modified" JavaScript from Chapter 14 is an easy way to accomplish this.

- **Don't have several links to the same content on the same page.** It is horribly confusing for your user to see links to _interesting material_, _more material that is interesting_, _even more interesting material_, all of which point to exactly the same page. In fact, you should beware of using too many links as a general principle. A page that is filled with many links of any type can be confusing for the user. Link to important sites, but don't overdo the links—unless you are creating a page of links, that is. A page of links is usually not a good use for a Web page, but in specialized cases it can be useful. If you are going to have a page of links, consider putting them in a table to better arrange them for your user.

- **Make sure your page is unique.** Okay, this sounds like a social issue, not a style issue, but your page should exist only if it supplies some unique content to the Net. It is not sufficient to be a page of links, or a page of quotes from other pages, or a page of images, ahem, "borrowed" from other sites. Your page should provide something unique to the world. If it doesn't, why should it take up space on the Net? Perhaps the only thing unique about your page is your history, your vision, and a collection of your holiday pictures. Well, let's forget that last bit—but the first two items are reason enough to create a Web page. No one else has your exact history and vision.

  The point is, your page should provide something new to the Web, something that is available only on your pages. Without that, all the rest of these issues become merely smoke.

Style in the \<HEAD>

- **Use a title, and make it a meaningful one.** Often the title is all a potential user has to go on to determine if she wants to go to your page. Make your title descriptive and accurate. A good title is usually less than 50 characters long. Remember, if users save your page in a Bookmarks file, your title is the description that will be stored to help them find your page again.

- **Include \<META> tags that contain complete and accurate data.** An example of a good \<META> tag follows:

  ```
  <META name="KEYWORDS" content="Keywords like style guide,
  excellent">
  ```

  These tags help indexing packages like AltaVista search your page and create accurate links to it. The list of keywords will often be displayed by the search engine as well.

- **Use external resources when possible.** It is usually more maintainable to link to style sheets and JavaScripts than to code them in the \<HEAD> container. If you use a style sheet or JavaScripts in more than one page, make them external and link to them.

The \<BODY> of Style

- **Don't use frames unless you must.** While there are some good uses for frames, which we have discussed, as a general rule, you shouldn't use them. They take up screen real estate, they can slow processing, and they functionally disable some useful browser tools like the "Back" button and bookmarking. If you absolutely must use them, be sure to provide your users with a prominently displayed way to exit from the framed document lest they be trapped in your frames.

- **Use headings in level order.** \<H1> headings are for important, main ideas. \<H2> should come next, then \<H3>, and so on. Always use headings in order. Don't skip a level unless your design forces you to. And if it does, consider changing your design.

- **Use the cascading styles.** The HTML 4.0 specifications gave us cascading style sheets. You have seen numerous examples of how those are used throughout this text. To summarize our advice, when possible,
  1. If you are providing style data for more than one page, use an external style sheet and link to it.
  2. Use document-level style data.
  3. Use inline style for specific, unique style changes that happen only once on a page.
- **Put equal spacing between elements of equal importance.** Add extra spacing between elements that are of distinct categories.
- **Use horizontal rules to separate different elements on the page.** Horizontal rules, <HR>, provide a good visual break. But don't code them with too large a **size** attribute. According to some Web weavers, it is considered bad form to code more than one <HR> in succession. Others use a series of two or three <HR>s of different sizes to create an interesting border or divider. If you code more than one <HR>, don't go overboard.
- **Keep your pages to a reasonable length.** There is great debate on what is a "reasonable" length for a page. It is like when Abraham Lincoln was asked how long a man's leg should be, and he gave the famous reply, "Long enough to reach the ground." Your Web page should be long enough to reach the ground, too. Hmmm . . . okay, how long would that be? How about long enough to cover the concept or idea you are presenting? If the page is too short, the user wastes time waiting for it to paint up. (However, sometimes it is an excellent idea to have small pages that serve as footnotes to your larger page.) If the page is too long, users may not want to view all of it. There is some evidence that most users will not scroll down more than one or at the most two screens on a page. That is a good measure for your home page, as well as for index pages or pages at the head of a set. Yet, it makes little sense to break up the posting of a scientific paper that runs to 15 screens just for the sake of brevity. If you are putting a book on the Net, it is usually a good idea to break it down by chapters, or even by large sections. But don't break a book into 20-line chunks and force your reader to flip from page to page to follow your narrative. The proper length, then, depends on the content.
- **Always have a table of contents for your site.** If you have a complex site with several different areas of interest, try to have a main *table of contents* (TOC) that links to the sublevel TOCs. This way your user can navigate about your site more easily. Each page should have a link back to the sublevel TOC at a minimum. It is good to also have a link to the main TOC. A series of pages should have links from each one to the next. It makes little sense to force the user to bounce back to the TOC to see each successive page of a document. The pages should have "Next" and "Back" links to help the user navigate.

  This is not to say that your TOC must look like a TOC! It is easy to create a little table of links that serves as a TOC. This way the user has a navigation tool, but you don't sacrifice the "look and feel" of your page. Figure A.2 provides an example.

Navigation Tools									
Student Pages	Linux	Educational	Shareware	Search	Special Interest	Books	Tools	Unix Instructors	Mad Doc G.

Figure A.2 Table of contents as navigation element.

- **Test your page with the Lynx browser.** Lynx is available for download to your server (check with your systems manager) or for use from several sites. The Web page for this book has a link to Lynx in case you can't find one closer to home.
- **Print your page.** This sounds like a simple test, but it is sometimes amazing how bad a page can look when printed. A good Web weaver will always consider the printed version of their page even though the Web is designed to save trees.
- **Always indicate the status of your page.** Some pages are created for a specific purpose and require no updating. You should tell your user when the data on your pages are final versions and not subject to revision. On the other hand, most pages are constantly under revision. If that is the case, tell the user so, and give him some idea as to when the next update will happen. However, don't use the cute "under construction" GIFs or, worse, the "under construction" *animated* GIFs. Everybody knows that everyone's pages are almost always "under construction"; you don't need to include those graphics.
- **Always use the shortest URL you can get away with when referencing pages within your site.** Remember that the browser will complete the left portion of the URL if you allow it to. Use relative URLs whenever possible.
- **Don't use <BLINK>!** There really isn't any compelling reason to, now, is there?
- **Don't change the URL of your page unless you absolutely must.** Cruising the Net, one finds the "page not found" message far too often. It seems that people just move their pages from place to place. Plan where you are parking your page, and keep it there. Moving pages is really a disservice to your users.
- **Make sure the text within an <A> container explains the target of the link.** Remember, some text-only browsers display link text just like any other text, so the explanation is critical.
- **Ensure that each image element contains a descriptive "alt".** Every image must be described by a line of text. This rule allows nongraphical browsers and browsers with the image loading turned off to know the content of the images. Creative use of the **alt** value allows the user with the nongraphical browser to get the general idea in some cases. For example, if you have a graphic for "New," you can code the **alt** attribute like this: alt=">NEW<". A graphical bullet could be coded this way: alt="*" or alt="@".
- **Use the new, nonvisual styles as they are developed.** Creating pages that can be heard, not just read, will bring your content to more users. As the multisensory techniques and tags evolve, make an effort to use them so as to allow the widest audience possible to enjoy your efforts.

- **Use a good HTML validation program to test your page.** Several good HTML validation packages are available that will check the code on your site. The one we recommend is located at: http://validator.w3.org/. Don't be surprised if this validation package finds many little errors.

Ethical/Moral Considerations

- **Leave your eyepatch and Jolly Roger at home when you cruise the Web and when you design and code Web pages.** A plethora of wonderful images and applets and animated GIFs and backgrounds are out there that people have spent a great deal of time and effort to create. Don't pirate them for your site. Take only those that are clearly marked as free, and always give credit to the site where you found them.
- **Don't link to images or multimedia across the Net unless the owner of the site requires it.** Linking will slow the loading of your page and create additional congestion on the Net as well. Always harvest the images or other resources you are going to use and host them locally. Of course, you must have permission from the owner of the resource before you harvest it. Don't make the mistake of thinking that if you find a copyrighted image, you can link to it rather than copy it. The actual display of that image is controlled, and the owner of the copyright won't appreciate your using it without permission.
- **Be careful about the content of your pages.** In the United States we have the Constitution to protect our right to free speech. This is not a universal right. Some countries restrict the content of any material allowed across their borders. In addition, many organizations and parents are beginning to use blocking software to limit access to sites on the Net. If you have valuable content to share—and why else would you have a Web page—you don't want access to your site blocked because you have used offensive language or graphics. If you are compelled to use language or graphics that a significant portion of your audience may find offensive, put them on a page or pages of their own, and tell your users what they are linking to. Remember as well that unless you own your own Internet feed and the computer hosting your page, somebody else may feel responsible for what you post.
- **Pay attention to the people who take the time to comment on your page.** For every one that writes, there will have been dozens who left your page in frustration and will not return.

Language and Writing

- **Write in gender-neutral language whenever possible.** However, the line, "A wise Web weaver always checks *his/her* links," is gender-neutral but seems clunky, obvious, and interrupts the text flow. A better choice might be, "Wise Web weavers always check *their* links."
- **Spell-check your pages!**

- **Proofread your pages.** A spell checker checks only spelling. As you cruise the Web, you will notice sites where the Web weaver did use a spell checker but probably never reread the page. Eye yam shore ewe no thee kinks of problems eye yam tanking abut! My spell checker had *no* problem with the preceding line.
- **Now proofread it again; then have somebody else proofread it.**
- **Avoid regional slang.** You are writing for an international audience, and using slang can cause serious problems for non-native speakers of your language. As regional dialects continue to evolve, non-native speakers may include people from the other half of your country as well as folks from outside your national borders.
- **Don't use the phrase "click here."** Not only is the effect obnoxious, but the phrase assumes the user has a mouse.
- **Try to avoid politically inflammatory, racist, or religiously biased language on your page.** If you feel compelled to use any of this kind of language, put it on pages that your users can choose to link to, and be sure to tell users what they are linking to. For example:

These are my <u>feelings</u> about the UNIX operating system. Note: I'm a UNIX aficionado!

That line tells users that they will be linking to a page that is probably a pro-Unix rant. If they don't want to read it, they don't have to. Don't put rants on your home page, forcing users to see them when first seeing your page.

- **Avoid specifying fonts by name if possible.** With the new style attribute in the HTML 4.0 specifications, it is very tempting to find some "fun" fonts on your machine and incorporate them into your page. While this can result in a very vibrant page, it can also cause two different problems:
  1. If the user's platform doesn't have the particular font you requested, it will default to its "normal" font. That may not give the results you desire.
  2. If the user has a font on her system that has the same name but different glyphs than the one you specified, the page may well be unreadable when displayed. For these reasons, we recommend the following restrictions when specifying the "font-family":
     a. If you must use a named font, like "New Century Schoolbook," follow it with a generic style that will also work, like serif, sans-serif, or monospace. (Avoid cursive and fantasy.)
     b. Test your page with the generic font to ensure that it looks correct.
     c. The named fonts of "New Times Roman," "Helvetica," and "Courier," are probably generally available. Others are subject to the whims of the users and their platform.
- **Create pages you are proud of, and then keep them that way.** Regularly scheduled maintenance will keep your car running longer and your Web pages fresh and exciting. Don't let your content get stale. Stay aware of the changes and improvements in the specifications, and keep your pages up to date with those suggestions. And, finally, have fun!

The following sites contained style guides at the time this book was written. With the rate of change on the Net, some of these sites will have disappeared by the time you read this. However, other sites will have come online. Searching with a search engine like AltaVista or HotBot will allow you to find others.

www.mcs.net/~jorn/html/net/checklist.html
www.useit.com/alertbox/9612.html
www.sun.com/960416/columns/alertbox/index.html
www.tlc-systems.com/webtips.shtml
www.sysmag.com/web/html-style.html
www.w3.org/Provider/Style/All.html
www.anybrowser.org/campaign/

The most important thing you must do as a Web weaver is be considerate of your users—first, last, always—and design your pages for them.

style properties and values

These properties and values were defined in the CSS2 specifications of May 1998. They may not all work with your browser.

PROPERTY	DESCRIPTION	VALUES	SPECIAL NOTES
azimuth	Changes the left/right orientation of the sound within a 360 degree surround-sound environment.	[angle] | left-side | far-left | left | center-left | center | center-right | right | far-right | right-side | behind | leftwards | rightwards | inherit	[angle] is set from –360 to 360 degrees (deg) with center = 0deg, right = 90deg, behind = 180deg, and left = 270deg or –90deg. Rightwards = +20deg and leftwards = –20deg.
background-attachment	Determines whether the background moves when the window scrolls.	scroll | fixed | inherit	
background-color	Sets background color.	[color] | transparent | inherit	[color] is six-digit hexadecimal code or color keyword (found on the insert in the back of this book).
background-image	Loads background graphic from designated URL.	[url] (path/filename) | none | inherit	A background image takes precedence over the color.

PROPERTY	DESCRIPTION	VALUES	SPECIAL NOTES
background-position	Provides x,y coordinates for positioning image within page.	%	[length]	top, center or bottom	left, center or right	inherit	[length] measurements can be in either inches (in) or centimeters (cm).
background-repeat	Determines if small background images repeat horizontally (x) or vertically (y).	repeat	repeat-x	repeat-y	no-repeat	inherit	Using repeat means image repeats vertically and horizontally.
border-color	Changes the color of the border.	[color]	transparent	inherit	Alternatives: border-top-color, border-right-color, border-bottom-color, or border-left-color
border-collapse	Applies to table borders as they relate to a column or column group.	collapse	separate	
border-spacing	Specifies the distance that separates adjacent cell borders.	length	Lengths may not be negative. Default value equals 0.
border-style	Changes the look of the border line.	none	hidden	dotted	dashed	solid	double	groove	ridge	inset	outset	Alternatives: border-top-style, border-right-style, border-bottom-style or border-left-style
border-width	Changes thickness, style, and color of border line.	thin	medium	thick	absolute value	Alternatives: border-top-width, border-right-width, border-bottom-width or border-left-width
border-bottom	Changes thickness, style, and color of bottom border.	thin	medium	thick	[length]	hidden	dotted	dashed	solid	double	groove	ridge	inset	outset	[color]	transparent	
border-left	Changes thickness, style, and color of left border.	thin	medium	thick	[length]	hidden	dotted	dashed	solid	double	groove	ridge	inset	outset	[color]	transparent	
border-top	Changes thickness, style, and color of top border.	thin	medium	thick	[length]	hidden	dotted	dashed	solid	double	groove	ridge	inset	outset	[color]	transparent	
border-right	Changes color, style, and thickness of right border.	thin	medium	thick	[length]	hidden	dotted	dashed	solid	double	groove	ridge	inset	outset	[color]	transparent	
caption-side	Specifies the position of the caption with respect to the table.	top	bottom	left	right	inherit	Captions inherit properties from the table.

PROPERTY	DESCRIPTION	VALUES	SPECIAL NOTES
clear	Breaks off the `float` property's control of the text flow.	none | left | right | both | inherit	
clip	Defines the portion of an element's rendered content that is visible.	[shape] | auto | inherit	An element's original size is the default clip size. The only valid shape value is "rect".
color	Changes typeface's color.	Color keyword or associated hexadecimal number.	See the color insert in the back of this book for color options.
cue-after	Provides sound after event as auditory icon.	[url] | none | inherit	
cue-before	Provides sound before event as auditory icon.	[url] | none | inherit	
cursor	Specifies the type of screen pointer to be displayed.	url | auto | crosshair | default | pointer |move | e-resize thru w-resize | text | wait | help | inherit	e-resize, ne-resize, nw-resize, n-resize, se-resize, sw-resize, s-resize and w-resize indicate that some edge (where e is for east, and ne is for north-east, etc.) is to be moved.
direction	Specifies the base writing direction of blocks of text.	ltr | rtl | inherit	
elevation	Changes up/down orientation of sound.	[angle] | below | level | above | higher | lower | inherit	[angle] is set from 90 to −90 degrees (deg) with level = 0deg, above = 90deg, and below = −90deg. Higher = +10deg and lower = −10deg.
empty-cells	Controls the rendering of borders around cells that have no visible content.	show | hide | inherit	If all the cells in a row have a value of "hide" and have no visible content, the entire row is not displayed.
float	Allows other elements to be aligned to the left or right of the object.	left | right | none | inherit	

PROPERTY	DESCRIPTION	VALUES	SPECIAL NOTES
font	Shortcut option for changing the glyph used by the browser.	[font-style] | [font-variant] | [font-weight] [font-size] | [line-height] | [font-family] | caption | icon | menu | message-box | small-caption | status-bar | inherit	All font-related properties are first reset to their initial values, then explicitly set based on the values assigned to this property.
font-family	Controls typeface used by the browser.	serif | sans-serif | cursive | fantasy | monospace | others	Specific family names, like Arial or Times New Roman, are acceptable. Names with embedded spaces must be enclosed in quotes.
font-size	Controls the size of the font as measured in points (1/72 of an inch).	pt | 1-100% | larger | smaller | xx-small through xx-large | inherit	Absolute sizes include xx-small, x-small, small, medium, large, x-large, and xx-large.
font-style	Determines if glyph is displayed on a slant or not.	normal | italic | oblique | inherit	
font-stretch	Determines the width of the glyph.	normal | wider | narrower | ultra-condensed through ultra-expanded | inherit	Absolute sizes include ultra-condensed, extra-condensed, condensed, semi-condensed, normal, semi-expanded, expanded, extra-expanded and ultra-expanded.
font-variant	Determines if glyph is displayed in short uppercase characters or not.	normal | small-caps | inherit	If a small-caps font is not available, the browser can use scaled-down versions of standard uppercase characters.
font-weight	Determines the thickness or darkness of the glyph.	normal | bold | bolder | lighter | 100-900 | inherit	Normal text is 400 and bold text is 700.
letter-spacing	Increases (+) or decreases (–) spacing between letters.	normal | [length] | inherit	[length] is measured in em or cm. Decimals are acceptable.
line-height	Determines the vertical space set aside for a line of text.	normal | [number] | [length] | [percentage] | inherit	[number] is the value to be multiplied by the text height.

PROPERTY	DESCRIPTION	VALUES	SPECIAL NOTES
list-style	Shortcut option for changing the marker and the maker location within a list.	[list-style-type] I [list-style-position] I [list-style-image] I inherit	
list-style-image	Sets the image used as the list item marker.	[url] I none I inherit	Replaces marker set with the "list-style-type" marker.
list-style-position	Specifies position of the marker in the list.	inside I outside I inherit	
list-style-type	Specifies appearance of the list item marker.	disc I circle I square I decimal I decimal-leading-zero I lower-roman I upper-roman I lower-greek I lower-alpha I lower-latin I upper-alpha I upper-latin I hebrew I armenian I georgian I cjk-ideographic I hiragana I katakana I hiragana-iroha I katakana-iroha I none I inherit	There are three types of markers: glyphs, numbering systems, and alphabetic characters. The value specified by the list-style-image overrides marker set by list-style-type.
margin	Shortcut option for defining all four transparent areas (margins) that surround the CSS box.	[margin-width] {1,4} I inherit	When one value is used, all margins are the same; for two values, the top/bottom are the same and left/right are the same; for three values, the first value is the top, the second value is the right and left, and the third value is the bottom; four values are assigned to the top, right, bottom, and left, respectively.
margin-bottom	Defines transparent area at bottom of CSS box.	[length] I [percentage] I auto I inherit	[length] is measured in em, cm, or in.
margin-left	Defines transparent area at left side of CSS box.	[length] I [percentage] I auto I inherit	[length] is measured in em, cm, or in.
margin-top	Defines transparent area at top of CSS box.	[length] I [percentage] I auto I inherit	[length] is measured in em, cm, or in.
margin-right	Defines transparent area at right side of CSS box.	[length] I [percentage] I auto I inherit	[length] is measured in em, cm, or in.

PROPERTY	DESCRIPTION	VALUES	SPECIAL NOTES
max-height	Sets maximum height for an object.	[length] | [percentage] | none | inherit	[length] is measured in em, cm, or in.
max-width	Sets maximum width for an object.	[length] | [percentage] | none | inherit	[length] is measured in em, cm, or in.
min-height	Sets minimum height for an object.	[length] | [percentage] | inherit	[length] is measured in em, cm, or in.
min-width	Sets minimum width for an object.	[length] | [percentage] | inherit	[length] is measured in em, cm, or in.
outline	Shortcut option to create outline around visual objects such as buttons, active form fields, image maps, etc.	[outline-color] | [outline-style] | outline-width] | inherit	
outline-color	Sets color of the outline that surrounds an object.	[color] | invert | inherit	[color] is six-digit hexadecimal code or color keyword (found on the insert in the back of this book).
outline-style	Sets style of the outline that surrounds an object.	none | hidden | dotted | dashed | solid | double | groove | ridge | inset | outset | inherit	Similar to border-style.
outline-width	Sets width of the outline that surrounds an object.	thin | medium | thick | absolute value | inherit	Similar to border-width.
overflow	Works with "clip" property to determine how overflow is clipped.	visible | hidden | scroll | auto | inherit	
padding	Shortcut option for defining the white space that separates the contents from the border or outline.	[padding-width] {1,4} | inherit	When one value is used, all padding is the same; for two values, the top and bottom are the same, and left and right are the same; for three values, the first value is the top, the second value is the right and left, and the third value is the bottom; four values are assigned to the top, right, bottom, and left, respectively.

PROPERTY	DESCRIPTION	VALUES	SPECIAL NOTES
padding-top	Changes thickness of white space between the top of the contents and border line.	[padding-width] I inherit	[padding-width] is measured in %, em, cm, mm, or in.
padding-right	Changes thickness of white space between the right of the contents and border line.	[padding-width] I inherit	[padding-width] is measured in %, em, cm, mm, or in.
padding-bottom	Changes thickness of white space between the bottom of the contents and border line.	[padding-width] I inherit	[padding-width] is measured in %, em, cm, mm, or in.
padding-left	Changes thickness of white space between the left of the contents and border line.	[padding-width] I inherit	[padding-width] is measured in %, em, cm, mm, or in.
pause	Shortcut option for setting time before or after speaking an element's content.	[time] I [percentage] {1,2} I inherit	If two values are given, the first value is pause-before, and the second is pause-after.
pause-after	Sets time after speaking an element's content and before starting next text.	[time] I [percentage] I inherit	Time is measured in milliseconds (ms) and seconds (s).
pause-before	Sets time before speaking an element's content.	[time] I [percentage] I inherit	Time is measured in milliseconds (ms) and seconds (s).
pitch	Adjusts frequency (pitch) of speaking voice.	[frequency] I x-low I low I medium I high I x-high I inherit	[frequency] is given in hertz (Hz), with low being a lower frequency than medium.
pitch-range	Specifies variation in average pitch.	[number] I inherit	[number] ranges from 0 to 100, with 0 being flat and 100 being animated.
play-during	Specifies sound to play as background while element's content is spoken.	[url] mix I repeat I auto I none I inherit	When mix is used, the url sound is played along with background sound.
richness	Identifies how a voice will carry in a large room. Rich carries well while smooth does not.	[number] I inherit	[number] ranges from 0 to 100, with 0 being smooth and 100 being rich.

PROPERTY	DESCRIPTION	VALUES	SPECIAL NOTES
speak	Determines how text is rendered aurally.	normal | none | spell-out | inherit	Normal means language-dependent pronunciation rules are used. Spell-out means each letter is spoken.
speak-numeral	Controls how numerals are spoken. Pronunciation is language-dependent.	digits | continuous | inherit	Digits means 123 would be spoken as "one, two, three." Continuous means 123 would be spoken as "one hundred twenty-three."
speak-punctuation	Determines if punctuation is spoken.	code | none | inherit	Code means punctuation is spoken.
speech-rate	Adjusts speed at which words are read.	[number] | x-slow | slow | medium | fast | x-fast | faster | slower | inherit	[number] is given in words per minute, with x-slow = 80, medium = 180, x-fast = 300, faster = +40, and slower = –40.
stress	Specifies intonation peaks within voice inflection.	[number] | inherit	[number] ranges from 0 to 100, with the meaning of the numbers depending on language.
text-align	Orients text left and/or right or in the middle of a screen.	left | right | center | justify | [string] | inherit	[string] applies to cell alignment in a table based on a string value.
text-decoration	Draws horizontal line through text area or turns area on and off.	none | underline | overline | line-through | blink | inherit	Applies only to text and has no impact on images.
text-indent	Moves start of first line to the left or right of text area's default edge.	[length] | [percentage] | inherit	[length] is given in em. Negative numbers move text left.
text-shadow	Overlays another character image left or right (x), up or down (y).	none | color | x y blur | inherit	Coordinates and blur are given in pixels (px): –x goes left and –y goes up.
text-transform	Standardizes the case of the text.	none | capitalize | uppercase | lowercase | inherit	Capitalize converts first character of each word to uppercase.
vertical-align	Orients text up and down within the vertical line space assigned to each line of text in the text area.	baseline | sub | super | top | text-top | middle | bottom | text-bottom | [percentage] | [length] | inherit	Baseline = "0%" or "0cm". Positive values raise text above baseline, and negative values lower text.

PROPERTY	DESCRIPTION	VALUES	SPECIAL NOTES
voice-family	Sets the tenor of the speaking voice. *You could even use your own voice.*	[specific-voice] I [generic-voice] I inherit	Generic voices include male, female, and child.
volume	Adjusts a sound's dynamic range.	[number] I [percentage] I silent I x-soft I soft I medium I loud I x-loud I inherit	[number] ranges from 0 to 100 with x-soft = 0, medium = 50, and x-loud = 100.
white-space	Determines how tabs and repeated spaces are handled.	normal I pre I nowrap I inherit	Both pre and nowrap recognize "\A" as a line break symbol.
word-spacing	Increases (+) or decreases (–) spacing between words.	normal I [length] I inherit	[length] is measured in em or cm.

appendix **C**

comm**on** character set

The following table presents a common set of characters that are recognized by most browsers. The glyph that appears on the screen is listed under "Symbol." The numeric value must always be preceded by an &# and end with a semi-colon. The three-digit numeric values and related name, when available, can appear in an HTML document instead of the typed character. These characters represent the Latin-1 character set that is also known as by the International Standards Organization code ISO 8859-1. Furthermore, this is the base character set for the Unicode characters (ISO 10646-1) identified in the HTML 4.0 specifications. The numeric values 128-159 are not used in the Latin-1 or Uni-code character sets of HTML.

Latin 1 (ISO 8859-1)

NUMERIC VALUE	SYMBOL	NAME	DESCRIPTION
				Horizontal tab

			Line feed

			Carriage return
 			Space
!	!		Exclamation point
"	"	"	Quotation mark
#	#		Octothorp

NUMERIC VALUE	SYMBOL	NAME	DESCRIPTION
&#036;	$		Dollar sign
&#037;	%		Percent sign
&#038;	&	&amp;	Ampersand
&#039;	'		Apostrophe
&#040;	(		Left parenthesis
&#041;	)		Right parenthesis
&#042;	*		Asterisk
&#043;	+		Plus sign
&#044;	,		Comma
&#045;	-		Hyphen
&#046;	.		Period
&#047;	/		Slash
&#048;	0		Zero
&#049;	1		One
&#050;	2		Two
&#051;	3		Three
&#052;	4		Four
&#053;	5		Five
&#054;	6		Six
&#055;	7		Seven
&#056;	8		Eight
&#057;	9		Nine
&#058;	:		Colon
&#059;	;		Semicolon
&#060;	<	&lt;	Less than
&#061;	=		Equal sign
&#062;	>	&gt;	Greater than
&#063;	?		Question mark
&#064;	@		Commercial at sign
&#065;	A		Uppercase A

Numeric Value	Symbol	Name	Description
&#066;	B		Uppercase B
&#067;	C		Uppercase C
&#068;	D		Uppercase D
&#069;	E		Uppercase E
&#070;	F		Uppercase F
&#071;	G		Uppercase G
&#072;	H		Uppercase H
&#073;	I		Uppercase I
&#074;	J		Uppercase J
&#075;	K		Uppercase K
&#076;	L		Uppercase L
&#077;	M		Uppercase M
&#078;	N		Uppercase N
&#079;	O		Uppercase O
&#080;	P		Uppercase P
&#081;	Q		Uppercase Q
&#082;	R		Uppercase R
&#083;	S		Uppercase S
&#084;	T		Uppercase T
&#085;	U		Uppercase U
&#086;	V		Uppercase V
&#087;	W		Uppercase W
&#088;	X		Uppercase X
&#089;	Y		Uppercase Y
&#090;	Z		Uppercase Z
&#091;	[		Left square bracket
&#092;	\		Backslash
&#093;	]		Right square bracket
&#094;	^		Caret
&#095;	_		Underscore

Numeric Value	Symbol	Name	Description
&#096;	`		Grave accent
&#097;	a		Lowercase a
&#098;	b		Lowercase b
&#099;	c		Lowercase c
&#100;	d		Lowercase d
&#101;	e		Lowercase e
&#102;	f		Lowercase f
&#103;	g		Lowercase g
&#104;	h		Lowercase h
&#105;	i		Lowercase i
&#106;	j		Lowercase j
&#107;	k		Lowercase k
&#108;	l		Lowercase l
&#109;	m		Lowercase m
&#110;	n		Lowercase n
&#111;	o		Lowercase o
&#112;	p		Lowercase p
&#113;	q		Lowercase q
&#114;	r		Lowercase r
&#115;	s		Lowercase s
&#116;	t		Lowercase t
&#117;	u		Lowercase u
&#118;	v		Lowercase v
&#119;	w		Lowercase w
&#120;	x		Lowercase x
&#121;	y		Lowercase y
&#122;	z		Lowercase z
&#123;	{		Left curly brace
|	|		Vertical bar
&#125;	}		Right curly brace

Numeric Value	Symbol	Name	Description
&#126;	~		Tilde
			Non-breaking space
&#161;	¡	&iexcl;	Inverted exclamation mark
&#162;	¢	&cent;	Cent sign
&#163;	£	&pound;	Pound sterling sign
&#164;		&curren;	General currency sign
&#165;	¥	&yen;	Yen sign
&#166;			&brvbar;	Broken (vertical) bar
&#167;	§	&sect;	Section sign
&#168;	..	&uml;	Umlaut
&#169;	©	&copy;	Copyright sign
&#170;	a	&ordf;	Feminine ordinal indicator
&#171;	«	&laquo;	Left angle quote
&#172;	¬	&not;	Not sign
&#173;	–	&shy;	Discretionary hyphen
&#174;	®	&reg;	Registered sign
&#175;	–	&macr;	Macron accent
&#176;	°	&deg;	Degree sign
&#177;	±	&plusmn;	Plus-or-minus sign
&#178;	2	&sup2;	Superscript two
&#179;	3	&sup3;	Superscript three
&#180;	´	&acute;	Acute accent
&#181;	μ	&micro;	Greek mu
&#182;	¶	&para;	Paragraph sign
&#183;	·	&middot;	Middle dot
&#184;	،	&cedil;	Cedilla
&#185;	1	&sup1;	Superscript one
&#186;	°	&ordm;	Masculine ordinal indicator
&#187;	»	&raquo;	Right angle quote
&#188;	¼	&frac14;	Fraction one-quarter

Numeric Value	Symbol	Name	Description
&#189;	½	&frac12;	Fraction one-half
&#190;	¾	&frac34;	Fraction three-quarters
&#191;	¿	&iquest;	Inverted question mark
&#192;	À	&Agrave;	Uppercase A, grave accent
&#193;	Á	&Aacute;	Uppercase A, acute accent
&#194;	Â	&Acirc;	Uppercase A, circumflex accent
&#195;	Ã	&Atilde;	Uppercase A, tilde
&#196;	Ä	&Auml;	Uppercase A, umlaut
&#197;	Å	&Aring;	Uppercase A, ring
&#198;	Æ	&AElig;	Uppercase AE ligature
&#199;	Ç	&Ccedil;	Uppercase C, cedilla
&#200;	È	&Egrave;	Uppercase E, grave accent
&#201;	É	&Eacute;	Uppercase E, acute accent
&#202;	Ê	&Ecirc;	Uppercase E, circumflex accent
&#203;	Ë	&Euml;	Uppercase E, umlaut
&#204;	Ì	&Igrave;	Uppercase I, grave accent
&#205;	Í	&Iacute;	Uppercase I, acute accent
&#206;	Î	&Icirc;	Uppercase I, circumflex accent
&#207;	Ï	&Iuml;	Uppercase I, umlaut
&#208;	_	&ETH;	Uppercase Eth, Icelandic
&#209;	Ñ	&Ntilde;	Uppercase N, tilde
&#210;	Ò	&Ograve;	Uppercase O, grave accent
&#211;	Ó	&Oacute;	Uppercase O, acute accent
&#212;	Ô	&Ocirc;	Uppercase O, circumflex accent
&#213;	Õ	&Otilde;	Uppercase O, tilde
&#214;	Ö	&Ouml;	Uppercase O, umlaut
&#215;	×	&times;	Multiplication sign
&#216;	Ø	&Oslash;	Uppercase O, slash
&#217;	Ù	&Ugrave;	Uppercase U, grave accent
&#218;	Ú	&Uacute;	Uppercase U, acute accent

Numeric Value	Symbol	Name	Description
&#219;	Û	&Ucirc;	Uppercase U, circumflex accent
&#220;	Ü	&Uuml;	Uppercase U, umlaut
&#221;	Ý	&Yacute;	Uppercase Y, acute accent
&#222;	Þ	&THORN;	Uppercase Thorn, Icelandic
&#223;	ß	&szlig;	Lowercase sz ligature, German
&#224;	à	&agrave;	Lowercase a, grave accent
&#225;	á	&aacute;	Lowercase a, acute accent
&#226;	â	&acirc;	Lowercase a, circumflex accent
&#227;	ã	&atilde;	Lowercase a, tilde
&#228;	ä	&auml;	Lowercase a, umlaut
&#229;	å	&aring;	Lowercase a, ring
&#230;	æ	&aelig;	Lowercase ae ligature
&#231;	ç	&ccedil;	Lowercase c, cedilla
&#232;	è	&egrave;	Lowercase e, grave accent
&#233;	é	&eacute;	Lowercase e, acute accent
&#234;	ê	&ecirc;	Lowercase e, circumflex accent
&#235;	ë	&euml;	Lowercase e, umlaut
&#236;	ì	&igrave;	Lowercase i, grave accent
&#237;	í	&iacute;	Lowercase i, acute accent
&#238;	î	&icirc;	Lowercase i, circumflex accent
&#239;	ï	&iuml;	Lowercase i, umlaut
&#240;		&eth;	Lowercase eth, Icelandic
&#241;	ñ	&ntilde;	Lowercase n, tilde
&#242;	ò	&ograve;	Lowercase o, grave accent
&#243;	ó	&oacute;	Lowercase o, acute accent
&#244;	ô	&ocirc;	Lowercase o, circumflex accent
&#245;	õ	&otilde;	Lowercase o, tilde
&#246;	ö	&ouml;	Lowercase o, umlaut
&#247;	÷	&divide;	division sign
&#248;	ø	&oslash;	Lowercase o, slash

Numeric Value	Symbol	Name	Description
&#249;	ù	&ugrave;	Lowercase u, grave accent
&#250;	ú	&uacute;	Lowercase u, acute accent
&#251;	û	&ucirc;	Lowercase u, circumflex accent
&#252;	ü	&uuml;	Lowercase u, umlaut
&#253;	ý	&yacute;	Lowercase y, acute accent
&#254;	þ	&thorn;	Lowercase thorn, Icelandic
&#255;	ÿ	&yuml;	Lowercase y, umlaut

As mentioned before, the numeric values 128-159 are not used in the Latin-1 or Unicode character sets of HTML. However, these numeric values are recognized by some browsers, like Internet Explorer, and are referred to as the Code Page 1252 (CP1252) or C1 superset. The following table identifies the C1 and Unicode numeric values assigned to this character set. The numeric values used by Unicode, like those of Latin-1, must always be preceded by an &# and end with a semicolon.

Sample HTML Recognized Unicode (ISO 10646-1)

Unicode	Symbol	C1 Superset	Description
&#8218;	‚	&#130;	Low single quote
&#402;	ƒ	&#131;	Florin
&#8222;	„	&#132;	Low double quote
&#8230;	…	&#133;	Ellipsis
&#8224;	†	&#134;	Dagger
&#8225;	‡	&#135;	Double dagger
&#710;	ˆ	&#136;	Circumflex
&#8240;	‰	&#137;	Per Mille sign
&#352;	Š	&#138;	Uppercase S, caron
&#8249;	‹	&#139;	Single left angle quote
&#338;	Œ	&#140;	Uppercase OE ligature
&#8216;	'	&#145;	Left single quote

Unicode	Symbol	C1 Superset	Description
’	'	’	Right single quote
“	"	“	Left double quote
”	"	”	Right double quote
•	•	•	Bullet
–	–	–	En dash
—	—	—	Em dash
˜	˜	˜	Small tilde
™	™	™	Trademark
š	š	š	Lowercase s, caron
›	›	›	Single right angle quote
œ	œ	œ	Lowercase oe ligature
Ÿ	Ÿ	Ÿ	Uppercase Y, umlaut

using file transfer protocol

File transfer protocol (ftp) is an Internet protocol for copying files from one computer to another. Software that supports ftp is the tool most often used to *publish* a new Web page—that is, to copy an HTML document on an active Web server for public access. You can use ftp to copy interesting files from other places on the Net to your computer. Or you can use ftp to copy files on your local machine to other computers on the Internet. You can retrieve or send text files, images, icons, and other information with ftp.

Ftp software is available for most operating systems, but it was originally a Unix tool, so the commands for standard ftp look very Unix-like. In the first part of this discussion we will look at the Unix ftp commands used if you are working on a Unix-based computer. Other operating systems also support this command-line version of ftp. In addition, many enhanced ftp software packages are available to make it easy to transfer files. We will take a look at these graphical alternatives at the end of this appendix.

Table D.1 shows some of the common ftp commands. You may choose to use more graphical ftp software, which will do more of the work for you, but even then, the steps described here must be accomplished for ftp to work.

Ftp software can operate in one of two transfer modes, either ASCII or binary. If you are copying images, sounds, or programs, you need to copy them as binary files. Binary transfers take a little longer, but they are usually copied without errors. Use ASCII only for copying text files. If you try to copy a binary file in ASCII mode, ftp will try to convert the binary to an ASCII representation. This often involves padding with extra zero bits, which will corrupt a binary file. If you download a program and it doesn't seem to work, chances are you downloaded it in ASCII rather than binary. Download it again, using binary transfer mode, and it will probably work.

CONNECTION COMMANDS	
open	Open a specific connection using ftp.
close	Close the current connection (ftp continues to run).
bye	Close the current connection and quit ftp.
?	Show a list of all the commands.
help	Give a one-line explanation of the command that follows help.
SWITCHES (TOGGLES)	
prompt	A switch that turns on or off confirmation of each file move.
verbose	A switch that gives you statistics on the transfer.
hash	Presents a set of #s to indicate the file transfer is in progress; this lets you know that ftp is really working. It does slow down the transfer slightly, but may save your sanity if you are moving a large file.
TRANSFER MODES	
ASCII	Turns on ASCII file transfer mode; use only for text.
bin(ary)	Turns on binary file transfer mode; safe but a little slower.
NAVIGATION COMMANDS	
cd	Changes the remote directory.
pwd	Shows the directory on the remote computer.
lcd	Shows or changes the *local* directory.
ls	Lists the files in the current directory on the remote computer.
dir	Produces a longer version of ls.
FILE TRANSFER COMMANDS	
put	Sends a file to the remote machine.
get	Retrieves a file from the remote machine.
mput	Sends a series of files to a remote machine (multiple put).
mget	Retrieves a series of files from a remote machine (multiple get).
delete	Removes a file from the remote machine (dangerous!). This command is not usually enabled, but you should *never* take chances.

Table D.1 Common ftp commands.

A normal ftp session is shown in Figure D.1. It starts with the ftp command to initiate a connection between the local computer (the one you are sitting at) and a remote computer (the one that either has the files you want or is where you want to send files). In this screen, the user *ttg* has connected to *phred,* a Unix-based computer that has an ftp server set up for registered users only. Other ftp sites are set up to allow *anonymous ftp* connections in which the user can use the name "anonymous" and thus need no password. In the case of Figure D.1, the user was required to enter his name and then a password. This is the way it will most likely be when you move pages up to your Web server.

```
clyde% ftp phred
Connected to phred.dccd.edu
220 phred dcccd.edu FTP server (Version wu-2.4.2-academ[Beta-12] (1) Fri Dec 31
23:59:21 EST 1999) ready
Name (phred:ttg): ttg
331 Password required for ttg.
Password:
230 User ttg logged in.
ftp> cd web-pages
250 CWD command successful.
ftp>
```

Figure D.1 Starting an ftp session.

In Figure D.1, *ttg* types his user ID, then his password. The ftp server on *phred* responds with the "logged in" message. Notice that the prompt changes to ftp>, indicating that the ftp program is now active. Next, the user changes directories with the cd web-pages command, making the *web-pages* directory active. This is where the Web pages for that user are stored. Each time the user enters a command, ftp tells him whether the command worked or not. This is an important feature of ftp; the user is always provided with immediate feedback.

Now that *ttg* is in the correct directory, the real work can begin. Since *ttg* knows that he wants to download a file that starts with an "h," he asks the computer to list the files in the current directory that begin with "h," using the command ls h*, as shown in Figure D.2. After looking over the list of files, *ttg* decides that the file he really wants is htmllab4.html, a file containing the exercises for the fourth lab in his HTML class.

```
ftp> ls h*
200 PORT command successful.
150 Opening ASCII mode data connection for file list.
htmlextra1.html
htmllab1.html
htmllab2.html
htmllab3.html
htmllab3.old
htmllab4.html
htmllab4.old
htmllab5.html
htmllab5.old
htmllab6.html
htmllab7.html
226 Transfer complete.
remote: h*
164 bytes received n 0.027 seconds (5.9) Kbytes/s)
ftp>
```

Figure D.2 Listing files on the remote computer.

Figure D.3 shows the screen capture after *ttg* downloads `htmllab4.html` to his local PC. First, the user issues a `get htmllab4.html` command. The ftp program informs him that the file is 2325 bytes long. Then ftp begins to download the file. As it is a rather small file, there was no need to turn on the hash function. Notice that the ftp program tells the user the name of the file on both the local and remote computers. Finally, all of 0.0097 seconds later, ftp reports that 2362 bytes have been downloaded. On close examination the file seems to have grown by 37 bytes in the download! Why? Because *ttg* forgot to set the transfer mode to *binary*! Even though the file is actually an ASCII file, as are all HTML files, the ftp program pads the file with some bytes of binary zeros to round things out. The zeros won't make any difference in this case, as we will see in a moment.

```
ftp> get htmllab4.html
200 PORT command successful.
150 Opening ASCII mode data connection for htmllab4.html (2325 bytes).
226 Transfer complete.
local: htmllab4. html remote: htmllab4.html
2362 bytes received in 0.0097 seconds (2.4e+02 Kbytes/s)
ftp> bin
200 Type set to I.
ftp> put htmllab4.html
200 PORT command successful.
150 opening BINARY mode data connection for htmllab4.html.
226 Transfer complete.
local: htmllab4.html remote: htmllab4.html
2325 bytes received in 0.0028 seconds (8.1e+02 kbytes/s)
```

Figure D.3 Downloading a file from a remote server.

This scenario serves only as an example of how to retrieve a file with ftp. Usually the user would modify the file in some way before putting it back. In this case nothing was done to the file, but *ttg* decides he should set the transfer mode to binary. That is the next line in the code. Then he sends the file back to the server with the `put` command. Notice that ftp moves exactly the right number of bytes this time.

This is the normal sequence of events using ftp. It is not a complex tool to use. The biggest problem most students have with ftp is figuring out where the files should come from or where they went after they were uploaded or downloaded, and that problem disappears with a little practice.

FTP Software

Many software tools are available to make the ftp process more intuitive. The one we will use in the remaining figures is called CuteFTP. It was designed to run in Microsoft Windows' mouse-oriented "point and click" environment. CuteFTP is a very powerful program with lots of options. At this time, however, we will look at only the bare bones of this tool. CuteFTP is on the CD that comes with this text. It is also available for download from www.cuteFTP.com with a 30-day trial. CuteFTP is *shareware*. If you use the product after the 30 days of free trial, you are obligated to pay the author, GlobalSCAPE Inc., $34.95 for the time and effort necessary to create this product.

The screen captures in Figures D.4 through D.8 show the steps in setting up and using CuteFTP. The first screen shows how to set up CuteFTP to find a particular computer. Here we set up "*Phred*" at IP address 144.162.120.233. This may or may not be a valid IP address; it is for demonstration purposes only. Notice that we can set the user ID and the secret password as well, so CuteFTP can go to the site and log in for us. In the box below UserID, we can set the radio button to use anonymous ftp if that is the type of site we intend to access.

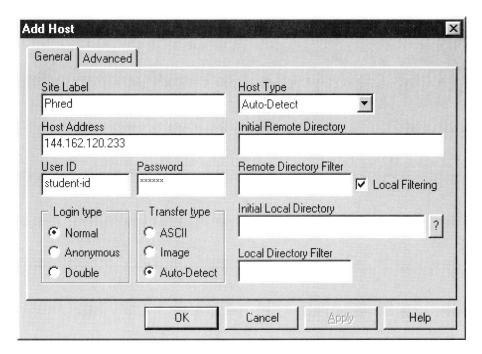

Figure D.4 Setting up an ftp site using CuteFTP.

Figure D.5 shows the first screen we normally see when starting CuteFTP. It allows us to select a site from a series of folders. When we click on a site, CuteFTP will connect us to it.

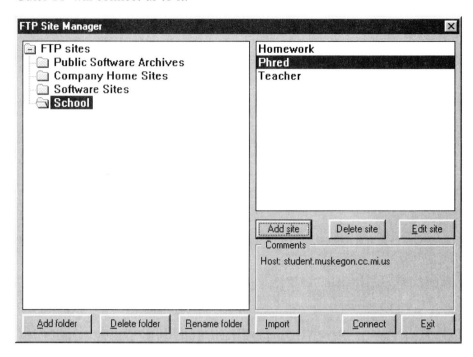

Figure D.5 Initial Cuteftp screen to select a site.

In Figure D.6, CuteFTP has connected to *phred,* and we have clicked on the *web-pages* subdirectory to open that set of files. Notice that the interface is a complete mouse-oriented graphical interface. In this example we want to download a file from *phred* to our local computer.

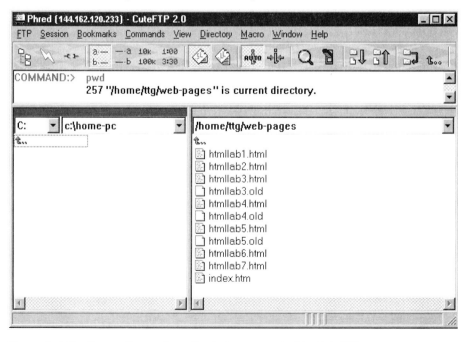

Figure D.6 Starting an ftp session after being connected by CuteFTP.

As Figure D.7 shows, the file we want to download is htmllab4.html from *phred*. To download, we simply double-click on the filename. If we click on the server side, CuteFTP will download the file to our PC. If we click on the local side (left), CuteFTP will upload the file to the server. It really makes the ftp process simple.

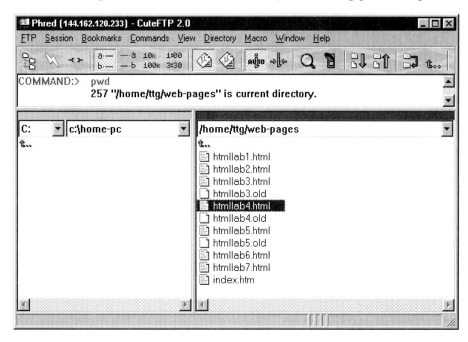

Figure D.7 Selecting a file to download.

In Figure D.8, CuteFTP has successfully downloaded the file from *Phred* to our home PC in .01 seconds. Programs like CuteFTP make it much easier to move files across the Net. Even old command-line pros like your humble authors use graphical ftp software on their home computers. It is a great tool that makes ftping much easier.

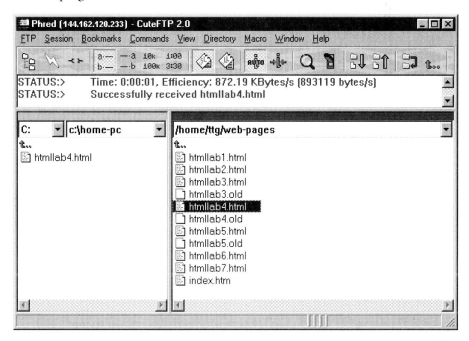

Figure D.8 File successfully downloaded.

glossary

Note: This glossary contains words beyond those indicated as key words in the text. It is designed to be a bit more comprehensive than the run-of-the-mill glossary. If you have any words that you think should have been included, please send your suggested additions to ttg@phred.dcccd.edu. We will consider any additions that will make this glossary more complete, and more fun! We look forward to your suggestions.

A

Absolute path name—also called **absolute URL,** the complete description of the path to a resource.

Absolute width—width measured in pixels. *See also* Relative width.

Abstract Window Toolkit (AWT)—includes user interface features like windows, dialog boxes, buttons, checkboxes, menus, scroll bars, lists, and text fields.

Abstraction—results from taking the essential characteristics out of an object and creating data to represent those characteristics.

Access—to retrieve data from a storage medium like a tape or disk.

Access time—the time it takes the read/write head to find requested data on a storage medium.

ACM. *See* Association for Computing Machinery (ACM)

Active directory—the directory or subdirectory that the operating system or application program uses as a default when accessing programs or data files from disk.

Address—unique number assigned to each memory location within a computer's processing hardware.

AI. *See* Artificial intelligence (AI)

AIFC. *See* AIFF Compressed Format (AIFC)

AIFF. *See* Audio Interchange File Format (AIFF)

AIFF Compressed Format (AIFC)—sound format developed by Apple because AIFF required so much storage space. Compression is lossy.

Algorithm—statement of the steps to be followed in solving a problem or performing a process.

Alphanumeric data—another name for textual data.

American National Standards Institute (ANSI)—group that develops programming language standards for use by industry and computer manufacturers.

Analog signals—signals representing data as patterns of frequencies, like sounds.

Analog sound—sound in which values flow from one to another continuously.

Anchor name—the anchor container with the name attribute, serving as a target anchor.

Animated GIF—a series of GIF images that are quickly changed in order to create simple animation.

Animation—visual images of motions produced by rapid presentation of drawn or computer-generated graphics.

Anonymous ftp—allows use of ftp without entering password; users give "anonymous" as name and their e-mail address as a password.

ANSI. *See* American National Standards Institute (ANSI)

Append—to attach additional material to a data stream or file, usually adding data to the end of the file or data stream.

Applet—small program, usually written in the Java language, that runs within a window inside the browser.

Applet viewer—allows user to view applets without a browser.

Application software—class of programs that solve specific user-oriented processing problems like word processors, spreadsheets, or browsers.

Arithmetic operation—ability of a computer to do mathematical functions like addition and subtraction with numerical data.

Artificial intelligence (AI)—software application that simulates human thought and judgment by the use of heuristic problem-solving techniques.

American Standard Code for Information Interchange (ASCII)—code for storing data that uses 7 bits to a byte and is commonly used in microcomputers; an extended version of ASCII uses 8 bits per byte.

ASCII editor—produces an ASCII file; also called a *text editor*.

Attributes—HTML elements that modify tags; they are coded within the open tag of a container.

Audio icons—used like graphical icons to delimit parts of the text, to highlight specific phrases, and to call attention to changes in content, but they are composed solely of sound.

Audio Interchange File Format (AIFF)—sound format developed by Apple and used most often by Macintosh and Silicon Graphics to store high-end audio data. It has an uncompressed format, and it supports stereo.

Audio Video Interface (AVI)—provided by Internet Explorer for inline movies.

Audiovisual data—data that people can hear or see, like voice, music, drawings, photographs, and video sequences.

AVI. *See* Audio Video Interface (AVI)

AWT. *See* Abstract Window Toolkit (AWT)

B

Backup—extra copy of data or programs on a disk or tape that is kept for use in case the original is destroyed or corrupted.

Backup procedures—making a copy of important files and programs on another tape or disk. This is essential to prevent loss of your work in the event your system or disk is damaged.

Base URL—the URL of the page that invokes an applet, image, or new page (unless the <BASE> attribute is coded).

Baseline—imaginary line that runs across the bottom of the text letters, not including descenders.

Benchmark test—compares software and hardware performance against a minimum standard agreed upon by management and the application development team.

Berners-Lee, Tim—invented the World Wide Web in late 1990 while working at CERN, the European Particle Physics Laboratory in Geneva, Switzerland. He wrote the first WWW client and the first WWW server, along with most of the communications software, defining URLs, HTTP, and HTML. A graduate of Oxford University, Tim is now the overall director of the W^{3}C.

Beta releases—experimental versions of software that test new features before they become part of the current release.

Beta test—prerelease testing of commercial software by potential outside users.

Binary—code pattern of on/off bits used to represent data or computer operations.

Binary digit—the on or off state of a single computer circuit, represented as one and zero, respectively; also known as *bit*.

Binary file—file of machine-readable code composed of ones and zeros.

Bit—the on or off state of a single computer circuit, represented as one and zero, respectively; also known as *binary digit*.

Bit mapping—pattern of pixels making up a graphic image; also known as *pixel graphics*.

Bits per pixel (bpp)—determines the number of colors in an image.

Bits per second (bps)—a measurement of data transmission speed.

Bleeding—when color from one pixel affects an adjacent pixel.

Block-level element—an element, like the <HR>, that automatically forces a new line before and after it.

BMP—standard Microsoft Windows image format, usually created by Paintbrush program and used for the wallpaper in Windows. It supports 1, 4, 8, and 24 bits per pixel. It is usually not compressed.

Bogon—analogous with proton/electron/neutron and doubtless reinforced after 1980 by the similarity to Douglas Adams's "Vogons"; see the bibliography in Appendix C of the "Hacker's Dictionary," and note that Arthur Dent actually mispronounces "Vogons" as "Bogons" at one point. 1. The elementary particle of bogosity (see quantum bogodynamics). For instance, "The Ethernet is emitting bogons again" means that it is broken, or acting in an erratic or bogus fashion. 2. A query packet sent from a TCP/IP domain resolver to a root server, having the reply bit set instead of the query bit. 3. Any bogus or incorrectly formed packet sent on a network.

4. By synecdoche, used to refer to any bogus thing, as in, "I'd like to go to lunch with you but I've got to go to the weekly staff bogon." 5. A person who is bogus or who says bogus things. This was historically the original usage, but it has been overtaken by its derivative senses (1–4). *See also* Bogosity; bogus

Bogosity—1. The degree to which something is bogus. At CMU, bogosity is measured with a bogometer; in a seminar, when a speaker says something bogus, a listener might raise his hand and say, "My bogometer just triggered." More extremely, "You just pinned my bogometer" means you just said or did something so outrageously bogus that it is off the scale, pinning the bogometer needle at the highest possible reading (one might also say, "You just redlined my bogometer"). The agreed upon unit of bogosity is the microLenat. 2. The potential field generated by a bogon flux.

Bogotify—to make or become bogus. A program that has been changed so many times as to become completely disorganized has become bogotified. If you tighten a nut too hard and strip the threads on the bolt, the bolt has become bogotified, and you had better not use it any more. This coinage led to the notional *autobogotiphobia,* defined as "the fear of becoming bogotified"; but is not clear that the latter has ever been "live" jargon rather than a self-conscious joke in jargon about jargon. *See also* Bogosity; bogus

Bogue out—to become bogus, suddenly and unexpectedly. "His talk was relatively sane until somebody asked him a trick question; then he bogued out and did nothing but flame afterwards." *See also* Bogosity; bogus

Bogus—1. Nonfunctional. "Your patches are bogus." 2. Useless. "OPCON is a bogus program." 3. False. "Your arguments are bogus." 4. Incorrect. "That algorithm is bogus." 5. Unbelievable. "You claim to have solved the halting problem for Turing Machines? That's totally bogus." 6. Silly. "Stop writing those bogus sagas." Astrology is bogus. So is a bolt that is obviously about to break. So is someone who makes blatantly false claims to have solved a scientific problem. (This word seems to have some but not all of the connotations of *random*—mostly the negative ones.) It is claimed that *bogus* was originally used in the hackish sense at Princeton in the late 1960s. It was spread to CMU and Yale by Michael Shamos, a migratory Princeton alumnus. A glossary of bogus words was compiled at Yale when the word was first popularized. The word spread into hackerdom from CMU and MIT. By the early 1980s it was also current in something like the hackish sense in West Coast teen slang, and it had gone mainstream by 1985. A correspondent from Cambridge reports, by contrast, that these uses of *bogus* grate on British nerves; in Britain the word means, rather specifically, "counterfeit," as in "a bogus 10-pound note."

The bogon has become the type case for a whole bestiary of nonce particle names, including the *clutron* or *cluon* (indivisible particle of cluefulness, obviously the antiparticle of the bogon) and the *futon* (elementary particle of randomness, or sometimes of lameness). These are not so much live usages in themselves as examples of a live meta-usage: that is, it has become a standard joke or linguistic maneuver to "explain" otherwise mysterious circumstances by inventing nonce particle names. And these imply nonce particle theories, with all their dignity or lack thereof (we might note parenthetically that this is a generalization from "[bogus particle] theories" to "bogus [particle theories]"!). Perhaps such particles are the modern-day equivalents of trolls and wood-nymphs as standard starting points around which to construct explanatory myths. Of course, playing on an existing word (as with *futon*) yields additional flavor.

Boilerplate—partially completed document with spaces or codes for specific fields that are added later.

Boole, George—(1815-1864) developed two-state (true or false) logic theory for mathematical expressions during the nineteenth century. His theories later became the basis for binary code.

Bpp. *See* Bits per pixel (bpp)

Bps. *See* Bits per second (bps)

Browser—software that translates the HTML codes into a presentation on the screen; used to cruise the World Wide Web.

Browser pane—the part of the screen that is normally visible to the user.

Buffer—internal memory set aside for temporary data storage.

Bug—an error within a computer program. The first bug was a moth that was trapped in a relay in one of the first computers. Grace Hopper taped the moth in the log book and explained how they had "de-bugged" the computer. Actually the term *bug,* in entomology, refers to the family Hemiptera. Computer bugs fall into two classes, syntax errors and logic errors. A *syntax error* is an actual error in the formation of the computer code. A *logic error* is correct syntactically but produces an incorrect answer. For example, coding <HR width="5%"> when you want a line half the screen width would be a logic error (you should code it "width="50%".)

Bulleted list—list with items bulleted instead of numbered or lettered.

Buttons—elements that perform some action when clicked with a mouse button or activated with the Enter key.

Byron, Augusta Ada—(Countess of Lovelace, 1815-1852) annotated and published Charles Babbage's work in the 1840s. Her detailed instructions for operation of the Analytical Engine are considered a precursor to modern programming. Actually Ada was really the first programmer. She was also the daughter of Lord Byron, the famous poet.

Byte—a group of bits representing a single character or digit of data, usually 8 bits.

C

C—high-level programming language used in system programming and graphics. It is portable and easy to structure but is a complex language to learn.

Cache—to store data that may be needed again, either on disk (in the case of caching pages) or in memory.

CAI. *See* Computer-assisted instruction (CAI)

Call—request for a program.

Calling document—page that contains the link that brings up a search page.

Camera-ready copy—a printed document ready to be photographed for a traditional printing plate. Its current meaning is a document ready to be copied.

Cards—HyperCard pages.

Carriage-return line feed (CrLf)—new line of text, usually the result of touching the Enter or Return key. Called a *newline* in Unix parlance.

Case sensitivity—recognizing the difference between uppercase and lowercase letters.

Cathode ray tube (CRT)—an output peripheral by which a visual display is shown on a screen; also known as *monitor.*

CD. *See* Compact disc (CD)

CD-ROM (*compact disc read-only memory*)—a high-capacity removable optical disk that permanently stores data and cannot be changed; also known as *CD* or *compact disk.*

CD-RW (compact disc read/write)—a high-capacity optical disk with a surface that can be written upon, then erased and rewritten upon.

Cell—intersection of a row and column in a table.

Central processing unit (CPU)—processing hardware of a computer, containing a processor and memory.

CGA.—*See* color graphics adapter (CGA)

CGI script—a program, running on a server, written in any one of several popular languages, most often Perl or a Unix shell language, to process data sent from an HTML form.

Channel—division of audio data representing a single voice or instrument.

Character—smallest unit of data, a single digit, letter, or symbol.

Chip—small silicon wafer on which resides integrated circuits and other processing circuitry.

Checkboxes—type of input item that allows a user to make more than one selection by activating boxes next to each choice.

Click—to press a mouse button once to select a menu option or icon.

"Click here"—sentence to be avoided. Anyone who has read this book will *never* use this outmoded and vulgar phrase.

Client/server—network design in which the client—that is, any end-user's computer—takes on processing tasks traditionally handled by a network server.

Client software—program that is resident on your computer but interacts with other programs or data across the Net.

Client-side mapping—image map controlled by client rather than server. This is the preferred type of mapping because it reduces the load on the Net.

Clip art—graphics and images on paper or disk that are purchased for use by designers.

Close box—icon found in the top right corner of a window. Clicking on the close box deactivates the associated window, which usually returns the window back into its original icon.

Code—written program instruction.

Coding—writing a computer program or HTML page.

Color graphics adapter (CGA)—color monitor standard that displays 640 by 200 pixels in 16 colors.

Comments—documentation of choices made while writing a program or HTML page, including explanations of why those choices were made.

Common Gateway Interface (CGI)—program that processes the information sent in on a form.

Compact disc (CD)—removable disk that permanently stores data and cannot be changed; also known as *CD-ROM.*

Compiler—high-level language translator that checks an entire program for errors while it is translating all the code into machine language. If there are syntax errors, a list of errors is output by this program.

Computer architecture—the physical characteristics of the computer, for example, a 450 MHz Pentium processor with a graphics card of 64 million colors and a stereo graphics card.

Computer-assisted instruction (CAI)—Using the computer to present material to students. A type of self-paced learning popular in the 1980s that is making a resurgence through the use of Web-based training.

Concatenation—adding to the end of an element or file.

Container elements *See* Containers

Containers—used to modify the contents placed within them. They consist of a beginning and closing tag. Although the closing tag can sometimes be inferred, it should never be eliminated.

Content—what a document says versus how a document looks (layout).

Content-based style. *See* Logical style

Cookie—a small quantum of data, stored by the browser, that is associated with a particular HTML page on the Net. Usually cookies are used to store and retrieve information about the user. In most cases, cookies live only for the life of the browsing session and disappear when the browser is closed. The reason for the term *cookie* is lost in the mists of antiquity, but there are a couple of good possibilities. First, the term *magic cookie* was used to describe a small chunk of data that allowed access to some special functions of a computer program. These small data elements were used in the mainframe days. Another rendition of the cookie was the cookie-monster program. That was arguably one of the first computer virus programs. The user would be working along and all at once the computer would clear the terminal screen and say "Give me a cookie." If the user responded with any input except the word "cookie," the program would continue to demand a cookie. The absolutely proper name for a cookie is a *persistent client state HTTP cookie,* but the term *magic cookie* is much more fun.

CrLf. *See* Carriage-return line feed (CrLf)

CPU. *See* Central processing unit (CPU)

Crash—term generically used to describe a computer failure but can also be used to describe the failure of any part of a computer system or a software failure.

CRT. *See* Cathode ray tube (CRT)

Cursor—blinking line or box that highlights where the computer is going to display the next keyboard entry.

Cursor control—use of keys on keyboard to move the cursor up, down, left, or right through a document.

Cut and paste—process of changing the location of data or formulas within a document or page; also known as *Move*.

D

Data—facts, figures, and images, the stuff of data processing. Note: Data is a *plural* word; the singular is datum.

Data compression—to reduce data storage space by replacing data redundancies with special notations that take up less space. Data compression can be lossy, meaning some of the data in the sound or image are lost, or lossless, meaning all the data are preserved in the compression.

Debug—to remove the errors from a program. *See* Bug.

Default value—the choice that the program will make for you if you fail to specify a value.

Definition list—list formatted like a dictionary or glossary.

Deprecated tags—tags that are still supported by software but are targeted for replacement and will become obsolete in the near future.

DHTML. *See* Dynamic HTML (DHTML)

Dialog box—window that prompts the user to enter text, select options from a list, or click on an icon to initiate or cancel some program option.

Digital sound—sound in which values are represented by numbers rather than by a continuous stream.

Digital video—created by capturing analog video at regular intervals and saving each capture as a distinct image called a *frame*. Frames can then be played back to give the appearance of motion, that is, to create a movie. Digital video files may have audio tracks associated with the frames.

Direct call—process of retrieving a file by name.

Discrete data—data represented by numbers (digital data).

Distributed program—program that runs on computers across the Internet, such as an HTML browser.

Dithering—replacing one uniform color with repeating patterns of other colors that approximate the initial color, or blending two colors to create a third color. Dithering can reduce compressibility and usability.

DNS. *See* Domain Name Server (DNS)

Document—the HTML code for a page.

Document-level style sheet—establishes formatting rules that affect all elements in a document's <BODY> container.

Domain—the computer that runs the server software.

Domain name—substitutes for the numeric IP address; an alphabetic name, such as "www.McGraw-Hill.com."

Domain Name Server (DNS)—program that translates domain names into IP addresses.

Downloading—copying a computer-readable file from another computer to your computer.

Drag—to move an object on the screen by pointing at it and holding down a mouse button while you move it to a new screen location.

Driver—master document that builds the frames of a framed document.

Drop-down menu—menu options that stay hidden in a menu bar at the top of the screen until the user selects it. When the menu is selected, the menu opens to list program options. Once an option is selected, the menu rolls back up into the menu bar. Also known as *pull-down menu.*

Dublin Metadata Core Element Set (Dublin Core)—standard for the META tag.

Dynamic content—refers to the spectrum of active features, including images, sound, animation, and interactivity.

Dynamic document—document with active features that could include images, sound, animation, and interactivity.

Dynamic HTML (DHTML)—provides the capacity to perform some of the animation features formerly available only through Java.

E

Echo—the Unix command that sends a data stream to the output device.

Empty element. *See* Empty tag

Empty tag—a tag that does not enclose any text, so it has no closing code—for example, <BR>.

Encapsulation—feature of object-oriented programming in which data and the operations necessary to manipulate those data are collected together into a usable module.

End user—person who can use computer technology to organize data, stimulate new ideas, solve problems, and communicate the results to others. This individual is also called a *user*. In HTML parlance, the user is that individual for whom we create pages.

Executable file—binary file.

Extended graphics adapter (EGA)—color monitor standard that displays 720 by 350 pixels in 16 colors.

Extended graphics array (XGA)—color monitor standard that displays 1024 by 768 pixels in 65,536 colors.

External image—an image that is placed on a page by itself, and a link is provided to it.

F

Field—related group of letters, numbers, and symbols, as in a name or address.

File Transfer Protocol (ftp)—allows you to move files across the Net.

Filename—unique set of letters, numbers, and symbols that identifies a data file or program.

Filename extension—a combination of three or four letters that is added to the end of a filename, preceded by a period, to identify the file format. For example, hypertext markup language files are identified by the filename extensions .htm or .html.

Firewall—program that protects one or more computers from attack from the Net.

Flagitious—According to *Webster's Dictionary of the English Language,* flagitious comes from the Latin *flagitiosus* and means grossly wicked. Rhetorically it means guilty of enormous crimes. Perhaps a bit strong to apply to the <BLINK> tag, but it is a fun word, and after you have looked at as many blinking pages as we have, well, they do seem grossly wicked at that.

Floating image—an image that can be placed by the browser in either margin.

Floating-point number—a number with a decimal point.

Flood filling—creating a large colored area by using height and width attributes to expand a very small image across the screen.

Focus—identifies the currently active control that is able to receive input.

Font—the typeface, weight, style, and size of the text.

Form—an HTML document, or part of an HTML document, that allows the user to provide input and then returns an HTML document in response, either giving requested information or simply thanking the user.

Frame—1. The division of a framed page. Each frame contains an HTML document. 2. Created by capturing analog video at regular intervals and saving each capture as a distinct image. Frames can be played back to create a movie.

Freeware—software in the public domain.

Ftp. *See* File Transfer Protocol (ftp)

Full justification—both right and left margins of a document are aligned. Full justification is not often seen in HTML documents.

Function—predefined formula or code segment that performs common mathematical, financial, or logical operations. We often use JavaScript functions in HTML pages.

Function keys—keyboard keys that activate special software features (the F1–F12 keys on most keyboards.)

G

GIF. *See* Graphic Interchange Format (GIF)

Gigabyte—1 billion bytes of memory.

GIGO—"garbage in, garbage out," meaning errors in data produce useless information.

Global variable—a value stored at a location known to all the functions on a page.

Glyphs—symbols, letters, and numbers.

Graphic Interchange Format (GIF)—the most common image format on the Web, supporting 8-bit color and having lossless compression. The three types of GIF are plain, transparent, and animated.

Graphical user interface (GUI)—program that uses images to facilitate users' selections of commands by means of a pointing device like a mouse.

Grep—a Unix tool used to find particular lines in one or more files. Stands for Global Regular Expression Print.

Grunt work—also called *scut work*. The boring part of any task. In building an HTML document, coding the <HTML>, <HEAD> . . . skeleton could be considered grunt work.

GUI. *See* Graphical user interface (GUI)

H

Hacker—self-taught computer expert who tends to try to find unauthorized ways to access computer systems.

Hard return—a carriage return entered into the text when the user presses the Return or Enter key.

Hardware—computer and other associated equipment. Generally, if you were to kick the hardware with your bare foot, it would hurt.

Harvest—to collect resources from the Net, such as images, sounds, and applets.

Hierarchical model—model in which data items and their references are organized in a top-down fashion; larger parts are composed of smaller parts.

High-level language—programming language that resembles human language. Programs written in high-level languages, like BASIC and Pascal, must be translated into the computer's machine language before being used.

Highlight—to increase the intensity of certain characters on a screen for emphasis.

Home page—the highest level page on a Web site.

Horizontal rule—tag that places a horizontal line, or rule, on a page.

Hosting—making a Web page available on a known domain.

Hot spots—areas in image maps that can be selected to invoke associated HTML documents.

Hoze—to completely break or mess up. Often used to describe the results of a logic error. For example one might say, "I forgot to code the closing tag on the italics container and it hozed the rest of the page."

HREF. *See* Hypertext reference (HREF)

HTML. *See* HyperText Markup Language (HTML)

HTML author—the person who creates a Web page.

HTML editor—software used to produce HTML code.

HTML text-file converter—converts existing word-processor files to HTML code.

HTML verifier—makes sure your links are valid and your HTML syntax and grammar are correct.

HTML viewer—lets you see what your document may look like on a browser.

Http. *See* Hypertext Transport Protocol (http)

HyperCard—forerunner of HTML; Macintosh feature that allowed users to create buttons that would perform certain actions.

Hyper document—document that contains links.

Hypertext document—document that contains links.

HyperText Markup Language (HTML)—the tool used to build Web pages; not a true programming language.

Hypertext reference (HREF)—a required attribute of the LINK tag; it points to some valid http address.

Hypertext Transport Protocol (http)—the protocol used to send HTML documents across the Net.

I

Icon—picture of item, action, or computer operation.

IF . . . THEN—programming statements used to perform actions based on the value of a given condition. IF a particular condition is true, THEN perform the associated action(s).

Import—to add graphics, images, or text created by other software to a document.

Image editor—allows you to modify images, add special effects, and convert from one file format to another.

Image map—image that serves as a map in that users can click on various parts (links) of the image to retrieve information. There are two types: server-side maps and client-side maps.

Infinite loop—a series of instructions within a computer program that are repeated continuously without exit.

Information—knowledge derived by processing data, usually in the form of a printed report or screen display. The only reason we build Web pages is to provide information.

Inheritance—feature of object-oriented programming in which one class can receive data structures and methods or procedures from a previous class.

Inline element—part of an HTML page that is placed within the current line of text.

Inline image—an image that occurs within the line of text. In HTML, images are placed inline unless the author codes one of the **align** attribute values.

Integer—a whole number, without a decimal point.

Intellectual property—material resulting from ideas, or mental processes; usually protected by a copyright.

Interactivity—exists when the user can input information to a page and receive a response. Java provides a degree of interactivity that allows users to play games, live, on the Net.

Internet address. *See* Internet Protocol (IP) address

Internet Protocol (IP) address—numeric address assigned to each machine on the Internet. Consists of four sets of one, two, or three octal digits separated by periods. *See also* Domain name

Internet Service Provider (ISP)—company that specializes in providing access to the Internet.

Interpreter—translates source code into binary code, one line at a time.

Intersystem link—link to an item in a different system.

Intranet—computer network like the Internet except that it contains only the computers of a specific company.

Intrapage link—link to an item located within the current document or page.

Intrasystem link—link to an item within the current system.

Intrinsic events—mouse activities, like clicking, and document changes, like loading.

IP address. *See* Internet Protocol (IP) address

ISP. *See* Internet Service Provider (ISP)

Iteration. *See* Loop

J

Jacquard, Joseph Marie—(1752-1834) developer in 1801 of mechanized looms using punched cards for patterns.

Java—high-level programming language that uses object-oriented techniques, works across the Internet, is translated line by line, is safe and hard to crash, runs on many different computer platforms, and does powerful things quickly.

Java applet—a small program written in the Java language that serves as an extension to an HTML document, providing visual and other effects, including animation. Applets are a subset of Java. They are called from an HTML program and run on a browser.

Java compiler—translates Java source code into bytecode; called Javac.

Java development kit (JDK)—includes a Java compiler (Javac), Java bytecode interpreter to run stand-alone programs, a Java debugging tool, and an applet viewer.

JavaScript—specialized programming language for building programs that are embedded in an HTML document and perform simple tasks; not related to Java. JavaScript gives the HTML programmer tools such as looping and conditional statements.

JavaScript editor—software package that helps Web authors create JavaScripts, taking much of the grunt work out of creating JavaScript.

Java Virtual Machine—Java interpreter.

Javac—Java compiler; translates Java source code into bytecode.

JDK. *See* Java development kit (JDK)

Joint Photographic Experts Group (JPEG)—image format on the Web that supports 8-bit and 24-bit color and is available on all browsers. Compression is lossy. *Progressive JPEGs* create an effect similar to an animated GIF.

JPEG. *See* Joint Photographic Experts Group (JPEG)

Just-in-time programming—involves multithreading, in which a program can start running before all of it is downloaded.

Justification—the alignment of text along the margins.

K

K. *See* Kilobyte (K)

Kerning—adjusting the spacing between printed characters according to the shape of the characters.

kHz. *See* Kilohertz (kHz)

Kilobyte (K)—consists of 1024 bytes of memory, or 2^{10} bytes.

Kilohertz (kHz)—roughly a thousand samples per second.

L

Late binding—choosing the correct method to handle an object at run time.

Latin-1 character set—list of common letters, numbers, symbols, and punctuation marks used in Western languages, each with a numeric value and some also with names; designed by the International Standards Organization (ISO).

Layout—how a document looks versus what it says (content).

LCD. *See* Liquid crystal display (LCD)

Left justification—alignment of text in a document along only the left edge.

Line break—tag to end a line on a page and start a new one.

Linear programming—type of programming wherein an optimum solution for a problem is found for a given set of requirements and constraints using a top-down method.

Liquid crystal display (LCD)—monitor in which an electric field causes configurations of molecules to align and light up, producing characters.

Link—specially marked place on the screen that will cause something to happen when you activate it. Links can open another HTML document, move you to another place in the current document, display a picture, play a sound, or run a video clip.

List box—displays a list of names or options. When the list is too long to fit in the box, scroll arrows move the list up and down to display different items within the list box.

Local action buttons—buttons that cause the browser to perform specific actions within the client (browser), instead of involving a CGI script on the server.

Local area network (LAN)—privately owned collection of interconnected computers within a confined service area.

Local variable—a value known only to the function in which it was created.

Logic error—program error that is translatable but does not produce correct results.

Logical operation—ability of a computer to compare two values to see which is larger or if they are equal.

Logical operator—symbol (<, >, =) indicating which logical operation is to be used in an IF . . . THEN statement.

Logical style—using specific style containers that describe the way the text within a container is used rather than simply how it looks.

Loop. *See* Iteration

Lossless compression—compression that keeps all the data bits in the image so that image or sound quality does not degrade.

Lossy compression—compression in which some pixels are discarded, causing image or sound quality to degrade.

Lynx—the most common text only browser.

M

Machine code—an operating language unique to each computer that is made up of bits (0 or 1) representing electronic switches (off or on); also known as *machine language.*

Mailto—refers to a directive in a form that causes data to be sent to an electronic mail (e-mail) address rather than being sent to be processed by a CGI script.

Maintaining state—term used to describe the process of storing some aspect or aspects of user information for later retrieval. Examples include color choices, last time visited, places visited at the site, and other data that may be important to the user. Most often cookies are used to maintain state in a browser.

Maintenance—keeping one or more of a computer system's components or programs up to date.

Maintenance programmer—a person who modifies programs or Web pages already in use in order to reflect a change in content.

Marker—bullet used in an unordered list.

Marquee—display of animated (moving) text that scrolls horizontally or vertically on the page.

Maximize button—Windows icon with two overlapping boxes found in the top right corner of the title bar next to the minimize button. Clicking on the maximize button expands the related window to fill the screen.

McLuhan, Marshall—(1911-1980) author of books relating technology to society. His ideas have influenced present-day data communications and multimedia.

Megabyte (MB)—1 million bytes of memory.

Megahertz (MHz)—1 million clock cycles per second; a measurement of processing hardware speed.

Memory—computer circuitry that temporarily stores data and programs. Usually grouped by storage capacity of thousands (K) or millions (M) of characters; for example, a computer with 8M of memory can store up to 8 million letters, numbers, or symbols.

Menu—list of program options that allows a user to activate an option by highlighting it or by entering a single letter or number.

Menu bar—horizontal area that runs across the top of a window and displays menu titles.

Method—In object-oriented programming, a method is a way of manipulating data. Objects have methods associated with them to process the data, which are called *properties* of the object. Some of the methods are things like getMonth() or write(). One way to identify a method is that it will usually return a value or values, and it usually ends with parentheses. Methods can also act on data that are passed to them through parameters contained in the parentheses. For example, document.write("Hello World") will write the phrase "Hello World" to the current document.

Microsecond—one millionth of a second; used to measure the speed of a computer's processing.

Millisecond—one thousandth of a second; used to measure the access time of a computer's disk drive.

Minimize button—Windows icon with an underscore found in the top right corner of the title bar next to the maximize/restore button. Clicking on the minimize button converts the window back into an icon or sends it to the taskbar.

MIPS—1 million instructions per second; a measurement of a computer's processing speed.

MIME. *See* Multipurpose Internet Mail Extensions (MIME)

Modal—term usually meaning to have modes or be associated with a particular mode. However, in this instance we will use the Microsoft definition. In MS-speak, a modal window will stay on the screen and claim any input the user enters until it is closed. You can access other windows only after the modal window is closed. Such a window would typically be used to warn the user of an error or problem. The alert( ), confirm( ), and prompt( ) dialog boxes are all examples of modal windows in JavaScript.

Modular—a modular language, like JavaScript, allows the coder to create small sections of code that perform one task.

Monaural sound—single-channel sound as opposed to multiple-channel (stereo).

Monitor—an output peripheral by which a visual display is shown on a screen; also called a *screen* or *CRT.*

Monochrome monitor—single-color monitor, that is, a monitor that shows one color against a black background.

Monospaced font—font in which each letter takes up the same amount of space. *See also* Proportionally spaced font

Movie—digital video file, sometimes accompanied by audio file. *See also* Audio/Video Interleave (AVI)

Moving Picture Experts Group (MPEG)—video or audio format with the best compression algorithms, providing high-quality online files.

MPEG. *See* Moving Picture Experts Group (MPEG)

Mu-law (μ-law)—sound file originally developed for Unix, now an international standard for compression voice-quality audio, supported by almost all operating systems. Does not support stereo. Extension is ".au."

Multimedia—includes sound, pictures, and animation.

Multiprocessing—linking several computers together to work on a common problem.

Multipurpose Internet Mail Extensions (MIME)—tells the browser what kind of file data are being sent across the Net.

Multitasking—one computer running two or more independent programs concurrently.

Multithreading—allows access to different parts of the same program at the same time. This allows a program to begin execution before it has completely downloaded from the Net.

N

Nanosecond—one billionth of a second; used to measure the speed of a computer's processor.

Nesting lists—lists within lists; lists with sublists.

Netcology—conservation of Net resources; coined from the term *ecology*.

Newline—term used in Unix to describe a carriage-return line feed.

Null—no value. Literally, binary zeros in a field.

O

Object—section of program code in object-oriented programming that contains both the processing code and descriptions of related data to perform a single task. Each object is an instance of a class; it has a state and a behavior. It is the term used to describe an element, like a button, form, the actual browser, the document, or even the current date. The data contained within the object are called the *properties,* and the instructions for manipulating the data or causing the object to interact with other objects are called *methods.*

Object instance—a particular occurrence or use of a class (in object-oriented programming).

Object-oriented programming (OOP)—programming methodology whereby a program is organized into objects, each containing both descriptions of the data and processing operations necessary to perform a task.

Obsolete tags—tags that are no longer supported by updated browsers.

OCR. *See* Optical character recognition (OCR)

Offline—state of hardware when it is not communicating with the computer. This is also used to indicate a process that happens when the computer is not connected to the Internet, for example "offline viewing."

Online—direct input and processing of data by a computer.

OOP. *See* Object-oriented programming (OOP)

Open standard—a standard that is still developing; anyone is free to use it and make suggestions about inclusions.

Operating system—a collection of system programs that oversees the execution of application programs, manages files, and controls the computer system's resources—monitor, keyboard, disk drives, memory, etc.

Optical character recognition (OCR)—process in which a device like a scanner is used along with special software to take a picture of a page of text, analyze the picture, and produce a file of machine-readable data from the analysis. For example, if you were to process this page of the glossary using OCR, you would end up with a file containing all of these words that you could process with a word processor.

Ordered list—list with items numbered or lettered.

P

Package—set of directory names, starting from the URL, with each element of the package separated from the others by a dot. Or, something you get at Christmas or on your birthday. (I like the second definition better than the first . . . oh, well.)

Padding—white space around elements such as cells, tables, or images.

Page—what you see when a document is displayed on your screen by a browser.

Page footer—appears at the end of an HTML document and provides basic information about the creator of the page plus a list of the navigation links used. Should contain the date last modified as well.

Palette—displays the color options available in a graphics package.

Pane—*See* Browser pane

Paragraph—identifies a continuous string of text within a page; used to break up text into smaller units. In HTML, defined by the <P> . . . </P> container.

Parameters—attributes that give the Web weaver some control over applets.

Parent class—a superclass in object-oriented programming; a feature of inheritance.

Parent window—the window containing the hypertext reference to another page.

Parse—to divide into component parts. We parse a sentence into words using white space and punctuation. The browser must parse HTML code into its components so it can interpret it.

Password—special combination of letters, numbers, or symbols that is theoretically known only to the user, and allows access to protected computer systems and data.

Path—set of directory names that lead to a specific document.

PCX—image format on the Web that was developed by Zsoft for the PC Paintbrush program. Supports 1, 4, 8, and 24 bits per pixel but does not seem to support compression.

PDA. *See* Personal digital assistant (PDA)

PDF—image format on the Web that is created with a special software package called Acrobat from Adobe. PDF documents can look like a magazine page, with multiple columns. PDF documents support "on page" searching.

Perl—an elegant little programming language developed by Larry Wall, often used to write CGI scripts. Perl stands for Practical Extraction and Report Language.

Personal digital assistant (PDA)—class of devices like the PalmPilot III, the Avigo, or any of a series of small, usually palmtop devices used to manage personal information.

Physical style—describes the way the text within a container is supposed to look when displayed by a browser. *See also* Logical style

Picosecond—one trillionth of a second; used to measure speed within a computer's processor.

Pitch—the number of characters printed per inch in a document.

Pixel—stands for "picture element"; one of the many tiny dots that make up the display on your screen. In a color monitor, each pixel is actually three small dots, one each red, blue, and green. (No, we don't know where the "x" came from.)

Platform—describes the specific type of computer and its operating system, browser, and so forth.

Platform independence—can be run on a variety of platforms; this is an important goal for HTML code.

Plug-in—additional software program that works with a browser and is required to display multimedia or other special formats.

PNG. *See* Portable Network Graphics (PNG)

Point—unit of measure for type size. One point equals 1/72 of an inch.

Pointers—variables that contain the addresses of other data.

Polymorphism—having the same name for more than one, usually related, method. The two types of polymorphism are overloading and overriding.

Port number—must be specified when the server is set up to receive http traffic on a network port other than the default port.

Portability—characteristic of being viewable by all sorts of computers.

Portable Network Graphics (PNG)—relatively new but important image format on the Web that supports 8-bit and 24-bit color but is an open standard and is not supported by all browsers. Compression is lossless. Compression is excellent, so there are many Web weavers that are trying to help PNG become the standard on the Net.

Pragma—normally used to indicate information a compiler uses. In this instance it means "extra data the browser uses."

Prepend—to add data to the beginning of a file, variable name, or data stream. For example, accessing the data stored at a memory location in Unix is accomplished by prepending a dollar sign ($) to the variable name.

Preventive maintenance procedures—running diagnostic checks and cleaning computer hardware to prevent a crash from occurring; running diagnostic checks, link-viability checks, and the like to ensure that a Web page is healthy, wealthy, and wise.

Primary storage—another name for a computer's internal memory.

Procedural approach—traditional approach to program design in which data are separate from instructions and the programmer lists the steps needed to solve a problem.

Progressive image—a file saved as layers that display the image data in several passes, each pass making the image better.

Property—object-oriented term used to describe the data associated with an object. Some examples of properties are the colors of the text, links, and background of a document, or the current date and time. Properties are the data that an object's methods use or modify.

Proportionally spaced font—font in which some letters take up more space than others. *See also* Monospaced font

Protocol—tells the browser what kind of resource it is accessing and allows different machines or programs to communicate. HTTP and plain text are two examples.

Pseudocode—a method of representing program logic by using English phrases in an outline form.

Public—available to other applications, either as a direct call or through the import statement.

Public domain—not copyrighted; can be used for free, without obtaining permission. It is always a good idea to give credit to the source of public domain material—that is just polite.

Publish—to move a Web page to the server that will host it, making it available to the world.

Pull-down menu—menu options that stay hidden in a menu bar at the top of the screen until the user selects it. When the menu is selected, the menu opens to list program options. Once an option is selected, the menu rolls back up into the menu bar. Also known as *drop-down menu.*

Pull technology—starts with the client requesting data from the server. Almost all HTML screens are "pulled." The client is in control.

Push technology—starts with the server deciding to send data to the client without a request from the client. This is still rare on the Net. Broadcast televison is an example of push technology. The client (your TV) doesn't request the data; it is just sent by the server (the TV station), and your client can use it if so desired.

R

Radio button—type of input item that ensures that only one of a series of choices can be selected by the user. So called because it resembles an old-fashioned pushbutton radio.

Readability—how easy a page is to read. Two of the factors that determine readability are (1) the proper use of white space to separate design elements and (2) starting new lines of code where appropriate. Not only is the readability of a page important, but so is the readability of the HTML code.

Relative path name—as opposed to *absolute path name,* does not start with a right slash, because it starts with the current position in the file structure. The browser fills in all of the missing data to the left of the information provided.

Relative width—width measured as a percentage of the screen. *See also* Absolute width

Resolution—a measure of graphic image sharpness in bits (pixels) per inch or bits per line. The higher the resolution, the sharper the graphic image is.

RGB number—number representing a specific mixture of red, green, and blue colors; expressed as a six-digit (hexadecimal) number in HTML. An example is #FFCC99.

Resource Interchange File Format Waveform Audio Format (RIFF WAVE)—proprietary sound file format sponsored jointly by Microsoft and IBM and most commonly used on Microsoft Windows products. It is supported by most operating systems, has uncompressed format, and supports stereo. File extension is ".wav."

Reverse video—putting text into the opposite colors expected on a screen; done for emphasis. For example, white characters on a black background would be reverse video.

RGB monitor—monitor using red, green, and blue (RGB) pixels in combinations to form a variety of colors.

RIFF WAVE. *See* Resource Interchange File Format Waveform Audio Format (RIFF WAVE)

Right justification—alignment of text in a document along the right edge.

Rollover—a feature on a page that changes as the mouse pointer moves over it.

Robust—strongly constucted.

Rules—part of a style sheet. The rules in a style sheet provide the direction for the browser as it builds specific elements of the page.

S

Sans-serif type style—a type style in which the printed characters lack tails, resulting in a simple block style of text.

Scalar—one of the two ways information can be accessed in a computer program. With scalar values, the data are present in the command, without ever being stored in a specific location in memory. For example, the following print statement uses a scalar value:

```
print "Hello World".
```

The character data string "Hello World" is a scalar value.

The other choice is to use *variables*. A variable is a handy name for a location in memory. In the following example, the data are stored in the variable string:

```
string = "Hello World"
print $string
```

Then the contents of that variable are printed. (Note: this is a Unix example, so the $ that precedes the variable name is required. What it is saying is, "Print the contents of the variable 'string,' not the word 'string.' ")

Screen pointer—an icon, usually an arrow, on a screen that moves when the mouse or some other pointer device is moved. Program options are activated by using a mouse to move the screen pointer over the desired icon and clicking the mouse button.

Script—a program, usually written in a scripting language like Perl or JavaScript or one of the Unix shells. A script usually has one well-defined function and is relatively small.

Scripting language—a language used to write scripts, for example, JavaScript, Perl, or Unix shell languages.

Scroll—to roll data up, down, and sideways on a screen for viewing long or wide documents.

Scroll arrows—arrows found at both ends of a scroll bar. Users change the view of a window or list box by clicking on one of the scroll arrows.

Scroll bar—area that appears on the right or lower edges of a window or list box when only a partial view is available. A scroll bar contains a scroll box and scroll arrows.

Scroll box—square within a scroll bar that identifies which portion of the window or list box is currently being viewed. Users can change the view by dragging the scroll box within the scroll bar.

Search site—specialized Web page designed to help people find data from other pages by means of one or more keywords.

Searchable document—document containing ISINDEX tag; it allows the user to search one or more files on the server.

Secure environment—created by a programming language that cannot write to disk drives or cause overflow errors; an environment safe from viruses.

Security manager—runs at all times in Java to enforce the rules of applet behavior.

Selection—basic structure in a computer program that allows execution of one of two different sets of code based on some condition; often called an *IF-THEN structure.*

Sequence—basic structure of a computer program whereby instructions are executed in the order they appear in the program.

Serif type—a type style in which short line segments are added to print characters to help the reader's eye flow across the page.

Server redirection—technique for returning a CGI script in which a Location: header is coded instead of a Content-type: header.

Server-side mapping—image map controlled by server; that is, the server decides what client should do.

SGML. *See* Standard Generalized Markup Language (SGML)

Shareware—software that you can legally copy and use but for which you should register and pay the registration fee.

Shell script—A program, often a small program, written in one of the Unix shell languages. Most scripts are written to run in the Bourne shell.

Snail mail—regular postal service.

Source—origin of a link.

Stacks—HyperCard documents.

Stand-alone program—runs on a single, local machine and is complete on that machine.

Standard Generalized Markup Language (SGML)—language for coding Web pages that can be viewed by all types of computers, all across the world. HTML is a subset of SGML.

Static Web page—page containing no links.

Status line—area of a browser pane that displays pertinent information about what is happening within the browser. Often the status line shows the address to which a link points.

Stereo sound—multiple-channel sound as opposed to single-channel (monaural).

Storyboard—diagram illustrating how two or more Web pages relate to one another.

String—a series of characters enclosed in either single or double quotation marks that are displayed as ASCII text.

Style—describes a way to set off a group of characters from the surrounding text block.

Style sheets—added in the new HTML standard to give the Web weaver more control over the placement and appearance of various elements on the page and to allow the creation of aural entries. There are two types of style sheets: *external,* which are files called when the browser opens the page, and *internal,* which usually apply only to the page in which they occur.

Super VGA monitor—color monitor standard that displays 1024 by 768 pixels in 256 colors.

Syntax—word order, spacing, abbreviations, and special symbols used by a command-driven interface or programming language.

Syntax error—an error in the formation of the computer code.

T

Table—data arranged in rows and columns.

Tagged Image File Format (TIFF)—image format used to exchange documents between different computer platforms. Supports 1, 4, 8, and 24 bits per pixel.

Tags—HTML codes that are enclosed in angle brackets and are used to format the text. *See also* Containers

Target—end of a link; the place from which data are being transferred.

Telnet—allows you to work remotely on computers across the Net.

Template—an HTML skeleton with labels and scripts, but no test or pictures, that is formatted for a specific application where it is copied and reused. Templates are very useful to increase efficiency and reduce grunt work.

Terabyte—1 trillion bytes of memory.

Text—nongraphical data composed of ASCII characters.

Text box—accepts keyboard entries from user to identify new filenames or disk locations. Text boxes are often used within a dialog box.

Text file—file consisting of just text, with no embedded word-processing codes; consists of only ASCII characters. Also called a *plain ASCII file.*

Thumbnail image—very small version of the actual image, created using special thumbnailing software.

TIFF. *See* Tagged Image File Format (TIFF)

Tile—to repeat an image; for example, you can use a small image as the background of a Web page by tiling it, or repeating it to fill the screen.

Title bar—horizontal area across the top of a window that displays the window's title. A window can be moved by clicking on the title bar and dragging it to a new screen location.

Toggle—switch; turns a preset feature on and off.

Turing, Alan—(1912-1954) developed the Turing test for artificial intelligence and provided some basis for computer science theory.

U

Unicode—modeled on the ASCII character set, but it uses 16-bit encoding to support full multilingual text. No escape sequence or control code is required to specify any character in any language. According to the Unicode standard, any glyph in any language should be able to be represented.

Uniform Resource Identifier (URI)—the most general identifier for Web resources; the URL is a component of the URI.

Uniform Resource Locator (URL)—the Internet address, or location, of a resource, whether it is a Web page or a specific part of a Web page.

Universal Resource Name (URN)—a more general identifier for Web resources, not yet completely defined.

Unordered list. *See* Bulleted list

Uploading—sending data or programs directly to another computer.

URI. *See* Uniform Resource Identifier (URI)

URL. *See* Uniform Resource Locator (URL)

URN. *See* Universal Resource Name (URN)

User friendly—term for an attribute of computers meaning "easy to use" that is horribly overused. It is included here to beg you not to use it when describing your pages!

Utility applets—useful, practical applets usually designed for commercial sale.

Vaporware—computer programs that have been promised but do not exist.

Variable name—a generic way of referring to a location in the computer's memory.

Variable value—the data stored at the location in memory specified by a variable name.

Verification program. *See* HTML verifier

VGA. *See* Video graphics array (VGA)

Video display terminal (VDT)—a screen that provides temporary output of information.

Video graphics array (VGA)—color monitor standard that displays 720 by 400 pixels in 256 colors.

Virus—harmful software that destroys other software on the target machine and can reproduce itself and spread from machine to machine.

Void—will not return a value.

Web administrator—person who maintains a Web server.

Web master—person responsible for a collection of pages on a Web site.

Web server—computer on the Internet with a recognized domain name or IP address that runs one of the Web server packages like Apache.

Web site—a series of related Web pages.

Web weaver—person who creates a Web page.

What You See Is What You Get (WYSIWYG)—started as a tool for word processing and desktop publishing to show what the end result would look like. Now it has come to refer to any application that shows the user what the output will look like as the code is being generated.

White space—spaces, tabs, and blank lines; those areas on the screen that are not covered by text or graphics.

Wizard—program that helps you code and will identify errors in your code.

Word wrap—feature in which the word processor senses the margins and moves words to the next line as needed without carriage returns being necessary.

World Wide Web Consortium (W^{3}C)—international organization that sets standards for HTML protocols and tags (www.w3c.org).

Workaround—term used to describe an action or set of actions that take the place of some other, often broken, action. Usually a workaround is less than elegant but does provide the user with a way to accomplish the desired task.

W^{3}C. *See* World Wide Web Consortium (W^{3}C)

WYSIWYG. *See* What You See Is What You Get (WYSIWYG)

Your Mileage May Vary (YMMV)—an expression that indicates that there are differences between browsers and platforms. For example, "The page looked good on my machine at home, but YMMV."

Z

Zipped file—compressed file.

Zorro—Ok, so he has nothing to do with HTML, he was still a neat historical figure.

index